INTRODUCTION TO LAW

AUSTRALIA AND NEW ZEALAND
The Law Book Company Ltd.
Sydney : Melbourne : Perth

CANADA AND U.S.A.
The Carswell Company Ltd.
Agincourt, Ontario

INDIA
N. M. Tripathi Private Ltd.
Bombay
and
Eastern Law House Private Ltd.
Calcutta and Delhi
M.P.P. House
Bangalore

ISRAEL
Steimatzky's Agency Ltd.
Jerusalem : Tel Aviv : Haifa

MALAYSIA : SINGAPORE : BRUNEI
Malayan Law Journal (Pte.) Ltd.
Singapore and Kuala Lumpur

PAKISTAN
Pakistan Law House
Karachi

INTRODUCTION TO LAW

SECOND EDITION

BY

L. A. RUTHERFORD, LL.B., B.C.L., A.I.B.
Principal Lecturer in Law, Newcastle-upon-Tyne Polytechnic

I. A. TODD, LL.B., B.C.L., Grad. Cert. Ed.
Vice Principal, College of Arts and Technology, Newcastle-upon-Tyne

M. G. WOODLEY,
B.A. (Law/Econ.), M.Sc. (Management Studies)
Senior Lecturer in Law, Newcastle-upon-Tyne Polytechnic

Published in association with the Institute of Legal Executives

LONDON
SWEET & MAXWELL
1987

First edition 1982
Reprinted 1983
Reprinted 1985
Second edition 1987

Published by
Sweet and Maxwell Ltd. of
11 New Fetter Lane, London
Computerset by Burgess & Son,
Abingdon, Oxon
Made and printed in Great Britain by
Richard Clay Ltd.,
Bungay, Suffolk

British Library Cataloguing in Publication Data
Rutherford, L.A.
  Introduction to law.—2nd ed.
  1. Law—England
  I. Title   II. Todd, I.A.   III. Woodley, M.G.
  IV. Institute of Legal Executives
  344.2   KD660
  ISBN 0-421-36760-1

Dedicated

to

Catherine, Helen, Jenny, Keith,
Mark, Patrick and Stephen

PREFACE TO THE SECOND EDITION

The preface to the first edition of this book pointed to the separate treatment afforded by the text to the needs of the individual law consumer and those of the commercial/industrial consumer. This dual focus remains the central rationale for the structure of the book. There have, however, been modifications to accommodate the amendments which have been made, since 1982, to the Law syllabus of Part 1 of the membership examinations of the Institute of Legal Executives.

In the years which have passed since publication of the first edition the law makers have continued to legislate and adjudicate and, in so doing, perpetuate that process which, through the slow march of attrition, renders inoperative and irrelevant the content of all legal textbooks. A new edition provides the authors of legal texts with an opportunity to remove that which is redundant, add that which is new and re-consider basic principles and concepts. This, we have attempted to do.

It may be too much to hope that the "labour we delight in physics pain" (Lady Macbeth) but we do hope that our readers will at least abstain from the chorus—

"another damned, thick, square book!
Always scribble, scribble, scribble!"

(Duke of Gloucester 1743–1805)

To our families, who may well be tempted to join with the Duke's chorus, we once again express our sincere appreciation for their support and encouragement.

January 1987

L.A.R.
I.A.T.
M.G.W.

PREFACE TO THE FIRST EDITION

This book is intended primarily for use by those studying for the Associate level examinations of the Institute of Legal Executives. The authors trust, however, that others too may find it of assistance and, dare one hope, of interest.

In recognition of the increased demand for legal services by a newly emergent class of individual or private law consumers, who in former times would have regarded the services of the legal office as being of little relevance to themselves or their families, the book affords separate treatment to that body of law which is of more relevance to the needs of the individual and that which is of greater significance to the commercial or industrial law consumer. For the term "law consumer" we are, of course, indebted to Llewellyn's *Bramble Bush*. We have sought to provide a comprehensive consideration of areas traditionally found in introductory legal texts. Thus a detailed account is given of criminal law, contract, tort and property. We have, however, also recognised the movement which has resulted in increased importance, at this level, of areas of law which were previously thought to be the concern of the specialist. These areas include labour law, consumer law, taxation and the law relating to individual freedoms.

To lighten the task of those coming into contact with law for the first time, no use has been made of footnotes or legal citations. A Table of Cases has, nevertheless, kindly been prepared by our publishers, who have also undertaken the burden of preparation of the index. We are indebted to them on each count. We should also like to acknowledge our indebtedness to our long-suffering wives and children who endured the preparation of the manuscript.

Students are particularly directed towards Sweet & Maxwell's *Students' Law Reporter* as a means of updating the book.

May 1982   L.A.R.
                                                                 I.A.T.
                                                                 M.G.W.

CONTENTS

TABLE OF CASES

TABLE OF STATUTES

xxi

UNIT ONE
THE GENERAL LEGAL ENVIRONMENT

In primitive societies, individuals living in a village community maintain relationships with their neighbours which fully recognise the extent to which the members of the community depend upon and relate to one another. An individual in such a community will assist a neighbour with his work, help him build his home and barter produce with him. The neighbours may spend their leisure time together and it is possible that, through marriage, they form part of a family group. In these circumstances, it is clear that it would be difficult to isolate the separate threads of their relationship for, in the eyes of the villagers, the relationship is meaningful only in its totality, based, as it is, upon respect, loyalty, trust and affection. (Social scientists refer to this kind of society as the *Gemeinschaft*.) In more advanced societies, individuals have wider horizons and enter into relationships with a greater variety of people. Like the villager in the more primitive society, they marry and form friendships which are based upon feelings of affection and respect, but, unlike the villager, they enter into many relationships which are more limited in the extent of their commitment. Thus, the individual may enter into a contract of employment and view his relationship with the employer solely in terms of contractual rights and obligations rather than in terms of the virtues of loyalty and co-operation which might develop if the parties to the contract did not interpret their responsibilities so narrowly. Similarly, the individual in a modern, complex, trading society will enter into contracts for the sale of goods or the provision of services which, to his mind, create a relationship which extends only so far as is provided for by the terms of the contract. (Social scientists recognise the role of contract in isolating aspects of human relationships and identify the society which emerges from such transactions as the *Gesellschaft*.) In the Gesellschaft the law must provide rules for a variety of single faceted relationships, for these relationships have significance only in law. The law must also, of course, maintain the sanctions which exist in any society to deter those who do not conform with the accepted norms of the society. Thus, the law makes provision for the punishment of those who steal from others, fight with others, cause damage to others or commit other "anti-social" acts.

The law may be seen to have a variety of aims and objectives in a developed society:
   (a) through the sanctions of criminal law it provides a framework of rules which determine, or recognise, "acceptable" patterns of behaviour within society;
   (b) it provides mechanisms by which the providers of the factors of production (land, labour and capital) can be encouraged to invest those factors for reward (rent, wages and interest);
   (c) through the concept of contract it encourages trade and commerce and facilitates their development on a vastly greater scale than would otherwise be possible;
   (d) it acknowledges that even in relationships based upon affection, (*e.g.* those between husband and wife or parent and child) there is a

1

need for clearly defined rights and obligations and provides for this need;

(e) it sets out the rules which determine the relationship between the citizen and the state and, in so doing, it provides for the limits of individual freedom;

(f) it provides a "safety valve" by which conflicts within society can be resolved within the existing social, economic and political structure. Its role is, thus, one of "system maintenance" for it preserves the existing order of things by resolving conflicts before they lead to revolutionary change.

The substantive areas of law which arise out of these aims and objectives will be considered in *Units Two* and *Three*. *Unit One* will focus not upon substantive areas, but rather upon the way in which rules become recognised as law, the categories into which they fall and the way in which English law has developed. Consideration will also be given to the processes by which conflicts in society are resolved and to the institutions involved. A picture will gradually emerge of the general legal environment which provides a base for the substantive areas of law set out in the later units. The extent to which this environment permeates the life of individuals within society will become manifest and these individuals will be seen to be in need of specialist advice and assistance in order that they can cope with the complexities of this significant, but intangible, feature of their general environment. This need has been identified as creating a market for legal services which ought to be as well developed, and as well provided for, as those for groceries or consumer durables. To appreciate the nature of this market, it is necessary to examine the nature of the suppliers of services to the "law consumer" and, that being so, the Unit will include a section which analyses the provision of legal services. The Unit is, thus, designed to describe and explain:

(a) the sources of English law;
(b) the classification of laws;
(c) the historical development of English law;
(d) the structure and composition of courts in England and Wales;
(e) other institutions and processes for the resolution of conflict; and
(f) the provision of legal services.

Part One

THE SOURCES OF ENGLISH LAW

There are, basically, three sources of English law:
- (a) the law which emerges from the parliamentary process (known as *statutory law*);
- (b) the law which emerges from bodies to whom legislative power has been delegated (known as *delegated legislation*);
- (c) the law which emerges from the law courts (known as *case law*).

Section A: Statutes and Statutory Interpretation

The United Kingdom is a *Parliamentary democracy* and statutes are passed by a process which does not require the consent of a majority of the citizens within the state (by, for example, a referendum), but rather the consent of the *Queen in Parliament* (*i.e.* the consent of the members of the House of Commons and the House of Lords and the assent of the Queen).

The great majority of Acts of Parliament are *public* Acts (*i.e.* sponsored by the government). Their initiation results from policy determinations made by the government of the day, which may, for example, wish to pass an Act to give a statutory right to council tenants to purchase their houses, to provide the police with greater powers, to require secret ballots before trade unions begin industrial action, or to protect consumers from "small print" in the agreements by which they purchase their goods. The task of preparing the *Bill* will be given to a parliamentary draftsman, a lawyer trained in the preparation of statutes. Once prepared, the Bill is then subject to a process which involves it passing through the House of Commons and then the House of Lords prior to its being presented to the Monarch for Royal Assent. If it passes through this process and receives the Royal Assent the Bill will have become an Act of Parliament. The process is set out in *diagram 1*.

Whilst the passing of an Act is the culmination of one process, the Parliamentary process, it is only the beginning of another, that of statutory interpretation (the process by which a meaning is attached to the Act).

Statutory interpretation: why is there a problem?

We have seen that most legislation is sponsored by the government. The Bill will have been initiated by a minister who would, no doubt, have been aware of his policy objectives and could, if asked, explain the purpose of the Act *as he intended it*. We have also seen that the Act will have been created by a Parliamentary draftsman who could, similarly, explain the meaning that *he* intended his words to have. However, neither the minister nor the draftsman were responsible for their Bill becoming law for the Bill became law only when it was passed by Parliament. Having secured this

Diagram 1

HOW A BILL BECOMES AN ACT

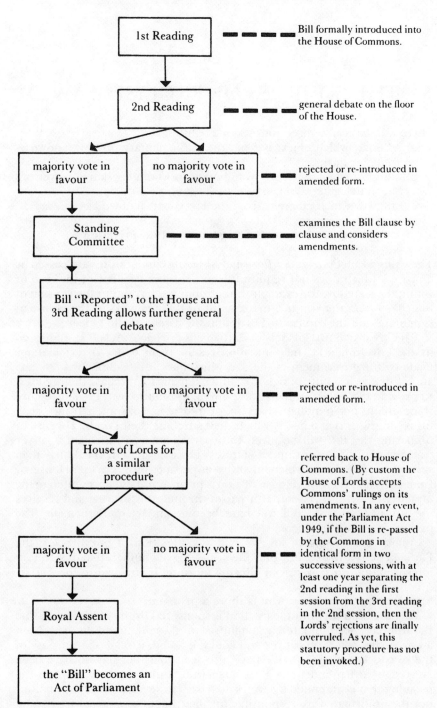

1st Reading	Bill formally introduced into the House of Commons.
2nd Reading	general debate on the floor of the House.
majority vote in favour / no majority vote in favour	rejected or re-introduced in amended form.
Standing Committee	examines the Bill clause by clause and considers amendments.
Bill "Reported" to the House and 3rd Reading allows further general debate	
majority vote in favour / no majority vote in favour	rejected or re-introduced in amended form.
House of Lords for a similar procedure	referred back to House of Commons. (By custom the House of Lords accepts Commons' rulings on its amendments. In any event, under the Parliament Act 1949, if the Bill is re-passed by the Commons in identical form in two successive sessions, with at least one year separating the 2nd reading in the first session from the 3rd reading in the 2nd session, then the Lords' rejections are finally overruled. As yet, this statutory procedure has not been invoked.)
majority vote in favour / no majority vote in favour	
Royal Assent	
the "Bill" becomes an Act of Parliament	

support, the Bill is, literally, *an Act of Parliament* or, in other words, a manifestation of the will of Parliament. As Parliament consists of over 600 members of the House of Commons, the members of the House of Lords and the Queen, there is no *one* person who can, with authority, state the nature of that will. The intention of Parliament, when passing the Act, is quite separate from the intention of any one person, or any group of persons, who supported the Bill in its passage through Parliament.

When seeking the meaning of a statutory provision, therefore, an individual judge cannot seek assistance from anyone within Parliament. Until a judge has indicated his view of the meaning of a statutory provision, other individuals (*e.g.* civil servants, policemen, lawyers or ordinary citizens) are, likewise, in a situation in which there is no "authority" to turn to. As a result any ambiguity in a statutory provision cannot be resolved in the certain knowledge that the outcome selected is the "correct" one.

The complexity of the task facing a court required to apply a statute, and thus determine the intention of Parliament, is revealed when one considers the problem which was presented to the court in *Hobson* v. *Gledhill*. After a series of incidents in which children had wandered onto building sites and had been mauled by unsupervised guard dogs, Parliament passed the Guard Dogs Act 1975. Section 1(1) of the Act provides that:

> "A person shall not use or permit the use of a guard dog at any premises unless a person ('the handler') who is capable of controlling the dog is present on the premises and the dog is under the control of the handler at all times while it is being so used except while it is secured so that it is not at liberty to go freely about the premises."

The parliamentary draftsman who drafted the sub-section would, when performing this task, be primarily concerned with avoiding doubt and ambiguity in relation to the offence created therein. He was not, however, successful and the court, in this case, was confronted with the inherent ambiguity in the section. A handler had chained a guard dog so that its range of movement was severely restricted and then left the dog to roam, unsupervised, on the premises. Had the handler committed an offence under the section? The answer to this question depended upon whether the words "*except while it is so secured that it is not at liberty to go freely about the premises*" applied to the sub-section as a whole. The sub-section was capable of being interpreted in either of two, conflicting, ways. The sub-section provided, on one interpretation (*alternative A*), that the offence was *not* committed if:

(i) the handler was present on the premises *and* was in control of the dog, or,

(ii) the handler was present on the premises *and* the dog was chained or otherwise secured.

The alternative interpretation (*alternative B*) would provide that there was *no* offence where:

(i) the handler was present on the premises *and* was in control of the dog, or,

(ii) the dog was chained or otherwise secured *whether or not the handler was present.*

The court, adopting *alternative B*, decided that if a dog was chained, or otherwise secured, there was no legal requirement for a handler to be present. The reason for this decision was not that the court considered *alternative B* to be the only logical interpretation, nor that the court considered it to be the "better" alternative, the court was, quite simply, persuaded that where a man stands accused of a criminal offence, any ambiguity in an Act of Parliament should be resolved in his favour. Cases such as this raise an obvious problem. How effective are Acts of Parliament as vehicles for implementing the wishes of Parliament? Is it not possible, bearing in mind the reason for passing the Guard Dogs Act 1975, that Parliament intended that a guard dog should *always* be accompanied by a handler, who was either in control of it or capable of controlling it should it break free of its chain or rope? As the law now stands, after *Hobson* v. *Gledhill*, a handler need not be present on premises if the dog is secured. Who has decided this, Parliament or the judiciary?

Identifying the "intention of Parliament": the "rules" of statutory interpretation

The courts have evolved so-called "rules" of interpretation to assist them in the task of determining the intention of Parliament. These rules are referred to as:

(1) the "literal" rule;
(2) the "golden" rule;
(3) the "mischief" rule.

The literal rule

This rule provides that if the words of a statute are clear they should be applied as they stand. The words should be given their strict literal meaning and sentences should be given their grammatical meaning. In *R.* v. *City of London Court Judge*, Lord Esher asserted that as long as there is no ambiguity words convey a clear meaning: only ambiguity makes words unclear. This proposition is, he maintained, unaffected by the fact that the words may result in absurdity:

> "If the words of an Act are clear, you must follow them, even though they lead to manifest absurdity. The court has nothing to do with the question whether the legislature has committed an absurdity. In my opinion the rule has always been this—if the words of an Act admit of two interpretations, then they are not clear; and if one interpretation leads to an absurdity and the other does not, the court will conclude that the legislature did not intend to lead to an absurdity, and will adopt the other interpretation."

In its starkest form, therefore, this rule is clear. If the words of a statutory provision are not ambiguous they must be applied in accordance with their ordinary and natural meaning, *whatever the outcome*. The rationale of this rule is that the best way to discover the intention of Parliament is to look at what it has said in the Act it has passed: "The intention of Parliament is not to be judged by what is in its mind, but by its expression of that mind in that statute itself" (*per* Lord Thankerton in *Wicks* v. *D.P.P.*). An example of this approach can be found in the decision in *R.* v. *Vaccari*. Section 157(1) of the Bankruptcy Act 1914 provided that any adjudged bankrupt would be guilty of a criminal offence if, at the time of the receiving order, he had "debts contracted in the course and for the furtherance of trade or business" and had contributed to his insolvency by gambling. The accused, who had gambled, owed the Inland Revenue arrears of tax amounting to £7,000. He could not pay this sum. He was charged with an offence under section 157(1), but was acquitted on the grounds that whilst his gambling had certainly contributed towards his insolvency, his debt arose out of his statutory obligation to pay tax and was not a debt "*contracted* in the course and for the furtherance of trade or business."

The golden rule

Sometimes an application of the literal rule will result in an absurd result. Section 57 of the Offences Against the Person Act 1861, for example, provides that, "whosoever being married shall marry another person during the life of the former husband or wife" is guilty of bigamy. A literal interpretation of the section would result in the conclusion that nobody could ever commit bigamy, for if a person is married it is impossible for him to *marry* another. All that a married person can do is to *purport* to marry another, the second "marriage" is totally invalid. In *R.* v. *Allen* the court applied the golden rule and interpreted the section so that it read, "whosoever being married shall *go through a ceremony of marriage* with another during the life of the former husband or wife" is guilty of bigamy. Clearly this approach can be justified, for the courts are, allegedly, attempting to discover the intention of Parliament. An application of the literal rule in *R.* v. *Allen* would have been tantamount to a finding that Parliament enacted a section of an Act which had no meaning at all.

A clear statement of the principles underlying the golden rule is provided by Baron Parke in *Becke* v. *Smith*:

"It is a very useful rule in the construction of a statute to adhere to the ordinary meaning of the words used, and to the grammatical construction, unless that is at variance with the intention of the legislature to be collected from the statute itself, or leads to any manifest absurdity or repugnance, in which case the language may be varied or modified so as to avoid such inconvenience, but no further."

This approach appears, at first sight, to be incompatible with that advocated by Lord Esher in *R.* v. *City of London Court Judge* and may very well be at variance with the literal rule. The two approaches are not, however, necessarily irreconcilable. If one interprets the word "absurdity" so as to relate it to a curious or undesirable outcome of the application of the statutory rule which clearly results from interpretation, then the approaches are at odds, for a hard literal approach would lead to the conclusion that such an outcome is irrelevant to the construction of the statute, whilst the golden rule would acknowledge that the outcome was a vital factor to be taken into consideration. If, however, "absurdity" is taken to relate rather to the outcome of the attempted interpretation of the statute and is confined to the structural, grammatical, exercise, then the approaches are not incompatible. Thus, the decision in *R.* v. *Allen* that the wording of section 57 of the Offences Against the Person Act 1861 could not be applied literally without absurdity, can be seen to relate to the interpretation of the section rather than to the outcome of the particular case before the court. The fact that the accused would, upon a literal interpretation of the section, have been acquitted of bigamy was not the absurd outcome. The absurdity was rather contained in the conclusion, inherent in a literal approach to the section, that Parliament had taken the trouble to give legislative effect to words which had absolutely no legal impact.

Thus, it may be that the literal and golden rules together provide that:

(a)   if the words of a section are clear and provide an outcome to the case before the court, those words must be applied and that outcome adopted even though it is thought to be "peculiar" or "unfair";

(b)   if the words, whilst clear, lead to an outcome which is, equally clearly, *not* the intention of Parliament (as in *R.* v. *Allen*), then the words must be varied, but only to the extent that is necessary to provide the outcome that Parliament must be taken to have anticipated.

The mischief rule

According to this rule of interpretation, the intention of Parliament is best ascertained by reference to the problem, or mischief, that induced the legislation. Discover the mischief, it is argued, and one has discovered what Parliament intended to do in the Act, which can then be interpreted appropriately. In *Smith* v. *Hughes*, the court was called upon to consider section 1(1) of the Street Offences Act 1959, which made it an offence for a prostitute to solicit men "in a street or public place." The accused prostitute had tapped on a balcony railing and "hissed" at men as they passed below. Had she committed an offence under the section? Lord Chief Justice Parker referred to the mischief and found the prostitute guilty:

"I approach the matter by considering what is the mischief aimed at by this Act. Everybody knows that this was an Act intended to clean up the streets, to enable people to walk along the streets without being molested or solicited by common prostitutes. Viewed in that way, it can matter little whether the prostitute is soliciting while in the street or standing in a doorway or on a balcony."

Many consider the mischief rule to be the most satisfactory approach to the problem of statutory interpretation. The *21st Report of the Law Commission*, for example, asserted that the mischief rule provided a "somewhat more satisfactory approach to the interpretation of statutes" than the literal rule, for, in the opinion of the Law Commission, "to place undue reliance on the literal meaning of the words of a provision is to assume an unattainable perfection in draftsmanship . . . such an approach ignores the limitations of language." Some observers of the judiciary would, however, point to the flexibility this rule gives to judges, for it leaves them free to identify the mischief which will support the interpretation they wish to advance. The mischief of the Guard Dogs Act 1975, for example, could either be:

(a)   the fact that guard dogs were left without *supervision*, which would advance the interpretation set out in *alternative A* (see page 5);

(b)   the fact that guard dogs were left in a situation in which they were not *controlled*, which would advance the interpretation set out in *alternative B*.

By a sophisticated approach to the "ascertainment" of the mischief, it is argued, the judge can deviate from the true intention of Parliament.

The relationship between the rules

It has been argued that the "rules" of interpretation are not rules in a strict sense. A judge can, it is said, adopt whichever "rule" he considers suitable and there is no rule to tell him which "rule" he should use in any given situation. It is argued that it is this flexibility which gives the judiciary an opportunity to influence the effect of legislation. In an article entitled "Statutory Interpretation in a Nutshell" (*Canadian Bar Review* 1938), Professor J. Willis asserted that a court will invoke "whichever of the rules produces a result which satisfies its sense of justice in the case before it."

The modern approach, however, is to accept that whilst judges have discretion when interpreting statutes, there is only a limited discretion. The following speeches by Lord Reid sum up this approach:

(a) "In determining the meaning of any word or phrase in a statute the first question to ask always is what is the natural or ordinary meaning of that word or phrase in its context in the statute. It is only when that meaning leads to some result which cannot reasonably be supposed to have been the interpretation of the legislature that it is proper to look for some other possible meaning of the word or phrase" (*Pinner* v. *Everett*).

(b) "Then (*i.e.* where there is doubt) rules of construction are relied on. They are not rules in the ordinary sense of having some binding force. They are our servants, not our masters. They are aids to construction, presumptions or pointers. Not infrequently one "rule' points in one direction, another in a different direction. In each case we must look at all relevant circumstances and decide as a matter of judgment what weight to attach to any particular "rule' " (*Maunsell* v. *Olins*).

(c) "It is a cardinal principle applicable to all kinds of statutes that you may not for any reason attach to a statutory provision a meaning which the words of that provision cannot reasonably bear. If they are capable of more than one meaning, then you can choose between those meanings, but beyond that you must not go" (*Jones* v. *D.P.P.*).

Taking these three statements together, the modern approach is:
  (1) that the ordinary (literal) meaning of the statute must be adhered to, *unless* it is clear that to do so would not result in the advancement of that which Parliament intended;
  (2) that where the literal approach is not appropriate other rules may be applied *but only to the extent* that they result in an outcome *which can be supported by the words of the statute.*

Identifying the "intention of Parliament": seeking assistance from rules of language

When interpreting statutes the courts will apply ordinary rules of communication.

Noscitur a sociis . . . the maxim noscitur a sociis ("a thing is known by its companions") is a reminder to the courts that words must be interpreted in context. In *Pengelly* v. *Bell Punch Co. Ltd.* the court was called upon to apply section 28(1) of the Factories Act 1961, which provided that all "floors, steps, stairs, passages and gangways" had to be kept free of obstruction. Did the section apply to parts of a factory floor used for storage? The court held that it did not, for the words "steps, stairs, passages and gangways" all related to parts of the factory along which workmen were intended to pass. A more bizarre illustration of this principle was provided in *R.* v. *Ann Harris*. In that case Ann Harris was charged with a statutory offence as a result of her having bitten off the end of a prostitute's nose. The statute provided that the offence was committed by a person who had "stabbed, cut or wounded another." Had Ann Harris wounded the prostitute? The court decided that she had not, for the words "stabbed" and "cut" implied the use of an implement and, by implication, the word "wound" carried a similar requirement. (The court may have arrived at this conclusion mechanically, as a result of the application of the *noscitur a sociis* principle, but one suspects this was not so. The case was determined in 1836 and one may wonder whether it would have been similarly determined, in that era, if the prostitute had bitten off the end of Ann Harris' nose.)

Ejusdem generis ... where a list of specific items forming a category is followed by a general concluding clause, this general clause is taken to refer only to things of the same kind as those specified. This rule is based on a commonsense communications rule. If a mother asks her child to run to the corner shop and buy "a large cut white loaf, a large uncut white loaf, a small cut brown loaf or *anything else*," she would be far from pleased if the child brought back a tin of peaches. She has, indeed, instructed the child to buy "anything else," but this general phrase has been preceded by specific examples and must take colour from them. The *ejusdem generis* rule was applied in *Powell* v. *Kempton Park Racecourse Co.* Section 1 of the Betting Act 1853 prohibited the keeping of a "house, office, room or other place" for the purposes of betting. Did section 1 apply to Tattersall's ring at a racecourse? The House of Lords held that it did not, for the specific examples given in the section were all *indoor* places and the phrase "or other place" had to be interpreted in that light. In *R.* v. *Payne*, a person who took a crowbar into a prison with a view to passing it to a prisoner, was charged under a statute which made it an offence to "convey into a prison, with intent to facilitate the escape of any prisoner any mask, dress or other disguise, or any letter, or any other article." It was argued that he was not guilty for, interpreted *ejusdem generis*, the words "*or any other article*" did not include a crowbar. This argument was rejected, for the specific words not creating a clearly defined category, the *ejusdem generis* rule did not apply and the words "*or any article*" were unrestricted. The outcome might have been different but for the inclusion within the statute of the words "or any letter."

It would appear that the *ejusdem generis rule* must give way to an interpretation which clearly advances the mischief of a statutory provision. In *Skinner* v. *Shew* the court considered section 32 of the Patents, Designs and Trademarks Act 1883 which granted a right to an injunction against the continuation of *unjustified* threats of legal proceedings relating to patent rights. The Act stipulated that the right to an injunction existed, in certain circumstances, "where any person claiming to be a patentee of any invention, *by circulars, advertisements or otherwise* threatens any other person with any legal proceedings." Did the section grant a right to an injunction where a threat was made *by letter*? There were two conflicting approaches:

(*a*)   interpreted *ejusdem generis,* the words "or otherwise" clearly related to written material which was intended to reach a wide, public, audience (and, therefore, not to letters);

(*b*)   the mischief of the Act was the use of threats by those who knew they would not succeed in any legal action against the person threatened. The letter clearly fell within this mischief.

The court adopted a mischief approach to the section. Bowen L.J. asserted, in relation to the conflict between the two principles of interpretation:

"But there is an exception to that rule (*i.e. ejusdem generis*), if it be a rule and not a maxim of common sense, which is that although the words immediately around and before the general words are words which are prima facie confined, yet if you can see from a wider inspection of the scope of the legislation that the general words notwithstanding that they follow particular words, are nevertheless to be construed generally, you must give effect to the intention of the legislature as gathered from the entire section."

Expressio unius . . . it is a common sense rule of communication that "*expressio unius est exclusio alterius*" (*i.e.* that express reference to one thing excludes other things which are not similarly referred to). Thus, where a statute referred to "lands, houses and coalmines, it was held that mines other than coalmines were not covered by the statute and did not fall within the general term "lands" (*R. v. Sedgley Inhabitants*). Sometimes, however, the express reference to one thing is a reflection of Parliament's desire to make it certain that the thing is included within the provision, rather than any wish to exclude other things. Thus, section 14 of the Rent and Mortgages Interest (Restriction) Act 1920 provided that where a tenant had paid excess rent he could recover that rent from the landlord *or his personal representative* (*i.e.* the person who administers the landlord's estate upon his death). It was argued that, *expressio unius,* there was no right of recovery granted to the personal representative of the tenant. Jenkins L.J. said, in *Dean v. Wiesengrund*:

"The argument for the landlord is summed up in the *maxim expressio unius est exclusio alterius* which, applied to the present case, is said to compel the conclusion that the express reference to the legal personal representative of one of the parties excludes any implied reference to the legal personal representative of the other. But this maxim is after all no more than an aid to construction and has little, if any, weight where it is possible to account for the *inclusio unius* on grounds other than an intention to effect the *exclusio alterius*."

Section B: Delegated Legislation

Parliament is, according to constitutional theory, legislatively supreme. This means that Parliament may legislate on any matter and is the only body with this legislative power. Often, however, Parliament delegates its law-making powers to other agencies who may then make *delegated* or *subordinate* legislation. It is increasingly common for Parliament to debate and enact "skeleton" provisions which are to be "filled out" by government departments. The reasons for this are as follows:

(a) Parliament lacks expertise in technical areas and is not able readily to legislate for matters of detail. Parliament is, however, recognised as an excellent forum for debate and it best uses the time available to it by debating the principles involved in legislative proposals and delegating to a department the task of preparing *statutory instruments* which contain detailed provisions. (The Act that Parliament passes is called an *enabling* Act, for it is the provisions of this Act which permit, or enable, the government department to make rules which have the force of law. The Act may also be referred to as the *parent* Act).

(b) Regulations relating to detailed, technical, matters are often such as to require constant amendment. It is easier to amend, or withdraw, statutory instruments than it is similarly to alter the effect of Parliamentary, or *primary*, legislation.

(c) Often, the state needs to respond quickly and effectively to an emergency situation. Parliamentary procedures are not appropriate in such circumstances and a more efficient response can often be provided for, in advance of the emergency, by Parliament granting law-making powers to the body it wishes to deal with certain contingencies. Thus, for example, a government department may be given statutory power to make regulations dealing with the closure of farms and the disposal of infected animals in the event of an outbreak of foot and mouth disease.

Ministers and government departments are not the only bodies capable of making delegated legislation. Local authorities may make *bye-laws* and the Privy Council may make *Orders in Council*. During the 1939–45 war, for example, vast powers were conferred upon the Privy Council by the Emergency Powers (Defence) Act 1939, and, as a result, the government of the day was given power to deal speedily with problems of the utmost urgency.

The ability to bypass Parliament in an emergency situation, or whenever speed is important, is, no doubt, a considerable advantage. It is, however, also a source of concern. The doctrine of *separation of powers* identifies three functions of government, the *legislative* function, the *executive* (or administrative) function and the *judicial* function: the doctrine provides that where one branch of government exercises not only its own function but also that of another branch, then arbitrary government is likely to result. Where a government department, or a local authority, possesses delegated power to make law this potential for abuse obviously exists. Moreover, the powers vested in the administration are wide-ranging and clearly capable of causing serious distress to the individual. Thus, for example, non-elected local authority employees can draft a compulsory purchase order which may result in a person having to sell his home to the local authority against his wishes. The existence of executive legislation was stigmatised by Lord Chief Justice Hewart as an aspect of "The New Despotism" and has resulted in the development of Parliamentary and judicial safeguards which form that area lawyers now identify as "administrative law."

Since the accession of Britain to the European Communities, we are now subject to *regulations, directives, decisions and recommendations* flowing from the *Council of Ministers* and the *European Commission*. Article 189 of the Treaty of Rome provides that " . . . a regulation shall have general application. It shall be binding in its entirety and directly applicable in all member states." Regulations are quite clearly part of our body of law. Article 189 also provides that a directive is " . . . binding as to the result to be achieved, upon each member state to whom it is addressed, but shall leave to the national authorities the choice of the form and methods." As a result, a directive binds the British government, which has discretion only in relation to the manner in which it implements the directive. The existence of this body of "community law" appears to directly contradict the doctrine of *Parliamentary Supremacy*, by which Parliament is recognised as being legislatively supreme. One possible approach to this apparent conflict is contained in the proposition that Parliament, when passing the European Communities Act 1972 to give municipal effect to the Treaty of Accession to the Communities, provided for yet another source of delegated legislation and that European regulations should be viewed in this light. By passing another Act of Parliament, it is argued, Parliament could rescind the authority it has given to the European agencies and invalidate the effect of their rules. (The existence of directives poses fewer problems to the advocates of Parliamentary Supremacy, for directives are only given municipal force by legislation passed by Parliament.)

Section C: Case Law

When an English judge hears a case he does two things:
  (a) he determines the issue before him when, for example, he awards damages to the plaintiff in a civil action;
  (b) he states a principle of law, when he states his reasons for awarding damages to the plaintiff.

The determination of the issue before him is obviously the most important matter for the parties to the dispute and, for them, the determination of the case renders the matter *res judicata*. This means that the issue cannot be reopened in any further legal proceedings. The decision of the judge may be appealed against but once any appeal has been determined, or the time for lodging an appeal has passed, the issue is settled once and for all.

   To a lawyer, the determination of the issue is of little direct interest, for him the most important aspect of the case is the judge's reasoning, for this reasoning creates a legal principle which is, within certain limits, *binding* on later judges hearing similar cases. The system by which one decision stands as a precedent for later courts is known as the system of *stare decisis* (the decision stands) and the principle of law which emerges from the case is known as the *ratio decidendi* of the case. The consideration of a hypothetical example may help to illustrate the nature of the *ratio decidendi*. Let us assume that A, a workman at a factory owned by B, is ordered to perform a welding task by C, the foreman, and is not supplied with goggles. He begins the task, but loses the sight of one eye as a result of a spark damaging it. He sues B for damages. Let us further suppose that there is no existing case or statute on the point to assist the judge. The judge cannot say that there is no answer to the problem, for the law *must* have an answer, either B is liable to A in this situation or he is not. The judge decides that, in these circumstances, B is liable to A. What has he decided for the future? The answer to this question is to be found in establishing the *ratio decidendi* of the case. Obviously in any future case a worker required to do welding work without goggles by his foreman can sue his employer if he is injured. The injured worker's advocate would simply cite *A* v. *B* as authority for the proposition that his client should succeed. Can we extend this principle further? Would a crafts teacher in school be able to cite *A* v. *B* as authority for the proposition that he should be able to obtain damages against the local authority which employs him if he were to be injured as a result of his headmaster having instructed him to use machinery which was not adequately fenced? Yes, if the court hearing the teacher's claim could be convinced that the *ratio decidendi* of *A* v. *B* was wide enough to cover a claim by any employee who has been instructed, by someone in authority over him, to perform a task which is unnecessarily dangerous. How far can the principle of a case be extended? The answer may be that a principle can be extended as far as the judge in the subsequent case will allow it to be. A judge can thus restrict a precedent he does not approve of by refusing to extend the principle of the case beyond the particular facts of that case. He can, conversely, advance a precedent he does approve of, by allowing an extension of the principle.

Sometimes, in the course of his judgment, a judge may make comments "by the way." Such comments are *obiter dicta* and have no binding authority. A comment is an *obiter dictum* when it has not affected the outcome of the case. In *Rondel* v. *Worsley*, for example, the House of Lords was called upon to determine whether a barrister could be liable in Negligence as a result of his careless handling of a case. The House of Lords asserted that a barrister could not be sued in Negligence for work undertaken as an advocate and also expressed the view that a solicitor would be similarly immune if he was involved in advocacy. The comments made by the House of Lords in relation to solicitors are clearly *obiter*, for the outcome of *Rondel* v. *Worsley* would not have been different if the House had not expressed that view. To say that the remarks are *obiter* is not to deprive them of any influence. Such remarks are not, strictly speaking, *binding* on later courts, but they can be highly *persuasive*. *Obiter dicta* of appellate courts, particularly the House of Lords, are treated with great respect and, in most circumstances, would be followed by a judge in an appropriate case.

The binding force of a precedent depends upon the status of the court which made it. As a general principle a court is only bound by a precedent of another court if that other court has superior status.

The hierarchy of courts

(a) *The House of Lords* (The Judicial Committee of the House of Lords)... is the court at the top of the hierarchy and it binds all other courts by its decisions. It is not, however, bound by its own decisions.

(b) *The Civil Division of the Court of Appeal*... precedents of the Civil Division of the Court of Appeal are binding on all inferior courts. In *Young* v. *Bristol Aeroplane Co.* it was established that the Civil Division is bound by its *own* previous decisions. Prior to his retirement Lord Denning M.R. (Master of the Rolls), the most senior judge in the court, constantly attempted to alter this situation and to free the Civil Division from what he considered to be "a self imposed limitation." His campaign has, however, been described by Lord Diplock as a "one man crusade" and he was unable to persuade other members of the court that this was either desirable or possible.

(c) *The Criminal Division of the Court of Appeal*... precedents of the Criminal Division are binding on all inferior courts (including the Divisional Court of the Queen's Bench Division—see page 37). The court will usually follow its own decisions and those of the Civil Division. It is not, however *bound* by its own previous decisions where to do so would cause injustice to the appellant (who may well be languishing in prison).

[Why is the Civil Division of the Court of Appeal bound by its own precedents whilst the Criminal Division is not? The answer lies in an appreciation of the different objectives of civil and criminal law (see page 21). That the accused be treated fairly is vital in the area of criminal law, where a man's freedom can be taken away from him. This factor may not be so significant in civil law. The prime objective in this area is to provide a framework by which persons can regulate their affairs and it would be a poor framework indeed if a particular court could frequently alter it, thus throwing into disarray contracts which had been settled and trusts established on the basis of existing precedents.]

(d) *Divisional Courts of the High Court* (see page 34) ... such courts are bound by decisions of the House of Lords and Court of Appeal. In *civil* cases divisional courts are also bound by their own previous decisions. The Divisional Court of the Queens's Bench Division (which hears criminal cases) will follow its own decisions unless it considers that to do so would unjustly affect the appellant and, thus, is in a similar position to the Criminal Division of the Court of Appeal.

(e) *Judges of the High Court sitting at first instance* ... these trial judges are bound by decisions of the House of Lords and Court of Appeal. They are also bound, in civil cases, by a decision of the divisional court of *their division*. High Court judges bind inferior courts (*e.g.* county courts) but not other High Court judges. A High Court judge would, however, normally follow a decision made by another.

(f) *Magistrates' Courts and County Courts* ... these courts are bound by all courts above them in the hierarchy, but their own decisions are not binding.

(g) *The European Court of Justice* ... is not bound by its previous decisions but it will, in order to achieve consistency, follow them wherever possible. In all matters of community law the courts of the United Kingdom *must* defer to any relevant decision of the European Court of Justice (section 53(1) of the European Communities Act 1972).

It should be noted that whilst a precedent is only binding on *inferior* courts, the decision of *any* court may influence another, even though that other court has superior status. Thus, Court of Appeal decisions may influence the House of Lords.

Avoiding a precedent

A judge is only bound by a precedent if his case is *similar* to the one he is being urged to follow. A judge who does not wish to follow a precedent may *distinguish* it by pointing to a difference in the material facts (*i.e.* the facts that matter). If we revisit the hypothetical example set out on page 13 we could appreciate that *A* v. *B* could be distinguished in a subsequent case in which a worker had performed welding work, not at the request of his foreman, but as a favour to a workmate who had failed to hand over goggles which were available. A judge who does not wish to follow a precedent should, usually, be able to point to some difference in the facts of the case before him. The only limitation on this process would seem to be the judge's own inhibitions, for judges would not wish to be seen to be making meaningless distinctions.

Where there are conflicting decisions of courts of *equal* status, a judge in an inferior court may choose which precedent he wishes to follow.

(There cannot, of course, be conflicting decisions of courts of *unequal* status, for the decision of the superior court would always prevail).

A judge may refuse to follow a decision on the grounds that it was made *per incuriam*, or mistakenly, in that the court which made the decision overlooked a statutory provision or a precedent by which it was bound. Thus, in *R.* v. *Northumberland Compensation Appeal Tribunal, ex p. Shaw*, a Divisional Court of the King's Bench Division declined to follow a Court of Appeal decision on the grounds that the Court of Appeal had, when arriving at its decision, overlooked a precedent of the House of Lords.

A judge of a superior court can always *overrule* the decision of an inferior court and an appellate judge can *reverse* the decision. What is the difference between overruling and reversing a precedent? None, so far as the doctrine of precedent is concerned, the difference lies in the effect upon the parties. Thus:

(1) In *X* v. *Y* a decision is made in favour of X. Y pays X damages. Twenty years later in *P* v. *Q* a superior court overrules the precedent established in *X* v. *Y*. Result:
  (a) *X* v. *Y* is no longer good law, it has been replaced by *P.* v. *Q.*
  (b) X does not need to repay to Y the damages he recovered, for as between X and Y the matter is *res judicata*.

(2) In *X* v. *Y* a decision is made in favour of X. Y is ordered to pay X damages. Y appeals and the appellate court reverses the decision made at first instance. Result:
  (a) *X* v. *Y* is no longer good law, it has now been replaced by *Y* v. *X*
  (b) X will not now receive damages from Y.

Codification

The Law Commission has stated that the object of a code is to set out, in a statute, all of the law relating to a given area. On the continent all areas of law have been codified (*e.g.* the *Code Napoleon*). There has been no such general codification, in England, though various branches of the law have been codified (*e.g.* Bills of Exchange Act 1882, Theft Act 1968, Sale of Goods Act 1979, Forgery and Counterfeiting Act 1981).

When our system of case-law is considered, its advantages and disadvantages are usually gauged by reference to codified systems of law.

Advantages and disadvantages of the doctrine of precedent

It has been suggested that the advantages of the system of precedent are:
  (a) certainty;
  (b) flexibility and aptitude for growth;
  (c) greater detail than is possible in a codified system; and
  (d) practicability.

(a) *Certainty* . . . "It provides at least some degree of certainty upon which individuals can rely in the conduct of their affairs, as well as the basis for an orderly development of legal rules" (House of Lords *Practice Statement 1966*, see page 18). American research has, however, shown the limitations of this argument. R. C. Lawlor attempted, with the aid of a computer, to forecast the decision of the U.S. Supreme Court in a civil rights case. He programmed the computer with data relating to the relevant precedents and he also fed in data relating to the attitudes of the judges who were to hear the case. He then made two predictions of the outcome of the case, one based on the precedents, one based on the personal information. His second prediction was more successful than his first.

(b) *Flexibility*... the doctrine of precedent permits some degree of flexibility. A judge in an inferior court can distinguish an unpopular precedent and a judge in a superior court can overrule it.

Some academic writers would assert that it is not possible for case law to lead to certainty *and* flexibility.

(c) *Detail*... there are approximately 400,000 decided cases and, it is argued, the wealth of detail contained therein cannot be rivalled by any code.

(d) *Practicability*... it is more convenient to follow a precedent than argue each point on its merits every time it arises. Why, lawyers would ask, should it be constantly necessary to "invent the wheel"?

The disadvantages of the system of precedent are commonly thought to be:

(*a*) rigidity;
(*b*) over-subtlety; and
(*c*) bulk and complexity.

These disadvantages are, of course, the "mirror image" of the advantages.

(a) *Rigidity*... it is argued that an English judge has little discretion when determining cases. In *Olympia Oil Cake Co.* v. *Produce Brokers Co. Ltd.*, for example, Lord Justice Phillimore, when following a decision of the Court of Appeal, stated, "With reluctance, I might almost say sorrow, I concur in the view that this appeal must be dismissed. I trust the case will proceed to the House of Lords." Such a situation led Professor Geldhart to conclude that "the English judge is a slave to the past and a despot for the future."

(b) *Over-subtlety*... over-technical distinctions often arise as a result of judges finding differences between the case they are determining and others they are being asked to follow. The practice of distinguishing precedents also leads to a great deal of *uncertainty*.

(c) *Bulk and complexity*... there is no index to all the precedents contained in our law reports. Precedents are discovered by trial and error. When discovered they often reveal other precedents. As a result of this "snowballing" effect a court can be faced with a great many precedents which it has to follow or distinguish.

Because of the disadvantages of precedent, critics argue that English law should be codified. A codification would, however, leave the problem of whether precedents of interpretation would be binding. Would a judge be bound by an interpretation of the code made by a judge in a superior court?

The judiciary and law reform

Case-law has always been subject to constant review by the judiciary. A decision may be overruled by a judge of appropriate status and unpopular, isolated, decisions are, in practice, ignored by the judiciary or distinguished and restricted until, eventually, the ratio is limited to the particular facts of the case. Prior to 1966, however, there was one serious impediment to such review. If a principle came from a decision of the House of Lords it could only be distinguished, it could not be overruled, for a decision of the House of Lords could not be overruled by a court of inferior status and the House itself was bound by its own decisions. A decision of the House could thus only be altered by statute. In 1966, however, a *Practice Statement* by the Lord Chancellor indicated that the House of Lords would, in appropriate cases, refuse to follow an earlier decision. Since that time, it has been possible for the judiciary to change any precedent. The House of Lords has shown itself to be willing to apply the *Practice Statement* and depart from its own precedents. In *R. v. Shivpuri*, for example, it overruled its decision in *Anderton* v. *Ryan* made only one year previously. Lord Bridge, who made speeches in each case, made no apology for his change of mind and stated that "the *Practice Statement* is an effective abandonment of our pretension to infallibility." He pointed to the fact that if the House discovers that its earlier decision has "distorted" the law then "the sooner it is corrected the better." Potentially, therefore, the common law provides an inbuilt agency of law reform where outmoded legal principles emerge from cases.

An example of the exercise of this potential may be found in the attitude of the courts towards the liability of an occupier of land to child trespassers. In *Addie & Sons* v. *Dumbreck* (1929) the House of Lords refused to give judgment in favour of a four-year-old trespasser who had been crushed by machinery belonging to the defendants, despite the fact that servants of the defendants were aware that children often played near to the machinery. The House refused to find for the plaintiff, simply because he was a trespasser, taking the view that the only duty owed by an occupier of land to such a trespasser was a humanitarian duty not to act recklessly with regard to children known to be on the premises. This case represented the law in 1957 when Parliament passed the Occupiers' Liability Act. Whilst imposing upon an occupier a common duty of care to his *lawful* visitors, Parliament did *not* take the opportunity of altering the law relating to trespassers and *Addie's* case survived the Act. Despite the fact that Parliament had apparently preserved the common law rule, the House of Lords in *British Railways Board* v. *Herrington* (1972) abandoned the principle in *Addie's* case and gave judgment in favour of a child injured whilst trespassing on property belonging to the Board, even though the child was not known to be present when the injury occurred. Fully aware that "there might be some force in an argument that for this House to depart from *Addie's* case would, in effect, be to legislate where Parliament has abstained," Lord Wilberforce nevertheless asserted that "the common law is a developing entity as the *judges* develop it, and so long as we follow the well-tried method of moving forward in accordance with principle as fresh facts emerge and changes in society occur we are surely doing what Parliament intends we should do." Support for the view that this particular application of principle was, indeed, an act which would secure the approval of Parliament was provided in 1984 when Parliament enacted the Occupiers' Liability Act of that year and adopted the framework established by *Herrington*.

The approach of the House of Lords in *Herrington's* case has, however, been criticised. Professor P. S. Atiyah points to the way in which the House took it upon itself to speculate as to Parliament's intention in 1957 in *not* legislating for liability to trespassers and questions the constitutional propriety of so doing. Lord Reid, for example, had expressed the view that Parliament's "pointed" omission to alter the rule established in *Addie's* case revealed an intention to affirm that rule, but then conceded that it was "just possible" that Parliament had been unable to make up its mind in relation to this issue. Atiyah asserts that there is a variety of reasons for Parliament not changing a common law rule (lack of parliamentary time, lack of ministerial energy, lack of agreement as to the alternatives, satisfaction with the existing law) and concludes that it is a "constitutional mistake to ask the question at all." He is equally critical of the decision of the House of Lords in *La Pintada*, in 1984, to refuse to depart from the common law rule that interest is not generally payable on an overdue debt on the basis that Parliament had failed to enact legislation giving effect to the Law Commission's recommendations relating to the issue. Again, he warns it is "quite wrong to treat the failure of Parliament to pass a Bill as though it were an actual enactment to the opposite effect."

Reform by the judiciary can provide an effective method of keeping case-law abreast of changes in society, but it hardly seems fair that a litigant should have to bear the cost of bringing a case to court, and possibly taking it as far as the House of Lords, in the hope that an outmoded principle will be changed by a basically conservative judiciary. There has, therefore, been a demand for a more systematic process of law reform.

Law reform agencies

In 1952 the *Law Reform Committee* was appointed "to consider, having regard especially to *judicial decisions*, what changes are desirable in such legal doctrines as the Lord Chancellor may from time to time refer to the Committee." Since 1952 the Committee has produced many reports, most of which have been implemented by legislation. The report of the Committee on *Innocent Misrepresentation* led, for example, to the Misrepresentation Act 1967. It may be noted, however, that in its report on *Occupiers' liabilty to invitees, licensees and trespassers* (1954) the Law Reform Committee recommended that the law governing liability to trespassers should *not* be altered (see above), which recommendation may be considered to have been accepted by Parliament, but not by the judiciary. (See, however, Professor Atiyah's view set out above).

In 1959, the *Criminal Law Revision Committee* was established "to examine such aspects of the criminal law of England and Wales as the Home Secretary may from time to time refer to the Committee to consider whether the law requires revision and to make recommendations." Probably the most important report prepared by the Committee was that on *Theft and related Offences* (1966) which was largely implemented by the Theft Act 1968.

Most important of all the permanent agencies of law reform is the *Law Commission*, established by the Law Commissions Act 1965. Section 3(1) of the Act provides that the Commission should "keep under review *all the law* . . . with a view to its systematic development and reform, including in particular the *codification* of such law, the elimination of anomalies, the repeal of obsolete and unnecessary enactments, the reduction of the number of separate enactments and generally the simplification and modernisation of the law." The existence of such a body is absolutely vital if any extensive programme of codification is anticipated. One of the greatest drawbacks to codification is that the code tends to be "frozen" in the economic and social climate prevailing at the time of its enactment. A "review body" is essential and in this role the Law Commission has already been responsible for a major amendment to one code, the Sale of Goods

Act. The Act, which implied terms relating to the quality and identity of goods into contracts for their purchase, was passed in 1894 and thus emerged from the laissez-faire attitude prevailing in Victorian England. Inherent in the philosophy was the idea that contracting parties should be free to agree on the terms of their agreement, even though one of the parties might be foolish in agreeing to the terms proposed. There was, therefore, provision in the Act for the parties to exclude the operation of the very terms implied by the Act. Such a notion may well have seemed appropriate in the nineteenth century when most of the cases determined by reference to the Act concerned contracts entered into by businessmen, but it became increasingly inappropriate during the twentieth century. Consumers purchasing motor cars and other expensive items would, invariably, be invited to sign a standard form of contract with "fine print." As most suppliers inserted the same terms into their contracts the consumer was faced with a "take it or leave it" situation. Few consumers would appreciate the significance of a term excluding liability for "all conditions or warranties implied by common law or by statute." Consumers signing such agreements were bound by them and lost the protection of the terms implied by the Sale of Goods Act, but it was not realistic to maintain that there had been real agreement to this. In 1969 the Law Commission reported on exclusion clauses in contracts and, as a result, the Supply of Goods (Implied Terms) Act 1973 was passed, an Act which, amongst other provisions, made it impossible to exclude the modified implied terms of the Sale of Goods Act in a "consumer sale." (The Unfair Contract Terms Act 1977 and the Sale of Goods Act 1979 have, largely, adopted these provisions).

Other Acts of Parliament passed as a result of Law Commission reports include the Animals Act 1971, the Criminal Damage Act 1971, the Defective Premises Act 1972, the Criminal Attempts Act 1981 and the Matrimonial and Family Proceedings Act 1984.

In addition to the permanent agencies of law reform, royal commissions and departmental commissions are set up, from time to time, to investigate a particular branch of law. Thus, the Police and Criminal Evidence Act 1984 followed upon the *Report of the Royal Commission on Criminal Procedure* (1980) and the *Crowther Report on Consumer Credit* (1971) led to the passing of the Consumer Credit Act 1974.

It has to be said that there is no clear model by reference to which the respective roles of Parliament, the judiciary and the major law reform agencies may be identified. There is a particular need for clarification in areas of law which are continuously subject to change. Thus, in 1982, the editor of the *Criminal Law Review* called for "a fundamental reappraisal of the roles of the courts, the legislature and law reform agencies in the development of our criminal law." It is likely that specialists in other branches of the law would endorse this view.

Part Two

THE CLASSIFICATION OF LAW

Legal rules can, for convenience be divided into two categories:
(a)   the rules of criminal law; and
(b)   the rules of civil law.

Section A: Criminal Law

Some offences are regarded as being so serious that they are offences against society as a whole. Society has an interest in offences such as theft, murder and arson, for if they are not checked a civilised society cannot function. Society's interest is reflected in the fact that such offences fall within the jurisdiction of the *criminal law*.

The involvement of the state can be seen in the following features of criminal law:
(a)   the police will attempt to apprehend criminals;
(b)   the state will pay the costs involved in the prosecution of those accused of criminal offences; and
(c)   if the accused is found guilty of the offence with which he has been charged he will be punished by the state (*e.g.* by a fine or imprisonment).

Offences such as rape and murder are obviously not the kind of offences which are committed by commercial undertakings or public bodies, but it should not be thought, from this, that criminal law is an area which is individual, rather than organisation, orientated. Since the Second World War a new type of criminal offence has emerged as a result of the development of a body of *regulatory* criminal law which recognises *quasi-criminal* conduct (*e.g.* conduct which harms the environment or abuses consumers). Thus:
(a)   the Trade Descriptions Act 1968 provides that it is a criminal offence to attach a false trade description to goods;
(b)   the Unsolicited Goods and Services Act 1971 provides that it is a criminal offence to demand payment for unsolicited goods which have been delivered to the consumer; and
(c)   the Control of Pollution Act 1974 provides that anyone who deposits poisonous waste on land (other than a designated site) so as to create an environmental hazard commits a criminal offence.
The above offences are obviously of a type which may be committed by commercial and public undertakings as well as by individuals. The enforcement of these "regulatory" criminal offences is not normally entrusted to the police, but rather to specialist enforcement agencies (*e.g.* trading standards officers).

Criminal law is considered in greater detail in Unit Two.

Section B: Civil Law

Some offences are not regarded as being of direct interest to society as a whole, but rather a matter of personal interest to the parties involved. Thus, if a party to a contract will not perform his obligations, the state accepts that enforcement of the obligation should be left to the other contracting party. The state provides a system of courts in which the plaintiff (the party who sues) may bring his action and it will, through these courts, provide a judgment on the dispute and, if necesssary, enforce his judgment. Legal costs, attendance of witnesses and other such matters are, however, within the responsibility of the parties to the dispute.

Civil matters may be divided into three categories:

(a)   those which relate to a *contract* which has been entered into by the parties to the dispute;

(b)   those which relate to a *trust*—where, for example, A has left property to B (a trustee) on the basis that he should use that property for the benefit of C (the beneficiary); and

(c)   those which relate to neither a contract nor a trust. A person may, for example, sue an organisation in *Nuisance* as a result of that organisation's continued unreasonable use of its land. A company secretary or a council official may be sued for *Defamation* by a party who resents statements they have made in relation to him. These offences, and others (*e.g. Negligence* and *Trespass*), have little in common. They are, as a result, categorised into a "rag bag" collection of offences known simply as *wrongs* (or, in Norman French, *torts*).

Relationship between civil and criminal law

Civil Law	*Criminal Law*
i) the *plaintiff* initiates the proceedings.	i) the *Crown* initiates the proceedings.
ii) the plaintiff *sues*.	ii) the Crown *prosecutes*.
iii) the person sued is the *defendant*.	iii) the *accused* is prosecuted.
iv) the object of civil proceedings is to provide the plaintiff with a *remedy* (damages/specific performance/injunction) if the defendant is found to be *liable*.	iv) the *accused*, if found guilty, is *punished* (*e.g.* by a fine or imprisonment).
but—*punitive damages* may be awarded in civil actions in tort.	*but*—a criminal court may make a *compensation order* in favour of a person who has suffered loss.

A person or an organisation is subject to criminal law whether or not he wishes to be. This is not necessarily the case in relation to civil law. An individual may only be sued in contract where he has elected to enter into a contract. Contractual liability is, therefore, undertaken voluntarily and arises out of agreement rather than by law. A person who commits a tort, however, has not necessarily elected to enter into a relationship with his "victim." Tortious liability, like criminal liability, arises by law, not by agreement.

A person will, normally be guilty of a criminal offence only if he commits that offence with *mens rea* (*i.e.* "guilty mind"). He must normally be blameworthy and must have *intended* to commit the offence or, perhaps, have been *reckless*. (Thus, a motorist who kills a pedestrian may be guilty of manslaughter even though he did not *intend* to kill his victim.) Sometimes, however, it would be so dificult for the state to prove the necessary mental element that an offence will be created which is of *strict liability*. If so, a person will be guilty if he conducts himself in a certain, prohibited, way (*e.g.* by selling tainted meat) even though he was not, in any way, to *blame* (perhaps the defect in the meat was not detectable and resulted from fault earlier in the chain of distribution). Liability in contract is normally *strict*. Thus, a retailer who sells defective goods to a customer is liable even though he was not at fault. Liability in tort usually depends upon *fault*, although there are some instances of strict liability (as in *Rylands* v. *Fletcher,* see page 352), and commercial undertakings and public bodies are strictly liable for their employees in that they will be liable for any tort committed by an employee in the course of his employment (see the section on vicarious liability, page 319).

Part Three

THE HISTORICAL DEVELOPMENT OF ENGLISH LAW

Section A: Common Law

Prior to the Norman Conquest there was no common law, in the sense of a law that was common to the whole of England. A unified legal system requires a strong central administration and, in Anglo-Saxon England, this was not the case. The law consisted of customary rules which were local in application and often based upon principles which had been handed down from one generation to another by word of mouth rather than in written form.

With the Normans came a strong central government and a will to centralise all aspects of administration. As part of this process *itinerent* (or travelling) justices toured the country hearing *pleas of the Crown*, or offences in which the Crown had a direct interest (*e.g.* offences relating to public order), and, in time, *common pleas*, matters which did not directly affect the interests of the Crown. The justices brought uniformity to the law, for they tended to adopt those customary rules of which they approved and apply them generally irrespective of locality. In this way a body of common law began to emerge. The justices were part of the *Curia Regis* (a term used to describe a close circle of advisers to the King) and suitors who were not prepared to await the itinerent justices in their locality began to look to the *Curia* for redress. In 1178 a royal ordinance provided that five of the justices should be permanently located in Westminster Hall. From the *Curia Regis* emerged the great Common Law Courts:

- (*a*) the Court of Exchequer;
- (*b*) the Court of Common Pleas; and
- (*c*) the Court of King's Bench.

(a) *Court of Exchequer* . . . it was in this court that the King would proceed against his debtors and originally the jurisdiction of the court was limited to fiscal matters. The Exchequer writ of *Quominus* was used, however, to extend the court's jurisdiction by means of a fiction. The plaintiff would plead that he was a debtor of the King and that unless he could recover a debt from the defendant he would not be able to discharge his indebtedness to the Crown. By this device the Court of Exchequer heard cases that properly fell within the jurisdiction of the Court of Common Pleas.

(b) *Court of Common Pleas* . . . during the Middle Ages the Common Pleas was the busiest of the Common Law Courts hearing, as it did, actions which would now be seen as actions in contract and tort. Of all the actions heard in the court that of *Debt* was heard most often. For all actions to recover a debt in excess of 40 shillings had to be heard in Common Pleas. Gradually, however, Common Pleas lost its pre-eminence to the other Common Law Courts which adopted processes which were cheaper and speedier than those of Common Pleas and usurped its jurisdiction by means of legal fictions (see, for example, the writ of Quominus, above, and Latitat, below).

(c) *Court of King's Bench* ... originally the jurisdiction of the King's Bench was limited to criminal matters and actions of trespass. In addition, the Court exercised a supervisory jurisdiction over inferior courts through the prerogative writs of *habeas corpus* (see page 43), *mandamus, prohibition* and *certiorari* (for an account of the modern prerogative orders bearing these names see page 41). It had no real civil jurisdiction. The court extended its jurisdiction, however, by use of fictions. Thus, the court, like all others, had jurisdiction to try any matter relating to one of its prisoners. If, then, a person was in custody subsequent to an allegation of trespass, the court had the right to hear an action against him for, say, debt. Some litigants were prepared to bring an action of trespass in relation to a defendant who owed a debt and, upon recovering the debt, abandon the allegation of trespass. If the bill of trespass, which could only be issued if the cause of action arose in Middlesex, could not be served because the defendant did not live in Middlesex, the sheriff of Middlesex would return it to the court, whereupon the King's Bench issued a writ of *Latitat* to the county where the defendant "lurked and ran about." Gradually, the practice developed by which the alleged trespass did not need to be stated and proceedings were commenced by Latitat. By the end of the sixteenth century the King's Bench was hearing as many civil cases as the Common Pleas.

Alongside the Common Law Courts there was an *assize* circuit. The Statute of Westminster II, 1285, permitted the practice by which juries could be summoned to Westminster to give their verdicts "unless before" (*nisi prius*) that time, the royal justices should arrive, on circuit, in the county. These justices were empowered to act by the following royal commissions:

- (*a*) *assize,* which authorised the justices to determine disputes relating to real property;
- (*b*) *nisi prius,* which authorised the justices to take verdicts from juries;
- (*c*) *oyer and terminer,* which authorised the hearing and determination of certain classes of criminal offence; and
- (*d*) *general gaol delivery,* which authorised the justices to clear the prisons by hearing all of the cases against the prisoners.

The writ system

Actions at common law were commenced by a writ. There were different writs for each form of action and if no writ existed then that was an indication that the law did not recognise a cause of action. Thus, there were, for example, writs for trespass, debt, detinue and covenant. A writ of trespass would assert that "by force of arms and against the King's peace" the defendant had interfered with the plaintiff's land or goods or, indeed, with his person. Debt and detinue lay to recover money or goods from the defendant and covenant lay to enforce a promise made under seal in a deed. In 1258, the Provisions of Oxford stipulated that no new writs could be issued. If, then, a cause of action had not been recognised and a writ formulated, the common law could not recognise the plaintiff as having legally enforceable rights.

In 1285, the Statute of Westminster II provided that new writs could issue providing they were analogous to existing writs. Plaintiffs after 1285 had to show that either:

(*a*)   there was an existing writ which covered their claim; or

(*b*)   that there was no such writ, but that their claim was *in consimili casu* ("in like case") to that recognised in an existing writ and, in consequence, a new writ should issue.

This provision resulted in a great many new writs coming into existence, many of them based on the old writ of trespass (which became known as "that fertile mother of actions"). There were, nevertheless, many potential actions which were neither recognised in old writs nor analogous to previously accepted causes of action. These grievances remained without any form of redress.

Section B: Equity

The rigidity of the common law after 1250 led those who were dissatisfied with it to petition the Lord Chancellor as *Keeper of the King's conscience*. In particular, there was concern that:

(a) the common law did not recognise the concept of a trust. If A settled property on B, the trustee, to hold for the benefit of C, the beneficiary, then the common law recognised B's rights to the property and ignored C's.

(b) the common law was preoccupied with the *form* of transactions. Thus, if A wished to mortgage his land to B and effected a sale of the land to B subject to a right to redeem within a stipulated time period, then, if A had not discharged his indebtedness by the date of redemption, the common law acknowledged the sale and ignored the true intent of the parties which was that the land was only to be used as a security for a loan.

(c) the common law remedy of *damages* was inadequate in certain circumstances.

The Lord Chancellor showed a willingness to modify the harshness of the common law and to approach disputes with a view to finding a just, or *equitable* solution. His decisions, and those of the *Court of Chancery* which subsequently came to exercise his role, gave rise to a body of rules known as the rules of *Equity*. At first, the determining factor for the petitioner was the Lord Chancellor's view of the merits of his claim. The lack of consistency which resulted from this flexibility led to the accusation that "equity varies as the Lord Chancellor's foot." Gradually, however, some element of certainty was provided by the emergence of the so-called *maxims* of equity, these being, in effect, guidelines for the benefit of those administering equitable relief. These maxims include the following:

(a) *Equity will not suffer a wrong to be without a remedy* . . . thus equity recognised and enforced the rights of a beneficiary under a trust;

(b) *Equity looks to the intent rather than the form* . . . thus equity recognised the true nature of a mortgage and provided an *equity of redemption* to mortgagors who had failed to repay their loans on the date of redemption as a result of fraud or misfortune;

(c) *He who comes to equity must come clean hands* . . . thus there could be no assistance to, say, a beneficiary who had been party to a fraud; and

(d) *Delay defeats equity* . . . and so a plaintiff coming to equity would be required to act with some degree of urgency or he would be presumed to be in no need of equitable relief.

This process hardened to such an extent that the Court of Chancery came to accept that it was bound by a system of precedent in the same way as were the common law courts. In *Gee* v. *Pritchard* (1818) Lord Eldon asserted that . . . "Nothing would inflict on me greater pain . . . than the recollection that I had done anything to justify the reproach that the equity of this court varies like the Chancellor's foot," and in 1878 Sir George Jessel, M.R. stated that " . . . this court is not, as I have often said, a court of conscience, but a court of law."

The contribution of equity

Equity developed as a modification of the common law and has been described as "a gloss on the common law." The extent of this modification can be seen in:

(a) Equity's *exclusive* jurisdiction, where equity recognised rights which were not enforced at common law (*e.g.* the rights of a beneficiary under a trust);

(b) Equity's *concurrent* jurisdiction, where equity provided new, discretionary, remedies (*e.g. specific performance* of a contract, see page 157, and the *injunction*, see page 157);

(c) Equity's *auxiliary* jurisdiction, where equity provided for new procedures to assist plaintiffs (*e.g. discovery of documents*, by which a plaintiff can require his adversary to produce documents relevant to the case).

Section C: The Relationship Between Common Law and Equity

Where equity and common law came into conflict, as with their different approaches where a mortgagor did not redeem on the appointed date, the Chancellor issued a *common injunction* which, in effect, limited the jurisdiction of the common law. This device was bitterly resented by the common law judges and in 1615 Lord Chief Justice Coke held that where a common law court had arrived at a decision in a case, any appeal to the Chancellor would result in the appellant's imprisonment. The conflict between the two systems having been brought to a head, the dispute was referred to the King who, in the *Earl of Oxford's* case (1615), decided that in a case of conflict equity should prevail.

The Judicature Acts 1873–1875

The Acts abolished the old common law courts and the Court of Chancery and created, in their place, a Supreme Court of Judicature which could administer both common law and equity. The Chancery Division and the Queen's Bench Division of the High Court emerged from these reforms and, largely, the Chancery Divison will consider matters involving the jurisdiction of equity whilst the Queen's Bench Division primarily administers common law. Both divisions can, however, grant relief in equity or provide a common law remedy.

Thus, whilst common law and equity still exist as separate entities, each based on a body of case law, their administration is fused. In that light it is now possible to define common law and equity in the following terms:

(*a*)   common law is that body of law which is based upon rules developed prior to 1873, by the common law courts;

(*b*)   equity is that body of law which is based upon rules developed, prior to 1873, in the Court of Chancery.

It is important to note that equity and common law have not ceased to develop since 1873 and that the above definitions refer to the *origins* of the two systems rather than to the source of *all* their rules.

Part Four

THE STRUCTURE AND COMPOSITION OF COURTS IN ENGLAND AND WALES

In any developed society structures will be established to process the disputes which arise as a result of the competing interests of its members or even as a result of a disagreement between the state itself (the *administration*) and its members. These structures ensure that such conflicts do not lead to tensions which may threaten the stability of the settled order (which is accepted, or, at least, acquiesced in). The nature of these disputes will vary. A trading company may be aggrieved because another has not performed, or has misperformed, a contractual undertaking. A motorist may claim that a haulage contractor should pay for damage that has resulted from a road accident. An inventor may claim that another has infringed his patent rights or a manufacturer may claim that another has interfered with his trade mark. The state may accuse individuals of criminal offences and an individual may claim that the Department of Health and Social Security should be paying him industrial injury benefit. A taxi driver may be aggrieved because his licence has been taken away from him and a ratepayer may insist that a local authority should maintain the pavement outside his home. Whatever their differences, however, all these disputes have one common feature: there are, in all of these instances, two parties and thus two sets of interests. One way of resolving disputes with this central feature is to recognise the parties as *adversaries* and to provide a forum in which they may vigorously advance their case and, in so doing, bring the characteristics of the dispute into sharp focus. This having been done, the dispute may be *adjudicated* upon by an independent umpire representing the state. (Where the state is, itself, a party to the dispute the judiciary would still provide the necessary independent element for they represent a branch of the administration not involved in the dispute.) This is the process which has been adopted in the United Kingdom and it is seen at its most formal in the system of courts established to determine civil and criminal disputes. Included within the civil court system is a distinctive procedure for handling disputes with the state where they relate to matters of public law. In recent times this judicial review of administrative action has, with increased levels of state influence over the affairs of its citizens, assumed great significance and it is given separate treatment.

In this Part we will describe:
- (a) those who are involved in determining disputes brought before the courts (*i.e.* members of the judiciary, magistrates and juries);
- (b) the structure of courts and of appeals;
- (c) the process of judicial supervision over *administrative* action; and

(*d*)   the system of legal aid and advice which is designed to reduce the inequality between the parties which results where one has greater financial resources than the other.

Section A: The Decision-Makers

THE JUDICIARY

The judiciary is the collective name for the body of judges who preside over our courts. The individual judges may be:

(a) *Recorders* . . . who are part-time judges (expected to serve a minimum of 30 days a year). They are appointed from barristers or solicitors of ten years standing, by the Queen on the advice of the Lord Chancellor. The compulsory retiring age is 75 and appointment may be terminated for incapacity or misconduct.

(b) *Circuit Judges* . . . who are appointed by the Queen, on the advice of the Lord Chancellor, from barristers of 10 years standing or recorders who have held judicial office for at least five years. (As solicitors are eligible for appointment as a recorder, it is possible for a solicitor to become a circuit judge.) The retiring age is 72, though a circuit judge may be asked to remain in office until he is 75. A circuit judge may be removed from office by the Lord Chancellor on the grounds of "incapacity or misbehaviour."

(c) *Puisne Judges* (High Court Judges) . . . who are appointed by the Queen on the advice of the Lord Chancellor, from barristers of 10 years standing. They hold office "whilst of good behaviour" but can be removed from their judicial office by resolution of both Houses of Parliament. Puisne judges must retire at 75.

(d) *Lords Justices of Appeal* . . . who are appointed by the Queen, on the advice of the Prime Minister, from barristers of at least 15 years standing or from the ranks of the existing body of puisne judges. They retire at the same age as puisne judges and may be dismissed under the same circumstances.

(e) *Lords of Appeal in Ordinary* . . . who are appointed as life peers by the Queen, on the advice of the Prime Minister, from barristers of 15 years standing or members of the judiciary who have held high judicial office for two years. Usually, Lords of Appeal in Ordinary are appointed from the ranks of Lords Justices of Appeal. They retire at the same age as puisne judges and Lords Justices of Appeal and may be dismissed in the same circumstances.

Lords of Appeal in Ordinary sit only in the Judicial Committee of the House of Lords. They are, in theory, entitled to sit in the Court of Appeal but they never do. Lords Justices of Appeal sit only in the Court of Appeal although they may, again in theory, be requested to sit in other courts. These judges are, therefore, in all but theory, exclusively appellate court judges. They do not determine cases, they hear appeals from the decisions of other judges. Because they are removed from the "hurly-burly" of the trial court, having no jury to superintend or witnesses to consider, they can concentrate upon the issue before them without distraction. The issue will usually be a question of law rather than of fact and, as a result, these appellate court judges have an opportunity to develop the law which is disproportionate to their number (20 or so). Because of this, Lords

Justices of Appeal and, particularly, Lords of Appeal in Ordinary have acquired high status.

The other judges, puisne judges, circuit judges and recorders, are called first instance judges (although puisne judges may sit in the Court of Appeal). They hear and determine civil claims in county courts and the High Court and criminal charges in the Crown Court. The Courts Act 1971 anticipated a situation in which any first instance judge could be available to hear a claim or charge in any first instance court (other than a magistrates' court). Thus, puisne judges will normally sit in the High Court or Crown Court, but they can be asked to sit in a county court. Similarly, a circuit judge will normally sit in either the Crown Court or a county court, but may be invited to hear cases in the High Court. Such a flexible situation obviously facilitates maximum use of scarce judicial manpower but, one suspects, it could result in loss of expertise. A judge who always sits in the Crown Court hearing criminal cases would, obviously, have a firmer grasp of the criminal process than an equally able judge whose expertise lay in the commercial area and who normally sat in the High Court. Because first instance judges must devote much of their attention to the orderly conduct of the trial, their ability to influence the law they are administering is not as great as that of the appellate court judges.

Criticism of the judiciary

The judiciary has often been subject to criticism, not least for its composition. With the sole exception that a solicitor may become a circuit judge, by virtue of his experience as a recorder (not, it should be noted, because of his status as a solicitor), all judicial appointments are made from the Bar. This may appear unexceptional, for barristers specialise in advocacy and are, as a result, familiar with the workings of the courts. To qualify as a barrister, however, one must have served a period of pupillage with a "master," and, for at least part of this time, the pupil receives no income. Having qualified, a barrister is not allowed to open an office and attract clients, he must have his clients introduced to him by solicitors and is thus, initially at least, dependent upon his "connections." These factors, taken together, result in a Bar which consists of a disproportionate number of members from the middle and upper classes. It follows from this that the judiciary is drawn from a narrow socio-economic band. To its credit the judiciary has not been unwilling to recognise this fact and the accompanying dangers. Lord Justice Scrutton, for example, admitted that, "the habits you are trained in, the people with whom you mix, lead to your having a certain class of ideas. . . . It is very difficult sometimes to be sure that you have put yourself into a thoroughly impartial position between two disputants, one of your own class and one not of your class." Some concern is also expressed at the age at which a judge must retire. The earliest age for retirement is 72 and many judges are entitled to remain in office until 75.

THE ROLE OF LAYMEN

It is a basic principle of English law that a man alleged to have committed a criminal offence may only be tried by his peers. Generally speaking, therefore, everyone who appears before an English criminal court will have the question of his guilt or innocence determined by laymen. If he is tried in a magistrates' court, the question of his guilt will, normally, be determined by lay magistrates. If he is tried in the Crown Court the question will be determined by a jury.

Magistrates

Magistrates are appointed by the Crown on the advice of the Lord Chancellor. The Lord Chancellor is, in turn, guided by local advisory committees. Magistrates receive no remuneration although they are entitled to be re-imbursed for loss of earnings and other necessary expenditure. They have no legal qualifications but they are required to undertake a course of training. A Royal Commission, in 1948, suggested that the instruction they receive should relate to the nature of their task, rather than to the details of law. In particular, the Commission recommended, magistrates should know how to *act judicially*. This is a very difficult task and would, for example, involve the assimilation of the notion that decisions should be based on admissible evidence. A magistrate will often, during the course of a trial, hear evidence which he ought not to take into account. To be able to make a decision, based on admissible evidence, that a person is innocent, whilst fairly sure, because of inadmissible evidence that has come to the notice of the bench, that the person is guilty, involves a high degree of sophistication. It is, however, important that magistrates should appreciate the nature of the judicial task for, as Lord Goddard C.J. asserted when giving evidence to the Commission, justices of the peace (lay magistrates) are not censured by appellate courts if they make a mistake of law, but a failure to act judicially is a reason for criticism. Magistrates are assisted by legally qualified clerks who advise on matters of law.

Some of the larger cities use full-time, salaried and legally qualified *stipendiary magistrates*. Such magistrates can, it is alleged, deal with criminal cases far more quickly than their lay counterparts. Moreover, it is asserted, the fact that a stipendiary magistrate, rather than a rotating body of lay justices, is presiding over the court leads to consistency in sentencing.

Juries

The Juries Act 1974 provides that to be eligible for jury service a person must be between the ages of 18 and 65, be registered as a parliamentary or local government elector and have been resident in this country for five years (since the age of 13). Certain people are not eligible for jury service (*e.g.* judges and solicitors) and some, because of their criminal record, are disqualified. The Juries (Disqualification) Act 1984 provides that a person is disqualified from jury service if:

(a)   at any time in the last ten years, he has, in the United Kingdom, served any part of a sentence of imprisonment, youth custody or detention; or been detained in a borstal institution; or had passed on him a suspended sentence of imprisonment or order for detention; or had made in respect of him a community service order; or

(b)   at any time in the last five years he has been placed on probation.

A jury of 12 will be selected for a criminal trial, but a trial, once begun, may continue so long as the jury is not reduced (*e.g.* by sickness,) below nine. A unanimous decision is not now necessary so long as the jury, having deliberated for at least two hours, reach a majority verdict (of ten out of 11 or 12, or nine out of ten). The jury is required to determine questions of fact, matters of law being the concern of the judge.

[In civil cases juries have all disappeared. In the Queen's Bench Division, for example, less than one per cent. of cases are heard by juries.]

Criticism of juries . . . critics of the jury system point to the following perceived weaknesses in the use of juries:

(a) juries are not selected on the basis of intelligence (nor are they disqualified for lack of it) and many members of a typical jury might find it difficult to follow the complicated evidence that would be presented in, say, an alleged case of fraud;

(b) juries are inexperienced and, in consequence, likely to be unduly influenced by others in the trial proceedings (*e.g.* barristers or the trial judge), by dominant individuals within the jury or even by the appearance or demeanour or the accused;

(c) juries are not always sufficiently sophisticated as to be able to understand the true nature of their role and, as a result, they may be prepared to find in favour of an accused whom they believe to be guilty but who they do not wish to be punished (*e.g.* a policeman or prison officer who has assaulted a child molester); and

(d) some jurymen (*e.g.* the owners of a small business) may resent being forced into jury service and may be concerned to return to their other interests as quickly as possible, this being an unfortunate state of mind for anyone required to make decisions involving the liberty of an accused and the protection of society.

Section B: The Courts

THE CIVIL COURTS

A civil dispute will come before one of the two civil courts of first instance:
(*a*) The High Court, or
(*b*) a county court.

The High Court

The High Court was created by the Judicature Acts 1873–1875 and it now consists of three divisions:
(*a*) The Queen's Bench Division;
(*b*) The Chancery Division; and
(*c*) The Family Division.

The Family Division hears, as its name implies, cases involving the family unit. It deals, for example, with defended divorce cases, applications relating to legitimacy and certain probate matters. The Chancery Division deals principally with trusts, mortgages, revenue cases and the winding-up of companies. The Queen's Bench Division hears all matters not expressly allocated to the other divisions (*e.g.* actions in contract and tort). In theory any division of the High Court can hear any type of case, but, in practice, the cases are allocated between the divisions so that they can specialise in the manner outlined above. This practice is so well-established that if a case is begun in the "wrong" division it will be transferred and the plaintiff will have to bear the costs incurred by his failure to select the appropriate division. Some statutes actually specify that certain types of action are to be heard in a particular division.

County courts

The County Courts Act 1846 created a system of county courts to hear minor civil disputes, which system now operates under the provisions of the County Courts Act 1984. County courts basically hear the same type of case as the High Court, the criteria for determining which court has jurisdiction being the amount of the claim or matter. In contract and tort actions, for example, the cut-off point is £5,000. Claims involving more than this amount go to the High Court whilst those involving less go to a county court. This is not an automatic cut-off, however, for:

(a) it is possible for county courts to hear cases involving claims in excess of the prescribed financial limits if both parties agree (as may well happen, for costs are lower in a county court than in the High Court); and

(b) it is possible for a plaintiff to bring before the High Court a claim which falls within the jurisdiction of the county courts. If so, he may, if he succeeds, recover only county court costs (even though he has incurred High Court costs) and, in some circumstances, he may recover no costs at all.

County courts have been given, by statute, exclusive jurisdiction in some matters. The Consumer Credit Act 1974, for example, gives exclusive jurisdiction to county courts in relation to civil disputes arising out of the provisions of the Act.

The judge in a county court is assisted by a *registrar* (a solicitor of at least seven years standing) and the registrar may hear cases where the amount involved does not exceed £500. The 1984 Act provides for the appointment of part-time registrars who will practise as solicitors when not invoved as registrars. In an attempt to strengthen the ability of county courts to act as genuine "small claim" courts, the Administration of Justice Act 1973 extended the power of county courts to refer disputes to arbitration. A county court may order any proceedings to be referred to arbitration to whomsoever and on such terms as the court thinks "just and reasonable." Either the judge or the registrar is empowered to make an order of reference to arbitration. County court rules provide however, that the registrar may only make such an order if the amount involved does not exceed £500, or, if the parties consent to the reference. Judges and registrars may themselves sit as the arbitrator and in most cases the arbitrator is the registrar. The award of the arbitrator is entered as judgment and takes effect as if given by the judge. County court rules provide that costs (other than the cost of the summons) are generally not recoverable on a claim which does not exceed £500, so the winner will not be compensated for his expenditure. This provision discourages the use of legal representation in such claims and helps to ensure the speedy settlement of the dispute at arbitration which, because of the absence of legal representation, tends to be inquisitorial in nature. The introduction of county court arbitration has been most beneficial and provides a consumer with a small claim a genuine opportunity to pursue that claim.

Appeals in civil cases

Some civil appeals are heard by *Divisional Courts of the High Court*. A divisional court is a court consisting, usually, of two or more judges of the division, whereas a first instance court of the division is presided over by a single judge. The *Divisional Court of the Chancery Division* hears appeals from county courts in bankruptcy matters and the *Divisional Court of the*

Family Division hears appeals from magistrates' courts in family law matters.

The normal appeal, in a civil case, is, however, to the *Court of Appeal* (*Civil Division*), though the parties can, prior to the hearing of their case at first instance, agree to exclude the right of appeal. Appeal lies to the Court

Diagram 2

APPEALS IN CIVIL CASES

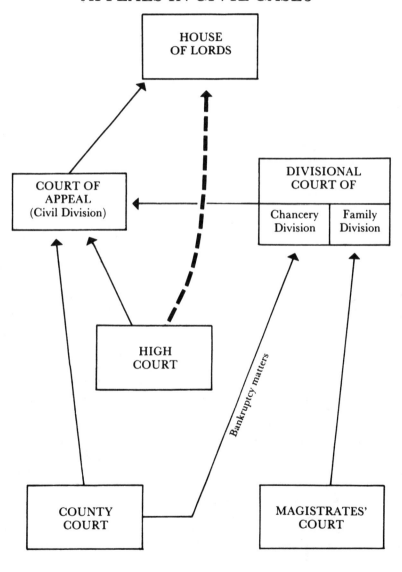

"Leap-frogging" appeal

of Appeal on questions of law or fact, though in small claims in the county court there is no appeal to the Court of Appeal on a factual issue.

There is further appeal, on points of *law*, to the *House of Lords* (which, when sitting as the Judicial Committee of the House of Lords, consists only of judges drawn from the ranks of the Lords of Appeal in Ordinary, the Lord Chancellor and any ex-Lord Chancellors and peers who have held high judicial office). It is possible for a civil appeal to *leapfrog* the Court of Appeal and come to the House of Lords directly from the High Court. This can only happen, however, where the appeal relates to a matter of statutory interpretation or a precedent of the Court of Appeal or the House of Lords. (If there was no such appeal it would, in some cases, be necessary to appeal to the Court of Appeal in the knowledge that the appeal would be dismissed and a further appeal to the House of Lords would be necessary. For, as the Court of Appeal is, in civil cases, bound not only by the House of Lords but also by its own previous decisions, there are some points of law which can only be effectively considered by the House of Lords). The structure of appeals in civil cases is set out in *diagram 2*.

The High Court and the Court of Appeal, together with the Crown Court comprise the Supreme Court. The composition, jurisdiction and procedures of these courts are provided for by the Supreme Court Act 1981. The House of Lords is not part of the Supreme Court.

THE CRIMINAL COURTS

A person accused of a criminal offence will either be tried in a magistrates' court or in the Crown Court. The Criminal Law Act 1977 and the Magistrates' Courts Act 1980 provide that some offences are always to be tried in a magistrates' court, some, because of their seriousness, are always to be tried in the Crown Court and some may be tried in either court depending upon whether the magistrates decide that a case should go to the Crown Court.

Magistrates' courts

A magistrates' court will consist of two or more justices of the peace assisted by a legally qualified clerk, or a legally qualified stipendiary. All cases begin in a magistrates' court and 95 per cent. are determined there (by summary trial). If magistrates hear a case which could have been tried in the Crown Court (*i.e.* a case triable either way) and, upon discovering the accused's criminal record, find that their powers of sentencing (a maximum fine of £2,000 and a maximum term of imprisonment of six months) are inadequate they may commit the accused to the Crown Court so that he be sentenced there.

In the case of offences triable only in the Crown Court (on indictment), a single magistrate, acting as an examining justice, will hold a preliminary enquiry to see if there is a prima facie case against the accused. If as a result of these *committal proceedings* such a case is established, the accused will be committed to the Crown Court for trial.

(Magistrates' courts also have a limited civil jurisdiction involving, for example, the hearing of affiliation proceedings and the making of separation and maintenance orders. Because of the intimate nature of the evidence, the public are excluded when such cases are being heard.)

The Crown Court

The Crown Court has jurisdiction over the whole of England and Wales. There are 24 *first tier centres* in which the Crown Court is presided over by a High Court judge or a circuit judge (and at which the High Court also sits). In the 19 *second tier centres*, High Court judges and circuit judges preside (but the High Court does not sit) and in the 46 *third tier centres* the Crown Court is visited only by circuit judges. Within the various centres the work is allocated between judges on the basis of the seriousness of the offence, criminal offences having been divided, for this purpose, into four categories. First class offences must be tried by a High Court judge. Second class offences should also be tried by a High Court judge unless the presiding judge of the circuit releases the case for trial by either a circuit judge or a recorder. Third class offences may be tried by any judge and fourth class offences will normally be heard by a circuit judge or recorder.

The Crown Court hears the more serious criminal offences (which are triable only in the Crown Court) and, if a magistrates' court so decides, those offences which may be tried either in the Crown Court or in a magistrates' court. The Crown Court also sentences offenders committed for this purpose by a magistrates' court.

Appeals in criminal cases

As well as being a first instance court, the *Crown Court* hears appeals from magistrates' courts. Normally only the accused may appeal against the decision of the magistrates, though certain statutes give the prosecution a right to appeal. An appeal by the accused against his conviction involves a complete re-hearing in the Crown Court, an appeal against the sentence imposed by the magistrates involves only a consideration of matters relevant to the sentence. Sitting as an appellate court, the Crown Court will consist of a judge and two to four lay magistrates (this also being the composition of the court when it sentences offenders committed for that purpose). The court may, having heard an appeal, impose any sentence which is within the limits imposed on magistrates' courts and can, thus, impose a sentence heavier than that actually imposed by the magistrates.

The *Divisional Court of the Queen's Bench Division* hears appeals "by way of case stated" from magistrates' courts, or from the Crown Court (but only where the Crown Court was itself acting as an appellate court). An appeal by way of case stated is not, in reality, an appeal, it is an application to the Divisional Court for a *review* of a decision made by lay justices (who, in addition to presiding over magistrates' courts, sit in the Crown Court when that Court is sitting as an appellate court). The "appeal" by way of case stated is a check on the limited legal expertise possessed by magistrates and, as such, it is an appeal only on a point of law. If the Divisional Court considers that the accused did not, in law, commit the offence charged, it will remit (send back) the case to the magistrates and direct an acquittal.

Where the Crown Court has been acting as a court of first instance, appeals lie to the *Court of Appeal (Criminal Division)*. Appeals against conviction, on questions of *law*, lie to the Court of Appeal as of right. An appeal against conviction, on a question of *fact*, does not (the accused must obtain leave to appeal from the Crown Court judge or the Court of Appeal

Diagram 3

APPEALS IN CRIMINAL CASES

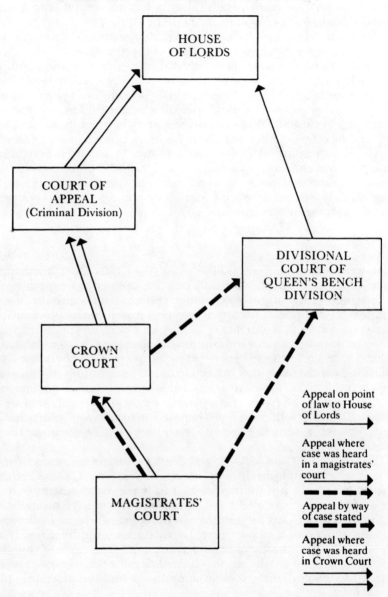

itself). An appeal against sentence lies only with the leave of the Court of Appeal and there is no such appeal if the sentence is fixed by law.

An appeal against sentence lies to the Court of Appeal so long as the sentence was imposed by the Crown Court and, as a result, the Court of Appeal hears appeals from the Crown Court where the case was determined by a magistrates' court which then committed the accused to the Crown Court for sentence.

The final court of appeal is the *House of Lords*, which hears appeals from the Court of Appeal (Criminal Division) where the Court of Appeal certifies the matter to be a point of law of general public importance and either the Court of Appeal or the House of Lords gives leave to appeal. There is a similar right of appeal to the House of Lords from the Divisional Court of the Queen's Bench Division, for it would be futile for an appeal to lie from that Court to the Court of Appeal as, in criminal cases, the composition of the Court of Appeal and the Divisional Court of the Queen's Bench Division can be similar (*e.g.* the Lord Chief Justice and two High Court judges).

Only a handful of criminal cases each year are appealed to the House of Lords, which raises the question of which court in the hierarchy is the most important. It will be recalled that English courts perform two functions:
(*a*) they determine the issue before them and, in doing so they . . .
(*b*) create judicial precedents.
Lawyers, preoccupied by the status of the House of Lords (and the Court of Appeal) in relation to the weight given to their precedents tend to lose sight of the fact that, in relation to the issue-determining function, the most important criminal courts, without doubt, are the magistrates' courts.

The structure of appeals in criminal cases is set out in *diagram 3*.

Section C: Judicial Supervision of Administrative Action

This section considers the role of the courts in the process of supervision over administrative action. In this context the term "administration" refers to the departments of central government, local authorities and other bodies concerned with the implementation of the policies approved by Parliament. Although the administration is generally subject to the same law as others, there has developed a discrete system for dealing with matters of "public law." Thus, for example, should it be alleged that the Revenue has failed in its duty to collect taxes, this would be a public law matter. On the other hand, a claim that a local authority had without permission dumped toxic chemicals on another's land would be dealt with in the same way as any other action in trespass. In the leading case of *O'Reilly* v. *Mackman* the House of Lords ruled that the special procedure of review provided by the Divisional Court of the Queen's Bench Division should be exclusively used in matters of public law rather than an ordinary civil action brought in other courts. A fundamental freedom, deriving from the basic right to live according to the "Rule of Law," may be expressed as incorporating:
(a) a positive right to the proper conferment or management of benefits where duties are imposed upon the administration; and
(b) a negative right not to be subjected to arbitrary interference by the administration.
Thus where, for example, the state has undertaken duties to provide for the welfare of citizens, there is a right that benefits should be administered

strictly in accordance with the enabling legislation. On the other hand, where, for example, the state has introduced controls over the development of land, there is a right that only those uses prescribed by statute as requiring planning permission should be inhibited. In short, the administration is required to conform precisely to the prescriptions of the law. To this end, the administration:

(a)   seeks to keep its own house in order (*e.g.* through the system of tribunals, discussed at page 46);

(b)   provides avenues for the resolution of conflict (*e.g.* through the use of public inquiries, discussed at page 210); and

(c)   is subjected to the ultimate supervisory jurisdiction of the courts.

This Section will focus on the supervisory jurisdiction of the courts.

THE SUPERVISORY FUNCTION OF THE COURTS

The courts have a constitutional role as "interpreters of the written law and expounders of the common law and rules of equity." This *supervisory* function, commonly referred to as *judicial review* may be exercised upon appeal to the High Court (as provided by some particular statutory scheme) or simply through the inherent jurisdiction of the court. The application *for review* procedure is adjudicated upon through the Divisional Court of the Queen's Bench Division.

Ultra vires

The principle underlying the system of judicial review is the doctrine of *ultra vires* (the term means "beyond the powers"), which requires that a body must act within its powers (*intra vires*). Administrative bodies derive their powers from Parliament and they can only undertake those tasks assigned to them by Parliament. They must keep within the sphere of activity delegated to them; they must follow the procedures laid down by Parliament for the exercise of their powers; in determining any issue they must take into account only those matters which Parliament has intended them to take into account; they must not fail to take into account those matters which Parliament has intended they shall take into account; and they must not act for an improper purpose.

When delegating a power Parliament may fail to make plain the limits of that power. It is the task of the courts to interpret and give effect to the wishes of the legislature. In interpreting the wishes of Parliament, the courts have implied the principles of *natural justice* which, normally, must be observed whenever a person or public body has a power to reach a decision affecting the rights of subjects. The principles of natural justice were originally developed in relation to the supervisory jurisdiction of the superior courts over the activities of inferior courts. Inferior courts were required to hear both sides of the case (the *audi alteram partem* rule) and were not to be biased in favour of one side or the other (the rule of *nemo judex in causa sua potest*—no man must be judge in his own cause). However, in the famous case of *Cooper* v. *Wandsworth Board of Works* (1863) the principles of natural justice were extended to the activities of the administration. Here the court considered that although a local board had a power to demolish buildings erected in breach of statute, nevertheless, Parliament could not have intended demolition to take place without the Board first giving the owner an opportunity to explain his actions. The court ruled that to demolish without affording this opportunity was outside the powers of the local board. Since that time, the *audi alteram partem* principle has been widely applied to the acts of the administration. The principle requires, broadly, that the parties must be fully informed of any case they must answer and, must be given a proper opportunity to prepare and present a case. Thus in *Errington* v. *Minister of Health* where, after the close of a public inquiry into slum clearance proposals, a minister had discussions with a local authority "behind the backs" of the objectors the court found a breach of natural justice. Clearly the objectors had not had an opportunity to deal with the points raised by the local authority in the private discussions.

The doctrine of *ultra vires* applies to any statutory body and requires the body to remain within its powers, otherwise any purported act will be null and void. Traditionally the doctrine of *ultra vires* is considered under various heads.

Substantive ultra vires... this term is used to denote the situation in which a body cannot justify its actions as falling within the statute authorising its function. In *White and Collins* v. *Minister of Health*, for example, a minister had power to confirm a compulsory purchase order except where the land "formed part of a park." The court held that the land in respect of which an order had been made was in fact part of a park and quashed the minister's confirmation.

Procedural ultra vires... if Parliament prescribes a procedure to be followed in the exercise of a power then, generally, failure to observe that procedure precludes the decision-maker from exercising the power. Thus, in *Howard* v. *Secretary of State for the Environment* a minister had power to consider an appeal in a planning matter if the appeal was lodged within a specified period of time. The court held that if the appeal was lodged after the period had expired, the minister could no longer consider the matter on appeal.

Other heads of error... equally fatal to the power of decision, are taking into account irrelevant considerations or using a power for an improper purpose. Thus in *R.* v. *Hillingdon B.C., ex parte Royco* a local planning authority, in granting a planning permission for a private residential development, attached conditions which required that the houses should be first let to persons on the local council house waiting list. The court held that the needs of the council to meet its obligations to those on the waiting list were not relevant to the grant of permission for the applicant's housing development.

Judicial remedies

The ways in which the courts may become involved in conflicts between the administration and subjects, and the remedies available, are somewhat varied. As previously indicated, the courts may become involved under statutory machinery enabling challenge to an order or decision (*e.g.* the Tribunals and Inquiries Act 1971 provides for appeals on points of law to the High Court from certain specified tribunals). In these cases the remedies available are prescribed by the relevant statute. This may provide, for example, that a compulsory purchase order which has been confirmed by a minister is to be quashed, so that the authority seeking to compulsorily acquire land is placed back at "square one."

Where the court is called upon to exercise its supervisory function in the absence of a statutory scheme for review once more there are several possible remedies. These remedies are the *prerogative orders* of *certiorari, prohibition* and *mandamus*; the *declaration*; the *injunction* and the actions for *damages.* The Supreme Court Act 1981 provides for a uniform procedure, the *application for review*, under which the various remedies may be sought either singly or in the alternative from the Divisional Court. The issue of the remedies (with the exception of damages) is discretionary and the court must be satisfied that the applicant has a sufficient interest in the matter under review (*i.e.* has *locus standi*) so that it is proper that a remedy should issue. Briefly, the order of *certiorari* issues to quash decisions which are erroneous in law. Thus it would quash a decision of a tribunal which has exceeded its jurisdiction. In theory, the order will only issue against bodies which are required to act judicially (in a court-like manner), although there has been a tendency to give a liberal interpretation to this requirement (*e.g.* in *R.* v. *Hillingdon B.C., ex parte Royco*, an order of certiorari quashed a decision of a planning authority granting planning permission). *Prohibition* is an order issued to prevent an inferior body from exceeding its jurisdiction or acting contrary to natural justice. In practice, in most cases, decisions have been reached before the matter falls into dispute, so that it is too late to seek prohibition and the decision must be quashed by certiorari. *Mandamus* is an order whereby the court will compel the performance of a public duty. Thus if a tribunal declines to consider an application because it erroneously considers it has no jurisdiction to act, the court will direct it to consider the matter. The *declaration* is merely a statement by the court declaring what the law is. Although it is not a contempt of court to ignore a declaration, nevertheless, so far as public bodies are concerned, it is clear that they are anxious to observe the law and they will, as a result, observe such an order. The *injunction* is usually issued to order a person or body to refrain from some act and there is some degree of overlap with the order of prohibition. Finally, because public authorities who are in breach of contract or commit torts, such as trespass or negligence, are liable to be sued under the ordinary common law for *damages* such a course may be used to challenge a public authority's actions. In *Cooper* v. *Wandsworth Board of Works*, for example, a housebuilder brought an action for trespass against the local board, which was ordered to pay damages. The liability arose because an act of demolition undertaken by the public body was *ultra vires*, not authorised by statute and a mere trespass. It must be emphasised, however, that this method of challenging administrative action will, following *O'Reilly* v. *Mackman* (see earlier), only be available where there is an obvious infringement of a private right. Attempts to circumvent the application for review procedure will be struck down as an abuse of the process of the courts. This was done in *O'Reilly's* case where prisoners sought a declaration in an action commenced by writ as a means of gaining access to sensitive prison records. The action was struck out as it raised public law matters and to have proceeded in this way would have avoided the strict controls over access to pre-trial information imposed by the application for review procedure.

Because judicial review is based upon the principle of *ultra vires*, which itself depends upon the interpretation of enabling legislation, it is always possible, at least in theory, for Parliament to expressly exclude the courts' power of review. However, although "privative clauses" protecting compulsory purchase orders from judicial challenge outside the six-week period provided for statutory appeal as to their legality (see page 210) have been effective (*Smith* v. *East Elloe R.D.C.*), the courts are not readily excluded. Thus, in *Anisminic* v. *Foreign Compensation Commission* it was held by the House of Lords that a clause in the Foreign Compensation Act 1950 which provided "determinations by the Foreign Compensation Commission shall not be challenged in any legal proceedings whatsoever" did not prevent the issue of a declaration that as the Commission's purported determination was *ultra vires* it was null and void. A void determination was thus treated as not being a determination at all and was not protected.

The criminal process... gives rise to a particularly acute problem associated with procedural failure, that of unlawful detention and it deserves special mention in concluding our consideration of judicial supervision over the administration. A man who is held against his will without having been *lawfully* arrested, has various options open to him:

  (a) he may use "reasonable force" to break free of the unlawful detention;
  (b) he may sue for damages;
  (c) he may, in appropriate cases, apply for a writ of *habeas corpus*.

An application for a writ of *habeas corpus* may be made by the person detained, or by others acting for him if there is good reason why the individual cannot apply, to the Divisional Court of the Queen's Bench Division or, in vacation time, to a single judge. The writ is an order, by the court or judge, to the person having custody of the individual concerned to bring him before the court, or the judge, so that the legality of the detention can be determined. Professor Harry Street pointed out (in *Freedom, the Individual and the Law*) that the significance of this writ "... cannot be measured by the frequency with which men are set free by it." He contended that "... what counts is that police and others are aware that it is immediately available to prevent illegal imprisonment."

It may happen that the police, as agents of the state, may bring an individual before a court in circumstances in which there is no question of their having broken the law, but in which it is apparent that the case ought not to have been brought. In these circumstances, the individual may ask the court to make an award to cover the costs he has incurred in his defence. An award of costs in these circumstances will often be seen to be a criticism of the fact that the prosecution has been brought. Where there is evidence that a prosecution was brought maliciously and without reasonable cause, the individual who has been prosecuted may, upon acquittal, bring an action for damages for *malicious prosecution*. (See page 100 for a consideration of powers of arrest.)

Section D: Legal Aid and Advice

It is clearly unacceptable that access to specialist legal assistance should be denied to those who are financially disadvantaged. In an attempt to provide for this mischief the state has recognised that the provision of legal aid and advice is as much its responsibility as the provision of education or health care services.

Legal aid and advice in civil cases

A state financed *legal aid* scheme was established in 1949, and this is now regulated by the Legal Aid Act 1974. The scheme, which is administered by the Law Society, extends to all civil courts. The country is divided into areas, each area having its own committee. An application for legal aid is first made to a district committee, with an appeal to an area committee if the application is refused. Where an application is made in respect of proceedings before an appeal court, it is made directly to the area committee.

Legal aid is not available for certain actions (such as defamation of character) and in all cases an applicant must satisfy the committee that it is reasonable to take or defend proceedings. It is also necessary for the applicant to establish that he falls within the set income and capital limits. Even if granted legal aid, the applicant may be required to pay a contribution towards his costs.

Part I of the Legal Aid Act 1974 makes provision for *legal advice and assistance* to be given by solicitors to those found, by the solicitor, to be financially eligible. The scheme covers advice given by the solicitor and covers anything which is accepted as being within the solicitor's normal range of activities *except* for litigation (for which a *legal aid* order is necessary). Legal advice and assistance would, for example, be granted to an applicant (who falls within the financial limits) in order that he might have a will drafted. A solicitor may also, under this scheme, negotiate on his client's behalf in an attempt to settle a claim, or, if the claim can not be settled, the solicitor may, under the scheme, give advice relating to an application for legal aid. The scheme was originally called the "£25 scheme" as the solicitor could claim no more than £25 for his costs and expenses. The limit has been increased and it is now referred to as the "Green Form" scheme.

Legal aid and advice in criminal cases

In criminal cases the *legal aid* scheme is administered by the courts themselves. Legal aid can be obtained in all criminal proceedings but a fresh application must be made at every stage in the hierarchy of courts. An application would, for example, be made to the magistrates' clerk, in relation to proceedings before a magistrates' court, and to the Registrar of the Court of Appeal in relation to proceedings before the Court of Appeal and the House of Lords.

The Legal Aid Act 1974 requires the court awarding legal aid to satisfy itself that "it is in the interest of justice" that an order be made (which is usually taken for granted) and that the applicant's financial resources are such that he requires assistance. The Act does not set strict financial limits in relation to the applicant's means, as it does in relation to civil cases, but the courts have been notified by the Home Office that they should observe the same limits. The court making the order may require the applicant to pay a contribution.

A person accused of a criminal offence may also obtain legal assistance under the *legal advice* scheme, during the post-arrest but pre-trial stage. The Legal Aid Act 1982 provides for a "duty solicitor" scheme by which those accused of criminal offences in a magistrates' court may secure representation.

Part Five

OTHER INSTITUTIONS AND PROCESSES FOR THE RESOLUTION OF CONFLICT

There is only one process by which a person accused of a criminal offence can have his guilt or innocence established: that process involves the determination of the charges brought by the prosecution by a court of criminal jurisdiction (*i.e.* the Crown Court or a magistrates' court). In relation to non-criminal matters, however, alternative processes have developed because of the limitations of an action in a civil court. Such actions are formal, time-consuming and expensive. Because of these factors a non-criminal dispute may now be resolved:

(*a*)   by arbitration;
(*b*)   by an out-of-court settlement;
(*c*)   by a tribunal; and
(*d*)   by an administrative process.

Arbitration
Disputes may be referred to an arbitrator, rather than to the courts if:

(*a*)   a statute so requires; or,
(*b*)   the parties have so agreed.

Arbitration is attractive to businessmen as the proceedings are conducted in private and the award is published only to the parties. The proceedings are also, certainly in straightforward cases, cheaper and quicker than litigation. Perhaps the main advantage, however, is that the arbitrator selected by the parties will often be an expert in the area involved. He may well, as a result, be better equipped than a judge to determine complicated commercial disputes.

Section 1 of the Arbitration Act 1979 provides that there may be an appeal from the arbitrator to the High Court on a question of law providing both parties consent or the court gives leave. The court may not, however, grant leave to appeal if the parties have entered into an *exclusion agreement* which excludes the right to appeal (section 3). In any event, the High Court may grant leave to appeal only if it considers that the determination of the question of law could *substantially* affect the rights of one or more of the parties.

Settlement
The vast majority of civil disputes never actually come before a judge, they are settled by the parties at an earlier stage. The settlement takes effect as a contract between the parties. The present system in England gives every encouragement to the parties to settle. If the plaintiff wins he will be awarded costs, but these costs will not re-imburse his actual

expenditure and there is always the fear of losing. Even if the plaintiff is successful at first instance, the defendant may appeal to the Court of Appeal and, possibly, from there to the House of Lords. The costs involved, paid for by the loser, are phenomenal. The *Evershed Committee* (on *Supreme Court Practice and Procedures*) noted that "a litigant of moderate means, faced with a wealthy opponent who is prepared to fight his case extravagantly, may be forced to abandon his just claim for fear that in the event of losing his case he may be ruined." The Law Society Annual Report for 1963–64 notes that "the odds are, therefore, stacked against the litigant opposed by a rich man or a wealthy company." Nothing has changed since the date of the report to alter that conclusion and one can only guess at the number of "settlements" that are forced upon plaintiffs by wealthy defendants.

Tribunals

The burst of governmental activity and the adoption of the concept of the paternal state (in the form which we now recognise as the *Welfare State*) which followed the First World War, necessitated the setting up of a large number of tribunals to deal with disputes relating to various welfare benefits. These tribunals are known as *administrative* tribunals because of their connection with various parts of the administration, but their decisions are, nonetheless, in the main, of a judicial character (*i.e.* they find facts and apply the appropriate law to these facts). Indeed the *Franks Committee on Administrative Tribunals and Enquiries,* which reported in 1957, considered that tribunals ought to be regarded as a part of our system of adjudication, rather than as an adjunct to the administration. Tribunals may be described as bodies, other than courts of law, with statutory jurisdiction to determine claims, usually, but not necessarily, between an individul (or business organisation) and a government department. Whereas the ordinary courts, in addition to the determination of individual disputes, seek to lay down a coherent system of law through the system of precedent, tribunals do not. The reasons given for the existence of tribunals were given by Lord Pearce in the case of *Anisminic* v. *Foreign Compensation Commission* as, "speed, cheapness and expert knowledge." In short, tribunals form a suitable means of dealing with small repetitive matters, not involving great sums of money nor dealing with matters of great principle.

All tribunals, without exception, owe their origin to statute. Apart from this common feature and the nature of their task, tribunals exhibit few common features. However, certain basic elements were considered desirable by the *Franks Committee* and, in the main, it is possible to distinguish features in tribunals which are referable to an attempt to achieve these. Franks considered "openness, fairness and impartiality" should be watchwords for tribunals. By "openness" they meant that hearings should be in public and publicity should be given to reasoned decisions. "Fairness" should be ensured by appropriate rules, allowing, for example, the calling of witnesses, and requiring that participants should be adequately informed of the administration's case. "Impartiality," of course, is essential to any judicial body, but Franks considered that tribunals should be free from not only real but also apparent influence of government departments. Many today feel concern that individuals attending tribunals should be obliged to attend the hearing in buildings occupied by the department with whom they are in dispute. Moreover, tribunals are frequently supported by clerical and administrative staff drawn from the department concerned in the dispute. This cannot be viewed with satisfaction.

Most tribunals have three members for a\ hearing (*e.g.* industrial tribunals are presided over by a legally qualified chairman, selected from a panel drawn up by the Lord Chancellor, and two other members selected from panels which the appropriate minister has drawn up after consultation with bodies representative of employers and employed persons). Some appointments are full-time and salaried but most are part-time, with provision merely being made for the payment of expenses. Members are normally only dismissable by the appropriate minister and only after he has obtained the consent of the Lord Chancellor. Normally, the decision of a tribunal is final as to fact but there may be challenge upon questions of law either by means of judicial review (see page 40) or by appeal.

The advantages which have been claimed for tribunals are many, not least of which are cheapness and accessibility. Tribunals are often conveniently situated, normally no fees are payable for hearings and parties are encouraged to appear in person. (Legal Aid is not generally available to pay for legal representation before a tribunal, although Legal Advice may be obtained to assist in the preparation of a case prior to the hearing itself). In practice, members of trade unions are often assisted and represented by trade union officials. However, most citizens are not members of trade unions and clearly the inarticulate and less able individual may be placed at a disadvantage when confronted with a case presented by an official of a government department who may be employed mainly to deal with cases before a particular tribunal. Nevertheless, the encouragement of informal procedure and the expertise of the tribunal members may be expected to overcome, in some measure, such disadvantages. Frequently, cases can be brought and disposed of very quickly through the tribunal system, tribunals normally announcing their findings immediately following the hearing. Undoubtedly tribunals lift a considerable burden from our overworked courts.

Although all tribunals depend upon particular statutes for their existence and the statute will determine their composition and jurisdiction, there is one important general statute in this sphere. This is the Tribunals and Inquiries Act 1971, which is a consolidating statute, the forerunner of which, the 1958 Act, implemented most of the important recommendations of the *Franks Committee on Administrative Tribunals and Enquiries*. This legislation provided for the setting up of the *Council on Tribunals* as a statutory body, consisting of 10 to 15 part-time members, with the principal task of keeping under review the working of those tribunals (and inquiries) specified by Parliament. The Council submits an annual report to the Lord Chancellor, which he in turn lays before Parliament. These reports are published and provide an insight into the work of tribunals and any current problems as seen by the Council. The Council has provided a valuable service in securing improvements in the procedures of tribunals (and inquiries), for it must be consulted in the making of delegated legislation governing rules of procedure. The Act also provides for a right of appeal to the High Court, from certain specified tribunals, on a point of law. Section 12 of the 1971 Act provides that tribunals must, if requested, provide reasons for a decision. This requirement is of singular importance in the event of a challenge to a decision either on appeal or by judicial review. Moreover, a requirement to give reasons for a decision may be felt to provide a most desirable impetus to good decision-making.

Administrative process

The rights of citizens have increasingly been seen as extending beyond basic legal rights to encompass fair treatment and, to this end, a number of *extra-judicial* remedies have been provided. The office of the *Parliamentary Commissioner for Administration* was established under the Parliamentary Commissioner Act 1967. The Commissioner's task is to investigate complaints of "injustice in consequence of maladministration" made by members of the public against central government departments. The terms *injustice* and *maladministration* are not defined but the late Mr. Crossman in introducing the Act said that the government had preferred the term "injustice" to the terms *loss* or *damage*, for they would have had legal overtones and could have been held to exclude "one thing which I am particularly anxious shall remain within the meaning of the word—the sense of outrage aroused by unfair or incompetent administration even where the complainant has suffered no loss." "Maladministration," he suggested, "might include such things as bias, neglect, inattention, delay, incompetence, perversity, turpitude, arbitrariness, ..."

Not all complaints of maladministration fall within the jurisdiction of the Parliamentary Commissioner, for the Act excludes, for example, the spheres of local authorities, public corporations and the National Health Service. Most significantly, the Commissioner shall not conduct an investigation into "any action in respect of which the person aggrieved has or had a right of appeal, reference or review to or before a tribunal . . . [or] a remedy by way of proceedings in any court of law." The Commissioner does have a discretion to waive this provision "if satisfied that in the particular circumstances it is not reasonable to expect the complainant to resort or have resort to it." Thus the non-availability of Legal Aid to support an action may provide grounds for the Commissioner to exercise his discretion, even though the complainant does, in theory, have a legal remedy. Probably, the accessibility of a process of appeal to tribunals will preclude the Commissioner from undertaking investigations in appropriate circumstances.

The Parliamentary Commissioner cannot award damages to a complainant, but, in practice, he has often obtained *ex gratia* payments from government departments (although he has not always been successful). The administration has not always been willing to accept his reports (the Inland Revenue has, on occasion, refused to waive arrears of tax where the burden has built up due to maladministration on its part). The Commissioner may issue special reports to Parliament if his investigation reveals serious matters and Parliament may then, of course, take action.

Although the Health Service and Local Government, Police and Water Authorities are excluded from the jurisdiction of the Parliamentary Commissioner these areas are governed by the *Health Service Commissioners* and the *Commissioners for Local Government*. Further, although the Public Corporations fall outside the jurisdiction of the Parliamentary Commissioner there are avenues of redress provided by the various statutes setting up these public bodies. The constituent statutes frequently provide for consumer bodies to act in a consultative capacity (*e.g.* Electricity

Consultative Councils). These bodies undertake a most valuable function in frequently mediating between consumers and the corporations and do undertake fairly wide ranging investigations, as well as considering individual complaints.

The least formal remedy against the administration is by way of complaint to elected representatives, be it Members of Parliament or local councillors. These elected representatives can frequently achieve much through their intimate knowledge of the administration. However, the efficacy of such avenues of redress does depend upon the energy, expertise, aptitude and workload of the individual representative.

Finally, perhaps the most vivid illustration of the triumph of fairness over strict legal rights lies in the sphere of deprivation of liberty. It is, unfortunately, possible for an innocent person to be convicted of a criminal offence and to lose his appeal against this conviction. In such an event, the individual will be unjustly punished and may even be unjustly imprisoned. Where cases of this type come to light the Crown, acting on the advice of the Home Secretary, will exercise its prerogative to grant a free pardon, which sets aside the individual's sentence and his conviction. It is likely, in such cases, that the state would also attempt to compensate the unfortunate individual by making an *ex gratia* financial award. It should be noted that whilst these victims of the criminal process have been wrongly convicted they have not been unlawfully imprisoned, for they have been deprived of their liberty in a way which is procedurally correct.

Part Six

THE PROVISION OF LEGAL SERVICES

Like the Ritz, the courts of this country are open to all. However, in practice, those who wish to litigate are obliged to engage the services of lawyers. Similarly, the law serves all, but although it is generally true to say that no one will benefit from pleading his ignorance of the law, its deeper mysteries are in practical terms only accessible to those trained in law. It is, therefore, to the *legal office*, in its various forms, that those faced with legal problems of a substantial nature are likely to turn. This book is primarily directed towards a consideration of legal principles and rules but an adequate appreciation of the law requires, in addition, a view of the lawyers and the offices in which they toil in the service of others.

The legal profession is divided into two quite distinct branches, *solicitors* and *barristers*, and membership has been increasing at unprecedented rates throughout the past decade. There are some 5,500 practising barristers and about 45,000 solicitors, in around 6,500 firms, conducting private practice. In addition, the profession is served by a further significant body of legally trained personnel, 6,000 *Fellows* (together with 8,000 *Associate* and student members) of the Institute of Legal Executives employed mainly in solicitors' offices in private practice, the legal departments of public or local authorities, or in industry and commerce. The Report of the Royal Commission on Legal Services (*The Benson Report*), published in 1979, concluded that "The legal profession should continue to be organised in two branches, barristers and solicitors" and that following its most detailed investigation " . . . the profession should have a period of orderly development free, so far as possible, from external interventions." Despite this conclusion there has been a lively and, indeed, a continuing debate as to the form of profession which will best serve the community. There is, as yet, no clear indication as to likely changes and, as it may be fairly claimed that the Benson Report found the profession to be basically satisfactory, a brief description of its current profile is likely to remain helpful for a time. It is instructive to consider the profession in the light of the five characteristics which Benson identified as denoting the status of a profession. These are: (i) a central governing body representing the profession with powers of control and discipline over its members; (ii) the function of giving advice or service in a specialised field of knowledge (and in the case of the legal profession, a direct responsibility to the court for the administration of justice); (iii) specified standards of education and training as prerequisites of memberships; (iv) the obligation of members to observe high standards of conduct over and above strict legal requirement; and (v) an obligation to act in the interests of clients so as to discharge duties in such a manner as a client would himself have acted had he possessed the knowledge and means.

Section A: The Legal Profession

Barristers

The origins of the legal profession have been traced to the end of the thirteenth century when a restriction was placed upon the clergy from acting on behalf of others in matters not relating to canon law. From this time a number of societies of lawyers formed and had their accommodation (known as chambers) within easy access of the courts, in London, around which their business revolved. Four of these societies of barristers remain today, the Inner and Middle Temples (names associated with the Crusading Order of Knights Templar whose buildings were taken over by the lawyers on dissolution of the Order) Lincoln's Inn and Gray's Inn. For many centuries the profession was undivided and barristers dealt directly with their lay clients although it became common for clients to appoint agents of "attorneys" to act on their behalf and in these instances the barristers took instructions from the attorneys. In the seventeenth century the right to practise as an advocate in the Royal Courts became restricted to members of the Inns of Court and by the nineteenth century the practice of accepting instructions to appear in court only from a solicitor acting for a lay client was finally established. The seventeenth century also introduced the system of "taking silk" under which barristers of standing may become *Queen's Counsel*, entitled to wear a silk gown, and lead a "junior" barrister in court. Juniors are involved in both advocacy and preliminary paper work but *Q.C.'s* specialise in advocacy although they do provide opinions as part of their basic task. Appointment as a *Q.C.* follows application but is entirely within the discretion of the Lord Chancellor.

The Inns of Court were originally not only disciplined associations of lawyers but also centres of learning, providing an academic environment within which members could practise, study and enjoy a communal social life. There is still a residual element of this blissful ideal, for the Inns provide libraries and halls in which members take their refreshments together and, indeed, dining with colleagues is an essential part of the training of a barrister. However, the institutions of the Bar have undergone an evolutionary process whereby today the education of barristers is principally the concern of the Council of Legal Education and the Inns of Court School of Law. Control over the Bar is now vested in the Benches of the Inns of Court and the body which is representative of the profession as a whole is known as the Council.

Solicitors

As has been previously indicated, lawyers from the earliest times formed themselves into associations. Certain of these associations came to mark formal divisions in the profession, barristers forming one, attorneys, representing and advising clients, another. There were also notaries, scriveners, proctors and solicitors, the latter two specialising in matrimonial matters and land, respectively. The Judicature Act 1873 merged the functions of solicitors, attorneys and proctors and adopted the common title of solicitor which is now reserved to those qualified in this branch of the profession. From early times solicitors have been recognised as officers of the court and the Master of the Rolls (who presides over the Civil Division of the Court of Appeal) has the function of approving the rules governing their conduct and practice within the profession. The Law

Society was formed by Royal Charter in 1831 and as the representative and controlling body has as its objectives "promoting professional improvement and facilitating the acquisition of legal knowledge." The Solicitors Acts confer wide powers upon the Law Society which is responsible for the examination and training of those entering the profession. Only those who have been admitted by the Society, entered upon the Roll, and hold a current practising certificate are entitled to act as solicitors. Professional conduct is also the concern of the Society but because of the status of being officers of the court, solicitors are subjected not only to a disciplinary jurisdiction of the Society but also to that of the Supreme Court and any of its judges.

Legal executives

In the nineteenth century, before the introduction of copying machines and typewriters, solicitors and attorneys employed considerable numbers of clerks, mainly for the purpose of handwriting documents. In addition to the menial clerks whose laborious tasks have been superseded, there was a class of senior clerks undertaking legal fee-earning work and these were the forerunners of the present "legal executives." In 1892 the Solicitors' Managing Clerks' Association was founded to represent their interests. Unfortunately the Association did not achieve its aim of raising the calibre, status and level of earnings of managing clerks and its qualifying examination, leading to a managing clerk's certificate, was not widely supported. In 1963, following discussions between the Law Society and the Association, a new, independent, examining and qualifying body for unadmitted staff, *The Institute of Legal Executives*, was formed. Membership of the Institute is not a condition of employment in solicitors' and other legal offices but the Institute seeks to improve the number and quality of unadmitted staff. The title "legal executive" is widely used to identify members of a solicitor's staff who whilst not qualified as solicitors perform professional work but, in proper use it refers to *Fellows of the Institute*. These legally trained personnel must have completed at least eight years employment with a solicitor and have passed the Institute's qualifying examinations. The examinations are of a high standard, laying particular emphasis upon the practical as well as academic aspects of legal work, and the final, Fellowship, examinations are recognised by the Law Society as earning exemption from equivalent papers in the first qualifying examination for solicitors.

The Royal Commission on Legal Services concluded that "all solicitors should acknowledge the valuable contribution which may be made by legal executives to the work of the profession and, in recognition of the advantage to themselves in doing so, should encourage their staff to join the Institute and attempt its qualifications." Moreover, it was indicated that the close links between the Law Society and the Institute should be maintained and "wherever possible and appropriate the Law Society should bring the Institute into preliminary discussions of policy issues affecting its members' interests."

Functions within the profession

The basic task of a solicitor is to give general legal advice and to conduct the daily legal affairs of his clients. Surveys of consultations undertaken for The Benson Report revealed that by far the greatest single category related to conveyancing, which accounted for 30 per cent. Other categories were: estates of deceased persons, 11 per cent.; making or altering wills, 10 per cent.; family matters (including divorce and custody disputes), 12 per cent.; motoring offences four per cent. and other offences, three per cent.; road accidents and work-place accidents, three per cent. each and other accidents, one per cent.; faulty goods, buying and selling businesses and self-employment, two per cent.; and a miscellaneous number of problems accounting for one per cent. including those arising from landlord and tenant relationships, neighbours, employment, insurance and revenue matters. Solicitors have long had a number of statutory monopolies over certain types of work whereby only they (together with barristers) might, by way of business, create documents relating to legal proceedings and the disposal of property. However, the Administration of Justice Act 1985 makes provision for the establishment of a profession of "licensed conveyancers." The members of this new profession are to be exempted from the restraints imposed by the solicitors' "monopoly" over the preparation, for reward, of contracts and deeds relating to the sale of land.

Barristers are retained by solicitors to undertake specified tasks as and when necessary to the conduct of their clients' affairs. These tasks may consist of the drafting of documents, provision of specialist advice, preparation of documents with a view to litigation, or actually representing a client in court. The barrister's work is somewhat remote for he is not in regular contact with his clients and he does not normally communicate with others on behalf of his clients. At the time of The Benson Report, of the 4,363 barristers practising in 303 sets of chambers, 3,080 operated in London and the remaining 1,283 were in 104 sets in 28 provincial centres. Although there has been an increase to some 5,500 practising barristers, the percentage operating in the provinces has remained constant at around 30 per cent. and the number of sets of chambers has remained below 350. Practising women barristers remain below 700. There is considerable overlap in the work undertaken by the two branches of the profession for both provide legal advice and both act as advocates. However, only barristers have full rights of audience in all courts. Solicitors may appear before magistrates' and county courts (where most civil and criminal cases are dealt with) and have limited rights before the Crown Court but they must normally engage the services of a barrister before the High Court. In practice, many solicitors frequently instruct counsel even where they have rights of audience, as a matter of convenience, relying upon counsel's expertise in advocacy or in a specialised branch of law. Nevertheless, there is a continuing and vigorous debate over what are commonly referred to as the restrictive practices maintained by the Bar which preserve their pre-eminence in advocacy. It is fruitless to speculate as to the eventual outcome but already minor inroads have been made whereby solicitors are afforded rights to appear before the High Court.

It may be an over-simplification to regard solicitors as general practitioners and barristers as specialists but it does at least afford a rough guide to the basic scene. Some solicitors specialise in particular areas of law and, indeed, may even make advocacy their specialism within their firms but most are general practitioners and not advocates. Most barristers, however, do have specialisms and regard themselves as specialist advocates, yet some barristers, particularly those specialising in Chancery matters, rarely see a court, spending their days drafting documents and advising upon the technicalities of company law, property and wills. Although there are no surveys of the work undertaken by the Bar it is reasonable to conclude that crime and personal injuries account for the greatest proportion, with a substantial amount of time devoted to divorce. To a considerable degree these are the categories of work financed out of legal aid. The survey of sources of barristers' income undertaken for The Benson Report revealed that 24 per cent. of the earnings of silks were attributable to public funds and of juniors, 52 per cent. Barristers were also shown to be consulted in four per cent. of all the matters on which solicitors were consulted and about half of those instances involved a barrister appearing on behalf of a client before a court or tribunal.

Licensed conveyancers

The profession of licensed conveyancer is at the embryo stage. Under Part II of the Administration of Justice Act 1985 machinery is established whereby a profession may be created but its shape remains obscure. The task of giving definition to the profession is in the hands of the Conveyancing Council and until its work is completed speculation as to the impact of the new profession upon the existing professions is unhelpful. In simple terms, section 11 of the 1985 Act provides that the so-called "conveyancing monopoly" created by section 22 of the Solicitors Act 1974 shall extend to licensed conveyancers. Only conveyancing services, as defined by the legislation, will be subject to regulation which will, of course, leave the licensed conveyancer free to additionally prepare wills or short-leases not under seal as these may be done by anyone.

Section B: The Legal Office

PRIVATE PRACTICE

Both branches of the profession employ staff but their differing functions impose a requirement for quite dissimilar specialist staff and office organisations. Each type of office is now briefly described together with a consideration of personnel.

The solicitor's office

A solicitor requires an organisation which can efficiently handle, on a continuing basis, his clients' files, records and money. Obviously firms vary in size but The Benson Report revealed a movement towards amalgamations and that the number of one partner firms was falling. This trend has continued so that today there are less than 4,000 solicitors practising on their own account. In 1979, 34 per cent. of firms had one principal solicitor; 24 per cent., two principals; 24 per cent., three to four principals; and 18 per cent. had five or more principals. The Law Society in its evidence to the Royal Commission indicated that the typical firm was situated in a provincial town and was composed of three principals, five other fee-earners of whom one was an assistant solicitor, two were legal executives, one an articled clerk and one a junior clerk. In addition, the firm would employ ten full-time and three part-time staff consisting of accounts clerks, secretaries, a telephonist and receptionist. Thus the total staff would be 21 and the Law Society claimed that two-thirds of all firms were of this size or smaller. Out of his gross fees, a principal is likely to pay around 70 per cent. towards the running of his office, with about 25 per cent. of his time being spent upon "non-productive" activities such as administration.

Of course the organisation of legal offices varies considerably but a useful account, directed towards practice efficiency, is to be found in *Organisation and Management of a Solicitor's Office*, by P. J. Purton *et al*. New work in a firm sufficiently large to allow specialisation may be typically broken down into such categories as: (a) conveyancing; (b) probate; (c) matrimonial; (d) litigation; (e) commercial; (f) town planning and compulsory purchase; (g) taxation; and (h) general business including the drafting of wills. Allocation of work within a specialism is of course a further matter and delegation to legal executives and articled clerks is an essential facet of an efficient operation. The Benson Report revealed that of the time spent on conveyancing 70 per cent. was that of qualified solicitors and 30 per cent. that of others. Indeed, in 17 per cent. of cases qualified solicitors were not involved at all! Moreover, Fellows of the Institute of Legal Executives do have certain rights of audience, the County Courts (Rights of Audience) Direction 1978 allows such rights in regard to unopposed applications for adjournment and applications for judgment by consent where there is no question as to the applicant's entitlement to judgment or its terms. However, it must always be borne in mind that sole responsibility lies upon the solicitor for the work done in his office and by his authority. Basic office routines are described in our companion book, *Huddy: Introduction to Legal Practice I*, by Charles Blake.

Barristers' chambers

The term "a set of chambers" is used to describe a group of barristers who, being prevented by the custom of their profession from operating a partnership, nevertheless work together as a professional practice sharing accommodation and the services of a clerk. Barristers do not employ other fee-earners and spend only approximately 30 per cent. of their gross fees upon administrative expenses but they do employ specialist, although not legally trained, staff. In their evidence to the Royal Commission on Legal Services the Senate explained the misleading title of the administrative lynch-pin of any chambers, the barrister's clerk. Although the general description "clerk" covers a wide range of employees engaged in paperwork and book-keeping it is inadequate to describe the unique post of office administrator and accountant, business manager and agent, which this senior employee holds. His duties provide a fair guide to the operation of a barristers' chambers and may be catalogued under three heads:

(a) *Office administrator and accountant* . . . in the exercise of this function the senior clerk operates on behalf of all members of his chambers and may be expected to supervise secretarial and typing support staff, instruct and supervise junior clerks and oversee the accounts and preparation of an annual statement of income and expenditure.

(b) *Business manager* . . . this function is undertaken on behalf of each member of the chambers as a separate principal and entails the maintenance of a diary of professional engagements, which is a highly skilled task for it requires not only vigilance in checking court lists but experience in assessing appropriate caseloads. The clerk also negotiates upon fees and manages his principal's accounts with solicitors.

(c) *Agent* . . . in this capacity the duties are diverse but may generally be taken to include ensuring that new entrants to chambers receive appropriate work, advising solicitors upon which barrister may best undertake particular briefs and, indeed, giving impartial advice to solicitors on the allocation of work to his own or other chambers.

There are some 300 senior barristers' clerks who, although being represented by the Barristers' Clerks' Association, operate upon an autonomous basis making generalisations extremely difficult. Indeed, 75 per cent. of the clerks responding to a survey by their Association had no formal contracts of employment.

There are as previously indicated, two basic classes of work undertaken by a barrister, advocacy and paper-work. When papers are forwarded by a solicitor to chambers they are accompanied by written instructions as to the work required, where a court appearance is indicated the instructions are known as a *brief*. Both forms of instructions have backsheets giving the names of counsel and solicitor, the nature of the work and, normally, the name of the client, together with the title of the case and court if appropriate. Where routine paper-work is involved a fee is not usually agreed until the work is completed but in the case of briefs there is normally a provisionally agreed fee marked although in all cases a revision may be made after scrutiny of the papers. Barristers must not appear in court on behalf of fee-paying clients unless a fee has been marked on the brief so as to avoid any suspicion that counsel may have a financial interest in the outcome of a case. Where counsel is to be remunerated out of public funds the fees are not agreed between the solicitor and the barristers' clerk but are determined at the conclusion of the proceedings for here the fees allowable are settled on *legal aid taxation*. Where counsel are instructed to prosecute they normally simply accept the fees allowed by the Crown Court on taxation of costs out of central funds.

The relationship between a barrister, solicitor, and client may be summarised as follows:

(*a*) there is a contractual relationship between the solicitor and his lay client;

(*b*) the solicitor has responsibility for retaining a barrister and agreeing fees; and

(*c*) the barrister cannot sue to recover his fees but the solicitor is obliged to recover the fees from the lay client, and may bring proceedings to this end, being professionally responsible to pay over the fees to the barrister.

Gaps in the provision of legal services

The nature of legal education and, in consequence, the scope of the provision of legal services, has largely been determined by reference to the traditional demands made of law offices. Thus, solicitors have tended to acquire expertise relating to private sector housing, the administration of estates, the law relating to business organisations and commercial transactions and the law relating to accidents and industrial injuries. They often have no training or expertise in the areas of public sector housing or welfare law. Although such areas are just as likely to require the individual to seek legal advice as the more "traditional" areas of concern to lawyers, they are not areas which have, in the past, brought clients into the legal office for, without doubt, consulting a solicitor has been, for many years, a practice which simply did not present itself as feasible to many of the less fortunate within society (precisely those, in fact, who would have brought problems associated with the "missing" areas of expertise). The fact that providers of legal services have not been able to meet this latent, but nonetheless real, demand is reflected in the geographical location of law offices, which are rarely found in the poorer urban areas. To meet this need there has been a movement towards the creation of "neighbour-hood" law centres staffed by lawyers with appropriate expertise and located mainly in the older residential areas of our big cities. The centres all rely upon public funding and in times of financial stringency their continued development remains problematical.

LEGAL OFFICES IN INDUSTRY, COMMERCE AND THE PUBLIC SERVICE

There are a great many lawyers engaged other than in private practice, being qualified as either solicitors or barristers. Although estimates of their numbers vary there are at least as many barristers employed outside as are engaged in private practice and probably in excess of 10,000 solicitors similarly engaged. The work of these employed barristers and solicitors is similar, although there are certain restrictions placed upon barristers as to the work which they may undertake in connection with the transfer of property because of the solicitors' statutory monopoly noted earlier. A barrister in employment is basically a legal adviser but a solicitor may be engaged to work as a solicitor as well as a legal adviser. In *Crompton Amusement Machines Limited* v. *Commissioners of Customs and Excise*, Lord Denning, M.R., explained the position of salaried solicitors in these words: "They are regarded by the law as in every respect in the same position as those who practice on their own account. The only difference is that they act for one client only, and not for several clients." The relevance of this distinction is that because the salaried lawyer relies upon his employer for his livelihood he may be faced with pressures from within his employer's organisation which strain his loyalty to his profession. The traditions of the legal profession require independent and objective attitudes and sensitivity to internal organisational interests and policies may run counter to this desirable position. As a balance to the problem of independence it must be noted that The Benson Report did caution that "independence and self regulation can breed insularity and complacency and a narrow attitude of mind."

The legal department in industry and commerce

It is possible that one cannnot identify a typical legal department of a commercial or industrial undertaking. Even some of the largest organisations operate without salaried legal advisers, preferring to rely upon a favoured practice as the fount of their legal knowledge. Again many organisations operate on a shoestring requiring a sole adviser to display the insight associated with the combined wisdom of the whole legal profession. However, certain classes of employer have an established policy of maintaining their own legal staff and a short reflection upon two of these is perhaps worthwhile. Banks, for example, employ professionally qualified personnel within their executor and trustee departments. The services provided by such staff encompass the obtaining of probate of wills and generally administering the estates of deceased persons, giving effect to their expressed wishes. This may require the management of stocks and shares, sale and purchase of land, various contractual negotiations and the management of trusts in the service of beneficiaries. Insurance companies also normally operate their own legal departments with staff engaged in drafting policies of insurance, assessing and settling claims. However, most commercial and industrial legal departments simply undertake the tasks normally associated with private practice. Of course, it is unlikely that divorce will feature on the menu but routine conveyancing and contracting are likely to be meat and drink. Other more specialised activities may be the formation of subsidiary companies, and advising upon the rights and duties of employers, insurance, patents, trademarks, copyright and all manner of intellectual property rights.

The civil service legal department

Before considering legal offices within the civil service in detail it is helpful to note certain office holders whose functions have wide impact upon government legal departments generally. The office of *Attorney-General* is a political appointment as Chief Law Officer of the Crown, he is also Head of the Bar. His functions include: advising the Queen in her private capacity; answering questions in the House of Commons upon legal matters; representing the Crown in court in matters of constitutional significance; advising the government; and advising government departments. The *Solicitor-General*, despite his title, is also a barrister and acts as deputy to the Attorney-General. Operating under the general supervison of the Attorney-General (although appointed by the Home Secretary) is *The Director of Public Prosecutions*. This is a non-political post and its holder may be either a solicitor or barrister. The D.P.P., who is assisted by a considerable staff of solicitors and barristers, holds a significant place in the administration of criminal justice. Under the Prosection of Offences Act 1985 the D.P.P. is the head of the *Crown Prosecution Service* established by that Act and is responsible to the Attorney-General. All prosecutions, other than those undertaken privately, are now conducted by the D.P.P. through the Crown Prosecution Service. The D.P.P. retains the power of decision over whether to prosecute in cases of serious crime and his consent is required, by statute, before prosecutions for certain offences may be instituted. He also undertakes a co-ordinating or harmonising role for he is advised of all cases within the categories specified in regulations emanating from the Attorney-General and may offer advice as to whether a matter should be pursued or dropped. Thus, should a local police prosecutor, for example, decline to prosecute then the D.P.P. may take over. In the event of a prosecution going ahead against the advice of the D.P.P. then he may advise the Attorney-General who has power to *enter a nolle prosequi* withdrawing the proceedings under the royal prerogative.

Finally, the *Lord Chancellor* in addition to his political and judicial duties has responsibility for the administration of the Supreme Court and the county courts (magistrates' courts are administered by the Home Office). He has also a general responsiblity for the state of the civil law and to a lesser extent for the criminal law (primarily within the responsibility of the Home Office). A specific duty is to oversee legal advice and assistance generally, and to undertake direct responsibility for legal aid in civil cases. The Lord Chancellor's Department is responsible for expenditure of about £600 million a year. It has a staff of 10,000, running a court system which in total deals with well over two million cases, criminal and civil, in a year. The Department consists of a number of offices employing lawyers but the Department is treated as a single unit within which staff are likely to move. For ease of administration of the 400 or so courts that fall within the Department's responsibility England and Wales has been divided into six areas, known as circuits. Each circuit is under the control of a "circuit administrator" to whom "courts administrators" are responsible for the courts in their areas. The Lord Chancellor also has responsibility for three other government departments: the Land Registry, the Public Record Office and the Northern Ireland Court Service. These are known as "sister" departments but are largely autonomous. In addition, the Department has a number of "associated offices" which lie outside the circuit system. The London headquarters' staff deal with all facets of the administration and legislation for which the Lord Chancellor is responsible, including: the Legal Aid and Advice Scheme; and the rules of the Supreme Court, county courts and certain tribunals. Associated offices include:

(a) *The Law Commission* . . . established in 1965, in which legal staff are concerned with detailed schemes to reform the law in all its aspects, both civil and criminal, together with maintaining an overview of the implications of law deriving from the European Economic Community.

(b) *The Council on Tribunals* . . . which deals with the constitution and working of most tribunals, including rules of procedure.

(c) *The Official Solicitor's Office* . . . in which staff support the Official Solicitor who has numerous tasks as an Officer of the Supreme Court. For example, he represents children and mentally disabled persons ensuring that they are properly represented in various legal processes. These would include proceedings before the Court of Protection or any of the situations in which a *guardian ad litem*, or next friend, is required.

The civil service provides employment for over a thousand professionally qualified legal staff ranging through various departments such as the Charity Commission, Department of Trade and Industry, Office of Fair Trading and the Office of the Public Trustee. The latter is a large Civil Service office which falls within the overall responsibility of the Lord Chancellor as an associated office.

The *Public Trustee* is a trust corporation set up under the Public Trustee Act 1906 to undertake the business of executorship and trusteeship. He may act as executor or administrator of an estate, or as trustee of a will or settlement under original appointment or later transfer. The original underlying scheme was that the office should provide a trustee of strength and independence for family trusts in cases of dissension and also where testators envisaged particular difficulties. Fees are charged for services but the department is intended to be non-profit making, the fees merely meeting departmental expenses. The department is organised into sections dealing with trust administration, accounting, property management, taxation and investment. Professionally qualified staff act as trust officers in cases demanding professional skills or as advisers to other staff.

The county court, which also falls within the overall responsibility of the Lord Chancellor, provides an example of a *court office* and is selected for consideration as the most widely used civil court. The chief civil servant in a county court is the *registrar*, a solicitor, who is responsible for the staff and also acts as an assistant judge. The non-legally qualified staff may typically be pictured as headed by a chief clerk and a court administrator, who works under a circuit administrator, arranging court sittings. Responsible to the chief clerk may be three higher executive officers presiding over a number of administrative sections staffed by, perhaps, 20 clerical officers. These sections reflect the wide ranging civil jurisdiction of the county court and may, for example, specialise in (a) undefended divorce; (b) issuing warrants enforcing judgments; (c) bankruptcy and chancery matters; and (d) miscellaneous general business.

The legal department in local government

The work of a legal department within a *local authority* is likely to be extremely varied for local government provides an almost endless range of services. The tasks commonly associated with an office within a substantial authority include basic contracting, conveyancing and accident claims as well as specialised aspects, such as public health, education, housing, planning, compulsory purchase, highways, transport and social welfare services. A picture of a typical legal department could take the form of a senior solicitor at its head with three deputies, two of whom may be qualified solicitors and the other a senior administrator. Within the department there may be six assistant solicitors serving four sections with specialisms such as: (a) housing, social services and committees; (b) highways, planning and building regulations; (c) hackney carriage, street trading and general licensing; and (d) staffing. Each of these sections may require up to six staff, some being legal executives (designated legal assistants).

The staff of *magistrates' court offices* are local authority employees and not civil servants. A magistrates' court revolves around the holder of the post of *Clerk to the Justices* who is not only responsible for advising the lay magistrates on law and procedure but also for the running of the court office. The justices' clerk must today be qualified as either a solicitor or barrister and is appointed by the Magistrates' Court Committee for the county, although his selection is confirmed by the Home Secretary. A few justices' clerks appointments are part-time but it is more usual for them to be full-time. A magistrates' court has not only a wide criminal jurisdiction in minor matters but also an extensive civil role. The latter encompasses: domestic proceedings (*e.g.* making maintenance and affiliation orders; the collection of certain debts (*e.g.* sums due in respect of electricity, gas, water and rates); and duties as licensing justices. This wide jurisdiction necessitates multiple sittings in the larger courts with justices sitting perhaps in juvenile courts, domestic courts, normal criminal courts and in licensing sessions. The organisation of the office will reflect the diverse functions of the court. Although generalisations are difficult, a medium sized magistrates' court office is likely to take something of the following form. Working under the justices' clerk will be a deputy clerk and, perhaps, six court clerks who may *take courts*, acting as justices' clerks, but subject to the overall control of the office holder. The administrative staff may consist of four ushers and 15 to 20 clerical officers. The number of divisions within the office varies but may typically be seen as including:

(a) *Money Payments* (in up-to-date offices being centred upon a computer), which records the collection of fines, fees and witness expenses, generated by the criminal sessions, together with maintenance and affiliation payments from the civil jurisdiction. From the sums collected appropriate disbursements are made and follow-up procedures instituted in cases of non-payment.

(b) *Process Issue*, which issues summonses following the receipt of information.

(c) *Legal Aid*, which advises and makes appropriate arrangements in the interests of those appearing before the court.

(d) *General Court Administration*, which attends to sittings and makes arrangements for lay magistrates to attend for duty.

THE INDIVIDUAL (PRIVATE) CONSUMER

Part One

STATE, CRIME AND INDIVIDUAL FREEDOMS

The visitor to the legal office, or the *law consumer* as we have described him, may be someone who has been drawn into dispute not with another individual, but rather with one of the institutions representing the state. The state has, this century, increasingly acquired decision-making powers and responsibilities. This has inevitably brought it into conflict with individuals within the society it governs. These new areas of state responsibility have been added to the more traditional functions of the state which encompass, for example, the obligation to preserve public order and, of course, these traditional areas of state concern still retain their potential for bringing the state and the individual citizen into dispute.

Before any attempt is made to identify potential areas of dispute, it may be useful to define "the state" and to indicate some of its functions.

The state

"The state" is a term which conveniently brings together all the agencies involved in government and public sector administration. It includes all the policy-making bodies (*e.g.* the office of Prime Minister, the Cabinet, Parliament, government ministers and local government councils) and a variety of bodies involved in the implementation of policy (*e.g.* the civil service and local authority and hospital administrators). It covers, in effect, all the bodies involved in the provision of services for which there is no direct payment, or minimal direct payment (*e.g.* law and order, health services, education, defence, water and sewerage). The term is, however, a flexible one and is also used, at times, to embrace other public bodies who do not provide "free" services but sell them commercially at market price. Used in this way "the state" is a term wide enough to cover, for example, all the nationalised industries.

The authority of the state

The state not only has *power* to influence the activities of individuals within society, it also has *authority* to do so. Individuals within society are aware of the extent to which their freedoms are curtailed by the actions of the state (which thus has power over them) and, generally speaking, *accept* that it is legitimate for the state to exercise such power (thus recognising the authority of the state). Individuals may not welcome the exercise of state power, or even approve of it, but they tend to accept it. Whilst accepting the legitimacy of state involvement, however, individuals may, at times, suspect that particular officers or agencies of the state have overstepped their powers or exercised them irregularly. It is in such instances that the individual may turn to the legal office for advice and assistance.

Functions of the state

In relatively unsophisticated societies, the state confines itself to straightforward and fairly non-contentious activities. It seeks to defend society from external threat (in the form of invasion by foreign armies) and, internally, to protect individuals from particularly gross instances of abuse to themselves (*e.g.* murder, assault and rape) or to their property (*e.g.* theft and arson). Our own society has developed in such a way that the state has, in addition to the exercise of such functions, thought it proper to intrude into other areas of activity. The state has, thus, from time to time, attempted to preserve "appropriate" moral standards by prohibiting certain "unacceptable" behaviour (*e.g.* soliciting on the streets for the purposes of prostitution, homosexual conduct, attempts to commit suicide, publication of obscene material and blasphemy). It has, further, displayed in recent years a recognition that it should enforce new, "public," concepts of morality. It accepts, for example, that it should protect the general body of consumers within society from commercial abuse and exploitation. Similarly, it would not seek to avoid responsibility for the protection of an environment increasingly at risk from the consequences of unrestrained economic activity.

We may, perhaps, classify these three areas of state concern and of criminal activity as:

   (a) conduct which is traditionally and almost universally recognised as criminal;
   (b) conduct which offends entrenched notions of morality; and
   (c) conduct which is, in contemporary terms, anti-social and in need of regulation.

In all of the above areas, the state prohibits various forms of conduct and invokes criminal sanctions against those who ignore its strictures. A *crime* can now be seen, perhaps, to be nothing more nor less than activity which the state wishes to prevent and is prepared to penalise. As moral, social and economic views change within society, so too does the attitude of the state and its approach to certain types of activity. Thus, whilst homosexual conduct between consenting male adults in private was formerly a criminal offence, the state has determined that this shall no longer be the case. Similarly, the state has decided that it is no longer a criminal offence to attempt to commit suicide. Instances such as these which reveal the changing attitudes of both society and the state merely illustrate a more basic fact, that no conduct is inherently criminal (although some behaviour is prohibited in virtually all societies — *e.g.* murder, rape, theft). Equally, conduct which is non-criminal in nature at the present time need not necessarily remain so (and there are, for example, powerful lobbies presently campaigning for the imposition of general criminal sanctions to deter smoking in public places and to encourage dog owners to take steps to prevent their pets fouling areas to which the public has access). Whether conduct is to be criminal or non-criminal depends, then, partly upon the expectations of society and partly upon the attitudes of the officers and agencies who, at any particular time, comprise the collective entity known as "the state."

Once the state has determined that conduct is to be regarded as "criminal," it has inevitably interfered with the freedom of action of individuals within society who will, for example, no longer be free to murder others or steal from them, to pollute rivers with waste material from a manufacturing process, or to drive a motorcycle without wearing a helmet. Thus, activity which has been designated as criminal ceases to be within the range of activities which may be exercised by the individual citizen as of right or, to use a well-known, and perhaps somewhat overworked phrase, as part of the "freedom of the individual." State activity and individual freedoms may, as a result, appear to be constantly in conflict. As on a child's see-saw, as one side rises the other must inevitably fall. This is, however, arguably an unduly pessimistic view of state activity for such activity brings with it a multitude of freedoms (*e.g.* freedom from assault, freedom from pollution and freedom from commercial abuse). Nevertheless, there are many who view with suspicion the increased range of state activity because of their support for the "freedom of the individual."

It can now be seen that the visitor to the legal office may have made his appointment because of:

(a) his concern that the state is preparing to punish him for having committed a criminal offence; or

(b) his concern that the state is interfering with the freedom of the individual, in general, and with his own personal rights in particular.

Section A: The Individual and Criminal Offences

We have seen that an individual may find that he is accused of certain conduct which has been designated as "criminal" because it:

(a) falls within one of the "traditional" categories of criminal conduct; or

(b) offends entrenched notions of morality; or

(c) falls foul of the "regulatory" role which the state has adopted in relation to certain categories of anti-community activity.

It may be helpful to separate these categories of criminal conduct and to examine each in turn. Prior to doing so, however, an outline will be provided of general principles relating to criminal liability. This outline will introduce the reader to:

(a) the concepts of *actus reus* and *mens rea* which, together, form the basis of criminal liability;

(b) the pragmatic development of notions of *strict liability* and *vicarious liability*;

(c) the categories of persons who may be regarded as being parties to a crime;

(d) the inchoate offences of *attempt, incitement* and *conspiracy*.

A separate outline will then be provided of general defences to criminal liability.

GENERAL PRINCIPLES OF CRIMINAL LIABILITY

Actus reus and mens rea

It is fair to say that an individual may do anything he wishes to do, and may refrain from doing anything he does not wish to do, unless there is a rule which provides to the contrary. Such a rule, which may be statutory or common-law based, will define the conduct which is prohibited and this definition will prove the *actus reus* of the offence. The *actus reus* of any offence is the totality of fact which must be established by the prosecutor if the accused is to be found guilty, save only for the state of mind of the accused which does not form part of the *actus reus*.

The accused's state of mind is not, however, irrelevant. A criminal offence is only committed if the accused brings about all of the acts and outcomes which form the *actus reus* of the offence with *mens rea* (*i.e.* the appropriate state of mind). Some offences expressly indicate the state of mind required of the perpetrator of the *actus reus*. Thus:

(a) it may be necessary to show that the accused "intended" his act to have certain consequences. Section 1(1) of the Theft Act 1968, for example, provides that a person "is guilty of theft if he dishonestly appropriates property belonging to another *with the intention of permanently depriving the other of it . . .*";

(b) it may not be necessary to show that the accused ever intended his conduct to have the consequences which have arisen and may be sufficient to show that he was of a "reckless" frame of mind at the time of the incident. Section 2 of the Road Traffic Act 1972, for example, provides that a person "who drives a motor vehicle on a road *recklessly* shall be guilty of an offence";

(c) in some instances, a lower level of moral culpability will suffice. For the purposes of section 3 of the Road Traffic Act 1972, for example, it is sufficient that "a person drives a motor vehicle on a road *without due care and attention . . . .*"

Often, however, there is no such express indication and, in these cases, the court must satisfy itself that the accused has acted with a "guilty mind." Normally, a court will only accept that such is the case if it concludes either that the accused *intended* to bring about the *actus reus* of the offence, or that he was *reckless* as to the consequences of his actions.

It may be helpful, at this stage, to consider one particular offence and to determine both the *actus reus* of the offence and the mental element necessary to establish that the accused has acted with *mens rea*. The offence to be considered arises out of section 4 of the Public Order Act 1986. The section provides that:

"A person is guilty of an offence if he
(a) uses towards another person threatening, abusive or insulting words or behaviour, or
(b) distributes or displays to another person any writing, sign or other visible representation which is threatening, abusive or insulting,
with intent to cause that person to believe that immediate unlawful violence will be used against him or another by any person, or to provoke the immediate use of unlawful violence by that person or another, or whereby that person is likely to believe that such violence will be used or it is likely that such violence will be provoked."

In order to establish whether such activity has taken place a court may be required to determine what is meant by "threatening," "abusive" or "insulting" words or behaviour. In *Brutus* v. *Cozens*, for example, the Court had to grapple with the meaning of "insulting behaviour." In that case, an anti-apartheid demonstrator entered Number 2 Court at Wimbledon whilst a South African was playing, blew a whistle and attempted to distribute leaflets. As a result of his actions, play was disrupted for some considerable time. He was arrested and charged with the offence now provided for by section 4. The Divisional Court of the Queen's Bench Division asserted that "insulting behaviour" was that which affronted other people and evidenced a disrespect for their rights. On this basis, the demonstrator had clearly committed an offence. The House of Lords, however, rejected this approach and, whilst accepting that spectators would have been justifiably angry at the accused's actions, felt that the spectators could not have felt that they were being insulted. That being so, the *actus reus* of the offence was not committed and, as a result, the accused could not be guilty of the offence.

The *actus reus* of section 4 may involve more than activity. In the absence of any intention to cause a belief that immediate violence will be used or to provoke the immediate use of such violence, it must be established that, in the circumstances in which the accused used his threatening, abusive or insulting words or behaviour, there was a likelihood of violence or a likelihood of the "victim" believing that violence would occur, whether or not such violence was likely.

The requirement of mens rea . . . if there is no likelihood of violence or belief that there will be violence, an offence can only be committed by a person who *intends* to cause such a belief or to provoke actual violence. This requirement follows from the express wording of section 4. The general principle that the accused must have acted with a guilty mind would also imply that the state would need to establish that the accused intended to use the words or behaviour that he did use and that either he intended such words or behaviour to be threatening, abusive or insulting or was reckless as to whether his words or behaviour could be interpreted in this way. In the case of this offence Parliament has sought to avoid any doubt by expressly providing, in section 6 of the 1986 Act, that:

> "A person is guilty of an offence under section 4 only if he intends his words or behaviour or the writing, sign or other visible representation, to be threatening, abusive or insulting, or is aware that it may be threatening, abusive or insulting."

Some statutes, particularly modern statutes, will be equally explicit in relation to *mens rea*, others will not and the courts will need to refer to general principles.

Strict liability

Sometimes, particularly in the case of "regulatory" criminal offences, the burden of proof that would fall upon the state, if it had always to prove that all aspects of the *actus reus* of the offence had been committed with *mens rea*, would be unduly onerous. In *Alphacell Ltd.* v. *Woodward*, for example, a company was charged with the offence of causing polluted matter to enter a river. The company's processing system was such that polluted matter ought not to have entered the river, for pumps had been installed to prevent this very occurrence. The pumps had, however, failed to operate, as a result of their being blocked by vegetation, and the *actus reus* of the offence was committed. A conviction would have been very difficult, in these circumstances, had it been necessary to establish that the company had intended to pollute the river or had been either reckless or negligent. This problem was avoided by the determination of the court that the offence charged was one of *strict liability* (*i.e.* an offence for which it is not necessary to establish *mens rea* in relation to at least one aspect of the *actus reus*). Having made this determination, the court was able to indicate that the offence could be committed by "innocent" polluters of the river. The intention is not, of course, to punish those who bear no moral responsibility for their acts, but rather to create a situation in which those who are minded to run the risk of prosecution, on the basis that the state may not be able to establish that they were at fault, will be deterred from such an approach. Thus, in the *Alphacell* case, Lord Salmon asserted that if " . . . it were held to be law that no conviction could be obtained . . . unless the prosecution could discharge the often impossible onus of proving that the pollution was caused intentionally or negligently, a great deal of pollution would go unpunished and undeterred to the relief of many riparian factory owners. As a result, many rivers which are now filthy would become filthier still and many rivers which are now clean would lose their cleanliness."

In *Pharmaceutical Society of Great Britain* v. *Storkwain* another objective for the use of strict liability in crime was identified, that of providing for strict control of those who have a great responsibility. In this case a retail chemist was found guilty of selling medications which could only be sold under prescription in circumstances in which there was no prescription, even though the customer had produced a forged prescription which the chemist believed to be valid. In justifying this decision the House of Lords adopted the rationale provided by Farquarson J. in the Divisional Court:

> "It is perfectly obvious that pharmacists are in a position to put illicit drugs and perhaps other medicines on the market. Happily this rarely happens but it does from time to time. It can therefore be readily understood that Parliament would find it necessary to impose a heavier liability on those who are in such a position, and make them strictly accountable for any breaches of the Act."

Vicarious liability

Just as an employer may be liable for civil offences committed by his employees whilst acting in the course of their employment (see page 319), he may also be liable for activities which contravene criminal law.

An employer will be vicariously liable for the criminal acts of his employee where:

(a) the act in question is taken to be the act of the employer; or

(b) the employer is taken to have delegated performance of a statutory obligation to the employee.

Act of employee taken to be act of employer . . . a number of statutes, such as the Trade Descriptions Act 1968, the Unsolicited Goods and Services Act 1971 and the Consumer Credit Act 1974, create criminal offences which may be committed by those involved in selling goods or services to consumers. Such sales and the negotiations preceding them are, of course, often undertaken by an employee of an individual or corporate employer. To the consumer, however, the transaction is not one which involves the employee, he is merely carrying out a mechanical function for the principal actor in the transaction, the employer. A consumer who agrees with Mr. A, an employee of a garage run by Mr. B, to purchase a car, has no difficulty in appreciating that his contract is with Mr. B, not Mr. A. Should not, therefore, Mr. B be liable for Mr. A if Mr. A negotiates or sells in a way prohibited by criminal law? The current approach would be to answer this question in the affirmative.

In *Coppen* v. *Moor (No. 2)* a shop owner instructed his staff to sell American hams by the description "breakfast hams." Unknown to him, and without anyone's permission, an assistant sold one of the hams as a "Scotch ham." The shop owner was convicted of selling goods to which a false trade description had been attached. This decision is in line with the view that liability ought to attach to the contracting party rather than to the party at fault. Such an approach is broadly supportive of the interests of the consumer in that it:

(a)   encourages the owners of enterprises to recruit wisely;
(b)   encourages the owners of enterprises to devise a programme of training for their employees;
(c)   encourages the owners of enterprises to ensure that their staff are properly supervised; and, ultimately;
(d)   throws the risk of mistakes upon the seller rather than on the buyer.

Effective though such an approach may be, however, it cannot be denied that it may be inherently unfair. A realisation of this has led in modern statutes to "saving clauses" which will, in certain circumstances permit the employer to escape liability. Thus, for example, section 24(1) of the Trade Descriptions Act 1968 provides for a defence where the offence results from the "... act or default of another person ..." and where the employer "took all reasonable precautions and exercised all due diligence to avoid the commission of such an offence by himself or any person under his control." The employer may, of course, have difficulty in establishing that the offence resulted from the act of "another person." In *Tesco Supermarkets Ltd.* v. *Nattrass,* however, the court was sympathetic to the problem facing employers and accepted that a store manager was "another person" to the company which employed him and which was accused of the offence. Not being a member of the senior management team of the company, the store manager was not part of the company's "directing mind and will" and was, in consequence, "another person."

Delegated performance of statutory duty ... it is a long established principle of criminal law that where Parliament has imposed upon a person a duty to do, or to refrain from doing, certain acts, that person cannot escape his liability for breach of that duty by delegating his responsibilities to another. Thus, for example, the Metropolitan Police Act 1839 stipulated that it was an offence for anyone "who shall have or keep any house" to "knowingly permit or suffer prostitutes ... to meet together and remain in a place where refreshments are sold and consumed." In *Allen* v. *Whitehead* a café proprietor was found guilty of the offence even though he did not himself run the café but, instead, employed a manager who had been expressly instructed not to permit prostitutes on to the premises.

The justification for this approach is that, without this liability, those who are traditionally regarded as bearing responsibility for the conduct of their businesses and the use made of their premises (*e.g.* licensees of public houses, managers of hotels and shopkeepers) would be able to evade liability by the simple expedient of delegation.

Parties to a crime

The person who brings about the *actus reus* of the offence is the *principal offender*. Thus, the person who, distributes or displays any writing or sign which is threatening, abusive or insulting in such a way that it is likely that violence will be provoked is the principal offender for the purposes of the offence committed by virtue of section 4 of the Public Order Act 1986 (see page 109). There may, indeed, be more than one principal offender, as where two men jointly hold a banner which is abusive and likely to provoke violence.

Often, however, where more than one person plays a part in the commission of an offence, one of the parties will bring about the *actus reus* of the offence and others will not. Were it not for the actions of the principal offender the more limited activities of the others would not result in the commission of the *actus reus* of the offence. These others are not, then, principal offenders, but their undesirable activities may result in them being *secondary offenders*.

The Accessories and Abettors Act 1861 provides that:

"Whosoever shall aid, abet, counsel or procure the commission of any indictable offence . . . shall be liable to be tried, indicted and punished as a principal offender."

Thus, where the offence is an indictable offence, this statute provides that a secondary offender is liable to the same penalty as the principal. The Magistrates' Courts Act 1952 contains similar provisions where the offence is a summary one (as is the case, for example, with section 5 of the Public Order Act).

It has become so common to refer to a person "aiding *and* abetting" another that there has been uncertainty as to whether these words are necessarily mutually supportive or whether they can be used to denote two separate offences. In *Attorney-General's Reference (No. 1 of 1975)*, the Lord Chief Justice made clear his view that Parliament, having used four separate words in the 1861 Act, must be taken to have intended to identify four separate activities. If so, the words probably have the following meaning:

(a) *aiding* a principal offender involves active assistance to that principal in the commission of the *actus reus* of the offence (as where one person holds another while that other is killed by the principal);

(b) *abetting* a principal offender and *counselling* the commission of the offence are different terms which relate to the same activity, that of inciting or encouraging the offender in relation to the particular offence. The distinction between the terms is, it would appear, one of timing. A secondary party abets the principal where his encouragement to that principal is contemporaneous with the commission of the offence, but where the encouragement precedes the offence it amounts to counselling;

(c) *procuring the commission* of an offence involves some act which causes the offence to be committed (as where the procurer "spikes" the principal offender's drink and causes him to "drive a motor vehicle . . . having consumed alcohol in such a quantity that the proportion thereof in his blood . . . exceeds the prescribed limit . . . ").

The secondary offences described above are committed only where the principal offender brings about the *actus reus* of the offence charged. Thus, if it is decided that an accused has not committed an offence, others cannot be liable for, say, aiding or abetting the accused. (The situation is different, however, where the principal has committed the *actus reus* of the offence but is found to have a defence, such as insanity.)

Attempt to commit a crime

Section 1(1) of the Criminal Attempts Act 1981 provides that it is an indictable offence to attempt to commit an indictable offence. By section 4(1) of the Act, the attempt is punishable to the same extent as the substantive offence.

The term "attempt" implies a certain state of mind, that of intending to commit the offence. Thus, even where the substantive offence can be committed without intention, as where it can be committed by a person who is reckless or careless, a person can only be found guilty of attempting to commit that offence if it can be established that he intended to do so. Where intention forms no part of the substantive offence, as, for example, in section 2 of the Road Traffic Act 1972 which provides for the offence of reckless driving, there can clearly be no question of the law recognising the possibility of an attempt to commit the offence.

The word "attempt" also invokes images of an act which is not far removed from commission of the substantive offence. An assassin who seeks to murder someone by shooting him, has clearly attempted murder when he squeezes the trigger of his rifle, fires a bullet, and fails to kill his target only because a policeman or bodyguard has, at the last moment, propelled himself at the target and taken him out of the line of fire. That final, outrageous, act of the assassin is, however, only one stage, the final stage, in a process which will have involved many other acts. The assassin may have purchased his rifle. At the time of purchase he may have intended to use the rifle to kill the man he narrowly failed to shoot. He may, however, have had no particular target in mind and may have purchased the rifle simply as a tool of his trade, as a joiner would purchase a plane or a screwdriver, ready to be used in whatever assignment may subsequently be offered. Having purchased a rifle and agreed to kill the target, the assassin may have had to make arrangements to travel to the place of the intended assassination. He may have entered into a contract with an hotel in order to secure a room from which to fire the rifle and he may have had to construct a makeshift support for his rifle to steady his aim and enhance his prospects of success. Could these acts be construed as amounting to attempts to murder? Clearly, a distinction may be drawn between acts which are *preparatory* to the commission of the offence and acts which amount to an *attempt* to commit that offence. The firing of the rifle would obviously amount to an attempt to commit murder, the reservation of a seat on a train to carry the assassin to the place of intended assassination would not. In *R.* v. *Robinson* a jeweller, intending to make a fraudulent claim against his insurer, set about convincing the police that items of stock had been stolen. In order to give credibility to his story he tied himself up and called for assistance. He was found not to have made an attempt to obtain money by false pretences, the court accepting that, no claim on his policy ever having been made, his elaborate pretence remained a preparatory act and stopped short of an attempt. The case, which has been criticised, reveals the difficulties which may arise when determining whether, as a fact, the accused's act is sufficiently proximate to the substantive offence to amount to an attempt. Section 1(1) of the 1981 Act provides expressly that a person can only be guilty of an attempt if he does an act which is more than merely preparatory to the commission of the offence.

Formerly, difficulties were caused by the situation in which the accused had attempted to commit an act which was impossible (*e.g.* attempting to steal from a man with no money). Section 1(2) of the 1981 Act now provides, however, that " . . . a person may be guilty of attempting to commit an offence to which this section applies even though the facts are such that the commission of the offence is impossible." Similarly, section 1(3) of the Act provides that a person shall be taken to intend to commit an indictable offence if he would have been so regarded had the facts of the case been as he believed them to be. This section has proved difficult to apply for it covers a variety of different circumstances. Thus, for example, it covers each of the following situations:

(a) that in which an objective observer of the act would see it as entirely innocent (*e.g.* where a person purchases goods which are not stolen, believing them to be stolen or where a person has consensual intercourse with a girl over the age of 16 believing her to be under that age);

(b) that in which an objective observer of the act would see it as being culpable (*e.g.* where a person puts his hand into the pocket of another's jacket believing it to contain money which he will steal, but the pocket is empty).

In *Anderton* v. *Ryan* the House of Lords asserted that there was a criminal attempt, under the provisions of the 1981 Act, in the latter case but not in the former case, where there was "objective innocence." In consequence, it allowed an appeal against conviction by a person who had purchased a television mistakenly believing it to be stolen. In *R.* v. *Shivpuri*, however, the House changed its mind, denied any distinction between situations (a) and (b) above and found a person guilty of "attempting to be knowingly concerned in dealing with and harbouring a controlled drug (heroin)" even though the powder he possessed was, unknown to him, not heroin but, instead, a vegetable material akin to snuff.

Incitement

To *incite* another to commit an offence is, itself, an offence. The Criminal Law Act 1977 provides that:

(a) incitement to commit an indictable offence is triable on indictment;

(b) incitement to commit an offence triable either way is itself triable either way; and

(c) incitement to commit a summary offence is triable by summary proceedings.

(See page 36 for an explanation of the distinction between offences triable on indictment, those triable by summary proceedings and those triable either way.)

It will be recalled that a person who *counsels* an offender is equally liable to punishment as a secondary offender. The distinction between incitement, on the one hand, and counselling on the other is twofold:

  (a) incitement probably requires a greater degree of forcefulness than is necessary for counselling and involves, perhaps, some degree of persuasion rather than mere encouragement;
  (b) a party may be found guilty of inciting another even though that other does not commit the substantive offence; a party cannot, however, be liable as a secondary party (for counselling the principal) where the accused is found not to have committed the substantive offence and there is, thus, no principal offender.

The same conduct may, of course, amount to both counselling or incitement. Thus, if A persuades B to steal from C, A will be guilty of counselling should B commit the offence, and of incitement if he does not.

Conspiracy

By section 1(1) of the Criminal Law Act 1977, as amended by the Criminal Attempts Act 1981, the offence of *statutory conspiracy* is committed " . . . if a person agrees with any other person or persons that a course of conduct shall be pursued which, if the agreement is carried out in accordance with their intentions, either

  (a) will necessarily amount to or involve the commission of any offence or offences by one or more of the parties to the agreement, or
  (b) would do so but for the existence of facts which render the commission of the offence or any of the offences impossible."

In order that the offence be committed, it must be established that:

  (a) there has been an agreement between two or more people; and
  (b) a course of conduct has been agreed upon which, if carried out, *must* lead to an offence being committed (or would, but for the fact that commission of the offence is impossible . . . as where A and B agree to shoot C who, unknown to them, has died); and
  (c) the offence which must be committed (or would be committed but for its impossibility) would be committed by one (or more) of the parties to the agreement.

Where an offence is one of strict liability and can, thus, be committed by a person who has no *mens rea* in relation to an aspect of the *actus reus* of the offence, a person can only be guilty of a conspiracy to commit that offence where he has *mens rea*, for section 1(2) of the 1977 Act provides:

"Where liability for any offence may be incurred without knowledge on the part of the person committing it of any particular fact or circumstance necessary for the commission of the offence, a person shall nevertheless not be guilty of conspiracy to commit that offence . . . unless he and at least one other party to the agreement intend or know that fact or circumstance shall or will exist at the time when the conduct constituting the offence is to take place."

Consider, for example, the offence created by section 20 of the Sexual Offences Act 1956, that of taking, without lawful authority or excuse, an unmarried girl under the age of 16 years out of the possession of her parent or guardian against his will. This offence is one of strict liability in so far as a mistaken belief that a girl was over the age of 16 would not provide a defence to a person charged with the offence. In order that a person could be found to be guilty of a *conspiracy* to commit the offence, however, it would be necessary to establish that the accused (and one other party to the agreement) was aware of the fact that the girl was under the age of 16.

In addition to the statutory offence created by section 1(1) of the 1977 Act, it is, at *common law,* an offence to:

(a) conspire to defraud; or

(b) conspire to corrupt public morals (see page 95).

GENERAL DEFENCES TO CRIMINAL LIABILITY

Sometimes a party who has brought about the *actus reus* of an offence may avail himself of a defence which is available only to a person accused of that particular offence, as where a person accused of murder pleads diminished responsibility. Where appropriate, defences of this type will be discussed in the sections of this book devoted to the individual offences. Some defences, are, however, more general in nature, and may be raised in relation to a variety of specific offences. It is these general defences that are outlined below.

Capacity

Some individuals are deemed to be incapable of committing a criminal offence, or are considered to have limited capacity. Their incapacity may result from:

(a) their age;

(b) their mental condition;

(c) their state of drunkenness at the time of the offence.

Age . . . a child under the age of 10 is deemed to be incapable of committing a criminal offence. This presumption cannot be rebutted by evidence which reveals that a child was fully aware of the nature of his act and of the inevitable or likely consequences of it. The child has complete immunity (though he may be subject to "care proceedings" in a juvenile court). Indeed, the immunity is so extensive that the child is not considered to have a defence available to him, rather he is considered not to have committed an offence. Thus, if A, being nine years old, conducts himself in a way that would be criminal were he to be over 10, an offence has not been committed and, as a result, others who might have been drawn into criminal liability as secondary parties cannot be so liable. They will either attract primary liability as principal offenders or they will escape liability.

Children between the ages of 10 and 14 years are presumed to be incapable of forming a criminal intent, but this presumption can be rebutted by evidence showing that a child appreciated that his act was wrong. Evidence of such awareness would include evidence which pointed to the fact that the child had been careful to ensure that there were no witnesses to his act or had attempted to escape responsibility for his act by, for example, telling lies.

Children over the age of 14 have full capacity, that is to say they are treated as being as responsible for their actions as would be an adult. There are, of course, certain procedural differences in that a *young person* (*i.e.* someone between the ages of 14 and 17) would appear before magistrates only in a specially constituted *juvenile court.*

For both children (*i.e.* someone under the age of 14) and young persons, *care proceedings* are an alternative to prosecution.

Mental capacity . . . an accused may be so mentally confused as to be unable to cope with the role expected of him in a criminal trial. He may not, for example, understand the charge or he may be unable to appreciate the significance of pleading either guilty or not guilty. If so, he may be found unfit to plead under the Criminal Procedure (Insanity) Act 1964 and ordered to be detained in an institution during Her Majesty's pleasure.

An accused who is able to cope with the formalities of a criminal trial may, nonetheless, wish to establish that he was insane at the time of the offence. Under the *McNaghten Rules* the accused will be presumed to be sane and to have sufficient capacity to be responsible at law for his actions unless he can establish that, at the time of the offence, he was " . . . labouring under such a defect of reason, from disease of the mind, as not to know the nature and quality of the act he was doing, or, if he did know it, that he did not know he was doing what was wrong."

Thus, under the rules, the accused must establish:

(a) that his defect of reason arose from a *disease of the mind* . . . It would appear that any disease which affects the mind will suffice, the disease does not have to be a brain disease. Thus, for example, diabetes may result in a disease of the mind. A defect of reason which results from some external factor is not a defect which results from a disease of the mind. In *R.* v. *Quick*, for example, it was asserted that a diabetic who committed an offence whilst suffering from hypoglycaemia, induced by insulin, was not suffering from a disease of the mind. His defect of reason resulted from the insulin (an external factor) rather than the diabetes. (The fact that the court will not accept that a person is insane does not, of course, mean that he will be guilty of the offence charged. He may be able to plead another defence, such as the defence of automatism, or he may be acquitted on the basis that his state of mind was such that *mens rea* cannot be established. Indeed, it is not necessarily in the accused's best interests that he be found to be insane, for if acquitted he will be a free man whereas, if insane, he will be detained in an institution.)

(b) that the defect of reason resulted in a situation in which the accused *either* did not know the nature and quality of the act he was doing, *or* did not know that what he was doing was wrong. . . . An accused will be taken to have been ignorant of the nature and quality of his act where he believes that he was doing an act quite different to the act actually committed (*e.g.* where he kills his wife with a hammer, but believes, at the time, that he is hammering a nail into wood). An accused will be taken to know that his act is wrong if he is aware that it is contrary to the law. The fact that the accused believed his action to be morally right is irrelevant if he is aware that it is unlawful.

Drunkenness . . . that a drunken person is incapacitated, to a greater or lesser extent, is undeniable. That this self-inflicted incapacity should always excuse him from the consequences of a criminal action is, however, a notion that would attract little popular support.

In *D.P.P.* v. *Beard* it was established that drunkenness was only a defence if it resulted in the accused not having the appropriate *mens rea*. It would not be sufficient, for example, for a person accused of murder to state that he had intended to kill his victim, but would not have formed such an intention had he not been under the influence of drink. It would appear, further, that the principle stated in *Beard* generally applies only to crimes of *specific intent,* that is to say crimes which involve the state in establishing that a particular intention has been formed by the accused. In these circumstances the accused may assert that he was so drunk that he did not form the intention necessary for commission of the offence. If, for instance, we return to the example provided by section 4 of the Public Order Act 1986 (see page 69), we discover that the offence may be committed by a person "with intent to . . . provoke the immediate use of unlawful violence . . . " Clearly, a person could be so drunk that he could use threatening, abusive or insulting words or behaviour without ever having formed such a specific intention. His drunken state would, therefore, be a defence to this offence if it was always necessary to establish such intent. It will be recalled, however, that no intent to provoke violence need be established where it can be shown that the accused's conduct resulted in a situation arising in which "it is likely that such violence will be provoked." If, therefore, the accused can be shown to have acted in a way likely to have led to violence being provoked he could be found guilty of an offence under section 4 of the 1986 Act even though he can establish that, at the time, his mind was a blank (because of drink) and that he had formed no specific intent. Where, however, violence was not likely, he could only be convicted if it could be established that he intended to provoke violence and here he could point to the fact that intoxication prevented the formation of such intent and, if he could convince the court that this was so, escape liability.

The proposition that drunkenness negativing *mens rea* can be a defence only in the case of crimes of specific intent whilst broadly correct is, it must be admitted, not one of universal application. As a result of policy, the courts have accepted that intoxication can negative *mens rea*, and thus provide a defence, to crimes which do not require a specific intent and have refused to accept that drunkenness negativing *mens rea* can be a defence to other offences which might appear to involve the formation of a particular intent (*e.g.* rape). Where the intoxication of the accused is raised as a defence, therefore, it appears that there are two classes of offence. One class consists of those offences in relation to which the court will accept drunkenness as a defence, providing it can be established that intoxication was so severe that the accused did not form the appropriate *mens rea*. The other consists of those offences for which drunkenness will not be a defence, no matter how incapable the accused was in relation to the formation of intent. In the former classification are included most of the offences of specific intent and some other offences which have been brought into this category by the courts, largely on the grounds of expediency. In the latter classification are to be found most of the crimes of basic (*i.e.* non-specific) intent, together with some crimes of specific intent which, again, have been so classified on the basis of expediency. What can be said with certainty is that an accused who, charged with an offence in the latter category, pleads that he was so drunk that he formed no *mens rea*, will meet with short shrift. In effect, his plea will simply relieve the state of the burden of establishing *mens rea*.

Where an accused claims that he was so drunk as to have been incapable of *mens rea* and that his intoxication was *involuntary* (as where "friends" have "spiked" his drinks) it seems clear that he will, if he can establish these facts, have a defence to *any* offence (whether the offence is one of specific intent or not).

Intoxication is not, of course, the only form of self-induced incapacity. In some circles drunkenness has been considered rather passé and self-abuse by drugs considerably more sophisticated. A series of cases involving crimes committed by such sophisticates has established that the same rules apply to a person incapacitated by drugs as to a person befuddled by drink. Where, however, a person takes a sedative drug (*e.g.* Valium) it may be that a court would be sympathetic to a claim that there should be no conviction for an offence committed whilst under the intoxicating influence of the drug, for takers of these drugs would not normally anticipate such an outcome.

Mistake

Mistake is a defence to criminal liability in the same way that it vitiates contractual liability (see page 119). Mistake will enable a party to escape liability in contract where it can be shown that, as a result of the mistake, the parties have not reached true agreement, or, in other words, have not actually made a contract upon which they may be liable. Similarly, a party who brings about the *actus reus* of an offence whilst under a mistaken belief will escape liability if he can establish that, because of the mistake, he did not form the appropriate *mens rea* or, in other words, that he did not commit the crime. Thus, where an offence can only be committed by an accused who *intends* to bring about the *actus reus,* or who is *reckless*, any mistake which operates upon the mind of the accused so as to negative intention or recklessness must provide a defence. Where, however, an offence can be committed *negligently,* only a *reasonable* mistake will protect the accused, for an unreasonable mistake will, by definition, reveal negligence.

Necessity

There are, perhaps, two situations in which an accused may wish to plead that he should not be considered liable at criminal law because his acts were brought about by necessity:

(a) that in which the accused asserts that he, or his family, would have suffered but for his criminal act;

(b) that in which the accused asserts that others would have suffered but for his criminal act.

For policy reasons, the courts have generally refused to accept necessity as a defence in situation (a). Thus, hunger is unlikely to be accepted as a defence to a charge of theft, just as homelessness has not been accepted as a defence to a civil action in trespass. In *R.* v. *Dudley and Stephens* shipwrecked sailors at sea in an open boat killed and ate a cabin boy in order that they might stay alive. They were rescued four days later and the jury accepted that, but for eating the boy, the sailors would have perished before that time. The accused sailors, were, however, convicted of murder (though sentence was commuted to six months' imprisonment) by a court which thus rejected the notion that their crime should be excused because it was necessary.

The courts appear to be more willing to excuse criminal acts which are committed for the benefit of others where it can be shown that the benefit secured outweighs the culpability of the offence committed. Such an approach is, no doubt, one which would have the full support of the public, who would clearly expect an ambulance driver or fire appliance driver to "crash" a red traffic light (with care) if such an act would help to reduce the risk to death or serious injury to a patient or fire victim. Such an approach can, at least in the case of statutory offences, be justified by recognising that it must be a reasonable principle of statutory interpretation that Parliament intended that the offences that it creates should apply in all circumstances save those in which observance of the statutory provision will demonstrably lead to greater harm to the community. (Such a presumption would, of course, have to give way if the clear words of the statute indicated the contrary).

Duress

Where an accused commits an offence because he has received threats from another that death or serious injury will be inflicted upon him or upon a third party if he does not commit the offence, should the accused have a defence? Should the state punish, for example, a bank manager who steals from his own bank because his family is being held hostage?

The accused is in much the same position as a man who pleads necessity. The man who claims that it was necessary to commit a crime accepts that he had a choice, that he could have elected not to carry out the criminal act, but claims that his "choice" to commit the crime was, in reality, the only option available to him because of force of circumstances. The man who pleads duress asserts the same, save that his choice results not from force of circumstances but from force of threat.

Recognition of the pressure that is placed upon an individual by threats of violence has led the courts to accept that duress may be raised as a defence to virtually all crimes. Duress will not, however, avail a party accused of being the principal party to murder, though it is a defence to a party charged with aiding and abetting a murder (*R.* v. *Howe*).

Coercion is a particular form of duress and is available as a defence to a wife who has committed a crime " . . . in the presence of, and under the coercion of, her husband" (Criminal Justice Act 1925). The defence is not available where the wife is charged with treason or murder, but may be wider than the defence of duress in that "coercion" might not be a term limited only to threats of physical violence (*e.g.* it may cover a threat to desert the wife and her children).

Automatism

In the case of necessity or duress, an accused will admit that he had a choice whether or not to commit the *actus reus* of the offence, but will seek to convince the court that the element of choice was, in the circumstances of the case, hypothetical. Occasionally, however, an accused may argue that he should not be considered responsible for his actions because *he did not will them.* Rather than pointing to pressures which forced him to act in a particular, criminal, fashion he will seek to establish to the satisfaction of the court that, his mind not accompanying his actions, he should not be treated as having "acted" at all. Thus, for example, in *Hill* v. *Baxter,* a driver of a motor car pointed to the fact that he had been attacked by a swarm of bees and was, as a result, not responsible for his involuntary reactions.

In essence, automatism is not so much a defence as a factor which negatives liability. We have seen that mistake does not, in reality, excuse criminal conduct but, rather, by its operation upon the mind of the accused, prevents the formation of *mens rea* and thus the commission of the offence. Similarly, an accused who can establish that he did not will his act has established that he did not commit the offence with which he is charged.

Automatism is not normally available to a person who has induced his own incapacity. Thus, a driver who recklessly continues to drive knowing that he is tired cannot claim that he is not responsible for his actions when finally he falls asleep at the wheel. Nor can a drunk claim that his criminal acts are not willed (though his intoxication may, as we have seen, in certain circumstances provide a defence). It is, however, possible for self-induced automatism to arise in circumstances in which there is no culpability. Thus, for example, a diabetic may fail to take sufficient food after his last dose of insulin and suffer a malfunctioning of mind caused by hypoglaecemia. Providing he was not aware of this risk it is likely that the diabetic would be able to rely upon the defence of automatism should he injure someone during this period of instability.

SPECIFIC CRIMINAL OFFENCES

Having considered general principles of criminal liability and the general defences available to a person accused of a criminal offence, it is now appropriate to consider details of a selection of specific offences.

It will be recalled that, earlier, a threefold classification of offences was adopted:

(a) those which are "traditionally" regarded as falling within the boundaries of criminal law;

(b) those which are regarded as criminal because they offend entrenched notions of morality; and

(c) those which are regarded as criminal because they are harmful to the physical and commercial environment of the individual within society.

The first of these three categories contains all of the offences that most people would immediately identify as prohibiting conduct which must not, in a civilised community, be allowed to be undertaken without threat of sanction. It is traditional to classify such offences into those which are offences against the person and those which are offences against property. On the basis of this classification, the following specific offences against the person will be considered:

(a) murder;

(b) manslaughter; and

(c) assault in its various forms, including rape.

Of the many offences against property which may be committed, the following will be considered:

(a) theft;

(b) robbery;

(c) burglary;

(d) handling stolen goods; and

(e) criminal damage.

The second category of offences, those that offend entrenched views of morality, is one which is constantly subject to critical analysis. Few would question that murder ought to be classified as conduct which is criminal, but there is no similar consensus in relation, for example, to drug offences, pornography or prostitution. In some societies such conduct is proscribed, in others it is not. Equally, it is possible to contemplate that many of the offences included in this category will, in this country, cease to be criminal in due course. These offences tend, therefore, to be "marginal."

Of such marginal offences, the following will be considered in some detail:

(a) offences relating to prostitution;
(b) offences relating to homosexual conduct; and
(c) obscenity.

The nature of "regulatory" criminal offences, which form the third of our three categories of criminal conduct, will be illustrated by a consideration of the steps taken to control:

(a) false trade descriptions; and
(b) demands for payment for unsolicited goods.

"TRADITIONAL" CRIMINAL OFFENCES

Murder

Murder is an offence at common law. It is committed when a person unlawfully kills a reasonable creature under the King's peace, with malice aforethought, so that the victim dies within a year and a day.

Unlawfully kills . . . the offence is not committed merely by the killing of another, it must be shown that the killing was unlawful. A coroner's verdict of *justifiable homicide* would, for example, reveal that an inquest believed that A had not murdered B even though it accepted that A had killed B.

A reasonable creature . . . human beings are the only creatures with reason that count for the purposes of murder. Determining whether a human being has acquired or retained reason at the time of his death is, however, a matter which has often concerned courts and academic writers alike. It is not murder to kill a child before it leaves its mother's womb (though it may amount to *child destruction* or to unlawful abortion) and the courts have accepted that a child may only be murdered if the child has attained an existence independent of its mother. Determination of the fact of separate existence is, of course, a task which may tax the court. Similarly, in this age of advanced medical techniques, determining the point at which a person is already dead is a task fraught with difficulty and one which raises major medical, moral and philosophical questions. Is a person now to be treated as dead, for example, when his heart ceases to function or when his brain ceases to operate or, indeed, when both organs cease to function (even though, in each case, his bodily functions can be artificially stimulated)?

Under the King's peace . . . now that there is no question of individuals being declared "outlaws," all persons within the jurisdiction of English courts are "under the King's peace," unless they are enemies killed by act of war (as would be the case, for example, where the pilot of an enemy bomber is shot down or an enemy paratrooper is killed in a gun battle). Moreover, where the offence is committed by a person entitled to live in the United Kingdom, an English court may try the case regardless of the nationality of the victim or the country in which the offence took place.

With malice aforethought . . . unless there is "malice aforethought" the accused can only be convicted of manslaughter. "Malice aforethought" is a generic term which embraces all of the states of mind which, separately, will suffice to constitute the *mens rea* of murder. It would appear, from *R.* v. *Moloney* that an accused will be taken to have had malice aforethought where:

(a) he intended to kill; *or*
(b) he intended to cause grievous bodily harm (*i.e.* "really serious injury").

In *R.* v. *Hancock and Shankland* the Court of Appeal asserted that an *intention* to cause death or really serious injury may be inferred in circumstances in which a jury is satisfied that the accused's act was "highly likely" to cause death or really serious bodily injury and the accused appreciated that this was so. In these circumstances, the fact that the accused did not *desire* that result is irrelevant. It should be noted, however, that on appeal from the Court of Appeal to the House of Lords, Lord Scarman reminded trial judges that where *foresight* of a consequence is part of the evidence relied upon by the prosecution to show that the accused *intended* the consequences, the trial judge must emphasise that this is only one factor, though it may be a very significant factor, for the jury to consider.

Death within a year and a day . . . the seemingly antiquated rule that the accused can only be guilty of murder if his victim dies within a year and a day can, perhaps, be defended on the basis that, in the case of an offence as serious as murder, the threat of prosecution must not hang indefinitely over the accused. At some stage the risk of prosecution for murder must end. Whether the relatives and friends of the victim would agree with such sentiments is, or course, another matter.

Causation . . . the rule that death must occur within a year and a day was, of course, originally intended to relate to the problem of causation. If a person died later than this how could it be established that it was the accused's act that led to the victim's death? The development of medical science has, no doubt, diminished the extent to which lapse of time is, in itself, a problem. Modern medical techniques have, however, raised other problems of causation. What, for example, is the responsibility of an accused who assaults another who then dies in hospital, not as a result of his injuries, but as a consequence of the administration of drugs or the application of some other form of treatment? The problem is a difficult one, but, nevertheless, one which is quite clearly defined. The accused is either to be considered liable for his victim's death, on the basis that but for his assault the accused would not have been in hospital, would not have been administered drugs and would not have died; or, he is not to be considered liable, on the basis that his act did not cause his victim's death. However, no matter how clearly a problem is defined, the answers provided by the courts are often, of necessity, complex. So it is in this situation, where it would appear that the accused will sometimes be considered to be liable and sometimes not. It would appear that where the injury was manifestly not the cause of death, but merely provided the reason why the victim was subjected to treatment which kills him, then the accused is not liable for murder. Thus, in *R.* v. *Jordan* the Court of Criminal Appeal (as it then was) was prepared to quash a conviction for murder upon hearing evidence that the victim, who had been stabbed by the accused, was probably killed by treatment which, in the circumstances of the case, was clearly wrong. Where, however, the injury inflicted by the accused is still a major threat to the victim's life, then, even though it appears likely that the operative cause of death was medical treatment (which was, perhaps, negligent, though not grossly so), the accused will be guilty of murder. In *R. v. Smith*, for example, a soldier who had been stabbed by another became the victim of an unfortunate, and for him tragic, series of events. He was dropped by a friend carrying him to a doctor and was then treated in a way which, with hindsight, was most unhelpful. The soldier who had inflicted the wounds was found guilty of murder. (It is, perhaps, easy to see a distinction between *Jordan* and *Smith*; in one case the wound was clearly not the cause of death, whilst in the other, the wound was the cause of death, albeit a wound which, perhaps, ought not to have led to death. It would seem, however, that the courts are not prepared to adopt an approach which depends entirely upon determining the operative cause of death; and it appears that a court would find the accused guilty even where the wound was not, in itself, the operative cause of death, so long as the treatment given to the victim was not grossly negligent).

Similar problems of causation arise where:

(a)   the victim does not seek medical assistance and dies as a result;

(b)   the victim commits suicide because he cannot bear the pain of the wound inflicted by the accused;

(c)   the victim is wounded by another after the accused has injured him.

In all cases the court will have to consider the particular facts before it and address itself to the problem of determining whether the assault was the operative cause (or, at least, *an* operative cause) of death.

Diminished responsibility ... an outline has already been provided of general defences to criminal liability, many of which may be raised by a person accused of murder. The Homicide Act 1957 introduced a different kind of defence, one which is a particular defence in that it is only applicable to cases in which the accused is charged with murder. The defence is that of *diminished responsibility* and it has the effect of reducing the accused's liability from that for murder to that for manslaughter where " ... he was suffering from such abnormality of mind (whether arising from a condition of arrested or retarded development of mind or any inherent causes or induced by disease or injury) as substantially impaired his mental responsibility for his acts and omissions in doing or being a party to the killing."

The defence is available to those who would not be able to establish that they are insane within the meaning of the McNaghten Rules (see earlier) but who can establish that through "abnormality of mind" they have great difficulty in exercising normal restraint over their emotions. It covers, in effect, those who are insane within the meaning that would be attached to that term by the general public.

Infanticide ... section 1(1) of the Infanticide Act 1938 provides that:

"Where a woman by any wilful act or omission causes the death of her child under the age of twelve months, but at the time of the act or omission the balance of her mind was disturbed by reason of her not having fully recovered from the effect of giving birth to the child or by reason of the effect of lactation consequent upon the birth of the child, then, notwithstanding that the circumstances were such that but for this act the offence would have amounted to murder, she shall be guilty of . . . *infanticide.*"

In the event of a woman being found to be guilty of infanticide she will be punished as though she were guilty of manslaughter.

Penalty for murder . . . prior to 1957 the mandatory sentence for those convicted of murder was death by hanging. A distinction was then made between *capital murder* to which the death sentence still applied and non-capital murder which was punished by life imprisonment. The Murder (Abolition of Death Penalty) Act 1965 ended capital punishment and provided that life imprisonment was the penalty for all murders.

The trial judge may, when passing sentence, recommend to the Home Secretary the minimum period of imprisonment that the accused should serve before being released on licence.

Manslaughter

There are two forms of manslaughter:
(a) voluntary manslaughter; and
(b) involuntary manslaughter

Voluntary manslaughter . . . in the case of voluntary manslaughter the accused has the appropriate *mens rea* for murder but, by virtue of a provision contained in a statute or at common law, his conduct will be considered to amount to manslaughter rather than murder. It has been explained (see above) that an accused who can establish *diminished responsibility* will have committed manslaughter and not murder. Similarly, the Homicide Act 1957, which introduced the defence of diminished responsibility, also provided that the survivor of a "suicide pact" will, if he has killed the other, be guilty of manslaughter rather than murder.

The only instance of voluntary manslaughter recognised by common law was where the killing resulted from *provocation*. Section 3 of the Homicide Act 1957 now provides that:

> "Where on a charge of murder there is evidence on which the jury can find the person charged was provoked (whether by things done or things said or both together) to lose his self-control, the question whether the provocation was enough to make a reasonable man do as he did shall be left to be determined by the jury; and in determining that question the jury should take into account everything both done and said according to the effect which, in their opinion, it would have on a reasonable man."

To establish that he falls within the defence of provocation the accused must, therefore, establish:
(a) that he was provoked;
(b) that he lost his self-control; and
(c) that, as a result, he acted in a way that a reasonable man might have acted (which will be left to the jury to determine).

These three constituent parts of the defence contain a complex amalgam of subjective and objective considerations. It must be shown that the accused was provoked and that, as a result, he actually lost self-control. This requirement is subjective; it would not, for example, be sufficient to establish that the accused did not lose his self control but that a reasonable man would have done. Having established this, however, an objective test is then made of the accused's actions; the jury must consider whether a "reasonable man" might have acted in this way. The problem then arises, of course, of determining the nature and characteristics of the "reasonable man." In *Bedder* v. *D.P.P.*, a case which was determined in 1954 and so prior to the passing of the Homicide Act, the court considered the actions of a man who killed a prostitute who taunted, punched and kicked him after his unsuccessful attempt at intercourse with her. The accused was sexually impotent and, as one might reasonably expect, was concerned and embarrassed by this fact. The trial judge directed the jury that, when considering the likely reaction of a reasonable man, they must take into account the possible reaction of an *ordinary* man (*i.e.* one who was not impotent). Such an approach is, perhaps, tinged with eccentricity. Now that the 1957 Act recognises that things *said* to the accused may constitute provocation, it would be odd if the courts were to continue to ignore the characteristics of the accused which made the words offensive to him. In *D.P.P.* v. *Camplin* (1978) the House of Lords accepted that this was so and Lord Diplock proposed that:

> "The judge should state (to the jury) what the question is, using the very terms of the section (which states that " . . . the jury shall take into account *everything* . . . according to the effect it would have on a reasonable man"). He should explain to them that the reasonable man referred to in the question is a person having the power of self-control to be expected of an ordinary person of the sex and age of the accused, *but in other respects sharing such of the accused's characteristics as they think would affect the gravity of the provocation to him . . . .*"

This liberal approach has, however, been somewhat qualified by the decision of the Court of Appeal in *R.* v. *Newell* that a *temporary* state of mind (*e.g.* depression) should not be regarded as a "characteristic" of the accused. Thus, a man, like the accused in *Newell*, depressed by the fact that the woman that he has lived with has left him cannot expect the court to take into account his depressed state when he kills a friend who speaks disparagingly of her.

Involuntary manslaughter . . . we have seen that *malice aforethought* is the *mens rea* of murder, but that, in some circumstances, a person who has killed another with malice aforethought will be guilty only of voluntary manslaughter. Where there is an unlawful homicide and it can be shown that the accused did not kill with malice aforethought, he is liable for manslaughter and, there being no *mens rea* for murder, the manslaughter will be involuntary. To constitute manslaughter the homicide must be "unlawful" and the offence falls, therefore, between acts which constitute murder and those which will be regarded as lawful homicide (as where the accused killed in self-defence or by the use of reasonable force to prevent a crime or, in certain circumstances, to effect an arrest). There must, therefore, be some degree of culpability. In some cases the accused will be clearly "blameworthy" as where he is grossly negligent or reckless (though not reckless in a situation in which it is highly probable that someone will be killed or suffer grievous bodily harm, for that would, in most circumstances, be taken to constitute malice aforethought). Thus if, as in *R.* v. *Pike*, a party was to administer potentially harmful drugs or a gas as a stimulant to his partner in sexual activity and that partner was to die as a result, it may not be possible to establish that the accused knew that there was a high probability of death or really serious injury but it is quite likely that he could be shown to have been reckless. The accused would, in such case, be guilty not of murder but of voluntary manslaughter. Presumably the public at large would support such a finding for, in its view, the accused has "nearly" murdered. What, however, of the situation in which the accused's state of mind is such that the offence is at the other end of the range of activities which constitute manslaughter, where it is "nearly" an accident? At one time an accused would be considered to be guilty of (at least) manslaughter where he committed an unlawful act which led to death. Thus, for example, where (in *R. v. Fenton*) an accused threw stones down a mine shaft and damaged equipment so that a basket being lowered down the mine overturned, causing the death of a miner, the court accepted that such an act could amount to manslaughter. No doubt the accused was, in that case, culpable but equally there was in all probability no question of his having anticipated the kind of consequences that ensued. The attitude of the courts has mellowed over the years and now a court must be satisfied not only that the accused committed an unlawful act, but also that the act was *dangerous* (in the sense that a reasonable person could have recognised that the act carried with it the possibility of *some* immediate risk of personal injury even though he may not have appreciated that there was a risk of serious injury). It must, in effect, be shown that the act was directed at *a person*. Thus, in *R. v. Dalby* a person who supplied Diconal tablets to a friend was found to be not guilty of manslaughter when the friend died as a result of injecting himself, for the accused had not directed his act against the person of the deceased. Where, however, a person struck another, A, violently, causing him to fall against B, a frail old lady, who sustained injuries and subsequently died, the accused was found to be guilty (*R. v. Mitchell*). The act in question had *not* been directed against the victim but it had been directed against a person.

Assault

The term "assault" is often used to refer to two quite distinct offences, that of *assault* and that of *battery*.

An assault is committed when the accused acts in such a way as to make another reasonably fear that personal violence will be inflicted upon him. Where the accused threatens another, but it is clear that he cannot, or will not, bring his threats into effect, there is no assault. In *Tuberville* v. *Savadge* the accused laid his hands on his sword (an action which alone is, in appropriate circumstances, sufficient to constitute an assault) and said "if it were not Assize time I would not take such language." The court determined that there was no assault, for the accused had made it clear that, it being Assize time, he would take no action. A battery occurs when personal violence is actually inflicted upon another. The slightest touch against the victim's consent will be sufficient to constitute a battery. Assault and battery are also torts (see page 162) and may form the basis of a civil action for compensation.

There is no assault or battery where the "victim" consents. Thus, the raising of a fist by a boxer may well cause his opponent to fear that he is to be subjected to personal violence, but there is no assault. Equally, the fast bowler who attempts to draw a batsman into an unwise shot by use of a "bouncer" does not commit a battery even though the missile that he aims at the batsman renders him unconscious. There are, however, limits to the extent to which consent negatives the commission of an offence. Thus, a party to a duel would not be able to point to the consent of the other, nor would public policy permit the infliction of force for sexual gratification.

Parents, teachers and others in *loco parentis* have a power to chastise by reasonable use of force.

Some forms of assault (using that term in its widest sense as a generic term which embraces a battery) are, by statute, identified as offences more serious than a common assault. Thus:

(a) Section 51(1) of the Police Act 1964 provides that: "Any person who assaults a constable in the execution of his duty, or a person assisting a constable in the execution of his duty, shall be guilty of an offence"; the offence is a summary offence punishable by up to six months' imprisonment or a fine of up to £1,000 or both.

(b) Section 47 of the Offences Against the Person Act 1861 provides that a person who assaults "occasioning actual bodily harm" commits an offence. The offence is triable either way and is punishable by up to five years' imprisonment.

Sections 18 and 20 of the Offences Against the Person Act 1861 create the even more serious offences of wounding and causing or inflicting grievous bodily harm (*i.e.* really serious injury):

(a) Section 18 provides that: "Whosoever shall unlawfully and maliciously by any means whatsoever wound or cause any grievous bodily harm to any person with intent to do some grievous bodily harm to any person or with intent to resist or prevent the lawful apprehension or detainer of any person shall be guilty of an (indictable) offence, and being convicted thereof shall be liable to imprisonment for life";

(b) Section 20 provides that: "Whosoever shall unlawfully and maliciously wound or inflict any grievous bodily harm upon any other person, either with or without any weapon or instrument shall be guilty of an offence (triable either way) and being convicted thereof shall be liable to imprisonment for five years."

Rape

Section 1(1) of the Sexual Offences Act 1956 provides that: "It is an offence for a man to rape a woman." The Sexual Offences (Amendment Act) 1976 provides that "a man commits rape if:

(a) he has unlawful sexual intercourse with a woman who at the time of the intercourse does not consent to it; *and*

(b) at that time he knows she does not consent to the intercourse or he is reckless as to whether she consents to it."

Rape is punishable with a maximum sentence of life imprisonment.

Unlawful sexual intercourse . . . sexual intercourse is *unlawful*, for the purposes of this offence, where it takes place between parties who are not married. Thus, any illicit sexual intercourse is unlawful, though it will not, of course, amount to rape where the woman consents. It would appear that sexual intercourse may also be regarded as unlawful where, the wife not consenting, intercourse takes place following a formal separation of the parties (*i.e.* one effected by agreement or by order of a court).

The courts will accept that sexual intercourse has taken place where it can be established that the man has penetrated the woman.

Consent . . . a woman will not have been raped if she consented to
intercourse. Such consent cannot have been given where the woman was
not in a position to exercise choice. Thus, convictions for rape have been
secured where intercourse has taken place with women who were asleep or
in a state of drunken stupor. The fact that a woman *submits* to intercourse
does not necessarily indicate that she *consents* to it, for, whilst not
consenting to the act, she may be fearful of violence should she resist.

The apparent consent of a woman to intercourse will not be treated as
genuine consent where:

(a) the woman has been deceived as to the nature of the act that is
taking place. Thus where, in *R.* v. *Flattery*, a girl was told that the act
was a surgical operation she was not taken to have consented to the
intercourse;

(b) the woman has been deceived as to the identity of her partner.

The 1976 Act provides that where the woman does not consent to
intercourse, the accused is, nonetheless, not guilty of rape if:

(a) he does not know that she does not consent; *and*

(b) he is not reckless as to whether or not she consents.

Thus, if, as in *Morgan* v. *D.P.P.*, a husband informs friends that his wife is a
willing partner to intercourse and that her acts of resistance are merely
part of a "game," then, if the jury can be convinced that the accused
actually believed that there was consent, the accused cannot be found to be
guilty.

Theft

Section 1(1) of the Theft Act 1968 provides that a person commits *theft*
where:

" . . . he dishonestly appropriates property belonging to another with the
intention of permanently depriving the other of it . . . ."

A person guilty of theft may be sentenced to a term of imprisonment not
exceeding 10 years.

Dishonest appropriation . . . in order that there be a "dishonest appropriation," it is clear that there must be an *appropriation* and that this
appropriation must be made *dishonestly*. Let us first consider the meaning
of the term "appropriation."

Section 3(1) of the 1968 Act provides that:

"Any assumption by a person of the rights of an owner amounts to an
appropriation, and this includes, where he has come by the property
(innocently or not) without stealing it, any later assumption of a right to
it by keeping or dealing with it as owner."

An accused will clearly have made an appropriation of goods where he
takes them, and this will be the act that, in most cases of theft, constitutes
the required appropriation. There are, however, other instances of
appropriation. A person may be entrusted with goods in a certain capacity
and may *act in a manner inconsistent with the terms upon which he has received
the goods*. Thus, an agent may be given goods with express instructions to
sell them only at a certain, minimum, price. A sale at a price lower than that
authorised by the principal will amount to theft. To *use* goods in a manner
inconsistent with the intention of the owner may also constitute an
appropriation. Thus, if a motorist leaves his car at a garage in order that it

be repaired there would clearly be an appropriation if a mechanic used the car to transport himself to and from his home, at lunch time, other than for the legitimate purposes of testing it. (There would, of course, be *no theft* in this particular example, for the mechanic does not intend to permanently deprive the owner of his car.) *Destruction* of goods would also constitute an appropriation of them, for only the owner, or someone acting with his authority, has the power to destroy the goods. All of these examples of appropriation are, of course, merely instances of a general concept and there will be other acts which will fulfil the definition contained in section 3(1) and thus constitute an appropriation for the purposes of theft.

The appropriation will only result in theft if it is *dishonest*. Section 2(1) of the Theft Act provides:

"A person's appropriation of property belonging to another is not to be regarded as dishonest—
(a) if he appropriates the property in the belief that he has *in law* the *right* to deprive the other of it, on behalf of himself or of a third person; *or*
(b) if he appropriates the property in the belief that he would have the *other's consent* if the other knew of the appropriation and the circumstances of it; *or*
(c) if he appropriates the property in the belief that the person to whom the property belongs cannot be discovered by taking reasonable steps."

Thus, if a seller of goods despatches goods to a buyer, only to discover that the buyer has not paid for them on the contractually agreed date, he may well believe that he has every right to stop the goods in transit and recover possession of them. This view may not, however, be correct. Ownership of the goods may, by virtue of agreement between the parties or as a result of the operation of provisions in the Sale of Goods Act 1979 have passed to the buyer, so that they no longer belong to the seller. If so, the seller only has a legal right to stop them in transit if the buyer is insolvent. In the event of the buyer not being insolvent the seller will, if he has recovered the goods, have committed the tort of conversion because of his wrongful interference with the goods but, believing that he has a right to recover, his appropriation of the goods will not be considered to be dishonest and he will not be guilty of theft. Similarly, if the accused notices a magazine sticking out of the letter box of his neighbour's home he may, if he knows that the neighbour is away on holiday, believe that the neighbour would willingly consent to his taking the magazine from the letter box. He may, indeed, believe that he was doing his neighbour a favour by removing an indication to others that the house is empty. The fact that his neighbour had a particular interest in articles in the magazine, looked forward to reading it on his return and certainly would not have assented to the appropriation is neither here nor there. The belief of the accused is the factor that is significant. Few people today would, if they found valuable lost property, believe that the owner of the property could not be found. If, therefore, they found such property and kept it, it is unlikely that they would be able to convince the court that they appropriated the property "in the belief that the person to whom the property belongs cannot be discovered by taking reasonable steps." Where, however, the property found has little monetary value many people might suspect that the loss would not be reported, that it would not be worth the trouble involved in taking the item to a police station and that it would be in order to keep the item, for the next passer-by would certainly do so. Such people are, most people would agree, not "dishonest" and ought not to be treated as such.

Section 2(1) does not, of course, provide a test for use in determining whether an appropriation has been dishonest. It merely provides instances of appropriations which will *not* be taken to be dishonest. It is for a jury to determine, in any particular case, whether or not the accused has been dishonest. In doing so they must take into account the state of mind of the accused rather than apply an objective test of honesty.

Property belonging to another . . . to commit theft the accused must dishonestly appropriate "property" and that property must "belong to another."

Section 4(1) of the 1968 Act defines "property" as including " . . . money and all other property, real or personal, including things in action and other intangible property" (see pages 191 and 213 for an explanation of these terms). To be meaningfully included within the definition of "property" it is obvious that a thing must be capable of being appropriated. Concern that *electricity* could not be appropriated led to the passing of a section of the Theft Act to deal with this problem. (Section 13 provides that: "A person who dishonestly uses without due authority, or dishonestly causes to be wasted or diverted any electricity shall on conviction on indictment be liable to imprisonment for a term not exceeding five years." This offence would, for example, be appropriate where a householder attempts to by-pass the electricity meter in his home and, presumably, where employees make private calls on their employers' telephones despite instructions to the contrary).

It might appear trite to say that there is only theft where the property stolen *belongs to another*. Normally, of course, there is no problem in determining that this is so. In some situations, however, difficulties may arise in establishing that the property stolen belongs to someone other than the accused. Consider, for example, the situation in which a member of a working men's club takes a bottle of beer from the bar without paying for it. Has he appropriated property belonging to another? As a member of the club he is a part owner of the stock and, in part, the bottle was his. He has, however, by his appropriation deprived other members of their share and by appropriating their rights he has taken from them a chose in action which, as we have seen, falls within the definition of property; clearly he has committed theft. Consider also the situation in which the accused pledges goods with a pawnbroker (an act which does not take away his ownership of the goods) and then, without redeeming the pledge, takes the goods from the pawnbroker's shop without the knowledge of the pawnbroker. Has our accused in these circumstances appropriated property "belonging to another"? The answer, again, is in the affirmative; by the agreement between himself and the pawnbroker the accused has created rights which may be exercised by the pawnbroker and, in unlawfully recovering possession of the goods, he has, at least, compromised these rights. Such a sophisticated approach is not, however, necessary, for the provisions of section 5(1) of the Theft Act would result in the accused having stolen the goods themselves, rather than having merely appropriated rights relating to them. Section 5(1) provides that:

"Property shall be regarded as belonging to any person having possession or control of it, or having in it any proprietary right or interest . . . ."

Thus, to return to our examples, the other members of the working men's club have a proprietary right in the stock of the club and the pawnbroker has possession and a proprietary right in the goods pawned. In each case, therefore, the goods appropriated clearly belong "to another" and have, as a result, been stolen.

With the intention of permanently depriving the other of it . . . the accused will only be guilty of theft if, at the time of his dishonest appropriation of goods belonging to another, he intended to permanently deprive the victim of the goods.

Because of the difficulty in establishing such an intention where the accused has taken another's car (did he intend to permanently deprive the owner of the car or did he intend to use the car only to get him home late at night and then to abandon it in circumstances in which it would, in all likelihood be recovered by the owner?) the specific offence of *taking a conveyance without consent* was introduced by section 12 of the Theft Act 1968.

Robbery

Section 8(1) of the Theft Act 1968 provides that:

"A person is guilty of robbery if he steals, and immediately before or at the time of doing so, and in order to do so, he uses force on any person or puts or seeks to put any person in fear of being then and there subjected to force."

A person who commits robbery, or an assault with intent to rob, is liable to a sentence of life imprisonment.

If he steals . . . commission of theft is part of the *actus reus* of robbery. Thus, if the accused can show that he has not committed theft then he cannot be convicted of robbery. We have seen, for example, that it may not be possible to show that a person who takes a motor car from another is guilty of theft. If, when taking the car, the accused threatens the owner with violence, it would be equally difficult to establish robbery.

Uses force on any person, etc . . . the feature which makes robbery a more serious offence than theft is the use or threat of force. It is not necessary that the force should have been used against the victim of the theft, or that the threat of force should have been directed at him. The section clearly states that the offence is committed where the accused " . . . used force *on any person* or puts or seeks to put *any person in fear* . . . ." Thus, if A wishing to steal from B, a schoolchild, threatens C, the child's teacher, A is guilty of robbery.

It is, of course, necessary that the use of force, or the threat of it, took place *at the time* of the theft or *immediately before it*. It is also necessary that the force should be used or threatened *in order to effect the theft*. Thus, if the accused discovers, in the process of stealing from his victim, that the victim holds strong religious or political beliefs which are repugnant to the accused, and he uses or threatens force as a reaction to this discovery, then the accused may well be guilty of an assault *and* theft, but he will not have committed robbery.

Burglary
Section 9 of the Theft Act 1968 provides that a person commits burglary if:

(a)   he enters any building or part of a building as a trespasser and with intent to steal or to inflict grievous bodily harm on any person, or to rape, or to cause unlawful damage; *or*

(b)   having entered any building or part of a building as a trespasser he steals or attempts to steal or inflicts or attempts to inflict grievous bodily harm on any person.

The offence carries a term of imprisonment not exceeding 14 years.

Enters any building as trespasser . . . to commit burglary, the accused must commit the tort of trespass (see page 357) but, the offence of burglary being a criminal offence, he must also trespass with *mens rea*. Thus, he must be aware of the trespass or, at least, be reckless as to whether or not he enters the premises with consent. A person who enters premises lawfully may *subsequently* become a trespasser if he then acts in a manner inconsistent with the occupier's consent to his entry. Thus, in *Harrison* v. *Duke of Rutland* a lawful visitor to land became a trespasser when he attempted to frighten game so as to frustrate a shooting party organised by the owner of the land. If, therefore, a person enters premises for a lawful purpose, as would a police constable who wishes to investigate the circumstances of a burglary, then, if that person, having entered the premises, decides that he will steal property he finds there and does so, he is guilty of theft. Not having *entered* as a trespasser, however, he would not commit burglary.

Section 9(3) of the 1968 Act provides that inhabited vehicles (*e.g.* caravans) or vessels are to be treated as "buildings," for the purposes of burglary.

Entry with intent to steal, etc./stealing, etc., having entered as trespasser . . . having established that the accused entered the building as a trespasser, it is then necessary to establish that he *either*:

(a)   intended, at the time of entry, to steal, or inflict grievous bodily harm, or to rape, or to cause unlawful damage (whether or not he actually did so); *or*

(b)   proceeded to steal, or attempt to steal or inflict or attempt to inflict grievous bodily harm (even though he did not enter with this intention).

Aggravated burglary . . . section 10 of the Theft Act 1968 provides that:

"A person is guilty of aggravated burglary if he commits any burglary and at the time has with him any firearm or imitation firearm, any weapon of offence or any explosive."

Aggravated burglary is punishable by a maximum sentence of life imprisonment.

Handling stolen goods
Section 22 of the Theft Act 1968 provides that a person handles stolen goods if:

"(otherwise than in the course of the stealing) knowing or believing them to be stolen goods he dishonestly receives the goods, or dishonestly undertakes or assists in their retention, removal, disposal, or realisation by or for the benefit of another person, or if he arranges to do so."

Stolen goods . . . a person can only be convicted of handling stolen goods if the goods have been stolen, that is to say if there has been a theft. Thus, where there is no theft there can be no conviction for handling. If, therefore, A sells B's goods to C in the mistaken belief that B would have consented to the appropriation of his goods by A had he known of it, C cannot be guilty of handling even though he believes the goods to be stolen (see page 87).

Goods which have been stolen may, at some time, cease to be regarded as stolen goods. Thus, section 24(3) of the 1968 Act provides that " . . . no goods shall be regarded as having continued to be stolen goods after they have been restored to the person from whom they were stolen or to other lawful possession or custody, or after that person and any other person claiming through him has otherwise ceased as regards those goods to have any right to restitution in respect of the theft." If, therefore, a bona fide purchaser buys stolen goods in *market overt* (open market) he will acquire title to the goods which, from that time onward, cease to be stolen goods.

Just as goods which have been stolen may cease to be so regarded, goods which have not been stolen may be deemed to have been stolen. Section 24(2) provides that goods will be regarded as stolen where:

(a) they represent the proceeds of any disposal or realisation of the stolen goods by the thief (as where the thief exchanges the stolen goods for other goods);

(b) they represent the proceeds of a disposal or realisation of the stolen goods by the handler (as where a handler exchanges the stolen goods for other goods).

Handling . . . a person handles goods for the purposes of section 22 where he:

(a) receives them; *or*

(b) arranges to receive them; *or*

(c) undertakes or assists in their retention, removal, disposal or realisation by or for the benefit or another person; *or*

(d) arranges to act as in (c) above.

Thus, if A buys stolen goods from B and takes possession of them he *receives* stolen goods and thus handles them. Equally, if he *makes arrangements* to receive stolen goods, he handles them even though he does not receive them. If A helps B to hide stolen goods he *assists in their retention*. If he helps B to carry stolen goods from one place to another, he *assists in their removal*. If he sells them for B, he *undertakes the realisation* of stolen goods and if he destroys them for B, he *undertakes their disposal*. In all of these cases A has handled stolen goods even though he has not received them.

Knowing or believing them to be stolen . . . if the accused *knows* that he is handling stolen goods he clearly commits an offence. So too where he *believes* that they are stolen and they are in fact stolen. It would appear that it is not sufficient to show that the accused *suspected* that the goods were stolen (as might be the case where goods are sold at a very cheap price off trade premises by someone other than a retailer). So long as the accused thought there was a *possibility* that the goods were not stolen, he presumably does not *believe* that they were stolen.

Criminal damage

Section 1(1) of the Criminal Damage Act 1971 provides that:

"A person who without lawful excuse destroys or damages any property belonging to another intending to destroy or damage any such property or being reckless as to whether any such property would be destroyed or damaged shall be guilty of an offence."

The offence created by section 1(1) is punishable by a maximum term of imprisonment of ten years.

Without lawful excuse . . . some forms of wilful damage to property will not constitute a criminal act. Thus, a fireman who smashes the window of a burning house or rips off the door of a car in order that he may effect a rescue is clearly acting lawfully. So too is the doctor who, in an emergency, tears a patient's trousers in order to treat his leg or a policeman who, armed with a warrant, finds that he needs to force a door in order to enter premises and effect an arrest.

In addition to such situations, section 5 of the Criminal Damage Act provides that an accused will be deemed to have a lawful excuse where:

(a)   he believed that he had consent to effect the destruction or damage, or that he would have had such consent had the person who was in a position to give such consent (or who appeared to be in such a position) known the circumstances; *or*

(b)   the destruction or damage was effected in order to protect property and the accused believed that an immediate act was necessary and that the act taken was reasonable in the circumstances (even though the steps taken were, from an objective standpoint, unreasonable).

Thus, if A, whilst burning garden rubbish, decides that he will burn materials in his neighbour's garden in the mistaken belief that his neighbour, who is at that time on holiday, would welcome the act, A does not commit criminal damage. Similarly, if A believes that B's parked motor car, which is on fire, is likely to explode and damage his house, he would not commit the offence if he broke into the car in order to release the handbrake so that he could push it away.

Destroys or damages any property belonging to another . . . normally it is clear when property has been either destroyed or damaged. In marginal cases, however, the court may have to determine whether such is the case. In *"A" (Juvenile)* v. *R.* for example, the court was called upon to consider whether damage was caused to a policeman's raincoat as a result of it being spat upon by the accused. Immediately after the incident the wearer of the coat had removed the spittle with tissue paper but had taken no further steps to remove traces of it. The court was presented with a coat bearing a faint mark and required to pronounce upon it. The court decided that criminal damage had not been caused. Spitting, it was accepted, could cause damage to some garments (made, perhaps, of satin or velvet), but it was noted that, in this particular case, all traces of spittle, and therefore all damage, could easily be removed by a simple process (*i.e.* the application of soap and water). It would appear, therefore, that the degree of permanency of the damage and the steps that need to be taken to "repair" it are relevant factors. *Destruction* would appear to be a word which has an unequivocal meaning. However, commercial lawyers have, for years, struggled with the meaning of the word *perished* as used in the Sale of Goods Act. No doubt similar problems arise in relation to the 1971 Act.

Have, for example, potatoes been destroyed when they still exist and are recognisable as such, but have been rendered inedible? Such difficulties of definition are, however, difficulties of terminology rather than of substance in this context, for if goods have not been *destroyed* it is highly likely that they will, at least, have been *damaged*.

For the purposes of the 1971 Act, section 10(1) provides that "property" means: " . . . property of a tangible nature, whether real or personal, including money . . . ." Thus, land may be the subject of criminal damage but intangible property cannot. *Damage* and *destruction* are, thus, clearly to be regarded as terms relating to *physical harm* caused to the property of another.

Criminal damage arises only where the damage is caused to property "belonging to another." Section 10 of the Act provides that property shall be taken to belong to another when:

(a) he has custody or control of it;
(b) he has a proprietary right or interest; or
(c) he has a charge on it.

Intending to destroy or damage/being reckless as to destruction or damage . . . the accused must either *intend* to destroy or damage the property or be *reckless* as to whether the property is destroyed or damaged. He must also be aware (and thus have *intention*) that the property belongs to another, or be reckless as to whether it belongs to another.

CRIMINAL OFFENCES WHICH OFFEND ENTRENCHED NOTIONS OF MORALITY

Most societies attempt to use law to promote moral standards, or, rather to penalise deviance from such standards, by the use of criminal law. The nature of the standards, and thus the characteristics of the legal provisions, will, of course, differ from society to society. Indeed, with changing moral standards, the legal provisions within any one state will alter with the passage of time and conduct which was once "criminal" will cease to be such and vice versa. The specific offences described below are presented not because they are "special" or particularly important, but simply because they provide examples of one type of criminal offence, that which has been specified to be criminal because it offends entrenched notions of morality.

Offences relating to prostitution

The law relating to prostitution, is perhaps, paradoxical. Prostitution itself is not a criminal activity. Virtually every way in which a potential client may be contacted by a prostitute, is, however, likely to lead to the commission of an offence. A prostitute commits a criminal offence where she *solicits* on the street, a pimp who finds clients for her will commit the offence of *living on the immoral earnings of a prostitute,* it is an offence for a person to *keep a brothel* and, since the decision in *Shaw* v. *D.P.P.* an offence may be committed when prostitutes advertise their services in a magazine. It is, moreover, an offence to *persuade* a woman to become a prostitute.

Loitering or soliciting . . . section 1 of the Street Offences Act 1959 provides that:

"It shall be an offence for a common prostitute to loiter or solicit in a street or public place for the purposes of prostitution."

The offence is a summary one punishable by a fine. Section 71 of the Criminal Justice Act 1982 abolished imprisonment for soliciting.

A prostitute *loiters* when she "hangs about" or lingers in a particular place, she *solicits* when she makes an invitation to men. In *Smith* v. *Hughes* the court was called upon to determine whether a prostitute had solicited men *in a street* by tapping on the window of her room and inviting them in. The court found that she had, even though she was not herself in the street. Lord Chief Justice Parker did so by an application of the *mischief rule* (see page 8), pointing out that the mischief to passers-by was the same whether or not the girl was in the street. Hilbery J. did so by an application of the *literal rule* (see page 6), pointing out that a person is only solicited when he receives the communication and, he being in the street at that time, he was therefore solicited in the street.

Living on immoral earnings . . . section 30 of the Sexual Offences Act 1956 provides that:

"It is an offence for a man knowingly to live wholly or in part on the earnings of prostitution."

The offence carries a maximum penalty of seven years imprisonment.

For the purposes of the section any man who:
(a) lives with or is habitually in the company of a prostitute; or
(b) exercises control, direction or influence over a prostitute's movements in a way which shows he is aiding, abetting or compelling her prostitution with others,

is *presumed* to be knowingly living on the earnings of prostitution, unless he proves the contrary.

When it is recalled that prostitution is not unlawful, it may be considered unfortunate that a prostitute's boyfriend (who will, no doubt, be "habitually in the company" of the prostitute) is, by that fact alone, presumed to have committed an offence carrying with it up to seven years imprisonment.

Keeping a brothel . . . section 33 of the Sexual Offences Act 1956 provides that:

"It is an offence for a person to keep a brothel, or to manage, or act or assist in the management of, a brothel."

It is also an offence, under the 1956 Act, for a landlord to let premises in the knowledge that they are to be used as a brothel and for an occupier to permit his premises to be used as a brothel.

Premises will only be regarded as a brothel where at least two prostitutes use the premises to ply their trade. (Where only one prostitute uses the premises there is every likelihood that the occupier of the premises, whilst not keeping a brothel, will be guilty of living on the earnings of prostitution.)

Conspiracy to corrupt public morals . . . in *Shaw* v. *D.P.P.* the accused published a magazine, called the *Ladies Directory*, containing the names and addresses of prostitutes and an indication of the "services" they were prepared to offer. The court found that the accused had conspired to *corrupt public morals* and asserted that " . . . there remains in the courts of law a residual power to enforce the supreme and fundamental purpose of the law, to conserve not only the safety and order but also the moral welfare of the state."

Offences relating to homosexual conduct

The Sexual Offences Act 1956 provides that:

"It is an offence for a person to commit *buggery* with another . . . ."

Section 13 of the same Act provides that:

"It is an offence for a man to commit *an act of gross indecency* with another man . . . or to be a party to the commission by a man of an act of gross indecency with another man, or to procure the commission by a man of an act of gross indecency with another man."

Both of these sections must be read subject to section 1 of the Sexual Offences Act 1967 (passed as a result of the *Report of the Committee on Homosexual Offences and Prostitution*, 1957) which provides that a man does *not* by acts committed with other men, commit either offence where:

(a)   the parties consent;
(b)   they are both 21 or over; and
(c)   the act is done in private.

One bizarre consequence of the 1967 Act is the fact that if A buggers B, another man, in private, then, providing B consented and both A and B are at least 21, neither A nor B commit an offence. If, however, A, being over 21, buggers B, his wife who is also over 21, in the privacy of their home, both commit an offence. Indeed, in the latter situation A faces a possible term of life imprisonment.

It remains an offence for a man to commit buggery or gross indecency with another man under the age of 21, or with a consenting man over 21 in a public place. For the purposes of homosexual offences no act is done in private if:

(a)   there are other persons present; *or*
(b)   the act is done in a lavatory to which the public have access.

Whilst it is no longer an offence for adult men to undertake homosexual acts in private, it was held in *Knuller Ltd.* v. *D.P.P.* that there is a *conspiracy to corrupt public morals* where a publisher produces a magazine which contains advertisements by which homosexuals attempt to contact potential partners. This approach has been criticised on the basis that it is illogical of the state to prosecute a person because he facilitates the making of an invitation to indulge in lawful activity. Another view, however, presented by Lord Reid in *Knuller*, is that " . . . there is a material difference between merely exempting certain conduct from criminal penalties and making it lawful in the full sense." According to this view the 1967 Act states, in effect, that " . . . even though it may be corrupting, if people choose to corrupt themselves in this way that is their affair and the law will not interfere. But no licence is given to others to encourage the practice."

Section 32 of the Sexual Offences Act 1956 provides that:

"It is an offence for a man persistently to solicit or importune in a public place for immoral purposes."

Obscenity

Section 1 of the Obscene Publications Act 1959 provides that:

" . . . an article shall be deemed to be obscene if its effect . . . is, if taken as a whole, such as to tend to *deprave and corrupt* persons who are likely, having regard to all the relevant circumstances, to read, see or hear the matter contained or embodied in it . . . ."

The definition contained in the 1959 Act is not restricted to material which is sexual in nature and, for example, would embrace material which pointed to the "merits" of drug-taking. Normally, however, prosecutions related to material which is likely to lead to sexual depravity.

Section 2(1) of the 1959 Act provides that it is an offence *to publish an obscene article*, whether for gain or not. The same subsection, as amended by the Obscene Publications Act 1964, provides that it is an offence *to possess an obscene article for publication for gain*.

Publishing an obscene article . . . the 1959 Act provides that a person "publishes" an article where he:

(a)   distributes it;
(b)   circulates it;
(c)   sells, lets or hires it;
(d)   gives or lends it; or
(e)   offers it for sale or for letting or hiring.

Where the article contains material to be looked at, or is a record, then a person publishes it when, otherwise than on television or radio, he:

(a)   shows it;
(b)   plays it; or
(c)   projects it.

The accused will only be guilty of the offence if it can be established that:

(a)   the person to whom the article was published was a person who was, at least to some extent, susceptible to the article's potential to deprave and corrupt (not, as in *R.* v. *Clayton and Halsey,* an experienced police officer who was able to testify that because of his experience the article had no effect upon him); *or*
(b)   it was likely that others could have seen or heard the material and that the material was such that it would tend to deprave and corrupt such persons; *or*
(c)   it has been published to a person whom it is likely to deprave or corrupt (though not by the accused) and this publication could reasonably have been expected to follow from publication of the material by the accused.

Being in possession of an obscene article for publication for gain . . . as a result of the 1964 Act an accused who cannot be charged with publishing an obscene article, because the only person to whom it has been published is a policeman (see *R.* v. *Clayton and Halsey,* above), may now be charged with possession of such an article.

Defences . . . the accused will have a defence (by virtue of sections within both the 1959 Act and the 1964 Act) where:

(a)   he had not examined the article; *and*
(b)   he had no reasonable cause to believe that it was obscene.

Thus, if A a bookseller sells or has possession of a normally respectable magazine which happens to contain, unknown to him, an obscene article, he will be able to claim the defence. If, however, the magazine is notorious for such material his ignorance of the particular article will be no defence.

Where a book is obscene, the 1959 Act provides a defence where it can be established that it can be "justified as being for the public good on the ground that it is in the interests of science, literature, art or learning, or of other objects of general concern."

The Indecent Displays (Control) Act 1981 provides that it is an offence to make, cause or permit the public display of any indecent matter. Under the provisions of the Act, designed to protect the public from displays they cannot avoid (*e.g.* displays in the windows of "porn" shops) a display *inside* a shop constitutes an offence unless customers gain access to the shop only by passing a warning notice.

"REGULATORY" CRIMINAL OFFENCES

The so-called "regulatory" criminal offences represent, perhaps, the "high-water mark" in the state's use of criminal sanctions. Having attempted to deter citizens in respect of the "traditional" criminal offences and having attempted to prevent activity which society would view as grossly immoral (*e.g.* prostitution and homosexual conduct), the state has now indicated that it feels itself free to pass legislation which regulates commercial activities in order to safeguard the economic or social interests of individual members of society. It has, for example, promoted legislation which seeks to deter commercially immoral conduct and legislation which inhibits, by use of criminal sanctions, the despoilation of the environment. The Trade Descriptions Act 1968 and the Unsolicited Goods and Services Act 1971 provide examples of legislation designed to prevent undesirable trading practices.

Trade Descriptions Act 1968

Section 1 of the Act provides that:

"Any person who, in the course of a trade or business —
(a) applies a false trade description to any goods; *or*
(b) supplies or offers to supply any goods to which a false trade description is applied,
shall . . . be guilty of an offence."

In the course of a trade or business . . . the Act is not intended to apply to transactions between private individuals. It operates, therefore, only when a person sells in the course of a trade or business. It is not, however, necessary to show that the business has been established for the express purpose of selling goods. Thus, in *Havering London Borough* v. *Stephenson* a car with a false speedometer mileage reading was treated as having been sold in the course of a business when it had been sold by a car hire firm.

Where the goods are actually sold to the consumer he will often have a right to sue the seller under section 13 of the Sale of Goods Act 1979 (see page 363) and it may be wondered why this criminal sanction has been provided. The answer, of course, is that a civil action may, in many cases and for a variety of reasons, appear unattractive to the consumer. The passing of criminal legislation in this area is, therefore, an attempt to protect the consumer by deterring those who would abuse him, in the same way that breathalyser laws seek to protect road users.

Applies a false trade description . . . a false trade description is a trade description which is false. A "trade description" is defined, in section 2 of the Act, as an indication, by whatever means, of any of the following:
(a) quantity or size, (*e.g.* "20 metres");

(b)   method of manufacture or production (*e.g.* "built by robots");
(c)   composition (*e.g.* "solid gold");
(d)   fitness for purpose (*e.g.* "paint suitable for internal or external use");
(e)   other physical characteristics (*e.g.* colour);
(f)   testing by any person (*e.g.* "tested on the production line by quality controllers");
(g)   approved by any person (*e.g.* "approved by doctors");
(h)   the place or date of manufacture or production (*e.g.* "Sheffield Steel");
(i)   the person by whom manufactured (*e.g.* "Parker Pen").

A trade description will be false if it is false *to a material degree* (*i.e.* false enough to matter). A statement that a person was receiving 20 tonnes of coal would not, for example, be false within the meaning of the Act if the consumer found that the consignment was 1kg. short of 20 tonnes.

Section 4 of the Act provides that the accused "applies" a false trade description where he:

(a)   affixes or annexes it to or in any manner marks it on or incorporates it with—
   (i)   the goods themselves, *or*
   (ii)   anything in, or with which, the goods are supplied;
(b)   places the goods in, on, or with anything which the trade description has been affixed to or annexed to, marked on or incorporated with, or places any such thing with the goods; *or*
(c)   uses the trade description in any manner likely to be taken as referring to the goods.

Supplies or offers to supply any goods to which a false trade description is applied . . . a retailer who sells goods to which another person (*e.g.* the manufacturer) has applied a false trade description commits an offence. So too if he "offers to supply goods" to which a false trade description is applied. Section 6 of the Act provides that a person exposing goods for supply is *deemed* to offer to supply them and thus, for the purposes of this Act, avoids the difficulty that normally goods exposed for sale would not be an offer but would, rather, constitute an *"invitation to treat"* (see page 115).

Defences . . . section 24 of the Act provides for a defence where:

(a)   the commission of the offence was due to a *mistake* or to *reliance on information* supplied to him or to the *act or default of another person*, an *accident* or some other cause beyond his control; *and*
(b)   he took all *reasonable precautions* and exercised all *due diligence* to avoid the commission of such an offence by himself or any person under his control.

Thus, in *Naish* v. *Gore* a car dealer who had purchased a *"low-mileage car,"* obtained an A.A. Report indicating that the condition of the car was consistent with the recorded mileage and then sold the car only to discover that the mileage reading had been tampered with, was able to claim a defence.

Other offences . . . the Act contains other provisions relating to false indications of price and false descriptions relating to *services*.

Unsolicited Goods and Services Act 1971

In an attempt to combat the evil of "inertia selling" (by which goods which have not been requested are delivered to the consumer and payment required), the Unsolicited Goods and Services Act 1971 provides for the passing of title in the goods to the consumer (in certain circumstances). This is, of course, a provision which affects the position in *civil law* of the sender and recipient of the goods rather than one which has any significance in criminal law. In the same Act, however, there are several criminal sanctions. In particular, it is stated to be an offence:

  (a) to demand payment for unsolicited goods;
  (b) to threaten legal proceedings or the placing of the consumer's name on a default list;
  (c) to threaten any other collection procedure.

Section B: Freedom of the Individual

English law provides a positive presumption of freedom. An individual is free to undertake any activity he wishes, or to refrain from complying with any request made of him, unless there is in existence a legal rule which expressly stipulates to the contrary. This bias in favour of the individual in his relationships with the agencies of the state creates an environment which appears to be supportive of the "freedom of the individual" and to buttress basic rights or "civil liberties." Some commentators point, however, to the passive nature of the state's approach to this area of concern. The state recognises rights only in so far as it does not proscribe the relevant behaviour, but it has not taken general steps to ensure that ordinary citizens are granted more positive rights, such as freedom of information or, in other words, free access to information used by the state in relation to decisions which affect the individual (*e.g.* as to entitlement to state-provided benefits). From time to time there are calls for a statutory "Bill of Rights" which will provide for such positive rights and which will act as a constant reminder to the various agencies of the state that individuals within society possess freedoms which ought not to be transgressed. Such a Bill would make reference to "fundamental" principles which could not be violated, even by legislation. Any Act of Parliament which was found to be at variance with basic rights would be "unconstitutional" and void. In *English Law—The New Dimension*, Lord Justice Scarman called for " . . . entrenched or fundamental laws protected by a Bill of Rights—a constitutional law which it is the duty of the courts to protect even against the power of Parliament . . . ," and stated that he saw " . . . no reason why a curb should not be placed on Parliament itself when the issue is one of human rights." Whilst there is an obvious attraction to the concept of a Bill of Rights, there is some force in the argument raised by opponents of such a measure, that once a comprehensive statement of individual rights had found its way into statutory form, the law might be seen to have moved to a positive presumption against freedom. It would, perhaps, be logical to argue that any activity not expressly identified in the Bill of Rights as being one of the statutory freedoms, does not form part of the freedom of the individual and may be restricted on that basis.

Whilst the state has not provided a comprehensive framework of positive rights it has been willing to introduce legislation (*e.g.* the Data Protection Act 1984 and the Local Government (Access to Information) Act 1985) which grants positive rights in specific situations. The Local Government (Access to Information) Act, for example, provides that the public have a right to:

(a) attend, subject to specified exceptions, the meetings of local authority councils and those of their committees and sub-committees;

(b) receive notice of council, committee and sub-committee meetings;

(c) inspect copies of the agenda and reports for meetings;

(d) inspect the minutes of meetings, which right is available for six years after the meeting;

(e) inspect, both before a meeting and up to four years after a meeting, a list of all background papers (*i.e.* documents other than published works) referred to in the preparation of any report which is open to public inspection and a copy of each document listed (and there is a corresponding duty upon the officer preparing the report to prepare a list of the background papers he has used);

(f) inspect a register showing the name, address and ward of every council member and the name and address of every member of each committee and sub-committee; and

(g) inspect a list of delegated powers exercisable by officers.

This Act grants to individuals in society a powerful range of rights. Its limited focus makes it, however, a far cry from an all-embracing Bill of Rights, even in relation to access to information.

Until such time as a Bill of Rights finds its way on to the statute book, the position at common law will remain one of negative recognition of rights. Although such an approach accepts that any action may be undertaken unless it is specifically prohibited, it is, for the purpose of analysis, convenient to identify certain activities which are regarded as so significant that they are traditionally referred to when consideration is given to individual freedoms. Whilst the relative significance of areas of freedom will vary according to the values of individuals within society, most members of society would recognise, and value, the worth of the following:

(a) freedom from interference with personal liberty;

(b) freedom of speech;

(c) freedom to protest and demonstrate;

(d) freedom of religion; and

(e) freedom from discrimination.

FREEDOM FROM INTERFERENCE WITH PERSONAL LIBERTY

Magna Carta (1215) provided that "... no free man shall be taken or imprisoned ... or any otherwise destroyed, nor will we pass upon him nor deal with him but by lawful judgment of his peers, or by the law of the land." It has, since that time been a basic principle of common law that an individual can only be detained and deprived of his liberty if the person seeking to detain him can prove that he has, at law, a right to do so. This principle holds true even where the person wishing to detain the individual is a police officer. A policeman may, of course, lawfully deprive a subject of his liberty by arresting him and he may effect an arrest where:

(a) he is empowered by warrant to do so; *or*

(b) he has a common law or statutory power to arrest without warrant.

A police constable has a *common law* power to arrest without warrant anyone committing a breach of the peace. Under the *statutory* provisions of section 24 of the Police and Criminal Evidence Act 1984 he may also arrest without a warrant any person whom he either reasonably suspects to be in the act of committing an arrestable offence or to have committed an arrestable offence. The term *arrestable offence* includes offences for which the sentence is fixed by law (*e.g.* murder) and offences for which a person aged 21 or over may, upon a first conviction, be sentenced to a term of imprisonment of five years or more. By virtue of section 25 of the 1984 Act a police constable may arrest, without warrant, a person he reasonably suspects to be committing, or attempting to commit, a non-arrestable offence or to have committed or attempted to commit such an offence where it appears to him that the service of a summons is impracticable or inappropriate because any one of the *general arrest conditions* is satisfied. The general arrest conditions are:

(a) that the name of the person is unknown to, and cannot be readily ascertained by, the constable;

(b) that the constable has reasonable grounds for doubting whether a name furnished by the person as his name is his real name;

(c) that the person has failed to furnish a satisfactory address for service or the constable has reasonable grounds for doubting whether an address furnished by the relevant person is a satisfactory address for service;

(d) that the constable has reasonable grounds for believing that arrest is necessary to prevent the person causing physical injury to himself or any other person; suffering physical injury; causing loss of or damage to property; committing an offence against public decency; or causing an unlawful obstruction of the highway;

(e) that the constable has reasonable grounds for believing that arrest is necessary to protect a child or other vulnerable person from the person he plans to arrest.

Once arrested a person must be taken by the constable to a police station "as soon as practicable" (s.30(1)). This police station may be any police station unless it appears to the police constable that it may be necessary to keep the arrested person in police detention for more than six hours, in which case the arrested person must be taken to a *designated* police station (*i.e.* one designated by the chief constable as having sufficient accommodation to be used for the purpose of detaining arrested persons). Should the police constable realise, before arriving at the police station, that there are no grounds for keeping under arrest the person he has arrested (*e.g.* there are no longer grounds for believing that the accused has failed to furnish a satisfactory address) he must release him (s.30(7)). When an arrested person arrives at a police station the custody officer (*i.e.* an officer of at least the rank of sergeant who has been given this role by the chief constable) must determine whether he has before him sufficient evidence to charge the accused. Should he discover that he does not, he must release the accused unless he has reasonable grounds for believing that his continued detention is necessary to secure or preserve evidence relating to an offence for which the accused has been arrested or to obtain such evidence by questioning him (s.37). Further, should the custody officer become aware, at any time, that there are no longer grounds for detaining the accused in custody he has a *duty* to order his *immediate* release (s.34(2)).

The 1984 Act creates a duty to *review* the need for the continued detention of those in police custody. This review must be undertaken, in the case of a person who has been arrested and charged, by the custody officer. In the case of a person who has been arrested but not charged it must be undertaken by an officer of at least the rank of inspector. The Act provides that the first review must take place not later than six hours after the detention was first authorised, that the second must take place no later than nine hours after the first and that subsequent reviews must take place at intervals of not more than nine hours. There are, additionally, limits upon the time that a person may be detained without being charged. Normally a person must be released if he has not been charged within 24 hours of his arrival at the police station or of the time of his arrest, whichever is the *earlier.* Where a person has been arrested for a *serious* arrestable offence (*i.e.* the more serious offences such as murder, treason, manslaughter, rape and kidnapping; any arrestable offence which consists of making a threat and the carrying out of that threat would be likely to lead to specified consequences, such as the death of any person or serious injury to any person; or any arrestable offence which would, if committed, have led to those specified consequences or where its commission is intended or likely to have those consequences) then, providing the police officer in charge of the station, who must be of the rank of superintendent or above, believes that the continued detention of the accused is necessary to secure or preserve evidence relating to an offence for which the accused is under arrest or to obtain such evidence by questioning him *and* that the investigation is being conducted diligently and expeditiously, the accused may be detained for a period of 36 hours. Further detention, up to 96 hours, requires an order of a magistrates' court, which can, subject to the overall limit of 96 hours, authorise further periods of detention for 36 hours.

Any detention of an individual who has not been arrested is, prima facie, unlawful. In *Kenlin* v. *Gardiner* policemen noticed two schoolboys going from house to house on an estate; the boys were reminding members of their rugby team that a game had been arranged, although the officers could not, from their observations, know that this was the case. Wishing to question the boys about their behaviour, the officers approached them and identified themselves as policemen; the boys were not, however, prepared to co-operate and made as if to run away, whereupon the officers took hold of the boys, not for the purpose of arresting them but rather to facilitate their questioning. The boys reacted violently to the actions of the policemen and were, as a result, charged with assaulting police officers in the execution of their duty. The Divisional Court of the Queen's Bench Division found that the actions of the police officers were unlawful, on the basis that there is no power to detain a citizen who has not been arrested. That being so, the boys were justified in their use of force to break free from the unlawful detention. Similarly when, in *Ludlow* v. *Burgess,* a police officer put his hand on the shoulder of a youth to prevent him from walking away, the Divisional Court held that the youth was not guilty of assaulting a police officer in the execution of his duty when he punched and kicked the constable. As the detention was unlawful, there being no attempt made to arrest the youth, the police officer was clearly not acting in the execution of his duty. Cases such as these are of great importance, for they reveal that an English court will be prepared to uphold an individual's right to preserve his personal liberty even in difficult circumstances in which the sympathies of the court, and perhaps, those of a majority of the public, might not lie unequivocally with the person whose rights have been transgressed.

A police officer in England can, therefore, be seen to have no power to "detain for questioning" a person who has not been arrested and this position is unaffected by the fact that the individual concerned may be in a police station. If he has not been arrested the individual is, by virtue of section 29 of the Police and Criminal Evidence Act 1984, free to leave the premises if he so chooses (though there are statutory powers of detention in relation to those suspected of terrorist activities).

We have seen that, having been arrested, an individual cannot be deprived of his liberty indefinitely. He must be charged or released within the time periods specified above. Once charged he must be brought before the magistrates' court "as soon as practicable" and, in any event, not later than the first sitting after he is charged with the offence. If the offence is not one which may be tried in a magistrates' court, the magistrates must determine whether the accused should be remanded in custody or granted bail. Remand in custody is a particularly serious limitation upon the freedom of the individual, for the accused has not yet been tried and must, at that stage, be presumed to be innocent. In consequence, the Bail Act 1976 provides that bail *should* be granted unless the court believes that a grant of bail will result in:

(a) the accused absconding; *or*
(b) the accused committing a further offence; *or*
(c) interference with witnesses or some other obstruction of the course of justice.

The question of bail can be raised at an earlier stage in the criminal process, for the police may release the accused on bail where the offence is not serious and the accused has been arrested without warrant.

Thus, throughout the pre-trial stages of the criminal process there is a presumption in favour of personal liberty. A policeman cannot detain the individual *unless* he has arrested him and magistrates should award bail to the individual *unless* they can identify specific reasons for not so doing.

Whilst most people who are deprived of their liberty are detained by police officers, personal freedom may be compromised by others within society. Security guards, shop assistants, caretakers or, indeed, ordinary householders are among the groups of people who may be drawn into situations in which they seek to detain someone against his will. Like the police, however, all these people would be required to point to lawful authority for their actions, for anyone who, without such lawful justification, compels another to stay in a particular place or with a particular person, so that the other is not free to go as he pleases, commits the tort of false imprisonment (see page 163).

FREEDOM OF SPEECH

Because of the general presumption in favour of freedom of the individual, it is a basic principle that people are free to say and write whatever they please and this freedom is one that democratic societies value particularly highly, in the belief that it marks a clear difference between government and administration in a "free society" and those processes in more oppressive regimes. Freedom of speech, is not, however, a freedom without fetters. In our society the individual is not free to express himself in a completely uninhibited way. He may not, for example:

(a) defame another;

(b) commit a contempt of court;
(c) express seditious or treasonable views; *or*
(d) publish obscene material.

Defamation

In *Sim* v. *Stretch* Lord Atkin asserted that defamation is the publication of a statement which tends to lower a person in the estimation of right-thinking members of society generally. As a result of cases such as *Youssoupoff* v. *Metro-Goldwyn-Mayer Pictures Ltd.* (see page 165) a statement would also be regarded as defamatory if it tended to make members of society shun or avoid the person at whom the statement was directed. A written defamatory statement constitutes *libel*, whilst the spoken word amounts to *slander*. Although a libel which is likely to cause a breach of the peace may constitute *criminal libel*, defamation is basically a civil wrong rather than a criminal offence. (See pages 164–167 for a more detailed discussion of defamation).

Contempt of court

Any act which hinders the administration of justice or diminishes the authority of the law is a contempt of court. Sometimes a contempt will be gross, as in *Morris* v. *Crown Office* where a group of Welsh students interrupted judicial proceedings, shouted slogans, distributed pamphlets and sang songs. Often, however, the offence will be committed by those who are less clearly culpable. In *R.* v. *Border Television, ex p. Att.-Gen.* Border Television and the Newcastle Evening Chronicle published material which revealed that a person on trial for theft and related offences had a record of similar convictions. They argued that public policy required free reporting and that there were dangers in placing restrictions upon the Media. The court refused to accept this view, however, and, pointing out the likely effect of the published material upon members of the jury and thus upon the accused's right to a fair trial, found that a contempt had been committed. When considering a case such as this it is necessary to bear in mind that the curbs upon freedom of speech are imposed not for arbitrary or authoritarian reasons, but rather to safeguard another freedom, that of the accused who is in danger of losing his liberty and who is entitled to a fair trial by a jury who have not been influenced by information which would not have been allowed in evidence.

This concern for the interests of the accused has led to the recognition of that aspect of contempt of court which penalises conduct prejudicial to particular legal proceedings as an offence of *strict liability* (see page 66). Section 1 of the Contempt of Court Act 1981 refers to the "strict liability rule" and defines it as "the rule of law whereby conduct may be treated as contempt of court as tending to interfere with the course of justice in particular legal proceedings regardless of intent to do so." By section 2 of the Act the strict liability rule applies only to:
(a) a publication;
(b) which creates a *substantial* risk that the course of justice in particular proceedings will be seriously impeded or prejudiced;
(c) where the particular proceedings are *active* at the time of the publication (*i.e.* where, in a criminal case, there has been an arrest without warrant, the issue of a summons or warrant, the service of an indictment or an oral charge or, in a civil case, where

arrangements for the hearing are made or, in the absence of such arrangements, from the time the hearing begins until it ends).

There are circumstances in which the strict liability rule could be applied in a harsh and oppressive manner (*e.g.* where a newspaper editor is unaware of the fact that a person who is the subject of an article in his newspaper has been arrested without warrant) and so section 3 of the Act provides that a person is not guilty under the rule where:

(a) the publisher of the material has taken all reasonable care but, despite this, is unaware, at the time of publication, that the rule applies and has no reason to suspect that proceedings are active;

(b) a distributor of material has taken all reasonable care but is unaware, at the time of distribution, of the offending item and has no reason to suspect that such an item may be present.

Section 7 of the 1981 Act provides that proceedings for contempt which are based upon the strict liability rule may only be commenced by, or with the approval of, the Attorney-General or upon the motion of a court which has jurisdiction to consider cases of contempt.

The law relating to contempt of court is potentially a significant inhibition upon free speech. It would, for example, be particularly unfortunate if general issues of public concern could not be openly discussed for fear that such discussion should incidentally prejudice a particular case which is active. In recognition of this, section 5 of the 1981 Act provides that:

"A publication made as or as part of a discussion in good faith of public affairs or other matters of general public interest is not to be treated as a contempt of court under the strict liability rule if the risk of impediment or prejudice to particular legal proceedings is merely incidental to the discussion."

The provisions of section 5 were applied by the House of Lords in *Attorney-General* v. *English*. During the trial of a doctor accused of unlawfully terminating, by starvation, the life of a handicapped baby the *Daily Mail* published an article in support of a parliamentary candidate fighting on a "sanctity of life" platform. The candidate had herself been born handicapped and the article concluded that times and attitudes had changed and that she would not now have survived, for someone would surely have "recommended letting her die of starvation." The House of Lords accepted that the article created a substantial risk of prejudice to the doctor but accepted that section 5 of the 1981 Act applied. Lord Diplock asserted that: " . . . such gagging of bona fide public discussions in the press of controversial matters of general public interest, merely because there are in existence contemporaneous legal proceedings in which some particular instance of those controversial matters may be in issue, is what section 5 of the Contempt of Court Act 1981 was in my view intended to prevent."

Sedition and treason

In *R.* v. *Burns* it was asserted that a statement is seditious if it is made with an intention:

"to bring into hatred or contempt, or to excite disaffection against the person of, Her Majesty . . . or the government and constitution of the

United Kingdom, as by law established, or either House of Parliament, or the administration of justice, or to excite Her Majesty's subjects to attempt, otherwise than by lawful means, the alteration of any matter in church or state by law established, or to raise discontent or disaffection amongst Her Majesty's subjects, or to promote feelings of ill-will and hostility between different classes of such subjects."

Criticism of the state is not, in itself, seditious and the present view seems to be that a conviction for sedition can only be secured when it can be established that the person making the statement *intended* to promote violence and disorder in a matter of state.

The Treason Act 1351 provides that it is treason to:

(a) "compass or imagine the death of our lord the King or our lady his Queen or their eldest son and heir";

(b) "violate the King's wife or the King's eldest unmarried daughter or the wife of the King's eldest son and heir";

(c) "levy war against our lord the King in his realm";

(d) "be adherent to the King's enemies in his realm giving to them aid and comfort in the realm, or elsewhere";

(e) "slay the chancellor, treasurer or the King's justices . . . ."

Whilst these offences obviously range widely, it is clear that they have implications for freedom of speech. It is now established that an individual is guilty of "compassing or imagining" the death of the King or his family only if he manifests his intention in some way and the spoken word would appear to be a sufficient manifestation. Similarly, there will be situations in which the spoken or written word may be considered to be "aiding and comforting" the King's enemies in the realm. The existence of such provisions may not be thought to be a major restraint on freedom of speech, but it ought to be appreciated that the offence of treason is still regarded as sufficiently important, being an offence against the state itself, to carry with it the death penalty.

Closely associated to sedition and treason are the offences provided for by the Official Secrets Acts. Section 1(1) of the 1911 Act provides for several offences, including publishing or communicating documents or information which is calculated to be of use to any enemy. Clearly, most individuals within society would accept that this is a legitimate curb upon freedom of speech. More contentious, however, are the offences contained in section 2 of the Act. In this section, it is, for example, an offence to communicate information which the individual has obtained "owing to his position as a person who holds or has held office under Her Majesty" to anyone except:

(a) a person to whom he is authorised to communicate it;

(b) a person to whom it is, in the interests of the state, his duty to communicate it.

A former Attorney-General has pointed out that the section "makes it a crime, without any possibility of a defence, to report the number of cups of tea consumed per week in a government department, or the details of a new carpet in a minister's room . . . ."

Obscene material

We have already seen that the freedom of the individual does not extend to a right to publish material which is considered to be obscene (see page 95).

FREEDOM TO PROTEST AND DEMONSTRATE

Recognition of freedom to protest is regarded by many as the most meaningful indication that the state is prepared to permit open and, perhaps, vigorous criticism of its policies. The existence of such a freedom is, however, often directly at odds with the right of individuals within society to enjoy public order and tranquillity. In his report upon the Red Lion Square incident in 1974, Lord Justice Scarman starkly presented the tension which exists between these two interests:

"Civilised living collapses—it is obvious—if public protest becomes violent protest or public order degenerates into the quietism imposed by successful oppression. But the problem is more complex than a choice between extremes—one a right to protest whenever and wherever you will and the other, a right to continuous calm upon our streets unruffled by the noise and obstructive pressure of the protesting procession. A balance has to be struck, a compromise found that will accommodate the exercise of the right to protest within a framework of public order which enables ordinary citizens who are not protesting, to go about their business and pleasure without obstruction or inconvenience. The fact that those who at any one time are concerned to secure the tranquillity of the streets are likely to be the majority must not lead us to deny the protesters their opportunity to march: the fact that the protesters are desperately sincere and are exercising a fundamental human right must not lead us to overlook the rights of the majority."

The freedom to protest and demonstrate is, in reality, comprised of two separate, and quite different, freedoms:
(a)   the right to attend static meetings; and
(b)   the right to join in a procession.
The individual is free to organise and attend meetings subject to the provisions of section 14 of the Public Order Act 1986 which empowers the police to impose conditions on public assemblies. The conditions which may be imposed relate to the place at which the assembly is to be held, its duration and the maximum number of persons who may attend. These conditions may be imposed where it appears that the assembly may result in serious public disorder, serious damage to property or serious disruption to the life of the community. They may also be imposed where it is believed that the purpose of the assembly is to intimidate others so that they will do an act they have a right not to do (e.g. join a trade union) or not do an act they have a right to do (e.g. present themselves for work during an industrial dispute). There is, however, no right to hold a meeting on the highway, for the individual has only a right of passage along a highway and, manifestly, attendance at a static meeting does not constitute an exercise of that right of passage. Thus, in relation to static meetings on the highway, the normal presumption in favour of freedom is reversed, such meetings are only legal where there is in existence a legal provision permitting them. One example of such a provision is section 15 of the Trade Union and Labour Relations Act 1974, as amended by the Employment Act 1980, which states that;

"It shall be lawful for a person in contemplation or furtherance of the trade dispute to attend—
(a) at or near his own place of work; *or*
(b) if he is an official of a trade union, at or near the place of work of a member of that union whom he is accompanying and whom he represents, for the purpose only of peacefully obtaining or communicating information, or peacefully persuading any person to work or abstain from working."

The courts have, when interpreting the unamended provisions of this section, been careful to point out that the legislation has a very limited objective, it does not create a statutory right to picket but rather it creates a statutory defence to charges which otherwise could be brought against the pickets in consequence of their very presence on the highway. In *Broome* v. *D.P.P.* Lord Salmon asserted that:

"The words make it plain that it is nothing but the *attendance* of the pickets at the places specified which is protected, and then only if their attendance is for one of the specified purposes. The section gives no protection in respect of anything the pickets may say or do whilst they are attending if what they say or do is itself unlawful. But for the section the *mere attendance* of pickets might constitute an offence . . . ."

The limited scope of this statutory defence can be seen from the fact that it is only available where "those attending" are doing so *in contemplation or furtherance of a trade dispute*. Thus in *Hubbard* v. *Pitt* a group of tenants protesting outside an estate agent's office were held to be acting outside the statutory defence. It was held at first instance that their actions amounted to an unreasonable obstruction of the highway and as such a public nuisance (see page 182). Such groups may also find themselves facing a further charge, if they, without lawful authority or excuse, in any way wilfully obstruct free passage along a highway. Indeed, this was the offence with which the accused was charged in *Broome* v. *D.P.P.*, when his picketing progressed from mere attendance to standing in front of lorries wishing to pass along the highway. (It is at least arguable that if the general right to picket is as limited as this brief discussion would suggest, then the law has failed to meet the obligation to secure freedom of peaceful assembly under Article 11 of the European Convention on Human Rights).

In the case of a procession, the activity is prima facie lawful as it represents no more than a synchronised exercise by the marchers of their individual right of passage and re-passage along the highway. Organisers of a procession may find, however, that they are not completely free to do as they wish.

Section 11 of the Public Order Act 1986 provides that written notice must be given to the police of any proposal to hold a public procession which is intended to demonstrate support for or opposition to the views or actions of any person, to publicise a cause or campaign, or to mark or commemorate an event. The notice must specify the date and time of the procession, the proposed route and the name and address of the organiser or one of the organisers. Upon receipt of this notice the police may, in certain circumstances, impose directions upon the organiser or organisers of the procession relating, for example, to the route to be taken. Where the chief constable reasonably believes that the power to impose conditions will not be sufficient to prevent serious public disorder he must apply to the local authority for an order prohibiting the holding of processions or any specified class of processions. It is a criminal offence to fail to give notice, knowingly to fail to comply with directions imposed by the police or to hold a procession in defiance of an order which has imposed a ban.

Even where a meeting or procession is initially lawful, it may become unlawful. The statutory offence of *affray* is committed when a person uses or threatens unlawful violence towards another and his conduct is such as would cause a person of reasonable courage to fear for his personal safety (Public Order Act, s. 3). In the case of a meeting or procession it may be that a group of people collectively use or threaten violence. If so, it is the conduct of the group which is considered, not that of the individuals within the group. For the purposes of affray words alone cannot constitute a threat. Where three or more persons, who are present together, use or threaten unlawful violence and the conduct of them, taken together, is such as would cause a person of reasonable courage to fear for his personal safety each of the persons using or threatening violence is guilty of the offence of *violent disorder* (Public Order Act 1986, s. 2). The offence of violent disorder becomes that of *riot*, in the case of any person using violence, where there are 12 or more persons using or threatening violence for a common purpose. Short of these extremely serious offences (affray being punishable by a term of imprisonment of up to three years, violent disorder by a term of up to five years and riot by a term of up to 10 years), a person at a meeting or procession may commit the summary offences of *causing fear or provoking violence* (Public Order Act 1986, s. 4 or *causing harassment, alarm or distress* (Public Order Act 1986, s. 5). Where a meeting or procession is held to stir up racial hatred it is likely that an offence will be committed under section 18 of the Public Order Act 1986. This section provides that a person who uses threatening, abusive or insulting words or behaviour, or displays any written material which is threatening, abusive or insulting, is guilty of an offence if:

(a) he intends thereby to stir up racial hatred, or
(b) having regard to all the circumstances racial hatred is likely to be stirred up thereby.

Further, even though a meeting or procession does not become unlawful, police officers have, at common law, power to take reasonable steps to prevent a breach of the peace. This may give a police officer the right to move a meeting, even though the threat to the peace comes from others and not from the persons attending the meeting. In *Duncan* v. *Jones*, Mrs. Duncan wished to hold a meeting in the street. A previous meeting had been followed by disturbances and, knowing this, a police officer informed her that she could not hold her meeting at that place, but could hold it some 175 yards away. She would not move and began the meeting, whereupon she was arrested for obstructing a police officer in the execution of his duty. She could, of course, only be guilty of this offence if the officer was acting within his duty. The court accepted that he was and Humphreys J. expressed a view that:

" . . . it is the duty of a police officer to prevent apprehended breaches of the peace. Here it is found as a fact that the respondent reasonably apprehended a breach of the peace. It then . . . became his duty to prevent anything which in his view would cause that breach of the peace."

A police officer's preventive power may even permit him to enter and remain upon private premises. In *Thomas* v. *Sawkins* a public meeting was called by opponents of the Incitement to Disaffection Bill. The police believed that the meeting was likely to become an unlawful or even a riotous assembly. They entered the premises and refused to leave. Upholding their right to do so, Lord Hewart C.J. asserted:

" . . . it is part of the preventive power and, therefore, of the preventive duty of the police, in cases where there are . . . reasonable grounds (for apprehending a breach of the peace) . . . to enter and remain on private premises."

Finally, it may be noted that the right to protest or demonstrate does not extend to quasi-military activity. Section 1 of the Public Order Act 1936 provides that an offence is committed by "any person who in any public place or at any public meeting wears uniform signifying his association with any political organisation or with the promotion of any political object." As a result of this section it was possible in *O'Moran* v. *D.P.P.* to secure convictions against eight men who marched behind a hearse wearing black berets, dark glasses and dark clothing.

FREEDOM OF RELIGION

In the past the law has imposed disabilities on non-conformists, Roman Catholics, Jews and other dissenters from the views of the established church. These disabilities (*e.g.* disqualification from public office) have long since been removed. The law has also sought to protect religious beliefs (or practices based upon those beliefs) in other circumstances. Thus an individual employee's religious beliefs may permit him to refuse to become a member of a trade union despite the existence of a "closed shop" agreement between his employer and a trade union, and still retain his statutory protection against unfair dismissal (see page 323). Moreover, where the individual's religious beliefs require him to display certain symbols of that faith (for example, dress or personal appearance) the law may indirectly prevent discrimination against him on those grounds.

The law is, however, potentially less tolerant to those who profess no religious views and who wish to criticise, in intemperate terms, facets of accepted religious views. A prosecution for blasphemy may still be brought against an individual, though no longer may such a prosecution result simply because an individual denies or criticises Christian beliefs. In *Bowman* v. *Secular Society Ltd.* Lord Sumner said:

"Our courts of law . . . do not . . . punish irreligious words as offences against God. . . . They deal with such words for their manner, their violence, or ribaldry, or more fully stated, for their tendency to endanger the peace then and there, to deprave public morality generally, to shake the fabric of society, and to be a cause of civil strife. . . . In the present day reasonable men do not apprehend the dissolution or the downfall of society because religion is publicly assailed by methods not scandalous . . . ."

Prosecutions for blasphemous libel are rare, but they are not unknown. In *R.* v. *Lemon; R.* v. *Gay News* a successful prosecution was brought in respect of a poem entitled "The Love that Dares to Speak its Name" published in "Gay News." The poem, and an accompanying drawing, indicated that Christ had been involved in promiscuous homosexual practices with the Apostles and other men and described sexual acts with the dead body of Christ. Lord Scarman thought it inappropriate to speculate "whether an outraged Christian would feel provoked by the words and illustration . . . to commit a breach of the peace" and suggested that the true test is whether the words are "calculated to outrage and insult the Christian's religious feelings" and that "in the modern law the phrase 'a tendency to cause a breach of the peace' is really a reference to that test."

FREEDOM FROM DISCRIMINATION

Under various international and European conventions attempts have been made to eliminate actions being taken which discriminate against individuals on the basis of race, colour, sex, religion, political opinion, national extraction or social origin. Whilst the common law made notable attempts to establish certain basic principles with reference to formal equal status, it was unable to adequately reconcile these "rights" with another basic principle, that of freedom of contract. Thus, it could state that all were equal before the law irrespective of race, colour or sex, but it could not (or would not) require that an employer, for example, should agree to employ married women or that a landlord should lease his property to a coloured person. Although the courts did eventually exhibit greater awareness of changing social and political attitudes towards such issues, it was left to Parliament to take the major steps to remove such discrimination.

At present, the principal legislative measures in this area are the Equal Pay Act 1970, the Sex Discrimination Act 1975 and the Race Relations Act 1976. The impact of this legislation in the employment field is examined in greater detail in *Unit 3, Part 2,* but the effects of the latter two Acts extend beyond mere employment. Thus, these Acts, also cover discrimination in relation to:

(a) the provision of educational opportunities;
(b) the provision of other goods, facilities or services (such as transport or entertainment);
(c) the disposal or management of premises;
(d) the granting of a licence or consent by a landlord for assignment or sub-letting of a tenancy.

Both statutes are framed in the same manner; first, they provide a definition of the term discrimination (see page 300), and secondly they set out the broad reasons in respect of which it is unlawful to "discriminate." Thus, it is unlawful to discriminate against an individual on the grounds of sex or married status, or on the grounds of colour, race, nationality or ethnic or national origins. In *Quinn* v. *Williams Furniture* it was held that retailers, who refused to provide a married woman with credit facilities unless her husband entered into a guarantee in circumstances in which they would not have imposed such a requirement on a married man, were acting unlawfully.

Even where a prima facie case of unlawful discrimination can be made out the "discriminator" may be able to bring himself within one of the general exceptions provided by each statute. Both Acts, for example, allow the defendant to point to compliance with a statutory provision as justification for an otherwise unlawful act. Both also, in their different ways, make participation in sporting activities an area outside their protection. Thus, discriminating between competitors on the ground of sex is not rendered unlawful for that reason alone. In one case, for example, the Football Association was held to be lawfully pursuing a policy under which girls could not play football alongside boys in games organised under its auspices.

Ultimately, only time will tell whether such legislation will prove any more effective than the courts have been in removing discrimination. Even the statutory structure has its weakness, not least the emphasis within the scheme upon enforcement by aggrieved individuals, upon whom the onus lies to pursue any claim before the courts and tribunals. In the employment field discrimination on racial grounds or on the ground of sex is actionable by way of complaint before an industrial tribunal (see page 326). Complaints about discrimination in other fields should be brought before a county court, which may grant any remedy which would have been available in the High Court. The proceedings will be conducted as for any other claim in tort, and damages awarded accordingly (see page 185). In addition, it is specifically provided that such damages may include compensation for injury to feelings whether or not they include compensation under any other head.

Further powers of enforcement lie in the hands of the Equal Opportunities Commission for Racial Equality which may investigate and seek to eliminate unlawful practices within their respective jurisdictions. To this end, each may, upon discovery of an unlawful discriminatory practice, serve a non-discrimination notice requiring the recipient to cease such practices.

Part Two

THE INDIVIDUAL IN DISPUTE

The law consumer's visit to the legal office may be occasioned by his complaint that he has suffered injury or loss because of another's failure to meet obligations. Individuals incur certain obligations simply by reason of belonging to the state, thus there is an obligation not to become involved in *criminal* activity. These obligations have been considered in Part One of this Unit. However, the state also imposes *civil* restraints upon activity which take the form of obligations placed upon citizens not to cause loss to others in certain circumstances. Where the actions of one citizen infringe the rights of another so that the state stigmatises the activity as amounting to a civil "wrong" it is said that a *tort* has been committed. The relationship between the *tortfeasor* (the party who breaks the obligation imposed by law) and his "victim" is one which exists not because the parties have agreed that they shall owe one another obligations but because the state acting through the courts has determined that it is proper that such obligations (or *duties*) shall arise. Thus, for example, the law consumer may have been injured in a road traffic accident due to another's careless driving. Whilst the state may, through criminal law, penalise the "guilty" party for having caused the accident, the "victim" may wish to seek separate redress for his injuries (not merely his personal injuries but also those to his property). This claim for *damages* would be based upon the tort of *Negligence*.

A further area of complaint in which a party asserts that there has been a failure to meet obligations due to him arises because of agreement. Where parties mutually agree that they should enter into a legally binding agreement it is said that their relationship is based upon a *contract*. If one of the parties fails to meet his contractual obligations then he is in breach of contract. Here the relationship has arisen because the parties have agreed that they shall create obligations between themselves. However, because all citizens operate within limits imposed by law their agreement will only be recognised in so far as it is not objectionable to the state.

These twin notions of contractual and tortious liability underpin much of our law and are given extended consideration in this Part.

Section A: Contract

Legally binding agreements are known in law as contracts. They provide the basis for commercial transactions and relationships, and also have a significant role in private arrangements. However, the notion of contract, familiar as it may be to the sophisticated, is not well understood. The very word contract is evocative, creating images of printed forms drafted by lawyers for use by large commercial, municipal or public undertakings, or, perhaps, of handwritten deeds painstakingly prepared by Dickensian clerks

113

in gloomy offices. The law consumer, influenced by such images, recognises that he enters into contracts when he signs a hire-purchase agreement in the showrooms of a motor dealer or when he makes a special visit to a solicitor's office to sign a house conveyance. He would, in all probability, fail to appreciate that he is also entering into a contract when he buys his daily newspaper and when he pays at the turnstile of his local football club. He would, no doubt, be surprised to discover that he could be bound by an agreement rashly made over a pint of beer.

Some contracts are required to be made under seal as a deed, but these contracts (*specialty* contracts) form only a fraction of the millions effected each day. The vast majority of contracts (*simple* contracts) are not normally subject to any particular requirement as to form and may be made orally, in writing or may even involve neither words nor writing. The consumer who serves himself with petrol at a filling station, for example, may never exchange words with the attendant but he has, nevertheless, a contract with the garage. What, then, is a simple contract? When can it be established that one exists?

If two parties make an agreement which they intend to be legally binding they will, normally, have entered into a simple contract, provided something of value, known as *consideration*, moves from each of them. The constituent elements of a simple contract are, then:
    (a)   an agreement between the parties;
    (b)   an intention that the agreement be legally binding; and
    (c)   the furnishing of consideration.
Each element will now be considered in turn.

AGREEMENT

The parties to a contract reach agreement when there is *consensus ad idem* (a "meeting of the minds"). It is difficult to establish, of course, what is in a person's mind and so the courts, when determining whether or not there has been agreement, look for a manifestation of the intention of the parties in their conduct. A court will be satisfied that agreement has been reached if, having considered the conduct of the parties, it can establish that:
    (a)   one party made an *offer* to the other which;
    (b)   that other *accepted*.

OFFER

The making of an offer by one party, the *offeror*, to the other, the *offeree*, is the first stage in the formation of a simple contract. The court will find that a party has made an offer whenever it is convinced that the offeror has indicated to the offeree that he is prepared to enter into a transaction on particular terms. No special form of words is required and the circumstances in which an offer is made are often mundane. The customer who points to a bar of chocolate in a display case in a shop, whilst handing his money to the shop assistant, is clearly offering to enter into a contract for the sale of goods. The football fan who proffers money to the attendant at a turnstile is, equally clearly, offering to purchase the entertainment provided by the club. Neither the football fan nor the customer of the confectionery shop would, if asked to explain their actions, be likely to admit to having made a contractual offer, for they would not recognise their action as such. This is not important. What matters is that a court would conclude that they had made an offer which is capable of being accepted, so as to bring the parties into a contractual relationship. Sometimes, however, a court will not conclude that there has been an offer made simply because a party has indicated that he is willing to transact generally, on particular terms. In *Pharmaceutical Society of Great Britain* v. *Boots Cash Chemists (Southern) Limited*, the court was called upon to determine when an offer was made in a self-service store. The defendant retailers operated a self-service chemist's shop, on the shelves of which were displayed goods which, by statute, could only be sold in the presence of a qualified pharmacist. A pharmacist sat at the check-out. If goods were taken from the shelves by the customer, placed in a basket and presented to the cashier at the check-out then where were the goods sold? If they were sold when picked up by the customer, they were not sold in the presence of a pharmacist as required by statute. If they were sold at the check-out, they were sold in the presence of a pharmacist and the statutory provisions would have been observed. The point at which goods are sold depends upon where they are offered for sale. If the display of goods on shelves amounts to a contractual offer, the offer will be accepted by the customer when he places the goods in his basket and the sale will take place there. If, however, goods are offered for sale at the check-out, the sale will take place there. It was held in this case that the display of goods was not an offer of the goods for sale, it was, in fact, an invitation to the customer (an *invitation to treat*) to make an offer for their purchase. No offer was made, and no sale effected, until the goods were presented at the check-out. This case establishes that a display of goods in a shop does not constitute an offer (even though the goods may be described as a "special offer"). It dispels the notion that a customer, having proffered the price indicated on a "tag" or label fixed to goods, can demand that the goods be sold to him at that price even though the tag or label has been incorrectly marked and under-prices the goods. The customer is, in this situation, merely making an offer in response to an invitation to treat, and the retailer is under no obligation to the customer unless he elects to accept it, which in the case of, say, under-priced goods, he may well do to maintain goodwill. The fact that the courts are not willing to find that a display of goods amounts to an offer to sell them is, however, not necessarily contrary to the interests of consumers. If a display of goods did amount to an offer of sale, the consumer would probably be taken to have accepted the offer when he placed the item in his basket or trolley. At that stage there would be a binding contract of sale between the retailer and his customer and, in theory, the customer would not then be free to change his mind, even should he see a cheaper brand on another shelf in the shop.

Who makes the offer and to whom is it made?

An offer can only be accepted by someone if it was made to him. If, therefore, an offer is made to a specific person, only that person can accept so as to bring himself and the offeror into a contractual relationship. Similarly, if an offer is accepted on the basis that the person making the offer has a certain identity, there will only be a contract between the parties if the offeror has that identity. In most cases of mistaken identity one of the parties, usually the offeror, will have been fraudulent and the mistake will have resulted from his deceit. Fraud always renders a contract *voidable* (or terminable at the option of the innocent party), but it will not necessarily prevent a contract being formed and, at any time prior to the innocent party terminating the contract, the fraudulent party may dispose of the goods which form the subject-matter of the·contract and divest the innocent party of his *title* (ownership) to the goods. Where there has been a mistake as to the identity of the offeror (or offeree) the courts will, when determining the validity of the "agreement," adopt certain criteria depending upon whether the "agreement" was:

(a)   negotiated *face-to-face*; or
(b)   at *arms length*, by correspondence.

Where an agreement is negotiated *face-to-face*, the court may attempt to ascertain the time at which the false identity was raised. If the agreement was made prior to the false claim of identity, it follows that the innocent party cannot have been influenced by this claim when he entered into the agreement. Clearly his intention was to make a contract with the person with whom he negotiated, whoever he may have been. This situation arose in *Phillips* v. *Brooks*. A rogue, intending to defraud a jeweller, entered the jeweller's shop and selected some items of jewellery. The jeweller agreed to sell the goods but, upon the rogue indicating that he wished to pay by cheque, made it clear that he would only transact on the basis of a cash payment. The rogue informed the jeweller that he was "Sir George Bullogh" and gave an address which the jeweller checked in a directory. Having found an entry in the directory which corresponded with the name and address supplied, the jeweller relented and allowed the rogue to take a ring in return for a cheque. The rogue immediately pawned the ring with a pawn-broker and disappeared with the proceeds. The jeweller, upon the cheque being dishonoured, attempted to recover his goods from the pawn-broker and the issue before the court was to determine who had title to the ring, jeweller or pawn-broker. Because of the legal maxim *nemo dat quod non habet* ("no one can give that which he has not"), the pawn-broker could only acquire title to the ring if the rogue had title to the ring. The rogue, of course, could only have title to the ring if he had entered into a valid contract with the jeweller. The jeweller denied the existence of such a contract, asserting that he had accepted an offer made by "Sir George Bullogh" and that if he did not have a contract with Sir George Bullogh he did not have a contract with anyone. The court rejected this assertion and found that the jeweller did have a contract with the rogue, who thereby acquired title to the ring. As this contract had not been *avoided* (terminated) at the time of the disposition of the ring to the pawn-broker, title passed to the pawn-broker who was, thus, owner of the ring. As the rogue had not mentioned the name "Sir George Bullogh" at the time the jeweller agreed to sell the ring, it followed that he could not have had an intention to accept only an offer made by Sir George Bullogh. With whom, then, did he intend to contract? There could only be one answer, he intended to contract with the person with whom he negotiated, the rogue. No doubt the jeweller's decision to surrender possession of the ring was influenced by the rogue's deceit, but this was immaterial to the question of whether or not there was a contract between the jeweller and the rogue.

Where the false claim of identity has been raised prior to the conclusion of the "agreement" the position is less certain. In *Ingram* v. *Little*, a rogue obtained a car from its owners and sold it to a third party. Like the rogue in *Phillips* v. *Brooks*, he gave a false name and address, which was checked by the owners prior to their allowing him to take possession of the goods in return for a cheque. Unlike the bogus "Sir George Bullogh," however, the fraudulent "purchaser" in *Ingram* v. *Little* made his false claim of identity *prior* to the making of the contract. When the agreement was entered into, therefore, the owners of the car were aware of the alleged identity of their purchaser. The court concluded that the owners had made an offer to P.G.M. Hutchinson, the man the rogue purported to be, which could only be accepted by that person. As P.G.M. Hutchinson had not accepted that offer, the owners of the car had not contracted to sell it and, accordingly, they, and not the subsequent purchaser from the rogue, had title. The decision of the court in *Ingram* v. *Little* has been much criticised for, whilst the owners of the car may well have believed, at the time of entering into the "agreement," that they were dealing with P.G.M. Hutchinson (a person they had never previously heard of), it is not easy to appreciate that Mr. Hutchinson's identity was material to them. They would, presumably, have made the offer to anyone whose name and address had been given to them and confirmed by a check in a directory. Had the rogue given another name and address the situation would not, surely, have developed differently. How, then, can it be maintained that the offer was made only to P.G.M. Hutchinson? In *Lewis* v. *Averay*, the Court of Appeal doubted that there was a genuine distinction between *Phillips* v. *Brooks* and *Ingram* v. *Little* and asserted that where parties negotiate face-to-face, "the presumption in law is that there is a contract, even though there is a fraudulent impersonation by the buyer representing himself as a different man than he is." It is likely that *Ingram* v. *Little* would not now be followed.

Where the parties have negotiated at *arms length*, the courts appear to draw a distinction between:

    (a) a mistake as to the *identity* of the other party; and

    (b) a mistake as to the *attributes* of the other party.

In *Cundy* v. *Lindsay*, a rogue named Blenkarn, writing from an address in Wood Street, Cheapside, offered to buy a consignment of goods from the plaintiffs. When signing the letter containing the offer, the rogue signed his name in such a way that it appeared to have been signed by "Blenkiron and Company," a reputable company which traded from an address in Wood Street, Cheapside. The goods were dispatched to Blenkarn and promptly sold, by him, to a third party. The issue before the court was, then, the familiar issue of determining which of the two innocent parties was to lose; the original owner, who had not been paid, or the ultimate purchaser. The title of the purchaser depended upon Blenkarn's title and, of course, the plaintiffs asserted that Blenkarn had no title for they had not contracted with him. The court concluded that the plaintiffs had not accepted an offer made by Blenkarn for, when they accepted the offer, the plaintiffs had in mind the person they were contracting with, the reputable firm of "Blenkiron and Co." They were accepting an offer apparently made by that company. They would, no doubt, have accepted offers made by offerors other than Blenkiron and Co., but, equally, there were others with whom they would not have traded. The identity of the offeror was material to them and, as a result, they did not have a contract with anyone not of that identity. In *King's Norton Metal Company Ltd.* v. *Edridge* the rogue, Wallis, was, perhaps, even more inventive than Alfred Blenkarn. On notepaper containing a picture of a large factory and a statement that the offeror had premises in Belfast, Lille and Ghent, Wallis ordered goods from the plaintiffs, signing the letter "Hallam and Company." The situation then developed along all-too-familiar lines and the ensuing litigation was between the unpaid seller and a purchaser from the rogue. This time, the court found for the purchaser, holding that the plaintiffs, from whom Wallis obtained the goods, had contracted with him and had, as a result, transferred title to him, which title (being voidable for fraud) had not been avoided at the time of the subsequent disposition to the purchaser. Why, in this case, did the court find that the plaintiffs had contracted with the rogue? The court was impressed by the fact that, unlike the situation in *Cundy* v. *Lindsay*, there was no separate entity with whom the plaintiff could have contracted, for Hallam and Company did not exist. Had the letter been signed by "Jones and Company" or "Edwards and Company" or any other similar name, the outcome would, in all probability, have been the same. It was not, in reality, the name (or identity) of the offeror that had persuaded the plaintiffs to enter into the contract, it was the fact that they believed that they were dealing with a wealthy offeror. The identity of the offeror was, thus, not material to the plaintiffs and they were in fact mistaken merely as to the attributes of the offeror. Such a mistake was insufficient to convince the court that the parties had not reached *consensus ad idem*. In *Cundy* v. *Lindsay*, on the other hand, the name (or identity) of the offeror had impacted upon the plaintiffs albeit, admittedly, because of the attributes of that known entity.

The courts are, then, willing to find that an offer has been made to only one person (or that an offer is accepted only on the basis that it has been made by a particular person). They are, however, equally willing to find that an offer has been made to a number of people, or even to the world at large. In *Carlill* v. *Carbolic Smoke Ball Co.*, the defendants, as part of a promotion campaign for their product, offered, by advertisement, a reward of £100 "to any person who contracts the increasing epidemic influenza, colds or any disease caused by taking cold, after having used the ball three times daily for two weeks according to the printed direction supplied with each ball." The defendants informed the public that, "£1,000 is deposited with the Alliance Bank, Regent Street, showing our sincerity in the matter." The plaintiff, relying upon the advertisement, purchased and used a ball as directed. She nevertheless contracted influenza and sued to recover the reward. Normally the courts are willing to accept that a statement made in an advertisement is a *mere puff* which is neither intended by the supplier, nor accepted by the public, to be a statement which can ultimately harden into a contractual promise. In this case, however, the promise of the reward and the indication that a fund had been set aside to meet claims, convinced the court that the public would expect the Carbolic Smoke Ball Company to be making a binding promise. To whom was this offer of a reward made? The court, when finding for the plaintiff, concluded that it was made to the world at large.

An offer must be certain and it must be communicated

In *Carlill* v. *Carbolic Smoke Ball Company*, it was argued by the defendants that they could not have been making a contractual offer as the terms of the offer were too vague. What was the nature of their promise? Did they promise that consumers, once having used a ball, would never again contract influenza or cold? Or, did they merely promise that the consumer would be so immune for a reasonable time after his use of the ball? The court rejected this argument and asserted that the terms of the offer would appear clear to a reasonable member of the public, he would expect that he would have immunity only for a reasonable period after his having last used a ball. The terms of the offer were certain and could be accepted so as to bring offeror and offeree into a contractual relationship. Where, however, the terms of an offer are uncertain, they cannot lead to the formation of a contract. Thus, in *Scammell* v. *Ouston* the House of Lords found that there was no contract where the offeror had indicated that he wished to take a motor van "on hire-purchase terms." There are no universal hire-purchase terms and the phrase used by the offeror needed further clarification. The parties had, accordingly, not yet arrived at a situation in which a clear unequivocal offer had yet been made. There could, therefore, be no contract between them.

Even where the offeror has made an offer which is sufficiently precise as to be capable of acceptance, there can be no contract where there is "acceptance" in ignorance of the offer. An offer must be communicated to the offeree before it can be accepted. Mrs. Carlill knew of the offer which had been made by the Carbolic Smoke Ball Company when she accepted their offer. Had she been ignorant of the offer she would not have been entitled to the reward.

The offer and acceptance must correspond

There may be a failure of *consensus* when there are two things which could form the *subject* of an agreement and one is in the mind of the offeror whilst the offeree has in mind the other. *Raffles* v. *Wichelhaus* concerned the sale of a cargo of cotton "to arrive ex Peerless from Bombay." There were, unfortunately, two ships of this name both due to sail from Bombay. That which the plaintiff had in mind was due to arrive in December, but the defendant had in mind the other, due in October. The court held that the parties were mistaken, there was objectively no agreement and therefore no contract. Had it been possible for an "officious bystander" to have looked objectively at the facts and reasonably asserted that the contract must have been intended to cover a particular ship then the situation would have been different. A mere subjective error by one party would be immaterial and he would be bound to the assumed "bargain."

Where there is a mistake as to the *nature* of an agreement the consequences are more difficult to determine. For example, if one party forms a mistaken impression of the nature of the other party's offer, believing that a painting being offered is an original whereas it is a copy, then basically the contract stands. It is objectively based upon consensus. However, should a seller *know* of the buyer's mistake, then he may be held to be "snatching" at the bargain which will be void as the offer made and the offer accepted do not correspond.

In short, when parties fall into mutual mistake of a fundamental kind, as in *Raffles* v. *Wichelhaus*, there is no contract; where there is mutual mistake, not of a fundamental nature, but merely of a qualitative nature, the basic agreement is sufficient; and where there is a unilateral mistake (one party is mistaken and the other knows of that mistake) then there is no sufficient agreement. Where a court finds there is no contract due to lack of consensus it is frequently said that the contract is *void*. This is of course a contradiction in terms but gives an accurate picture of a fundamental defect in formation having a more serious effect than mere fraud, which produces a voidable contract.

An offer may terminate prior to its acceptance

Once an offer has been accepted it ceases to exist as an offer, having merged into the agreement made with the offeree. An offer may, however, terminate prior to this time, as a result of:

(a) the passage of time;

(b) the offeror revoking his offer;

(c) the offeree rejecting the offer; and

(d) the death of either offeror or offeree.

(a) *Time* . . . an offer is made at a particular point in time and the offeror normally expects that the offer will either be accepted or rejected within a certain period of time. If the offer is expressed to be valid only until a certain date then, quite clearly, it terminates on that date and cannot subsequently be accepted. Where there is no express reference to a time limit the court will, nevertheless, require the offer to have been accepted within a reasonable time of the offer having been made. In *Ramsgate Victoria Hotel Company* v. *Montefiore*, for example, an offer to buy shares in the plaintiff company was made on June 8, 1864 which offer was "accepted" on November 23, 1864. The court held that there was no contract between the parties as the offer was not open to acceptance in November, having lapsed through passage of time. This case does not establish a general rule that a five-month period is one which must result in an offer lapsing. The value of shares may fluctuate on a daily basis and, quite clearly, an offeror expects that his offer will be accepted, if at all, within a very short space of time. It is quite possible that an offer made by one commercial undertaking to another may be so complex and important that a considerable time for consideration of its terms and implications would be expected. What, then, is a "reasonable time"? In many cases the offeror can only be certain that his offer has lapsed through passage of time when a court has so determined as a result of litigation. It would be inconvenient if the law provided no means of terminating the period of uncertainty. Where an offer has been in existence for a period of time which the offeror considers sufficient for it to have been either accepted or rejected by the offeree, the offeror can ensure that the offer is no longer open to the original offeree by revoking his offer. He will then be able to contract with someone else.

(b) *Revocation* . . . an offer can be revoked at any time prior to its being accepted. It is not, however, sufficient that the offeror forms an intention that his offer should no longer be open to acceptance, he must actually communicate this intention to the offeree. In *Byrne* v. *Van Tienhoven*, for example, the offeror posted a letter to the offeree which indicated that the offer was no longer open, the letter being posted prior to acceptance. The letter was, however, not received by the offeree until after he had accepted. The court held that there was a valid contract, for revocation takes effect only upon its communication to the offeree and can only be effective prior to acceptance. If the intention of the offeror that his offer be no longer open to acceptance is communicated to the offeree, the offer is revoked even though it was not the offeror who informed the offeree. In *Dickinson* v. *Dodds*, the defendant offered to sell his farm to the plaintiff and then, without informing the plaintiff, sold it to someone else. The offeree, having been informed of the sale by a friend, subsequently purported to accept the offer which had been made to him. If this acceptance had been valid he would have had a contract with the defendant. In such a situation the offeror will be unable to perform the contract and will, accordingly, be liable in damages to the offeree. The court held that there was no contract between the plaintiff and the defendant for, at the time of his purported acceptance, the offeree knew that the offeror no longer intended to contract with him. (It should be noted that the offer made to the plaintiff was revoked not by the subsequent sale to a third party, but by the communication to the offeree of the offeror's change of intention.)

Sometimes an offeror will undertake that he will not revoke his offer until the offeree has had time to consider the terms of the offer. Such an undertaking is referred to as an *option*. The promise given to the offeree should be seen as a separate offer. In effect, the offeror offers to keep his principal offer open for a certain period of time. The offeree may accept this parasitic offer, but he will only be able to enforce the promise contained therein if he can show that this ancillary agreement is, in itself, a contract. He must, therefore, show that there was an intention that the parties be legally bound by the parasitic agreement and that he, the offeree, furnished consideration. It is the lack of separate consideration for the option that often renders such promises meaningless. In *Dickinson* v. *Dodds*, for example, the offeror had undertaken to keep his offer of sale open for two days and had, in fact, revoked within that time period. The plaintiff was unable to enforce the undertaking, however, for he had provided no consideration.

(c) *Rejection* . . . should the offeree reject the offer that has been made to him, the offer will terminate. If the offeree subsequently changes his mind and indicates that he is willing to transact on the original terms he will, in effect, be making an offer to the original offeror. He has not accepted the original offer for, as we have seen, that offer terminated upon his rejection.

Where an offeree responds to an offer by making a counter-offer (an offer to enter into the transaction, but on terms which are different to those contained in the original offer) the counter-offer will operate as a rejection of the original offer which will, as a result, terminate. In *Hyde* v. *Wrench*, an offer was made for the sale of a farm for £1,000. The prospective purchaser made a counter-offer of £950 but, upon rejection of the counter-offer, purported to accept the original offer. The court held that there was no contract for the sale of the farm for £1,000, the original offer of sale had terminated upon the counter-offer being made. The subsequent indication that the prospective purchaser would be willing to pay £1,000 amounted to an offer which the vendor could accept or reject. The original offer only terminates, however, where it is rejected by a counter-offer. Where the offeree asks for further information but does not indicate that he is not prepared to transact on the offeror's terms, there is no counter-offer and the original offer stands and may be accepted.

In *Stevenson* v. *McLean*, the following situation arose:

1. The defendant offered to sell to the plaintiff a consignment of iron, at 40 shillings per ton.

2. The plaintiff offeree telegraphed to ask if the offeror would "accept

forty shillings for delivery over two months, or if not, longest time you would give."

3. Having received the offeree's telegram, the offeror sold the iron to a third party and sent a telegram to the offeree to notify him of the sale.

4. The offeree, having received no reply to his telegram, and being unaware of the sale to the third party, sent another telegram in which he accepted the terms outlined in the offer. This telegram of acceptance became effective before the offeror's revocation was communicated to the offeree.

The court had to determine whether there was a contract between the offeror and offeree. It held that there was such a contract, for:

(i)   the offeror's revocation was ineffective;

(ii)   the first telegram sent by the offeree did not amount to a counter-offer, it was a mere request for further information; and

(iii) the second telegram sent by the offeree was an unequivocal acceptance of an offer which had been neither revoked nor rejected.

(d) *Death* . . . the death of either offeror or offeree may cause an offer to terminate. There is little direct authority and the cases that do exist are contradictory. It appears likely, however, that if an offer is made to a particular offeree it terminates upon his death and cannot be accepted by his executors. There is clear authority for the proposition that an offeree cannot accept an offer if he is aware of the death of the offeror. It is, however, possible that the executors of an offeror would be bound by an acceptance made in ignorance of his death.

ACCEPTANCE

Before the parties will be considered to have a binding agreement there must be an unequivocal acceptance of the offer. There will not be an unequivocal acceptance if the offeree:

(a)   adds new terms; or

(b)   qualifies existing terms.

In *Brogden* v. *Metropolitan Rail Company*, the defendant sent a draft agreement to the plaintiff for his approval. There was a blank space on the draft so that the name of an arbitrator could be inserted. The plaintiff inserted the name of an arbitrator and returned the draft, marked "approved," to the defendant. The court held that there was not, at that stage, agreement on the terms of the draft, for the offeror was unaware of one of the terms of the alleged contract (the name of the arbitrator) and, as a result, it could not be said that there was *consensus ad idem*. The common practice of dealing on the basis of standard printed terms of business has given rise to a particular problem often referred to as the "battle of forms." A prospective buyer may, for example, offer to buy goods from another by sending an order on a form which either contains or refers to his own standard conditions of trade. The prospective seller "accepts" the offer by confirmation of the order on a form which refers to his own standard terms of business. The problem arises if the two sets of standard terms materially differ. Whose standard terms should then prevail? In *Butler Machine Tool Co. Ltd.* v. *Ex-Cell-O Corporation (England), Ltd.* the Court of Appeal indicated that the seller's confirmation amounts to a counter-offer which is capable of acceptance by the buyer. For example, the buyer may impliedly accept the counter-offer by receipt and acceptance of the goods. This illustrates the "last shot in the battle" analysis by which the last set of terms to be exchanged will be taken as the contract terms. A difficulty which this presents is that unless and until the counter-offer is deemed to be accepted there is technically no contract even though both the seller and buyer may believe that a contract has been concluded. In such a situation it is possible that the courts may be obliged to fall back on quasi-contractual principles to resolve problems. (See page 160).

When selling land, it has, in England, become common practice for the vendor to accept the prospective purchaser's offer "*subject to contract*," a form of words which, the courts accept, indicates that the vendor does not regard himself as being legally bound by the agreement he appears to have made with the offeror. Because he has not made an unqualified acceptance of the offer, there is, in law, no acceptance and, as a result, no contract between the parties. The vendor is, as a result, free to contract with other parties. It was this contractual principle which enabled vendors, during the explosion of house prices in the early 1970s, to renege on their "agreements" with purchasers and sell their houses to third parties who were prepared to pay higher prices. This dishonourable, but perfectly legal, practice which became known as *gazumping* still has a tendency to develop whenever rapid increases in house prices occur.

Communication of acceptance

Normally an acceptance of an offer is only effective when it is communicated to the offeror. In *Entores* v. *Miles Far East Company*, Lord Justice Parker provided the example of a man who "accepts" an offer by telephone, unaware of the fact that the line had gone dead prior to his informing the offeror of his acceptance. Quite clearly there is no acceptance and no contract in this situation.

There are, however, situations in which two parties will be considered to have a contract even though the offeror is unaware that his offer has been accepted. In *Carlill* v. *Carbolic Smoke Ball Company*, for example, the offeror was not informed by Mrs. Carlill that she wished to accept the offer and the first that the offeror knew of the acceptance was when the reward was claimed. The courts have accepted that in cases such as this (known as *unilateral agreements*), where the offeror indicates that *performance of an act* (*e.g.* purchasing and using a smoke ball, finding a dog or giving information to the police for a reward) will constitute acceptance of the offer, the acceptance is complete upon performance of the act even though the offeror is unaware of this fact. If the offeror does not wish to contract on these terms he can easily frame his offer so that communication of acceptance is necessary. In the situation in which performance of an act will constitute acceptance, each of the parties is in control of his own contractual position. The offeror has elected to waive communication of acceptance and the offeree is free to perform the act or refrain from performance. The situation would be quite different if an offeror was able to impose upon an offeree a situation in which non-performance of an act would constitute acceptance of the offer. An attempt to create such a situation was made in *Felthouse* v. *Bindley*. The plaintiff, in this case, wrote to the defendant, offering to purchase the defendant's horse at a certain price. He indicated that "if I hear no more about him, I consider the horse mine at that price." The court held that the defendant's failure to reply to the plaintiff's letter did not amount to an acceptance of the offer contained therein. The offeror cannot gain for himself the advantage of the offeree's inertia.

An offeror may find that he is bound by a contract of which he was unaware where the offeree has accepted the offer by post. It was established in *Household Fire Insurance* v. *Grant* that, where post is the normal means of communication, an acceptance is valid upon posting of a properly stamped and addressed letter of acceptance. The later loss or destruction of the letter is immaterial and, in such circumstances, the offeror will be bound by a contract of which he has no notice. This may appear hard on the offeror. What, however, is the alternative? If a posted acceptance was valid only upon its receipt by the offeror, the acceptor would be vulnerable to fraudulent denials of receipt. In any event, the offeror can safeguard his own position by expressly framing his offer so that acceptance will only be valid upon communication. The *postal rule* has not been extended to acceptances which are sent by telex, such acceptances are valid only upon receipt by the offeror. Thus in *Brinkibon Ltd.* v. *Stalag Stahl* when London buyers accepted an offer made by sellers in Austria, it was held by the House of Lords that the telexed acceptance was effective on its receipt in that country. However, their Lordships indicated that where communication is not instantaneous (perhaps, in the case of a telex sent out of office hours or via a third party's telex machine) the position should be resolved by reference to the parties' intentions, sound business practice and perhaps a judgment on where risk should lie. It may be that because the postal rule previously extended to telegrams it will extend to their replacement, the telemessage. If so, acceptance would be complete, in appropriate circumstances, when a message of acceptance was dictated to an authorised person for onward transmission to the offeror. (It should be noted that the "postal rule" applies only to letters of acceptance and not, for example, to letters of revocation.)

The postal rule will not, of course, apply where the offeror has stipulated that acceptance must be effected by some means of communication other than post. The offeror may expressly indicate the required means of communication, but it is possible that he may also do so by implication. An offeror who sends an offer by telex is probably indicating that the offeree must reply by some speedy method of communication and, presumably, reply by post would be unacceptable. Where, however, the offeror indicates that the offeree should accept in a certain way, it has been said (*e.g.* in *Manchester Diocesan Council for Education* v. *Commercial and General Investments*) that a reply by a different, but equally expeditious, means of communication will be valid.

Acceptance of tenders

Commercial and public undertakings often advertise for the submission of tenders for a particular project. In this situation normal contractual principles must be applied to determine the party who makes the offer and the party who brings the contract into existence by his acceptance. Basic principles indicate that the invitation to submit tenders is not a contractual offer which can be accepted by submission of tender. It is, rather, the tender which constitutes the offer. When, then, is this offer accepted? Where the invitation to tender was for a precise amount of materials, which will definitely be required from the person who submits the most acceptable tender, it is clear that acceptance of a tender brings a contract into existence. Where, however, the invitation to tender indicates only that the materials referred to might be required over a certain period of time, acceptance of the tender does not amount to an acceptance of the offer to supply goods. The offer will, in such circumstances, only be accepted when the goods are ordered. The tender constitutes, in fact, a standing offer and, unless the offer is revoked, the person who has submitted the tender is bound to deliver the goods which are ordered pursuant to the tender. Whilst the offer stands, a separate contract is entered into each time such an order is made.

FORM OF THE AGREEMENT

As we have seen, a simple contract may normally be made orally or in writing and may even arise from conduct. Some simple contracts, however, are subject to statutory provisions which require formalities.

The Consumer Credit Act 1974, for example, provides that consumer credit agreements (agreements under which non-corporate debtors borrow amounts not in excess of £15,000) are subject to the following stringent requirements:

(a) the agreement must be in writing and must be legible;
(b) the agreement must be signed by the debtor and by, or on behalf of, the creditor;
(c) the written agreement must contain the information specified by the Secretary of State (relating, for example, to the true rate of interest and to details of the statutory protection afforded to the debtor); and
(d) the debtor must be given a copy, or in some circumstances two copies, of the agreement.

If these formalities are not complied with the agreement is unenforceable. Some contracts must, then, be in writing. Others need only be *evidenced* in writing. Section 40(1) of the Law of Property Act 1925 provides that the "sale or other disposition of land or any interest in land must be evidenced in writing," and, as a result, all contracts for the sale of land (which includes things attached to land) must be supported by written evidence, signed by the defendant, which identifies:

(a) the contracting parties;
(b) the subject-matter of the agreement; and
(c) the consideration.

The 1925 Act does not require a contract for the sale of land to be written, an oral agreement is sufficient providing the necessary written evidence is produced to show that there was a contract. It will be recalled that an acceptance stated to be "subject to contract" does *not* create a binding agreement. The question of whether a document expressed to be "subject to contract" can be used as written evidence of an *actual* agreement has led to conflicting decisions of the Court of Appeal in *Law* v. *Jones* (1974) and *Tiverton Estates* v. *Wearwell* (1975). However, the Council of the Law Society has expressed its view that the *Tiverton* case vindicates the traditional approach so that correspondence expressed to be "subject to contract" cannot be used to satisfy section 40(1). In the absence of a House of Lords ruling, the buyer's protection against a vendor who deals with more than one prospective purchaser in a "contract race" rests on a Law Society Guideline. This requires that a vendor's solicitor must, by written communication, disclose the existence of a contract race to the solicitors acting for each prospective purchaser. It is not necessary for all the required information to be contained on one piece of paper and in *Pearce* v. *Gardner* a letter was linked with its envelope so that the names of both contracting parties could be established. Similarly, in *Elias* v. *George Sakely* a receipt (containing the names of the parties, and the amount of deposit received by the vendor as 10 per cent. of the purchase price) was linked with a letter containing the essential terms of the contract. Without written evidence the agreement is *unenforceable* (see page 132 for the meaning of unenforceable).

A contract of guarantee is also unenforceable if not evidenced in writing. The statute which requires written evidence, the Statute of Frauds 1677, provides that a contract of guarantee is one in which one party, the *guarantor*, agrees to be answerable for the "debt, default or miscarriage" of another. Under such a contract the guarantor makes himself secondarily liable, the party guaranteed having *primary* liability. If, under the terms of the agreement, the party who appears to be a guarantor is, in fact, primarily liable, the contract will not be one of guarantee and will be enforceable even though not evidenced in writing. Thus, in *Lakeman* v. *Mountstephen* it was held that there was no need for written evidence when the chairman of the Brixham local board of health encouraged a contractor to undertake the connection of house-drains to a sewer by saying to him, "Go on, Mountstephen, and do the work. I will see you paid." The work not having been authorised by the board, the promise made by its chairman amounted to an undertaking of primary liability.

CAPACITY TO MAKE A LEGALLY BINDING AGREEMENT

Minors

Not everyone has full capacity to make a legally binding agreement. Minors constitute one group of persons not fully bound by their agreements. Prior to 1969 the contractual rules relating to agreements made by minors were relatively important, for the age at which one ceased to be a minor was then 21 and persons under that age, in full-time employment and, perhaps, married, formed a significant section of the total body of consumers. Since the passing of the Family Law Reform Act 1969, which lowered the age of majority to 18, and with the raising of the school leaving age to 16, minors now form a relatively less significant contracting group and the law which governs their transactions has, as a result, assumed less importance. Briefly stated, minors are now bound by their contracts as follows:

(a) they must pay a *reasonable* price, which will not necessarily be the *contract* price, where they have, under a contract, received goods or services which are regarded as *necessaries*. (So far as goods are concerned, they will be necessaries if satisfying the definition contained in the Sale of Goods Act 1979, which requires them to be "suitable to the condition in life of such minor . . . and to his actual requirements at the time of sale and delivery.")

(b) they are not bound by contracts for goods which are not necessaries.

(c)	they are not bound by contracts for services which are not necessaries. (Necessary services have not been defined by statute, but the courts, when attempting to determine whether services are necessaries, adopt an approach similar to that used to identify necessary goods.) Minors are, however, bound by contracts under which they obtain education, training or experience relevant to their intended trade or profession.

(d)	they are bound by contracts under which they acquire a continuing obligation (*e.g.* a lease or a partnership agreement), though they can avoid such contracts during their minority, or within a reasonable time of attaining majority, and so avoid all liability other than that incurred prior to avoidance.

(e)	if they are not liable in contract they cannot be sued in another action which would result in substantially the same liability. Thus, if a minor obtains, on credit terms, goods which are not necessaries by fraudulently representing himself to be of the age of majority, he cannot be sued for his deceit.

[N.B. *Mental patients* and *drunkards* who enter into contracts under which they receive necessaries must also pay their supplier a reasonable price. Otherwise their contracts are voidable, at their option, providing the other party was aware, at the time of making the contract, that they were incapacitated by drink or mental illness. Mental patients and drunkards are bound in the ordinary way by contracts made with persons who were unaware of their incapacity.]

Companies

Nowadays, the most important type of incapacity is corporate incapacity. Corporations are legal persons having, in law, an identity and a contractual capacity different from that of their members. The contractual capacity of a corporation depends upon the manner of its creation:

(a)	*Chartered* corporations (created by royal charter) have unlimited contractual capacity;

(b)	*Statutory* corporations (created by Act of Parliament) can contract only within the powers granted to them by statute; and

(c)	*Registered* companies (incorporated by registration under the Companies legislation) can contract only so far as is necessary to further their objects as set out in their *memorandum of association.*

A contract made by a statutory or registered corporation which is outside its capacity is, at common law, *ultra vires* (beyond its powers) and void. Thus, in *Ashbury Railway Carriage Company* v. *Riche* it was held that a company was not bound by a contract, entered into by its directors, for the purchase of a railway as its memorandum of association provided that its objects were only " . . . to make, sell or lend on hire railway carriages and rolling stock, and all kinds of railway plant, fittings, machinery and rolling stock; to carry on the business of mechanical engineers and general contractors; to purchase, lease and sell mines, minerals, land and buildings; to purchase and sell as merchants, timber, coal, metals or other materials and to buy and sell any such materials on commission or as agents." The agreement negotiated was clearly *ultra vires*, void and, therefore, not enforceable by either party. Now, however, section 35 of the Companies Act 1985 provides:

"In favour of a person dealing with a company in good faith, any transaction decided on by the directors shall be deemed to be one which it is within the capacity of the company to enter and a party to a transaction so decided on shall not be bound to enquire as to the capacity of the company to enter into it . . . and shall be presumed to have acted in good faith unless the contrary is proved." As a result of this provision, originally introduced by the European Communities Act 1972, a registered company can no longer rely upon the *ultra vires* doctrine when sued upon an *ultra vires* contract. The doctrine still exists, however, as a defence available to the party with whom the corporation has "contracted." Agreements made by statutory corporations are unaffected by the 1985 Act.

AGREEMENTS WHICH THE LAW WILL NOT ENFORCE

The courts will not enforce agreements which are:
  (a) void by statute;
  (b) contrary to public policy;
  (c) illegal;
  (d) unenforceable by statute; and
  (e) entered into under duress or undue influence.

Agreements which are void by statute

Some contracts are rendered void by the provisions of a particular Act of Parliament and, as a result, are completely ineffective. The Resale Prices Act 1976, for example, renders void any agreement between manufacturer and retailer by which the retailer indicates that he will only re-sell the goods at a minimum price (unless the agreement is approved by the Restrictive Practices Court).

Agreements which are contrary to public policy

Where a court feels that enforcement of a contract would be contrary to the public interest it may refuse enforcement on grounds of *public policy*. There exist several *heads*, or categories, of public policy and the House of Lords has indicated that it would be unwilling to extend these heads though, no doubt, it would recognise new heads if necessary. The existing heads include:
  (a) contracts which oust the jurisdiction of the courts; and
  (b) contracts in restraint of trade.
  (a) *Contracts which oust the jurisdiction of the courts* . . . the basic position is that parties cannot, by contract, take away the right of either to submit questions of law to the courts. However, the parties can agree that questions of fact be finally determined by arbitration and that an arbitrator or tribunal shall make an initial finding as to law. The Arbitration Act 1979 abolished the jurisdiction of the High Court to set aside arbitrations on the grounds of error of fact or law on the face of the record but provided for an appeal to the High Court on a question of law provided both parties consent or the court gives leave. The court may not, however, grant leave if the parties have entered into an *exclusion agreement* which excludes the right to appeal. Moreover, the High Court can only grant leave to appeal if it considers that the determination of a question of law could substantially affect the rights of one or more of the parties. Exclusion agreements are basically designed to encourage *foreign* parties to arbitrate in this country

and exclusions relating to *domestic* agreements are only effective if entered after the commencement of the relevant arbitration.

(b) *Agreements in restraint of trade* . . . a contract in restraint of trade is one which restricts a person's freedom to carry on his trade or profession in the manner of his choosing. The courts are called upon to apply common law principles to contracts in restraint of trade in three situations:

(i) where the seller of a business agrees with the purchaser that he will not compete with him;

(ii) where an employee, as a term of his contract of employment, promises his employer that he will not, upon leaving his employment, work for a rival employer; and

(iii) where a supplier of goods restricts his customer to the distribution only of goods supplied by himself.

The common law assumes that such agreements are *void* and that the promisor is, as a result, free to trade or enter into employment in a manner inconsistent with his promise. Agreements in restraint of trade are, however, valid and enforceable when they are *reasonable*. They must, however, be reasonable:

(a) as between the parties; and

(b) in relation to the public interest.

When determining whether the restraint is reasonable, the courts will take into account:

(a) the geographical area covered by the restriction;

(b) the duration of the restriction;

(c) the interest protected by the person who has imposed the restriction; and

(d) the consideration provided by that person.

In *Mason* v. *Provident Clothing Company* a canvasser, employed by the Provident Clothing Company, agreed that he would not, upon leaving that employment, engage in any similar activity within a 25-mile radius of London. The restriction was to operate for a period of three years. The court, when asked to determine the validity of this agreement, took into account the interest which the employer was seeking to protect. As a result of his having engaged in door-to-door canvassing, the employee acquired a list of names of those persons willing to transact with his employer. Such a list would be useful to rival businesses and the goodwill developed by the canvasser could easily be exploited for the benefit of those rivals and to the detriment of the original employer. The court was, nevertheless, of the opinion that the restraint which had been imposed was much wider, geographically, than was necessary to protect this interest and, as a result, the restraint was found to be unreasonable and void. This meant that the former employee was free to canvass in the area in which he had previously operated on behalf of the Provident Clothing Company. A narrower restraint might well have been considered to have been valid and, if so, would have given the employer the protection it sought. Thus, in *Fitch* v. *Dewes*, a solicitor was able to enforce an agreement made with his managing clerk by which the clerk undertook that he would not, upon leaving the solicitor's employment, engage in similar work within seven miles of the solicitor's office. Because of the contacts made, and goodwill developed, between the clerk and his employer's clients, the court was satisfied that his employer had a legitimate interest to protect. It was of the opinion that the restriction was no wider than it needed to be to protect this interest, even though it was to operate for the remainder of the clerk's working life. In *Nordenfelt* v. *Maxim Nordenfelt Gun and Ammunition Company*, an agreement was held to be valid even though it resulted in the promisor being totally prohibited from trading in the field in which he had expertise. Nordenfelt sold his business and his patent rights, for a fortune, to a company which then employed him. He agreed that he would not, for a period of 25 years, engage in the manufacturing of armaments other than under his employment with the company. The court, taking into account the vast sum of money paid to him and the world-wide market for armaments, accepted that this agreement was valid, even though the restraint contained therein was unlimited geographically and, in effect, in duration. The court was also satisfied that the restraint was in the public interest as it resulted in a British company holding important patent rights. Theoretically, a restraint which is reasonable *vis-à-vis* the parties may yet be contrary to the public interest. Thus if a restraint which reasonably protected an employer's interest had the effect of depriving the community of scarce professional skills it could be unlawful. However, the Court of Appeal has recently held in *Kerr* v. *Morris*, overruling an earlier decision, that a restraint which deprived a community of the services of a particular medical practitioner was not contrary to the public interest. Clearly the notion of public interest is, in this sphere, somewhat capricious.

The courts are, generally speaking, more willing to accept and enforce a restriction contained in an agreement made between vendor and purchaser of a business than one contained in a contract of employment. When a business is sold the parties normally arrive at a price on the basis that goodwill is to be transferred and the restraint on future competition is merely a means of ensuring that goodwill is in fact transferred. The parties to the sale of a business may, moreover, be in a position where they can make a true bargain, whereas the person seeking employment may feel constrained to accept whatever terms he is offered.

The *solus agreement* (under which a supplier insists that his customers should deal only with him) has, in recent years, required the courts to consider restraints on trade in a context divorced from the sale of a business or the entering into a contract of employment. In *Esso Petroleum* v. *Harpers Garage*, the owner of two garages agreed, in return for a loan (which was secured by a mortgage) and for the advantages of Esso's *dealer co-operation plan* (one of the advantages of which was guaranteed deliveries) to sell only motor products supplied by Esso. He tied one of his garages for a period of four years and the other for a period of 21 years. The court accepted the first restriction as valid, but would not enforce the second as they considered the duration of the tie to be unreasonable. Cases such as this illustrate the dilemma faced by the courts which must observe the following, conflicting, legal principles:

(a) parties must be free to enter into contracts on terms they themselves negotiate; and

(b) those involved in commerce must be free to trade.

It should not be thought that the second of these freedoms should always prevail. In *Morris* v. *Saxelby*, Lord Shaw asserted that: "The delicacy of the operation of law in settling the bounds of either freedom has long been familiar. In these cases . . . there are two freedoms to be considered . . . and . . . it is a mistake to think that public interest is only concerned with one, it is concerned with both."

Whilst the *Esso Petroleum* case established that the doctrine of restraint of trade could extend even to a covenant contained in a mortgage of land, a majority of their Lordships sitting in the House of Lords considered that the doctrine had no application to covenants contained in leases or conveyances on purchase. On this basis, a man purchasing a petrol station or taking it on lease from a petrol company would be unable to challenge a petrol *solus agreement* contained in the conveyance or lease. Lord Reid explained the reason for this technical point thus: "Restraint of trade appears to me to imply that a man contracts to give up some freedom which otherwise he would have had. A person buying or leasing land had no previous right to be there at all, let alone to trade there, and when he takes possession of that land, subject to a negative restrictive covenant he gives up no right or freedom which he previously had." In *Alec Lobb (Garages) Ltd.* v. *Total Oil Great Britain Ltd.* an unsuccessful attempt was made to gain the benefit of this technical exception to the doctrine. The owner–operators of a petrol filling station got into financial difficulties and arranged with a petrol company that the company should take a lease of the station for 51 years in return for a payment of £35,000 and a nominal rent. On the same day the petrol company leased-back the station to the operators at a rent of £2,500 per annum for 21 years by an underlease with a solus tie in favour of the petrol company. It was held that the lease and lease-back were to be treated as a single transaction under which the owner–operators gave up their existing freedom to trade, in a qualified fashion for the first 21 years and totally for the last 30. The transparent device was not permitted to circumvent the doctrine of restraint of trade. However, certain types of agreement have become so much part of the commercial scene that it is unlikely that the doctrine could be extended to control them. For example, the tied public house and the sole agency agreement (under which a person is given the sole right to supply a manufacturer's goods within a certain area) have probably been established beyond the reach of the common law and lie solely within the province of legislative competition policy. (See page 380 for a consideration of legislative controls over competition.)

Where contracting parties make an agreement which is in unreasonable restraint of trade, and therefore void, the whole contract, or, indeed, the whole of the restraint, may not be void. The courts may be prepared to *sever* the unacceptable part of the contract and enforce the remainder. In *Goldsoll* v. *Goldman*, for example, the defendant, who was engaged in selling imitation jewellery in London, sold his business to a rival. He undertook that he would not deal in "real or imitation jewellery in the County of London or any part of the United Kingdom of Great Britain and Ireland and the Isle of Man or in France, the United States, Russia, or Spain or within 25 miles of Potsdamerstrasse, Berlin, or St. Stefans Kirche, Vienna." The court considered the restraint over the whole of the United Kingdom to be reasonable, but that relating to areas outside the United Kingdom to be unnecessary and, as a result, unreasonable. It was similarly hostile to the restraint relating to trade in real jewellery, for the business sold dealt only in imitation jewellery and there were separate markets for real and imitation jewellery. The court did not, however, declare the agreement to be void, instead it struck out:

(a) the references to areas outside the United Kingdom; and

(b)   the references to real jewellery.

The remaining provisions, which now related to dealing in imitation jewellery in the United Kingdom, were reasonable and enforceable. Whilst the courts will delete objectionable parts of a contract, they will not rewrite the contract and will only be prepared to sever the agreement if the remainder of the contract stands by itself. In the *Alec Lobb* case the invalid solus tie could readily be severed and the lease and underlease were allowed to stand.

Illegal agreements

Some agreements are not merely contrary to public policy, they are positively illegal. Such contracts will obviously not be enforced by the courts. Thus, the court in *Everet* v. *Williams* would not enforce an agreement between highwaymen as to the division of their booty when one, unbelievably, sued the other (and was later hanged!). A contract for a criminal venture is clearly illegal. For the purposes of the law of contract, however, a court will also consider the following contracts to be illegal:

(a)   contracts to commit a civil wrong;
(b)   contracts leading to corruption in public life;
(c)   contracts prejudicial to the security of the nation; and
(d)   contracts which promote sexual immorality.

As a result, the court would not, in *Pearce* v. *Brooks*, enforce an agreement under which a prostitute hired a coach from a firm which knew that she intended to use it to ply her trade. Not only are such contracts void, in the same way as contracts contrary to public policy, the courts will, in relation to illegal contracts, also refuse to order restitution of money paid or goods delivered. Nor will the courts sever such agreements, for the illegality taints the whole agreement. A contract containing an illegal provision is, therefore, void in its entirety.

Agreements which are unenforceable by statute

We have already seen that some contracts are, by statute, unenforceable (see page 126). As a result of their unenforceability a court will not award damages, or any other relief, should the contract be broken. This does not mean, however, that such agreements have no effect. In *Monnickendam* v. *Leanse*, the plaintiff agreed, orally, to purchase the defendant's house and paid over a deposit. He then changed his mind about the purchase and requested the return of the deposit. As we have seen, an oral contract for the sale of land is unenforceable and as a result the plaintiff could not have been sued for his failure to perform. The contract was not, however, void and it was effective in every way, save that it could not be sued upon. The plaintiff had, therefore, paid over money under a valid contract and he could not recover.

Part performance... although an agreement not satisfying section 40(1) of the Law of Property Act 1925 is unenforceable at common law, section 40(2) preserves the equitable *doctrine of part performance*. This doctrine, based upon the maxim that "Equity does not allow a statute to be used as an engine for fraud," provides that if one party to a contract has performed wholly or a substantial part of the bargain the other should not be allowed to evade his obligations by pleading the lack of a written memorandum. In the light of the most recent consideration of the doctrine by the House of Lords in *Steadman* v. *Steadman* it may be said that there are four requirements to be satisfied by the plaintiff pleading part performance:

(a) an act of part performance (such as giving up secure accommodation elsewhere in order to enter into possession under the alleged contract) which is at the very least compatible with the existence of the alleged contract;

(b) that it would be fraudulent for the defendant to rely upon the lack of written evidence as a defence;

(c) that the contract is of a nature that the courts will order specific performance (discussed page 157), which, here means that the doctrine is restricted to contracts concerning interests in land;

(d) that other evidence can be adduced to support the act of part performance in proving the actual contract.

In *Steadman's* case a mere payment of money was held to be a sufficient act of part performance, Lord Reid saying, "the rule must be that you take the whole circumstances, leaving aside the evidence about the oral contract, to see whether it is proved that the acts relied on were done in reliance on a contract: that will be proved if it is shown to be more probable than not." (See page 26 for a consideration of equity and equitable maxims.)

Agreements entered into under duress or undue influence

Where a person enters into a contract only under threat of violence to his person or as a result of the administration of violence to his person, the agreement may be avoided for duress. Indeed, there is some authority for the proposition that such extreme coercion renders a purported contract void.

Any coercion which does not amount to duress will constitute undue influence. A contract entered into under undue influence is voidable at the option of the party coerced and, if avoided, will not be enforced by the courts. In some relationships there is a presumption of undue influence which may be rebutted. Thus, if a solicitor makes a contract with a client, or a doctor with a patient, the burden of proof will be upon the party denying undue influence. The presumption may be best rebutted by evidence that the party allegedly coerced received independent advice from a qualified person as to the nature and effect of the transaction in dispute. If no sufficient evidence can be shown to rebut the presumption the court will not enforce an agreement and completed transactions may be set aside. However, it should be noted that the House of Lords has recently ruled in *National Westminster Bank plc* v. *Morgan* that the court only has power to set aside transactions where they are disadvantageous to the person seeking relief. In this case a mortgage in favour of a bank which had repaid a building society mortgage was not set aside as the transaction had allowed the mortgagor to keep a roof over her head.

In *Universe Tankships Inc. of Monrovia* v. *International Transport Workers Federation* (1982) the House of Lords recognised the existence of a new form of duress, *economic duress*. In that case the I.T.W.F., in pursuit of a policy of "blacking" ships sailing under a flag of convenience, required a ship's captain to enter into an agreement by which a certificate exempting the ship from the blacking policy would be issued. Under the terms of the agreement the ship, which was stranded at Milford Haven, would be allowed to leave port if a large sum of money was paid to the I.T.W.F. The

House of Lords concluded that this money was paid over under economic duress and was recoverable. The House indicated that contracts entered into under economic duress were *voidable*. Lord Diplock explained the rationale of this new concept as being the unwillingness of the law to accept pressure exerted on one contracting party by the other which is not "legitimate." Defining the limits of legitimacy may be a difficult task, for, as Lord Diplock accepted, "commercial pressure, in some degree, exists wherever one party to a commercial transaction is in a stronger bargaining position than the other party." He was not, however, prepared to speculate as to the circumstances in which "commercial pressure, even though it amounts to a coercion of the will of a party in the weaker bargaining position, may be treated as legitimate."

In 1983 the concept of economic duress was further debated in *Alec Lobb* v. *Total Oil Company* where the court was called upon to consider a restraint clause in a lease and lease-back arrangement (see page 131). The arrangement had been entered into by a petrol company and the owner/operators of a filling station at the request of the operators who were under severe financial pressure. The court found the restraint unreasonable and struck it out but would not set aside the lease and lease-back arrangement on the grounds of economic duress. To set aside an agreement on this ground, the court asserted, a court would have to be satisfied that:

(a) the party wishing to have the agreement set aside had entered into it unwillingly;
(b) he had no alternative but to submit to the other's demands;
(c) his agreement was apparent rather than real and resulted from improper pressure; and
(d) he had repudiated the agreement as soon as the pressure was relieved.

In the case before the court the pressure had not been exerted by the oil company, but by other creditors; the operators had themselves requested the agreement and had regarded it as binding for several years without ever indicating that they wished to repudiate it; and there was no evidence that the petrol company had taken any advantage of the operators' situation.

INTENTION TO BE LEGALLY BOUND BY THE AGREEMENT

An agreement reached by offeror and offeree will only constitute a legally binding contract if the parties intended that they should be legally bound by the agreement. For evidential purposes the courts classify agreements into the following categories:

(a) *social and domestic agreements*, which are made between friends or members of the same family; and
(b) *business agreements*, which are all those agreements which are not social or domestic agreements.

Social and domestic agreements

Relatives engaged in conversation in the security of the family home make promises to one another which they may well intend to honour but which they would never expect to be legally binding. Friends are similarly uninhibited when they converse with one another and would be equally aghast at the suggestion that they intended their agreements to be binding. Recognising social realities, the courts will presume, in the case of social or domestic agreements, that the parties did not intend to be legally bound by their agreement and that there is no contractual relationship between them. This does not mean that the courts will not be prepared to find that a social or domestic agreement has hardened into a contractual agreement, it means, simply, that the burden of proving that a contract exists rests with the party who maintains that there was an intention to be legally bound. In *Parker* v. *Clark* such an intention was established. An elderly couple invited their niece and her husband to live with them, on the basis of shared expenses. The older couple promised to leave the niece their house when they died and, at their suggestion, the niece and her husband sold their own cottage. Subsequently relations between the two couples became less than friendly and litigation ensued. The court, impressed by the fact that the younger couple had elected to rely upon the agreement to the extent of selling their home, concluded that the parties had intended their agreement to be legally binding.

Business agreements

Where an agreement is not a social or domestic agreement, the courts presume that the agreement reached was one which was intended to be legally binding. Again, this does not mean that every business agreement constitutes a legally binding contract, but rather that a party asserting that there was no intention to be legally bound has the burden of proof in relation to this assertion. In *Rose and Frank Company* v. *Crompton Bros.*, the fact that the parties had not intended their agreement to be legally binding was established by bringing to the attention of the court a clause in the agreement which provided that it was not entered into as a "formal or legal agreement, and shall not be subject to legal jurisdiction in the law courts." Here the clause was obviously unambiguous, the parties quite clearly had not intended to create legal relations. Where, however, there is ambiguity in such a clause then the ambiguity will normally be resolved in favour of the party who asserts that the agreement was intended to be legally binding. In *Edwards* v. *Skyways*, the defendants promised to make an *ex gratia* payment to one of their employees who was to be made redundant. They then contended that they were not bound by their promise. The court accepted that the use of the words *ex gratia* indicated that the defendants were not admitting to any *pre-contractual* liability, but, the court concluded, the words were not sufficient to prevent liability arising on the contract. The defendants had not rebutted the presumption that they intended to be bound by their agreement.

Collective agreements in industry form a very specialised category of agreements and are given separate consideration in *Unit Three, Part Two* as part of the employment relationship.

CONSIDERATION MUST SUPPORT THE AGREEMENT

A bare promise (that is one which is made by the promisor in circumstances in which he is to receive nothing in return) is, in English law, enforceable only if made under seal as a *deed*. To constitute a simple contract an agreement must amount to a bargain, each of the parties paying a *price* for that which he receives from the other. This "price" is referred to as *consideration.* What can constitute consideration? In *Currie* v. *Misa* consideration was defined as "some right, interest, profit or benefit accruing to one party, or some forbearance, detriment, loss or responsibility given, suffered or undertaken by the other." If, therefore, one party *gives* a right, an interest, a profit or a benefit, he gives consideration. If he *incurs* or *undertakes* a forbearance, a detriment, a loss or a responsibility he also gives consideration.

Where a person has performed that which amounts to consideration, the consideration is said to be *executed*. If, therefore, A agrees to sell a car to B for £2,000, then A executes his consideration when he delivers the car and B when he pays the price. Until the execution of the consideration all that exists is a promise; A has promised to deliver the car and B has promised to pay the price. Such promises are themselves sufficient to constitute consideration; *executory* consideration. A and B have, therefore, a legally binding agreement as soon as they exchange promises, for each has thereby furnished executory consideration. Executed consideration must be distinguished from *past* consideration, which is not sufficient to support a contract. Past consideration, like executed consideration, is consideration which has been performed, but, unlike executed consideration, past consideration is performed prior to the making of the agreement. If B, having been given a car by A, promises to give A £2,000 for the car, there is no consideration furnished by A so as to make B's promise binding. That which A has given, delivery of a car, had been given prior to the making of B's promise. It is, therefore, past consideration and, as such, does not amount to contractual consideration.

The exception to the requirement of consideration, the promise contained in a document known as a deed which has been sealed and delivered, is known as a *specialty* contract as opposed to the *simple* contract supported by consideration.

There must be sufficient consideration

In *Thomas* v. *Thomas,* an executor agreed with the deceased's widow that she should be allowed to reside in the deceased's house at a "rent" of £1 per year. The executor made this agreement because he knew that it had been the deceased's wish that his widow should reside in the house so long as she should remain unmarried. The agreement between executor and widow was held to constitute a valid contract, but *only* because of the agreement to pay a rent of £1 per annum. The fact that the executor was motivated to act in a certain way did not, in itself, give any rights to the widow. Upon her agreeing to pay rent, however, she was committed to the payment of something of value, no matter how inadequate this payment might appear when gauged in the light of the market value of the tenancy. She had, as a result, furnished consideration so as to make the executor's promise binding. It is, therefore, clear that consideration need not be *adequate.*

Consideration must, however, be *sufficient* in that it must have some value. If a party promises to do only that which he is already contractually obliged to do, he is, in reality, giving nothing of value to the promisee. In *Stilk* v. *Myrick,* for example, it was held that the crew of a ship could not enforce a promise made by their captain to share amongst them the wages of two members of the crew who had deserted during the voyage. The court was of the opinion that the crew had, " . . . undertaken to do all that they could under all the emergencies of the voyage. They had sold all their services till the voyage should be completed . . . the desertion of a part of the crew is to be considered an emergency of the voyage as much as their death; and those who remain are bound by the terms of their original contract to exert themselves to the utmost to bring the ship in safety to her destined port." The crew were, thus, already under a contractual obligation and a subsequent promise to discharge that obligation could not amount to consideration for a fresh promise made by their employers.

If, however, the party who is contractually bound does more than merely re-affirm his original undertaking, he may well furnish consideration which will enable him to enforce any promise made to him subsequent to his having entered into the original contract. In *Hartley* v. *Ponsonby*, the facts were substantially the same as in *Stilk* v. *Myrick*, save for the very important difference that the court concluded that "the ship was so short-handed . . . that it would have been dangerous to life to proceed . . . so dangerous to life that the plaintiff and the other seamen were not bound to re-embark under their articles . . . and so were free men and at liberty to make a fresh bargain." In undertaking to perform the task they had originally undertaken, but in different circumstances and on different terms, the crew had provided consideration for the promise made to them of additional reward.

It would appear that there is one situation in which a party will be taken to have provided consideration when he undertakes to perform merely that which he is already contractually obliged to perform. If A contracts with B, it would appear that A provides consideration to C, in return for a promise made by C, if A promises C that he will perform his contract with B. In *New Zealand Shipping Co. Ltd.* v. *A.M. Satterthwaite & Co. Ltd. (The Eurymedon)* the Judicial Committee of the Privy Council held that the unloading by stevedores of goods from a ship (which the stevedores were already bound to do by a contract with the shipowners) was consideration for a promise by the owners of the cargo to the stevedores that they should not be liable in respect of damage to the goods in the unloading process. Moreover, in *Pao On* v. *Lau Yiu Long* the Privy Council declined to distinguish between *executed* and *executory* consideration. Lord Scarman said, "Their Lordships do not doubt that a promise to perform, or the performance of a pre-existing contractual obligation to a third party can be a valid consideration."

Consideration must move from the promisee

If a person has not furnished consideration he cannot enforce a promise made to him. Where, however, the promisee does furnish consideration it is immaterial that the consideration does not move to the promisor, so long as the consideration moves at his request. Thus, if A promises to pay B provided that B will perform a service for C, B can, by performing that service, ensure that he will be entitled to recover from A.

Privity of contract . . . it follows from the principle of consideration that the legal relationship created between the parties to a contract is exclusive to them. Only those who are *privy* (or parties) can sue on a contract so as to participate in its benefits and similarly only those who are privy can incur contractual liability. Thus, in *Tweddle* v. *Atkinson* a prospective bride's father agreed with the prospective groom's father that each would make payments to the happy couple. Unfortunately the bride's father failed to pay and it was held that the groom could not sue him in respect of the breach of contract, even though it was made for the groom's benefit, for there was no privity between them. In more common circumstances this rule may be seen to operate where a customer buys a new car from a garage and it proves to be of defective manufacture. The buyer's remedy is against the garage, for he has privity with the seller, but there is no *contractual* remedy against the manufacturer. (In practice motor manufacturers give specific "warranties" with new cars which, under a *Code of Practice* agreed with the Director General of Fair Trading, they will honour directly not only with the buyer of the car but also with a subsequent purchaser during the "warranty period.") Similarly, in *Adler* v. *Dickson*, it was held that a crew member could not take advantage of a clause in a contract between a shipowner and a passenger which was intended to benefit not only the shipowner but also his crew. The crew member was not privy to the agreement and was therefore a stranger to the contract.

There are exceptions to the general rule. For example, a lease of land may create rights and obligations which are treated as belonging to the land itself so that not only are the original parties to the lease bound but also future assignees (or owners) of the lease (see page 347). (Assignment of contracts effects a change in the basic rule, by agreement, and is considered in more detail under *Personal Property*.) An example of a statutory exception is provided by the Resale Prices Act 1976 under which, in exceptional circumstances following approval by the Restrictive Practices Court, a manufacturer who sells goods to a wholesaler subject to a *minimum price agreement* may enforce that agreement against any trader who subsequently takes the goods with notice of the restriction upon price-cutting. The Consumer Credit Act 1974, s.75, also provides a most significant exception and is dealt with later in detail as an aspect of consumer protection (see page 371).

OBLIGATIONS ARISING FROM CONTRACTS

Contractual terms

Consider the situation in which one party addresses another and asks, "Will you sell me your car for £1,000?" and the other replies "Yes." This agreement represents a contract of the most straightforward nature and the undertakings of each party (the *terms* of the contract) are easily determined. However, contracts are not normally concluded in such a straightforward fashion. Commercial contracts are generally much more complex and are created only after a period of negotiation. The agreement eventually concluded will normally consist of multiple promises or undertakings by each party. These mutual undertakings, or terms, may require careful analysis in order to determine their legal significance.

Classification of terms . . . the terms of a contract may be divided into two major classes, *conditions* and *warranties*. There may also be, additionally, an intermediate class which may be designated as the class of the *innominate term*.

A *condition* is a term of major importance in a contractual agreement. It is of such a nature that it may be said to "go to the root" of the undertaking. In short, if a condition of a contract is not performed it may be said that the whole basis of the contract is destroyed. A *warranty* is a term of only minor significance. It may be said to be collateral to the main purpose of the contract. Should a warranty not be performed this breach may be regarded as something of an irritation, but it would not destroy the essential character of the undertaking embodied in the contract.

Where a term of a contract is broken, the courts will need to determine whether the term is a condition or a warranty, for the remedies available for breach of contract vary according to this classification. A breach of condition is a more serious matter than a breach of warranty, providing the innocent party with a right to repudiate (set aside) the contract and/or claim damages (see page 156 for a consideration of damages). For example, if a seller was to undertake to transport a load of perishable goods to their buyer upon a particular day, a failure to transport upon the day would clearly amount to a breach of condition. The failure to transport as required by the contract would be a matter of great concern to the buyer and would go to the root of the undertaking. The buyer would be entitled to refuse a future delivery and sue for damages. If, however, the buyer had further required in his contract that the seller should prepare the invoice of the goods to be delivered in a particular form to facilitate checking by the buyer upon receipt, then a failure to comply with this requirement would, no doubt, annoy the buyer and, indeed, inconvenience him, but, this breach would appear to be a less significant breach of contract and, therefore, only a breach of warranty. For breach of warranty, the innocent party may claim damages in respect of loss incurred but may not repudiate the contract. Clearly, in many cases, as in the above examples, the question of whether a term is a condition or warranty may be easily determined from the nature of the undertaking. However, it may not always be possible to proceed in this way. Frequently, undertakings are so complex and interrelated that the seriousness of a breach of an undertaking (and the appropriate remedy for the innocent party) may only be determined after the breach has occurred. It is almost meaningless, in such contracts, to initially classify the particular obligations as either conditions or warranties. Such an unreal classification would often result in inappropriate remedies being available to the innocent party, for, if the term was to be identified as a warranty, he would have to carry on with the contract even though he may have suffered particularly severe consequences arising out of the breach. In some contracts it may be more realistic to consider the consequences of the breach rather than the initial significance of the term. In *Hong Kong Fir Shipping Co. Ltd.* v. *Kawasaki Kisen Kaisha Ltd.* such an approach was suggested to deal with this taxing situation. The Court of Appeal accepted that rigidly classifying all terms as either conditions or warranties (and then merely applying the appropriate remedy for breach of such terms without reference to the actual consequences of the breach of contract) was unduly restrictive. Upon this unconventional approach it may be necessary to treat some terms as *innominate* or *intermediate* in nature, the appropriate remedy only being ascertainable after a breach has occurred. Thus a breach resulting in serious consequences would entitle the innocent party to those remedies available for a breach of condition, whereas less serious consequences would entitle that party to only damages for breach of warranty. Here, therefore, the determining factor in relation to the availability of remedies would be the consequences of the breach, rather than the status of the term broken. These consequences may, of course, only be determined "after the event." In less complex contracts the approach of the courts would remain the conventional one of initial classification of terms, thus alerting the parties, from the outset, as to the remedies available in the event of breach.

However, another, subsequent, Court of Appeal decision, *The Mihalis Angelos*, has suggested that the approach of the court in the *Hong Kong Fir* case may not be entirely suited to the commercial world. Businessmen, it was suggested, require *certainty* in their contracts and prefer to know from the outset whether a term is a condition or a warranty so as to enable them to order their affairs accordingly. In short, they may prefer to be able to predict with certainty what the consequences will be of a breach of contract. Most recently in *Bunge Corporation* v. *Tradax S.A.* the House of Lords has emphasised that in many commercial contracts the nature of a particular term has for long been well settled leaving no room for the "wait and see" approach. For example, stipulations as to the time of performance are normally conditions irrespective of the degree of loss suffered following a breach (see *Hartley* v. *Hymans*, page 366). The *Bunge* case recognised the merit of flexibility in the approach taken in the *Hong Kong Fir*, it emphasised however that this flexibility does not extend to a freedom to classify the terms themselves by reference to a "wait and see" approach. The terms of a contract must be capable of classification *from the outset*, the flexibility granted by a "wait and see" approach arises rather in relation to the identification of an *appropriate remedy* for breach of a term which has been identified, using normal principles of construction, as an innominate term.

Implied terms . . . the terms of a contract are normally "express" terms, in the sense that the parties have expressed their agreement as to particular undertakings. But it may come to pass that one party does not perform the contract as the other party had anticipated it would be performed and that this aspect of performance may not be expressly provided for in the agreement. In this case the court may be called upon to decide whether it would be proper to imply a term into the agreement which would, effectively, result in one party being in breach of a term to which he had not expressly agreed. This issue is essentially a question of determining whether a party has done, or failed to do, something which the parties would have expressly agreed upon as a term, had they envisaged the circumstances which arose. In short, the question of whether to imply a term is essentially a question of "business ethics" and "business efficacy." The leading illustration of this principle is *The Moorcock*. Here the defendants agreed to allow the plaintiffs to use their wharf to discharge and load a steamship. The defendants had not checked whether the bed of the river was safe. The vessel grounded at low tide and was damaged. The court found that a term was to be implied into the contract that the defendants had taken care to check that the river bed would be safe, as this must have been the real, but unexpressed, intention of the parties. There was, of course, a breach of this term.

Apart from implication of terms by a court, there are other implied terms of the greatest importance which have been provided by statute, particularly in relation to sales of goods and more recently in contracts for the supply of services. These terms are considered in *Unit Three* as an aspect of consumer protection.

Representations
    The terms of a contract are the undertakings which form the content of
a legally enforceable agreement. However, as has been indicated, contracts
are normally concluded after a period of negotiation. That negotiation
may involve the parties in a dialogue which, although not forming part of
the contract itself, may have a legal significance which impinges upon the
contract. Where one party, at or about the time of the making of a
contract, makes a statement of fact which, although not intended to
become a "term" of the contract, nevertheless induces the other party to
enter into the contract, that statement of fact is classified as a *representation*.
Should the statement of fact be false, then it is a *misrepresentation*. Thus,
terms of a contract are essential stipulations of a contract and any failure
to satisfy these undertakings involves a *breach of contract*. Representations,
on the other hand, do not form part of the contract itself but stand apart,
outside the contractual link. Should a mere representation be untrue (a
misrepresentation) this does not give rise to a breach of contract.
However, the party who is misled by the misrepresentation is not
remediless, his remedy is simply not that for breach of contract.

MISREPRESENTATION

A misrepresentation may be defined as a false statement of fact, made by
one party to a contract before the contract is completed, which, whilst not
amounting to a term of the contract, is intended to induce and does induce
the other party to enter into the contract. Each part of this definition is
important and must be considered in turn.
    Statement must be of fact . . . an expression of a personal assessment of a
factual situation is not a statement of fact, but rather an *opinion* and, as
such, cannot amount to a misrepresentation. An opinion genuinely held
cannot be said to be false even though it is shown to be erroneous or
misconceived. In *Bissett* v. *Wilkinson*, B, in negotiations leading to the sale
of his farm to W, said that the land would support 2,000 sheep. Both
parties were aware that the land had never been used as a sheep farm. W
bought the land only to discover that it was incapable of supporting so
many sheep. It was held that B's statement, although inducing the
purchase, was merely a statement of an (erroneous) opinion and could not
amount to a misrepresentation. However, a statement of opinion by
implication involves a statement that the opinion is genuinely held after an
assessment of known facts. In *Edgington* v. *Fitzmaurice*, Bowen L.J. said:
"The state of a man's mind is as much a fact as the state of his digestion. It
is true that it is very difficult to prove what the state of a man's mind at any
particular time is, but, if it can be ascertained, it is as much a fact as
anything else." Thus, in *Smith* v. *Land and House Property Corporation*, a
seller of an hotel stated that it was, at that time, "let to Mr. Frederick Fleck
(a most desirable tenant)." In fact, Fleck was in arrears with the rent and
he never paid unless he was pressed to do so. The court held that the
description of Fleck was not a mere expression of opinion, but a
misrepresentation, for "if the facts are not equally well known to both sides
then a statement of opinion by the one who knows the facts best involves
very often a statement of material fact, for he impliedly states that he
knows facts which justify his opinion." (Contrast *Bissett* v. *Wilkinson* where
both parties knew the land had never been used to keep sheep.) A

reasonable man could not genuinely have held the favourable opinion of Fleck and the statement must have been a misrepresentation as to the state of the seller's mind.

Silence as a misrepresentation ... just as parties are basically free to agree upon whatever terms they wish, so also there is no obligation to make representations. Hence, it is a basic rule that there is no duty of disclosure of relevant facts placed upon contracting parties. Silence is, therefore, not normally capable of amounting to a misrepresentation. If a contracting party wishes to be informed of facts within the other party's knowledge, then he must ask for information. There are, however, three situations which may be considered as exceptions to the general rule. First, there is a duty to correct statements which, although true when made, subsequently become false or misleading before the contract is completed. For example, in *With* v. *O'Flanagan*, the defendant, in the course of negotiations leading to the sale of a medical practice, truthfully informed the plaintiff that the practice was worth £2,000 per annum. Before the contract was completed the defendant became ill and during his illness the value of the practice fell catastrophically. The court found that the failure to amend the earlier statement amounted to a misrepresentation. Secondly, if a statement is made, it must constitute a full disclosure, for a half-disclosure, although true in itself, may create a false impression. For example, in *Coles* v. *White City (Manchester) Greyhound Association*, a company described land which it proposed developing as a greyhound stadium as "eminently suitable" for development. It was not disclosed that the land had already been scheduled under local authority proposals for a "town planning scheme." The failure to disclose the proposal was found to constitute a misrepresentation, for although literally true, the description was misleading. Finally, in certain circumstances the law imposes a duty to disclose material facts. In these circumstances contracts are known as contracts *uberrimae fidei* ("of the utmost good faith"). The reason for this special requirement is that in some situations one party is in a particularly advantageous position so as to best know the material facts. The most common example of this type of contract is the contract of insurance. Here the law imposes a duty upon the insured party to disclose "all material facts which would influence the judgment of a prudent insurer in fixing the premium or determining whether he will take the risk."

Statement must induce the contract ... in order to be actionable, the misrepresentation must actually have the effect of inducing the person to whom it is made to enter into the contract. Thus, if a party is unaware of the existence of a misrepresentation, then the false statement cannot affect the contract. Similarly, if, although aware of the statement, a party takes steps to check its truth, which check fails to reveal the fact that the statement is false, the misrepresentation has not been relied upon so as to induce the contract. Reliance has instead, been placed upon the party's own investigations. For example, in *Attwood* v. *Small*, following exaggerated claims by the seller of a mine as to its capacity, a purchaser commissioned his own survey. This survey failed to reveal the falsity of the seller's claim. It was held that the false statement had not been relied upon and was not actionable. However, if an invitation to check the accuracy of a claim is not accepted, the mere opportunity to make an independent assessment will not deprive the misled party of his remedy.

Types of misrepresentation

There are three types of misrepresentation; fraudulent, negligent and innocent. Although, generally speaking, a misrepresentation makes a contract *voidable* (it is valid until set aside) at the option of the party misled, the consequences of misrepresentation, in some measure, vary in accordance with classification.

Fraudulent misrepresentation occurs when a false statement of fact is made (i) knowingly, or (ii) without belief in its truth, or (iii) recklessly (*i.e.* careless whether it be true or false). Thus, in the absence of honest belief in its truth, when made, a false statement is fraudulent. *Innocent* misrepresentations constitute those representations which, although false, are made honestly, with reasonable grounds for belief in their truth. *Negligent* misrepresentations are false statements made, honestly, yet without reasonable grounds for belief in their truth. This distinction between innocent and negligent misrepresentations is derived from the Misrepresentation Act 1967 and clearly requires that the reasonableness of the belief should be assessed in accordance with the standards of the "reasonable man." Thus, the honest but stupid or credulous person will, although not careless by his own standards, be objectively considered negligent in law. Accordingly, if an accountant, for example, when selling his own business, misunderstood or misinterpreted his own accounts and thereby misrepresented the finances of the business to a purchaser, he could not, because of his alleged expertise, claim reasonable ground for belief in the statement. The misrepresentation, made honestly, would be negligent. The same statement made by a shopkeeper might well be innocent.

Representations and contractual terms

It has been explained that there is a distinction, of considerable significance, between representations and contractual terms. However, each may arise from negotiations conducted prior to the final agreement which forms the contract itself, so that statements made at that stage may be considered as either embryo terms or representations. The mystery of how to distinguish between terms, which fall within contracts, and representations, which lie outside, is not easily solved. The solution lies, essentially, in the intention of the parties. What did the maker of the statement intend? The test of intention is, however, objective; would a reasonable man have taken the statement to be meant as a contractual undertaking or a mere representation? In determining this question a number of guidelines have been suggested.

The strength of the statement . . . will be assessed by the court in assessing its impact. For example, where a seller stated that the subject of sale (a boat) was "sound," but advised the buyer to have it checked, there was found to be no contractual undertaking of soundness. On the other hand, where, when a buyer was about to examine a horse at a sale, the seller intervened and said: "You need not look for anything; the horse is perfectly sound," who could have doubted that this was such an undertaking?

The significance of the statement . . . for the person to whom it was made may be decisive. Thus, in *Bannerman* v. *White*, a prospective buyer of hops asked the seller whether the goods had been treated with sulphur, indicating that if they had he was not interested in them. An assurance that the hops had not been treated with sulphur was clearly a term of the contract of sale.

The relative expertise and knowledge of the parties . . . has an impact upon reasonable expectations. For example, in *Oscar Chess Ltd.* v. *Williams*, a private individual "traded-in" a car which he described as a 1948 model (it was so described in a log-book which had been fraudulently altered by some unknown person); in fact it was a 1939 model. The statement as to date of origin was found not to be a term of the contract, for the buyers, as car dealers, had greater expertise than the seller. In contrast, in *Dick Bentley Productions Ltd.* v. *Harold Smith (Motors) Ltd.*, a car dealer sold a car to a customer who had asked for a "well vetted" car, the dealer indicating that the engine had "only done 20,000 miles." In fact the engine had served 100,000 miles. This statement was a contractual term.

Written contracts . . . allow for a further factor to be considered. For where oral negotiations are eventually reduced into a written contract, should an earlier oral statement not be included in the written agreement, then this is an indication that the statement is not to be considered as a contractual term.

NON-CONTRACTUAL MISSTATEMENTS

Although misrepresentation, by definition, necessarily involves a statement by a *party* to a contract, if a false statement is made by a person who is not a party there may still be a remedy available to the person misled, under the principle of *Hedley Byrne & Co. Ltd.* v. *Heller & Partners*. In this case the House of Lords stated that a *duty of care* could exist in the making of statements where there is a "special relationship" between the parties. Where such a relationship exists, a negligent misstatement may form the basis of an action, in *Negligence*, in respect of loss suffered because of the misstatement. In *Esso Petroleum Corp. Ltd.* v. *Mardon*, the court considered that "when an inquirer consults a businessman in the course of his business and makes it plain to him that he is seeking advice and intends to act on it in a particular way, any reasonable businessman would realise that, if he chooses to give advice without any warning or qualification, he is putting himself under a moral obligation to take some care . . . such care as is reasonable in the whole circumstances." Indeed, it has since been held in *Yianni* v. *Edwin Evans & Sons* that where a valuer engaged by a building society negligently assessed the value of a house for mortgage purposes, the purchasers of the house, who had relied upon the valuation (although they had no contract with the valuer) could hold the valuer liable in Negligence.

CLASSIFICATION OF STATEMENTS

It is now clear that statements made during contractual negotiations may fall within different classifications. These classifications are set out in *diagram* 4 (p. 145).

EXEMPTION CLAUSES

Exemption clauses are terms of a contract which have been devised to exclude or limit liability for breaches of contract in certain circumstances. It has been a basic principle of our law that parties should be free to agree

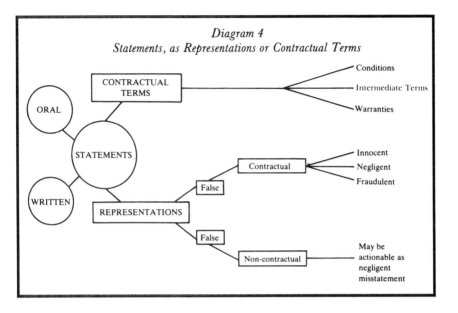

Diagram 4
Statements, as Representations or Contractual Terms

upon whatever contractual terms they may wish. However, in recent times there has been increasing statutory intervention to control exemption clauses. Nevertheless, there remain areas where there is no statutory control. Indeed, by application of basic principles one may discover that it is unnecessary to fall back upon statutory controls for, in many instances, apparently effective exemption clauses may be found to be ineffective. Thus, for example, whenever it is sought to place reliance upon any term of a contract, it is essential to determine whether or not that term actually forms part of the contract.

Agreement between the parties . . . an exemption clause cannot form part of a contract if it has not been agreed upon, but this is not to say that merely because one party is unaware of a term he will be able to avoid being bound by it. If, for example, a written contract contains exemption clauses and one party does not trouble to read the document which clearly sets out those terms, then that party will still be bound by them despite his ignorance of their provisions, for they form a term of his contract. A party is not, however, bound by provisions which are not a term of his contract. For example, in *Olley* v. *Marlborough Court Hotel* a guest booked in at the reception desk of an hotel. Upon entering her bedroom she saw, for the first time, a notice excluding the hotel from "liability for damage to or for loss of articles owned by patrons." Subsequently some of her belongings were stolen. The court found that as the guest had not seen the notice at the time of making the contract (*i.e.* at the reception desk), the notice could not form part of the contract between the hotel and guest and, as a result, could not be relied upon by the hotel. The rule may be simply expressed as a requirement that terms must be communicated. Where an attempt at communication has been made, but a party has not become aware of terms despite this effort, the question is whether what has been done was sufficient in the circumstances. For example, in *Chapelton* v. *Barry U.D.C.* the plaintiff hired a deck chair from the defendant and was handed a ticket stating that the council would not be liable for damage in the event of "any accident or damage arising from the hire of the chair." The chairs had been stacked adjacent to a notice indicating merely the price per hour. It was held by the court that the plaintiff could recover in respect of the injury which he suffered, when the deck chair collapsed, for it was not reasonable to expect the plaintiff to realise that the ticket sought to provide an additional contractual term. In contrast, however, a ticket issued as a receipt may be effective to carry a contractual term. In *Parker* v. *South Eastern Railway* the plaintiff deposited a bag in a railway station left-luggage department and received a ticket in return. The ticket carried an instruction "see back," and on the back was an exemption clause limiting liability. The court indicated that, in the circumstances, reasonable notice of the term had been given and the plaintiff was bound by the clause. It has been said that the more onerous the provisions of an exemption clause, the more must be done to bring it to the attention of a party affected. Indeed, Lord Denning has said that some exemption clauses would not be effectively communicated in the absence of being printed in red ink with a red hand pointing to them!

Overriding undertakings . . . another consideration, relevant when determining the effectiveness of exemption clauses, is any undertaking given in negotiations taking place at the time of the contract. Thus, in *Curtis* v. *Chemical Cleaning Company*, the plaintiff took a dress to the defendant's shop to have it cleaned. A form was presented, by the defendant, for signature. The form contained an exemption of liability for "any damage caused by the cleaning process." The plaintiff asked the counter assistant what the clause meant and was informed (incorrectly) that the clause only excluded liability for damage to sequins and beads. When the dress was returned it was badly stained. The court found that the defendant, when sued for damaging the dress, could not rely upon the clause because the assistant had misrepresented its provisions. Again, in *Couchman* v. *Hill*, a heifer was described in an auction catalogue as "unserved." The catalogue and conditions of sale contained a clause excluding liability for "errors of description." The plaintiff asked the owner and auctioneer whether they could confirm that the heifer was unserved and they confirmed the statement in the catalogue. The court found that no reliance could be placed upon the exclusion clause when the heifer was found to be in calf. The oral undertaking given at the time of sale had overridden the exclusion clause.

Interpretation by the courts . . . the courts will always interpret any exemption clause with great care. The principle which is adopted is known as the *contra proferentem* rule, which means that the courts will resolve any doubt or ambiguity against the person seeking to rely upon the exemption clause. Thus, in *Andrews* v. *Singer*, the plaintiff contracted to buy "new Singer cars" from the defendants. A clause excluded liability for breach of "all conditions, warranties and liabilities, implied by statute, common law or otherwise." One of the cars delivered was a used car, which constituted a breach of the express term that the car be new. The court found that the defendants could not rely upon the exemption clause, for the breach in question related to an *express* term whereas the clause related only to *implied* terms.

However, it must be emphasised that the common law does not allow the courts to override contracts freely entered. There are, today, statutory controls over exemption clauses but Parliament has refrained from legislating so as to interfere with freely negotiated contracts. Thus, in *Photo Production Ltd.* v. *Securicor* the House of Lords indicated that when parties of equal bargaining strength contract so as to apportion risks, the courts will not strive to avoid an exemption clause but will simply give effect to the wishes of the parties as expressed in their contract. In this case Securicor was employed to guard the plaintiff's factory. An exemption clause provided that "under no circumstances shall Securicor be responsible for any injurious act or default by its employees." A guard deliberately lit a fire which destroyed the factory. It was held that Securicor was protected from any liability for the guard's action. Commercial organisations may thus be seen to be free to apportion the risks inherent in their operations, for the factory owners, having shouldered the burden of the risk of fire, could have passed that risk to insurers in return for payment of a premium. This approach to contract interpretation lays stress upon pre-contract negotiations where parties should decide as to which should insure against losses. Having decided this matter, the content of the contract, possibly including an exemption clause, will naturally follow. In keeping with recognition of a basic right of the parties to allocate risk is the ruling in *Ailsa Craig Fishing Co. Ltd.* v. *Malvern Fishing Co. Ltd.* that the courts will be more ready to accept that parties have intended to *limit* liability rather than *exclude* it altogether. Clearly a limitation of liability exhibits an intention to allocate risk.

It should be noted, however, that the House of Lords, in *Photo Productions*, emphasized that an exemption clause, no matter how widely drafted, will not excuse a party whose purported performance of a contract falls outside the "four corners" of the agreement: the classic illustration of this principle being that an exemption clause will not excuse the delivery of chalk under a contract for cheese.

(The highly significant statutory controls over exemption clauses are considered in *Unit Three, Part Five* as an aspect of consumer protection.)

COMPLETION OF CONTRACTUAL OBLIGATIONS

Performance

Having considered how contractual obligations arise, it is necessary to examine the performance of those obligations. Performance is, of course, the anticipated method whereby the parties to a contract should discharge their undertakings and complete the life of a particular contract. It is important to note that the performance which the law requires of parties to a contract is normally a precise fulfilment, in every respect, of the contractual undertakings. This principle is well demonstrated by *Bolton* v. *Mahadeva*, where the plaintiffs contracted to install a combined heating and hot water system in the defendant's house for £560. When sued for the price, the defendant claimed that the contract had not been performed. The installation had been undertaken, but the work was so inadequately performed that the house was not sufficiently warm and fumes were given out into the living room. To correct the defects would have cost £174, almost one-third of the contract price. The court asserted that entire performance of the contract was essential in order that there be an obligation to pay the contract price and held that the plaintiffs were entitled to no payment at all.

Exceptions to the basic rule . . . the basic rule, requiring complete performance, is subject to qualification. If a contract has been *substantially performed* then, even though some small part of the work has been badly done or not done at all, the contractor is entitled to the agreed contractual price less deductions necessary to remedy the inadequate performance. However, what amounts to a substantial performance will depend upon the facts of each case. For example, in *Hoenig* v. *Isaacs*, on a contract to furnish and decorate a flat for £750, defects in a wardrobe, bookshelf and bookcase amounted to nearly £56, yet the court held that there was, nevertheless, substantial performance.

Again, if parties have agreed upon a contract which has been divided into several separate parts, then performance of each part of the contract will entitle the contractor to payment in respect of that part. This type of contract is common in the construction industry where, for example, it is not unusual for payment to become due upon completion of various stages of a building (*e.g.* foundations, damp course level and first floor). Whether a contract is to be regarded as an entire contract which must be wholly performed, or as a severable contract under which performance of parts of the contract may be regarded as complete performances of those particular parts entitling payment, is a matter of no little difficulty. The answer in any given case lies essentially in the expressed or presumed intention of the parties. For example, in *Roberts* v. *Havelock*, a shipwright undertook to carry out immediate repairs to the defendant's ship which had been damaged whilst delivering a cargo. Before all of the repairs were completed the shipwright sued for payment in respect of the work which he had done. The court held that he must succeed, for there was no agreement that all of the work should be completed in return for a lump sum.

A further circumstance in which a partial performance may ground a successful claim for payment, is where one party prevents the other from completing his contractual performance. In *Planché* v. *Colburn* the plaintiff agreed to write a series of articles on ancient costume and armour. The work was to be published in serial form in a periodical magazine. When the greater part of the writing was complete, the defendant ceased publication of the magazine. It was held that the plaintiff was entitled to be paid in respect of the work which he had completed, not because he had performed the contract, but because he "was not to be deprived of the fruits of his labour." Such a claim is not based upon the contract but arises in "*quasi-contract*" which is discussed later.

Tender of performance . . . normally, a tender (or offer) of performance has the same effect as performance of a contract itself. Thus, if a seller of goods makes them available to the buyer and the buyer refuses to accept delivery, the seller will be treated as having performed his part of the contract of sale and will no longer be under an obligation to supply the goods. Where the contractual obligation consists of the payment of money, the principle of tender of performance still applies, though in modified form. Thus, if a tender of money is made but rejected, there is no need for a further tender to be made. The tender does not, however, extinguish a debt, and should an action be brought against the debtor, he should pay the sum tendered into court and plead the tender before the court. Should the creditor proceed with his action and be awarded no more than the amount tendered, he will be ordered to pay the debtor's costs in the action.

Agreement that performance is not required

Although performance of a contract is clearly the intention of the parties at the time of entering an agreement, such performance may become unnecessary should the parties reach a further agreement to that effect. A contract is created by agreement and, similarly, the performance which it demands may be dispensed with by agreement.

The requirement of consideration . . . one must, however, appreciate that an agreement to end a contract, if it is to be legally binding, must itself be a contract. Thus, an agreement to dispense with performance must itself be supported by consideration. Where the original contract remains entirely *executory* (*i.e.* the obligations have not been performed by either party and there remains only an exchange of promises) each party may agree to release the other from his obligation to perform, in consideration of being released from his own obligation. Where, however, one party has performed his obligations and the other has not, the party who has performed may still agree to release the other from his obligations. Such a release will only be binding if it is made under seal or supported by consideration. For example, if one party has performed his part of a bargain and the other party has yet to perform, the parties may agree upon a different performance in substitution for the outstanding obligation. In such a case, the binding effect of the substituted agreement is said to be in *accord and satisfaction.* The "accord" refers to the agreement and the "satisfaction" refers to the consideration.

Because of the requirement that there be consideration, it follows that a promise to accept a smaller sum than that due under a contract is not normally binding on the promisor. If A owes B £200 under a contract, he must pay that sum in full. If B agrees to accept a payment of a smaller sum, say £100, in "final settlement" of the debt, he may take that sum and then sue for the balance, despite his promise. B's promise to accept the smaller sum is only enforceable if A furnishes consideration (as, for example, where A undertakes to pay the smaller sum at an earlier date than that on which the larger sum becomes payable).

There are, however, two exceptions to the rule that a party is only bound by a promise to release the other from his obligations if consideration is given in return. The promisor will be bound by such an undertaking, even though the other party does not furnish consideration, where:

(a) he is a party to a *composition* agreement; or
(b) the promisee is able to obtain the benefit of the defence of *promissory estoppel.*

Composition agreements . . . where a creditor enters into a composition agreement, an agreement between a debtor and all his creditors under which each creditor is to receive part payment (*e.g.* 25p for each £1 owed) as final satisfaction of the debt, the creditor will be bound by the terms of the agreement. The debtor gives no consideration to his creditors in return for their agreeing to surrender their contractual claims against him and it would appear that the basis of this exception is that an action by any individual creditor to recover the balance "due" to him under his contract would amount to a fraud upon the other creditors. As the whole of the debtor's assets are being distributed under the agreement, a judgment for the balance due to a particular creditor could only be met out of funds earmarked for another.

The defence of promissory estoppel . . . where one party to a contract indicates that he will release the other from his contractual obligation, the promisor will be bound by this promise should the promisee change his position in reliance upon it. The promisor will be *estopped* (prevented) from denying his promise and will not be permitted to enforce his "rights" in contravention of his promise. In *Hughes* v. *Metropolitan Railway Company*, a tenant was served with notice by his landlord that he should perform his contractual obligation to repair the premises within six months or forfeit his lease. The tenant agreed to effect the necessary repairs, but suggested that the landlord might wish to purchase the tenant's interest in the property, that he, the tenant, would be willing to enter into negotiations for the sale of his interest and that if negotiations were to commence he would await their outcome before beginning the repairs to the property. The landlord entered into such negotiations, and, in the opinion of the court, thereby acquiesced in the non-commencement of the repairs. The negotiations were broken off after a period of two months and, upon the expiration of six months after service of the notice to repair, the landlord claimed that the lease was forfeit as the tenant had not completed the repairs. The court would not, however, permit the landlord to act in a manner inconsistent with his implied promise and indicated that the six-month period referred to in the notice to repair began to run only upon the termination of negotiations between the parties. It is important to note that the court in this case merely *suspended* the landlord's right to enforce the notice to repair, it did not *extinguish* it. Any failure on the part of the tenant to repair the premises by the end of the revised period would have resulted in the tenancy being forfeited.

It would appear, then, that the defence of promissory estoppel may protect a promisee only to the extent that it will *suspend* the right of the promisor to enforce his contractual rights where he has undertaken not to enforce those rights. However, the defence will *extinguish* the promisor's rights when the promisee has irreversibly altered his position. In *Hughes* v. *Metropolitan Railway Company* the promisee had not altered his position in a way which could not be rectified, the rights of the promisor were, therefore, merely suspended. Where, however, a contracting party undertakes that he will not enforce payment of part of the debt and, relying upon this promise, the debtor commits himself to expenditure that he would not otherwise have undertaken, the promisor's right to enforce payment of the debt will be extinguished and the debtor will no longer be under an obligation to make payment.

What, then, is the relationship between the defence of promissory estoppel and the general rule that a contracting party is not bound by a promise that he will not enforce payment unless consideration is given in return? It would appear that where the creditor makes a promise that he will not enforce payment:

(a) the promisee will not be able to resist a later demand for payment if he has neither provided consideration in return for the promise nor altered his position in reliance upon it;

(b) the promisor will not be able to enforce a later demand for payment, where the promisee has altered his position as a result of the promise, until he gives reasonable notice that he intends to act in a manner inconsistent with his original promise;

(c) the promisor will have no right to enforce a later demand for payment where the promisee has irretrievably altered his position in reliance upon the original promise.

Perhaps the most famous application of the principle of promissory estoppel is in the case of *Central London Property Trust* v. *High Trees House* where a tenant of a block of flats which had become unprofitable due to the Second World War retained the tenancy after the landlord promised to reduce the rent. Following the war, the landlord commenced charging the *full* rent and in an action he was held to be free to do so for the future as no consideration had been given for the earlier promise of a reduction. However, the court indicated, *obiter*, that no claim for the full rent would have been successful for the war-time period as the tenant had detrimentally altered his intended course of action in reliance upon the promise.

It must be emphasised that promissory estoppel is a "shield and not a sword." Whilst a contracting party can raise the doctrine of promissory estoppel as a *defence* to an action brought in contravention of a promise made without consideration, he cannot use the doctrine so as to *sue* the promisor for breach of his promise.

Waiver . . . as indicated above, consideration is normally necessary if there is to be a release of the obligations arising under a contract. To mitigate the severity of this rule, however, a doctrine of *waiver* has been developed in relation to variations of the obligations of the parties. Where one contracting party affords some latitude to the other a court may, under this doctrine, hold the party affording the indulgence to his undertaking, even in the absence of consideration. In *Charles Rickards* v. *Oppenheim*, a seller undertook to build coachwork onto a Rolls-Royce chassis. The completed car was to be delivered by March 1948. When the car was still unfinished at the stipulated delivery date, the buyer indicated that he was willing to extend the delivery date by a further three months. This indication amounted to a waiver and no action for non-delivery would have been entertained by a court before expiry of the three-month period. Unlike promissory estoppel, however, a waiver cannot in any circumstances totally excuse non-performance. It merely modifies the contractual undertaking.

Conditional contracts . . . a final form of agreement which may excuse performance of a contract may be found in the original contract itself. Contracts may be expressed to be subject to the fulfilment of a *condition precedent* or, indeed, subject to the occurrence of a *condition subsequent*. A condition precedent is the term adopted to refer to an event, the happening of which is expressed to be essential to contractual undertakings becoming legally binding. Thus, if an importer agrees to purchase goods from overseas, but indicates that the contract is subject to his obtaining an import licence then, should no licence be forthcoming, the contract will never come into existence. Similarly, a condition subsequent is an event, the happening of which will relieve the parties to a contract of their obligations. For example, an importer may agree to purchase a commodity at market price until the market price reaches a specified figure. Once the specified figure is reached, then further purchases are no longer required under the contract.

Impossibility of performance

Conditions precedent and subsequent take effect through express agreement. However, the common law may achieve similar ends by imposing solutions upon contracting parties where they have failed to address themselves to particular eventualities.

Initial impossibility ... a particularly striking illustration of such an imposed solution, whereby the courts ruled that parties were relieved from their contractual obligations, is to be found in *Couturier* v. *Hastie*. Here the parties contracted for the sale of a cargo of corn believed to be en route for England from Salonica. Unknown to the parties, at the time of the contract the cargo had ceased to exist as a commercial entity, for, due to overheating, it had become necessary for the master of the ship to sell the cargo at an intermediate port. Although the parties had not directed their attention to the possibility of non-existence of the subject-matter of the contract, the court considered that, impliedly, the contract was contingent upon such existence. In short, the parties were mistaken. The mistake was common to each and "the contract" could be considered as never having come into existence. Such an imposed solution, based upon the presumed intention of the parties, effectively relieved the parties of any contractual obligations which they believed they had undertaken. Indeed, subsequent to the decision in *Couturier* v. *Hastie*, the legislature enacted a provision now to be found in the Sale of Goods Act 1979 which may be said to embody the principle in that case. Section 6 of the Act provides that, "Where there is a contract for the sale of specific goods (goods identified and agreed upon at the time of the making of the contract of sale), and the goods without the knowledge of the seller have perished at the time when the contract is made, the contract is void."

Initial impossibility of performance because of non-existence of the subject-matter of a contract is a comparatively simple notion which, as has been seen, relieves parties from their obligations to perform. More difficult is the situation in which, subsequent to the formation of a contract, circumstances arise in which performance becomes impossible or would involve an undertaking of a wholly different character to that contemplated when the parties entered their agreement.

Subsequent impossibility ... when parties enter into contracts, they are, of course, in a position to guard against future contingencies by express stipulations. For instance, if a builder agrees to construct a house by a certain date he may guard against being unable to complete the work by that date, due to circumstances beyond his control, by an express stipulation. He may provide that if work is stopped due to inclement weather or labour disputes, then the date for completion will be changed. Because of this freedom to take account of events, there is a basic proposition that if a party enters into a contract to do a particular thing, then he is not excused from the consequences of non-performance even if performance turns out to be impossible or simply futile. This basic proposition reflects the absolute view of contractual undertakings, in that the liability for breach of contract is independent of fault and that parties to contracts are expected either to perform their obligations or pay compensation for having failed to do so (see page 156 for damages for breach of contract). Nevertheless, a doctrine of *frustration* has developed under which, in appropriate circumstances, the law will excuse parties from performance of their undertakings. Development of this doctrine may be traced to the case of *Taylor* v. *Caldwell*, which provides a basic illustration of the doctrine in action. Here, the defendants contracted to make their hall available to the plaintiffs for concerts. Shortly before the first concert the hall was destroyed in an accidental fire without any fault on the part of the defendants. The question arose as to whether the defendants were excused from performance of the contract or whether they were liable for breach of contract in not making their hall available. The court found that the defendants were relieved from performance, for the parties "must have contemplated the continuing existence (of the hall) as the foundation of what was to be done."

This case raises a question which has since remained at large. It is as to the legal theory underlying the doctrine of frustration. These are two basic possibilities:

(a) that the court intervenes in a situation which requires the imposition of a just and reasonable solution;

(b) that the courts will seek to discover the intention of the parties, imply a term giving effect to that intention and enforce that term.

Whichever approach is correct, a useful test to adopt, in any given situation in which frustration is in issue, is to consider whether, had the parties contemplated the situation which has arisen, they would, as sensible men, have said "if that happens, of course it is all over between us." Most certainly one must bear in mind that the doctrine of frustration can only come into play in the absence of an express contractual term dealing with the particular contingency. If the parties have expressed themselves as to a particular situation, then their agreement is paramount and the doctrine of frustration cannot displace their contractual obligations. Because of the uncertainty as to an underlying theory, it is difficult to identify the precise circumstances in which the doctrine of frustration will apply. However, consideration of a number of illustrations of its application may be a useful guide.

Instances of frustration . . . impossibility of performance, as in *Taylor* v. *Caldwell*, is perhaps the most simple situation in which to predict application of the doctrine of frustration. Indeed, section 7 of the Sale of Goods Act 1979 applies this rule to contracts for the sale of goods and provides that in relation to sales of specific goods where the goods perish after the making of the contract, but before ownership of the goods has passed from the seller to the buyer, the contract of sale is avoided. In short, the seller will be relieved of his obligation to perform the contract and deliver goods which no longer exist. This rule is subject to neither party being at fault. Thus, should either party be responsible for the destruction of the goods, then the rule will not avoid the contract. Either the seller, because of his fault, will be liable in damages for having failed to perform the contract or, the buyer, because of his fault, will be obliged to pay for goods of which he will not have the benefit.

Where the performance of a contract is legal at the time of the making of the contract, it may come to pass, because of a prohibition by government, that performance of the contract is illegal. Thus, in *Metropolitan Water Board* v. *Dick, Kerr & Co.*, the defendants undertook to build a reservoir within six years. The work commenced, but owing to a national emergency the defendants were ordered to cease work and instead, build a munitions factory. The plaintiffs sought to show that the defendants ought to continue with the contract to build the reservoir upon cessation of the national emergency. The court held that the illegality of further performance having intervened, such an interruption would result in the contract, if resumed, being entirely different from that originally agreed. In fact the prices of raw materials and labour had increased greatly and to have called upon the defendants to perform their contract would have been unjust. The defendants were, accordingly, relieved of further performance as the original contract was frustrated.

The significance of this latter case lies in the fact that the court was willing to apply the doctrine of frustration despite the fact that performance of the original contract was not impossible but merely more onerous. This leads to a class of cases in which frustration may apply, where there may be said to be *commercial* frustration, despite performance being theoretically possible. The difficulty of predicting the application of the doctrine to such cases is revealed by the contrasting cases of *Krell* v. *Henry* and *Herne Bay Steamboat Co.* v. *Hutton.* The cases both arose out of the illness of King Edward VII, which prevented the King attending his official engagements. In *Krell* v. *Henry*, rooms were rented overlooking the route of the King's coronation procession. The contract did not specifically refer to the purpose of the letting, but because of the specific date agreed the court formed the opinion that the opportunity to view the procession was the foundation of the contract. The contract was frustrated by cancellation of the coronation and performance was excused. In the *Herne Bay Steamboat* case, the plaintiff had chartered a steamboat in order to cruise round the fleet assembled at Spithead and also to witness the Royal review of the assembled warships. Again, the King could not oblige, but the court found that because the royal review was not the sole foundation of the contract, the contract was not frustrated.

Finally, it must be emphasised that mere additional expense or difficulty in performing a contract will not relieve a party from performance. Thus, in *Davis Contractors Ltd.* v. *Fareham Urban District Council* the plaintiffs undertook to build council houses for a fixed sum. The work took almost three times as long as anticipated owing to labour difficulties. This, of course, involved the contractors in considerable additional expense, but the court held that this alone did not frustrate the contract. Similarly, in *The Noblee Thorl*, it was held that when shippers were obliged, because of the Suez Canal crisis, to travel from the East to Europe via the Cape of Good Hope, a contract of shipment was not frustrated. It may be added that, in *The Eugenia*, where a ship became trapped in the Suez Canal by the war, no frustration could be claimed because the master of the ship had sailed into the hostile area and was "at fault." In short, *self-induced* "frustration" cannot discharge a contract.

Consequences of frustration . . . when a contract is frustrated, it is brought immediately to an end and the parties are relieved from performance. However, normally it is only performance by one party which is rendered impossible and it is commonly the case that the other party has already performed his obligation. An essential feature of the law relating to frustration is the regulation or distribution of loss arising out of the frustration. Thus, if one party has already performed his obligation and the other has been relieved of his, the court must determine whether it can compensate the party who has performed for loss of the reciprocal obligation. Perhaps the most simple illustration of the problem arises where one party has made a payment in advance and a frustrating event prevents his benefiting from the expected contractual performance. On the one hand, the party who has paid may feel that he ought to be able to recover his money. On the other hand, the other contracting party may have incurred expenses in preparation for his performance and may feel that he ought to be able to retain his fee as it was not his fault that he was prevented from performance. The old law was simple, "loss lay where it fell." For example, in the circumstances of a frustrated contract for a room overlooking the coronation procession, a deposit paid in advance was irrecoverable but money remaining payable after the frustrating event ceased to be payable. However, this rule was qualified in the *Fibrosa* case. Here, in July 1939, a Polish company agreed to buy machinery from an English company for £4,800. A thousand pounds was paid immediately and the balance was payable upon delivery. German forces invaded Poland rendering delivery impossible and this frustrated the contract. The buyers sued to recover the £1,000 paid in advance of delivery and the House of Lords, forsaking the old rule, held that they were entitled to recover, as the consideration for the contract had wholly failed. But the House of Lords indicated that if there had not been a *total failure of consideration* (for example if a small part of the machinery had been delivered) then the £1,000 would have been irrecoverable. This decision meant, of course, that the English company, through no fault of its own, was deprived of any payment despite the fact that it had incurred expense in preparation for performance of the contract. The ruling in the *Fibrosa* case served to emphasise the unsatisfactory nature of "all or nothing" solutions and the Legislature stepped in to remedy the inadequacy of the judge made law. The Law Reform (Frustrated Contracts) Act 1943 now provides four simple rules:

(a) all money paid before the frustrating event is recoverable;

(b) all money payable but not in fact paid, ceases to be payable;

(c) where a party has incurred expenses before the frustrating event, he may retain, or recover in respect of those expenses, a sum not exceeding any amounts paid or payable before the frustrating event; and

(d) where a party has obtained a valuable benefit under the contract, he may be required to pay a proper sum in respect of that benefit.

These rules are of general application, although certain types of contract are exceptionally excluded from their operation. In particular, where contracts for the sale of specific goods are avoided by frustration (see section 7 of Sale of Goods Act 1979 considered earlier) the old judge made rule, that "loss lies where it falls," remains. This is an area in which firmly established principles of great antiquity have been recognised and, therefore, normally, parties will know the nature of their risk and obligation. The same considerations underlie the exclusion of contracts of insurance and contracts for the carriage of goods by sea from the operation of the 1943 Act. It has long been the understanding of insurers that once a premium is paid and the risk undertaken by the insurer there should be "no apportionment or return of the premium afterwards," even though the subject-matter of the risk should disappear. "If I insure against sickness on January 1st and die on February 1st, my executors cannot get back $^{11}/_{12}$ of the premium."

REMEDIES ON BREACH OF CONTRACT

Damages

The basic objective in awarding damages to a party suffering loss consequent upon a breach of contract is to place the innocent party as nearly as may be in the position he would have been in had the contract been performed. Thus, damages are assessed as equal to the loss sustained by the breach of contract. The leading case laying down the basic principles for assessment of damages for breach of contract is *Hadley* v. *Baxendale*, where it was stated that "The damages ... should be such as may fairly and reasonably be considered as either arising naturally, that is according to the usual course of things, from the breach of contract itself, or such as may reasonably be supposed to have been in the contemplation of both parties at the time they made the contract, as the probable result of the breach of it."

When assessing damages the court will assess loss under various heads, being guided by the two limbs of the rule in *Hadley* v. *Baxendale*. The first limb allows for loss *arising naturally* from the breach of contract itself; for example, the difference in the value of a perfect article from the value of the defective article sold. The second limb allows for loss *reasonably supposed to have been in the contemplation of the parties* when they made the contract as being the likely consequence of a breach; for example, loss of profits. Where goods are sold in circumstances in which it is indicated that the buyer intends to re-sell, then the seller will be liable to compensate the buyer for loss of profit which he would have made upon resale. This profit will, however, only be the normal level of profit and if the buyer actually loses a particularly advantageous sub-contract he cannot recover this additional higher profit as damages (unless he has advised the seller of the unusual consequences of breach). In *Victoria Laundry* v. *Newman's Industries* the sellers failed to deliver a boiler which the buyers had ordered for their business. The buyers had not revealed that they anticipated an exceptionally high profit from immediate use of the boiler to perform an unusually lucrative contract. It was held that the buyers could recover, as damages for breach of contract, loss of normal profit but not the exceptionally high level of profit actually lost. In addition to the special damages, which can be precisely calculated, the court may also in appropriate cases award sums by way of general damages for distress, vexation or the like, arising from breach. These awards are, however, subject to the basic principles and must have been contemplated as likely to result from the breach. Thus, in *Jarvis* v. *Swans Tours Ltd.* a tour operator was held liable to a disappointed holiday-maker when his vacation turned out to be a pale shadow of that promised. Disappointment must have been contemplated when, for example, a swift burst on a homegoing workman's accordion was provided as a "traditional Swiss evening." But, the Court of Appeal in *Bliss* v. *South East Thames Regional Health Authority* has emphasised that such awards should only be made where pleasure, peace of mind or freedom from stress are objectives of the contractual undertaking.

The anxiety of the law to permit parties to regulate their own agreements naturally leads to the practice of parties agreeing in advance upon fixed (or *liquidated*) sums being payable in the event of specified breaches. However, should a sum be fixed as a "penalty" in an attempt to coerce a party to keep his agreement, then equity may step in to disallow the penalty should it greatly exceed the actual loss likely to result from breach.

Mitigation ... it is a general principle that the plaintiff must take reasonable steps to mitigate or minimise loss and this applies equally to claims in contract or tort. However, it should be noted that it has recently been held in *Basildon District Council* v. *J. E. Lessor (Properties) Ltd.* that the defence of *contributory negligence* (discussed at page 180) has no place in the law of contract.

Taxation ... in quantifying the damages in contract (and tort) the court will pay regard to the incidence of taxation. Thus, it was decided in *British Transport Commission* v. *Gourley* that, since the plaintiff ought not to make a profit out of the wrong done to him, the figure to be awarded under the head of loss of earnings should be his earnings *after* tax.

Specific performance and injunction

The most significant non-monetary remedies are those of *specific performance* and *injunction*. These equitable remedies are available at the *discretion* of the court for, unlike an award of damages, they are not available as of right. For this reason, a failure to seek redress promptly may result in a court refusing assistance because "delay defeats equity" (see page 27). Thus, these remedies may be lost even though statutory limitation periods have not expired (see page 161).

The remedy of specific performance is an order from the court directing that a particular obligation be actually performed; such an order will only be made where damages would be inadequate compensation. Thus, in most cases of breach of contract an award of monetary compensation will be sufficient to place the injured party into the position he would have been in had the contract actually been performed. However, where, for example, the contract was for the sale of an antique of unique quality, then only an order to actually transfer the ownership of the antique will meet the requirements of the situation. This remedy is most appropriate where there is a refusal to carry out a contract for the sale of land, for no two pieces of land are precisely the same, and in accordance with the principle of mutuality the remedy may be sought by either the seller or buyer. On the other hand, no such order will be made where the contract is one for the performance of personal services. Thus, in *Lumley* v. *Wagner* an order of specific performance was not granted to require an opera singer to perform a contractual undertaking to sing for a particular impresario.

An injunction is basically an order from the court directing that a particular course of action be restrained. In *Lumley* v. *Wagner* the impresario was awarded an injunction to prevent the singer from performing for anyone other than himself. "Equity follows the law" and an injunction, like an order for specific performance, will not normally be granted where damages are an adequate remedy. A court will not grant an injunction where its effect would be to compel the defendant to do something which he could not be compelled to do by an order for specific performance. Thus, in *Page One Records Ltd.* v. *Britton*, the plaintiff unsuccessfully sought an injunction to prevent a pop group from engaging as their manager anyone other than himself. Since it was found judicially that pop groups need managers, the grant of an injunction would have required the defendants to employ the plaintiff and as the contract was one

for personal services an order for specific performance could not have
been awarded.

REMEDIES FOR MISREPRESENTATION

As previously indicated, misrepresentations inducing parties to enter into
contracts may be either fraudulent or innocent. Innocent misrepresentation may be either:

(a) made by a party who had "reasonable ground to believe and did
     believe up to the time the contract was made that the facts
     represented were true," in which case the misrepresentation may be
     said to be *wholly innocent*; or

(b) made by a party who, although not fraudulent, is unable to show
     that he falls within the first category and may be considered to have
     made a *negligent* misrepresentation.

The remedies for misrepresentation derive from case law and the
Misrepresentation Act 1967. Following a misrepresentation, the party
misled has two remedies. He may *rescind* the contract (set it aside as though
it had never been entered into) and, *in addition*, he may claim damages.
Thus, if the misrepresentation related to a contract for the sale of goods,
then if the goods have been delivered, they may be returned and, if they
have not been delivered, then the buyer may refuse to accept them.
Damages will be assessed as for a breach of contract. However, the
equitable remedy of rescission is discretionary and if the court considers
that justice will not be best served by awarding rescission, then *damages*
may be awarded *in lieu of rescission*. For example, rescission might well be
refused where an individual has made an innocent misrepresentation
during the sale of his house and used the proceeds of sale to purchase
another residence. In such a situation rescission could cause considerable
hardship (possibly with a "chain reaction"). Of course the damages in lieu
of rescission could compensate the "victim" of the misrepresentation for
the lower value of the house which he bought. It must be emphasised that
an award of damages in lieu of rescission does *not* preclude an additional
award of damages which may be claimed whether or not rescission is
sought. Thus, in *Gosling* v. *Anderson* the purchaser of a house, who did not
claim rescission, was awarded damages for the seller's innocent but
careless misrepresentation that the property had the benefit of planning
permission for a garage. Where, however, in an action arising out of a
misrepresentation, the misrepresentor is able to show that he was wholly
innocent, then this will preclude an award of damages and the party misled
will be left to his remedy of rescission (or damages *in lieu of rescission*).
Where fraudulent misrepresentations are made, the party telling an
untruth commits the tort of *deceit*. The party misled, in addition to the
remedy of rescission, may sue for damages for deceit and these damages
may be upon a heavier scale than contractual damages and indeed, even
more generous than normal tortious damages. For example, in *Archer* v.
Brown a swindler was held liable to compensate his victim in respect of
injury to feelings. The payment was described as aggravated damages and
would have been difficult to sustain as a head of claim in an ordinary
contract action and would only rarely be sustainable in tort. However, in
such an action the plaintiff must prove the defendant's fraudulent
intention and the burden of proof is a heavy one. Today it is more likely

that a plaintiff will merely allege misrepresentation, and in this case the defendant must bear the burden of proving that he was not negligent in making the false statement if he is to avoid liability for damages for his misrepresentation. See *diagram 5* for a summary.

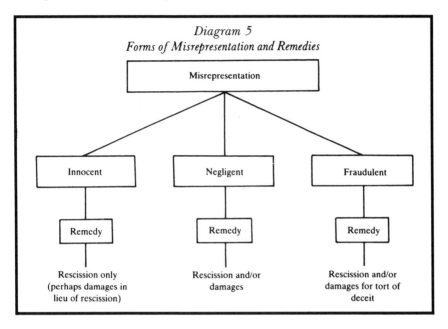

Diagram 5
Forms of Misrepresentation and Remedies

Exclusion of remedies for misrepresentation

If a contract contains a term which would exclude or restrict:

(a) any liability to which a party to a contract may be subject as a result of a misrepresentation; or

(b) any remedy which would otherwise be available to the other party to the contract as a result of the misrepresentation, then section 3 of the Misrepresentation Act 1967 provides that the term shall have no effect *except in so far as it is reasonable.* Moreover, it is for the party claiming that the term is reasonable to show that it is.

This control over terms seeking to avoid full responsibility for misrepresentation (unlike the provisions of the Unfair Contract Terms Act considered at page 367) does extend to contracts involving land. In *Walker* v. *Boyle* where a vendor in response to preliminary inquiries represented to the purchaser that she was not aware of any disputes regarding the boundaries of the property to be sold, although she ought to have been aware of such a dispute, it was held that a provision of the then *National Conditions of Sale* which stated that "no error, misstatement or omission in any preliminary answer concerning the property . . . shall annul the sale" failed the test of reasonableness. The judge said that just because an exclusion clause had been used for many years "did not entitle it to the automatic accolade of fairness and reasonableness."

However, where a contract is made by an agent on behalf of a principal, the principal can limit the agent's authority to make representations by a suitable notification. If the agent then nevertheless makes a representation, the principal can disclaim liability for the statement. There is no question of the disclaimer being subjected to the reasonableness test for, as the Court of Appeal held in *Collins* v. *Howell-Jones*, there is no attempt at avoiding liability. A principal could not incur liability for an unauthorised statement of which the other party had been warned.

Non est factum

A problem closely associated with misrepresentation arises where a signature has been obtained to a written contract under circumstances in which the signatory is fundamentally mistaken as to the consequences of his action. Normally, of course, if a party acts so that a reasonable man would believe that he has assented to terms put to him he will be bound even though he did not genuinely agree. Naturally a fraudulent party cannot enforce a contract, but should the fraudulent person have subsequently contracted with an innocent third party, then the problem arises as to whether the deceived person or the innocent third party should suffer. The usual principle is that the deceived person must shoulder the burden but, in exceptional circumstances, he may plead *non est factum* (it is not my deed), deny his signature and thus by this remedy avoid the consequences of his ill-fated act.

The conditions to be met for a successful plea were re-defined by the House of Lords in *Saunders* v. *Anglia Building Society*. Here a poorly sighted lady aged 86 was induced by her nephew to sign a document, which she was unable to read, transferring the lease of her home to a business associate of her nephew. She had been told that the document favoured her nephew. After the businessman had used the lease to raise a building society loan the old lady attempted to set aside the transaction and recover the lease from the building society by pleading *non est factum*. Her plea failed. The ground rules for a successful plea may be expressed as requiring the person signing a document, whether it is complete or blank to prove:

(a) that he was not negligent; and

(b) that the document signed was *fundamentally different* from that which he intended to sign.

In *Saunders'* case, the document did not differ greatly from that which the old lady envisaged for it was a document designed to raise money which could have been used to benefit her nephew in his business ventures. Only in rare circumstances will the plea be successful, for it would appear that the rules will require that persons at least read documents and do not rely solely upon statements made by others. The busy executive signing unread papers on the say so of his secretary must beware!

QUASI-CONTRACT

In a number of instances the law itself imposes obligations which arise not from contractual agreements but from situations related to contracts. These obligations are said to be *quasi-contractual* and have very complicated historical foundations. However, it may broadly be stated that today they have a common foundation in that each involves a restitution so that one party should not be unjustly enriched at another's expense. Despite the term quasi-contract, these claims involve obligations arising otherwise than under contracts. A brief consideration of two classes of quasi-contractual claims suffices to reveal the nature of this type of relief.

Actions for money paid under "failed contracts" . . . such an action lies to recover money paid over by mistake where in fact no money was due. Thus upon the facts of *Couturier* v. *Hastie*, discussed earlier as an illustration of initial impossibility (see page 152), should money have been paid over under the mistaken impression that a contract existed when in fact it did not, then that money would be recoverable under this head. Similarly, in the *Fibrosa* case (see page 155), considered under the heading of Frustration, the £1,000 was recoverable upon a "total failure of consideration."

Actions for services and benefits conferred . . . in *Planché* v. *Colburn*, discussed earlier as an example of partial contractual performance the plaintiff was unable to earn his contractual reward because of the defendant's default, yet he had rendered a valuable service. He was, under this head, entitled to a non-contractual reward by way of *quantum meruit* ("the amount he deserves"). Such a non-contractual award was made in *British Steel Corporation* v. *Cleveland Bridge and Engineering Co. Ltd.* where British Steel undertook work, at the request of the engineering company, so as to expedite performance of an anticipated contract which, despite protracted negotiations, was never concluded. Again, the supplier of "necessaries" to a minor cannot recover any contractual reward but he is entitled to a "reasonable" sum.

LIMITATION OF ACTIONS

Rights of action arising from breaches of obligations are not enforceable for ever, and after certain periods the pursuit of legal remedies becomes barred. Consolidating legislation, the Limitation Act 1980, sets out the basic rules.

The limitation period for a claim is:

(a) where the action is founded upon a *simple* contract, six years from the date at which the cause of action arises;

(b) where the action is founded upon a *specialty* contract, 12 years from the date at which the cause of action arises.

A cause of action arises at the time of breach and not when a contract is first made. There are a number of exceptions which interfere with the basic rules. Time does not begin to run against a minor until he reaches majority and not against a person of unsound mind until his disability ceases or he dies. Once time has begun to run an intervening disability does not postpone its impact. Perhaps the most significant exception is where an action arises from fraud, or the right of action is concealed by fraud, or the action seeks relief from the consequences of mistake. Here the limitation period only begins to run when the plaintiff discovers the fraud or mistake or could with reasonable diligence have done so. Fraud in this context is not strictly interpreted but covers any "unconscionable behaviour" even though it involves no moral turpitude on the part of the defendant. For example, an action could be maintained "out of time" against an electrical contractor whose employees had concealed faulty wiring in their haste to earn bonus payments.

A claim for a debt or other liquidated sum is subject to special rules. Here time begins to run afresh where the party in breach either makes a part payment or gives a written acknowledgment of the obligation.

Section B: Tort and Other Abuses (Injury to the Person)

The term *tort* is not one that admits of easy definition. A "tort" is a civil wrong, but then so is a breach of contract. The latter can only arise after a transaction entered into by the parties (such as a sale of goods contract or a contract of employment), the former may arise from an undesired and unlooked for course of events (*e.g.* a road traffic accident). On occasions, however, one set of circumstances can give rise to both contractual and tortious wrongs. (For example, an employer owes a duty of care to those employed by him under contracts of employment, actions for breach of that duty traditionally being brought, not for breach of the contract which gives rise to the duty, but based upon the tort of Negligence.) Indeed, where the individual law consumer is forced into an undesired relationship with another, more than one type of wrong may have been committed. (For example, the road traffic accident may involve both a criminal and a civil wrong, in the latter case based upon the tort of Negligence.)

The individual's visit to the legal office may, then, be prompted by an event which may involve both criminal and civil wrongs and which may arise from a desired or undesired relationship. In the examples used thus far, the civil wrong illustrated has been the tort of *Negligence* but, for all its ever-growing importance, the sort of occurrence that gives rise to an action in Negligence is not the only type of behaviour which the law of tort aims to "control." For example, an individual may seek advice about the behaviour of a neighbour which is causing him irritation and discomfort (*Nuisance*) or about a disparaging statement made in respect of himself by another (*Defamation*). In both these cases, unlike an action in Negligence where the desired remedy would be one of compensation for the loss suffered (*damages*), the allegedly wronged individuals may wish to know if they can have the harmful behaviour brought to an end (by an *injunction*). In some cases they may also seek damages. This, therefore, adds another element to our examination, namely that the law of tort may aim to prevent injuries arising as well as to compensate for those that do occur.

We must now consider some of the recognised heads of tortious liability.

TRESPASS TO THE PERSON

The tort of trespass to the person (out of which historically the tort of Negligence developed) is presently confined to various forms of intentional interference with the person, namely battery, assault and false imprisonment. All of these offences are, of course, crimes as well as civil wrongs.

Battery

This takes place where the defendant intentionally performs an act which directly and physically affects the plaintiff's person. It is the element of intention in the defendant's actions rather than its directness which distinguishes this tort from that of Negligence. In *Letang* v. *Cooper* the plaintiff was injured when the defendant's motor car ran over her whilst she was sunbathing on a grass car park. It was held that her case was one of Negligence, not trespass. The defendant had failed to see her lying on the grass, but there was no suggestion that his action was in any way intentional.

In *Wilson* v. *Pringle* the Court of Appeal held that an intention to *injure* is not an essential ingredient of an action for trespass to the person, rather it is the *act* which has to be intentional. However, the act has to be a hostile one. Whether an act is hostile is a question of fact and may be established by reference to a variety of factors. Thus, an act is likely to be accepted as being hostile where it is undertaken in anger or where it is unlawful, even though non-threatening, as in the case of a police officer who, acting beyond her powers, touches another in order to prevent that other from walking away (*Collins* v. *Wilcock*).

Assault

Assault arises, in contrast to battery, not from physical injury caused by the defendant's actions but as a result of the fear of immediate physical harm flowing from the defendant's actions. Normally when there is a battery this will have been immediately preceded by an assault (*i.e.* the fear of contact will have been in the plaintiff's mind before the contact actually takes place). This will not always be so. For example, a person who is attacked from behind and rendered unconscious would have no apprehension of contact and thus would suffer a battery but not an assault.

It is perhaps surprising that the law should have sought to protect an individual from the mental anxiety caused by an assault, whilst taking such an ambivalent attitude towards nervous shock caused by other tortious acts (see page 172). The explanation probably lies in the historical association of assault with breach of the peace and the criminal law.

False imprisonment

This, as suggested above, is a further form of trespass to the person, arising where the actions of the defendant restrict the plaintiff's freedom of movement. This restriction must be total, so that if the defendant locks a door behind the plaintiff as he enters a room but leaves another door unlocked, the tort has not been committed. Further, even if all doors are locked there may be a reasonable escape route available (a ground-floor window perhaps) and once more the tort of false imprisonment will not lie. But, the individual faced with an escape from such imprisonment may not be acting unreasonably if he is injured whilst attempting such an escape and may recover damages for those injuries from the defendant.

What actions of a defendant may constitute false imprisonment? Opinions differ, but broadly the defendant must act intentionally and directly to restrain totally the plaintiff's freedom of movement. Thus, the person who unwittingly locks another in a room is not liable under this head, although there may be liability under the tort of Negligence. Must the plaintiff know or believe that his freedom of movement is being restricted? There is some authority to support the proposition that if the plaintiff reasonably believes his movements to be restrained, then this is sufficient. There is even limited authority to the effect that the knowledge of the plaintiff is irrelevant, so that a person can sue upon the tort of false imprisonment even though he has no knowledge, at the time, of the restraint upon his movement should he have chosen to move.

Intentional physical harm other than trespass to the person

It is appropriate at this stage to make note of a further cause of action which, if not actually arising from trespass, nevertheless seems to lie somewhere between trespass and Negligence. In *Wilkinson* v. *Downton* the defendant falsely reported to the plaintiff that her husband had been seriously injured in an accident. The plaintiff, who suffered nervous shock and subsequently physical illness, was able to recover damages, even though the report amounted to no more than a misplaced joke. This case is apparently authority for a tort which consists of an act (or statement) wilfully done (or made) and calculated to cause physical harm to another, and which does in fact cause physical harm. This tort, although by no means as fully developed in this country as in America, is neither trespass (which requires directness) nor Negligence (which normally involves a careless rather than a deliberate act).

DEFAMATION

If the tort of trespass to the person seeks to protect an individual from physical harm, the tort of defamation aims to protect his reputation in the eyes of others. As such, without adhering to any particular principles, the law (a mixture of common law and statutory rules) seeks to strike a balance between freedom of speech on the one hand and an individual's reputation on the other. Traditionally the tort of defamation is considered to consist of two forms, *slander* and *libel*, although the *Committee on Defamation* did propose that this distinction should be removed. Slander constitutes the oral form of defamation, whilst libel will normally involve a written statement. But this breakdown is not totally accurate or helpful, and a better division would be to define slander as the non-permanent form of the tort, whereas a permanent statement (not necessarily just a written piece but also perhaps a film, painting or cartoon) will, if the other elements of the tort are satisfied, amount to libel. Those other elements are that a "defamatory statement," about an individual whose "reputation" can be defamed, has been "published," in which case, subject to various defences, liability is strict and damages may be high. However, before further consideration of these matters we must examine in a little more detail the distinction between slander and libel.

Slander and libel ... perhaps the most pressing justification for distinguishing the two forms of defamation is that libel is actionable *per se*, whereas in an action for slander the plaintiff must normally prove special damage suffered by himself (*e.g.* loss of employment or of a promise of future employment, or loss of membership of a club or society). Nevertheless, even slander is actionable *per se* in certain specified circumstances, including:

(a) an allegation by the defendant that the plaintiff has committed a crime punishable by imprisonment; and

(b) an allegation made about the plaintiff calculated to disparage him in respect of an office, profession, trade or business (*e.g.* a suggestion that his conduct of an office has been corrupt or dishonest).

Defamatory nature ... it should be said at once that not every statement which an individual finds hurtful or feels to be an attack upon his standing in society necessarily constitutes defamation. The context in which the statement is made must first be examined. Thus, swearing at a work-mate on a building site or chanting by a football-crowd in order to question the parentage of a referee does not amount to defamation. One test of the defamatory nature of a statement is whether it *lowers the plaintiff in the estimation of right-thinking members of society.* One difficulty, however, with this formula is that surely "right-thinking" people ought not to think less well of an individual simply because, for example, she has been raped. In *Yousoupoff* v. *M.G.M. Pictures Ltd.* it was suggested in the defendant's film that the plaintiff, a Russian princess, had been raped by Rasputin, the mad monk. Logically no worse ought to have been thought of the innocent victim of that attack, but as Lord Devlin said in another case, "logic is not the test." The film was accepted as being defamatory because it could have led to the plaintiff being "shunned and avoided."

In determining whether or not a statement is defamatory the words used must be looked at in their ordinary and natural sense. Occasionally, however, it may not be the words themselves (or the picture or whatever constitutes the material) but the *innuendo* that readers (or viewers) are likely to draw from them, which amounts to the defamatory statement. Where such an extended meaning is claimed, it is for the plaintiff to substantiate it. In *Tolley* v. *J.S. Fry & Sons* the defendants, a firm of chocolate manufacturers, published an advertisement for their products which included a cartoon featuring the plaintiff, a well-known amateur golfer. As such, any suggestion that the plaintiff ate chocolate would not in itself have been defamatory, but the innuendo that he had in some way infringed his amateur status by appearing in the advertisement was of a defamatory nature.

Civil actions alleging defamation hold something of a unique position in law in as much as certain issues are determined not by a judge but by a jury. The former's role is to decide whether the purportedly defamatory material is capable of bearing the meaning which the plaintiff has attached to it and thus whether it *can* be defamatory. The role of the jury is to decide questions of fact including (after judicial guidance) whether the statement *is* actually defamatory.

Whose reputation? . . . not every reputation earns the protection of this tort (the dead and trade unions—no innuendo intended!—being amongst those unprotected), but protection is not confined to human reputations, those of commercial undertakings, local authorities and other corporations are also covered. Whoever's reputation is at stake the plaintiff must be sufficiently identifiable as the subject, although it is not necessary that he was intended as the subject. For example, a fictitious character may be described in defamatory terms in a book, but in fact a person of that same name may actually exist. Such a passage would be defamatory of the latter. Moreover, a statement made about one person may be true as far as that person is concerned, but may be defamatory of another person of the same name. All that is apparently necessary is that some people believe the statement to refer to the latter and that the implication is false. In *Newstead* v. *London Express Newspaper Ltd.* a newspaper reported the trial for bigamy of one Harold Newstead, a 30-year-old Camberwell man, about whom the report was true. However, some readers wrongly attributed the report to another Harold Newstead, also of Camberwell and of about the same age, about whom it was untrue and, it was held, defamatory.

Publication . . . a further essential element of the tort is publication. Liability does not fall upon a man because he holds unexpressed thoughts about another, nor indeed where he tells that other person what he thinks. Publication does not even take place when the recipient is the defendant's wife (but does if the material is published to the plaintiff's wife). Otherwise, a statement may be deemed to have been published despite any lack of intention on the defendant's part. It is sufficient that the defendant could have foreseen the consequences. For example, a statement on a postcard sent to the plaintiff which would be seen by others or in a business letter sent to the plaintiff's office, and which the defendant ought to have realised would be opened by clerks, will be published. In the same way a message left on a telephone answering machine or a letter recorded on a dictaphone would be capable of being published.

Publication is not restricted to the initial communication and a person who repeats a defamatory statement, however innocently, is liable. Thus the author, publisher, printer and distributor (*e.g.* bookshops or libraries) may all have published defamatory material. But they may be able to rely upon one or more of the various defences available.

Defences to an action for defamation

The defendant may wish to raise one or more of the following defences.

Innocent defamation . . . may arise where the defendant's actions consist only of an unknown and non-negligent distribution of defamatory material (*e.g.* by libraries or newsagents). In such cases of unintentional defamation the printers and publishers may obtain a defence by making suitable apologies (section 4 of the Defamation Act 1952).

Justification . . . is a valid defence where the defamatory statement is true, despite the injurious affect upon the plaintiff's reputation. The onus of proof lies upon the defendant.

Fair comment . . . the defendant may be able to show that his statement constitutes fair comment on a matter of public interest (*e.g.* the conduct of public officials or of a public body). Such could be considered the price of public fame. It will be for the judge to decide whether or not a matter is of "public interest." Further, the comment must not be so blatantly unfair that no honest man could have made it.

Privilege . . . in certain cases the occasion upon which the purportedly defamatory statement is made may itself give rise to a valid defence. On such occasions the maker of the statement is said to have either *absolute* or *qualified* privilege. If the occasion attracts absolute privilege then the defendant has a defence even if his statement was motivated by malice. Such occasions of absolute privilege include parliamentary proceedings, media reports of judicial proceedings and solicitor–client communications. If, on the other hand, the occasion is one of qualified privilege (*e.g.* a fair and accurate report of a public meeting), the defendant may lose his protection if the statement is made with malice (*i.e.* with no honest belief in the statement).

Consent . . . where the plaintiff has consented to the publication of the defamatory material he cannot later base an action upon that material.

Remedies

As a general rule injunctive relief (see page 188) is not available in cases of defamation and the primary remedy is, therefore, one of damages. Libel and certain forms of slander, being actionable *per se*, attract damages "at large." Damages are at large where the interest wronged by the defendant's action may not have any ascertainable monetary value but the court is free to award substantial damages. The plaintiff may also recover damages under other heads:

Aggravated damages ... where the circumstances in which the statement is publicised (its manner or its frequency) may increase the harm to the plaintiff's reputation;

Parasitic damages ... where some interest other than reputation is harmed, for example, injury to feelings or loss of hospitality;

Exemplary damages ... where the defendant has published defamatory material (contained, for example, in a book) in the hope that the resulting publicity will provide him with profits greater than any damages awarded against him.

The defendant may seek to *mitigate* the award of damages by showing that the plaintiff's reputation is bad. In this case it is the established reputation of the plaintiff which is relevant and not that which he ought to have.

NEGLIGENCE

The law consumer may approach the legal office, not because another person has done him harm either by deliberate act against his person (trespass) or by a blow to his reputation (defamation), but simply because that other person's carelessness has caused him loss. In such circumstances his action will be based upon the tort of Negligence. However, he will not succeed merely because he can establish carelessness on the part of the defendant. In *Lochgelly Iron and Coal Co.* v. *McMullan*, Lord Wright asserted that, " ... In strict legal analysis, negligence means more than heedless or careless conduct, whether in omission or commission: it properly connotes the complex concept of duty, breach and damage thereby suffered by the person to whom the duty was owing."

In an action based upon the tort of Negligence the plaintiff must, therefore, establish:

(a)   the existence of a duty of care;
(b)   a breach of that duty; and
(c)   consequent damage.

Duty of care

The plaintiff must establish that the defendant was, in relation to the activity which has harmed the plaintiff, acting under a legal obligation to be careful. Where such an obligation exists the defendant is said to owe the plaintiff a *duty of care*.

The fact that the activities of the defendant have actually caused harm to the plaintiff will not necessarily result in the existence of a duty of care. How then is the existence of such a duty to be judged? In certain factual situations it is now so well recognised that a duty of care is owed that a court faced with a case on such facts will have no difficulty in finding for the plaintiff on that point. Thus, no one is likely to argue with the general proposition that the driver of a vehicle owes a duty of care to other road users. In the same way a manufacturer of goods owes a duty of care to the ultimate user of those goods where negligent manufacture renders the goods harmful to the consumer. The existence of this latter duty was clearly established in *Donoghue* v. *Stevenson*. The plaintiff and a friend went to a cafe where the friend bought ginger beer in a dark opaque bottle which concealed the contents. After the plaintiff had consumed some of the ginger beer, the friend poured out the remainder to reveal the remains of a decomposing snail. The plaintiff suffered gastro-enteritis from consumption of the ginger beer and the impurities it contained. The plaintiff could not, of course, sue the cafe proprietor in contract, as the contract of sale had been made by the friend. The court held that the manufacturer owed a duty of care to the plaintiff as ultimate consumer of his product.

The limited ratio of *Donoghue* v. *Stevenson* can be extended to other analogous situations. Thus, the repairer of a lift clearly owes a duty of care to users of that lift. But not every set of facts giving rise to loss by one party at the hands of another will fit so easily into this supplier–ultimate consumer framework. In particular, how are the courts to deal with new situations where there is no body of precedent to assist them? In *Donoghue* v. *Stevenson* Lord Atkin advanced a test, which he, at least, clearly intended to be of general application, to determine this question. By this test, commonly known as the "neighbour-test," an individual must take care not to injure his "neighbour." To the question "who is my neighbour?" Lord Atkin replied that one's neighbour is anyone who is "so closely and directly affected by any act that I ought reasonably to have them in contemplation as being so affected when I am directing my mind to the acts or omissions which are called in question." Thus, if I could have foreseen that my act or omission would have caused harm to another, then that other is my neighbour, and I owe him a duty of care.

The courts themselves have adopted an equivocal stance towards Lord Atkin's formulation. Whilst it has been stated on various occasions that the categories of negligence are never closed, the courts have not always been prepared to admit of the existence of a duty of care merely because the defendant's act would have foreseeably resulted in harm. The grounds for this reluctance to recognise a duty owed by defendant to plaintiff were once frequently hidden in legal argument, but more recently the judiciary has been prepared to admit openly that "policy" considerations have a role to play. Whatever the justification advanced in any particular case, it is possible to point to a number of exceptions to the "neighbour-test" where the courts have refrained from recognising, except perhaps to a limited extent, the existence of a duty of care (*no-duty situations*). But perhaps first it would be helpful to consider some of those cases where a duty of care has been held to exist (*duty situations*).

Duty situations

It was stated earlier that in certain factual situations it would not be difficult for a court to find that the defendant owed a duty of care to the plaintiff (*e.g.* the duty owed by an employer towards his employees for their safety—see page 314). In other cases such ready acceptance of a duty may not have been forthcoming, but even so a duty may have been acknowledged on the particular facts. In *Dutton* v. *Bognor Regis U.D.C.*, for example, a purchaser of a house was held to be the "neighbour" of a local authority who, through their building inspector, negligently approved the foundations prior to its being built. As a result, the purchaser was able to bring an action against the local authority when structural defects manifested themselves. In *Home Office* v. *Dorset Yacht Co.* the House of

Lords held that the Home Office, through its officers, owed a duty of care to the plaintiff, whose yacht was damaged when some borstal trainees escaped from an institution one night due to the alleged negligence of the officers. The majority of the House believed that Lord Atkin's neighbour principle had the status, if not of a statutory definition, then at least of a rule which ought to apply unless there was some justification or valid explanation for its exclusion. However, in Lord Diplock's opinion the issue did not rest solely upon foreseeability but also upon previous decisions and matters of policy, and he restricted the ambit of the duty of care to those (like the plaintiff) in the immediate vicinity of the borstal.

The issue of the basis for the existence of a duty of care was considered once more by the House of Lords in *Anns* v. *London Borough of Merton*. Lord Wilberforce, giving the leading judgment, stated that in order to establish that a duty of care arose in a particular situation, it was not necessary to bring the facts of that situation within those of previous situations in which a duty of care had been held to exist. Rather the court had to answer two questions. First, was there a sufficient relationship of proximity or neighbourhood between the defendant and plaintiff such that the former ought reasonably to have contemplated that carelessness on his part would be likely to cause damage to the latter? If so, then secondly, were there any grounds for negativing, reducing or limiting the scope of duty or the class of persons to whom it was owed or the damages to which a breach of it might give rise? In other words, even if the relationship of defendant and plaintiff was sufficiently proximate to give rise to a prima facie duty, were there any considerations, on grounds of policy or otherwise, which should exclude the plaintiff's claim?

In *Governors of the Peabody Donation Fund* v. *Sir Lindsay Parkinson & Co. Ltd.* Lord Keith held that such other grounds might include considerations of what is "just and reasonable." Here, the plaintiff developers sought to recover from the local authority for loss caused by delays in development which ensued because of a defective drainage system installed with the knowledge of the authority's inspector. However, the plaintiffs' own architects had instructed that the drains which were installed should be different from those shown in the approved plans. In Lord Keith's opinion it would be neither just nor reasonable to impose upon the authority a liability to indemnify the plaintiffs against their loss. It is clear that his Lordship believed that the ambit of the decision in *Anns* was restricted to cases where the apprehended injury was to the health or safety of owners or occupiers. In *Leigh & Sillavan Ltd.* v. *Aliakmon Shipping Co. Ltd.* Lord Brandon added the need for certainty as a reason for not extending duty situations. He also stated that in his opinion the *dicta* of Lord Wilberforce did not, and had not been intended to, provide a universally applicable test of the existence and scope of a duty of care. On the other hand, in *Emeh* v. *Kensington and Chelsea and Westminster Area Health Authority* the Court of Appeal rejected an earlier view that public policy in the support of the sanctity of life prevented a woman recovering the financial damage sustained by her as a result of a birth following a negligent failure to perform a sterilisation operation properly.

No-duty situations

In the same way that earlier decisions on analogous facts have established the existence of a duty of care, so the courts have developed certain situations where no duty of care will exist. Whilst there may not necessarily be any consistent thread of policy running through the cases, nevertheless it is possible to consider these cases under certain headings:

(a) economic loss;
(b) negligent misstatements;
(c) omissions to act;
(d) nervous shock; and
(e) trespassers to land.

Economic loss . . . it is well settled that there is no liability in the tort of Negligence where the *loss suffered* is purely economic or pecuniary loss. Thus, in *Weller* v. *Foot and Mouth Disease Research Institute* the court would not award damages, for "loss of commission," to auctioneers whose business it was to sell cattle, at a cattle market which was closed, as a result of an outbreak of foot and mouth caused by an escape of virus from a laboratory operated by the defendants. The reluctance to award damages to compensate for economic loss may appear unfair; it stems, however, from a perfectly acceptable premise, that there should be some limit to the liability arising out of a careless act. In *S.C.M.* v. *Whittall and Sons*, Lord Denning M.R. asserted that, " . . . the risk should be borne by the whole community who suffer the losses rather than rest on one pair of shoulders, that is, on the defendant who may, or may not, be insured against the risk." Would it have been reasonable on the facts of *Weller's* case to have awarded damages to the auctioneers (and to other auctioneers); to those butchers who normally bought their meat at the local market (and who, following the outbreak, had to buy more expensively, as a result of transportation costs and a swollen demand, at other markets); and to those consumers who, ultimately, paid more for their Sunday joints? There must, surely, be a point at which liability stops. The courts have identified this point as that at which loss is purely financial. However, if the defendant suffers physical injury and, in consequence, suffers financial loss resulting from, say, a loss of earnings, the damages awarded will compensate for his financial, as well as for his physical, loss. In *S.C.M.* v. *Whittall and Sons* the court held that loss of profits attributable to physical damage caused to factory machinery could be recovered. In that case the defendants negligently damaged a cable providing electricity to the plaintiff's factory, causing the factory to be without electricity for several hours. Molten metal in certain of the plaintiff's machines solidified and, in removing the metal, the plaintiff damaged his machinery. The court held that the plaintiff could recover in respect of the loss of profits resulting from this damage to the machinery. The court would not, however, award damages in respect of the loss of profit resulting from the inactivity of the undamaged machines whilst there was no power available, for such loss was purely economic.

In *Spartan Steel and Alloys Ltd.* v. *Martin & Co.*, the plaintiff's loss in similar circumstances consisted of a damaged production batch, the loss of profit on that particular batch and loss of profits on four more batches which could not be processed due to lack of power. In allowing the first two claims but not the last Lord Denning advanced various justifications in addition to the principle of risk-spreading asserted in *S.C.M.* v. *Whittall & Sons*. The type of hazard involved in cases such as these, Lord Denning suggested, was the sort that most people accepted and put up with, or at least took steps themselves to ameliorate the consequences. Such attitudes should be encouraged. Further, the law should not encourage the bringing of false or inflated claims for damages in cases such as interruptions to electricity supply, where proof would be very difficult. Whether Lord Denning's fears of a multiplicity of unreasonable claims are justified is arguable. It is clear, however, that the basic principle involved here, namely non-recovery of purely economic loss, applies even to those cases where there is only one potential plaintiff who has suffered solely financial loss, unless a court is willing to hold that the particular plaintiff is so proximate (see above) that there are no grounds of policy or otherwise upon which the duty owed or damages recoverable should fail (see *Ross* v. *Caunters*, page 175). In *Junior Books Ltd.* v. *Veitchi Co. Ltd.* it was held that just such a proximate relationship existed. The plaintiffs had contracted with a contractor for the construction of a factory and nominated a sub-contractor, as a specialist flooring contractor, to lay the floor. This task was performed negligently by the sub-contractor and the floor proved to be defective, although there was no risk of physical injury to persons or property. The House of Lords, by a majority, held that the sub-contractors were liable for the cost of repairing the floor and the profits lost in the meantime. Emphasis was placed upon the very close relationship between the parties, which fell only just short of a contractual relationship. Indeed later cases have sought to confine the ratio of *Junior Books* to its special facts. Thus in *Muirhead* v. *Industrial Tank Specialities Ltd.* a wholesale fish merchant decided to store lobsters in a storage tank installed by the first defendant. Sea water was to be pumped into, and recirculated around, the tank by pumps also installed by the first defendant but manufactured by a foreign manufacturer of electrical equipment. The pumps proved to be unsuitable for use in the United Kingdom and failed. As a result the merchant lost his stock of lobsters and sued to recover for that loss and for his lost profit, the cost of the defective pumps and the cost of servicing them (the last two heads being purely economic loss). In the event the first defendant went into liquidation and the action proceeded against the pump manufacturer with whom the merchant had had no contract and no contact and upon whom he had placed no reliance. The Court of Appeal reviewed *Junior Books* and concluded that the present case was no different from that of an ordinary purchaser of manufactured goods who, having suffered financial loss due to a defect in those goods, could only look to the vendor and not to the ultimate manufacturer to recover damages for purely economic loss. Thus, the fish merchant was confined to recovery in respect of his lost stock and the consequential loss of profit and not for the defective pumps which had caused those losses.

Negligent misstatements . . . there is in fact one class of negligent acts where the courts have been prepared to relax the apparently rigid rule for economic loss, that is where the financial loss is suffered as a result of a negligent misstatement on the defendant's part. But even here liability is by no means certain and the cases are capable of such subtle distinctions that they merit and receive separate treatment below (see page 173).

Omissions to act . . . in English law the basic rule is that a pure omission to act is not actionable in tort. To be actionable an omission must normally be based upon a special relationship between the parties such as that between employer and employee, or occupier and visitor. In any event, for a duty to lie the omission must relate to circumstances in which there is a positive duty to act. Lord Atkin in enunciating his neighbour-test clearly recognised situations in which there may be a duty to act when he stated that a person should avoid acts *or omissions* which would cause harm to another. It may be, for example, that a motorist, who fails to look for other traffic when turning at a road junction, is guilty of an "omission." However, no one would deny that a motorist owes a duty of care to other road-users and the "omission" in the above example is but one step in the negligent performance of that duty. On the other hand, where a person, seeing a man hanging from a ladder from which he has slipped, takes no steps to assist him even though he has the means to do so, there is no liability since there is no positive duty to act. But, should he attempt a rescue he is under a duty not to aggravate the plaintiff's position.

Nervous shock . . . in the same way, though for different reasons, that the law has been reluctant to compensate for purely economic loss, so the courts have only gradually recognised the causing of nervous shock as actionable. Indeed, the term "nervous shock" means in these circumstances, not distress or grief, but actual illness. This might be physical illness brought about by the shock or genuine mental illness. In these circumstances, at least, the courts were forced by medical evidence to accept the genuineness of the condition. Thus in *Dulieu* v. *White* it was accepted that the plaintiff could recover from nervous shock, even in the absence of other physical injury, where it resulted from fear for her own safety when the defendant's vehicle crashed into the public house where she was working. In *Hambrook* v. *Stokes* the Court of Appeal was ready to take this rule a step further by allowing recovery in respect of a mother who, on seeing a runaway lorry, feared not for her own safety but that of her children. Indeed, liability for nervous shock without physical injury has since been found in other situations where a special relationship has existed between plaintiff and victim or potential victims: a fellow employee in *Dooley* v. *Cammell Laird* and a rescuer in *Chadwick* v. *British Transport Commission*.

In *Bourhill* v. *Young*, in contrast, the plaintiff failed in a claim alleging that she suffered nervous shock as a consequence of "witnessing" an accident which had resulted from the defendant's negligence. In fact, whilst she had heard the collision, the plaintiff had not seen it, although she had later seen the blood left on the road after the defendant's body had been moved. The House of Lords held that the defendant owed her no duty of care since she herself had been in no danger nor had she actually seen the incident. In *Hinz* v. *Berry*, whilst the plaintiff also did not see the actual impact she both heard and saw the immediate result of an accident in which her husband was killed and her children injured when a motor car ran them down as they prepared a road-side picnic on the opposite side of the road. She was entitled to recover in respect of nervous shock.

If nervous shock has been recognised as actionable at least where there is risk of physical injury to the plaintiff, or a sufficiently close relationship between plaintiff and victim where the former "witnesses" the accident, should liability be extended to the plaintiff who neither sees or hears, nor is in the immediate vicinity of the accident, but who is informed about it later? In *Wilkinson* v. *Downton* such liability was upheld but there the defendant's act was a deliberate one and not merely a case of negligent action (see page 164). More recently in *McLoughlin* v. *O'Brian* the House of Lords was prepared to extend the duty of care to a mother whose husband and three children were involved in an accident caused by the defendant's negligence. One child was killed and the rest of the family badly injured. The plaintiff first heard of the accident from a neighbour before being taken to hospital where she saw the full extent of the tragedy. The House held that the test for liability was reasonable foreseeability of injury by shock as a result of the defendant's negligence. What was foreseeable, Lord Wilberforce added, was governed by three factors, namely the nature of the tie or relationship between the plaintiff and the injured person, the proximity of the plaintiff to the accident in time and space, and the means of communication by which the shock was caused. On the facts of the case all three factors operated in favour of the plaintiff. There was the obvious close tie between the mother and her family; she had come upon the "immediate aftermath" of the accident; and having done so she had witnessed the full horror of the injuries before treatment. It should be noted that as regards communication, his Lordship ruled out shock brought about by communication by a third party but left open the possibility that some equivalent of sight or hearing (for example, "through simultaneous television") might suffice. Also of interest is the fact that the Court of Appeal had rejected the plaintiff's claim on policy grounds. Lord Wilberforce stated the four policy arguments to be:

    (a)   the fear that too wide an extension of liability might lead to a proliferation of claims, some possibly fraudulent;

    (b)   that such an extension would be unfair to defendants as imposing damages out of proportion to the negligent conduct;

    (c)   increased evidentiary difficulties tending to protracted litigation; and

    (d)   that an extension of the scope of liability ought only to be made by the legislature, after careful research.

His Lordship believed that these arguments could be satisfactorily answered.

Trespassers to land . . . at one time it was believed that the only duty owed by an occupier of land to those who trespassed upon it was a duty not to wilfully harm them or to act with reckless disregard for their safety. It is now accepted, however, that an occupier owes even trespassers upon his land a limited duty of care (see page 357).

Negligent misstatements

It was indicated earlier that the one area where the courts have more readily relaxed the rule about liability for purely economic loss is in relation to misstatements. This is not wholly surprising since the type of damage that will usually, though not invariably, ensue upon a misstatement will be financial rather than physical. However, the attitude of the courts has not always been the same. From the end of the last century it was the common, but not universal, view that, in the absence of fraud, liability for making a misstatement rested upon a contractual or fiduciary relationship between maker and receiver (a *fiduciary relationship* is analogous to that existing between a trustee and the beneficiary under a trust). Where the misstatement was fraudulent then the plaintiff could recover damages under the tort of deceit. This view prevailed unchanged, if not unchallenged, despite the apparent liberalisation brought about by *Donoghue* v. *Stevenson* until a decision of the House of Lords in the early 1960s.

In *Hedley Byrne & Co. Ltd.* v. *Heller & Partners Ltd.* the plaintiffs, a firm of advertising agents, wanted information about the credit-worthiness of

"E," a potential customer. The plaintiffs' bankers therefore sought references from the client's bankers, the defendants in this action. The defendants gave favourable references about "E," but stated that they were made "without responsibility." In reliance on these references the plaintiffs made payments which they were unable to recover when "E" went into liquidation. The plaintiffs unsuccessfully brought an action claiming damages based upon the defendants' alleged negligence in giving the favourable references. But the plaintiffs' failure resulted from the defendants' express disclaimer of responsibility and not from any unwillingness on the part of the House of Lords to recognise the possible existence of a duty of care in making statements.

This much can be easily stated. It is more difficult to locate a thread that is common to all their Lordships' judgments, which dealt with broad principles rather than specific criteria. All agreed that liability for negligent misstatements differed from that for negligent actions, and thus the principles of *Donoghue* v. *Stevenson* were not directly relevant. In the former case it was said that the duty of care depended upon a special relationship between the parties, but different explanations were given as to the necessary nature of this relationship. In general terms it would seem that the duty of care will arise from an express or implied undertaking that the maker of a statement will exercise care in giving information or advice. This undertaking is not founded upon contract and need not therefore be supported by consideration.

In view of the significance of the *Hedley Byrne* decision to the development of the tort of Negligence it is not surprising that the House, on an issue which was essentially *obiter* given the disclaimer of responsibility, should step carefully and that, like their treatment of *Donoghue* v. *Stevenson*, the courts are still testing the limits of this head of liability. In one case, *Mutual Life and Citizens' Assurance Co.* v. *Evatt*, the Privy Council offered an opinion on this issue which appears to restrict considerably the ambit of *Hedley Byrne*. In *Evatt's* case the plaintiff, a policyholder with the defendant insurance company, sought advice from that company about the financial standing of an associated company, in which the plaintiff held shares. On the basis of the defendant's reply the plaintiff invested more money in the other company, which later collapsed. On a preliminary point the majority of the Privy Council believed that the plaintiff's claim disclosed no cause of action. For them the issue turned on the answers to the following questions:

(a) Was the defendant in the business of supplying information?
(b) Did the defendant claim to possess the necessary skill to give the information and to be prepared to exercise due diligence in giving reliable advice?

The answer to both questions, on the facts, was negative. Even where the answer to the first question is affirmative, few are likely to saddle themselves with the burden inherent in the second and accordingly the majority view in *Evatt's* case does appear to seriously limit the flexibility of the *Hedley Byrne* approach. However, the *Evatt* decision, whilst persuasive, is not of course binding upon English courts and has been viewed unfavourably in more than one later decision. It is true that the scope of the *Hedley Byrne* decision is such that the number of potential plaintiffs in some situations is endless. Thus there must be some limit, but rather than adopting a rigid criteria, it would seem more beneficial to leave the courts to find that no duty exists in certain circumstances (where, for example, the number of potential plaintiffs is great).

In the years since 1964 the issue of liability for negligent misstatements has arisen on various occasions apart from the *Evatt* case. For present purposes the cases can be considered in three arbitrary groupings, namely those involving:

(a) legal advisers;
(b) judges and arbitrators; and
(c) other professional men.

Legal advisers . . . it was held in *Midland Bank Trust* v. *Hett, Stubbs and Kemp* that a solicitor could be sued in the tort of Negligence as well as in contract by his client. Barristers, on the other hand, do not of course have any contractual relationship with their clients, for them any liability would perforce arise in tort, but at least in relation to the conduct of litigation a barrister (and, less frequently, a solicitor) owes no duty of care towards his client. In *Rondel* v. *Worsley* this immunity was justified by the House of Lords on the ground (*inter alia*) that a barrister could not properly fulfil his duty to the court or to the administration of justice with the threat of actions for negligence from clients hanging over him. In *Saif Ali* v. *Sydney Mitchell* the House extended this immunity to certain pre-trial work. However, even if the legal adviser is entitled to this privileged position compared to other professional men, there is no reason to protect him when it comes to "pure paperwork" such as the drafting of wills and settlements. Thus, in *Ross* v. *Caunters* a solicitor was held liable in negligence to a beneficiary under a will which, on the solicitor's advice, had been wrongly drawn up. Liability in this case, however, was not based upon *Hedley Byrne* but upon general principles of Negligence flowing from *Donoghue* v. *Stevenson*. Since the defendant had the plaintiff specifically in mind when advising the testator, there was a sufficient degree of proximity between the parties for a duty of care to arise, even though the plaintiff's loss was purely financial.

Judges and arbitrators . . . it is well settled that on grounds of *public policy* a judge has general immunity from suit (*Sirros* v. *Moore*). It has been argued that this immunity extends to arbitrators, although dicta of the House of Lords in *Arenson* v. *Casson Beckman Rutley & Co.* raise questions as to the existence or scope of any such immunity. There, on the facts, the arbitrator's function was not to settle a dispute but merely to value shares, he enjoyed no immunity and did owe a duty of care in respect of the valuation (to both seller and prospective buyer). In this respect he did not differ from any other professional man exercising his skill and judgment.

Other professional men . . . there is in principle no reason why injury which arises from a negligent statement should be treated differently from injury arising from a negligent action. In practice the potential scope of liability may force the courts to refuse to admit to a duty of care in a particular case. Nevertheless, on occasions liability has been found to be based upon some oral or written statement carelessly made. In *Sutcliffe* v. *Thackrah* an architect granting certificates of completion of work under a building contract was held to owe a duty of care to his client in respect of the certification. In *J.E.B. Fasteners Ltd.* v. *Marks, Bloom & Co.* it was stated that accountants preparing the accounts of a company in need of financial support ought reasonably to have foreseen that those accounts would be relied upon by persons proposing to give that support, possibly by means of a take-over. In *Yianni* v. *Edwin Evans & Sons* the plaintiffs, prospective house purchasers, relied upon a valuation report prepared by the defendants, a firm of valuers and surveyors, for the building society from which they hoped to obtain a mortgage. The plaintiffs, who had to pay for this valuation, did not seek an independent survey, although advised to do so by the building society, and accepted the mortgage offered. Serious cracks caused by subsidence were later discovered. Whilst admitting their negligence in preparation of the report, the defendants denied that they owed a duty of care to the plaintiffs. The court held, nevertheless, that the defendants ought reasonably to have had the plaintiffs in contemplation as persons who would rely upon their statement that the house provided adequate security for the proposed mortgage, notwithstanding the building society's warning. Thus a duty of care was owed.

In these three examples it can be seen that there was a sufficient relationship of proximity (see dicta of Lord Wilberforce in *Anns* v. *London Borough of Merton* above, page 169) for a duty of care to exist. The courts were not faced with potentially limitless numbers of plaintiffs and therefore were, perhaps, more willing to find against the defendants.

Breach of duty

Having established that a duty of care exists, the plaintiff must show that the defendant was in breach of that duty, or, in other words, that he did not observe the necessary *standard of care*. The standard against which the defendant's actions will be judged is that of *reasonableness*. In *Blyth* v. *Birmingham Waterworks Co.* Alderson B. asserted that, " . . . Negligence is the omission to do something which a reasonable man, guided upon those considerations which ordinarily regulate the conduct of human affairs, would do, or doing something which a prudent and reasonable man would not do." Whilst, however, the standard of care expected is normally that of the reasonable man, a defendant who has held himself out as having a particular expertise will be required to observe the standard of care expected of someone with that expertise. On the other hand, a householder who engages in D-I-Y (at least in relation to small tasks) is expected to show the standard of care of a reasonably competent amateur, not that of the professional. In *Nettleship* v. *Weston* by way of contrast, the Court of Appeal held that a learner-driver must reach the standard of a reasonably competent qualified driver. Failure to do so in the instant case resulted in liability for injury to a passenger (her driving instructor!). If such a result appears at first sight surprising, it no doubt turns on considerations relating to public policy and the existence of insurance against liability in road traffic cases. The same considerations underlie the decision in *Roberts* v. *Ramsbottom* where the defendant had unknowingly suffered a stroke, which so clouded his consciousness that from that moment he had been, through no fault of his own, unable properly to control his car or to realise that fact. Despite his physical condition the defendant was held liable in Negligence for a collision with another car.

In the case of treatment and diagnosis by a medical practitioner it was held in *Bolam* v. *Friern Hospital Management Committee* that a doctor discharges his duty if he acts in accordance with a practice accepted as proper by a body of responsible and skilled medical opinion. In *Sidaway* v. *Board of Governors of the Bethlem Royal Hospital and the Maudsley Hospital* the House of Lords held that the same test should be adopted when it came to advising a patient of the risks inherent in a proposed course of treatment. If this test allows the medical profession to be determiners of their own standards, it was side-stepped recently in *Gold* v. *Haringey Health Authority*. Here it was held that the *Bolam* test was an exceptional rule which did not apply to contraceptive counselling. Rather it was for the court to decide whether a person giving advice acted negligently in failing to warn of the risks of other forms of contraception. Current opinion and practice in the profession were merely two of the relevant considerations to be taken into account by the court in reaching that decision.

When determining whether or not the defendant has acted reasonably, the court will take into consideration factors such as:

(a) the extent to which it was likely that injury would be caused;
(b) the extent to which it was likely that if injury was to result, that injury would be serious; and
(c) the cost of ensuring that no injury would be caused.

Whilst these factors are here considered separately, a court would need to consider their interrelationship. Thus the likelihood of injury being caused may have to be balanced against the value to society in the defendant pursuing his activities.

The likelihood of injury being caused ... in *Fardon* v. *Harcourt-Rivington* Lord Dunedin asserted that, " ... if the possibility of danger emerging is only a mere possibility which would never occur to the mind of a reasonable man, then there is no negligence in not having taken extraordinary precautions...." The greater the likelihood of injury, then, of course, the greater the obligation to take sensible precautions. In *Bolton* v. *Stone* the plaintiff who was standing on the highway outside a cricket ground was struck by a cricket ball hit out of the ground. Whilst such an event had happened before, it was rare and the House of Lords considered that the likelihood of injury to a person in the plaintiff's position was so slight that the cricket club were not liable. In so deciding the House took into account the existence of a seven-foot fence, the distance from the pitch to the fence and the upward slope of the ground in that direction. No doubt the nature of the defendant's pastime also had a bearing (see *Miller* v. *Jackson*, page 183).

The likelihood of severe injury ... it may be that the defendant could have foreseen that his acts or omissions would injure someone who was particularly vulnerable to severe injury (*e.g.* a haemophiliac). That vulnerability makes it no more likely that the person will be injured, but it does mean that if injured, the consequences will be serious. Because of this, a reasonable man would take steps to ensure that such a person was not injured, even though he would not take steps to protect others who were not so vulnerable. In *Paris* v. *Stepney Borough Council*, the defendant employed a workman, with only one eye, who was blinded whilst carrying out the work for which he was employed. He claimed that he should have been supplied with goggles and that the failure of his employer to do so amounted to Negligence. The court accepted that the defendant was negligent, even though the risk to a two-eyed workman would not have been such as to have required the provision of goggles to all workers.

The cost of avoiding injury ... sometimes the cost of avoiding the risk of injury is such that society is better served by the risk being taken. Lord Justice Asquith made this point starkly when, in *Daborn* v. *Bath Tramways* he stated that, " ... if all the trains in this country were restricted to a speed of

five miles an hour, there would be fewer accidents, but our national life
would be intolerably slowed down." The case concerned the use of an
American made ambulance in war-time Britain. Being a left-hand drive
vehicle it could not be driven safely on British roads, for, when turning
right, the driver could not make the appropriate hand signal. The court,
nevertheless, held that the driver was not negligent in turning right
without making a signal, for the court appreciated that the cost (to the war
effort) of not using American vehicles would have been totally unacceptable. Similarly, in *Latimer* v. *A.E.C.* the court, when considering an injury
caused to a workman who had fallen on a factory floor which had become
slippery after a flood, rejected the assertion that the defendant should
have closed the factory until it was completely safe. The cost of such an
action, to employer and employee alike, would have been unacceptable. It
should be noted that whilst the courts are willing to balance the risk of
injury against the cost to society of prevention of injury, they are not
sympathetic to claims that the cost of prevention is too high when the
"excessive" cost is expressed only in terms of money. If an organisation
cannot afford to ensure that its commercial or industrial activities are safe,
it will have to terminate them.

Consequent damage
   Even though the plaintiff can establish that the defendant was under a
duty of care, and has not observed the necessary standard of care, he may
not be able to recover in respect of all the loss thereby occasioned. To be
recoverable that loss must have been *caused* by the defendant's breach of
duty and must not be too *remote* a consequence of it (*i.e.* it must be
foreseeable).
   Causation . . . before consideration is given as to whether or not the
plaintiff's loss is foreseeable it must be shown that the defendant's
negligent breach of duty did *in fact* cause that loss. This link can be
established if it can be shown that "but for" the defendant's actions the
loss would not have occurred. In *Barnett* v. *Chelsea and Kensington Hospital
Management Committee* the plaintiff's husband called at the defendant's
hospital early one morning complaining of vomiting after drinking tea. He
was not examined but told to consult his own doctor later that morning.
Later the same day he died of arsenical poisoning. Although it was held
that the lack of treatment amounted to a negligent breach of duty, this
breach was not found to have caused his death because even proper care
and treatment would probably not have saved his life. The use of this "but
for" test requires a hypothetical inquiry into the circumstances of the case.
On occasions this inquiry may involve putting hypothetical questions to a
party who is no longer able to answer. Thus, in *McWilliams* v. *Sir William
Arrol & Co.* the plaintiff's husband, a steel erector, was killed when he fell
from a tower which he was helping to erect. His employers had, in breach
of their duty to him, failed to provide a safety belt. Although it was
accepted that the belt would have saved his life, the plaintiff was unable to
establish on the evidence before the court that the defendant's breach
caused her husband's death. That evidence showed that even if the
employer had provided safety belts the deceased would not have worn one.
In *McGhee* v. *National Coal Board*, on the other hand, the defendants were
held to have been careless in not providing washing facilities for employees
who had been working in brick kilns. Washing would probably have helped

to prevent the dermatitis which the plaintiff contracted, although it was not certain. Nevertheless the defendants were held liable on the ground that their negligence materially increased the risk of injury.

Remoteness ... even when, by the test of causation, it can be shown that the plaintiff's loss has resulted from the defendant's action, this is not an end to the court's inquiry. The law does not seek to impose liability upon a defendant for all the consequences of his wrong, and thus a line must be drawn somewhere. In *Re Polemis* the line was drawn at liability for *all the direct consequences* of the defendant's negligence suffered by the plaintiff, whether they were foreseeable or not. This test was, however, replaced by that laid down in a later case, *The Wagon Mound*.

In *The Wagon Mound*, it was held that an award of damages would only compensate the plaintiff for loss which was *foreseeable*. The case concerned damage resulting from the negligent spillage of furnace oil into Sydney harbour. The oil spread under the plaintiff's wharf upon which the plaintiff was engaged in welding. A drop of molten metal fell from the wharf, ignited the oil and, in the ensuing fire, the wharf was destroyed. At that time it was commonly believed that furnace oil would not burn on water. The court held that damage by fouling would have been perfectly foreseeable, but that damage by fire was not. The defendant was, accordingly, not liable for that damage.

If the type of accident is foreseeable, however, the defendant will be liable for the full extent of the injury suffered, even though the full extent was not foreseeable. Thus, in *Hughes* v. *Lord Advocate*, the court awarded damages to a child who was badly *burned* when he entered a manhole shelter, tripped over a warning light and caused an explosion of vaporised paraffin from the light. The court accepted that the Post Office workers, who had left the shelter unattended, could not have foreseen the explosion; they could, however, have foreseen that the child would be *burned* by the lamp.

But if the type of accident was not foreseeable, the fact that a foreseeable occurrence would have resulted in similar injuries being suffered will not avail the plaintiff. Thus, in *Doughty* v. *Turner Manufacturing Co. Ltd.* the asbestos cover on a cauldron of acid was carelessly knocked into the cauldron. The plaintiff suffered burns, not because of a splash (which would have been foreseeable) but because of a delayed eruption caused by a chemical reaction between the lid and the acid (a reaction which was found to have been unforeseeable). The defendants were held not to be liable in Negligence.

Thin-skull cases ... it is clear that the consequences of the defendant's negligence will be more serious for the man with a weak heart or a thin skull, and it is a well-established principle that the defendant must take his victim as he finds him. In *Smith* v. *Leech Brain & Co.*, for example, the plaintiff was burned on the lip by a splash of molten metal due to the defendant's carelessness. The burn triggered off a form of cancer which had been present in a pre-malignant state. The defendants were held liable.

Novus actus interveniens ... even where the defendant's breach of duty causes the plaintiff's loss under the test outlined earlier, it is still possible that a court will find some other intervening event (*novus actus interveniens*) to have been the sole cause of that loss. Such intervening events may result from:

(a) a natural event (*e.g.* a storm at sea which worsens damage to a ship caused by a collision);

(b) the act or omission of a third party; or

(c) the act or omission of the plaintiff himself.

In *McKew* v. *Holland & Hannen & Cubitts Ltd.* the plaintiff had suffered a leg injury for which the defendants were liable. Shortly afterwards he attempted to descend a steep staircase which had no handrail, fell and sustained further injury. In refusing to hold the defendants liable for this further injury the House of Lords described the plaintiff's actions as unreasonable. He had known that his first injury occasionally caused him loss of control of his leg and, moreover, he had failed to make use of assistance from those accompanying him. Such conduct amounted to a *novus actus.* Here the intervening event was the plaintiff's own negligence, in *Lamb* v. *London Borough of Camden* it was the act of a third party. The defendants' negligence had caused the plaintiff's house to be unsafe and thus remain unoccupied for a period. Squatters moved in and caused substantial damage to the interior. The Court of Appeal held that this damage was too remote to be recoverable, even though the damage caused by the intervening human action may have been reasonably foreseeable in the present day. The court clearly believed that as a matter of policy some limit needed to be put upon the defendants' liability in order to keep it within reasonable bounds. Interestingly in *P. Perl (Exporters) Ltd.* v. *London Borough of Camden* the court dealt with similar circumstances on the basis that the defendant owed no duty of care to the plaintiffs to control the acts of an independent third party. As Lord Justice Oliver observed, "the question of the existence of a duty and that of whether the damage brought about by the act of a third party is too remote are simply two facets of the same problem. . . . Essentially the answer to both questions is to be found in answering the question, in what circumstances is a defendant to be held responsible at common law for the independent act of a third person which he knows or ought to know may injure his neighbour?"

Defences to an action in negligence

Even where the constituent elements of the tort of Negligence are satisfied, the defendant may be able to avail himself of the following defences:

(a) contributory negligence;

(b) *volenti non fit injuria.*

Contributory negligence . . . at one time it was a complete defence to show that the plaintiff had contributed towards his own loss. This is not now the position. Under the Law Reform (Contributory Negligence) Act 1945 the courts make an apportionment of damages in accordance with fault. Thus, if A negligently drives his car so that it crashes into a car driven by B, who was himself careless, the court will assess relative fault. If the court decides that A was 80 per cent. to blame, and B only 20 per cent., it will apportion damages accordingly. If, in the absence of contributory negligence, B would have been awarded £5,000, he will, after apportionment, receive only £4,000.

In assessing the relative fault of the parties the courts will consider all the surrounding circumstances. Thus, a lower anticipation for their own safety may be predicted for children, and lower standard of self-protection expected of those working in repetitive, noisy and fatiguing conditions.

The courts have, moreover, extended the principles of contributory negligence to situations where the plaintiff's conduct in no way contributes to the accident but where it does increase his loss. Thus in *Froom* v. *Butcher* it was held that failure to wear a seat belt was contributory negligence under the Act.

Volenti non fit injuria . . . if a person volunteers to take a risk he cannot bring an action if he is injured whilst taking that risk. However, the mere fact that a person has signed a contract containing a term which purports to exclude the defendant's liability for Negligence does not, in itself, indicate that he is a volunteer (section 2(3) of the Unfair Contract Terms Act 1977) and the term will have no contractual effect if it purports to exclude liability for death or personal injury (section 2(1)). Moreover, he is not a volunteer merely because he is aware of the risk. Thus, in *Smith* v. *Baker*, the court held that a man was not a volunteer merely because he *knew* that there was a risk of being injured by stones falling from a crane operating over his head. Lord Halsbury asserted that, " . . . in order to defeat a plaintiff's right by application of the maxim *(volenti non fit injuria)* . . . the court ought to be able to affirm that he consented to the particular thing being done which would involve the risk, and *consented* to take the risk upon himself." Nor is a person a volunteer if he acts, so as to attract the risk of injury, under a moral obligation. A policeman who prevented a horse from bolting down a busy street, in which there were children, was, accordingly, not a volunteer and could recover in respect of injuries.

DECEIT AND INJURIOUS FALSEHOOD

Where one party negligently makes a statement upon which another relies to his cost, an action in tort may lie upon the principle established in *Hedley Byrne* v. *Heller & Partners*. Where a person makes a statement about another person, impugning that person's reputation, an action may be founded in the tort of defamation. The torts of deceit and injurious falsehood are related, in part, to the torts of negligent misstatement and defamation respectively.

Deceit

A is liable in tort to B if he knowingly or recklessly makes a false statement to B intending that it shall be acted upon by B, who does act upon it and thereby suffers loss. This is the tort of deceit, of which the constituent elements are as follows:

(a) A must make a representation of fact;
(b) A must intend that B act upon that representation;
(c) A must either know his representation to be false or else must be reckless (*i.e.* not care whether it be true or false);
(d) B must rely upon the representation;
(e) B must suffer loss due to that reliance.

Injurious falsehood

Injurious or malicious falsehood arises where A makes a false statement to C about B, or his property, or his business, intending that the statement

will cause B loss and as a result of which B does suffer loss. The essential elements of this tort are:
  (a) a false statement about B, or his property, or his business;
  (b) the statement must be made to a third party, C;
  (c) it must be calculated to cause loss to B;
  (d) it must be made maliciously;
  (e) it must be shown by B that he has suffered consequent damage (this could be general loss of business and not necessarily loss of a particular customer, such as C).

NUISANCE

One of the issues that may prompt the individual law consumer to visit the legal office is his relationship with his physical, as opposed to his metaphorical (see *Donoghue* v. *Stevenson*), neighbours. His complaint may relate to interference with his *"right to privacy"* by excessive noise, smell or vibrations emanating from his neighbour's land. Indeed the interference may relate to something visible. The legal category for dealing with such problems is the tort of Nuisance. Nuisance is a special category in that the law must deal here not with the single, isolated actions so often involved in cases of Negligence, but with continuing relationships between parties whose complaints about each other may, objectively at least, be only trivial.

The term Nuisance covers two separate concepts, public and private nuisance.

Public nuisance

Public nuisance is a crime which may also give rise to a civil action where any individual can show that he has suffered special damage as a result of the defendant's criminal act. That act might be, for example, obstruction of the highway or polluting a public water supply. Indeed, any activity which materially affects the reasonable comfort and convenience of life of a class of Her Majesty's subjects will amount to a public nuisance (*i.e.* an activity will constitute a public nuisance if such a large group is affected that it would not be reasonable to expect any one person to bring proceedings to put a stop to it, but it should properly be controlled by the community at large—hence such activities involve commission of a crime).

Private nuisance

Private nuisance involves the unreasonable interference with another's use or enjoyment of his land. As such the interference may involve injury to the neighbour's land or to property thereon, or to chattels kept on the land. Moreover, the interference may not involve any physical damage but may affect the enjoyment of the land (including the plaintiff's ability to run his business). In the latter case, where no physical damage is caused, the interference must be substantial.

The tort of private nuisance provides protection against visible and invisible invasions of the plaintiff's enjoyment and use of his property. Thus vibrations, flooding, fire, smell, noise and dust may all amount to interference. In this Section the tort of nuisance will be considered only to the extent that it grants a *limited right of privacy* to the individual law consumer. Other instances of nuisance will be considered in *Unit Three, Part Four*.

The right to privacy, although limited, may cover a variety of interferences. Even an offensive sight may provide grounds for a successful action. In *Thompson-Schwab* v. *Costaki* the plaintiff obtained an injunction to restrain the activities of prostitutes who used the neighbouring property. In *Laws* v. *Florinplace Ltd.* the plaintiffs' complaint related to a "sex centre and cinema club" which had been opened in a predominantly residential area. The defendants' business activities would, it was claimed, constitute a material and unreasonable interference with the neighbouring residents' comfort and enjoyment of their property because of the instinctive repugnance that would be felt by ordinary decent people and because of the potential danger to young persons from the undesirable customers attracted to the area. In granting an interlocutory injunction (see page 189) the court clearly had in mind the fact that the material being sold was in the ordinary sense of the word, obscene, and was on the borderline of the criminal law. (On the role of the state in attempting to preserve "appropriate" moral standards by prohibiting certain "unacceptable" behaviour, see page 93.)

On occasions the view from the plaintiff's land may be, objectively at least, improved by the defendants' activities; for example, a householder whose garden looks on to a cricket field. That objective benefit may, however, be shattered by the invasion of the garden by cricket balls. In *Miller* v. *Jackson* a majority of the Court of Appeal were prepared to hold that this amounted to an actionable nuisance. It was said: "A balance has to be maintained between the individual's rights to enjoy his house and garden without the threat of damage and the rights of the public in general or a neighbour to engage in lawful pastimes." In a dissenting judgment Lord Denning M.R. argued that the public interest in the pursuit of communal and sporting activities outweighed any cost to the plaintiff householder. However, the view that an individual must suffer lack of enjoyment from the use of his land because of the benefit to the community as a whole from the defendant's use of his land has found only limited judicial acceptance.

There is, however, a limit to how far one should read these decisions as providing for some right to privacy. Privacy may be protected by an action in private nuisance but only indirectly, namely where the defendant's actions also amount to an unreasonable interference with the plaintiff's enjoyment of his land. The tort of nuisance of itself does not give a landowner the exclusive right to view his land or whatever activities are taking place on that land, nor does it give him the right to any particular view from his land.

The motive of the defendant . . . whilst no one would suggest that the batsman who hits a six out of the ground does so in order to spoil the householder's enjoyment of his garden, it may be that a bad motive on the part of one neighbour will transform conduct which would not otherwise amount to a nuisance into such. In *Christie* v. *Davey*, for example, an occupier of a semi-detached house was so enraged by the noise resulting from music lessons given by his neighbour, that he began to retaliate by knocking on the party wall, shouting, whistling, singing and beating upon tin trays during each lesson. The court accepted that each of the occupiers was irritated by the actions of the other, but found that only the irritation to the music teacher amounted to a nuisance, because of the malice of the neighbour.

Locality of nuisance . . . it is certainly true that the courts, in relation to nuisance as for many other torts, are far more willing to protect tangible injury (*e.g.* damage to the property itself) than intangible injury (*e.g.* personal discomfort or nervous shock). Where the loss suffered on account of the defendant's activities is damage to property, the locality in which those activities are pursued is not relevant (see *St. Helen's Smelting Co.* v. *Tipping* in *Unit Three, Part Four*). However, where the loss consists only of "sensible personal discomfort," the court must consider the locality where the activities are performed in order to decide whether the interference is substantial. Thus, in *Sturges* v. *Bridgman* an interference with the plaintiff's consulting room caused by the defendant's confectionery business had to be viewed in the light that the area consisted for the most part of medical consultants' surgeries.

Damage

Perhaps surprisingly, whilst damage to property is recoverable under the tort of private nuisance, there appears to be no direct English authority for a plaintiff to recover under this head in respect of personal injury caused by his neighbour's use of his land. In contrast, the loss suffered by the plaintiff who alleges public nuisance will most usually involve personal injury. The justification for this distinction is explained by the scope of private nuisance which aims to protect the plaintiff's interest in his land. His interest in his personal safety would be cared for by the tort of Negligence. This distinction is emphasised by the case of *Allen* v. *Gulf Oil Refining Ltd.* where one of the grounds of the plaintiff's claim was the fear under which she lived of an explosion at the defendant's refinery. Although the case was decided upon another point, it should be noted that the court was prepared to recognise at least a prima facie case based upon (*inter alia*) that fear and the subsequent anxiety and ill-health it was causing her. Such could be said to be affecting her enjoyment of her land. On the other hand, should the refinery have in fact exploded and the plaintiff have suffered injury, any action she might have had would be based upon the torts of Negligence and, possibly, *Rylands* v. *Fletcher* (see page 352).

Defences

To what extent can one party charged with causing a "nuisance" to his neighbour claim in his defence that he was pursuing the same activities without complaint long before that neighbour arrived, or that he is performing a socially useful function?

Coming to the nuisance . . . it is no defence for the defendant to show that the plaintiff came to the nuisance. In *Miller* v. *Jackson* it did not help the cricket club, which had played on its ground for the past 70 years, that the plaintiff had chosen to come to a place where there was a clear risk of interference (see page 188 for the unusual outcome of this case).

Utility of action . . . is no more a defence to a charge of nuisance than the previous grounds, although it may have a bearing on the remedy granted. In *Adams* v. *Ursell* a fish and chip shop owner was unable to resist a complaint made by a resident of the area, who found the smell of frying fish offensive, by pointing to the hardship which would be caused to the "poor people" who bought fish and chips at his shop, should he be obliged to stop frying. The court thought that "the answer to that is that it does not follow that the defendant cannot carry out his business in another more suitable place somewhere in the neighbourhood."

If neither of these claims will by themselves afford a successful defence, on what grounds can a defendant avoid liability?

Prescription . . . the right to pursue an activity, which would otherwise constitute a nuisance, may be acquired where the defendant has, to the plaintiff's knowledge, carried on that activity for 20 years or more. The activity must, however, have been an actionable nuisance for the full 20 years. Thus, in *Sturges* v. *Bridgman* the defendant's confectionery business, whilst established for well over 20 years, did not unreasonably interfere with the plaintiff's medical practice until the latter extended his surgery, and it was from this time that the 20 years had to run before a right by prescription could be claimed.

Statutory authority . . . it would be most unusual if this defence were to be available in a dispute between private householders, but occasionally the individual law consumer may approach the legal office with a complaint about the activities of a large public company or a public corporation. Such bodies may be pursuing their activities by virtue of statutory powers and may for that reason have a defence to any alleged nuisance. Everything will turn upon the construction of the particular statute. Thus, in *Allen* v. *Gulf Oil Refining* the defendant oil company was authorised by statute to acquire land for the construction of a refinery, but there was no *express* authority to operate it. However, in the opinion of the House of Lords, authority to construct had to carry with it *implied* authority to refine. Once it has been shown that the defendant's activity is *intra vires* the particular statute, the plaintiff must establish a nuisance and it is then for the defendant to prove that the nuisance was the inevitable consequence of the authorised activity. In the absence of negligence on the defendant's part this will be a sufficient defence.

In addition to the above defences it is open to a defendant to show that:

(a) the nuisance resulted from the act of a stranger of which he was unaware; or

(b) the nuisance was due to an unobservable act of nature or to an act of God; or

(c) the plaintiff consented to the activity.

DAMAGES IN TORT

Where an action is brought in tort, the principle governing assessment of recoverable damages differs somewhat from the rules applicable to contracts (see page 156). Here the courts seek to place the injured party into the position he would have been in had the tort not occurred. Thus, damages are assessed as equal to the loss caused by the tort. However, whereas parties to a contract may be expected to have intimate contact with one another and may discuss the likely damage which would result from a breach of contract, this is not so in the case of a tort. The law of tort seeks to regulate the relationship between parties where the rights of one party have been interfered with following a breach of a duty owed by another party. Although a manufacturer of goods owes a duty to the ultimate consumer of those goods, he does not have direct communication with that party so as to be informed of the particular loss which may be caused by breach of duty. As we have seen it was established in *The Wagon*

Mound that an injured party may recover in respect of loss which ought reasonably to have been foreseen as a consequence of the breach of duty. In the *Heron II, Koufos* v. *C. Czarnikow Ltd.* the House of Lords has confirmed that the distinction between contractual and tortious damages is a real one and that the degree of likelihood of loss required for a claim in contract exceeds that required under the foreseeability test in tort. The latter allows claims which are perhaps unlikely, but would be seen as possibilities by reasonable men, even though they would not succeed as contractual claims. In *Hadley* v. *Baxendale* the owners of a mill failed in their action for loss of profit when their business was kept at a standstill due to the failure of carriers to return a vital shaft. That the mill would totally cease production was not brought to the carrier's notice at the time of contract and therefore was not in their *contemplation as likely loss* (the mill could have had a spare shaft) but who can doubt that it was *reasonably foreseeable* that such loss could have resulted?

Even when in an action in tort it has been shown that the plaintiff has suffered loss which is not too remote, a further but different question must still be determined, namely "how much compensation should be awarded for that reasonably foreseeable loss?" We can examine this question by considering two types of actions:

(a)   actions for personal injury;

(b)   actions for loss of or damage to property.

Actions for personal injury . . . will lead, if successful, to an award of damages under various "heads," which can be categorised as *non-pecuniary* and *pecuniary*. The heads of non-pecuniary loss may include in a typical personal injuries case such as a road traffic accident:

(a)   pain and suffering;

(b)   loss of expectation of life;

(c)   loss of amenity (*e.g.* the loss of a pastime to the amateur birdwatcher who loses an eye);

(d)   the injury itself (*e.g.* the loss of a limb).

Whilst such losses by their very nature cannot be given specific monetary values, nevertheless damages are the only available form of compensation. In assessing the awards to be made under these heads the courts have tended to follow the patterns of awards from earlier cases so as to develop some consistency for different types of injury.

Pecuniary loss will usually consist of loss of earnings and expenses. Losses arising before the time the award is made present little problem since they can be relatively easily assessed. Future losses may depend upon issues such as, "how long will the plaintiff's physical injuries prevent him from re-entering full-time employment?" or "to what extent will the plaintiff's loss of limb reduce his future earning capacity?" These issues would raise no difficulties were it not for the practice in English law of awarding damages on a lump sum basis rather than by means of periodic payments. The former approach requires the courts to make various assumptions about the plaintiff's future position, often based on imprecise information. The latter approach, which was favoured by the *Pearson Commission (The Royal Commission on Civil Liability and Compensation for Personal Injury)*, would, particularly in times of rising unemployment and inflation, better meet the stated objective of compensation (namely, placing the injured party into the position he would have been in had the tort not occurred).

In determining the lump sum to be awarded under the present approach the courts use the so-called "multiplier": that is, they calculate the plaintiff's net annual loss (with no allowance for inflation) and multiply that by the likely number of years of disability. Thus,

lump sum award   =   net annual loss multiplied by 'y' years

The figure 'y' is unlikely to exceed 18 even where the plaintiff is young, since the courts have regard to the size of the lump sum and to the fact that it is received in advance of the time it would otherwise be earned and that interest may be paid upon it.

Actions for loss of or damage to property . . . in such actions it is easier to meet the principle of awarding damages equal to the loss caused by the defendant's tortious activities. Where property is destroyed damages will be assessed at the market value of a replacement at the time of destruction. In addition, a sum may be awarded to compensate for the lost profit-earning capacity of the property destroyed. Where property is merely damaged, damages will normally be calculated according to the cost of repair. Again a sum may also be claimed for loss of use whilst the damaged property is being repaired.

Non-compensatory damages . . . in exceptional circumstances there may be a non-compensatory or punitive element to an award of damages in tort. *Contemptuous damages* (usually the smallest coin of the realm) are awarded where the court believes that the plaintiff has a legal right but not one which was worthy of pursuit (see *Newstead* v. *London Express Newspaper*, page 165). *Nominal damages* are awarded when there has been an infringement of the plaintiff's legal right but no actual damage suffered. This is most likely to occur in the case of torts actionable *per se*, such as trespass or libel. An award of *exemplary* or *punitive damages*, on the other hand, reflects the court's view of the defendant's motive or conduct and is made to punish the defendant and to deter such behaviour in the future. The House of Lords has expressed a reluctance to make such awards, although in *Cassell & Co. Ltd.* v. *Broome* it was prepared to do so where the defendant, by publishing defamatory material in a book, stood to make a profit greater than the compensation awarded to the plaintiff.

Joint and several tortfeasors

The loss suffered by the plaintiff may have more than one cause (see page 178), and thus more than one party may bear liability. Where the parties commit the same tort they are said to be *joint tortfeasors* (*e.g.* in cases of vicarious liability an employer is a joint tortfeasor with his negligent employee, and the author, publisher and printer of a defamatory statement are joint tortfeasors). On the other hand, where the parties are responsible for different torts producing the same damage, they are termed *several or concurrent tortfeasors*. The distinction between joint and concurrent tortfeasors is now far less important than it once was.

Apportionment of damage . . . even though the plaintiff's loss has multiple causes to be laid at the door of more than one party, this does not prevent him from recovering in full from any one defendant. He, in turn, may be able to seek a contribution from the other tortfeasors. Where the plaintiff's loss can be separately allocated, apportionment of damage causes no difficulty, but this will not invariably be so. The issue is presently governed by the Civil Liability (Contribution) Act 1978, which provides that any person liable in respect of any damage suffered by another may recover *contribution* from any other person liable in respect of the same damage. The amount of the "contribution" is calculated on the same principle as that used for determining questions of contributory negligence (namely, degree of cause and culpability). Indeed, a contribution can be claimed from persons other than tortfeasors (*e.g.* where the other defendant's liability rests upon breach of a contractual obligation). Moreover, where two defendants (D_1 and D_2) have agreed by contract that D_2 will indemnify D_1 for any damages that D_1 has to meet whilst, for example, performing services for D_2, the 1978 Act does not affect the validity of any such agreement.

In theory the issue of contribution is a separate question from the plaintiff's claim, but in practice where the plaintiff sues only one of several defendants, the latter may utilise the *third-party* procedure and join those other defendants in the principal action.

Mitigation and taxation of damages

In actions in tort the issues of mitigation and of taxation of damages are the same as for actions in contract (see page 157).

NON-MONETARY REMEDIES

In addition to an award of damages there are various other remedies which may be sought before a court in appropriate circumstances (*e.g.* an application for *habeas corpus* in a case of false imprisonment). Indeed, in some cases (*e.g.* self-help) there may be no necessity to pursue an action before the court, rather the "wronged" party may be required to raise the "remedy" as a defence to any action brought against himself. (Where, for example, the owner of goods rightfully recovers those goods from another but, in so doing, trespasses upon that other's land and is subsequently sued for trespass to land.) But by far the most significant non-monetary remedies are those of *specific performance* and *injunction*. These equitable remedies are available at the *discretion* of the court for, unlike an award of damages, they are not available as of right. For this reason, a failure to seek redress promptly may result in a court refusing assistance because "delay defeats equity" (see page 27). Thus, these remedies may be lost even though statutory limitation periods have not expired (see page 189).

Injunction

This remedy is basically an order from the court directing that a particular course of action be restrained. Thus, an injunction may be awarded to prevent someone acting in a manner inconsistent with his neighbour's right of enjoyment of his land. An injunction will not normally be granted where damages are an adequate remedy. Where the defendant's wrongful act is a continuing one or repeated breaches are likely, damages will probably not be adequate. However, in *Miller* v. *Jackson* the Court of Appeal (whilst prepared to find that the six-hitting activities of village cricketers constituted a nuisance) refused to grant an injunction on the ground that the public interest should prevail over the private. In *Kennaway* v. *Thompson*, on the other hand, an injunction was granted by a differently constituted Court of Appeal to restrain the holding of motorboat racing and water-skiing activities on a lake next to the plaintiff's home. This restraint was not total, but merely sought to restrain such race meetings as could properly be said to constitute an *unreasonable* interference with the plaintiff's use of her land. The restraint was not total because the plaintiff had been aware of a lower level of such activities before she had built her house by that lake. But in *Tetley* v. *Chitty*, where the plaintiffs successfully complained that go-kart racing on the defendant's land amounted to a nuisance, the injunction granted was total. The court emphasised the fact that the plaintiffs had lived nearby that piece of land for some time prior to the commencement of the racing. It was also noted that the defendant had failed to take any steps to minimise the noise.

On occasions, the plaintiff may seek an injunction in proceedings which take place before the trial of the action. Injunctions granted provisionally by a court in such cases are termed *interlocutory injunctions*. It was held in *American Cyanamid Co.* v. *Ethicon Ltd.* that in order to succeed in such an application the plaintiff must merely show that there is a "serious question" to be tried. Where this is shown, the court must then determine where the *balance of convenience* lies. By this test (*inter alia*), the costs (in monetary terms) to the plaintiff in being refused the order are weighed against the costs to the defendant in not being able to pursue his allegedly wrong actions. An interlocutory action should be distinguished from an application for a *quia timet injunction*. In the latter case, the court will grant an injunction, even though no wrong has actually been committed, if the plaintiff can establish as a near certainty the imminent commission of a wrong which will cause him damage.

Where an injunction is issued after a trial of the action it will be a *perpetual* injunction and will be *prohibitory* or *mandatory*. A *prohibitory injunction* is an order to the defendant to stop committing a particular activity. A *mandatory injunction*, which would be less usual, is an order to the defendant to take specific positive steps to rectify some wrong he has already committed.

LIMITATION OF ACTIONS

Rights of action arising in tort are not enforceable for ever, and after certain periods the pursuit of legal remedies becomes barred. Consolidating legislation, the Limitation Act 1980, sets out the basic rules.

The right to bring an action in tort will be lost after the expiration of:
(a) six years from the date on which the cause of action accrues; or
(b) in the case of an action for personal injuries, three years from the date on which the cause of action accrues or from the "date of knowledge" (if later) of the person injured.
Where an action in tort includes claim for both personal injury and damage to property, both are subject to the shorter time period.

The date of accrual of the cause of action varies according to the nature of the tort. Thus, accrual arises:
(a) where the tort is actionable *per se*, on infliction of wrong;
(b) where the tort is actionable only on proof of damage, from the moment damage occurs;
(c) where the tort involves a continuing wrong (*e.g.* nuisance) independently for each action (*i.e.* each cause of action having its own limitation period).

In the case of torts actionable only on proof of damage, the moment of occurrence of damage has given rise to difficulties, particularly where that damage has been latent. Should the time period run from the moment of the breach of duty which causes the damage, even though that damage remains undiscoverable for many years? (For example, in *Dutton* v. *Bognor Regis U.D.C.* (see page 168) the plaintiff, whilst succeeding in establishing that a duty of care was owed to him under the *neighbour* principle, lost his claim on the ground that it was time-barred.) Or should the time begin to run only after the damage has been discovered or ought reasonably to have been? Despite the fact that judicial thinking on this issue was confused, the Legislature made no attempt to clarify the matter in the 1980 Act. However, in *Pirelli General Cable Works Ltd.* v. *Oscar Faber & Partners* the House of Lords seemingly resolved this debate by holding that the date of accrual of a cause of action in tort for damage caused by the negligent construction or design of a building was the date when the damage occurred, not when it was, or should have been, discovered. Moreover, it was held that time ran not only against the existing owner but also against his successors in title. In thus rejecting, albeit reluctantly, the doctrine of discoverability their Lordships called for remedial legislation. This call has been answered by the Latent Damage Act 1986 which provides for an extension of the ordinary six-year-period to allow a plaintiff three years from the date when the damage is discovered or is reasonably discoverable. However, there is a long stop barring actions more than 15 years from the date of the defendant's breach of duty. The Act also includes a right of action for a person who acquires property that is already damaged, when the facts about the damage are not yet known or could not have been known. Although not identical these measures will bring claims for damage to property more into line with personal injury actions in respect of which the position has been settled since 1963. In such cases statute provides that time runs from the date of accrual or from the "date of knowledge" (if later) of the injured person. The latter date is the date on which the plaintiff first has knowledge of four facts:

(a) that the injury is significant;

(b) that it is attributable in whole or part to the act or omission which is alleged to constitute negligence, nuisance or breach of duty;

(c) the identity of the defendant;

(d) where it is alleged that the act or omission is that of someone other than the defendant, the identity of that person and any additional supporting facts.

Knowledge that any acts or omissions did or did not, as a matter of law, involve negligence, nuisance or breach of duty is irrelevant.

As far as questions of fraud or fraudulent concealment and capability to sue are concerned, the rules are the same as for contractual actions.

Part Three

FAMILY MATTERS

Not all private law consumers will have been charged with a criminal offence. Nor will the majority ever be party to a civil action in contract or tort. Most people who visit the legal office will do so because of a concern relating to one of the more domestic matters considered within this Part.

The first Section, entitled "Property," is intended as a general introduction to the following two Sections which deal with the intricacies of real and personal property. These, for ease of exposition, have been loosely associated with the domestic scene but it will be readily appreciated that, in practice, they are not so confined. The remaining three Sections are more securely based within the family environment and have been treated as such.

Section A: Property

THE BASIC CLASSIFICATION OF PROPERTY

An individual law consumer seeking advice in relation to his property will normally express his needs or problems in everyday language without reference to lawyers' technical terms. He does not require an explanation in terms of "choses in possession," "choses in action" or "tangible" and "intangible property." Nevertheless, these and other terms are used by lawyers to describe distinctions of significance to legal analysis of everyday problems. Exposition through such terminology helps towards understanding of the underlying principles behind the legal rules governing property rights and also equips the lawyer to readily communicate with other professionals.

The meaning of property

Although the meaning of the word *property* changes with context, in this Section it is used to describe things that may be owned. The most *tangible* form of property is land, which is given a special place in our law, being known for historical reasons as *real property* (realty). All other forms of property are *personal property* (personalty) which may be either tangible or intangible. Tangible property is capable of physical possession, such as cars, horses or groceries. Intangible property is only capable of recognition as figments of the legal imagination, such as patents, debts or shares in a company.

Distinguishing real property from personal property

In the early development of our law, land was of peculiar significance in that at common law an action lay to enforce recovery of the thing itself

191

(known as a real action or action *in rem*). Freehold land is today known as real property. Rights over all other forms of property (collectively known as *chattels*, from the latin word for cattle), such as goods, were enforceable only by an action against the person (known as an action *in personam*) which would direct him to pay money should he refuse to return the actual goods. Hence the term *personal property*. There is one anomalous form of personal property which bears some similarity to land and some to goods, this is leasehold land. Leaseholds are known as *chattels real*, distinguishing them from other forms of personal property, *chattels personal*.

In the modern law, leaseholds and freeholds are considered as within the province of the law of real property, although for certain purposes of succession to property on death leaseholds still form part of personal property.

What is land?

Before embarking upon a consideration of the complexities which beset the law of real property, it is helpful to identify the legal meaning of *land*. It encompasses more than just the surface of the earth for, as was indicated in *Mitchell* v. *Moseley*, "the grant of land includes the surface and all that is above (houses, trees and the like) and all that is below—mines, earth, clay, etc." In addition to these tangible elements, a grant also includes certain intangible, or *incorporeal*, rights in land such as "easements," which confer on landowners rights over the land of others (*e.g.* a right of way over a neighbouring plot so as to afford a convenient means of access). The implication of land owning may be gathered from the latin expression *cuis est solum, eius est usque ad coleum et ad inferos* ("he who owns the surface also owns indefinitely upwards and downwards from the surface"). Whilst it should not be understood from this that the landowner's rights extend upwards to the heavens and downwards to the centre of the earth, which would lead to the view that a common law trespass occurred with each passage of a satellite through the projected airspace, there are rights associated with a certain limited degree of land projection. For example, in *Bernstein* v. *Skyviews and General Ltd.*, a case alleging invasion of privacy by over-flying for the purpose of aerial photography, it was assumed that an occupier's rights extend into the air so as to accommodate the ordinary use and enjoyment of his land. This would appear to encompass space in which to fly advertisements or to swing the jibs of cranes. The Civil Aviation Act 1949 adopts a cautious approach and prevents a landowner from claiming in either trespass or in nuisance for the mere fact of flight, provided that this is at a height which is reasonable, having regard to weather conditions. So far as minerals are concerned, the notion of projection is regarded as sound and exceptions have been specifically made by statute so as to remove rights in certain minerals, such as oil, gas and coal from private ownership (see, for example, the Coal Industry (Nationalisation) Act 1946).

Fixtures . . . it is a common belief that whatever is attached to the land becomes part of the land, but the law is much more sophisticated than this. Before one may assert that something which started life as a chattel has become part of the land to which it is attached one must consider two factors:

    (a)   the *degree* of annexation; and

(b)   the *purpose* of annexation.

Expressed simply this means that one must consider how firmly a chattel has become attached to land and the reasons for its attachment. The presumption is that if something is attached (or fixed) to land then it has become land, and the more securely it is fixed the stronger this presumption becomes. However, evidence of a different intention may be used to rebut the presumption. For example, in *Leigh* v. *Taylor* a tenant for life laid strips of wood over a drawing room paper and fixed them to the walls with two-inch nails. He stretched canvas over the wood and fastened a valuable tapestry onto the strips with tacks. Despite the sound workmanship, it was held that the tapestry had not become a fixture, and therefore part of the land, for it was found that the durable method of affixation was explainable as necessary for the proper enjoyment of the tapestry *as a chattel*. On the other hand, the attachment of chattels may be of such a nature as only explainable as being for the benefit and use of the land, thereby becoming part of the land. Such was found to be the case in *D'Eyncourt* v. *Gregory* with statues, stone seats and ornamental vases where they were part of the architectural design of a house or its grounds. However, the basic rule is that objects which are attached only by their own weight do not, without more, fall within the presumption associated with attachment so that in *Berkley* v. *Poulett* a white marble statue of a Greek athlete weighing half a ton and standing on a plinth was not a fixture.

Growing things . . . such as grass, plants and trees which, though they may need tending when first planted, do not require attention on a yearly basis so as to produce a crop, for example cherry trees, are known as *fructus naturales*. These form part of the land. But, cultivated crops, such as corn and roots, which are known as *fructus industriales*, do not form part of the land.

The significance of the definition of land

It is important to be able to determine whether something which is attached to, or growing on, land is to be treated as part of that land for several reasons. The basic rule is that a conveyance of land operates to pass to the purchaser all of the vendor's land including fixtures and *fructus naturales* but excluding *fructus industriales*. Again, a contract for the sale of land is required by statute to be evidenced in writing (see page 125) but this is not so in the case of a contract for the sale of goods. Finally, fixtures added by a tenant (who has only a limited interest in land) become part of the land and are therefore properly regarded as belonging to the freeholder (who has absolute ownership of the land). This principle is, however, modified in that a tenant is allowed to remove any "domestic" fixtures which he has attached and which can be removed without substantial damage to the fabric of the building. A similar rule applies in the case of "business" and "agricultural" fixtures.

Classification of real property

It is unhelpful to attempt a classification of real property divorced from the underlying substantive law but some non-technical explanation of the problems with which such a classification must cope may assist in appreciating its complexity. When land is bought and sold, the subject matter of the transaction extends far beyond the physical entity itself and encompasses other abstract interests. The special problems associated with real property arise, however, from the fact that it is possible for both present and future, absolute and limited, rights and liabilities to exist simultaneously in the same plot of land. By way of illustration, consider the following scenario: a father has an interest for his lifetime in certain land; his son has the right to enjoy the freehold or absolute ownership of the land on his father's death; the son's friend has possession of the land under a lease; a neighbour has the benefit of a covenant or promise which prevents the use of the land for certain purposes; another neighbour is entitled to cross over the land so as to reach his own property; and a building society has a security interest (a mortgage) over the leasehold in respect of money loaned for the purchase of that leasehold. The technical means of providing for the various "estates" and "interests" involved in these, not improbable, arrangements are considered in the following Section.

Classification of personal property

There are two basic categories of personal property. The first covers tangible or *corporeal* movables, which may be physically taken into control or possessed. These are known as *choses* or *things in possession* and are readily identifiable as the familiar goods (or chattels) of daily life such as books, television sets or chairs.

The second category is of *choses* or *things in action*. These are intangible or *incorporeal* property which cannot be physically taken into possession so that an owner's rights may only be secured by means of a legal action. Thus it is not possible to pick up a patent, debt or share in a company, although it is usual for such forms of property to be evidenced by some document which may, of course, be possessed. Some of the more nebulous forms of property, such as goodwill and copyright may not be evidenced in any documentary form but are well recognised as intellectual property and are dealt with at page 337. (See *diagram 6* for an outline of the classification of property).

Section B: Real Property

The visitor to the legal office, or law consumer, is likely to be visiting that office to discuss matters relating to real property. He may wish to purchase a new house for the family or he may be concerned as to the use that he, or others, may make of his premises. He may have been served a notice to quit his tenancy or he may wish to make an application for a fair rent to be determined. All these concerns and a variety of others are sufficiently important to convince most law consumers that they need the assistance of a specialist.

It is difficult to appreciate the legal provisions which apply in this area without having an understanding of the *estates* which may exist in land, and, that being so, this Section will begin with a consideration of this complicated, and conceptual, aspect of law. Consideration will then be given to the process by which land is bought and sold in England and Wales and to the law relating to leases. However, this Section does not complete our consideration of real property. The integrally linked areas of easements, profits and covenants have been given extended treatment in *Unit Three* with a view to better explaining their place and significance in the law of property.

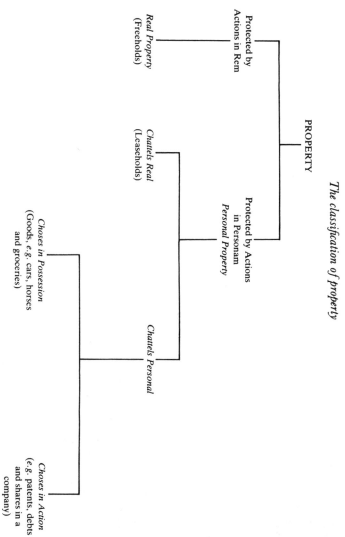

Diagram 6
The classification of property

ESTATES IN LAND

The position prior to 1925

Since Norman times it has been recognised that all land belongs to the Crown and that, accordingly, individuals may not own land. Individuals may, however, own an *estate* in land and the nature of a person's estate indicates the extent of his interest in the land. Prior to 1925 the estates described below were recognised at law.

A fee simple estate . . . the word "fee" indicates that the estate does not terminate upon the death of the tenant, but is inherited by his heirs, the word "simple" indicates that the fee is not restricted and that the estate may be inherited by any heir. Thus, if A purchased a fee simple estate from B he would have use of the land which was subject to the estate for his lifetime and, upon his death, that right would pass to his heir. *In effect*, A has purchased ownership of the land.

A fee tail . . . again, the word "fee" indicates that the estate is one which may be inherited; the word "tail" restricts the fee so that the estate can only be inherited by direct lineal descendants of the tenant (*e.g.* his son, daughter, grandson, great-granddaughter). The estate could be further restricted so that it could be inherited only by male descendants of the tenant.

An estate for life . . . such an estate is, obviously, not one of inheritance for upon the tenant's death his right to the estate terminates. The tenant could dispose of the estate during his lifetime and, if so, the purchaser would acquire an estate *pur autre vie* (*i.e.* an estate for the life of another). If A, having an estate for life, sold his rights to B, B would be able to exercise control over the land until A died, whereupon B's estate would terminate.

A leasehold estate . . . unlike the fee estates and life estates, which were *freehold* estates (of uncertain duration), the leasehold estate was for a fixed, and therefore certain, period of time. Thus, if A granted B an estate for 20 years, B acquired a leasehold estate. Similarly, if B entered into a tenancy renewable monthly he entered into an agreement of certain duration in that it could always be terminated by one month's notice and, therefore, acquired a leasehold estate.

The above estates could be granted *in possession* or *in remainder*. An estate was granted in possession when it took effect immediately. Thus, if A sold his fee simple to B, B would, upon completion of the sale, acquire the fee simple which was, accordingly, a fee simple in possession. An estate was granted in remainder when the granter created a succession of estates which resulted in rights to the land passing to another after the expiration of the first estate. If, therefore, A granted B a life estate and stipulated that C was to have a fee simple thereafter, B's life estate would be in possession and, until B's death, C's fee simple would be in remainder. In this example A has provided for C to have a fee simple and, in consequence, the land will never revert to A for upon the death of C his heir will inherit the estate. If, however, A had made no grant to C, the land would have reverted to A upon B's death. During B's life A would have had a fee simple *in reversion* (and, upon B's death, a fee simple in possession). It should be noted that a fee simple estate would still be in possession even though the tenant has granted a lease. Thus, if A, a fee simple owner, grants a lease to B, then, during the period of the lease A remains in possession of the fee simple.

Each of the estates recognised at common law could also exist, under a trust, in equity. (See page 27 for an outline of the relationship between common law and equity.) Thus, if A gave B an estate for life with remainder to C in fee simple, both B and C would receive legal estates: one (B's) would be in possession and the other (C's) in remainder. If, however, A gave D a fee simple on trust for B for life and thereafter for C in fee simple, D would have a legal fee simple (in possession), B would have an equitable estate for life (in possession) and C would have an equitable fee simple (in remainder). In these circumstances, D, as trustee, would not be entitled to use the land for his own benefit but would be required to hold the land for the benefit of B, in the first instance, and then for C. (This was not the common law position, for the common law recognised only the rights of the trustee and left him free to use the land as he wished. The development of equity, however, led to a recognition of the rights of the beneficiary under a trust, B and then C in this instance, and enforced these rights against the trustee.)

The position post 1925

Section 1 of the Law of Property Act 1925 provides that the only estates which are recognised in law are:

(a)   the fee simple absolute in possession; and

(b)   the term of years absolute.

These estates can *also* exist in equity under a trust, but all other estates can now *only* exist in equity (and are referred to as *equitable interests*).

The fee simple absolute in possession . . . we have already seen that a "fee" estate is one which is capable of being inherited following the death of the tenant and that the word "simple" indicates that the inheritance is not restricted as is the case with the fee tail. We have, further, seen that an estate is "in possession" when it takes immediate effect. It remains, then, necessary only to introduce the meaning of the term "absolute" in order that the full nature of the fee simple absolute in possession may be revealed. An estate is absolute when it is free from conditions. Thus, a grant of a fee simple to A "until he marries" would not create an estate which was absolute. Such an estate could not, therefore, exist in law, although it could exist in equity.

The term of years absolute . . . a grant of an estate to a tenant for a definite period of time (*e.g.* 99 years or 999 years) will, if the grant is unconditional, create a term of years absolute or, as it is often designated, a *lease*. Although a leasehold estate is known as a "term of years," the period may be for less than a year (*e.g.* one month or one week), such a short leasehold estate being referred to by convention as a *tenancy*. A lease is created only where the tenant is to receive exclusive possession of the land and, thus, a lodger does not obtain a leasehold estate when he enters into an agreement with the landlord.

Unlike a fee simple absolute, a term of years absolute does not have to be "in possession" to be a legal estate, thus a lease which is to commence in the future may result in the grant of a legal estate to the tenant.

Equitable interests . . . an estate in tail and a life estate may now exist only in equity. Similarly, a fee simple in remainder (*i.e.* not in possession) or a conditional fee simple or term of years cannot exist in law and are recognised only in equity.

Legal interests...legal estates are rights which are recognised by common law and which relate, in effect, to ownership of the land itself. In addition to the two legal estates, however, the 1925 Act recognised five *legal interests*, these being rights, recognised by common law, over the land of another. These legal interests include:

(a)   an easement, right or privilege in or over land for an interest equivalent to an estate in fee simple absolute in possession or a term of years absolute (see page 341 for a consideration of easements and similar rights);

(b)   a charge by way of legal mortgage.

Interests in land: protecting the purchaser

At common law a purchaser who bought land without notice that the land was subject to rights vested in another, took *subject to these rights* if they were recognised at law but *free of them* if they were recognised only by equity. Thus, the fewer the rights recognised by law then the greater the protection afforded to purchasers of land. Since 1925 there are only two legal estates which may exist in land and only five legal interests. The reduction of legally recognised rights is, then, a step which benefits purchasers.

As a further protection to purchasers the Land Charges Act 1925 (since replaced by the Land Charges Act 1972) extended the previously limited system of land charges. By virtue of this legislation some legal rights are now registrable and, if not registered, are void against a purchaser. Thus, a legal mortgage which is not protected by a deposit of the title deeds to the estate affected (such a mortgage being called a *puisne mortgage*) must be registered. In the event of non-registration, a purchaser will not be affected by the mortgage *even though he knew of it.* (A mortgage which is protected by a deposit of deeds is obviously no threat to a potential purchaser of the estate, for the mortgagor will not be able to complete the sale by transferring the deeds to the purchaser.) If a right is registrable and it is registered it will bind a purchaser of the estate even though he did not know of the right at the time of purchase. (Though, of course, if it is registered and the purchaser has secured the services of a solicitor, then he ought not to be unaware of it.) Similarly, certain equitable interests must now be registered. Thus a restrictive covenant made after 1925 by parties other than a lessor and a lessee must be registered. So must an equitable easement created after 1925. Prior to 1925 equitable rights did not bind a *bona fide purchaser* of the legal estate (*i.e.* a purchaser in good faith) providing he gave *value* (*i.e.* anything which would amount to consideration in contract, the satisfaction of an existing debt or a promise made in consideration of a future marriage) and had no *notice* of the relevant rights (this notice could be *actual* or *constructive*, where the purchaser would have known of the rights had he taken the steps that a reasonable man would have taken, or *imputed*, where an agent of the purchaser, such as his solicitor, had actual or constructive notice). This protection extended to the successors in title of the bona fide purchaser. Since 1925 failure to register a registrable equitable right will result in that right being void against a purchaser even though he has notice; equally a registered right will bind even a bona fide purchaser for value without notice. (Equitable rights which are not registrable still do not bind the bona fide purchaser who has given value and who has no notice.)

A purchaser is further protected against equitable interests existing in land by *overreaching* provisions which transfer the rights of a beneficiary to the proceeds of the sale. An example of the operation of this procedure may be helpful. If A grants B a life estate, C a life estate and D a fee simple absolute, then B, C and D all acquire equitable interests. B and C have been given a life estate which, since 1925, can only exist as an equitable interest and D has been given a fee simple absolute which is not in possession and which in consequence can, similarly, only exist in equity. C and D have, then, rights in the relevant land which will be compromised if the land is sold whilst B is exercising his life interest. B will hold his life interest under one of two types of trust: a *strict settlement*, in which case the land will normally be vested in him, or under a *trust for sale*, in which case the land will be vested in trustees. In either case, should the land be sold, the interests of C and D will be extinguished in so far as they relate to the land and, instead, C and D will be recognised as having a claim over the proceeds of sale. However, this transfer of rights from land to purchase price takes place only where the purchaser pays the price to trustees (these will be the trustees under the settlement in the case of a strict settlement). Given that he does this, the purchaser takes the land free of any claim by the beneficiaries even though he has notice of their interests.

THE SALE AND PURCHASE OF LAND

The contract

Land is acquired by contract. The purchaser who has identified the land he wishes to buy will negotiate with the vendor and, if negotiations are successfully concluded, enter into a simple contract to purchase. This contract may be oral or in writing but, if oral, it will not be enforceable unless evidenced in writing (see page 000 where consideration is given to the requirements of section 40 of the Law of Property Act 1925 and to the doctrine of part performance). Unlike a contract for the sale of goods, the subject-matter of a contract for the sale of land cannot be physically delivered to the buyer. The contract is, instead, performed by the seller executing a deed by which he transfers the estate to the buyer. The deed may be:

(a) a *conveyance*, by which the seller transfers a freehold estate; or
(b) a *grant* of a lease, by which the seller creates a leasehold estate in favour of the buyer; or
(c) an *assignment* of a lease, by which the seller transfers to the buyer an existing lease.

There are three main types of contract for the sale of land:

Open contracts . . . which set out only the essential terms of the contract, the other terms being those imposed by the provisions of the law (*e.g.* that the vendor must reveal a good title);

Formal contracts . . . containing specific conditions. In practice, standard forms of contract are used (*e.g.* the Law Society's Standard Conditions and the National Conditions of Sale);

Correspondence contracts... concluded by correspondence. Where an open contract is made in this way section 46 of the Law of Property Act 1925 provides that, subject to any contrary intention being expressed, the Statutory Form of Conditions of Sale (1925) shall apply.

A formal contract (by far the most common form of contract) will normally provide for the payment of a deposit by the purchaser and this will, in most cases, amount to 10 per cent. of the purchase price. Once the vendor has contracted to sell the land to the purchaser two consequences immediately follow:

(a) the purchaser carries the risk of destruction of the property by, for example, fire or flood (and, this being so, acquires an insurable interest in the property which will enable him to enter into a contract of insurance to cover this risk);

(b) the vendor becomes trustee of the land and holds it for the purchaser to whom he then owes the duty to manage and preserve the trust property. (The proceeds of any sale to a third party would, by reason of the trust, be regarded as being held on behalf of the purchaser.)

Prior to the contract being entered into the purchaser's solicitor will normally require the vendor, through his solicitor, to respond to *inquiries before contract*. These inquiries relate to the state of the property and are usually in standard form, though it is quite common for additional queries to be added to the list contained on the standard form.

The steps between contract and completion

The vendor must, between contract and completion, show that he can transfer a valid title to the purchaser. In the case of unregistered land, to establish a *good root of title* in an open contract the vendor is, by virtue of section 23 of the Law of Property Act 1969, required to show that his root of title is at least 15 years old. This means that he must be able to produce a document which is at least 15 years old and which disposes of the whole legal and equitable interest in the land. He must then, by the production of other documents, trace the title to himself. Thus, if a fee simple has been transferred entirely by a series of conveyances between vendors and purchasers, the vendor will need to produce all subsequent conveyances to that which forms his root of title. Imagine, for example, that a vendor has, in his possession, in 1987, conveyances showing a sale of the fee simple by A to B in 1925, by B to C in 1951, by C to D in 1973 and by D to himself in 1977, he must be in a position to produce the conveyances of 1951, 1973 and 1977. In a formal contract the length of title required to be proved will be provided for.

As a first stage in the process of establishing his title, the vendor must (through his solicitor) provide the purchaser with an *abstract of title* which sets out details of the documents by which the vendor will prove title. The purchaser may obtain further information on matters which concern him by delivering *requisitions on title*. The requisitions may, for example, seek confirmation that either a mortgage referred to in the abstract will be discharged prior to completion or that an agreement will be reached between the vendor and the mortgagee that the land will be sold free of the mortgage. The vendor will reply to the requisitions and, if necessary, the purchaser will make further requisitions. When finally satisfied the purchaser's solicitor will prepare a *draft conveyance* and submit it to the vendor's solicitor for approval and, when the draft has been agreed, the purchaser's solicitor *engrosses the conveyance* (*i.e.* he prepares a document which will become a deed when it has been executed by the parties). This document will normally contain.

(a) the *date*;
(b) the *names, addresses* and *occupations* of the parties;
(c) *recitals*, which commence with the word "*WHEREAS*" and describe the vendor's interest in the property;
(d) *testatum*, which commences "*NOW THIS CONVEYANCE WITNES-SETH*" and sets out the consideration, an acknowledgment of receipt of the purchase price by the vendor and the operative words of the conveyance ("*THE VENDOR AS BENEFICIAL OWNER HEREBY CONVEYS*") so called because they are the words which actually convey the property from vendor to purchaser. (The words "as beneficial owner" are significant for section 76 of the Law of Property Act 1925 provides that use of these words results in the vendor making a series of promises, or *covenants*, including promises that he has a right to convey the property, that the land is free from encumbrances not revealed in the conveyance and that the purchaser will acquire quiet enjoyment of the land);
(e) *parcels*, which describe the property conveyed;
(f) *habendum*, which reveals the purchaser's interest in the property conveyed (*e.g.* "To hold the same unto the purchaser in fee simple");
(g) a statement of *express covenants, conditions* and other special provisions;
(h) *testimonium*, a statement that the parties have signed and sealed the conveyance; and
(i) *attestation clause*, a statement indicating that a named witness was present when the vendor signed, sealed and delivered the conveyance.

Shortly before the date fixed for completion the purchaser will make *searches*. He will make a search of both the Land Charges Registry and the local land charges register to see if there are any registered land charges relating to the property. The Land Charges Registry will be able to advise the purchaser of entries showing, for example, that there is a restrictive covenant relating to the land or that a wife has registered a "right of occupation" to the marital home. The local registry will reveal charges acquired by the local authority (*e.g.* restrictions placed on the use of the land).

Completion

Completion usually takes place at the offices of the vendor's solicitor. The vendor's solicitor will hand over the engrossment of the conveyance signed and sealed (and now delivered) by the vendor (a *deed* being a document which is "signed, sealed and delivered") and the title deeds to the property. The purchaser's solicitor will, in turn, pay the purchase price (usually in the form of a *banker's draft*).

The conveyance of registered land

The Land Registration Act 1925 provides for the registration of *title* to land (a procedure which is quite distinct from that relating to the registration of *charges*). In certain areas registration of title is compulsory and, in such areas, the first sale of the fee simple following the designation of the area as a compulsory area must result in the title to the fee simple being registered. A leasehold estate must be registered upon a lease of 21 years or more being granted or a lease with 21 years still to run being assigned. A lease must also be registered if it is to run for 21 years and the freehold or leasehold estate from which it is granted has been registered. (This is so whether the land is in a compulsory area or not.)

The Register is divided into three parts:

(a) the *Property Register*, which describes the land, the estate to which the title has been registered and any interests in the land which are known to exist;

(b) the *Proprietorship Register*, which states the name, address and description of the registered proprietor;

(c) the *Charges Register*, which consists of entries adverse to the land (*e.g.* mortgages and restrictive covenants).

The registered proprietor is given a *land certificate* and any subsequent conveyance of the land requires only the preparation of a *transfer* following the submission of which to the Land Registry the purchaser's name is substituted for the vendor's on the Register. The purchaser cannot make a search of the Register without the registered proprietor's authority, but will normally seek this so that he can search for entries later than the date of the copy of the entries provided by the vendor in place of an abstract of title. In any event, section 70 of the Act lists certain overriding interests which bind the purchaser even though there is no entry in the Register (*e.g.* easements and profits à prendre . . . see page 341) and the purchaser must make separate enquiries relating to these.

Restrictions on use

The fact that a purchaser has bought the land, or more correctly an estate in the land, does not mean that he may use that land as he pleases. The restrictions which may constrain a private purchaser of land are, in essence, the same as those which operate upon commercial and industrial purchasers but discussion of these restrictions is postponed until we consider commercial and industrial law consumers in *Unit Three, Part Four*.

LEASES

Formalities

Since 1925 a lease will only be recognised as a legal estate if it grants a term of years absolute and is made by deed. If, however, the lease takes effect in possession (*i.e.* it starts to run immediately), the term does not exceed three years and it is at the best rent reasonably obtainable, then it may be made either orally or in writing and, in any event, a deed is not required.

A lease which does not satisfy the above requirements creates no legal estate. However, both common law and equity recognised an imperfect lease (*i.e.* one not complying with the appropriate formalities) as a contract to grant a lease providing it was for value and was evidenced in writing (see page 125) or, in the case of equity, evidenced by an act of part performance. Equity would then order specific performance of the contract and, once the lease had been granted to comply with this order, the tenant was in the position he would have enjoyed had the lease been granted by deed. Where an order of specific performance had not been sought by the tenant he was, clearly, in a different position. However, *equity looks on that as done which ought to be done* (this is one of the *maxims of equity* . . . see page 26) and, in equity, the parties were considered to be in the position they would have been in had the lease been granted. In *Walsh v. Lonsdale*, a landlord granted a lease of seven years on terms that a year's rent would be payable in advance upon demand. No deed was executed but the tenant took possession and paid rent, though not in advance. A year's rent in advance was then demanded and, upon the tenant refusing to pay, the landlord distrained for it. The tenant asserted that as distress was a legal, not an equitable, remedy the landlord could not distrain for the year's rent. The court held that he was mistaken in this assertion. Had the lease been granted by deed, distress would have been available to the landlord and, equity treating landlord and tenant as though this had been done, it would regard the distress as lawful. Where there is conflict between law and equity the rules of equity prevail (see page 27) and, in consequence, the tenant could not resist the distress *even at common law*. As a result of this case it may appear that the parties to an enforceable agreement to grant a lease, or to an imperfect grant of a lease which is enforceable as an agreement to grant a lease, are in the same position as if the lease had been granted by deed. This is not quite correct but, if the tenant's equitable rights have been registered as a land charge, he will, in effect, be in much the same position as if he had been granted a legal lease.

Types of lease

A tenancy may be:

(a) for a fixed term;
(b) yearly;
(c) weekly, monthly or for some other period;
(d) at will;
(e) at sufferance;
(f) for life;
(g) perpetually renewable.

A tenancy for a fixed term . . . is granted, for any period of certain duration and comes to an end at the expiration of the fixed term without need of the service of a notice to quit (though there are statutory exceptions to this rule).

A yearly tenancy . . . exists from year to year and will continue until one of the parties terminates it by notice. A yearly tenancy is assumed when a person occupies land with the landlord's consent and pays rent calculated by reference to a year. Thus, payment of a yearly rent by quarterly instalments will be a rent calculated by reference to a year and the payment of one quarter's rent will give rise to a yearly tenancy.

Tenancies for other periods . . . can be created in the same way as yearly tenancies, by express agreement or by the payment of rent calculated by reference to a particular time period (*e.g.* one week, one month or one quarter). Unless the parties have agreed to the contrary the period of notice required to terminate the tenancy is the same as the period of the tenancy. In the case of periodic tenancies of residential accommodation, section 5 of the Protection from Eviction Act 1977 provides that at least four weeks' written notice must be given.

Tenancies at will ... arise whenever a landlord permits a tenant to enter the land *as tenant* on terms that the tenancy may be determined at any time by notice. The courts are reluctant to identify a tenancy as a tenancy at will.

Tenancies at sufferance ... arise when a tenant holds over after the expiration of his tenancy without the consent of the landlord. The tenancy may be determined at any time or may be converted into a yearly tenancy or a tenancy for some other period by payment of rent. A tenancy at sufferance is not really a tenancy and is largely a legal device by which the tenant is not treated as a trespasser.

Tenancies for life ... are, by section 149(6) of the Law of Property Act 1925, converted into a fixed term of 90 years which can be terminated, following the death of the person specified, by one month's notice.

Perpetually renewable leases ... are created when a tenant is given a perpetual right to renew his tenancy (as where a tenant for a term of five years is given the right to renew this tenancy by service of notice). Section 145 of the Law of Property Act 1922 converts such tenancies into fixed terms for 2,000 years.

The obligations of the parties to a lease

In the absence of express provisions in the lease the landlord has the following obligations:

(a) he impliedly covenants that the tenant will have *quiet enjoyment* of the premises free from interference by himself or anyone claiming through him;

(b) he must not *derogate from his grant* (*i.e.* he must not act so as to make the premises unfit for the purpose for which they were let);

(c) where the premises are furnished, he impliedly promises that they are reasonably fit for human habitation at the beginning of the lease (*Smith* v. *Marrable*);

(d) where the premises are let at a low rent, there is an implied condition that they will be kept fit for human habitation (section 8 of the Landlord and Tenant Act 1985);

(e) where the premises are let on a short lease (less than seven years), there is an implied covenant by the landlord to keep the structure and exterior in repair and to keep in repair the installations in the premises for the supply of water, gas, electricity, for space heating or heating water and for sanitation (sections 11–14 of the Landlord and Tenant Act 1985).

The tenant would also have obligations. He would be obliged:

(a) to pay rent, rates and taxes;

(b) not to commit *waste* ... a tenant for a fixed term of years is liable for *voluntary waste* (*i.e.* any positive act which operates to the detriment of the land, such as felling trees) and *permissive waste* (*i.e.* permitting the land to deteriorate by neglect), a yearly tenant is also liable for both although his liability for permissive waste is limited to keeping the premises wind- and water-tight, a weekly tenant is not liable for permissive waste though he has certain obligations relating to the maintenance of the property, a tenant at will and a tenant at sufferance have no liability for permissive waste and no such positive obligations;

(c) to permit the landlord to enter the premises where he is under an obligation to repair (*e.g.* under sections 11–14 of the Landlord and Tenant Act 1985 . . . see above).

Sometimes, the parties will enter into a lease which provides that the "usual covenants" shall apply. In such an event, and where the lease does not specify the nature of these covenants, the obligations of the parties will depend, in part, upon local practices. The following covenants are, however, always usual:

(a) a covenant by the landlord that neither he nor anyone claiming through him will interfere with the tenant's quiet possession;

(b) a covenant by the tenant to pay the rent, rates and taxes;

(c) a covenant by the tenant to keep the premises in repair and to permit the landlord to enter the premises and view the state of repair; and

(d) a condition of re-entry for non-payment of rent.

The parties may actually specify certain express covenants which are to apply to their lease. The following are common examples of such express provisions:

(a) a covenant against assigning the lease . . . in the absence of such a covenant the tenant is entitled to assign without the landlord's consent. A simple covenant against assignment prohibits only an assignment of the *whole* lease and would permit an underletting of *part* of the premises. Often, however, the tenant will also be prevented from disposing of part of the premises by the terms of the covenant adopted. The covenant may prohibit an assignment *without the landlord's consent*, in which case section 19 of the Landlord and Tenant Act 1927 provides that the landlord must not unreasonably refuse this consent;

(b) a covenant to repair . . . such a covenant imposes upon the tenant only an obligation to *repair* not to *rebuild*, though the covenant does extend to the replacement of subsidiary parts of the premises which cannot be repaired (*e.g.* drainpipes);

(c) a covenant to insure . . . which compels the tenant to enter into a policy of insurance covering the specified risks for the duration of the tenancy.

Finally, under the Leasehold Reform Act 1967, a landlord may be obliged to confer fresh rights of occupation or even ownership on certain tenants. If the tenant has a long tenancy at a low rent, of property with a low rateable value, then, providing the premises is a house and he has occupied the house as his residence for the last three years or for periods amounting to three years in the last 10, he may serve a notice on the landlord in the prescribed form. By this notice he may elect either to:

(a) purchase the freehold at a price based upon the market value of the land (without regard to the value of the buildings erected upon it); or

(b) claim a new lease of 50 years at a rent based upon the current letting value of the site upon which the house is built.

Determination of tenancies

We have seen that a fixed term tenancy may terminate by *expiration of time* and that other tenancies may be terminated by *notice*. In addition, a landlord may *forfeit* a lease by enforcing a forfeiture of the lease because of the tenant's breach of one of his obligations. This right must be provided for in the lease and it will be lost if the landlord *waives* it by doing any act which reveals that, knowing of the breach, he wishes to treat the lease as still existing.

Section 146 of the Law of Property Act 1925 provides for certain formalities in the case of forfeiture for the tenant's breach of obligation other than payment of rent. The landlord must serve a statutory notice specifying the breach and give the tenant an opportunity to comply with it (by rectifying the breach). If the tenant complies he avoids forfeiture. The tenant may, before the landlord obtains possession, apply to the court for relief on such terms as the court thinks fit and, if this relief is granted, there will be no forfeiture. In any event section 2 of the Protection from Eviction Act 1977 provides that:

"Where any premises are let as a dwelling on a lease which is subject to a right of re-entry or forfeiture it shall not be lawful to enforce that right otherwise than by proceedings in the court while any person is lawfully residing in the premises or part of them."

A lease may also be terminated by *surrender* where the tenant gives up possession to the landlord and the landlord accepts.

Security of tenure

In the case of non-business tenancies, the tenant is protected by the provisions of sections 98 and 100 of the Rent Act 1977. In order to set out the nature of this protection it is necessary to define the following terms:

(a) protected tenancy; and

(b) statutory tenancy.

Protected tenancy . . . section 1 of the Rent Act 1977 provides that "a tenancy under which a dwelling house (which may be a house or part of a house) is let as a separate dwelling is a protected tenancy." Some premises do not fall within this classification even though they fit the definition. Thus, a tenancy will not be protected if the rateable value of the dwelling house exceeds certain specified limits. Nor is a tenancy protected if no rent is payable or a low rent (as defined in the Act) is payable. There are other exceptions covering, for example, tenancies where the rent includes payment for board or "attendance" (*e.g.* the provision of a valet or housemaid), tenancies between colleges and their students, and holiday lettings. There has been considerable judicial vacillation over the extent to which the courts might look behind agreements purporting to be licences and hence falling outside the statutory protection. Now, however, in *Street* v. *Mountford* the House of Lords has ruled unequivocally that where residential accommodation is offered and accepted with exclusive possession for a term at a rent the result will be a tenancy irrespective of the description of the agreement used by the parties.

Statutory tenancy . . . section 2 of the Rent Act 1977 provides that "after the termination of a protected tenancy of a dwelling house the person who, immediately before that termination, was the protected tenant of the dwelling house, shall, if and so long as he occupies the dwelling house as his residence, be the statutory tenant of it." The Act also provides rules for determining who, if anyone, is the statutory tenant following the death of the statutory tenant who was formerly the protected tenant. These rules would, for example, provide for his widow to be the statutory tenant providing she resided with him at his death.

Section 98 of the Rent Act 1977 provides that the court will not make an order for possession of a dwelling house which is subject to either a protected tenancy or a statutory tenancy unless the court considers it *reasonable* to make the order and the court is satisfied that *suitable alternative accommodation* will be available for the tenant. The court may, however, make an order even though it is not satisfied as to the availability of suitable alternative accommodation in certain circumstances:

(a) where rent has not been paid or any obligation of the protected or statutory tenancy has been broken;

(b) where the tenant or any person living with him has committed a nuisance or other annoyance to adjoining occupiers or has been convicted of using or permitting the use of the dwelling house for immoral or illegal purposes;

(c) where the condition of the dwelling house has deteriorated as a result of the acts or omissions of the tenant or any person living with him (providing the court is satisfied that the tenant has not taken reasonable steps to remove that other person);

(d) where the condition of furniture provided under the tenancy has deteriorated due to ill-treatment;

(e) where the tenant has served notice to quit and, in consequence, the landlord has contracted to sell or let the premises;

(f) where, without the landlord's consent, the tenant has assigned or sub-let the dwelling house or any sub-let part;

(g) where the dwelling house is reasonably required by the landlord for himself or an adult member of his family and the landlord had not become landlord by *purchasing* the dwelling house at a time when he ought to have been aware of the security afforded to the tenant;

(h) where the court is satisfied that the tenant is charging a rent for a sub-let part of the dwelling house, which is itself a protected or statutory tenancy, which is in excess of the maximum permitted by the 1977 Act.

There are situations in which the court *must* order possession including, in certain circumstances, that in which the landlord wishes to retire and occupy the dwelling house.

Section 100 of the 1977 Act provides that, in the case of protected or statutory tenancies, the court may adjourn proceedings for possession for such periods as it thinks fit. Further, it may make an order for possession and either stay or suspend operation of the order or postpone it for such periods as it thinks fit. If it wishes to exercise these powers it will normally impose conditions relating, for example, to payment of rent and rent arrears. Upon these conditions being complied with the court may then rescind the order for possession.

One effect of statutory protection affording security of tenure has been a reduction in the availability of private lettings. In order to encourage such lettings the Housing Act of 1980 introduced the *protected shorthold tenancy*. If the stringent requirements of the legislation, now to be found in the Housing Act 1985, are satisfied then at the end of the contractual term the landlord can obtain a mandatory order for possession.

Rent regulation
Section 18 of the Rent Act 1977 provides that protected and statutory tenancies are *regulated tenancies*. In relation to such tenancies a *fair rent* may be registered which then becomes the *contractual rent limit* and any rent in excess of this sum cannot be recovered from the tenant. If the fair rent is higher than the contractual rent the higher rent cannot be levied until the original contract has been terminated, which may be effected by service of a statutory *notice of increase*.

The country is divided into registration areas and, in each area, rent officers are responsible for keeping a *register of fair rents*. Applications for registration may be made by either the landlord or the tenant. If a party is not satisfied with the registered rent he may take his objection to a *Rent Assessment Committee* which may decide to visit the premises. The Committees have power to confirm or vary the decision of the rent officer.

Section 70 of the Rent Act 1977 provides that in determining *fair rent* regard should be had to all of the circumstances and, in particular, to:
(a)   the age, character, locality and state of repair of the dwelling house;
(b)   the quantity, quality and condition of any furniture provided for use by the tenant under the tenancy.

Public sector housing: the secure tenancy
The Housing Act 1985 provides for a special status in the field of public sector housing, that of the *secure tenancy*. There is a secure tenancy when a dwelling house is let as a separate dwelling and:
(a)   the "landlord condition" is satisfied; and
(b)   the "tenant condition" is satisfied.
The *landlord condition* is satisfied when the landlord is:
(a)   a local authority;
(b)   a new town corporation;
(c)   an urban development corporation;
(d)   the Development Board for Rural Wales;
(e)   the Housing Corporation;
(f)   a housing trust which is a charity; or
(g)   a housing association or housing co-operative as specified by the 1985 Act.
The *tenant condition* is satisfied where the tenant is an individual who occupies the dwelling house as his only, or as his principal, home: or where the tenancy is a joint tenancy, each of the joint tenants is an individual and at least one of them occupies the dwelling-house as his only or principal home.

Secure tenants are given security of tenure, statutory terms for their tenancy and, in certain circumstances, the right to buy their properties. Section 82 of the Housing Act 1985 provides that a secure tenancy for a term certain or for a weekly or other periodic tenancy cannot be terminated by the landlord except by order of the court. The court may not make an order unless it identifies certain specified grounds. These include situations where:
(a)   the tenant has defaulted in the payment of rent or any of his other obligations as tenant have not been performed;
(b)   the tenant, or someone living with him, has been guilty of conduct which is a nuisance or annoyance to neighbours or he has been

convicted of using or permitting the use of the dwelling house for immoral or illegal purposes;

(c) the tenant has acted in a way which has led to the condition of the dwelling house deteriorating, or someone living with him has (and the tenant has not taken reasonable steps to remove the other person);

(d) the condition of furniture provided under the tenancy has deteriorated owing to ill-treatment by the tenant or any person living with him (and the tenant has not taken reasonable steps to remove such person);

(e) the tenant induced the landlord to grant the tenancy by a false statement made knowingly or recklessly by the tenant;

(f) the tenant moved into the premises whilst his principal dwelling house was being improved and he accepted the tenancy of the present premises in the knowledge that he would be required to return to his principal dwelling house which is now available;

(g) the dwelling house is overcrowded.

In the case of (a)–(f) above the court must also consider it reasonable to make the order; in the case of (g) above the court must be satisfied that suitable accommodation will be available to the tenant.

The Housing Act 1985 provides for statutory rights to be incorporated as terms into a secure tenancy. Amongst these are the right to take in lodgers or to sub-let part of the dwelling house. Where the lodger or tenant under the sub-lease is a member of the tenant's family this right can be exercised without the consent of the landlord; in the case of others the right is subject to consent by the landlord, but this must not be unreasonably withheld.

Section 118 of the 1985 Act provides that a secure tenant may have the right to buy the freehold of his dwelling house if it is a house or a long lease if it is a flat. He may also have a right to a mortgage to finance the transaction. These rights are available to a secure tenant if he has been a public sector tenant for two years. The purchase price of the dwelling house will be based upon the market value at the time the tenant serves upon the landlord a notice of his intention to exercise his right to buy. There is, however, an entitlement to a discount of 32 per cent. of that value if the tenant's qualifying period is less than three years and the discount increases by one per cent. for each year of the tenant's occupation up to a maximum of 60 per cent. provided that it does not exceed £25,000. Any conveyance or assignment of the dwelling house within five years of its purchase by the secure tenant will involve the tenant in an obligation to repay at least part of the discount he has received.

COMPULSORY PURCHASE

Introduction

The sanctity of property rights has been a consistent theme of the common law. In the sphere of housing, as has been demonstrated, this is given particular support by statute. However, the inviolability of property has been severely dented by a wealth of legislation conferring powers of compulsory purchase of private land upon public authorities and other bodies. A consideration of real property would be incomplete without some recognition of the frailty which such property rights exhibit in the face of a demand by a public authority bent on their expropriation.

The compulsory purchase order

Powers of compulsory purchase of land have been granted by Parliament for a wide variety of purposes, for example for the purposes of building houses, roads, schools and hospitals. Indeed the list is almost endless, the possibilities inexhaustible. When a public body exercises a power of compulsory acquisition of land, then the land owner affected is eventually made an offer which he cannot refuse (*the notice to treat*). He is obliged to sell his land and is paid in accordance with a statutory scheme for assessment of compensation. In every scheme of compulsory acquisition, no matter by whom initiated (public or local authority), the *compulsory purchase order* must be confirmed by an appropriate minister who is in turn responsible to Parliament in respect of his decision to confirm. However, the normal procedure is that when notice of intention to apply for a compulsory purchase order has been given, and there is objection to the order, the minister, before confirming the order, must hold a *public local inquiry*. This inquiry which will be open to the public and held in the locality of the area concerned, will be presided over by a "person appointed" by the minister, commonly known as an *inspector*. The inspector will hear objections to the proposed order and will make findings of fact and a recommendation on the decision to the minister. The inspector will normally be a civil servant, professionally qualified in some relevant sphere (*e.g.* an engineer or surveyor), who will be attached to an appropriate department. He is employed, full-time, in the holding of inquiries and preparation of reports to ministers. The inspector's report (following recommendations of the *Franks Committee on Administrative Tribunals and Enquiries, 1957*) must be disclosed to the parties concerned and it is so disclosed when the final decision is made by the minister. The minister is not obliged to follow the recommendations of his inspector, but there are safeguards against arbitrary disregard of the inspector's recommendation. The minister is required to give reasons for any decision, if requested, and if the minister's reasons are inadequate, unintelligible, or not relevant to the issue then the decision may be subjected to review in the courts as being unlawful.

Although the *merits* of a minister's decision, taken after an inquiry, cannot be subjected to appeal it is normally the case that the relevant statutory scheme makes provision for appeal to the courts so as to ensure that if the minister has erred in law or failed to follow the correct procedure his decision may be corrected. These appeals on law must be made within a six-week period following the date of the decision, after which no further challenge may be made in the courts.

Following the Franks Report, the procedures relating to inquiries have been greatly improved and, indeed, under the supervision of the *Council on Tribunals* there has been a continuous review of procedures. The Council invites individuals to refer any matter relating to inquiries (and also tribunals) to it and this ensures close scrutiny of their day to day activities. It has devoted particular attention to advising upon and seeking improvements in procedures relating to inquiries. Typical of the procedural rules drawn up under its guidance are the *Compulsory Purchase by Public Authorities Rules 1976*. These prescribe that the minister must give not less than 42 days' notice of the date, time and place of the inquiry and, not less than 28 days before the inquiry is to be held, the body seeking to purchase must serve a written statement of its intended submission. The procedure at the inquiry is informal and the inspector has a wide discretion as to the conduct of the proceedings. Those directly affected have a *right* of appearance whereas others may be allowed to speak at the inspector's invitation. The normal practice is for the body seeking to purchase to open the case for the proposal in a manner somewhat similar to that adopted in a court action. This body makes an opening statement and calls witnesses to give evidence. These witnesses can be cross-examined by objectors and re-examined by the potential purchaser. The same procedure is followed wih the objectors' case. The inspector listens to these proceedings and at the close of the hearing he visits the site of the proposed acquisition accompanied by the parties. The inspector then closes the inquiry and prepares his report to the minister. If the minister differs from any recommendation made by the inspector because he differs over a finding of fact or receives new evidence (expert or otherwise) or considers a new issue of fact, he must give those entitled to appear at the inquiry 21 days' written notice before making a decision. They may, in that period, make written representations about the issue or, in the case of new evidence or a new issue of fact, demand that the inquiry be re-opened.

Section C: Personal Property

Introduction
Law consumers have traditionally had resort to the legal office at the first hint of a problem or transaction associated with real property. The technicalities surrounding personal property are, however, less well acknowledged and therefore are less likely to be the subject of specific professional consultation. Nevertheless, transactions and problems involving personal property are of common occurrence and an understanding of the relevant law is essential to the legal practitioner. The significance of this area of law extends beyond its obvious immediate application and frequently forms the basis for resolution of problems more naturally classifiable elsewhere. The central concepts of ownership and possession, for example, are integrally linked with the criminal law. This Section deals with basic principles of personal property which have wide application. At a more particular level, it also examines the law of cheques, primarily by way of explanation of the practices adopted in the use and processing of this most common yet complex form of personal property.

Basic concepts
In considering personal property rights there are two concepts which must be understood from the outset, these are ownership and possession.

Ownership . . . exists where the law recognises and protects certain rights over property. The owner has the complete right of use, enjoyment and disposal over his property except in so far as he is restricted by either the law itself or his own undertaking. Thus, an owner is free to allow his taxi to become rusty but the law would restrict him from allowing it to become a danger on the road or from carrying more passengers than the vehicle is designed to carry. Moreover, if he should agree to paint his taxi in another operator's livery and only to use it on that other's business then he has restricted his freedom to use the taxi as he pleases.

Possession ... requires both the right of control and an intention to exercise that control and it may be actual or constructive. An owner is in actual possession of his motor car when sitting in it, but if he should agree to loan the car to his friend and hand him the ignition key, then passing the key involves a constructive transfer of possession of the car to the friend because this is the intention. From that time on the friend is in possession even though a bystander would not have noticed any physical change.

Usually ownership and possession are vested in the same person but they may be separated. A car hire firm continues to own its vehicles whilst they are in the possession of hirers and indeed, should a car be stolen it would still be owned by the firm albeit in the possession of the thief.

Ownership is a question to be settled by application of legal rules. Possession is also ultimately determined by legal rules but is normally recognisable as a fact. Thus should property be lost, then the law provides that the owner will not normally be deprived of his rights of ownership but a finder will come into possession and that possession will carry legal consequences. The finder will be entitled to keep the property as against anyone other than the owner.

TRANSFER OF CHOSES

The basic rule is that an owner of a chose may transfer his property to another by way of a contract or indeed by the making of a gift. Detailed treatment of the transfer of personal property does, however, require that choses in possession should be considered separately from choses in action.

Choses in possession

The transfer of tangible movables is the meat and drink of everyday life in the form of contracts for the sale of goods. These transactions are governed by the normal principles of the law of contract together with certain specialised statutory rules mainly found in the Sale of Goods Act 1979. The statutory rules augment and modify the general principles, where appropriate, but normally there are no formalities required for a sale of goods contract.

The most basic rule of the general law governing the transfer of property is expressed in the latin maxim *nemo dat quod non habet* (no one can give that which he has not). In simple terms this means that a buyer (transferee) can take no better title to goods than that which the seller (transferor) had. Thus, if an owner sells goods then the buyer in turn becomes owner. But if a thief (who necessarily acquires no title to his booty), sells the stolen goods to a buyer, the general rule is that the owner may demand their return leaving the buyer to seek recompense from the thief. This principle demonstrates the sanctity of property rights in English law. Such a principle does of course tend to stifle trading because of the inherent difficulty in discovering whether a seller is in fact a true owner. Because of the needs of the trading community a number of exceptions to the *"nemo dat"* principle have been developed and these are considered in due course.

Choses in action

The transfer of intangible rights which, of course, can only be claimed or enforced by legal action is known as *assignment*. This is an area of law which has been the subject of a long, complicated, history which requires some explanation in order to make the present state of the law meaningful. Choses in action have no physical substance and depend upon legal rules for their very existence. It will come as no surprise to learn that the common law recognised some choses but the Court of Chancery (or equity) recognised even more. Thus a claim to a contract debt was recognised at common law but only equity would acknowledge a claim to a share in a trust fund, for trusts were creations of equity. In short, we now have recognition of *legal* choses in action and *equitable* choses in action.

The common law did not allow the holder of a chose in action to assign it so as to enable the assignee to sue on it in his own name. It was possible for an assignor to grant the assignee a *power of attorney* (a formal deed) enabling the assignee to sue the debtor in the assignor's name but the assignee could not insist upon this.

Equity, however, would enforce an assignment of a chose in action without insisting upon any particular formality. Moreover, it would enforce not only equitable choses in action but also legal choses in action. The procedure for enforcement was simply that equity required the assignor to join with the assignee in any action on the chose and in the event of the assignor refusing, he was treated as a defendant to the assignee's action. However, an assignee could only obtain such rights against the debtor as the assignor had. So that if a debtor would have had a defence to an action by the assignor, then provided the basis for the defence arose before the debtor was advised of the assignment, he had the same defence against the assignee. The assignment would be said to be *subject to equities*.

There have been many specific statutory provisions enabling assignment of particular contract rights but the most significant provision is section 136 of the Law of Property Act 1925 which provides that all debts and other choses in action are assignable. In order to effect a valid *statutory assignment* three conditions must be satisfied:

(a) it must be absolute;

(b) it must be in writing; and

(c) written notice must be given to the debtor.

An assignment satisfying these conditions enables the assignee to sue the debtor in his own name whether the assignment was for valuable consideration or merely gratuitous. However, the assignee still only acquires the same title or rights as his assignor for the assignment is, as always, subject to equities. Thus if X owed Y £100 and Y wished to transfer his right to Z, he could give effect to his wish by expressing his intention in writing making a complete transfer of the whole sum and giving notice to X. Should X have a set-off against Y of £10, then this could be set up as "an equity" against Z so reducing the effective value of the transferred right to £90.

Obviously an intending assignor ought ideally to comply with the provisions of the Law of Property Act but the question arises of dealing with instances in which the statutory provisions have not been fully observed. Once again equity may come to the rescue for an *equitable assignment* requires no formalities and may be made orally, or in writing, or by merely transferring possession of a document representing the chose assigned. But even here statute has intervened, for an equitable assignment of an equitable chose in action must, under section 53 of the Law of Property Act 1925, be in writing and signed by the assignor or his agent.

The question of *priority* is central to assignment and in all cases of assignment in order to secure priority it is wise to give notice to the debtor. Should an assignee fail to give notice, then a debtor may discharge his liability by paying the assignor or indeed by paying another assignee who has given notice. In the case of assignment of an equitable chose, it is provided by section 137 of the Law of Property Act 1925, that the notice in order to be effective must be in writing. Thus, if X should have an interest in a trust fund of which Y is trustee (and may be considered the debtor) and X wishes to transfer his interest to Z, then, because this is an equitable chose, should he fail to observe section 136 of the Law of Property Act 1925, even though the transfer may take effect as an equitable assignment it must be made in writing signed by X or his agent (s.53). Moreover, should there be no notice in writing given to Y, then, if X subsequently made a second transfer of the same interest to Q and notice of this transfer was given to Y, Q's interest should prevail over that of Z.

NEGOTIABLE INSTRUMENTS

Introduction

The original basic rule of common law that choses in action could not be transferred has, it should now be clear, been quite overtaken by statute and the work of equity. However, the principle of *"nemo dat quod non habet"* has remained in the notion that assignees take "subject to equities." There is one more significant historical development to relate which has a profound impact upon our present law.

The *law merchant* from early times recognised certain types of legal choses in action as being transferable and the law merchant was admitted as part of the common law thus providing an exception to the basic rule. These special choses in action were known as *negotiable instruments* because not only were they *transferable* but also in certain circumstances the transferee could acquire a better title than that possessed by his transferor. In other words, the significance of *negotiability* is that the rule that transferees take "subject to equities" may be avoided. The development of this exceptional class of negotiable instruments was essential to the existence of a trading community because the principal use of negotiable instruments is as a substitute for money. Obviously a trader wishing to pay a £100 debt would be seriously inconvenienced if he was obliged to carry that sum in coin to his creditor's premises. The custom of merchants enabled the settlement of such debts by mere transfer of a document which was recognised as being "as good as money." If someone steals your £10 note and you find it in the possession of someone else who has given change for it, quite innocently, then you cannot claim back your £10 note because it is negotiable and the thief, who had no title, has given the innocent party a good title. Similarly, if a thief was to steal a cheque (one of the commonest forms of negotiable instrument) for £10 which had been given to you, then *it would be possible* for him to "negotiate" the cheque to an innocent party thus depriving you of your property in the cheque.

The essential features of a negotiable instrument are that:

(a) it is recognised by law (either by custom or statute) as being of a class which enables a third party taking it in good faith and for value, being money or money's worth, to obtain a good title, even though the person from whom he received it had a defective title;

(b) it must be freely transferable either by mere delivery or by delivery and indorsement (which simply means placing a signature upon a document).

Common forms of negotiable instrument

Much of the law governing negotiable instruments is to be found in the Bills of Exchange Act 1882 and the Cheques Act 1957, together with appropriate case law. Bills of exchange are a somewhat outdated form of negotiable instrument, so far as inland commercial transactions are concerned, but the ubiquitous cheque is actually a type of bill of exchange. Only the cheque will be considered in detail. Most legal offices deal with a constant flow of cheques and confidence in their handling is only gained on understanding of some basic legal rules. It suffices to note the other principal forms of negotiable instrument:

(a) *Promissory notes,* which are simply written promises by one person to pay money to another at a future date. Bank notes fall into this class.

(b) *Bearer bonds,* which are documents issued by foreign governments or companies, which entitle the bearer (the person in possession) to claim repayment of a loan and in the meantime to present detachable coupons entitling the presenter to payment of interest.

(c) *Bearer debentures,* which are documents in which companies acknowledge a debt to the bearer where the debt is normally secured by a charge on the companies' assets given to trustees who are responsible for proper conduct of the transaction. These instruments are principally issued by continental companies but entry into the European Communities has resulted in more frequent appearances on the domestic scene.

Cheques

A consideration of cheques must commence with the definition of a bill of exchange, for a cheque is simply a special form of bill. Section 3 of the Bills of Exchange Act 1882 defines a *bill of exchange* and its provisions may be expressed as requiring:

(a) an unconditional order;

(b) in writing;

(c) addressed by one person to another;

(d) signed by the person giving it;

(e) requiring the person to whom it is addressed to pay (on demand, or at a fixed or determinable future time);

(f) a sum certain in money;

(g) to, or to the order of, a specified person or to a bearer.

By section 73 of the 1882 Act *a cheque* is:

(a) a bill of exchange;

(b) drawn on a banker; and

(c) payable on demand.

The net effect of these two definitions may be illustrated by an example in which a banker's relationship with his customer is also shown. David Debtor has opened a current account with the Corner Bank Limited which has issued him with a cheque book. When David Debtor opened his account with Corner Bank Limited he handed money to the bank so that it might be held on his behalf. At this stage the banker became a debtor, owing David the amount which he deposited and David became the bank's creditor. However, the bank also impliedly undertook to observe David's instructions as to the manner in which the money in the account should be repaid. These instructions are communicated by David in the form of cheques drawn on the Corner Bank Limited. Thus, if David Debtor should owe £60 to Chris Creditor then he would express his instructions to the Corner Bank Limited in the form of a cheque, being an unconditional order in writing addressed by David Debtor to Corner Bank Limited, signed by David Debtor, requiring Corner Bank Limited to pay, on demand, a specified sum of money (£60) either to Chris Creditor or to whomsoever Chris Creditor should order it should be paid. The form of the cheque would be as illustrated in the figure below.

7th JUNE 1987

CORNER BANK LIMITED
GREY STREET BRANCH

PAY   Chris Creditor   OR ORDER

Sixty Pounds   £60 ——————

DAVID DEBTOR

The names given to the parties to the cheque are the *drawer* (David Debtor), the *drawee* (Corner Bank Limited) and the *payee* (Chris Creditor). Moreover, the payee of the cheque is the first *holder* and should he wish to transfer it then he would *indorse* it (sign it, customarily on the back) and pass it to the transferee (or *indorsee*) who would become, in turn, the holder.

Negotiation . . . is the term used to describe the transfer of a cheque but the requirements for transfer differ according to whether the cheque is payable to a specified person or to bearer. A cheque payable to a specified person is negotiated by indorsement and delivery. A cheque payable "to bearer" is negotiated by mere delivery, there is no need for any indorsement.

Indorsements . . . may be either special indorsements, indorsements in blank or restrictive indorsements. A special indorsement specifies the transferee. Thus, a cheque payable to "Chris Creditor or order" would be specially indorsed by Chris Creditor signing it on the back and following his signature by the words "pay James Smith." This negotiation would be completed when Chris Creditor handed the cheque to James Smith.

An indorsement in blank specifies no indorsee (transferee). Thus a cheque payable to "Chris Creditor or order" would be indorsed in blank by the simple action of Chris Creditor signing his name on the back. The cheque would then become payable to bearer and as such any future negotiation would be made by mere delivery.

A restrictive indorsement prohibits further negotiation of the cheque and the effect is that no further transfer is possible. Thus, if Chris Creditor, the payee of a cheque, was to negotiate the cheque by restrictive indorsement, "Pay James Smith only," then only James Smith would be entitled to present the cheque for payment.

Crossed cheques . . . take a variety of forms and a cheque which has two parallel transverse lines across its face (often but unnecessarily enclosing the words "and company" or "and Co.") is said to be *crossed generally*. The effect of crossing is that the cheque ought not to be "cashed" over the bank counter but should only be paid by the drawee (paying) bank following its presentation for payment by another (collecting) banker (or after having been credited to an account with the drawee bank). The impact of crossing is therefore to handicap a person who has wrongfully obtained a cheque, for in the delay in obtaining payment the loss may be discovered and the cheque "stopped." Moreover, tracing the wrongdoer will be easier because the cheque must have been presented by someone holding a bank account who ought therefore to be discoverable.

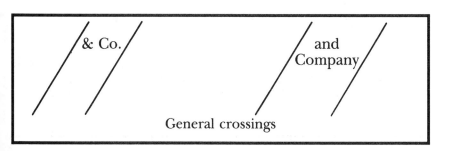

General crossings

Where the name of a particular banker (and often branch) is written across the face of a cheque (with or without transverse parallel lines) the cheque is *specially crossed*. The effect of this crossing is that the paying banker must only pay the cheque to the collecting banker named in the crossing. Such a special crossing may be used where a drawer wishes to pay a cheque to a person who is a well known customer of a particular bank or branch. By such a crossing the drawer will minimise the risk of successful impersonation should anyone steal the cheque. Because of the crossing the thief will have to present the cheque at the bank or branch at which the true owner is known.

Should a banker fail to observe the requirements of a general or special crossing he is liable to the true owner for any loss that person may suffer. Thus, if a bearer cheque is crossed and delivered to its payee from whom it is stolen, should the thief obtain payment over the counter, the paying banker would be liable to reimburse the payee with the amount of the cheque.

Neither general nor special crossings prevent negotiation of a cheque but should the crossed cheque have the words "not negotiable" added then although it remains *transferable*, it is not *negotiable*, and no one can claim to have a better title than the previous holder (1882 Act, s.81). In

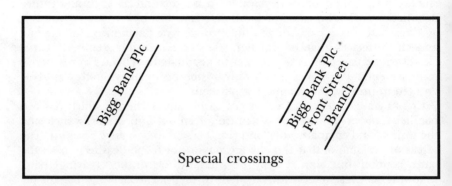

Special crossings

short, the instrument loses its essential quality as a negotiable instrument and holders take "subject to equities."

Cheques are frequently crossed "*A/C Payee*" or "*Account Payee only.*" These crossings are not recognised by statute and do not form part of a crossing, for the crossing is an instruction to the paying bank and these words can only be an instruction to the collecting bank as to how to deal with the funds represented by the cheque. The words do not prevent transfer nor negotiation of a cheque but do have significance in relation to "statutory protection for banks" which is considered below. In practice the collecting bank will only pay cheques written in this form into an account in the name of the person specified as payee or will make diligent inquiries before crediting an indorsee's account. The various crossings may be combined so as to bring together the several protections they give to the drawer.

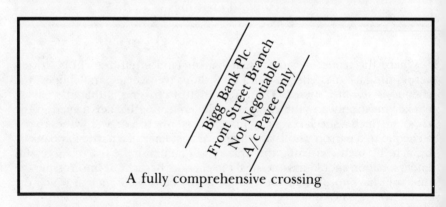

A fully comprehensive crossing

Statutory protection for banks . . . from liability in conversion is afforded because of the particular danger which banks run of innocently handling cheques for non-owners or paying cheques to non-owners so as to prima facie incur liability for this tort. (The tort of conversion is committed when a person deals with another's property as though it were his own . . . see page 221.) Some appreciation of this protection is valuable to those handling cheques on behalf of their organisations for it enables understanding of the procedures insisted upon by bankers.

If a bank pays the wrong person when paying one of its customer's cheques it is liable in conversion to the true owner of the cheque (*e.g.* the person from whom the cheque has been stolen) and cannot debit the customer's account. However, where the bank can claim the protection of the statutory provisions outlined below it will be entitled to debit its customer's account.

Section 59 of the Bills of Exchange Act 1882 provides that where a bank pays a holder of a cheque in good faith and without notice of any defect in title the bank is freed from liability. This section, however, only operates where the person paid is the *holder* (see page 000) and, a person in possession of an *order* cheque bearing a *forged indorsement* cannot be a holder (section 24 of the 1882 Act). Thus, section 59 only protects a bank which has paid on a *bearer* cheque which, of course, does not require indorsement for negotiation.

Section 60 protects a bank which pays an order cheque which has a forged indorsement provided:

(a) the bank pays in good faith; *and*

(b) in the ordinary course of business.

However, it is possible that a bank may pay the wrong person on an order cheque where there is no forged indorsement. If a thief, for example, stole a cheque which had already been indorsed and presented himself as the indorsee there would be no need for any forged indorsement. Section 60 would not protect the bank in this situation but section 80 may do so. Section 80 provides that where a banker pays a *crossed* cheque:

(a) in accordance with the crossing;

(b) in good faith; and

(c) without negligence.

it will be in the same position as if it had paid the true owner.

It will be noted that section 80 only applies to crossed cheques and this would appear to leave a bank vulnerable where it pays a thief who presents himself as the indorsee of an uncrossed cheque. However, section 1 of the Cheques Act 1957 provides that where a cheque is not indorsed, or is irregularly indorsed, and is paid in good faith and in the ordinary course of business, the bank does not incur any liability through the absence or irregularity of the indorsement. Prior to the passing of this provision banks, as a matter of course, required all cheques to be indorsed when paid in and went to considerable trouble to identify irregular indorsements. The 1957 Act relieved the banks of this time consuming process but had the Act not been passed the thief presenting himself as an indorsee would have been required to indorse the cheque which he had stolen. In the latter situation the bank would have relied upon section 60 for protection by reason of the forged indorsement and today it would call upon section 1 of the 1957 Act to protect it from liability which could have arisen by reason of the absence of the indorsement.

Finally, just as a paying bank is prima facie liable to the true owner should it pay the wrong person, the *collecting* bank may incur liability to the true owner should it collect payment for the wrong person. In this case, section 4 of the Cheques Act 1957 provides protection and the collecting bank will not be liable where it receives payment for a customer and does so in good faith and without negligence. It is in this situation that the words "account payee" written across a cheque could have significance (see earlier for crossed cheques). Should a collecting banker pay a cheque into an account of someone other than the payee and thereby collect the funds represented by the cheque for a non-owner, then he could be held to be negligent and lose his statutory protection. However, it has been held in *Lumsden & Co.* v. *London T.S.B.* that if the true owner's lack of care has contributed to the loss arising from the act of conversion then his damages may be appropriately reduced on account of contributory negligence (this principle has been maintained as an exception to section 11 of the Torts (Interference with Goods) Act 1977, which is noted below, by section 47 of the Banking Act 1979).

It can now be readily appreciated why banks take such care in paying and collecting cheques. Deviation from normal practice or negligence may leave a bank liable in conversion. For example, because cheques are normally presented for payment within a matter of days, those which have been in circulation for more than a week or two are regarded as stale and to pay them would be outside normal practice. In these circumstances a bank will take precautions and either decline to pay such cheques or make inquiries before doing so.

PROTECTION OF PERSONAL PROPERTY

The wide variety of personal property demands a range of remedies if the maxim *ubi jus, ibi remedium* (where there is a right, there is a remedy) is to be maintained. Protection of rights to chattels personal is achieved through the law of tort. Infringements of these rights give rise to liability to claims for damages and, in appropriate cases, to the issue of injunctions restraining the unlawful acts. In relation to certain property there is extensive legislation dealing with problems of infringement (*e.g.* for patents and copyright, Patents Act 1977, Copyright Act 1956). However, the most wide ranging protection is afforded through the law developed to deal with wrongful interference with goods. There are now two basic torts affording protection to personal property, namely *conversion* and *trespass to goods*. The Torts (Interference with Goods) Act 1977 does, however, acknowledge that an actionable interference with goods may also arise out of Negligence or any other tort, quite independently of the above two torts, in so far as damage is caused to goods. The 1977 Act did not codify the law governing interference with goods but merely dealt with certain deficiencies in the common law so that in large part the present law is to be found in the decisions of the courts.

Trespass to goods

Trespass to goods is merely a wrongful physical interference with goods. The usual form of this direct interference is damaging or removing goods. Thus, to slash a car tyre would amount to trespass, similarly to shift a parked car to another parking space would be a trespass. The slightest interference with goods will suffice to ground an action, such as the touching of an exhibit on display, but no doubt an award of substantial damages would only be made where actual loss had followed the trespass. The usefulness of an action for trespass to goods arises in cases of transitory interferences, more permanent interferences usually involve conversion.

Conversion

Conversion may take an almost endless variety of forms so that it appears impossible to provide a comprehensive definition. However, if one regards conversion as the civil equivalent of theft this would provide a broad picture of the tort. Yet, conversion need not involve any conscious wrongdoing, for the innocent purchaser of goods from a thief, who acquires no title to the goods, commits an action in conversion because he deals with the goods in a manner inconsistent with the rights of the owner. The tell-tale mark of an act amounting to conversion is that the wrong consists of either dealing with goods belonging to another so as to deny that other's rights or asserting rights which are inconsistent with those of another. The following are illustrative of wrongful acts amounting to conversion:

(a) *taking goods* belonging to another (*e.g.* where it is mistakenly believed that the taker is entitled to the goods);

(b) *withholding goods* belonging to another (*e.g.* where the withholder erroneously believes that he has good title to the goods);

(c) *destroying goods* belonging to another (*e.g.* in a case of criminal damage);

(d) *selling goods* belonging to another (*e.g.* where an auctioneer is handed goods to sell on behalf of a non-owner);

(e) where a banker *collects the proceeds of a cheque* for a customer who is not the true owner (see, however, the special statutory defences available to bankers discussed above);

(f) where a banker *cashes a cheque* over the counter to someone other than the true owner (see, however, the special statutory defences available to bankers discussed above).

In order to be able to bring an action for conversion the plaintiff must have been either:

(a) in possession of the goods; or

(b) entitled to call for immediate possession of the goods at the time of the wrong.

This means that a finder of goods, from whom they were withheld, can sue for their return, as in *Armory* v. *Delamirie* where a chimney sweep who had found a jewel in a flue was entitled to his claim against a jeweller to whom he had entrusted it for valuation. In contrast, if an owner has disabled himself from calling for immediate possession by, for instance, letting out the goods on hire, he may be unable to sue for conversion.

The usual remedy for conversion is an award of damages assessed as the value of the goods at the date of conversion but the court does have power to award delivery of specific goods and/or damages should this be appropriate (see page 222).

Defences

It must immediately be noted that mistake does not usually provide a defence to an action based upon wrongful interference with goods, for liability is strict. However, where the mistake causes an innocent party to purchase goods from a non-owner, then by one of the exceptions to the principle of *nemo dat quod non habet*, the innocent purchaser may acquire a good title to the goods so as to defeat the true owner's claim completely. The exceptions to the "*nemo dat*" principle have been developed as a compromise between the competing interests of owners (whose demand is that their property rights should be protected) and those of the trading community (whose demand is that commerce should be encouraged). There are many exceptions and two examples must suffice as illustrating the underlying nature of the compromise:

(a) Where an owner, having sold goods to a buyer, nevertheless remains in possession of the goods then sells and delivers them to a second buyer, the second buyer acquires ownership from the original seller. The first buyer who is thereby deprived of the title he originally received from the seller is left to pursue an action for damages against the seller.

(b) Where an owner places his goods in the hands of an agent who customarily has power to sell goods on behalf of others, then, even though the agent is not on this occasion authorised to sell the goods on behalf of the owner nevertheless a buyer may acquire ownership through the agent. Thus the owner would be deprived of his property and be left to sue the agent.

Finders too are afforded a defence to an action for wrongful interference with the goods which they take into their possession. The defence is available provided the finder acts reasonably in seeking to ascertain the true owner and does not intend to misappropriate the goods.

Contributory negligence has been firmly rejected as a defence to the mainstream actions of conversion and intentional trespass to goods by section 11 of the Torts (Interference with Goods) Act 1977. However, there has been a subsequent qualification upon this rule in order to meet the special needs of bankers and this has been noted above.

Finally, a *lien* may be relied upon as justifying an act which otherwise bears the marks of unlawful interference with goods. There are two main types, common law (or possessory) and equitable liens. The essence of a common law lien is that it entitles a party in possession of property to retain it until payment, operating as a form of security or "lawful blackmail." Thus, a repairer acquires the right to withhold repaired goods from the owner until payment is made for the work done. Moreover, of particular relevance to the legal practitioner, a solicitor has a lien over his clients' property for his professional fees, as does an accountant and also a banker.

An equitable lien attaches by law irrespective of possession and upon dissolution of a partnership a partner acquires a lien over partnership property for payment of money owed by the partnership. Of course, as there is no "thing" to be possessed an equitable lien may only be enforced following its recognition by order of the court.

Damages for interference with personal property

The usual remedy for wrongful interference with the goods (personal property) of a plaintiff is damages, assessed as the value of the goods at the date of conversion. In appropriate cases consequential loss (where, for example, the plaintiff cannot utilise his property in his business) may be recovered. Under the provisions of the Torts (Interference with Goods) Act 1977 a court may award the following forms of relief:

(a) an order for the delivery of the goods, and for payment of any consequential damages; or

(b) an order for delivery of the goods, but giving the defendant the alternative of paying damages by reference to the value of the goods, together in either alternative with payment of any consequential damages; or

(c) damages.

In an action for damages for wrongful interference payment of the damages (or settlement of the claim) extinguishes the plaintiff's title to the goods in question.

Actions for interference with personal property

These actions being tortious are subject to the general six-year limitation period discussed at page 189. Where, however, any cause of action has accrued in respect of the conversion of the plaintiff's goods and, before he recovers possession, a further conversion takes place, the limitation period runs from the original date of accrual. Moreover, the plaintiff will lose completely any title to those goods if he fails to bring an action before the expiration of the six years.

Section D: Marriage and Children

In most cases the reason for the law consumer's decision to acquire real property is that he is about to marry or, being married, his family has outgrown his present accommodation. Marriage is also likely to precipitate much activity in the acquisition of personal property. The property related aspects of marriage have, then, been dealt with in the preceding Sections. The present Section contains a consideration of marriage itself and of other matters which are generally regarded as related to marriage.

The classic definition of marriage in English law is that it is the "voluntary union for life of one man and one woman to the exclusion of all others." Marriage is, moreover, the institution upon which the family is built and to view it in the absence of children would be to risk a failure to appreciate its basic place in society. There are of course increasing numbers of "one parent" families, but the married family unit retains a special place in our law.

MARRIAGE

The mere event of agreeing to become married is of legal significance and upon marriage the parties acquire a legal status, that is, they enter a special class of persons with particular capacities and incapacities automatically imposed by law.

Agreements to marry

Frequently marriages are preceded by an "engagement" which the common law recognised as a binding contract if intended as such by the parties. However, it was obviously socially undesirable that the threat of a legal action should be used to drag an unstable marriage into existence and actions for breach of promise of marriage were abolished by the Law Reform (Miscellaneous Provisions) Act 1970. Section 1 of the Act simply provides that no agreement to marry has the effect of a legally binding contract. Yet, because engaged couples frequently pool resources and purchase property in preparation for their wedded bliss, disruption of the grand plan can leave a tangle of interests in property. Section 2 therefore provides that "where an agreement to marry is terminated, any rule of law relating to the rights of husbands and wives in relation to property in which either or both have a beneficial interest . . . shall apply in relation to any property in which either or both of the parties to the agreement had a beneficial interest while the agreement was in force...." Thus, if the prospective groom purchases a house in his own name using both his own money and that of his intended wife, and they both work so as to enhance the value of the prospective matrimonial home, the girl will be entitled to the same interest in it as she would have acquired had the parties been man and wife. As to that special piece of property, the engagement ring, section 3 provides that it is presumed to be an absolute gift and this can only be rebutted by evidence that it was intended to be returned in the event of no marriage taking place. On the other hand, wedding presents from third parties may be taken to be conditional gifts to be returned to the donors should the anticipated marriage fail to materialise.

The contract of marriage

In order to acquire the status of man and wife, parties must satisfy certain conditions which may be best appreciated by considering marriage (as did the common law) as a special form of contractual relationship. Thus the parties must have *capacity* to contract a marriage and they must observe appropriate *formalities*.

Capacity ... neither party must be already married and each must have attained the age of 16. Furthermore, the parties must not be within the prohibited degrees of relationship set out in the Marriage Act 1949, as amended. For example, a man may not marry his daughter nor indeed his wife's son's daughter. Finally, the parties must be respectively man and woman for as Ormrod J. expressed the matter in *Corbett* v. *Corbett* (a case arising from a "sex change") "the capacity for natural heterosexual intercourse is an essential element" of marriage. Biological sex is determined at birth and remains fixed, for the purposes of marriage, and it may be that those individuals who are sexually unclassifiable from birth are incapable of marriage with a true man or woman.

Lack of capacity to marry results in total failure of any purported marriage, which is *void* under section 11 of the Matrimonial Causes Act 1973.

Formalities ... the Marriage Acts 1949 to 1983 provide the formalities essential to a valid marriage which may be solemnised according to the rites of the Church of England before two witnesses after the publication of banns, or solemnised upon the authority of a superintendent registrar's certificate. The Jewish and Quaker communities have the privilege of solemnisation according to their own rites but other religious ceremonies must be underpinned by the superintendent registrar. If both parties are aware of a failure to comply with a procedural formality, for example, where the marriage is solemnised according to Church of England rites without proper publication of banns or appropriate dispensation, then the purported marriage will be void.

A marriage which is void is in fact no marriage at all, having never come into existence. The logical consequence is that there is no need for the parties to seek a judicial declaration of nullity but the court will consider such petitions and, simply in the interests of certainty, it may be advisable to obtain such a declaration.

Voidable marriages

Just as an apparently valid contract may be vitiated upon various grounds rendering it voidable, so too may a marriage. It must be emphasised, however, that a voidable marriage is to be treated as existing until it is set aside, and even then a decree of nullity only operates so as to annul it for the future. The grounds upon which a marriage may be voidable are set out in section 12 of the Matrimonial Causes Act 1973 (M.C.A.) and may be considered under five heads.

Non-consummation . . . a marriage is consummated upon "ordinary and complete" sexual intercourse after solemnisation. Mere non-consummation does not of itself form the basis for a petition of nullity but must be based upon either incapacity of either party or wilful refusal on the part of the respondent.

Lack of consent . . . duress, mistake as to identity, unsoundness of mind or other vitiating elements, have, in the past, been regarded as preventing a contract from coming into existence, and naturally affect a marriage contracted in such circumstances. However, because the parties could wish to ratify when able to give consent marriages are not today treated as totally void on these grounds. It has recently been held by the Court of Appeal in *Hirani* v. *Hirani* that duress is not restricted to fears of "immediate danger to life, limb or liberty" but extends to any overbearing of the will of the petitioner so as to destroy the reality of consent. In *Hirani* a Hindu girl, who had been associating with a Muslim boy, entered an arranged marriage with a Hindu having been told that unless she complied with her parents' wishes she must leave their home. The girl had nowhere else to go and no means of supporting herself and it was held that the threat had overborne her will.

Mental disorder . . . continuous or intermittent disorder (even though not depriving a party from giving consent to marriage) which renders a party "incapable of carrying out the ordinary duties and obligations of marriage" enables either the sufferer or the other party to petition.

Venereal disease . . . this provides grounds for a petition where the respondent suffered from it in a communicable form at the time of the ceremony.

Pregnancy per alium . . . a husband may petition where the respondent wife was pregnant, at the time of the ceremony, by someone else.

For all grounds, with the exception of the first, the court must normally be satisfied that proceedings were instituted within three years of the marriage (M.C.A., s.13(2)). Moreover, in the case of the last two grounds, the petitioner must have been unaware of the circumstances at the time of the marriage (M.C.A., s.13(3)). Under the Matrimonial and Family Proceedings Act 1984 a nullity petition may be presented after the three years' period if the petitioner has been suffering from a mental disorder (within the meaning of the Mental Health Act 1983) at some time during that period and it would be just for the court to grant leave. Finally, a decree of nullity may not issue avoiding a marriage should the respondent satisfy the court that the petitioner acted so as to lead the respondent reasonably to believe that he would not seek to avoid the marriage and that it would be unjust to grant a decree (M.C.A., s.13(1)).

The status arising from marriage

Following marriage the natural assumption is that the parties will commence sharing life together in the matrimonial home and this cosy picture is underlined by their mutual legal right to *consortium*. This is an abstract notion which revolves around the duty to cohabit. It may be illustrated by reference to a number of the incidents of consortium which are part and parcel of the relationship of husband and wife but also have an impact upon the rights and duties of the parties under the general law relating to crime, contract, tort and property.

Right to sexual intercourse... the duty of spouses to consummate a marriage stretches into a right of intercourse provided demands are not unreasonable. A spouse unreasonably insisting upon intercourse or wilfully and unreasonably refusing intercourse raises a situation in which the other party is entitled to withdraw from cohabitation without being considered in desertion and indeed the unreasonable spouse may be treated as having constructively deserted. The right to intercourse affects the criminal law, for a husband cannot normally be found guilty, as a principal, of rape of his own wife. However, if the parties have agreed to live apart or a court order has been made, then a conviction for rape would be possible and in any case obtaining intercourse by force could amount to a criminal assault. There was a basic rule that spouses were not permitted to give evidence against each other in criminal matters. But, under section 80 of the Police and Criminal Evidence Act 1984 spouses are now generally competent to give evidence for the prosecution. Indeed, in certain circumstances they may be compelled to do so, for example, in cases of assault by one spouse on the other.

Right to support or maintenance... at common law a husband has a duty to maintain his wife. This is reflected in a rebuttable presumption that a wife cohabiting with her husband has authority to pledge his credit for "necessaries," that is, for goods suitable to the husband's chosen life-style. Even if a husband has forbidden his wife to pledge his credit and the presumption is rebutted, the husband will still be liable on the contract of purchase if there has been an appearance of authority on the part of the wife as a result of a "holding out" (*e.g.* where a husband in the past has paid for goods supplied on credit to his wife so as to lead a tradesman into the belief that the wife was actually authorised to pledge her husband's credit, *Debbenham* v. *Mellon*). This one-sided duty has now been supplemented by various statutory provisions under which there are mutual obligations of maintenance relating to spouses and children. Thus, under section 17 of the Supplementary Benefits Act 1976, spouses are placed under a duty to maintain one another and their children. Supplementary benefit may be paid to assist those in need and then a claim may be made on behalf of the Secretary of State for Social Services in a magistrates' court to recover the sums paid from the defaulting spouse. Magistrates' courts are also empowered under the Domestic Proceedings and Magistrates' Courts Act 1978 to order a spouse to make financial provision (either periodic or lump sum payments) for the other party or children. The grounds for such claims are:

(a) failure to provide reasonable maintenance;
(b) unreasonable behaviour justifying the applicant in ceasing to cohabit; and
(c) desertion by the respondent.

The court is required to take account of the same factors as are considered upon marital breakdown under section 25 of the Matrimonial Causes Act 1973 (see page 232).

Marital communications... the intimate and confidential nature of the relationship of husband and wife has given rise to great reluctance to allow what passes between the parties to form the basis of legal liability. Thus, although since the Law Reform (Husband and Wife) Act 1962 each spouse has the same right of action against the other as if they were not married, the court has a power to stay an action if: (a) it appears no substantial benefit would accrue to either, or (b) the matter relates to property and could be better dealt with by an application under section 17 of the Married Women's Property Act 1882 (see below). For the purposes of the tort of defamation a communication between spouses does not amount to publication, and so far as contracts are concerned there is a rebuttable presumption against an intention to create legal relations. Moreover, in *Argyll* v. *Argyll* an injunction was granted in the court's general equitable jurisdiction to prevent the publication of secrets of the private married life of the parties.

Matrimonial home . . . the common law regarded a husband as head of the household with the duty to provide and choose a home, but today selection of the home is a matter for agreement between the parties. In the absence of agreement, the casting vote will probably be with the breadwinner as his or her base for operations is, next to consensus, the most relevant factor. Should it be impossible to say that either party is acting unreasonably in refusing to agree upon location of the matrimonial home then neither can allege desertion on the part of the other.

Ownership of the matrimonial home, and indeed other property held by spouses, has been the subject of considerable evolution. In early times it was normally assumed that a wife on marriage bestowed her husband with all her "wordly goods," but by the nineteenth century it became accepted that a wife retained her property interests. Of course, in practice during a harmonious marriage the parties tend to regard property as jointly owned, yet on breakdown more discriminating claims are likely to be made and the law has developed to take account of this fluid situation. The Married Women's Property Act 1882, s.17 (as amended), provides that "in any question between husband and wife as to the title to or possession of property" either party (and indeed parties to an engagement) may apply to the court, which "may make such order with respect to the property in dispute . . . " as is considered fit. After many years of uncertainty it is now established, following *Pettitt* v. *Pettitt* that the power of the court under this provision does not extend to varying existing interests nor does it confer any wider power to transfer or create interests in property than exists in any other proceedings. The section merely confers "a wide discretion as to the enforcement of the proprietary or possessory rights of one spouse in any property against the other" (*e.g.* the court may order property to be sold and direct how the proceeds are to be divided). Thus, one must look to other sources to discover the actual principles governing property rights of spouses which may then be enforced by the expeditious procedure of section 17.

The Married Women's Property Act 1964 deals with one common domestic arrangement leading to property acquisition. It provides that in the absence of contrary agreement money or property acquired through a housekeeping allowance made by a husband to a wife should be treated as belonging to the parties in equal shares. The Matrimonial Proceedings and Property Act 1970, s.37, provides that where one spouse makes a substantial contribution to the improvement of property in which the other has a beneficial interest, for example by undertaking refurbishment, then that spouse is to be regarded as having acquired thereby an interest (or greater interest) in the improved property. Indeed, in equity the court may apportion interests in jointly acquired property according to the contribution of the parties or, in the absence of evidence of precise contributions, as the court considers just. It ought to be noted that the court has extensive power, under the Matrimonial Causes Act 1973, ss.21–25, which may be used to disturb and reallocate existing property rights *upon divorce* (considered below).

The Matrimonial Homes Act 1983 affords statutory rights of occupation which extend to a right for those in occupation not to be excluded, and for those out of occupation a right to enter and remain in occupation of the matrimonial home (subject to the discretion of the court). The rights extend to a spouse, who has only a joint interest or, indeed, otherwise no interest affording a right to occupy. Registration of these rights as a Class F Land Charge or by notice, in the case of registered land, affords protection against third parties. Thus, during the currency of a marriage a deserted wife protected by registration could not be evicted, without a court order, from the matrimonial home even though the full legal and equitable rights were vested in the husband.

The Domestic Violence and Matrimonial Proceedings Act 1976 empowers the High Court or a county court to regulate the occupation of the matrimonial home (or quasi-matrimonial home, where parties are simply living together as husband and wife) and to protect spouses, cohabitees and children against family violence. Under section 1 the court is empowered to issue an injunction restraining one party from *molesting* the other (or "children living with the applicant") and also either excluding a party from the matrimonial home or requiring that the applicant should be permitted to enter and remain in the matrimonial home (or part of it). Although in theory there is an overlap between the 1976 and 1983 Acts as regards occupation by married couples, the House of Lords has indicated in *Richards* v. *Richards* that during the subsistence of a marriage exclusion from the matrimonial home should be dealt with under the Matrimonial Homes Act 1983.

The Domestic Proceedings and Magistrates' Courts Act 1978 gives magistrates' courts powers similar to those enjoyed by county courts under the 1976 Act but is restricted to *married couples*. Section 16 empowers magistrates' courts to make orders (a) against the use or threat of personal *violence* to the applicant or a child of the family (personal protection orders) and (b) prohibiting the respondent from entering, and/or requiring that party to leave the matrimonial home (exclusion orders). A *child of the family* is a child of both spouses or any other child who has been treated by both as a child of the family. Before making a personal protection order the court must be satisfied that violence has been used or threatened and that the order is necessary for protection. For the award of an exclusion order the criteria are that the applicant or child is in danger of being physically injured by the respondent who has (a) used personal violence against the applicant or child, or (b) threatened such violence *and* used such violence against some other person, or (c) contravened a personal protection order by threatening violence against the applicant or child.

Husband's surname . . . by custom a wife may take her husband's surname on marriage and may retain it even after divorce or her husband's death. In short, a husband has no property right in his name and his wife or former wife may only be restrained from using it where such use would be fraudulent or otherwise contrary to law as, for example, where an ex-wife held herself out as still being the lawful wife of her remarried former husband.

Breakdown of marriage

Magistrates' orders ... when a marriage breaks down the ultimate legal remedy is to formally terminate it by divorce proceedings. However, for many ailing marriages the matrimonial jurisdiction of magistrates' courts affords at least initial relief and although this may be simply a staging-post on the way to divorce many parties never go beyond a magistrates' court. Attempts at conciliation through probation officers appointed by the court are, perhaps, more likely to be successful at this stage than when divorce proceedings have been embarked upon. The Domestic Proceedings and Magistrates' Courts Act 1978 brought the jurisdiction of magistrates into line with divorce law. The grounds for the making of orders for financial relief between spouses are now similar to those situations considered in detail below as evidence in divorce proceedings of irretrievable breakdown of marriage but of course it is not necessary in proceedings before magistrates to show that the marriage has irretrievably broken down. Section 1 of the 1978 Act provides that the four grounds on which a magistrates' order for financial provision may be made are:

(a) failure to provide reasonable maintenance for the other spouse;
(b) failure to provide or make proper contributions towards reasonable maintenance of any child of the family;
(c) behaviour of such a nature that the petitioner cannot reasonably be expected to live with the respondent; and
(d) desertion.

Divorce ... although marriage is intended as a "union for life," and the Christian church directs that "those whom God hath joined together let no man put asunder," nevertheless divorce has a long and unhappy history. In the recent past the availability of divorce by judicial decree depended upon the "matrimonial offence" (*e.g.* adultery or cruelty) whereby one party would be adjudicated at fault in the breakdown of a marriage and this would afford the other party the opportunity to petition for termination of the marriage. Such an approach was in itself the cause of great stigma and unhappiness adding to an already unfortunate situation. The Law Commission in a reform paper published in 1966 suggested two aims for a good divorce law:

(a) to buttress, rather than undermine, the stability of marriage (*i.e.* divorce should not be so easy as to take away the incentive to make a marriage succeed and procedures should encourage reconciliation); and
(b) to enable the empty shell of a marriage which had irretrievably broken down to be destroyed with the maximum fairness and minimum bitterness, distress and humiliation.

Following considerable public debate the basis of the modern law was laid down in the Divorce Reform Act 1969 and is now to be found in a consolidating statute, The Matrimonial Causes Act 1973 (M.C.A.). The Church of England's favoured approach, that divorce should be available if a marriage has irretrievably broken down, has been accepted, but the Law Commission's view that proof of irretrievable breakdown should depend upon specific factual grounds may be seen as retaining the flavour of the "matrimonial offence." Whether the law meets the Law Commission's twin aims is a matter of opinion.

Section 1(1) of the M.C.A. 1973 provides that there is only one ground for divorce "...that the marriage has broken down irretrievably." However, section 1(2) provides that the court "shall not hold the marriage to have broken down irretrievably *unless* the petitioner satisfies the court of one or more of the following facts...." The factual situations are as follows:

(a) That the respondent has committed adultery *and* the petitioner finds it intolerable to live with the respondent. (The test is subjective: does *this* petitioner find it intolerable to live with this respondent? Both adultery and intolerability must be proved but the adultery need not necessarily be the cause of the intolerability.)

(b) That the respondent has behaved in such a way that the petitioner cannot *reasonably* be expected to live with the respondent. (Here the respondent's conduct must be considered by the court in relation to the petitioner's own conduct and all other relevant circumstances, for the question of reasonableness must be answered by the court as an objective test. Thus, a respondent need not be "at fault" and in *Thurlow* v. *Thurlow* a husband was granted a divorce under this head when his wife's severe neurological disorder rendered her bedridden and she had to be maintained in an institution.)

(c) That the respondent has *deserted* the petitioner for a continuous period of at least two years immediately preceding the presentation of the petition.

(d) That the parties have lived apart for a continuous period of at least two years immediately preceding the presentation of the petition *and* the respondent consents to the decree being granted. (This ground is in practice the most commonly relied upon and amounts to divorce by mutual consent.)

(e) That the parties have lived apart for a continuous period of at least five years immediately preceding presentation of the petition. (On establishing this ground a petitioner may divorce a respondent against his or her will. However, a respondent may oppose a decree on the ground that it would cause him or her grave financial or other hardship *and* that in all the circumstances it would be wrong to dissolve the marriage (s.5). This is very difficult to establish for the cause of the feared hardship must be the divorce and not simply the breakdown of marriage. Normally divorce does not add to the hardship of breakdown but may do so if, for example, a wife would be deprived of the opportunity of benefiting from a pension payable to a widow of her husband.)

Section 3 of the M.C.A. originally barred presentation of a divorce petition within three years of marriage except in cases of exceptional hardship or exceptional depravity. Now, following amendment by the Matrimonial and Family Proceedings Act 1984, it provides an absolute bar to the presentation of a petition before one year, removing judicial discretion to reduce the waiting period. The decree is made in two stages, first a *decree nisi* followed, normally after six weeks, by a *decree absolute*.

During the intervening period the Queen's Proctor may step in to show cause as to why the decree should not be made absolute. For example, in the case of (d) above, should it be shown that a petitioner misled a respondent, whether intentionally or not, into giving consent then the decree nisi may be rescinded. Further, under section 10, in the cases of both (d) and (e), a decree absolute will not be made unless the court is satisfied that the petitioner should not be required to make any financial provision for the respondent or that financial provision is made and is reasonable and fair.

A number of provisions of the M.C.A. seek directly or indirectly to promote reconciliation. Thus, by section 6, if at any stage it appears that a reasonable possibility of reconciliation has arisen, the court may adjourn the matter, referring the case to the court welfare officer. Further, in the factual situations of (c), (d) and (e) above, in determining whether a continuous period of separation has taken place no account is to be taken of any continuous period of six months (or non-consecutive periods not exceeding in aggregate six months) during which the parties have lived together, perhaps making a final attempt to live as man and wife.

It remains to mention what is perhaps the most significant rule of all, that the court may not grant a decree absolute unless it has made an order providing for appropriate welfare arrangements in respect of the children of the family. Should the court fail to make such an order then any decree absolute will be void.

Judicial separation . . . those who do not wish to bring their marriage to a formal end, perhaps because of religious beliefs, may nevertheless acquire the benefits of divorce short of being free to marry again. A judicial separation has the effect of leaving parties free to live apart, orders relating to maintenance, property and children may be made and even on death property will devolve as though the other spouse were dead. The grounds for judicial separation are the five factual situations provided in section 1(2) of the M.C.A. 1973, considered above, but there is no need to prove irretrievable breakdown.

Financial provision and property adjustment

A court hearing a petition for divorce, nullity or judicial separation, has wide powers to make appropriate orders dealt with principally under sections 21–25 of the M.C.A. 1973. At the outset of proceedings it may order *maintenance pending suit*, which is by way of a holding operation to support a spouse until full investigation and the making of orders following a decree. Orders following a decree may relate to both financial provision and property adjustment.

Financial provision . . . these orders are of two basic forms:
(a) periodical payments, being either unsecured, coming simply out of income, or secured upon capital so as to prevent a party from frustrating an order by disposing of assets; and
(b) lump sum payments.

These orders may be made so as to benefit both spouses and children of the family.

Property adjustment . . . these orders are directed towards a reallocation of property following a decree and are of two basic types:
(a) transfers to, or settlements of property for the benefit of, the other spouse or any children of the family; and

(b)   variations of ante-nuptial or post-nuptial settlements.

Express power is now given by section 24A of the M.C.A. to order sale of the matrimonial home.

Guidelines . . . section 25, as substituted by section 3 of the Matrimonial and Family Proceedings Act 1984, provides guidance to the court as to the exercise of its discretionary powers. Originally section 25 required that the court should seek "to place the parties, so far as is practicable and, having regard to their conduct, just to do so, in the financial position in which they would have been had the marriage not broken down and each had properly discharged his or her financial obligations and responsibilities to the other." However, following "serious and sustained criticism of the [then] law" the Law Commission, in 1981, recommended policy changes which recognised the demands of a changing society. In consequence the underlying assumption that each party to a marriage, notwithstanding divorce, should be able to look to the other for life-long maintenance has been swept away and greater emphasis has been placed upon the welfare of children following divorce. Section 25(1) now requires the court in exercising its discretion to have regard to all the circumstances of the case, "first consideration being given to the welfare while a minor of any child of the family who has not attained the age of eighteen." Section 25(2) sets out the other factors to which the court shall have regard as follows:

(a)   the income, earning capacity, property and other financial resources which each of the parties to the marriage has or is likely to have in the foreseeable future, including in the case of earning capacity any increase in that capacity which it would in the opinion of the court be reasonable to expect a party to the marriage to take steps to acquire;

(b)   the financial needs, obligations and responsibilities which each of the parties to the marriage has or is likely to have in the foreseeable future;

(c)   the standard of living enjoyed by the family before the breakdown of the marriage;

(d)   the age of each party to the marriage and the duration of the marriage;

(e)   any physical or mental disability of either of the parties to the marriage;

(f)   the contributions which each of the parties has made or is likely in the foreseeable future to make to the welfare of the family, including any contribution by looking after the home or caring for the family;

(g)   the conduct of each of the parties, if that conduct is such that it would in the opinion of the court be inequitable to disregard it;

(h)   in the case of proceedings for divorce or nullity of marriage, the value to each of the parties to the marriage of any benefit (for example, a pension) which, by reason of the dissolution or annulment of the marriage, that party will lose the chance of acquiring.

Section 25(3) provides a similar list of factors specifically directing the court towards the needs of the children of the family.

Section 25A provides what are commonly referred to as the "clean break" provisions. Subsection one imposes a duty on the court to exercise its powers so that the financial obligations of each party towards the other might be terminated as soon as is just and reasonable after the grant of the decree. Moreover, where the court decides to make a periodical payment order subsection two requires the court to have particular regard to whether it would be appropriate to limit the duration of those payments to a term considered sufficient to enable the recipient to adjust, without undue hardship, to the termination of his or her financial dependence on the other. The clean break principle is reinforced by subsection three which permits the court in dismissing an application for periodical payments to order that no further application be entertained.

The new guidelines introduced by the 1984 Act differ little from those originally provided by the 1973 Act and the discretionary nature of the court's power, combined with the diversity of circumstances which personal events throw up, render it fruitless to embark upon any review of the case law. It may, however, be instructive to note that although outright transfers of property are a possibility it is common for much more sophisticated arrangements to be ordered. For example, it is quite usual to order that occupation of the former matrimonial home should be enjoyed by the spouse with custody of the children until some future event, such as that spouse's re-marriage or the children reaching the age of 18. Thereafter, the house may be sold with the proceeds being distributed as appropriate.

CHILDREN

The importance which the law attaches to children, especially to their welfare in the event of marital breakdown, has previously been noted, yet it would be impossible to give any overall definition of "children." Even within a single statutory provision "children" of various ages may be accorded recognition (*e.g.* under section 41 of the M.C.A. 1973, directing the withholding of a decree unless the welfare of children of the family has been dealt with, children may be: (i) under the age of 16; (ii) under the age of 18 and in receipt of training; (iii) any other children when so merited by special circumstances). However, for many purposes "children" may, in law, be equated with "minors," that is, those under the age of 18 (Family Law Reform Act 1969). One point of overall impact is that a minor may not conduct litigation in person, but must be represented as a plaintiff by his "next friend" and as a defendant by his "guardian *ad litem*." Normally these representatives will be either a parent or guardian. The special position of children and young persons in the eyes of the criminal law was considered in some detail in *Part One* and that of minors in relation to contractual capacity in *Part Two* of this Unit. The remainder of the present consideration of children is directed mainly towards aspects of their welfare.

Custody and maintenance

Legitimacy and illegitimacy . . . a child is legitimate if his mother and father were married to one another at the time of his conception, birth or at any time between those events. The children of voidable marriages are also legitimate, as are those legitimated by such marriage (see later). Moreover, those born of a void marriage are legitimate should conception have occurred (or the ceremony of marriage have taken place, if later) at a time at which either or both parents reasonably believed the marriage to be valid.

The law presumes that children born to a married woman are legitimate as being her husband's children. This presumption is rebuttable upon proof that either (a) the husband and wife did not or could not have had sexual intercourse at the relevant time, or (b) the child was not the product of intercourse between the parties (*e.g.* where the husband is sterile).

Those born illegitimate may become legitimate. Section 2 of the Legitimacy Act 1976 provides that where the parents of an illegitimate child subsequently marry, then if the father is domiciled in England or Wales at the time of the marriage that child will be rendered legitimate from the date of the marriage. The effect of legitimation is that the child has virtually the same rights as a child legitimate from birth.

The Law Commission have recommended the removal of all the legal disadvantages of illegitimacy so far as they discriminate against the child. They suggest that the terminology be changed to marital and non-marital children as a means of eliminating alienation.

Children and parents ... a legitimate child benefits from his parents' marriage for he has a legal relationship with his father, enjoying until the age of majority (18 years), responsibilities placed upon both parents. If his parents should divorce, then his rights must be considered, as noted earlier. An illegitimate child has no automatic relationship with his father and, unless a court order varies the relationship, the mother enjoys parental rights and duties exclusively. However, fathers may, in "affiliation proceedings," be ordered to maintain their illegitimate children and, under the state welfare scheme a man adjudged to be the putative father is obliged, together with the mother, to maintain his child up to the age of 16.

Disputes as to custody ... in considering breakdown of marriage various references have been made to orders and arrangements concerning the welfare of children, ideally these should be amicably agreed but the court must settle disputes. Under the Matrimonial Causes Act 1973 orders may be made (in matrimonial proceedings for divorce, separation and nullity) awarding custody, care and control to either spouse or indeed to a third person, and "split orders" may be made awarding custody to one person, with care and control to another. Under the Domestic Proceedings and Magistrates' Courts Act 1978 the court may award custody to a parent or a party to the proceedings but, if it is considered appropriate that a third person should have custody, the court proceeds to deal with the matter as though an application for a custodianship order had been made under section 33 of the Children Act 1975 (see later). Under the Guardianship of Minors Act 1971 there need be no matrimonial proceedings and either parent (including those of illegitimate children) may apply for custody. The powers of the court extend to the making of: (a) split orders; (b) provision for access to either parent; (c) custodianship orders; (d) supervision orders involving a local authority or probation officer; or indeed exceptionally (e) committals into the care of a local authority.

Adoption ... the effect of a court order of adoption is to vest parental rights and duties relating to a child in the person or persons adopting. The governing legislation (not yet fully implemented) is a consolidating statute, the Adoption Act 1976, and under it adopters must always be at least 21 years of age and normally be either (a) a married couple or (b) an individual who is unmarried, although a permanently separated party may exceptionally adopt. Only children under 18 years of age, who have never been married may be adopted and they must normally have had their home with the adopter(s) for at least 12 months.

Section 22 of the Adoption Act provides that no order shall be made in respect of a child who was not placed with the applicant by an adoption agency unless the applicant has, at least three months before the order, given notice of intention to apply for an order to the local authority within whose area he resides. A local authority served with notice is obliged to investigate and report to the court. Moreover, no adoption may be made unless (a) the child's parent(s) or guardian unconditionally consent to the order or (b) the court dispenses with consent (*e.g.* where the parent has abandoned or neglected the child).

Perhaps the single most important principle relating to adoption is the "welfare principle." Section 6 provides that in reaching any decision a court or adoption agency shall have regard to all the circumstances but, first, consideration must be given to the need to safeguard and promote the welfare of the child and, so far as is practicable, the wishes and feelings of the child regarding any decision should be ascertained and given due consideration, having regard to his age and understanding. Any order may contain such terms and conditions as the court thinks fit and the making of an order may be postponed whilst an interim order gives custody to the applicants for a probationary period not exceeding two years.

The Registrar-General keeps a register of adoptions and it is possible, by using this register, to connect births and adoptions thus enabling an adopted child to discover his natural parents (Children Act 1975, s.26).

The Adoption Service . . . section 1 of the 1976 Act imposes a duty upon every local authority to establish and maintain a service to meet the needs, in relation to adoption, of children who have been or may be adopted, their parents or guardians, and those who have adopted or may adopt. The authority is required to provide appropriate services or ensure that they are provided by an approved adoption society. These services include: the provision of temporary board and lodging where needed by pregnant women, mothers or children; making arrangements for assessing children and prospective adopters; placing children for adoption; and counselling those with problems related to adoption.

Guardianship . . . at its widest the notion of guardianship involves both the relationship of parents with their children and also that of persons placed in the position of parents (*in loco parentis*) and the children under their care. A person may be so placed either by a parent (or parents) to act after his death or by court order. The relationship involves the custody of the "guardian" over his "ward" encompassing not only "actual possession" or physical custody but also "legal custody" conferring full control over property, education and general upbringing. At common law the custody of a legitimate child vested in the father but under the Guardianship Act 1973 the mother has the same rights as the father and these rights are exercisable by either of them without the other. In the event of disagreement the court may be called upon to give directions and indeed may, having regard to the welfare of the child, award a third person custody to the exclusion of the parents who may be ordered to pay for the child's maintenance.

Because of the difficulty involved in awarding custody to someone other than the parents (which will only normally be possible where a parent invites the exercise of the court's jurisdiction by taking proceedings under, for example, the Matrimonial Causes Act 1973 or the Guardianship Act 1973 as noted above) the Children Act 1975 provides for the *custodianship order*. By use of this order relatives or others looking after children on a long-term basis will be able to obtain legal custody of the children. This custodianship will not sever the legal relationship between parents and children as would adoption but it will confer legal status in relation to the children which is not afforded to those in the tenuous position of foster parents. *Foster parents* merely have *de facto* control and custody of those in their care, who are children under the upper limit of compulsory school age. The children must be visited on behalf of Social Services Departments which must satisfy themselves as to their well being and offer any necessary advice to the foster parents. Applications for custodianship orders may only be made by "qualified persons," that is:

(a)   a relative or step-parent with whom the child has had his home for three months preceding the application, provided consent is given by the person with legal custody;

(b)   any person with whom the child has had a home for at least 12 months, including the three months preceding the application, provided consent is given by the person with legal custody;

(c)   any person with whom the child has had his home for at least three years, including the three months preceding the application.

The requirement of consent in cases (a) and (b) is intended to maintain confidence in fostering, for only in case (c) can long-term fostering prejudice the position of parents.

Proceedings to make a child a *ward of court* may be brought by any interested person under the procedure laid down in section 41 of the Supreme Court Act 1981. The impact of an application is to immediately confer the status of ward of court, but unless the matter is promptly pursued this interim status will lapse. The effect of wardship (which may also be created under the court's inherent jurisdiction) is to vest parental rights in the court with physical possession being awarded to a parent or interested third party. An order ceases to have effect upon the ward reaching 18 years of age. This expeditious procedure may be used where, for example, parents of a handicapped baby refuse consent for a life-saving operation.

Financial needs of children ... as has been seen, orders for the maintenance of children may be made under various statutory provisions: (a) the Domestic Proceedings and Magistrates' Courts Act 1978; (b) the Matrimonial Causes Act 1973; (c) the Guardianship of Minors Act 1971; and (d) the Affiliation Proceedings Act 1957.

Duties of Local Authorities

To promote the welfare of children ... Part I of the Child Care Act 1980 deals with the general duty imposed upon local authorities to promote the welfare of children. Under section 1 a duty is imposed to provide such advice, guidance and assistance as may promote the welfare of children by diminishing the need to receive children into or keep them in care or indeed to bring them before a juvenile court in care proceedings. Under this provision assistance in kind or exceptionally in cash may be provided to those under the age of 18. As regards children under the age of 17, it is the duty of a local authority, where it is necessary in the interests of their welfare, to take them into its care provided the child:

(a) has neither parent nor guardian, has been abandoned, is lost; or

(b) has parents (or guardian) who are unable to provide for him due to mental or physical disability.

Moreover, a local authority may take over parental rights and duties (short of the right to consent or refuse to consent to adoptions) in respect of children in their care.

Treatment of those in care . . . in reaching decisions concerning children in their care, a local authority is bound by the "golden rule" of child care, that the first consideration must be to "safeguard and promote the welfare of the child." It is also bound, so far as is practicable, to ascertain the wishes and feelings of the child. Section 21 of the 1980 Act provides that a local authority shall discharge its obligation to provide accommodation and maintenance for children in its care in one of the following ways, as it sees fit:

(a) boarding out on terms as to payments by the authority;

(b) maintaining in a community or voluntary home; or

(c) making other suitable arrangements.

Where children are in care, orders, enforceable in the magistrates' courts, may direct parents to contribute to their maintenance and indeed children having attained the age of 16 who are engaged in full-time work may be directed to contribute to their own maintenance (s.45).

Care proceedings in juvenile courts . . . as has been noted (in *Part One* of this Unit) civil care proceedings before a juvenile court are an alternative to criminal proceedings in the case of those under 17 years of age. The Children and Young Persons Act 1969 imposes wide-ranging duties upon local authorities (and others) in relation to children (those under 14 years of age) and young persons (those between 14 and 17 years of age). Any local authority is under a duty to investigate and take appropriate action where there are grounds for bringing care proceedings. Proceedings may also be taken by a constable or authorised person (*e.g.* an officer of the N.S.P.C.C.) after notice to the local authority. Before making an order a juvenile court must find that one or more of the following conditions are satisfied in respect of the party before the court:

(a) the child's proper development is being avoidably prevented or neglected or his health is being avoidably impaired or neglected or he is being ill-treated;

(b) condition (a) will probably be satisfied because of findings in relation to another child of the same household;

(c) condition (a) will probably be satisfied having regard to the fact that a person who has been convicted of one or more specified offences is or may become a member of the same household;

(d) the child is exposed to moral danger;

(e) the child is beyond the control of his parent or guardian;

(f) the child is of compulsory school age and is not receiving efficient full-time education suitable to his age, ability and aptitude;

(g) the child is guilty of an offence other than homicide.

In addition, the court must be satisfied that the child is in need of care and control which he is unlikely to receive unless an order is made. The orders that may be made include the following:

(a) an order requiring the child's parent or guardian to enter into a recognisance to take proper care of him and exercise control over him;
(b) a supervision order placing the child under the supervision of the local authority or a probation officer;
(c) a care order committing the child to the care of a local authority;
(d) a hospital order under the Mental Health Act 1983.

Section E: Gifts, Trusts and Taxation

It may be a wish to make a transfer of property to other members of the family (or to a friend or other acquaintance) that prompts the consumer to visit the legal office. Such transfers may be effected by way of:
(a) a legally binding agreement;
(b) a gift; or
(c) a trust.
These are distinct and different methods for transferring property and the method chosen in any one case will be determined by the objectives of the transferor. One of the prime motivations for transfers, between the members of a family at least, will be tax considerations. Advice on the tax implications of a particular transfer may, therefore, be a reason for the consumer's visit.

LEGALLY BINDING AGREEMENT

It was noted earlier (see page 134) that an agreement reached by two or more parties will only constitute a legally binding contract if the parties intended that they should be legally bound by the agreement. Moreover, it was seen that the courts will presume, in the case of social or domestic agreements, that the parties did not intend to be legally bound by their agreement and that there is no contractual relationship between them. This presumption is, of course, rebuttable but it does mean that, where property is transferred between family or friends, care should be taken to make the contractual effect of the transaction unambiguous.

Where a transfer has taken place by means of a legally binding agreement, for full market value, the tax considerations and implications will normally be relatively straightforward, the only charge being one to Capital Gains Tax (see page 250).

GIFTS

Rather than make a sale at market value, one member of a family may wish to bestow a gift upon another member of the family (or indeed upon someone outside the family). The law recognises two classes of gifts:
(a) gifts *inter vivos*; and
(b) *donationes mortis causa.*

Gifts inter vivos
Before ownership of personal property can pass between two *living* parties the giver (donor) must *intend to give* and *deliver* the gift to the recipient (donee).
Delivery . . . may be effected by the transfer of possession of the subject-matter, by deed (an unequivocal statement under seal) or by declaration of

trust (if the donor declares himself to be trustee, this is sufficient to give the donee an equitable title). In the case of a gift of a chose in action delivery of the document by which it is represented may be insufficient and it may also be necessary to comply with special rules appropriate to that type of property (*e.g.* a transfer of shares in a company requires entry of the transferee's name in the company's register of members, see page 278).

Where delivery is by declaration of trust, an intention to create a trust is not enough, the trust must be completely executed, since equity will not, it is said, perfect an imperfect gift. Nevertheless, there is at least one exception to this rule, that is the principle in *Strong* v. *Bird*. This case holds that, where it is shown that a testator intended in his lifetime to forgive a debt, the intention continuing until his death, and by his will he has appointed the debtor his executor, the debt is released.

Intention to give . . . to be a valid gift of property the donor must have the intention to give, namely he must be fully aware of:

(a)   his objects (*i.e.* the recipients);
(b)   the nature and effect of the transaction;
(c)   the extent of the benefit being conferred; and
(d)   the amount of beneficial interest that he is losing.

Once a gift has been validly executed it cannot be revoked unless the right to revoke was reserved or there is some invalidating cause (*e.g.* fraud or mistake). Indeed, a gift may be made subject to conditions, precedent or subsequent; such, in order to be valid, must not be impossible of fulfilment, illegal or contrary to public policy (*e.g.* a gift made conditional upon a total restraint from marriage or a donation of money to a charity in return for a promise to procure the donor a title or honour). The courts are usually ready to find against such conditions for want of certainty. One occasion on which it is common practice to make gifts is upon an engagement to marry. As between the engaged parties the Law Reform (Miscellaneous Provisions) Act 1970 provides that gifts from one to the other made on condition that they be returned, if the engagement is broken, shall not be irrecoverable by reason only that the *donor* terminated the engagement. There is, however, a rebuttable statutory presumption that a gift of an engagement ring is absolute.

Donationes mortis causa

Gifts which are *donationes mortis causa* (*i.e.* made in expectation of death) lie between gifts *inter vivos* and legacies (see page 254). There are three essential conditions for such gifts to be valid:

(a)   the gift must be made in contemplation of the donor's death;
(b)   there must be a delivery of the subject-matter of the gift to the donee (or in certain circumstances a transfer of the means of getting at the property, *e.g.* delivery of a bank deposit book); and
(c)   the gift must be intended to take complete effect upon, but only upon, the donor's death.

By its nature, therefore, such a gift may be revoked before death. Moreover, the donee must not pre-decease the donor, otherwise the gift is ineffective.

Taxation of gifts

One of the principal inducements for gifts was the desire to avoid paying estate duty. The introduction of capital transfer tax reduced these savings, but this tax has itself been replaced by an inheritance tax which may once more confer these benefits (see page 251).

TRUSTS

A trust may be defined in essence as a relationship in which one person (a *trustee*) has property vested in him subject to an obligation to allow another person (the *beneficiary* or *cestui que trust*) to have the beneficial enjoyment of the property. Historically the trust (or *use*) was part and parcel of the development of Equity and the Court of Chancery (see page 26). It was used to overcome certain limitations on transfers of property which themselves were made to avoid feudal dues. Later purposes were to enable married women and unincorporated bodies to "hold" property through trustees. Today the uses of trusts are many and varied, and include the following:

(a) to enable those who cannot "hold" property themselves (*e.g.* trade unions) to hold it through trustees;

(b) to allow a person to make provision for another (*e.g.* a mistress) without publicity;

(c) to make a gift in the future, dependent on events that have not yet arisen (see below "discretionary trusts");

(d) to make provision for causes or non-human objects (*e.g.* pets), often by will;

(e) to enable two or more persons to hold land (the family home, for example, if in joint ownership, would be held upon a trust);

(f) to provide for the establishment of pension funds and unit trusts as means of investment of capital; and

(g) to facilitate schemes aimed at minimising a person's tax liability.

Trusts may be used for both real and personal property. However, as for any other transaction, a trust which is *wholly* illegal or contrary to public policy will not be enforced, and in the former case no assistance will be given to the settlor in recovering his property.

Classification of trusts

Trusts may be classified in various ways:

(a) by the targets of the trust
  (i) private; or
  (ii) charitable (public);

(b) by the method of creation
  (i) statutory (*e.g.* under the Administration of Estates Act 1925, upon intestacy, see page 256);
  (ii) express;
  (iii) implied; or
  (iv) constructive.

Other classifications are also used but, of those that are, the only distinction that will be noted here is that between *fixed* and *discretionary* trusts.

Fixed trusts . . . under these each of the beneficiaries is entitled to a specified (fixed) share of the property contained in the trust and those rights may be enforced against the trustees.

Discretionary trusts . . . allow the trustees to decide whether to distribute income, or to accumulate it. More importantly the trustees will be empowered to determine which beneficiaries (or group thereof) shall be entitled to receive any benefit at all from the trust. The discretionary trust is, therefore, useful where, for example, a parent wishes to make provision for his children dependent upon their future financial need. It was also the type of trust much favoured by tax planners since it allowed the trustees to minimise a beneficiary's tax liability by distributing or withholding trust income depending upon the beneficiary's other income. However, such schemes have been subject to fiscal attack which has led to their decline (and a corresponding rise in offshore tax havens). Given the discretionary power of the trustees, no rights may be enforced by the beneficiaries until that discretion has been exercised in their favour.

Express private trusts

A private trust is one which aims to benefit either one person or a specified number of persons. It is enforceable by that individual or that group.

Any person over the age of 18, who holds property that can be disposed of, has capacity to create a trust. There are few formalities of creation, although in some cases statute requires that certain formalities be met. (The Law of Property Act 1925, for example, requires that a declaration of a trust respecting any land or any interest in land must be evidenced in writing, and see page 252 for the formalities required for a trust created by a will). Otherwise the declaration of a trust may be by deed, in writing or oral. However, whichever means of creation is chosen, the law does require that there must be:

(a) certainty of words;
(b) certainty of subject-matter; and
(c) certainty of objects.

Certainty of words . . . the form of words (indeed the use of the word "trust") is not important, but the settlor's intention is. Thus, it is sufficient that an intention to create a trust can be ascertained from the words used in the instrument creating the trust. In *Comiskey* v. *Bowring-Hanbury*, for example, the settlor under his will left all his property to his wife "absolutely in full confidence that she will make such use of it as I would have made myself and that at her death she will devise it to such one or more of my nieces as she may think fit." The House of Lords held the words "in full confidence," when construed against the whole will, created a trust.

Certainty of subject-matter . . . it must be clear what property is being left otherwise the trust will fail at the outset (*e.g.* if a settlor gave "the bulk" of his property to be held on trust there would be uncertainty).

Certainty of objects . . . the objects (*i.e.* the persons who are to benefit) must be certain or capable of being rendered certain. At one time this last rule was restrictively interpreted to mean that the trustees had in effect to be able to make a list of the beneficiaries and, if they could not, the trust failed for uncertainty. However, in *McPhail* v. *Doulton* the House of Lords appears to have discarded this test in favour of one whereby the issue is: "Can it be said of any given person that he is a member of the class of objects under the trust?" If the answer is affirmative, the trust stands.

Implied trust

An implied trust is one which arises from the presumed intention of the settlor. Such trusts are often called *resulting trusts* because the beneficial interest may *result* to the settlor or his estate. The occasions when this may happen include:

    (a)   failure of the trust or beneficial interest;

    (b)   purchase of property in another's name; and

    (c)   sole ownership of matrimonial home.

Failure of the trust or beneficial interest . . . may occur, for example, for reasons of uncertainty (see above) or where a loan has been made to a company for a specific purpose and that purpose can no longer be achieved. In the latter case the loan would be held on a resulting trust for the lender.

Purchase of property in another's name . . . where a purchase of property is made in another person's name, a trust is presumed to result in favour of the person providing the finance (unless the purchase was made by way of a loan). Thus, where F provides money for T to purchase property, then T is presumed to hold the subsequently purchased property on a trust for F. However, it is a rebuttable presumption and one way in which it may be rebutted is by the *presumption of advancement*. This will apply where the true purchaser is the husband or father of the nominal purchaser, and in such cases the presumption of advancement (which is itself rebuttable) is that the transferor intended to advance the interest of the transferee by the making of a gift rather than by the establishment of a resulting trust.

Sole ownership of matrimonial home . . . the implication of trusts in relation to the matrimonial home has led to a division of judicial opinion between those who would favour strict application of traditional property rights and those who believe that such issues should be determined in the light of current notions of social justice. The problem arises where the matrimonial home stands in the name of one spouse only but the other has contributed in some way to its acquisition and/or up-keep. The answer to the problem is to be found in a combination of equitable principles and statutory rules. Under section 17 of the Married Women's Property Act 1882 where there is a dispute as to matrimonial property an application may be made to the court for an order with respect to the disputed property. But this provision is only procedural and the question of ownership must be determined according to traditional equitable principles. Further, and more importantly, where there are matrimonial proceedings (*e.g.* divorce) application may be made under the Matrimonial Causes Act 1973, as amended by the Matrimonial and Family Proceedings Act 1984, for a property adjustment order. Since 1984 the court, in deciding whether to exercise its powers, must have regard to all the circumstances of the case but must give first consideration to the welfare of any minor child of the family. Otherwise, as before, the court must have regard to certain specified matters, including the conduct of the parties and increases in earning capacity (the latter having been added to give greater weight to the parties becoming self-sufficient). Nevertheless, it may still be necessary, despite the court's wide discretionary powers under statute, for property rights to be ascertained according to equitable principles (*e.g.* where the parties are not married).

This task is most easily achieved where there has been express agreement as to the beneficial ownership of property, but failing that the courts must look to the implied or imputed intent of the parties. In *Pettitt* v. *Pettitt* a husband, and in *Gissing* v. *Gissing*, a wife, made financial contributions to property held solely in the name of the respective spouse but neither, in the opinion of the House of Lords, had acquired any rights as a result. To the extent that a common ratio was advanced in either case it seems to be that the court cannot ascribe to the parties intentions which they never had and that their intentions, whatever they were, must be ascertained at the date of purchase and not subsequently.

However, a more recent line of Court of Appeal decisions holds that the inference of a trust will arise where each spouse has made a substantial financial contribution to the purchase price (or mortgage payments). Even where there is no direct contribution but only an indirect payment (*e.g.* where one spouse pays for housekeeping and the other for the mortgage) this will suffice. Indeed, in *Hazell* v. *Hazell* and *Eves* v. *Eves*, Lord Denning M.R., at least, was ready to find for the "contributing spouse" even though there was no agreement, express or implied, giving rise to a resulting trust but rather, in his Lordship's view, a *constructive trust* (see below).

The principles (and difficulties) involved in ascertaining property rights as between married couples have been held to be applicable also to unmarried "spouses." Thus, in *Cooke* v. *Head*, the sledgehammer wielding mistress who contributed financially towards the mortgage payments and physically to the actual building of a bungalow, held in the name of the man alone, was found to be entitled to a one-third beneficial interest. On the other hand, in *Burns* v. *Burns* the mistress' contribution over a period of years to housekeeping, raising children and latterly to some household expenses was considered insufficient to entitle her to a share in the quasi-matrimonial home, held in the man's name and paid for by his money alone. Most recently the Court of Appeal has added to the uncertainty in this area by ruling in *Grant* v. *Edwards* that an unmarried woman could establish a beneficial interest in property held in the man's name alone if she could demonstrate a common intention that they should both have a beneficial interest and conduct which amounted to an acting upon that intention to her detriment. Such conduct could include substantial indirect contributions to mortgage repayments (*e.g.* by making payments for housekeeping and other expenses, without which the man would not have been able to make the mortgage repayments).

(For a further consideration of matrimonial property, see page 227).

Constructive trust

A constructive trust may be described as a relationship imposed by law in the interests of conscience, rather than one based on implied intention such as a resulting trust. The boundaries within which the law's (or more accurately equity's) conscience operates are not clear and, on one view at least, they have been left deliberately vague so as not to restrict the courts' approach to justice in any one case. As we have seen, use has been made of the constructive trust in determining property rights on the breakdown of marriage or termination of cohabitation. Additional uses of the concept include situations where:

(a) profits are made by a person in a fiduciary position; and

(b) a stranger intermeddles with trust property.

Profits made by a person in a fiduciary position . . . it is a basic principle that a trustee or person holding a fiduciary position (*i.e.* a position analogous to that of a trustee) should not place himself in a position where his duty and interest conflict. In *Keech* v. *Sandford* the defendant was a trustee of a lease for an infant. On the expiration of the lease the lessor would only renew it on condition that the trustee took the lease for his own benefit. Despite this stipulation it was held that the trustee must still hold the lease on trust for the infant. This general principle has since been extended beyond the strict trust relationship on many occasions. Thus, for example, a purchaser of property may be a constructive trustee for the person beneficially entitled to the property if he knew, at the time of transfer, that it was trust property.

It seems clear that "knowledge" (and the benefits which accrue from it) can be trust property. In *Boardman* v. *Phipps* a solicitor acted on behalf of trustees in connection with the affairs of a company in which the trust held shares. As a result he acquired knowledge which prompted him to purchase the remainder of the company's shares, from which he subsequently made a profit. It was held that the knowledge so acquired was trust property and that the defendant solicitor had to account for the profit so made.

Whilst it should not be thought that all information coming to trustees (or their agents) may give rise to a constructive trust, the *Boardman* v. *Phipps* principle has also been illustrated in the relationship between a company and its directors. This relationship is not in fact one of trustee–beneficiary, but directors clearly stand in a fiduciary relationship towards their company that in some ways resembles the position of trustees and in others the position of agents. Thus, in *Regal (Hastings) Ltd.* v. *Gulliver* and in *Industrial Development Consultants Ltd.* v. *Cooley*, directors who made use of knowledge which came to them when acting as directors were held accountable to their companies for the profits thereby made, even though they had exploited opportunities that were not open to those companies.

A stranger intermeddling with trust property . . . it was held in *Belmont Finance Corporation Ltd.* v. *Williams Furniture Ltd. (No. 2)* that if a stranger knowingly receives trust property with knowledge (actual or constructive) that the property comes into his hands through a breach of trust, he holds it upon a constructive trust. Even if a person does not receive trust property he will still be liable as a constructive trustee where he with knowledge participates in a dishonest and fraudulent design on the part of the trustees. In the latter circumstances it was held in *Selangor United Rubber Estates Ltd.* v. *Cradock (No. 3)* that "knowledge" was knowledge of circumstances which would indicate to an "honest reasonable man" that a dishonest and fraudulent design was being committed or would put him on inquiry whether it was being committed. Thus, actual knowledge would appear to be unnecessary. However, according to dicta in *Belmont Finance Corporation Ltd.* v. *Williams Furniture Ltd.*, actual knowledge of the fraud or reckless failure to make inquiries is required in order to place liability on a stranger by reason of his conduct.

Charitable trusts

The aim of a charitable trust is to benefit society in general or some considerable part of it, whereas the private trust is aimed at specified persons. Because of their public nature charitable trusts enjoy several advantages over the private trust (*e.g.* they will not fail for uncertainty and have certain tax advantages). The Charities Act 1960, under which charitable trusts must be registered with the Charity Commissioners, made radical reforms to the law relating to such trusts.

A comprehensive definition of the term "charity" has long proved elusive but perhaps the nearest was that set out in *Commissioners for Special Purposes of Income Tax* v. *Pemsel* which consisted of the following classification of charitable trusts:

(a) trusts for the relief of poverty;
(b) trusts for the advancement of education;
(c) trusts for the advancement of religion; and
(d) trusts for other purposes beneficial to the community.

In view of the last of these it should just be noted that, to be a charitable trust, a trust must in some way benefit the public (or a section of it). Moreover, the funds of such trusts must be used exclusively for charitable purposes. Nevertheless, in *Attorney-General* v. *Ross* it was held that it was not inconsistent with its status as a registered charity for a Polytechnic Students' Union, in order to achieve its own charitable purposes, to ally itself and contribute to the funds of a non-charitable organisation, the National Union of Students.

Trusts for the relief of poverty . . . are an exception, in fact, to the general requirement for a public element. Thus a trust for the relief of poverty amongst employees of a particular firm or company can be charitable. But in general terms trusts under this class must have among their objects the relief of the aged, the weak or the poor.

Trusts for the advancement of education . . . must have an element of teaching or education within their purpose and not be aimed merely at increasing public knowledge in a particular respect. The necessary element was found to be present in *Incorporated Council of Law Reporting for England and Wales* v. *Attorney-General*, since law reports accurately record the development and application of judge-made law and thus help to spread knowledge and understanding of that law.

Trusts for the advancement of religion . . . it seems that the advancement of all religions which are not "subversive of morality" will be held to be charitable, although certain "fringe" religions probably lack the necessary public benefit and would thus be excluded.

Trusts for other purposes beneficial to the community . . . form an unconnected residuary grouping which includes:

(a) trusts for the protection of animals;
(b) recreational trusts; and
(c) trusts for sport where connected to some other charitable body (*e.g.* a school).

In the case of recreational trusts the Recreational Charities Act 1958 provides that it shall be charitable to provide facilities for recreation or other leisure-time occupations if the facilities are provided in the interest of social welfare. Such trusts must of course be for the public benefit. On the other hand, trusts which at first sight have appeared to be in part educational have failed to secure the label "charity" on the ground that their primary object was political.

Cy-près doctrine . . . in contrast to the position where a private trust fails, charitable trusts are largely cushioned from failure by the cy-près doctrine and the trust property will not be held on a resulting trust for the benefit of the donor. Thus, where a trust has been established to further a particular charitable object but, *at the outset*, that object fails or becomes impossible, the funds of the trust will be applied to objects as near as possible to the original ones. However, for the cy-près doctrine to operate it must be shown that there was a general charitable intention in the original object. On the other hand, once the trust has taken effect but *failed later* for reasons of impossibility or impracticability, or the chosen object has not exhausted all the trusts funds, the doctrine operates without reference to the settlor's general intent (Charities Act 1960, s.13).

Trustees

Any adult individual, limited company or other corporation may be appointed a trustee subject to the power of the court to remove "undesirables" (*e.g.* persons convicted of offences involving dishonesty). There are no common law restrictions on the number of trustees for any one trust, although there are practical considerations. (For example, the beneficiaries are better protected if there are at least two trustees.) There are, however, certain statutory limitations on numbers (*e.g.* there must not normally be more than four trustees where land is settled or held upon trust for sale). A person need not accept appointment as a trustee and, in view of the onerous duties involved and the lack of a right to remuneration (unless provided for in the instrument establishing the trust), it would not be surprising if many refused appointment. Certain persons, however, specialise in this task.

Trust corporations . . . are corporate bodies such as banks and insurance companies which undertake the business of acting as trustee. To do so they must fulfil certain conditions, including meeting minimum capital requirements. The principal advantage of the trust corporation is that it can act as a sole trustee in circumstances where statute would otherwise require an act to be performed by two or more individual trustees.

Public Trustee . . . is a corporation sole (a corporation constituted in a single person who, by virtue of some office or function, has corporate status—see page 272). His main work involves the administration of the private trusts under which he has been appointed to act and which are charged for the services rendered on the basis of their size (see page 59).

The question of appointment and retirement of trustees may be governed in part by the terms of the trust deed and in part by the Trustee Act 1925.

Appointment of trustees . . . on the creation of a trust the trustees will often be appointed by the settlor, who may appoint himself. If no one is named, the court will appoint a trustee. During the trust, where an existing trustee retires or dies or an additional appointment is made, a new trustee may be appointed by the person empowered under the trust deed. If there is no provision for such eventualities in the deed, the Trustee Act specifies the order in which persons have the right to appoint.

Retirement of trustees . . . trustees may retire under the terms of the trust deed, by being replaced by a new trustee under section 36 of the Act, or without the need for replacement under section 39. Under this section a trustee may retire if:

(a)   after his retirement two or more trustees or a trust corporation remain;

(b)   the consent of remaining trustees is obtained;

(c) the consent of any one named in the trust deed as having the power to appoint new trustees is obtained; and

(d) the retirement is by deed.

Vesting of property . . . on appointment (or retirement) the property of a trust must be properly vested in the names of all trustees in the manner appropriate for the type of property involved (*e.g.* by conveyance for unregistered freehold land or by transfer and registration for shares in a company). Section 40 provides that where appointment or retirement is effected by deed most types of property automatically vest in the new or remaining trustees.

On their appointment, as well as ensuring that all property is properly vested, trustees should acquaint themselves with the terms of the trust and with the duties inherent in their position as trustees, including duties to:

(a) take care in administration of trust;

(b) avoid conflicts of interest;

(c) keep financial accounts and provide other information;

(d) ensure the right amount is paid to the right beneficiaries;

(e) invest trust funds.

Taking care in administration of trust . . . an *unpaid* trustee is bound to use only such due diligence and care in the management of a trust as an ordinary prudent man of business would use in the management of his own affairs. A higher standard is expected of a *paid* trustee. Acts or decisions in management should be those of all trustees unless, for example, the trust deed authorises otherwise. Where trustees are in doubt as to the manner in which to act, they should apply to the court for directions.

Avoiding conflicts of interest . . . trustees must not place themselves in a position where their duty to do the best they can for the beneficiaries might conflict with their personal interests. They should not, therefore:

(a) make payments to themselves for their services (unless authorised by the deed, the court or all the beneficiaries);

(b) carry on a competing business; or

(c) purchase trust property.

Investment of trust funds . . . trustees can only invest in those investments authorised by the trust deed or by the Trustee Investments Act 1961, and even then so as to reflect the needs of individual beneficiaries they must maintain a balance between those investments giving an income return and those providing capital growth. Since the 1961 Act the range of investments is wider than once was the case, but trustees must still keep a basic 50:50 split between so-called "narrower-range" investments (*e.g.* national savings certificates) and "wider-range" investments (*e.g.* shares in listed public companies). In the latter case expert advice must be sought before any investment is made. The Law Reform Committee has criticised the Act as out of date and due for revision. In the meantime the courts have shown a greater readiness to allow applications to extend the trustees' powers of investment.

Actions and remedies for breach of trust

A breach of trust occurs if a trustee does any act which he ought not to do or omits to perform an act which he ought to perform. Examples of such breaches include:

(a) investment of trust moneys in unauthorised investments;

(b)   taking an unauthorised profit; and

(c)   failing to exercise a proper discretion.

In such cases the beneficiaries may bring an action against one or more or all of the trustees. The liability of trustees is to compensate the trust fund for any loss sustained or to account for any unauthorised profit.

Limitation of actions . . . even if there has been a breach of trust the beneficiaries must be in time to sue. Where the action is in respect of fraud on the part of a trustee or is to recover property or proceeds thereof from the trustee's possession or use, there is no statutory period of limitation. Nevertheless, if a beneficiary delays bringing his action when in full knowledge of the facts he may be deemed to have acquiesced in the breach and thereby waived his claim.

Where the above exemption from the statutory period of limitation does not apply, actions to recover trust property or in respect of breach of trust in general must be brought within six years from the date on which the right of action accrued or, in the case of a future beneficiary not yet in possession of interest, six years from becoming entitled. However, actions for recovery of land or in respect of the personal estate of a deceased person may be brought within 12 years of the accrual of the right of action.

Relief or exemption from liability . . . may be gained by:

(a)   a suitably drafted clause in a trust instrument;

(b)   application to the court; or

(c)   waiver on the part of all beneficiaries.

Section 61 of the Trustee Act 1925 provides that the court may relieve a trustee from personal liability where he has acted honestly and reasonably and ought fairly to be excused.

Other remedies for breach of trust . . . as well as actions against the trustees themselves (who may in any event be insolvent), beneficiaries may pursue a remedy against trust property. Equity allows property or money to be *traced* (*i.e.* followed and recovered) into the hands of a recipient who has wrongly taken possession of it. Indeed, where money is used to purchase specific property, the beneficiaries may claim the property so purchased or a charge upon it. In all cases the property or money must be identifiable. This, in the latter case, would mean that money must continue to exist as a separate fund or as an identifiable part of a mixed fund or as identified property purchased by means of such a fund.

However, any claim of the beneficiaries would be extinguished as against a purchaser for value without notice.

TAXATION

At the outset of this Section it was suggested that one, if not the prime, objective behind property transfers within a family was the desire to minimise the family's total tax liability. The following passage is, therefore, a brief examination of the main charges that will be imposed, namely:

(a)   income tax;

(b)   capital gains tax; and

(c)   inheritance tax.

Income tax

Income tax is an annual tax which must be renewed each year by Act of Parliament. Thus, the Finance Act passed each year enacts those proposals from the Budget confirmed by Parliament. Amongst other matters these proposals will include the rate of tax and the amount of individual reliefs. The general approach in the taxation of income is to charge tax according to the source from which income arises. The Income and Corporation Taxes Act 1970, which is the principal Act charging income tax (and, in the case of companies, corporation tax), charges "all property, profits or gains" described or comprised in Schedules A–F of the Act and in accordance with the provisions applicable to each Schedule. Thus, for example, under Schedule A income tax is charged on annual profits or gains arising in respect of certain rents or receipts from land in the United Kingdom. The basis for computing such income is the rents or receipts to which the taxpayer becomes entitled in the year of assessment less the deductions authorised by the Act. Under Schedule B, on the other hand, the source taxed is income from the occupation of woodlands in the United Kingdom managed on a commercial basis and with a view to the realisation of profits. In this case tax is charged on one-third of the gross annual value for the current year of assessment.

The two Schedules which are most widely applicable, and thus recognised by the public at large, are Schedules D and E, both of which are further subdivided into Cases. Thus, Schedule D Case 1 charges the profits of a trade, whilst Case 2 of that Schedule charges profits of a profession or vocation, in each the normal basis for computation being the profits of the taxpayer's accounting year ending in the preceding year of assessment.

For example: S, a solicitor, draws up his accounts to end December 31 each year. The profits of his accounting year which ended December 31, 1986 will constitute his taxable income for the year of assessment 1987 to 1988.

Schedule E charges income arising from offices, employments and pensions (and certain other specified sources), and the basis of computation is the emoluments or other income of the current year of assessment.

A taxpayer may, of course, have more than one source of income but each must be charged under the appropriate Schedule. The basic rate charged on each source will be the same (pre-1973, earned and unearned income were charged differently) although, when the total income of an individual exceeds a certain figure, higher rates will be payable. For tax purposes the income of the family will usually be treated only in part as that of a single unit. Thus the separate incomes of husband and wife who are living together will be summed and charged to income tax as if the income of one person, but the income of an infant child will not normally be treated as if it were the income of his parent. In fact either husband or wife may apply to be *separately assessed* and each would pay his or her respective share of the tax charged, but the total bill would remain the same. On the other hand, where their total income is sufficiently high they may jointly elect to be *charged to income tax separately*, and this choice would result, in appropriate circumstances, in a tax saving.

There may be occasions when further savings may be made by one member of a family transferring part of his income to another. A grandparent or parent may choose to provide a source of income for the education of a child. (Indeed, divorce and separation may oblige a parent to make provision for other members of the family unit.) In such cases the transferor may arrange an *income settlement* (whereby a part of his income is transferred) or a *capital settlement* (whereby part of his capital is transferred). The former may be effected by entering a covenant to pay the transferee for a specified period (usually exceeding six years) a sum of money. Where the transferee's liability to tax is lower than that of the transferor a tax saving can be made. In the case of the capital settlement the transferor may by deed transfer part of his capital to trustees to be invested, the income thereby produced being paid to the beneficiaries. The income of such trusts will usually be treated as the income of the trustees who bear tax at the basic rate. When trust income reaches the beneficiaries they are also assessed to income tax but account is taken of the tax already paid by the trustees.

However, a significant limitation upon the tax-saving objectives of the transferor is that neither type of settlement will relieve the transferor of any liability where the settlement is upon the settlor's (transferor's) own, unmarried infant children. (Settlements upon grandchildren are not caught by this restriction.) Indeed, the legislation contains various anti-avoidance provisions which further limit the settlor's ability to minimise his own liability whilst gaining some direct benefit from the settlement.

Capital gains tax

Capital gains tax (CGT) was introduced by the Finance Act 1965 and amended by subsequent legislation. All this legislation was consolidated by the Capital Gains Tax Act 1979. CGT is levied on the sum of the *chargeable gains* which accrue to a person on the *disposal* of assets in a year of assessment (subject to the deduction of allowable losses).

Chargeable gain . . . is broadly the difference between the cost of the asset on its acquisition and the consideration in money or money's worth for its disposal. Where an asset was acquired before April 1965 the asset is treated as if it cost the amount it would have cost in the market in April 1965. Since 1982 a limited form of indexation allowance has accounted for inflation.

The rate of tax for individuals is 30 per cent. with an exemption for the first £6,300 of gains (for trustees only £3,150 is tax free). Chargeable gains of a married woman living with her husband are assessed on the husband unless election for separate assessment has been made.

Disposal . . . CGT arises on the disposal of an asset. The term "disposal" is not defined by the Act, but an asset will be disposed of whenever its ownership changes or whenever the owner divests himself of his rights or interests over that asset, whether by sale, exchange, gift or otherwise.

Where there is a disposal between husband and wife, that disposal is treated as if the asset was acquired, from the one making the disposal, for a consideration of such amount as would secure that, on the disposal, neither a gain nor a loss would fall to the one making the disposal. Where an asset is disposed of by way of gift or settlement, the disposal is deemed to be for market value (the same value being attributed to the person who acquires the asset for any future CGT liability). Disposals between connected persons (*e.g.* husband and wife and their relatives, and trustees and settlor) are assumed to be otherwise than by way of sale for full market value, and thus are subject to assessment at market value. Where property is put into a settlement this is treated as a disposal of the property and may give rise to a chargeable gain. Any disposal thereafter (*e.g.* the switching of trust investments) is a disposal by the trustees and the gains and losses are those of the trust.

Certain assets are not chargeable assets and thus no chargeable gain (or allowable loss) arises on their disposal. Such assets include private motor cars, winnings from prizes and the family home (*i.e.* the dwelling house which was the individual's only or main residence throughout his period of ownership).

Inheritance tax

In 1975 capital transfer tax (CTT) was introduced to replace estate duty. The latter was levied on the value of property which passed on the death of a person. CTT added to this a levy on all lifetime transfers of property subject to certain exemptions. In 1984 the various enactments relating to CTT were consolidated in the Capital Transfer Tax Act. However, the Finance Act 1986 changed the name of CTT to inheritance tax and, in relation to transfers made on or after March 18, 1986, reverted to the principle of charging lifetime gifts to tax only if they are made within the period of seven years before the donor's death. A new category of potentially exempt transfers was thereby created. In other respects the concepts outlined below have been retained for transfers falling within the seven-year-period, although such transfers are subject to a tapering charge. Thus, a transfer made between six and seven years before death would be taxed at 20 per cent. of the death rate, whereas one made within three years of death would be taxed at 100 per cent. of the death rate. For the purpose of inheritance tax transfers are cumulated and chargeable at progressive rates.

Chargeable transfers ... tax is charged on the value transferred by a *chargeable transfer*, which is any *transfer of value* made by an individual after March 1974 (other than an exempt transfer). A transfer of value is defined as any *disposition* made by a person as a result of which his estate immediately after disposition is less than it would be but for the disposition; and the amount by which it is less is the value transferred by the transfer.

It should be noted that tax is levied on the reduction in value of the transferor's estate, not on the increase in value of the transferee's estate. For example, if D gives to R a piece of jewellery from a rare collection, the reduction in value in D's collection will probably exceed the value of the single piece which R acquires.

The term *disposition* is not defined but would appear to involve any loss in value to the individual's estate, and such loss may follow either an act or omission. (For example, if P fails to pursue a just claim for damages against D, this may constitute a chargeable transfer by P.) On the other hand, where full consideration is provided in return for the disposition there is no diminution in value, and thus no transfer of value to be charged. What then is the position if the disposition is made for less than market value? If, in our earlier example, D sells the piece of jewellery to R for £5,000 but there is evidence that D could have obtained £7,000, D may have intended to confer a benefit on R or may merely have made a bad bargain. The legislation provides that the first situation would involve a chargeable transfer but the second would not.

On the death of any person tax is charged as if, immediately before his death, he had made a transfer of value and the value transferred by it had been equal to the value of his estate immediately before his death. The value of the estate is the price it would fetch if sold in the open market at that time, less liabilities.

Exempt transfers . . . certain transfers, even though of value, are exempt from CTT. Such include, in particular:

(a) transfers between spouses without limit and whether lifetime transfers or transfers on death;

(b) transfers up to the value of £3,000 in any one year by the transferor;

(c) gifts in consideration of marriage up to £1,000 (£5,000 if made by a parent to a child); and

(d) lifetime gifts to charities without limit.

Section F: Succession and Family Provision

In the previous Section discussion centred for the most part on transfers of property during the lifetime of the transferor. He may also wish to make provision for the transfer of his property upon his death and this he may do by making a *will*. Normally to be valid a will must be in writing and executed according to certain statutory formalities. As such, it will take effect as an expression of the *testator's* wishes upon his death, but not beforehand. It is possible, therefore, that the testator may before his death have disposed of the whole or part of his property by other means. A will is thus said to be *ambulatory* during the testator's lifetime, for the property subject to the will can only be identified upon death. However, for whatever reason, not everyone makes a will before his death and those who fail to do so are said to die *intestate*. Different rules by necessity apply to those who have and those who have not expressed their wishes for the devolution of their property upon death and these must be considered in turn.

TESTATE SUCCESSION

Capacity

Anyone of sound mind who is over the age of 18 years can make a valid will (*i.e.* have testamentary capacity). To be valid, however, the contents of the will must be known to, and approved by, the testator, who must not have been misled by the undue influence or fraud of another person. The time for judging the capacity and knowledge of the testator is usually the time when he executes the will, but it may be sufficient that these factors are proved to be present at the time when he gives instructions to a solicitor for the preparation of the will.

The motive of the testator is irrelevant. Thus his will is not invalid merely because he chooses to "disinherit . . . his children, and leave his property to strangers to gratify his spite, or to charities to gratify his pride." Where a duly executed will is rational on the face of it the testator is presumed to have had testamentary capacity.

Formalities

To be valid a will must conform to the requirements laid down by the Wills Act 1837, as amended by the Administration of Justice Act 1982, namely that it must be:

(a) in writing;
(b) signed by the testator; and
(c) "attested" by two witnesses.

In writing . . . a will must be in writing, although no particular form of words or style of document is required. Thus it could, for example, be typed or handwritten.

Signed by the testator . . . the testator (or someone else in his presence and by his direction) must sign the will with the intention to give effect to the will. It is not necessary for the testator's name to be signed, any mark will suffice so long as it is intended by the testator to be his signature.

At one time the position of the signature was also vital. The 1837 Act required the signature to be "at the foot or end" and, despite the apparently wider meaning given to this by the Wills Act Amendment Act 1852, the courts failed to consistently recognise a foot when they saw one. Under the latest amendments it is sufficient if "it appears that the testator intended by his signature to give effect to the will."

In any event an addition to a will even below a signature has always been a possibility if it is signed and attested in the same way as the will itself. Indeed a testator may often add to his will by codicils duly executed in the same manner as the will.

"Attested" by two witnesses . . . the testator's signature must either be made or acknowledged by the testator in the presence of two witnesses present at the same time. In the former situation it is, perhaps surprisingly, not necessary that the witnesses see the signature so long as they see the testator writing it. In the latter the will must already have been signed before the testator's acknowledgment, at which time the witnesses must see the signature or have the opportunity of seeing it. In both cases the simultaneous presence of at least two witnesses is essential. Prior to the amendments of 1982, as the cases showed, the order of events could be vital. The amended provision requires each witness either to attest and sign the will or to acknowledge his signature. This can be done separately if the witnesses so wish, but must be done in the presence of the testator. It is now possible for a witness who has signed the will before the testator has made his signature to put matters right by acknowledging his signature after the testator has signed (or acknowledged his signature) in the simultaneous presence of the witnesses. This relaxation reverses the effect of earlier decisons.

The witnesses themselves should be neither blind nor of unsound mental capacity. Indeed, by statute, a beneficiary (or his or her spouse) under a will who is an attesting witness loses that interest, although the attestation is valid. However the full strictness of this rule has been relaxed by the Wills Act 1968 which provides that the attestation of a will by a beneficiary is to be disregarded if the will is duly executed without that attestation (*e.g.* if there were three attesting witnesses and the beneficiary's attestation was superfluous). The aim of the rule which disqualifies attesting beneficiaries is to deter fraud. A similar policy lies behind the rule that a person who is convicted of murder or manslaughter is debarred from taking any benefit under the will (or intestacy) of his victim. However, in the case of unlawful killings, unless a person stands convicted of murder, the court has power under the Forfeiture Act 1982 to modify the effect of this forfeiture rule if the court is satisfied that the justice of the case so requires, having regard to the conduct of the offender and of the deceased and to any other material circumstances. In the same way the Act provides that such an offender may make an application under the Inheritance (Provision for Family Dependants) Act 1975 on the ground that there has been no reasonable financial provision made. But the court, in determining whether to exercise its discretion under the 1975 Act, will consider the conduct of the applicant (see below).

The above requirements of formality may in fact be relaxed in respect of certain privileged testators, in particular soldiers in actual military service and a seaman at sea. Liberal constructions have been given to both these phrases. Thus, seamen have been held to be "at sea" even though making their wills on land in the course of a voyage or just prior to a voyage. On the other hand, in *Re Rapley (deceased)* it was held that a seaman on leave who was not in receipt of instructions to join any particular ship was not "at sea" within the meaning of the Act. A privileged testator can make a valid will even though under the age of 18 years and without the will being written, signed or attested.

Classification of dispositions

It is necessary when considering the disposition of the testator's property to classify those dispositions since different rules apply to dispositions of real property (called *devises*) and of personal property (called *legacies*). Legacies may be further classified as:

(a) specific legacies;
(b) general legacies; or
(c) demonstrative legacies.

Specific legacies . . . such would be a gift by will of a specified thing that can be distinguished from the remainder of the testator's personal property; for example, "I give my painting by Picasso to A."

General legacies . . . are bequests (often sums of money) which are not distinguishable one from another; for example, "I give £300 to B" or "I bequeath a bicycle to C." It is not necessary that the testator's estate include £300 in cash or a bicycle at his death, merely that he has sufficient property which on realisation will enable the general legacies to be fulfilled.

Demonstrative legacies . . . are gifts which are general in nature but which are to come out of a specified fund or part of the testator's property; for example, "I give to D £500 out of my deposit account at the Co-operative Bank."

The term *residuary gift* should also be noted, such being a gift of the residue of the estate (or some part of it) once all other legacies and devises have been made and debts paid.

One of the reasons for differentiating between the various types of legacies (and devises) relates to the processes of *ademption* and of *abatement*.

Ademption of a legacy or devise . . . a legacy or a devise fails by ademption if its subject-matter no longer exists as part of the testator's estate at his death. By definition, ademption can only apply to a specific legacy or specific devise, since a general legacy and even a demonstrative legacy can always be satisfied if the testator has sufficient property at death.

Abatement . . . occurs where the burden of the testator's expenses, debts and liabilities has to be met by the beneficiaries under the will from the dispositions made to them. The order in which the testamentary dispositions "abate" (*i.e.* cease to take effect) is laid down by the

Administration of Estates Act 1925 for deaths after that year (subject to variation by the will). The statutory order of abatement is:

(a) property undisposed of by will, subject to the retention of a fund to meet *pecuniary* legacies (a pecuniary legacy for the purposes of the Act includes any general or demonstrative legacy which is to be met by a payment of money);

(b) property not specifically devised or bequeathed but included in a residuary gift, subject to the retention of a fund to meet the balance of the pecuniary legacies;

(c) property specifically appropriated or devised or bequeathed for the payment of debts;

(d) property charged with, or devised or bequeathed subject to a charge for, the payment of debts;

(e) the fund, if any, retained to meet pecuniary legacies;

(f) property specifically devised or bequeathed, rateably according to value;

(g) property appointed by will under a general power, including the statutory power to dispose of entailed interests according to value.

It should be emphasised that the above list is the statutory order in which beneficiaries are liable to lose their interests. Thus, those higher on the list are more likely than those lower down to recover none, or at best only part, of any disposition made to them. No distinction is drawn between real and personal property for these purposes, so all property within a particular paragraph abates rateably.

Revocation of a will

Given the ambulatory nature of a will which, for example, allows a testator before his death to dispose of property mentioned in the will in a manner inconsistent with that will, it follows that the testator may revoke that will at any time until his death. The Wills Act 1837, as amended, provides that a will may be revoked by:

(a) marriage;

(b) divorce;

(c) destruction;

(d) due execution of another will or codicil.

Marriage . . . normally acts as an automatic revocation of a will (unless the will has been made in expectation of marriage to a particular person and it appears that the testator intended the will not to be revoked by the marriage).

Divorce . . . a decree of divorce or of nullity now revokes any gift in a will to a former spouse and revokes any appointment of the former spouse as executor or as executor and trustee. However, this rule is subject to contrary intention and, in any event, does not prevent the former spouse from making an application under the Inheritance (Provision for Family and Dependants) Act 1975.

Destruction . . . of a will (or any part thereof) by "burning, tearing or otherwise destroying" revokes the will (or the part destroyed). However, the act of destruction must be performed by the testator (or by some person in his presence and by his direction) and there must be an intention to revoke at the time. An accidental destruction, whilst perhaps causing evidential problems, does not revoke a will.

Due execution of another will or codicil . . . where a new will or codicil has been executed according to the formalities required by the Act, this acts as a revocation of an existing will (or part thereof). The revocation may be express or implied. Express revocation occurs where, as is common, the new will contains a revocation clause by which the testator expressly revokes "all wills codicils and other testamentary dispositions heretofore made by me." An earlier will is impliedly revoked by a subsequent will to the extent that the latter contains provisions inconsistent with the former.

The Act also allows revocation by a written declaration, which states an intention to revoke and is duly executed in the manner required for a will.

INTESTACY

Where the owner of property has not drawn up a valid will disposing of his property on his death, the law steps in to provide for distribution of that property amongst his surviving relatives. The rules for distribution are contained in the Administration of Estates Act 1925, as subsequently amended. The same Act also deals with the administration of the intestate's property before distribution.

Administration of assets

The Act provides that the *personal representatives* (see page 259) of an intestate will hold all his property other than money upon trust for sale. This allows the personal representatives to hold the property prior to its sale and conversion into money, and subsequent distribution amongst the beneficiaries. Indeed they are empowered to postpone sale and conversion, and it may be that no sale ever takes place if any asset can be vested directly in the due beneficiary. It is the duty of the personal representatives to pay the intestate's expenses, debts and other liabilities out of the money arising from the sale and conversion. Any money or unsold property left over after these payments have been made is termed the "residuary estate."

Distribution of assets

The underlying assumption of the Act in relation to the distribution of the property of those who die intestate appears to be that they would, if so minded in advance, have intended their property to have devolved first to those closest to them (their spouses and any children), secondly to "close relatives" (parents, brothers or sisters of the whole blood), and last to relatives less closely tied (brothers and sisters of the half blood, grandparents, uncles and aunts).

Surviving spouse, no surviving children or close relatives ... entitles the surviving husband or wife to the whole residuary estate absolutely.

Surviving spouse and surviving children ... where the intestate leaves children who attain the age of 18 years or marry under that age, a surviving spouse is entitled to:

(a) the personal chattels absolutely (these include motor cars, books, jewellery and other household items, but not chattels used for business purposes nor money);

(b) a net sum with interest fixed by statute (*the statutory legacy*—for deaths on or after March 1, 1981 this sum is £40,000);

(c) a life interest in one half of the remainder of the residuary estate (*i.e.* the income produced by a half of the residuary estate once the personal chattels and the statutory legacy have been withdrawn).

The other half of the remaining residuary estate (if there is any) will be held on the *statutory trusts* for the surviving children, who will be equally entitled. After the death of the surviving spouse the surviving children will then be entitled to the whole of the remainder on the statutory trusts. But if none of the surviving children attain the age of 18 years or marry under that age, *and* there are no surviving close relatives, the surviving spouse will be absolutely entitled to the whole residuary estate (see above).

In a similar way, where there is no surviving spouse but surviving children the entire residuary estate is held on the statutory trusts.

Surviving spouse, no surviving children but surviving close relative ... whenever there is a surviving child the close relatives are entitled to no share of the intestate's estate. But, if there are no surviving children and whether or not there is a surviving spouse, the surviving close relatives will be entitled to a share (assuming there is anything left). In such a case, the surviving parent(s) will rank first in line, and only if there is no surviving parent will a brother or sister of the whole blood be entitled to any part of the remainder. It should be noted that where there is a surviving close relative but no surviving children the surviving spouse is entitled to:

(a) the personal chattels absolutely;
(b) the statutory legacy (here £85,000 for deaths on or after March 1, 1981);
(c) one half of the remainder absolutely.

Where no spouse or children survive the intestate, the entire residuary estate falls first to the surviving parents and, failing them, to any brothers or sisters of the whole blood.

Surviving relatives less closely tied ... will only become entitled when none of the above relatives survive so as to take a vested interest and even then only in the following order:

(a) brothers and sisters of the half blood;
(b) grandparents;
(c) uncles and aunts who are brothers or sisters of the whole blood of a parent of the intestate;
(d) uncles and aunts who are brothers or sisters of the half blood of a parent of the intestate.

In the absence of any of these relatives the estate passes to the Crown.

Two further general points should be noted. Where a relative who would otherwise have been entitled to receive a share dies *before* the intestate, he may in certain circumstances be "represented" by his own children if they survive the intestate. Thus, for example, P who has two children Q and R dies intestate. R also has two children S and T, but R dies before P. His share (whatever it may be—see above) in P's estate is divided equally between his two children, S and T (assuming R has made no valid will to the contrary).

The second point relates to the *hotchpot* rule. By this, certain benefits conferred on one of his children by the intestate during his lifetime have to be brought into account when his estate is being divided between all his children under the statutory trusts. However, whilst such prior benefits have to be set off against future settlement, there is no obligation to refund it to the estate.

FAMILY PROVISION

As we have seen, a testator may by his will dispose of his property as he wishes and may decide to make no provision for his surviving family. Where a person has made no will statute provides for distribution of his assets according to fixed rules, but these take no account of the survivors' needs. For these reasons the courts are empowered to order provision to be made for children and other applicants out of the deceased's net estate despite the deceased's intended or presumed wishes. Deaths after March 31, 1976 are governed by the Inheritance (Provision for Family and Dependants) Act 1975.

The benefit of the Act can only be claimed when the deceased died domiciled in England and Wales and the following may apply to the court for an order making provision for them:
   (a)   the deceased's wife or husband;
   (b)   a former wife or husband who has not remarried;
   (c)   a child of the deceased (whether legitimate, illegitimate or adopted);
   (d)   a child treated by the deceased as a child of the family in relation to any marriage of his;
   (e)   a "dependant" (*i.e.* any person who immediately before the deceased's death was being maintained by the deceased).

In *Leach* v. *Lindeman* it was held that "a child of the family" can include an adult where the deceased had assumed (expressly or impliedly) the position of parent towards the applicant. Any application to the court must be made within six months from the date on which representation is first taken out (see below). An application will only succeed if it can be shown that the disposition of property will not be such as to make "reasonable financial provision" for the applicant.

Reasonable financial provision . . . the Act sets two different standards for this. In the case of a surviving spouse, it is such financial provision as is reasonable in all the circumstances and this is not limited to maintenance. In any other case provision is limited to reasonable provision for maintenance.

In considering an application the court must have regard to certain specified matters, including the applicant's financial resources and needs, the size and nature of the net estate, and the applicant's conduct. Where the court believes that reasonable financial provision has not been made, the court may order (*inter alia*):
   (a)   periodic payments;
   (b)   lump sum payments; and
   (c)   transfer of property.

The Act contains anti-avoidance provisions to prevent a deceased from escaping from the Act's control.

THE ADMINISTRATION OF THE DECEASED'S PROPERTY

The preceding discussion has largely concentrated on the destination of the assets of the deceased and little has been said about the means and methods of distribution. Moreover, it has been assumed for the most part that the deceased's assets were destined for beneficiaries under the will or under the rules of intestacy. It is more than likely, however, that the deceased will owe and be owed various debts and liabilities, which must be settled before any distribution of the estate can take place. The process of administration is governed by the provisions of the Administration of Estates Act 1925 as amended.

Under this Act, the administration of the deceased's estate is the task of his *personal representatives*, whose duty is to administer the estate by gathering it in, paying creditors in order of priority and distributing the remaining assets to those who are entitled under the will or by the rules of intestacy. The personal representatives of a testator are called *executors*, whilst those of the intestate are termed *administrators*. In both cases a procedural step is necessary before the estate can be disposed of, namely the *grant of probate or of letters of administration*.

Grant of probate . . . confirms the authority of an executor and may be obtained by application to a district probate registry. The application must be accompanied by, amongst other things, a sworn affidavit (the "executor's oath") whereby the executor swears that (*inter alia*) he will carry out his statutory duties.

Letters of administration . . . a grant of letters of administration *confers* authority on an administrator. At one time it was necessary for an administrator to enter into an *administration bond* before letters of administration were granted. Since 1971, however, the court may only require a guarantee from one or more sureties and this requirement may not always be imposed.

Once the personal representatives have obtained the appropriate grant of authority they may proceed with their principal duties of collection, realisation and management of the deceased's estate. When the debts have been paid and liabilities satisfied the remaining estate can be distributed in the order that has already been discussed.

UNIT THREE
COMMERCIAL AND INDUSTRIAL CONSUMERS

Part One

TYPES, LEGAL STATUS AND STRUCTURE OF ORGANISATIONS

One of the principal reasons that may prompt the commercial or industrial consumer to visit a lawyer involves the choice of business organisation by means of which he may best run his enterprise. Even when this choice has been made (with or without the help of the legal office) advice and assistance may be sought in the formation of the business. Thus, the legal office may be called upon to draft a deed of settlement (partnership agreement) or to prepare documents to send to the Registrar of Companies. On other occasions an existing business organisation may seek advice about its liability arising from transactions into which it (or someone acting on its behalf) has entered. On the other hand, the advice sought may relate to possible legal action which the commercial or industrial law consumer wishes to bring, perhaps against one of its own participants or against another organisation, including those in the public sector. To be able to give such assistance involves a consideration of the different legal forms which organisations may take.

Section A: The Legal Form of the Organisation

Organisations can be divided into two types according to their legal status:
  (a)   corporate bodies; and
  (b)   unincorporated bodies.
The essence of a corporate body is that it has a legal personality distinct from the legal personalities of those persons who are its members (see page 272). A company such as I.C.I. is one example of a corporate body, a nationalised industry such as British Coal is another. It will be seen later that certain consequences flow from the gaining of corporate status which set this type of organisation apart from an unincorporated body. An unincorporated body has no separate identity at law but is comprised of the identities of each of its members individually. Examples of unincorporated bodies include partnerships (such as those formed by solicitors) and clubs and societies (such as those run for social or educational purposes).

THE FORMS OF BUSINESS ORGANISATION

The forms of business organisation at present operating in this country can be classified as:
  (a)   sole traders;
  (b)   partnerships;
  (c)   corporations; and

(d) special types of business organisations.

These, in turn, can be broken down into different types. This may be illustrated by reference to category (c), *corporations*. A corporation may gain its corporate status (*i.e.* be incorporated) either by Royal Charter or by Act of Parliament.

Incorporation by Royal Charter

At common law the Crown has power to create a corporation by granting a charter to persons agreeing to be incorporated. Early trading companies were created in this way and some are still in existence (*e.g.* the Bank of England). Other examples of chartered corporations are the British Broadcasting Corporation, which is formed by a Royal Charter that has to be periodically renewed, and the Institute of Chartered Accountants. One characteristic of a chartered corporation which sets it apart from any other type of corporation should be noted. This feature is the unrestricted capacity of the chartered corporation to make contracts, to deal with its property and to do anything else a human person can lawfully do. It will be seen later that this freedom of action does not extend to the other types of corporation.

Incorporation by Act of Parliament

Parliament may incorporate an organisation in one of three ways:
(a) by Private Act;
(b) by (special) Public Act; and
(c) by (general) Public Act.

Companies incorporated by Private Act . . . such companies (called *statutory companies*) were commonly formed during the latter part of the eighteenth and early part of the nineteenth centuries by the passing of Private Acts through Parliament by individual members (an expensive and sometimes lengthy procedure). Most of the companies formed in this way were railway, water, gas or electricity undertakings, which were later nationalised.

Companies incorporated by (special) Public Act . . . are the *public corporations*, the standard form of organisation operating in the public sector of the economy. Such corporations became particularly prominent with the expansion of nationalisation in the 1940s.

Companies incorporated by (general) Public Act . . . are by far the most common type of corporation and are formed by a simple registration procedure provided by the Companies Act 1985. Such corporations are correctly termed "registered companies" or "joint stock companies," but in common parlance this is shortened to the simple term "company."

Section B: Sole Trader

The framework for the modern forms of business organisation was developed during the period spanning the sixteenth and nineteenth centuries. Not surprisingly, therefore, the types and nature of the associations through which trade was carried on reflect contemporary times (*e.g.* the granting of charters by the Crown in the sixteenth and seventeenth centuries to companies such as the East India Company so that a virtual trade monopoly was secured). During the eighteenth century the rapid increase in the number of enterprises trading as unincorporated bodies without the grant of a charter was matched by an equally rapid increase in the number of business failures. The aftermath of one such spectacular failure (that of the South Sea Company) led in 1720 to the passing of the "Bubble Act" which made it unlawful to purport to trade as a corporate body or to raise transferable joint stock without legal authority. However, the effectiveness of this measure was restricted by the ingenuity of the legal profession which sought ways of avoiding the various disadvantages of trading as an unincorporated body.

Under the impetus provided by the first stages of the Industrial Revolution, Parliament first passed Private Acts in order to form incorporated bodies (the "statutory companies") and later, as the pressure for reform grew, allowed for the introduction of a simple method of incorporation by means of registration and publication of certain documents. It is this simple process which still lies at the heart of company law (see page 275).

Despite this simplified means of incorporation not all businessmen were attracted by the advantages of trading as a corporate body. Some preferred to continue to trade on their own as *sole traders*, others to join with fellow businessmen in *partnerships*.

SOLE TRADER

The term sole trader can be defined quite simply as a person engaged in business on his own. Examples of sole traders include the butcher, the grocer, the hairdresser, the electrician and, indeed, on occasions, the solicitor. The sole trader has no special legal status and no special laws apply to the person operating a business on his own account. There is no legal distinction between the commercial and the private transactions of the sole trader, nor between the legal status of the trader and that of any other citizen. Thus the issues which prompt the sole trader to visit the legal office will not differ in type (though probably in frequency) from those which concern the individual (private) consumer. Perhaps the most serious problem the sole trader is likely to face is that of bankruptcy.

Bankruptcy

Bankruptcy and liquidation . . . when an organisation can no longer trade profitably, it may face the prospect of insolvency (*i.e.* it may be unable to meet its current liabilities or persuade its creditors to await payment any longer). In such cases, the assets of the organisation must be gathered in and distributed amongst the creditors in accordance with their priorities. In the case of the individual trading on his own, or of a partnership, this process is termed *bankruptcy* and is conducted by the *trustee in bankruptcy*. In the case of a company, it is the process of *liquidation* or *winding up* conducted by the *liquidator*. The two processes are not dissimilar. Indeed, the system of liquidation (particularly the procedure followed) was modelled on that for bankruptcy. The two systems underwent major restructuring in the Insolvency Act 1985. The provisions of this Act and those of the Companies Act 1985 relating to corporate insolvency which were amended thereby have been consolidated to form something approaching an insolvency code by the Insolvency Act 1986. This provides that those engaged in insolvency proceedings in a capacity such as a trustee in bankruptcy or a liquidator must be qualified as members of duly recognised professional bodies.

Liquidation of a company may occur other than for reasons of insolvency, since the members of the company may decide voluntarily to bring their trading venture to an end. In this case, the company would be put into voluntary liquidation. If the sole trader or partnership decides to stop trading, there is no question of bankruptcy proceedings unless, of course, either is insolvent. But where a sole trader has become insolvent all his possessions are liable to be taken and distributed amongst his creditors, even though those possessions played no part in his business venture. He may, however, be able to reach agreement with his creditors that this should not happen. Under the Insolvency Act 1986 a new form of voluntary arrangement has been established whereby an individual debtor (whether or not he is a bankrupt) may conclude a composition of debts or a scheme of arrangement of his affairs with his creditors. This process is subject to supervision and to order of the court.

Bankruptcy petition . . . under the 1986 Act a petition for a *bankruptcy order* may be brought by a creditor on the ground that the debtor is unable to pay a debt in excess of £750. The debtor himself may also present a petition, accompanied by a statement of his affairs, on the ground that he is unable to pay his debts. In an appropriate case the court may decide that a voluntary arrangement would be more suitable.

Consequences of a bankruptcy order . . . the making of a bankruptcy order has the effect of rendering void any disposition of property made by the bankrupt after the presentation of the petition. The Official Receiver (an official of the Department of Trade and Industry) becomes receiver and manager of the bankrupt's estate until such time as a trustee in bankruptcy is appointed. His function is to safeguard and maintain the bankrupt's property during that period and to receive a statement of affairs, if one has not already been presented. The Official Receiver has a general duty to investigate the conduct and affairs of every bankrupt (reporting to the court if appropriate) but, under the 1986 Act, a public examination will only take place if the Official Receiver applies to the court for such to be held.

Trustee in bankruptcy . . . this role will be undertaken by the Official Receiver unless he decides to summon a meeting of creditors for the purpose of appointing a trustee in bankruptcy and that meeting appoints a person so to act. The creditors' meeting may establish a committee to perform various supervisory functions over the person appointed, who is in any event subject to the general control of the court. The duty of the trustee in bankruptcy is to gather in all the assets comprising the bankrupt's estate and to realise and distribute them amongst the creditors according to the rules as to priority (see page 284). Exempted from this realisation and distribution are such tools, books, vehicles and other items of equipment as are necessary to the bankrupt for use personally by him in his employment, business or vocation. Also exempt are items necessary to the basic domestic needs of the bankrupt and his family. In addition the realisation of the family home of the bankrupt may be subject, at least within the first year of bankruptcy, to consideration of the needs of the bankrupt's spouse, former spouse or children.

Preferential transactions . . . the 1986 Act contains a set of provisions parallel to those applicable to corporate insolvency (see page 285) which make certain transactions upon the application of the trustee in bankruptcy subject to a range of court orders. These provisions cover any transaction with any person at an undervalue (including transactions which are gifts or made in consideration of marriage) and any transaction which gives a preference to any person. In the former case a transaction is covered if it has been made in the two years prior to bankruptcy. This period is extended to five years if the individual was insolvent at the time of the transaction or became insolvent in consequence of the transaction. In the latter case a transaction made within six months of bankruptcy may be challenged as preferential if it puts a creditor into a better position in the event of the individual's bankruptcy and the intention to prefer the creditor influenced the individual in giving the preference. Where such a preference is given to a spouse or other close relative within the two years prior to bankruptcy the onus is upon the recipient to show that the bankrupt was not influenced by a desire to prefer him. In both cases to be a voidable preference the bankrupt must be insolvent at the time of the transaction or made insolvent in consequence of the transaction.

Discharge of bankrupt . . . persons adjudicated bankrupt for the first time will be automatically discharged three years after the commencement of the bankruptcy. Former bankrupts who have had the status of undischarged bankrupt within 15 years of the present bankruptcy may apply to the court for discharge not earlier than five years after the commencement of that bankruptcy. The effect of an order of discharge is to release the bankrupt from all debts and liabilities subject to certain exceptions, but does not affect the functions of the trustee in bankruptcy.

Section C: Partnership

THE NATURE AND DEFINITION OF PARTNERSHIP

Types of partnership

The law relating to partnerships is to be found in the Partnership Act 1890, the Limited Partnership Act 1907 and in the decisions of the courts. Partnerships governed by the 1890 Act are sometimes referred to as *ordinary partnerships*, whilst those subject to the 1907 Act are known as *limited partnerships*.

Under the Limited Partnership Act 1907 a distinction is drawn between *general partners* and *limited partners*. A general partner, of whom there must be at least one in every limited partnership, will be liable for all debts and obligations of the firm. A limited partner, on the other hand, will, on entering the partnership, contribute a sum of capital valued at a stated amount and will not be liable for debts and obligations beyond this fixed amount. The limited partner cannot withdraw any part of his capital contribution during the existence of the partnership, otherwise he becomes liable for the debts and obligations of the firm up to the amount withdrawn. The limited partner will lose his limited liability completely should he take part in management of the business. Inspecting the firm's books, examining the state and prospects of the partnership, and advising the partners thereon are not, however, acts of management and thus may be undertaken by the limited partner. Apart from such restrictions the price to be paid for the advantage of limited liability is the necessity to register with the Registrar of Companies certain particulars (including details of the contributions of limited partners). These particulars are open to public inspection. Otherwise, for the most part, the rules relating to partnership under the 1890 Act are equally applicable to the limited partnership. The limited partner, however, has no power to bind the firm.

Persons who have entered into partnership with one another are, for the purposes of the 1890 Act, called collectively a *firm*, and the name under which their business is carried on is called the firm-name. One of the basic distinctions between the partnership and the company as business organisations is that the partnership itself, unlike the company (see page 272), does not have, under English law, a legal personality distinct from that of the members comprising it. Nevertheless, the partnership does show certain "quasi-corporate" characteristics, and it is common business practice to think of the firm as carrying on the business, rather than the members (as is strictly the case). Indeed, the firm-name may be used in legal documents and, under the Rules of the Supreme Court, legal actions may be brought by and against the firm in the name of the firm, rather than in the names of all its members.

The choice of a name for the partnership is one for the partners, but they may not choose a name for their business which leads people to believe that their business is the business of another (see page 379).

Definition of partnership

Partnership is defined in section 1 of the Partnership Act 1890 as "the relation which subsists between persons carrying on a business in common with a view of profit." (Those carrying on a business as members of a company are specifically excluded from the definition of a partnership.) There are a number of elements to this definition.

The relation which subsists . . . although the Act does not state it, the partnership relationship is based upon a contract, express or implied, under which the parties carry on a business. Two or more persons wishing to carry on a business together may draw up an express contract regulating their relations. This document is called the *partnership agreement* or *deed of settlement*. On the other hand, the parties may draw up no express agreement but merely trade in common, in which case a contract will be implied from their conduct. In practice, the relationship between the partners will commonly be governed by a combination of express and implied contractual terms.

Between persons . . . every person (natural or legal) has the right to enter a partnership. Thus, a company may be a member of a partnership. Under the Companies Act 1985 there are restrictions on the maximum number of persons who may carry on a business for gain without registering that business as a company. In most cases the maximum number is 20, although partnerships consisting of professional persons (*e.g.* solicitors, accountants, surveyors, or estate agents) may exceed this limit. In the case of those carrying on the business of a bank, the maximum number is ten, although this may be raised to 20 with authorisation from the Department of Trade and Industry.

Carrying on a business in common . . . the term "business" is defined as including "every trade, occupation or profession." Essentially, the partnership relationship is an active relationship denoting a degree of continuity. However, under English law a partnership may be formed for a particular venture and dissolved on its completion.

With a view of profit . . . the Act requires that the business must be carried on *with a view* to making a profit. That is not to say that the business must actually make a profit. A business may be a partnership even though it trades at a loss.

THE RELATIONS OF PARTNERS TO OUTSIDERS

In its relationship to outsiders, the concept of agency is at the foundation of the law of partnership. Section 5 of the 1890 Act provides that "every partner is an agent of the firm and his other partners for the purpose of the business of the partnership." Under the law relating to principal and agent, an agent may fix liability upon his principal where the agent has acted:

(a) within the authority expressly given to him by his principal; or
(b) outside this express authority, but within the usual authority given to an agent in his position; or
(c) outside his express or usual authority, but within his apparent authority (*i.e.* where he is held out by the principal as having the authority to act in the way that he does, although he does not in fact have that authority).

Thus, a partner will bind the firm where he acts within:

(a) his express authority;
(b) his usual authority; or
(c) his apparent authority.

The partner's authority to act

In the case of the partnership the *express* authority of each partner will be set out in the partnership agreement. In addition, section 5 provides that each partner has authority to bind the firm and his partners by acts in the "usual course of business" for here he will have *usual* authority. However, the firm and the other partners will not be bound by the acts of any partner if he has no authority to act for the firm in a particular matter *and* the person with whom he is dealing either knows that he has no authority, or does not know or believe him to be a partner.

As well as being able to bind the firm by acts within his express authority or within the usual course of business, a partner may bind the firm where he acts within his *apparent* authority. If, for example, a partner is held out by his fellow partners to a third person as having the power to enter a particular contract with that person, then the firm will be bound even though the contract was not, in fact, one which he had express or usual authority to make.

Thus, if A, B and C are partners and A and B authorise C to purchase goods from Q on terms which would otherwise be outside C's express or usual authority, C will have express authority to so transact. By paying Q for the goods that C has bought for the firm, A and B would, additionally, hold C out as having that authority. In relation to Q, therefore, C has both express and apparent authority to transact on this basis. If A and B inform C that he may no longer transact with Q on the same basis, they will have terminated his express authority. But, unless they notify Q of this withdrawal of authority, C will still have his apparent authority to bind A and B.

A firm may also incur liability by *ratifying* the unauthorised acts of a partner, thus, retrospectively, granting him express authority.

Personal liability of a partner

Every partner is liable *jointly* with the other partners for all debts and contractual obligations incurred by the partnership while he is a partner. In the case of tortious liabilities, on the other hand, liability is *joint and several*. At one time the effect of this distinction was relevant to the procedural steps taken by a plaintiff. Where his action related to a debt or a contractual obligation he could only bring one action against the members of the partnership. If, for example, a partnership consisted of A, B and C, the plaintiff could choose to join all three to his action, sue just one of the partners or some combination of them. But where he did not join them all, he lost any rights against those he had omitted. Where, however, the plaintiff's action was in tort, he could sue the partners together (jointly) or each in turn (severally). In the latter case an unfulfilled judgment against one partner (who had perhaps become bankrupt) did not prevent further actions against the others. In practice any difficulty arising from the issue of personal liability could be avoided by suing in the name of the firm under the procedures provided by the Rules of the Supreme Court. In any event, the former common law rule that judgment against one wrongdoer extinguished the cause of action and thus barred further actions, has now been abolished by the Civil Liability (Contribution) Act 1978.

THE INTERNAL RELATIONS BETWEEN PARTNERS

Rights of partners

Section 24 of the 1890 Act provides that, *subject to the partnership agreement*, the interests of partners in the partnership property and their rights and duties in relation to the partnership must be determined by the following rules:

Sharing in profits and losses ... all the partners are entitled to share equally in the capital and profits of the business, and must contribute equally towards the losses, whether of capital or otherwise, sustained by the firm.

Right to indemnity ... every partner is entitled to be indemnified (compensated) by the firm in respect of payments made and personal liabilities incurred by him in the ordinary and proper conduct of the firm's business.

Participation in management ... every partner is entitled to take part in the management of the partnership business. This rule, however, is subject to modification where the partners have agreed that any one partner (a dormant partner) should not take part in management, or that a particular partner (a junior partner) should only have limited rights in the conduct of the business.

Remuneration for services ... no partner is entitled to a salary for acting in the partnership business. This rule is likely to be varied in the partnership agreement.

Introduction of new partners ... no person may be introduced as a partner without the consent of all the partners. However, too rigid an application of such a rule would have destroyed the continuity of many family businesses being run in partnership. Thus, the partners may by express agreement make allowance for the transfer of a partner's share.

Right to take part in decision-making ... any difference arising as to ordinary matters connected with the partnership business may be decided by a majority of the partners, but no change may be made in the nature of the partnership business without the consent of all existing partners.

Inspection of books and accounts ... the partnership books are to be kept at the place of business of the partnership, and every partner may, when he thinks fit, inspect and copy any of them. (Shareholders in a company do not have this right.)

Retirement of a partner

Where no fixed term has been agreed upon for the duration of the partnership (a "partnership at will"), any partner may end the partnership at any time by giving notice of his intention to do so to all the other partners. Such notice must be clearly stated, and cannot be withdrawn without the agreement of the other partners. Where the partnership was originally formed by deed, it may be terminated only by a signed notice in writing.

The retirement of a partner is prima facie an event leading to the dissolution of the firm. It would, however, be extremely inconvenient for the continued running of a business if, on the retirement of each partner, the firm's assets had to be realised and distributed amongst the members. Thus, the partnership agreement will (or at least ought to) make provision for this by requiring, for example, that a retiring partner agrees to receive his share of the partnership in cash, possibly payable over a period of months or years. By such a provision the worst of the disruption to the business may be avoided.

A relationship of the "utmost good faith"

The relationship between the partners is based upon the principle that they should exercise the utmost good faith in their dealings with one another. The duty of good faith exists not only during the life of the firm but also during its dissolution until its affairs are brought to a close. Under the Act, partners are bound to render true accounts and provide full information of all things affecting the partnership to any partner or his legal representative. Every partner must account to the firm for any benefit derived by him, without the consent of the other partners, from any transaction concerning the partnership, or from any use by him of the partnership property, name or business connection.

Without the consent of his fellow partners, a partner must not carry on a business which is of the same nature and competes with the firm. If he does, he must pay over to the firm any profits made from that competing business.

TERMINATION OF PARTNERSHIP RELATIONSHIP

Dissolution of partnership

In the case of a partnership, its assets will be disposed of when it is dissolved. A partnership may be dissolved with or without the aid of the court. No direct assistance from the court will be necessary if the partnership is one for a fixed duration and that period has been reached. Indeed, even if the partnership is one of indefinite duration, any partner may give notice of intention to dissolve the partnership at any time. Similarly, the death or bankruptcy of a partner serves to end the partnership. A partnership may also be dissolved by the court on various grounds, including:

(a) the insanity of one of the partners;

(b) the prejudicial conduct of one of the partners (*e.g.* a partner in a firm of solicitors who embezzles clients' money);

(c) the inability of the business to be carried on except at a permanent loss; and

(d) the opinion of the court that it would be just and equitable to do so (*e.g.* because the partners are in deadlock and refusing to communicate with each other).

But, whatever the cause of dissolution, the partnership will not be absolved from liability as regards third persons.

On dissolution, the property of the partnership must be gathered in and used in payment of the debts and liabilities of the firm. The assets will include the goodwill of the business (see page 340). Any surplus must be used to pay to the partners that which is due to them in accordance with the partnership agreement. In the absence of any such provision in the partnership agreement, the partners are entitled to be repaid the capital which they contributed. After that, again assuming no provision to the contrary, any remaining surplus profits will be shared equally between the partners. Consider the following example:

A, B and C contribute £300, £200 and £100 respectively to their partnership. On dissolution, the assets realise £1,400, but there are partnership debts of £500. After these have been paid off, the remaining £900 is applied in paying back to A, B and C their respective capital contributions. The £300 that is then left will be shared equally between the three partners.

If on dissolution there are losses, then these must be paid first out of profits, next out of capital and finally by the partners themselves in the same proportions as they would have shared in any profits.

For example, A, B and C contribute £300, £200 and £100 respectively to their partnership. On dissolution, the assets realise £1,000, but the partnership debts total £520. The distribution of assets will be:

(a) creditors are paid off, leaving assets of £480;

(b) the partners are paid their capital contributions, but there is a shortfall on capital of £120, which must be shared between the partners.

In the absence of any provision to the contrary, the loss will be borne equally by them. As a result—

Share of Net Assets

A brought in £300, less £40	£260
B brought in £200, less £40	£160
C brought in £100, less £40	£60
	£480

If, however, partners share trading profits and losses in the proportions in which they have contributed capital, any loss of capital will also be shared in this proportion. Thus, using the figures in the last example, A, B and C will share losses in the ratio 3:2:1 and the end result would be:

Share of Net Assets

A brought in £300, less £60	£240
B brought in £200, less £40	£160
C brought in £100, less £20	£80
	£480

A further problem arises where there are insufficient assets to repay the partners all their capital, but one of the partners is unable to contribute to the loss because he is insolvent. In the case of *Garner* v. *Murray*, it was held that the solvent partners were not obliged to make up the contribution of the insolvent partner, but that they would have to bear whatever deficiency was attributable to his insolvency in the proportion of their last agreed capital contributions before the dissolution.

For example, A, B and C are the members of a partnership to which they have contributed unequal amounts of capital, but in which profits and losses are shared equally. The last balance sheet for the partnership, drawn up before dissolution, is set out in table 1 (p. 271).

On dissolution of the partnership the assets will be gathered in and distributed as follows:

Assets are sold for £8,000.

Out of which creditors are paid £6,500 leaving £1,500 to be distributed to partners.

Loss after realisation of assets (£12,500–£8,000) = £4,500.

Under the rule in *Garner* v. *Murray* A and B only contribute to this deficiency their proper share (£1,500 each).

Surplus assets and solvent partner's contributions = £1,500 + £3,000
= £4,500

Division of this sum between solvent partners   A receives £2,700
in their capital contribution ratio (3:2)   B receives £1,800

Given that both A and B have made up the deficiency by £1,500, A will actually receive from the dissolution £1,200 (a loss on his original contribution of £1,800), and B will receive £300 (a loss on his contribution of £1,700).

Table 1

BALANCE SHEET

Capital Account		£	Fixed Assets	£
Contributions of			Premises	4,950
partners	A	3,000	Machinery	2,950
	B	2,000		
	C	1,000		
Current Liabilities			**Current Assets**	
Creditors		6,500	Stock	2,650
			Bank	1,950
		12,500		12,500

Bankruptcy and the partnership

There are two different situations that must be considered here. One partner may be declared bankrupt in respect of his separate personal debts, whilst his fellow partners remain solvent. Alternatively, it may be the partnership itself which is insolvent, because it is unable to meet the debts of the firm. In the first case the bankruptcy of one partner causes the partnership to be dissolved under section 33 of the Partnership Act 1890, and the share in the partnership of the bankrupt partner vests in his trustee in bankruptcy. Any partnership creditor is entitled to *prove* (*i.e.* make a claim) in that bankruptcy. In practice, however, there will normally be no such need, since the solvent partners will pay that creditor off and then seek a contribution towards such payment from the bankrupt partner by themselves proving in his bankruptcy.

Where it is the partnership itself which is insolvent, then normally all partners will be made bankrupt and bankruptcy proceedings may be brought, initially at least, in the name of the firm. The actual adjudication of bankruptcy must be made against each individual partner.

The one real difference between the bankruptcy involving a partnership or its members and that of any other individual is that there are two distinct groupings of creditors: those of the partner personally, and those of the firm itself. The basic principle, therefore, is to keep separate the property and debts of the partner as a private individual and those of the partnership itself. Where the two groups of creditors can be satisfied by the appropriate funds there is no difficulty. Where this is not so the following rules apply:

(a) the partnership property is applied as a *joint pool* in payment of the debts of the firm, and the separate property of each partner is applied as a *separate pool* in payment of his separate debts;

(b)   after such payment, any surplus of the joint pool is transferred to the separate pools of the partners in proportion to their rights under the partnership agreement; and, if the joint pool is deficient, any surplus of the separate pools will be dealt with as part of the joint pool and applied in payment of joint debts in proportion to the liability of each partner to contribute.

Consider the following example:

A, B and C are partners; A owes his separate creditors £200, and his separate pool is £350. B owes £450 personally, and has £900. C owes £100, and has nothing. The firm's debts are £1,000, and assets £700. The separate creditors of A take £200 of his £350, and those of B take £450 of his £900. The joint creditors take the £700 of the joint pool, but this is deficient by £300. Therefore, A's remaining £150 and B's £450 must go to make up this deficiency. If A and B are bound by their partnership agreement to contribute equally to any losses, A and B would both contribute £150 to the joint pool. B would then be left with £300, and this would not be available for C's separate creditors. (Indeed A and B would be entitled to prove in C's bankruptcy along with C's separate creditors in respect of their contribution towards C's liability to joint creditors.)

Section D: The Company

There are two concepts at the heart of any company:
(a)   the concept of legal personality; and
(b)   the concept of limited liability.

The concept of legal personality
Any person who has rights and duties at law is a legal person, but not all legal persons are human. Legal persons that are non-human are called *corporations*. A company is one type of corporation. Since a company is a legal person it enjoys rights and is subject to duties which are distinct from those which may be enjoyed or borne by its members. The property of the company (unlike that of the partnership) is held by and belongs to the company. The company has perpetual succession and is not affected by the death or retirement of any of its members.

The principle that a company has a legal personality distinct from that of its members was established by the House of Lords in the case of *Salomon* v. *Salomon & Son*. Salomon, a boot and shoe manufacturer, decided to transfer his business, which he had previously run as a sole trader, to a company which he had formed. His purpose, apparently, was to give his children a part in the business. Salomon sold the business to the company for £39,000, which was raised by issuing to Salomon 20,000 fully paid £1 shares in the company and £10,000 of debentures charged on all the assets, and by paying the balance in cash. However, the business did not prosper and soon the company was unable to pay its debts to its creditors.

The company was put into liquidation. The creditors claimed that Salomon was the real owner of the business and that he should meet their debts. But the House of Lords held that the company had been validly formed and was a separate legal entity. The business belonged to the company, not to Salomon himself, and the debts were the debts of the company and Salomon was not, therefore, personally liable to pay off the creditors.

The principle established by *Salomon's* case that a registered company is a legal person distinct from its members is sometimes referred to as "the veil of incorporation." As a general rule, the law will not go behind this veil and will treat a company as a separate legal person. However, in certain situations the courts have been prepared to "lift the veil" and look behind the corporate form to those who own and run the company. In *Gilford Motor Co. Ltd.* v. *Horne*, for example, an employee had agreed by covenant in restraint of trade that after the termination of his employment he would not solicit his employer's customers. After termination of that employment he formed a company which sent out circulars to the customers of his former employer. In granting an injunction against both the ex-employee and the company the court held that it would not allow the separate identity of the company to be used as a device to cover the breach of the restraint of trade clause. The employee was using the corporate form merely as a mask to hide behind and this the court would not allow him to do.

The concept of limited liability

This is the second concept fundamental to the company. As *Salomon's* case showed, the members of a company are not as such liable for the debts of the company. However, the law does not permit the members of a company to be completely free from liability.

The extent of the members' liability for the debts of the company will depend upon the way that liability has been limited, if at all. A company may be classified for this purpose as:

(a) a company limited by shares;

(b) a company limited by guarantee; or

(c) an unlimited company.

A company limited by shares . . . in this case the member's liability is limited to the amount unpaid on the shares that he holds. For example, if A agrees to buy 50 £1 shares in company X at £1 per share and pays the company 50p on each share (*i.e.* £25 in all), then £25 will be outstanding. This amount (the *uncalled* or *unpaid* amount on his shares) he can be called upon to pay at any later date during the company's existence. If the company trades unsuccessfully A may be made to pay his outstanding £25 but no more, no matter how great the debts of the company.

A company limited by guarantee . . . if a company has been formed as a company limited by guarantee (*e.g.* the Institute of Legal Executives) its members are under no liability to pay anything until such time as the company is wound up (*i.e.* its existence is brought to an end). At this time each member will be liable to contribute his *guaranteed* amount to the assets of the company. The guaranteed amount will be specified in the memorandum of the company on its formation.

Unlimited company... if a company has been formed as an unlimited company, then the members are fully liable for all the debts of the company. It is unusual for trading companies to be unlimited companies. The only advantage to be gained is that unlimited companies are exempted from certain disclosure requirements in respect of the filing of accounts and directors' and auditors' reports. This lack of publicity is sometimes sought by family-owned businesses.

Classification of companies

One way in which registered companies can be classified is, as we have seen, in terms of the way in which the liability of their members is limited. An alternative classification is into *public* or *private* companies. Before 1980 private companies were defined by reference to certain restrictive provisions contained in their Articles of Association (see page 276), and a public company was any company whose articles did not contain those provisions. The pendulum has now swung so that since 1980 it is the public company which is specifically defined and the private company which is the residual category.

A public company... is defined as any company:
(a) which is limited by shares (or limited by guarantee and having a share capital);
(b) whose memorandum states that the company is to be public;
(c) whose name ends with the words "public limited company" (p.l.c.); and
(d) which has complied with the registration provisions of the Companies Act (see below).

In some cases companies which were public companies before the 1980 legislation was passed will not wish to meet the last of these requirements and will re-register as private companies. Those companies that do choose the new public company status will be attracted by the advantage that their members will generally be able to freely transfer their shares and any member of the public willing to purchase them may normally become a member. In the absence of a market place, with adequate flows of information to both prospective sellers and buyers, the advantage of transferability would be less significant. The market place for transactions in the shares (and debentures) of public companies is provided by the Stock Exchange. Public companies whose shares are dealt in and "quoted" (or "listed") on the Stock Exchange are commonly referred to as *quoted public companies*. By no means all public companies are quoted companies. Those that are quoted have to meet certain strict requirements laid down by the Council of the Stock Exchange.

A private company... is any company which is not a public company. Whilst the former prohibition on the offering of shares to the public still applies, the other two requirements for a private company, which limited the number of members to 50 and required the articles to restrict the right to transfer shares, have been removed. Nevertheless, it is likely that where the private company is used as the vehicle for running a family business the right to transfer shares will still be restricted in order to retain family control over the business.

FORMATION

The law consumer who decides that he wishes to conduct his business by means of a company may approach the legal office for assistance in forming the company. All or some part of this task may be passed on by the legal office to an agency specialising in the formation of companies. Indeed, at a small cost a ready-formed company (often referred to as an "off-the-shelf company") may be purchased from such an agency. Whatever choice is made, the method of forming a company is very simple. Broadly, all that is required is for the person forming the company to send to the Registrar of Companies certain documents and to pay certain fees and duties. These documents will be examined by the Registrar and if they comply with the requirements of the Companies Act, the Registrar will duly register the formation of the company. The documents that must be sent to the Registrar are:

(a) the memorandum of association;
(b) the articles of association;
(c) a statement of the nominal share capital;
(d) a statement as to directors, secretary and registered office; and
(e) the declaration of compliance.

Memorandum of Association

This is a very important document in relation to the proposed company since, amongst other things, it will set out the objects for which the company is to be formed and the powers it will possess to achieve these objects. The memorandum contains six clauses:

(a) the name clause;
(b) the registered office clause;
(c) the objects clause;
(d) the limited liability clause;
(e) the capital clause; and
(f) the association clause.

The name clause . . . states the company's name and on incorporation this is the name the company will be given. If it is a public company the name must end with the words "public limited company." If it is a private company with limited liability then the word "limited" must appear as the last word of the name. The name of the company must be displayed outside every place of business, engraved on the company's seal (this will be used where necessary in authenticating the company's documents), and used in all the company's correspondence (*e.g.* letters, notices or orders for goods).

The registered office clause . . . must state whether the company's registered office is in England, Wales or Scotland, but there is no requirement to give an address (see below).

The objects clause . . . is particularly important since this determines what activities a company may lawfully pursue. This issue is discussed at greater length (see page 281).

The limited liability clause . . . in the case of a limited company must state simply that the liability of the members is limited. This clause acts as a warning to those dealing with the company.

The capital clause . . . in the memorandum of a company limited by shares must state the amount of share capital with which the company is to be registered (the *nominal capital*), the number of shares into which that amount is to be divided, and the amount of each share (its *nominal value*). Before 1980 there was in this country no fixed legal minimum or maximum figure at which the nominal capital had to be set. It was a question to be determined by the expected requirements of the business. In the case of public companies the amount of the nominal share capital stated in the memorandum must, since 1980, be not less than the *authorised minimum* (presently set at £50,000), of which at least one-quarter in value must be *paid up* (see page 278). However, as to the division of the nominal capital into shares of a fixed amount, there is no specific figure determined by law. The only requirement is that shares must have a fixed or nominal value, and this may, for example, be 5p, £100 or even £5,000. In practice, the nominal value of shares is usually set at a figure at which they can be easily bought and sold. Thus, shares with a nominal value of £1 are common.

The association clause . . . is the last clause in the memorandum and is a declaration by those signing the memorandum (*the subscribers*) that they wish to be formed into a company and that they agree to take the shares set opposite their names.

To form and register a company, whether public or private, it is only necessary for the company to have two members.

Articles of Association

These are the internal regulations for the conduct of the company's business. The articles will govern such issues as the holding of meetings, the rights of shareholders to vote at meetings and the powers of directors. Those engaged in the formation of the company (the *promoters*) may draw up for their proposed company its own set of internal regulations. For most purposes, however, such individuality is unnecessary and the promoters may adopt for the company a model set of articles contained in the Companies legislation. In the case of a company limited by shares, Table A, the Companies Regulations 1985 provides a model set of articles which will automatically apply, if no other articles are registered.

Alteration of articles . . . may be effected by the passing of a special resolution in general meeting (see page 279), subject to the right of the holders of 15 per cent. of the issued share capital to apply to the court (within 21 days) to have any such alteration cancelled.

Statement of nominal share capital

This is only necessary where the company has a share capital. Its function is to ensure that the requisite capital duty is paid on the shares issued on incorporation.

Statement as to directors, secretary and registered office

This must include the names and other personal details of the directors and secretary of the company, and their consent to act as such. It must also state the intended address of the company's registered office. The Registrar must not register the memorandum and articles unless this statement is delivered with them.

Declaration of compliance

This is a statutory declaration that all the requirements of the Companies Acts have been complied with. It must be made either by the solicitor engaged in the formation of the company or by a person named in the previous statement as a director or secretary of the company.

Once the above documents have been lodged with the Registrar, together with the £50 registration fee and any capital duty payable, they will be checked by the Registrar's staff. If everything is in order to the satisfaction of the Registrar, he will sign and issue the *certificate of incorporation* (the company's "birth certificate"). From the date stated in the certificate to be the date of incorporation, the company comes into existence as a legal person, a *body corporate*.

A private company may commence business (*e.g.* making contracts or borrowing money) from the date of incorporation. A public company, however, must comply with further requirements. In particular, it must obtain from the Registrar a *trading certificate* which will be conclusive evidence that the company is entitled to commence business.

MEMBERSHIP OF A COMPANY

Right to be a member

The right to be a member of a company is generally open to all persons natural or legal. Thus company X may hold shares in company Y. Indeed, if company X holds more than half of the "equity share capital" of company Y, then company Y is a *subsidiary* of company X, its *holding company*. (Equity share capital will generally be the company's issued ordinary shares.) In this case, one restriction upon membership of a company would be that company Y could not hold shares in company X, since the Acts provide that a subsidiary may not be a member of its holding company. Although it was a long-established rule that no company could purchase its own shares or be a member of itself, this policy has been modified to allow greater freedom, particularly to private companies, to buy back their shares. Similar relaxation has been granted in respect of a company which provides financial assistance to third parties to buy its own shares.

Becoming a member

There are three ways in which a person may become a member of a company:
(a) by subscribing to a memorandum of association;
(b) by agreeing, as a director, to take and pay for any shares which under the articles any director is required to hold; and
(c) by agreeing to become a member and having his name entered in the *register of members*.

By far the most usual way of becoming a member is the last method. It will be seen that this requires two steps:
(a) agreement to become a member; and
(b) entry of name in register of members.

Both steps must be completed before a person can be described as a member in respect of a particular holding of shares.

Agreement to become a member . . . the necessary agreement to become a member may arise in a number of ways, most commonly where a person has agreed to take shares on allotment or has contracted with an existing member for the transfer of ownership of his shares. Shares are taken on allotment where a person applies to a company in response to a *prospectus* (a document advertising to the public the company's shares) and shares are allotted to him by the company. In this situation the prospectus is an *invitation to treat*, the application for shares the *offer*, and the allotment of shares the *acceptance*. The *consideration* for the allotment is the payment for the shares. Payment in full is required, but this need not necessarily be made at the time of allotment. A company may only require part payment at this time, in which case the shares would be described as *partly paid*. The company may make *calls* upon the member to pay the outstanding (*unpaid*) amount on his shares in the future. It will be remembered that until a member has fully paid for his shares, he will remain liable for the company's debts to the amount, if any, unpaid on the shares (see page 273).

Entry of name in register of members . . . the second step in becoming a member is the entry of the purchaser's name in the register of members which every company must keep. The register of members will contain the names and addresses of members, a statement of the shares held by each member, the extent to which those shares are paid up, and the dates on which each person became, or ceased to be, a member.

INTERNAL MANAGEMENT

In the case of a sole trader, a partnership or a private company, ownership of the business is not divorced from the management function and the owners will not need to exert their control over a separate management team. This is not the situation in the case of a large public company, the shareholders of which may be concerned that their interests are protected. To ensure that management does not disregard the interests of shareholders, the internal structure of a company will consist of two organs, a board of directors and a meeting of shareholders.

Board of directors

The board of directors of a company will be a comparatively small group of persons who have been appointed directors by the general meeting. Under the articles of association of the company, the directors, as a board, will usually be given extensive powers, including control of the day-to-day management of the company. The board, in turn, may delegate all or any of these powers to one of themselves as managing director.

The division of responsibility for the control of management between the board and the general meeting will be determined largely by the articles. Where the board is given powers under the articles, the general meeting cannot interfere with the board's exercise of those powers. However, the general meeting will be able to exert some control over the board's use of its powers by removing directors from office. The general meeting can also act in areas reserved for the board if the directors are in deadlock or their number has fallen below that required for a quorum at board meetings. Moreover, if the directors exceed their powers, or use them for improper purposes, the general meeting may decide not to ratify their actions.

Meetings of shareholders

By exercising their rights to attend and vote at general meetings shareholders as a body may exert some control over the running of their company.

The Companies Act lays down various provisions for the calling, holding and conduct of general meetings. General meetings can be broadly classified as:

(a) annual general meetings (A.G.M.); and
(b) extraordinary general meetings (E.G.M.).

Annual general meeting . . . must be held every calendar year, with an interval of not more than 15 months between one A.G.M. and the next. This gives the shareholders the opportunity to question the directors on the company's performance each year. Twenty-one days' notice in writing must be given of an A.G.M. to every member specifying the place, date and hour of the meeting and, if there is to be any special business, the general nature of that business.

Extraordinary general meeting . . . is any general meeting of a company other than an annual general meeting. The calling of such meetings will depend upon the articles. Most provide that the directors *may* convene an E.G.M. whenever they think fit. Normally the articles require that they *must* call an E.G.M. if asked to do so by the holders of not less than one-tenth of the paid-up capital of the company carrying voting rights. Failure by the directors to do so within 21 days gives those asking for the meeting the right to convene the meeting themselves. Not less than 14 days' notice in writing must be given of an E.G.M. unless a *special resolution* is to be proposed, in which case at least 21 days' notice must be given. Notice of the business to be conducted must give the member such information as will allow him to make up his mind whether to attend or not and, at the same time, to appreciate the consequences if he decides not to go.

A company in general meeting acts by the passing of resolutions of which due notice has been given to the members. There are three types of resolution:

(a) the ordinary resolution;
(b) the extraordinary resolution; and
(c) the special resolution.

Ordinary resolution . . . is a resolution passed by a simple majority of the members present and voting (in person or by proxy) at the meeting.

Extraordinary resolution . . . is defined in the Act as a resolution passed by at least a three-fourths majority of the votes of the members present and voting (in person or by proxy) at the meeting.

Special resolution . . . is defined as a resolution passed by at least a three-fourths majority of the votes of the members present and voting (in person or by proxy) at a meeting of which at least 21 days' notice has been given.

The length of notice required for ordinary or extraordinary resolutions will depend on the kind of meeting being held.

In the absence of any contrary provision in the Act, or in the memorandum or articles, a company will act by ordinary resolutions (*e.g.*

on an increase of capital). However, special resolutions are required for any major constitutional change (*e.g.* alteration of memorandum or articles). Extraordinary resolutions are less common and are normally used where speed is essential (*e.g.* in winding-up proceedings). A printed copy of special and extraordinary resolutions must be registered with the Registrar of Companies within 15 days of their being passed.

DIRECTORS

Definition and qualifications

The term "director" has no special significance, and, for the purposes of the Act, the term includes any person occupying the position of director by whatever name called. The articles may provide that a person must hold a specified number of shares in the company to qualify for appointment as a director. However, this is unlikely to be so in the case of a public company, and in any event, in a private company the directors will probably have substantial shareholdings.

Register of directors and their interests

A company must keep at its registered office a register of directors, which must be open to inspection by members without charge. The register must contain details of the personal particulars of directors (including any other directorships held by them). A company must also keep and make available for inspection a register recording the interests of directors in the company's securities (shares or debentures). This information must be notified in writing to the company by the directors. If the company is one whose securities are quoted on the Stock Exchange, this information must also be relayed by the company to the Stock Exchange.

Appointment and removal

Every public company must have at least two directors and every private company at least one.

The power to remove directors is one exercised by general meeting. Under section 303 of the 1985 Act the general meeting may by ordinary resolution remove a director before the end of his period of office, notwithstanding anything in the articles or in any agreement between the director and the company.

The duties of directors

The position of directors towards the company is, in some respects, like that of trustees, in that they owe duties of good faith and of care to the company. Directors can be likened to trustees inasmuch as they hold the company's property on trust for the company and, if they misapply it in breach of that trust, they are liable to replace it.

The directors' duties of good faith are:
(a) to use their powers for proper purposes and bona fide for the benefit of the company as a whole; and
(b) to avoid situations where their duties to the company and their personal interests conflict.

Bona fide for benefit of company . . . it has been held that it is for the directors, not the court, to determine what is bona fide for the benefit of the company as a whole. Further, the 1985 Act provides that the interests of employees shall be included among those bona fide interests.

Conflict of interests . . . a director must disclose any interest he has in any contract with the company, otherwise that contract may be avoided at the option of the company. A director is deemed to have an interest for these purposes even if he is only a shareholder (and not a director) in another company which contracts with the company of which he is a director. In the case of certain property transactions in which a director is interested he must obtain the prior approval of the general meeting, otherwise the contract will be voidable.

The standard of care that a director must exhibit in his actions will vary from case to case. The standard expected of a director of a small private company will differ from that required of a director of a large public company. In the latter, a director, as well as being a member of the board, may also be an employee of the company with specific responsibilities for a particular aspect of the company's business (*e.g.* as personnel director or production director). As such he will be expected to exercise a high degree of skill and knowledge commensurate with his appointment.

The actions and remedies for breach of directors' duties are considered in *Part Three* of this Unit, see page 338.

LIABILITY OF A COMPANY TO OUTSIDERS

General principles

As a legal person, a registered company could have been allowed to have all the powers to act as if it were a human person. However, the law has not developed in this way. It has been established that a company can lawfully enter only those transactions which it is authorised to undertake by the Companies Acts and by its memorandum and articles of association. Any activity beyond this is, at common law, said to be *ultra vires* (beyond its powers) and void. At one time, an outsider who wished to enforce a contract against a company had to prove that the contract was:

(a) within the capacity of the company to make; and
(b) one which the director(s) with whom he had dealt had power to enter into.

It will be seen later that this position has been modified by statutory developments.

Ultra vires doctrine

The objects clause of the memorandum will set out the purposes for which the company has been formed and the powers which it has to achieve those purposes. If the company enters into a contract beyond the express or implied purposes as thus set down, that contract will, at common law, be *ultra vires* and prima facie unenforceable by either party. No rights will pass between the parties. It makes no difference that the general meeting has unanimously ratified the contract. The doctrine of *ultra vires* in relation to the company was justified on the grounds that it protected both shareholders and creditors from dissipation of their respective "investments" on unauthorised acts. However, the doctrine could work hardship, since outsiders contracting with a company were held to have *constructive notice* of the company's public documents (*i.e.* those documents which have to be registered with the Registrar of Companies and open to public inspection, such as the memorandum and articles of association). Thus, even if they had no *actual* knowledge, outsiders were deemed to know (have constructive notice) of any limitations upon the company's powers to act. As a result they would not be able to enforce their contracts against the company. In *Re Jon Beauforte (London) Ltd.* a company, which was authorised under its objects clause to manufacture ladies' dresses, began to make instead veneered panels, an unauthorised activity. The company entered various contracts in relation to this new line of business, including one with a coal merchant for the supply of coke. The coke was ordered on paper which described the company as veneered panel manufacturers and the coal merchant therefore had actual knowledge of the type of business for which the coke was to be used. Under the constructive notice doctrine, however, he had constructive notice of the contents of the company's memorandum and hence that this contract was *ultra vires* the company. Thus, it was held that he could not enforce his debts against the company.

European Communities Act 1972
   In order to bring company law in this country into line with that in the rest of the EEC, changes had to be made to the applicability of the *ultra vires* doctrine. These changes were introduced by section 9 of the European Communities Act 1972, which has subsequently been replaced by section 35 of the Companies Act 1985. Section 35(1) provides that in favour of a person dealing with a company in good faith, any transaction decided on by the directors shall be deemed to be one which it is within the capacity of the company to enter into, and the power of the directors to bind the company shall be deemed to be free of any limitation under the memorandum or articles of association. Further, section 35(2) states that a party to a transaction so decided on shall not be bound to enquire as to the capacity of the company to enter into it or as to any such limitation on the powers of the directors, and shall be presumed to have acted in good faith unless the contrary is proved. Thus, a person may in good faith enter a transaction with a company and enforce that contract even though the transaction was beyond the company's capacity. He is not bound to look into the objects clause in order to discover any limitations on the company's capacity or on the directors' powers to act. This provision is narrow in that it applies only to transactions "decided on by the directors" and not those made by lesser officers of the company. Indeed, it is unclear whether the term "directors" means the board of directors or whether it can also be taken to include transactions entered into by a single director. Where the board have delegated all or any of their powers to a single director (*e.g.* a managing director) it seems that this will be so.
   Section 35 does not affect the basis of the *ultra vires* doctrine. A company cannot itself enforce an *ultra vires* contract against a third person. If the directors make such contracts on the company's behalf, they act in breach of duty and are therefore liable to the company. An individual shareholder cannot prevent the performance of contracts already made with third parties who were acting in good faith, but he may obtain an injunction to prevent future *ultra vires* transactions.
   In 1986 a consultative document on the reform of the *ultra vires* doctrine proposed that a company should have the capacity to do any act whatsoever and that a third party dealing with a company should not, with

certain exceptions, be affected by the contents of a document merely because it is registered with the Registrar of Companies.

LIQUIDATION

The liquidation or winding up of a company is the process by which the company's existence is ended and its assets administered for the benefit of its creditors and members. The system of liquidation (particularly the procedure followed) is very similar to that for bankruptcy on which it was modelled. There are two types of liquidation:

(a) compulsory liquidation under an order of the court; and
(b) voluntary liquidation under a resolution of the company in general meeting.

In addition to these forms of liquidation the Insolvency Act 1986 provides two new procedures: the first, a simplified procedure for a company to make voluntary arrangements with its creditors; the second, an administration order procedure.

Administration order

The aim of this procedure, which may be used in conjunction with a voluntary arrangement, is to procure the rehabilitation and survival of the company as a going concern or, at least, to ensure a more advantageous realisation of assets than would follow from a winding up. Under this scheme an administrator may be appointed by the court upon application of the company, the directors or any creditor. However, such application must be dismissed by the court if a debenture holder has already exercised a contractual right to appoint an administrative receiver unless the debenture holder consents to the administration order.

The effect of an application is to impose a temporary moratorium over the company's affairs and property and, in particular, to prevent any resolution for, or order of, liquidation to be made. This moratorium is continued if the court makes an administration order and no steps to enforce any charge or security (including the appointment of a receiver) or to repossess goods will be possible except with the consent of the administrator or the leave of the court. Notification that an administration order has been made must be given to the company, all known creditors and the Registrar of Companies. All company documents must reveal the fact. A statement of affairs may be required from officers of the company. Within three months the administrator must send to all creditors, and submit to a duly convened creditors' meeting, a statement of his proposals to achieve the purposes that have been specified in the order. He must also notify the company's members. The creditors' meeting may approve the proposals, with or without modifications, and may, if it thinks fit, establish a committee which may seek further information from the administrator.

The administrator is charged with taking over management and control of the company's affairs, business and property. The powers of the directors are suspended during this period subject to the administrator's consent. The latter's duties will include the gathering in and realising of property (whether or not secured). However, the net proceeds of disposal must go first to secured creditors and, before disposal, the authorisation of the court may be necessary. The administrator's exercise of his duties and powers will be subject to the approved proposals and to subsequent approved revisions. Moreover, any creditor or member may petition the court on the ground that the company's affairs are being or have been conducted by the administrator in a manner which is or will be unfairly prejudicial to the general interests of creditors or members, or to the interests of some of them, including at least himself. The court has wide powers to give relief in such cases.

Compulsory liquidation

The court may order the winding up of a company when it is petitioned on any one of seven specified grounds, by far the most important of which is where a creditor petitions that the company is unable to meet its debts. A company will be deemed to be unable to pay its debts if:

(a) despite all his efforts, a creditor for more than £750 has failed to receive satisfaction; or

(b) the court is satisfied on all the evidence that the company is unable to pay its debts as they fall due.

Where the court grants the winding-up order, the Official Receiver is appointed provisional liquidator. He may request a *statement of affairs* from the directors or other officers of the company and must investigate, if the company has failed, the causes of that failure and the conduct of the company's business and report back to the court if he thinks fit. The Official Receiver, as provisional liquidator, may then call separate meetings of creditors and members. These meetings will decide whether a liquidator should be appointed to carry out the liquidation of the company and whether a *committee of creditors*, composed of representatives of both creditors and members, should be appointed to assist and supervise him. If no other person is appointed, the Official Receiver will act as liquidator.

The role of the liquidator is: to gather in and realise the company's assets; to distribute the proceeds among the creditors according to their entitlement; and to share out any surplus among the company's members according to their entitlement. In so doing, the liquidator will be closely supervised by the court and the committee of creditors (if any), and he must keep records and books of account. The order of distribution of assets is basically the same as in bankruptcy, and is as follows:

(a) secured creditors with fixed charges (to the extent that their securities are realised);

(b) costs and expenses of the winding up;

(c) preferential debts (*e.g.* certain taxes and wages and salaries over the last four months up to £800 per person);

(d) creditors whose debts are secured on a floating charge;

(e) ordinary unsecured trade creditors; and

(f) any balance of assets to the members, in accordance with their rights under the articles of association.

Once the winding up is completed, the liquidator must summon a final meeting of creditors and submit a report of the winding up to it. The dissolution of the company will follow three months after the liquidator notifies the Registrar of Companies that the final meeting has been held. A simpler (and in the past more used) procedure is for the liquidator to apply to the Registrar to have the company struck off the Register of Companies.

Voluntary liquidation

The voluntary winding up of companies is far more common than compulsory winding up, and may be effected by the company passing a special resolution. There are two types of voluntary liquidation:

(a) the members' voluntary liquidation; and
(b) the creditors' voluntary liquidation.

The former will occur where the directors are able to declare that the company will be able to pay all its debts within one year or less (the *declaration of solvency*). In this case, the members will appoint the liquidator and on his appointment the directors' powers cease, except so far as the liquidator or the general meeting sanction their continuance. In practice, the directors will usually ensure the appointment of a liquidator who will sanction that continuance. A creditors' voluntary liquidation will occur where the company is insolvent (*i.e.* when the directors are unable to make the declaration of solvency), in which case the creditors will have the greater interest in the conduct of the liquidation. A meeting of creditors must be called and may decide who is to be appointed as liquidator and whether a committee is to be appointed to oversee him. Otherwise, the conduct of the two types of voluntary liquidation is broadly the same, and the order of distribution of assets is no different from compulsory liquidation.

The protection of investors and creditors during liquidation

The Insolvency Act 1986 provides various measures designed to ensure that neither investors nor creditors are defrauded because of the liquidation of a company. However, the effectiveness of some of these measures depends upon the "independence" of the liquidator and, in the case of the members' voluntary winding up, this cannot necessarily be guaranteed since he is likely to be appointed by the directors or major shareholders. (Thus, for example, although the directors' powers cease upon appointment of liquidator, he may allow their control to continue.)

Nevertheless, certain civil liabilities (as well as criminal sanctions) may attend liquidation proceedings. Section 213 of the Insolvency Act 1986 enables the court to impose personal liability on any person who was knowingly a party to the continuation of the company's business with intent to commit a fraud or for any other fraudulent purpose. The weakness of this provision is the restricted meaning that has been given to the terms "fraud or . . . fraudulent purpose." In *Re Patrick & Lyon Ltd.*, fraud was held to mean "actual dishonesty involving according to current notions of fair trading among commercial men real moral blame." As a result, it is not difficult for a defendant to escape liability under this section, by claiming that the company continued trading merely so that existing creditors could be paid off.

However, under section 214 of the Insolvency Act 1986 a director may also face liability to contribute to the company's assets if the company has gone into insolvent liquidation and, at some time before, the director knew or ought to have concluded that there was no reasonable prospect that the company would avoid insolvent liquidation.

Further measures designed to prevent abuse of the limited liability of the company at the expense of the mass of ordinary creditors during both administration and liquidation proceedings are contained in the sections 238–241 and section 245 of the Act. Sections 238–241 provide that any transaction at an undervalue or which gives a preference to a person may be subject to a range of court orders if at the time the transaction is made or the preference given the company is insolvent or becomes insolvent in consequence of the transaction or preference. In the former case, to be valid, an undervalue transaction made within two years of liquidation must be shown to have been a genuine business transaction carried out in good faith in the reasonable belief that it would benefit the company. In the latter case a transaction made within six months of liquidation may be challenged as preferential if it puts a creditor into a better position in the event of the company's insolvent liquidation and the intention to prefer influenced the company in giving the preference. Where such a preference is given to a director (or an associate of his) within the two years prior to liquidation the onus is upon that director to show that the company was not influenced by a desire to prefer him. Under section 245 any floating charge created by a company within twelve months of liquidation will be invalid, unless it can be shown that the company was solvent at the time the charge was created and was not made insolvent in consequence of the transaction under which the charge was created. (The section does not apply to money paid or goods or services supplied to the company in consideration of the charge.) This provision is designed to prevent a company from selecting one of its existing unsecured creditors and, by granting him a floating charge, allowing him to rank in priority to other unsecured creditors. Such abuse would be particularly discreditable were the creditor so advantaged to be one of the directors (or an associate of theirs) and, therefore, in such cases any floating charge created within two years of liquidation will be invalid irrespective of a company's solvency at the time of creation.

Section E: The Choice of Legal Status for the Small Businessman, Partnership or Company

For those forming and running organisations the choice of legal status is, in many cases, already determined by factors beyond their control. For example, in the case of the solicitor, the controlling body for his profession (the Law Society) requires that if he carries on business with another person he must do so in partnership with that other person. Corporate status, is, therefore, not a choice available to him. In the same way the size and nature of the business carried on by an organisation may require the issuing of shares to the general public to raise capital. This will invariably mean that the numbers involved will exceed the permitted maximum for persons trading in partnership and the company will be the only available form.

However, for the small businessman the choice of legal status for his business is by no means so clear cut. He could, of course, trade on his own account as a sole trader, although this would generally prevent him from seeking others to invest their capital or skills and expertise in his business. More typically, the small businessman will wish to carry on his business along with other members of his family, or with friends or acquaintances. The partnership or the company will, therefore, be the available choices.

The factors which may influence the decision of the small businessman between these two legal forms are:
   (a)   the legal capacity of the business;
   (b)   the availability of limited liability;

(c) the raising of finance;
(d) the administrative burden;
(e) the right to participate in management;
(f) rights of membership and withdrawal;
(g) the allocation of income; and
(h) taxation.

The legal capacity of the business

One question that may concern the small businessman in choosing between a company and a partnership is the extent to which his activities may be restricted by any limitation on the legal capacity of either structure. The question of legal capacity may also concern those dealing with the business, since they may wonder whether their transactions with the company or partnership are valid. The small businessman may, therefore, wish to choose the form of business which will better put at ease the minds of those with whom the business deals.

The distinctions, if any, between the legal capacity of a company and that of a partnership are slight. The activities which a company may lawfully undertake will be set out in the objects clause of its memorandum. The company will be confined to its stated activities, subject to the right to amend or extend them. However, given this right of alteration and the fact that the objects clause may be widely drawn there should be no reason why a small businessman or those with whom he is dealing should ever be hindered by any restriction on the company's legal capacity. (The outsider dealing with the company is now given further protection by the provisions of section 35 of the Companies Act 1985.) The legal capacity of the partnership (or, more accurately, the partners) is equally wide, subject to any restrictions on a partner's right to bind the firm contained in the partnership agreement (which restrictions, to be effective against an outsider, must be known to him).

Thus, the outsider, on the one hand, may normally deal with either a company or a partnership, confident that any transaction into which he enters will be enforceable. The businessman, on the other hand, can make his choice between a company or a partnership in the knowledge that outsiders should be content to trade with either type of organisation and that neither type should restrict the scope of his business activities.

Limited liability

The limited liability afforded to the members of a company constitutes perhaps the most significant advantage of the company over the partnership. However, in practice, the owners of a company which has not yet established its own credit-worthiness with its suppliers of goods or capital finance, may be required to give personal guarantees to those suppliers or create charges on their own personal assets, such as their houses, in favour of the same. Where this is so, their liability for the debts of the company will, in effect, be no different from that of the members of a partnership. Nevertheless, the availability of limited liability is often the most important factor in influencing the choice between the company or the partnership.

The raising of finance

Once established and trading profitably, a business can hope to raise its finance internally by recirculating profits. However, whatever legal form is chosen for the business, a source of *initial* capital must be found.

For the small business, the first source will be the funds of the owners themselves and those of their families or friends. Further, it may raise capital by obtaining loans secured on the assets of business. Here, the company has an advantage over the partnership in the forms of security that it can offer to creditors. Both may grant fixed charges over property, but only the company may create a floating charge (see page 333). A third source of funds for the small business, which again is common to both partnership and company, will be to trade on credit (*i.e.* to obtain goods or services without paying for them until they have enabled the business to make a trading profit). Often the small business will acquire capital goods on hire-purchase. If the credit extended under such an agreement does not exceed £15,000, the partnership enjoys one advantage over the company, its agreements will be subject to the statutory protection afforded by the Consumer Credit Act 1974. This protection may be an attraction to a small businessman.

The administrative burden

In theory, a partnership may be formed by oral agreement or may be adjudged to exist because of a course of dealings by two or more persons and, therefore, there need be no formalities attending its formation. In practice, though, those wishing to trade as a partnership will generally have a formal partnership agreement. For the businessman wishing to trade by means of a company, there are companies available "off-the-shelf" and, in any event, the Companies Act provides a simple registration procedure for the formation of a company. Thus, the costs and formalities attending the formation of the business are probably not very different, whichever form is selected.

So far as running costs and other formalities are concerned, a partnership does have advantages. For example, it does not have to make an annual return to the Registrar or notify the Registrar of changes in its constitution. Further, whilst a partnership will need to keep accounts, those accounts will not be open to public inspection, unlike those of a company. The disclosure requirements imposed upon the small company were probably one of its greatest disadvantages in comparison with the partnership. This drawback has, however, been lessened by a reduction in the amount of accounting information such companies have to file.

Right to participate in management

In a partnership every member of the partnership has the right to take part in management. In a company a member has no such right where the articles place responsibility for supervising day-to-day management in the hands of directors. For the small businessman who is an owner-director, however, this distinction will not be important. Even if his fellow owners and directors try to exclude him from management, he may seek protection from the courts, which have recognised the right of an owner-director to take part in the running of his business by likening the small private company to the partnership.

Rights of membership and withdrawal

Each partner has the right to refuse the admittance of a new partner to the firm and can, therefore, choose with whom he will carry on business. He may also withdraw from the partnership at any time and recover the capital he has invested in the firm. Such rights may make a partnership appear attractive to, for example, a person who wishes to be in business only with those who are as industrious as himself. However, both these rights may be modified in the partnership agreement and the partner's freedom to choose his associates thus curtailed.

In a private company, whilst the removal of restrictions on transferability of shares may, in theory, have opened up membership, in practice a member may feel confident that membership of the business will not be subject to dramatic changes. The member may, however, find it difficult to withdraw his capital from such a business. Where a businessman has invested his money in a private company along with others, he must generally abide by the majority decisions. If in the future he can no longer accept the policies of the majority and decides to sell out, he may find it difficult to find an independent buyer and, in fact, may be required under the articles to sell to existing members. Sales in such cases will usually be based upon independent valuations, but, even so, the lack of a market for the shares will invariably depress the price he will receive. On the other hand, since 1981 the outgoing member may have been able to take advantage of the statutory power of a company to purchase its own shares.

The allocation of income

In both the partnership and the company the allocation of income is a contractual matter, to be determined, in the one case, by the provisions of the partnership agreement and, in the other, by the articles of association. Where the two types of organisation do differ is in the calculation of that which may be distributed. This matter is more rigidly controlled in relation to companies, which may not distribute dividends except out of *profits*. In a partnership the *capital* of the partners may be distributed amongst themselves.

Taxation

The main purpose of taxation is to raise revenue for the government and not to influence the choice between different legal forms for carrying on a business. Nevertheless, in so far as a partnership and a company are treated differently for tax purposes, then the choice of the small businessman may be influenced by tax considerations.

Broadly, a partnership (like a sole trader) is liable to income tax on its trading profits, whilst a company is liable to corporation tax. Where profits are low, the rate of tax paid by partners who have no other source of income will be lower than that paid by a company for corporation tax purposes. In these circumstances, the partnership will appear more advantageous than the company. Where partners do have other sources of income, then their rate of tax will rise on a graduated scale and may exceed the fixed rate of corporation tax. In these circumstances, a company will appear more attractive.

A partnership has a distinct advantage over the company in respect of taxation of profits inasmuch as the payment of tax, in the case of a partnership, can be delayed for a longer period after the accounting period in which the profits are made.

(In future the choice of business form open to the small buinessman may be widened if a government proposal to introduce an incorporated partnership is implemented.)

Section F: Special Types of Business Organisation

There are, in addition to partnerships and companies, other forms of industrial and commercial organisation operating in this country. Some of these, such as banks and insurance companies, adopt the same basic structure as the registered company and are subject to the Companies Act as well as to other specific statutory measures (*e.g.* the Insurance Companies Act 1982). Others, such as building societies, friendly societies and trade unions, have a different format and each is subject to its own legislative control and system of registration (*e.g.* the Building Societies Act 1986).

In the case of trade unions, whilst they do not have corporate status, they do have certain corporate attributes (*e.g.* they may sue and be sued and can make contracts). On the other hand, the transactions and activities of trade unions are subject to certain rules not applicable to other forms of business organisation. Thus, agreements between themselves and employers (*collective agreements*) are presumed not to be legally binding. Moreover, the actions of trade unions are subject to a restrictive legislative framework.

Section G: Public Bodies

The types of organisation falling within the term "public bodies" are wide ranging, but we can adopt, initially, a twofold classification into:
  (a) public corporations; and
  (b) local authorities.

PUBLIC CORPORATIONS

Public corporations are the standard form of organisation operating in the public sector. The most commonly known public corporations are probably the nationalised industries, such as British Coal or the British Railways Board. However, these are by no means the only types of public corporation. In fact, public corporations can be divided into three categories:
  (a) those concerned with industrial or commercial activities;
  (b) those providing social services; and
  (c) those performing regulatory and advisory functions.

Generally public corporations, whichever category they fall into, are corporate bodies, with perpetual succession, a common seal and power to hold land. Nevertheless, no two public corporations are alike and one must examine the individual statute under which a corporation has been formed in order to establish its true status, form, functions and powers and its subjection to control.

Industrial and commercial corporations

The government may decide to intervene in the running of industry and commerce for reasons that are economic, social or political. Taken to its ultimate stage, such intervention will involve the nationalisation of a whole industry (*e.g.* the electricity industry) or commercial service (*e.g.* the postal and communications services). Such total nationalisation became common in the years following the Second World War. The usual practice was to form a national board (*e.g.* the National Coal Board in 1946 and the Gas Council in 1948), which would acquire the assets of those companies operating in the industry to be nationalised in return for compensation paid to the companies concerned. The industry would then be run by this board, subject to the overall control of the appropriate government department. The national board created in this way usually consists of a chairman and other board members appointed by the appropriate government minister. Its duty is to carry out the day-to-day running of the industry subject to the overall direction and control of the minister. The latter will have power to control capital expenditure and borrowing, and to direct the use of surplus revenues. In practice, less use is made of these formal powers than of informal control over the national board. This has led to problems inasmuch as the separate responsibilities of boards and ministers have been blurred, and the latter have been accused of interfering in the functions of the former. This blurring of general policy making and day-to-day management also has consequences for the supervision of nationalised industries by Parliament, since a minister may only be questioned in the House on matters with which he is officially connected, whatever control he may have attempted to exert informally. Supervision of such bodies is also provided by debates in Parliament and, more particularly, by Select Committees which examine the reports and accounts of these corporations.

Public corporations have many of the qualities which belong to other types of corporation. However, the significant difference between the nationalised industry and the large public companies whose assets are acquired, is that the former has no shareholders to provide capital or to have any voice in its affairs. The public corporation does not raise its capital by issuing shares but by borrowing, which is guaranteed by the Treasury. If it cannot repay its borrowing, the loss falls ultimately on the taxpayer. In one important respect the public corporation and the registered company are no different. Neither organisation may exceed its stated purposes and powers. In the company those purposes and powers will be set out in its memorandum, whilst in the public corporation they will be defined in the Act which creates it. Any transaction beyond those purposes and powers will be *ultra vires* and unenforceable. However, the purposes and powers of public corporations are usually widely drawn and, in any event, the courts have adopted a liberal approach to the interpretation of those purposes and powers.

Social service corporations

Nationalisation need not be, and has not been, confined to those organisations producing goods or providing commercial services. The benefits to be gained from nationalisation (such as economies of scale) can be obtained by operating public services in other fields. In this country such nationalisation has taken place in, for example, the areas of health and education, although in neither case has there been complete nationalisation (note, for example, the existence of private medicine and the inappropriately named "public schools"). Responsibility for education has been given to local authorities, but in other cases executive bodies have been set up to manage such social services. These bodies are a further type of public corporation, whose purposes and powers will be determined by the Act which created them. An example of such a corporation is a Regional Health Authority.

The social service corporations are subject to closer direction and control than their counterparts in the industrial or commercial field. Their finance comes for the most part from government departments and thus they are subject to close auditory control.

Regulatory and advisory bodies

An example of a body with both regulatory and advisory functions is the Equal Opportunities Commission set up under the Sex Discrimination Act 1975. It works, on the one hand, towards the elimination of discrimination and the promotion of equality of opportunity between men and women generally, and, on the other, to advise the Secretary of State for Employment of any necessary amendments in the appropriate legislation. The Commission, which consists of a number of commissioners appointed by the Secretary of State, is a body corporate.

LOCAL AUTHORITIES

Under the constitutional framework of the United Kingdom much of the responsibility for government and administration has been taken from Parliament and given to bodies established at local levels (the *local authorities*). The structure of local government in England and Wales was reorganised under the Local Government Act 1972. However, one tier of that structure (the six metropolitan county councils) and the Greater London Council were abolished by the Local Government Act 1985 and their functions re-allocated.

Acquisition of powers

All the powers of local authorities are statutory, the main ones being those general powers granted under Local Government Acts, and/or the more specific powers granted under, for example, the Public Health Acts. (The general powers afforded to local authorities will include the rights to make contracts and to pass by-laws.) In addition, a particular local authority may be given specific powers under a private Act of Parliament promoted by that local authority.

Legal control of use of powers

In the exercise of their powers local authorities are subject to the *ultra vires* doctrine. Thus, for example, in *Attorney-General* v. *Fulham Corporation* a local authority had certain statutory powers to establish baths, wash-houses and open bathing places. It was held that these powers did not entitle it to conduct a laundry business and that it was acting *ultra vires* in washing customers' clothes rather than in providing facilities for persons to wash their own clothes. The willingness of the courts to control a local authority's use of its powers has been clearly evidenced in recent years by their role in the dispute between the Greater London Council (G.L.C.) and some of its ratepayers over its proposed transport policy. In *Bromley L.B.C.* v. *G.L.C.* the House of Lords found that the G.L.C. had exceeded its powers by acting unreasonably in reducing fares so that its transport system incurred large deficits.

A person may, in consequence of the *ultra vires* doctrine, discover that his contract with a local authority is void and unenforceable on the ground that the authority had no power to make it. However, a person entering into a contract with a local authority is *not* bound to inquire whether standing orders have been complied with, and his contract is not invalidated merely by non-compliance with standing orders.

The liability of a local authority in tort is broadly the same as that of any private individual, including liability for the torts of employees. Where local authorities exercise their statutory powers, there may be interference with the rights of individuals (*e.g.* the operation of a sewage works may constitute a nuisance) but as long as these powers have been properly exercised, no individual has any right to bring legal proceedings against an authority. Nevertheless, local authority powers must be exercised with reasonable care, otherwise an authority may be liable in Negligence.

Administrative control of use of powers

Central government control of the local authorities is now largely the province of the Department of the Environment. This Department (and other departments) exercises considerable administrative control over local authorities by various methods. It has wide powers to issue orders and regulations in respect of matters such as public health. The consent of the Secretary of State for the Environment is usually necessary before a local authority may raise a loan and the same minister has power to reduce the *rate support grant*, should there be any default in any aspect of local administration. The latter power is the most important financial control exercised over local authorities. Indeed, the present government has taken powers to penalise by loss of grant, local authorities which have overspent targets set centrally (*grant related expenditure assessments*) and to control the raising of rates by local authorities. As with companies, such bodies must make annual returns of income and expenditure and their accounts must be audited. The audit will normally be carried out by district auditors who are appointed by the Department of the Environment. Any person who is responsible for incurring any unlawful expenditure may, if the court so orders, have to repay that amount to the local authority.

In relation to the making of by-laws, the exercise of their powers by local authorities is subject to ministerial confirmation. In addition, they are subject to the control of the courts through the *ultra vires* doctrine (see page 40).

A further means of control over local authorities was introduced by the Local Government Act 1974. This Act established Commissioners for Local Administration to investigate and report on local government maladministration. However, these Commissioners have no powers to proceed against any authorities, and the latter might refuse to take action recommended by a Commissioner to remedy any maladministration (for a further discussion see *Unit One, Part Five*, page 48).

Part Two

LABOUR

In recent years, with growing statutory intervention in the employment field, the number of calls made upon the services of the legal office by industrial and commercial enterprises *as employers* has undoubtedly increased. The reasons for such requests are many and varied but the following examples will serve to illustrate the occasions on which an employer may come to the legal office seeking advice or assistance:

(a) in drafting documents;
(b) in response to a request from an employee;
(c) in response to workforce or trade union "pressure";
(d) in dealing with the government or government agencies;
(e) in relation to his employment policy in general;
(f) in response to legal action brought by another person; and
(g) in order to bring legal action against an employee.

Drafting documents . . . an employer who wishes to ensure that the relationship between himself and a worker is one of employer-independent contractor may require help from his legal adviser in drafting the terms of the contract between them in a form appropriate for that status. A more specific request may relate to covenants in restraint of trade. Thus, where the employeer wishes to include in the contract of a worker, who has knowledge of trade secrets, a term restricting his future employment opportunities, the expertise of the legal office will be sought in order to draft a clause which is effective both practically and legally. On the other hand, the document may not be part of the employment contract itself but be connected with the employer's recruitment policy. He may, for example, seek advice on job advertisements that he wishes to use or on the questions which he asks at interviews or in the application forms which he sends to prospective employees. Will it, for example, be lawful for an employer to advertise a vacancy for a "departmental manager" or to ask applicants for jobs whether they have children and, if so, who looks after them when they are ill?

Responding to requests from individual employees . . . an employer may be faced with a request from an employee for written details of his contract or a written statement of his pay. He could, therefore, approach the legal office to determine whether or not he is under any duty to provide such information. Advice may also be sought on other matters. If an employee asks for a reference, will his employer be obliged to provide it?

Responding to workforce or trade union "pressure" . . . where the employees of the industrial or commercial enterprise are unionised (and at times even when they are not) an employer may be asked to allow employees time off work. In seeking legal advice the employer may wish to know which employees are entitled to time off, the purposes for which they have a right

294

to take time off and the amount of time they must be granted. On the other hand, the workforce may have requested the employer to provide particular items of safety equipment or to establish a safety committee. In what circumstances will an employer be obliged to accede to such requests?

Dealing with the government or government agencies . . . an employer, whose factory has been visited by an inspector from the Health and Safety Executive, may need advice about an *improvement notice* served by the inspector subsequent to that visit. Another government agency with which an employer could have dealings is the Commission for Racial Equality. Where he has been notified of the Commission's intention to conduct a formal investigation into his recruitment policies, he may wish to exercise his right to make representations to the Commission through his lawyer. The contact with the state may, on the other hand, arise in relation to an employer's policy with respect to the employment of disabled persons. What proportion, if any, of his staff must consist of registered disabled persons?

General employment policy . . . there are clearly many reasons related to his employment policies that could prompt an employer to visit the legal office. Indeed some have been discussed under the previous headings. The inquiry may relate to a particular employee. Perhaps an employer, conscious of statutory rights on dismissal, wants advice on the best approach to adopt with an employee who is known to be a practical joker and whose antics have caused injury to others. In other instances the information sought may concern groups of employees. An employer who is proposing to take over another employer's business may consult his adviser in relation to the continuity of employment of any employees transferred to his employment as a result of the deal. On the other hand, an organisation employing both male and female workers may want assistance in formulating its pay policy. For example, what are the consequences for it of carrying out a job evaluation study?

Responding to legal action . . . often it will be the threat (or indeed the reality) of being faced with legal proceedings that will induce an employer to consult the legal office. He may have received a copy of an application form submitted to an industrial tribunal by a dismissed employee and may now wish to know what steps he should take. The proceedings may be criminal where, for example, the firm's vehicles have been used without current road tax licences. The employer may be faced with a civil action brought on behalf of a third party injured due to the negligence of one of his drivers. Will the employer be liable where the driver has made a detour from his authorised route and, whilst so doing, injured the plaintiff?

Bringing a legal action . . . consultations with lawyers may be prompted not only in response to legal proceedings commenced by others but also in order to bring an action. Thus, an employer may wish to start proceedings in order to enforce a restraint of trade clause against a former employee. Even where there is no such clause in the contract, he may inquire whether he can stop a former employee making use of information obtained whilst in the employer's employment. Will he, for example, be able to prevent that ex-employee from making use of a list of the employer's customers copied whilst in his employment?

These are simply some of the reasons that may induce visits by employers to the legal office. It is possible on occasions that an employer may not approach the legal office directly but through some third party such as an employer's association or a trade association of which he is a member. Indeed, it is not only employers or their representatives who may consult lawyers. Employees may also seek advice on their employment rights and duties for equally varied reasons. Whatever the reason for the consultation and whoever makes it, the first question that will need to be answered will almost invariably relate to the nature of the relationship between employer and worker.

Section A: The Employment Relationship

CONTRACT OF SERVICE OR CONTRACT FOR SERVICES?

The basis of the legal relationship between the industrial or commercial enterprise and its workers is contractual. The enterprise contracts with individual workers to secure their skills and expertise in return for some form of remuneration. For a lawyer a fundamental issue is the classification of this relationship, since it is the key to the rights and duties which the law grants to, or imposes upon, the parties to the contract. Traditionally lawyers have adopted a twofold classification of workers into *employees* and *non-employees* (*i.e.* the self-employed person or independent contractor). Various statutes define the term "employee" as meaning "an individual who has entered into or works under . . . a contract of employment . . . ." A "contract of employment" is, in turn, defined as a "a contract of service or apprenticeship, whether express or implied, and (if it is express) whether it is oral or in writing." An employee, therefore, is a person who works under a *contract of service*. The term independent contractor or self-employed person is not as such defined by statute but we can define it as meaning an individual who agrees to do work or provide services under a *contract for services*. Finally, the term *worker* is itself defined by statute as "including both a person who works under a contract of employment, and a person who works under any other contract to perform personally any work or services for another party to the contract who is not a professional client of his." It will be seen, therefore, that the term "worker" is wider than that of "employee," since all employees are workers, but not all workers are employees.

Both at common law and by statute the rights and duties as between employer and employee differ from those between employer and independent contractor. For example, the employer's duty to exercise care in relation to the safety of his employees is more demanding than that which relates to an independent contractor. Similarly, by statute an employee has a right not to be unfairly dismissed, a right not granted to the self-employed. It should be clear, therefore, why an employer may wish to ensure that the contracts which are drawn up with his workers result in the desired relationship between the parties. How can this be done? Unfortunately statute, whilst providing definitions of the various terms, does not provide any standard forms of contract appropriate for those who wish their relationship to be employer-employee or employer-independent contractor. Nor, indeed, does statute actually identify the contract of service or the contract for services. Thus it has been left to the courts to distinguish the former from the latter and thus to distinguish the employee from the self-employed person. In doing so the courts are traditionally thought to have used three tests:

(a) the control test;
(b) the organisation test; and
(c) the mixed or multiple test.

By examining these tests, advice can be given to the employer in order to ensure that the desired status is achieved in respect of each and every contract.

The control test

In *Yewens* v. *Noakes* it was said that if an employer could tell an individual worker not only *what* to do but also *how* and *when* to do it, then that individual worked under a contract of service. This test, the control test, proved useful in its own day in identifying employees in simple relationships (*e.g.* employer-domestic staff) but was hardly relevant to an increasingly complex and technological age in which an employer would not have the competence (or the desire) to instruct his skilled and professionally qualified employees how to do their work. It was to meet such changes that the so-called organisation test was introduced.

The organisation test

By this test, a person was said to be an employee if he was employed as a part of the business and his work was done as an integral part of the business. A chauffeur is, for example, clearly within an organisation, whereas a taxi driver used by the organisation is not. However, the organisation test, as an apparently single factor test, was of no more general application than the control test (what, for example, is the status of a "freelance" reporter who writes a regular column for a particular newspaper?) and it has been replaced by the mixed or multiple test.

The mixed or multiple test

This is the test currently most favoured by the courts and by it the courts will examine a wide range of factors (of which control is but one), weighting them according to the circumstances of the particular case and balancing them one against the other, before arriving at a final decision. For example, the courts will consider whether a worker pays tax by P.A.Y.E. (Pay-As-You-Earn), whether he is paid holiday pay and has a pension entitlement, whether national insurance contributions are paid in respect of him by his employer, and whether the employer may suspend or dismiss him. If the answer to each of these questions is in the affirmative, then the worker is likely to be an employee. Other questions that might be asked in any particular case are whether the worker has the chance to make a profit or suffer a loss from the provision of his services and whether the worker owns the machinery or equipment with which he is working. Here, if the answers are in the affirmative, the worker is more likely to be a self-employed person than an employee.

However, it is clear from the decided cases that there may be, in relation to a particular worker, factors which appear to lead to the conclusion that a person is both an employee and an independent contractor. Thus in *Ready-Mixed Concrete Ltd.* v. *Minister of Pensions and National Insurance* the worker was engaged in delivering concrete prepared by the company, in a lorry which he was buying from the company under a hire-purchase agreement. The lorry, which had to be painted in the company's colours, had not to be used to carry concrete supplied by any other producer. The worker, who had to wear the company's uniform, was also required to observe the company's rules whilst on the company's premises and to obey the orders of its foremen. These features of the relationship suggested that he was an employee. On the other hand, he had to maintain the lorry himself and to pay all his own running costs, including the preparation of accounts. He chose his own routes and paid his own income tax and national insurance contributions. These were indicative of a contract for services. The court held that, although he was subject to fairly strict control, he was, nevertheless, an independent contractor—"a small businessman" as the judge described him. The economic reality of the arrangement was that by purchasing the lorry the man had invested on his own account and that his profit depended on his own efficiency. He was in business on his own.

The *Ready-Mixed* case was unusual in that there was before the court a detailed document setting out the arrangement between the parties. Generally, there will be far less written evidence to consider. Often, indeed, the courts will be asked to determine the relationship between parties who have not even *discussed* the essential terms of their contract. This will be true, for example, of the casual employment of a labourer at a building site. In *Ferguson* v. *John Dawson & Partners Ltd.* the plaintiff was injured whilst working as a general labourer on one of the defendant company's building sites as a result of the defendant's failure to provide a guard rail as required by statute. To succeed in his claim for breach of statutory duty (see page 317) the plaintiff had to show that he was an employee of the company. On his engagement he had been told that he was working on the "lump" (as a self-employed, labour-only subcontractor). In other words, in return for providing his labour on a daily basis he would simply receive a rate for the job but would not be entitled to any of the fringe benefits that an employee might expect, such as sickness benefits or holiday pay. Nevertheless, the Court of Appeal held that the description attached by the parties to their arrangement could not alter the reality of the relationship, which was one of employer and employee.

Indeed, Parliament, foreseeing that employers might attempt to contract out of their statutory duties to employees, has provided that any such attempt in relation to individual employment rights (see page 311) shall be void. Not surprisingly, therefore, the Court of Appeal supported this protective approach and confirmed its decision in *Ferguson's* case in the case of *Young and Woods Ltd.* v. *West.* Here, the worker, a skilled machinist, chose to be treated as self-employed by his employer for tax reasons. Later, upon his dismissal, he claimed to be an employee for the purposes of statutory protection. The court upheld his claim on the ground that in reality the relationship had been that of employer-employee and it could not be said that the applicant had been in business on his own account. Even so the courts may not always be prepared to allow workers to choose a different employment status simply to suit their immediate need. Thus, in *Massey* v. *Crown Life Insurance Co.* a branch manager chose self-employment for tax reasons and, significantly as it later transpired, a detailed agreement to this effect was drawn up. His subsequent claim to be an employee was rejected by the Court of Appeal on the ground that, where the nature of the relationship was in doubt or was ambiguous, it was open to the parties to stipulate what their legal status was to be. Here, the reality of the situation did not clearly point to either status, thus the parties' own express stipulation was the decisive factor.

Casual workers

Increasingly tribunals and courts have been asked to examine the employment status of workers who do not work full time or on a permanent basis or at the employer's place of work. Such groups of part-time or casual or homeworkers have posed a particular problem because of the frequently flexible and irregular nature of their employment. This difficulty was resolved by the Court of Appeal in *O'Kelly* v. *Trusthouse Forte plc* by its finding that the law required mutual obligations (*i.e.* for the employer to have to offer work and the employee to have to do work) before there could be a contract of service.

Crown employees

It is unclear whether a Crown employee (*e.g.* a civil servant or a member of the armed forces) has a contract of employment as such. But it is clear that, as part of the rights, immunities and privileges granted by the common law to the Crown (its "Prerogative") the Crown employs its servants at its pleasure. A civil servant may, therefore, be dismissed at pleasure and have no common law remedy for wrongful dismissal. However, civil servants are fully protected under the provisions relating to unfair dismissal and are entitled to most other statutory employment rights.

LEGAL RESTRAINTS ON EMPLOYMENT

The traditional contractual notion of freedom of choice is only true in part as far as the contractual relationship between an employer and his workers is concerned. The law imposes certain constraints upon the employer. For example, a contract entered into by a minor (*i.e.* a person under the age of 18) is not enforceable unless it is, on the whole, substantially for his or her benefit. In *De Francesco* v. *Barnum* a minor was apprenticed to the plaintiff as a dancer. She agreed not to marry during her apprenticeship and to work only with the plaintiff's permission. For his part, the plaintiff was not obliged to provide her with work and, when he did, her pay was poor. The court held that the contract was void and could not be enforced by the plaintiff, since it was wholly unreasonable and not in the girl's interests. In any event such an attempt to restrict any worker's freedom to pursue his livelihood may also infringe the doctrine of restraint of trade.

Contracts in restraint of trade ... one consideration that a potential employer must bear in mind when engaging a worker to his employment is whether or not that worker has bound himself under the terms of his previous employment by a restraint of trade clause. On the other hand the employer himself may wish to place some control over his own workers' freedom to work for whomsoever and wheresoever they may desire after leaving employment with him. In such cases the employer may seek assistance in drafting a suitable valid restraint clause. Broadly, to be valid and enforceable such restraints must be reasonable as between the parties *and* in the public interest. In considering the reasonableness or otherwise of an agreement the courts will take into account a number of factors. The courts' approach to this issue has been examined (see page 129). It should be remembered that, paradoxically perhaps, the greater the protection the employer seeks (in terms of geographical area covered and duration of the restraint) the more likely it is that the restraint will be held to be too wide and thus invalid and unenforceable.

A further legal constraint on the employer's freedom to recruit whomsoever he wishes, is the requirement that organisations employing more than 20 employees must normally employ a proportion (3 per cent. of their total workforce) of registered disabled persons. This provision in the Disabled Persons (Employment) Acts 1944 and 1958 is, however, of only limited value. Employers tend to fill their quota with persons who, whilst registered as disabled, have learned to overcome their disability and are, in effect, fully fit. Moreover prosecutions for breach of the Act, though possible, are rare, but since 1980 companies have been required to state in their directors' reports their policy concerning disabled persons.

However, by far the most important legal constraints imposed upon employers in recent years are those that control employment policies with regard to female workers and coloured workers. In the case of two of those controlling measures amendments have been prompted by decisions of the European Court of Justice, thereby indicating the impact of community membership upon municipal law (see below).

Sex discrimination

Under the Sex Discrimination Act 1975 it is unlawful to discriminate against a person, on the grounds of sex, in the field of employment. Although this Act applies equally to men and women, by far the greatest use of its provisions has been by the latter, since it is the female section of the working population that has suffered from lack of equal opportunity. Discrimination against married persons on the grounds of marital status is also unlawful. The Act applies the term discrimination to three types of conduct: direct discrimination; indirect discrimination; and victimisation.

Direct discrimination . . . arises where a person treats a woman, on the grounds of her sex, less favourably than a man of the same marital status. Thus an employer who turns down a female applicant for a job on the ground that "the work is man's work" discriminates against her directly.

In *Ministry of Defence* v. *Jeremiah* men employed in a factory sometimes had to perform work which was particularly dirty and unpleasant, whilst female workers were excused from it. The Court of Appeal held that such uneven treatment amounted to unlawful direct discrimination which could not be excused on the ground of good motives or by the payment of premium rates for doing such work. In *Strathclyde Regional Council* v. *Porcelli* the court held that sexual harassment could amount to direct discrimination.

Indirect discrimination . . . arises where a person applies:
   (a)   a requirement or condition which, although it applies equally to a man, is such that a considerably smaller proportion of women than of men can comply with it; and
   (b)   which cannot be shown to be justifiable irrespective of sex; and
   (c)   which is to the woman's detriment because she cannot comply.
An example of indirect discrimination would be if an employer advertises a job for a "male or female clerk, who must be six feet tall," since a

considerably smaller proportion of women than men could comply with that requirement *and* it is unlikely to be justifiable irrespective of sex.

In *Price* v. *Civil Service Commission* the Commission operated a certain age bar which effectively ruled out many women of child-bearing age, including the applicant, for a particular job opportunity. It was held that this age bar amounted to a discriminatory requirement or condition since *in practice* the number of women who could comply was considerably fewer than the number of men, even though the proportion of men and women in the population of that age was the same and therefore *in theory* the proportion of each sex which could comply was the same. Nor could the age bar be justified merely because it was convenient for business reasons. At one time it was believed that to be justifiable a requirement or condition had to be shown to be necessary. However, in *Kidd* v. *D.R.G.(U.K.) Ltd.* the Employment Appeal Tribunal (E.A.T.) followed the approach of the Court of Appeal in a racial discrimination case, *Ojutiku* v. *Manpower Services Commission,* namely that an employer has to establish reasons which are "acceptable to right-thinking people as sound and tolerable reasons."

Victimisation . . . arises where a person is treated less favourably because that person has, for example, exercised his or her rights under the Sex Discrimination Act or the Equal Pay Act 1970.

It is unlawful for an employer to discriminate against an employee in recruitment arrangements, in the provision of promotion, transfer and training opportunities or any other benefits, facilities or services; or to dismiss or treat an employee detrimentally on the grounds of sex or marital status. In *Saunders* v. *Richmond upon Thames London Borough Council* the applicant claimed that she had been discriminated against in the manner in which her application for a post as golf professional at a municipal golf course had been considered. In particular, she complained that she had been asked questions at her interview which were not (or would not have been) asked of a man. The EAT held that it was not as such unlawful to ask applicants different questions. Indeed it might be desirable in certain circumstances to ask different questions according to an applicant's sex (*e.g.* a male applicant for a post at a girls' school). Nevertheless, the questions asked and information sought at interviews or on application forms might be of evidential value, since an employer might in this way reveal his true attitude and intent and, where that was to discriminate against a woman (or man) on the ground of her (or his) sex, such action would be unlawful.

In some cases discrimination may be allowed where a person's sex is a "genuine occupational qualification." For example, it would be lawful for a drama company to advertise for an actress to play a female lead part in a play. On the other hand, it is unlawful for an employer to advertise in a way which indicates, or might reasonably be understood as indicating, an intention to discriminate. A job description such as "waiter" or "salesgirl" is deemed under the Act to be discriminatory unless the advertisement indicates otherwise. Even so, in *Equal Opportunities Commission* v. *Robertson* a tribunal held that the term "departmental manager" did not indicate an intention to discriminate, since the word "manager" did not have a sexual connotation.

In 1986 legislation was enacted to give effect to the decision of the European Court in *Marshall* v. *Southampton and South West Hampshire Area Health Authority* that to dismiss a woman simply because she had reached state pensionable age, where that was different for men and women, contravened the Equal Treatment Directive. Furthermore, a person could rely upon the Directive in an action against a state authority acting as an employer. Under the Sex Discrimination Act 1986 it is unlawful for any employer to dismiss a woman on the ground of age in such circumstances. The Act also repeals the exemptions from the provisions of the 1975 Act which previously applied to employers with five or fewer employees and to private households. Finally, it removes all the significant restrictions on the working hours of female workers contained in legislation such as the Factories Act 1961.

Racial discrimination

It is unlawful for an employer to discriminate against a person on racial grounds. Under the Race Relations Act 1976 a person is discriminated against on racial grounds if he is discriminated against on the grounds of his colour, race, nationality or ethnic or national origins. In *Mandla* v. *Dowell Lee* the House of Lords held that Sikhs constituted an ethnic group for the purposes of the Act. The 1976 Act is largely modelled on the Sex Discrimination Act 1975 and, as under that Act, three types of conduct constitute discrimination: direct discrimination; indirect discrimination; and victimisation. These terms have the same meaning as under the 1975 Act, with appropriate amendments for the reason for discrimination. Thus direct discrimination arises where a person treats another person, on racial grounds, less favourably than he treats other persons. The Act stipulates that segregating a person from other persons on racial grounds is treating him less favourably than they are treated. For example, if an employer provides separate (though equal) canteen facilities for Asians and non-Asians, that would be direct discrimination.

Indirect discrimination is similarly given an identical meaning to that relating to sex. Thus, in *Singh* v. *Rowntree Mackintosh Ltd.* a rule prohibiting the wearing of beards by production workers indirectly discriminated against Sikhs, but was held to be justifiable in the interests of hygiene in the case of a food manufacturer. On the other hand, in *Mandla* v. *Dowell Lee* a "no turban" rule in a school was held not to be justifiable on the facts. In another case it was held that exam regulations which gave wider exemptions to graduates with degrees from British and Irish universities than to those from overseas universities discriminated indirectly and unlawfully against the latter on the grounds of nationality. A requirement that applicants for jobs must fill in application forms in English in their own handwriting has been held to amount to racial discrimination.

In the employment field the Act makes it unlawful for an employer to discriminate against a person on racial grounds in recruitment, training, provision of benefits and so forth. However, in *De Souza* v. *The Automobile Association* the Court of Appeal held that this did not include racial insults by a fellow employee unless the effect of the insult was to damage the working environment of the reasonable employee. As with the 1975 Act, there may be situations where a "genuine occupational qualification" may offer an exception. (For example, it would not be unlawful for the proprietor of an Indian restaurant to employ only Indian waiters.)

Equal pay legislation

The issue of equal treatment for women who have obtained employment is dealt with by the Equal Pay Act 1970 and by Article 119 of the Treaty of Rome (as amended by two later EEC Directives) providing for equal pay and conditions for work of equal value. The exact relationship between the UK legislation and the EEC provisions has not yet been settled, but undoubtedly the latter adds to the protection provided by the former (see below).

The Equal Pay Act itself did not come into force until the end of 1975 but under its provisions a woman is entitled to be treated equally with a man as regards all terms and conditions of employment (not just pay) where she can show that she is employed on "like work" or on "work rated as equivalent" with that of a man in the same employment.

To determine whether a woman's work is rated as equivalent, reference must be made to a job evaluation study. But, because there is no obligation on an employer to carry out any such study, these provisions have been little used. Since 1984, however, it has been possible for a woman to pursue a claim of *equal pay for work of equal value* as a result of additional regulations passed after a decision of the European Court requiring the United Kingdom to meet its obligations under the Treaty of Rome. Claims under these regulations may be referred by a tribunal to an independent expert for evaluation.

Women have had more success where they have been able to show that they are employed on like work with a man *in the same employment*. In *MacCarthy's Ltd.* v. *Smith*, after reference to the European Court, it was held that, by virtue of the EEC provisions, comparison could be made not only with a man doing like work at the same time as the woman applicant, but also with her predecessor in that position.

A woman is regarded as being employed on "like work" to a man if, but only if, her work and his are of the same or a broadly similar nature, and the differences (if any) between the things they do are not of practical importance in relation to terms and conditions of employment. In making such comparisons the tribunals and courts have made it clear that they will attach little weight to differences that are more apparent than real. In *Electrolux Ltd.* v. *Hutchinson*, for example, male employees had, in theory, different contractual duties (such as working compulsory overtime and working night-shifts). There was, however, little evidence that they were ever asked to perform such duties and the EAT held that female employees were entitled to the same basic rate of pay.

Once a woman has shown that she is entitled to equal treatment, the employer may raise the defence that any variation in terms and conditions is genuinely due to a material difference (other than the difference of sex) between her case and the man's. Factors which may be adjudged to amount to genuine material differences include academic qualifications, length of service, age, and differences in the place of work. The onus of showing such differences to be valid defences rests upon the employer. In *Jenkins* v. *Kingsgate (Clothing Productions) Ltd.* where an employer claimed that a difference in pay was based upon the fact that the women worked part-time, he was only able to succeed if he could show that the lower rate for part-timers was reasonably necessary to achieve some objective (probably economic) unrelated to sex. In *Fletcher* v. *Clay Cross (Quarry Services) Ltd.* a male applicant for a vacancy would only accept the position, for which he was the only suitable candidate, if he received a salary no less than his existing salary. As a result he was paid more than a longer serving female doing like work. The Court of Appeal held that this difference could not be justified on the ground of market forces, since to accept such extrinsic economic factors as a valid defence would render the Act inoperable.

The remedy for a woman (or a man if he is being treated less favourably than a woman) who feels that she is entitled to equal treatment in this respect, is by way of complaint to an industrial tribunal. If her complaint is well-founded, an *equality clause* (implied into the contract of employment of every woman employed at an establishment in the United Kingdom) will operate. Thus, any term of her contract which is less favourable to her than a term of a similar kind under the man's contract is automatically modified so as not to be less favourable. Moreover, the tribunal may award payment for arrears of remuneration or damages.

FORMATION OF THE CONTRACT

Whilst the basis of the employment relationship is the contract of employment, the law requires no particular form or formality in the making of that contract. Thus the contract may be written or oral; indeed, often the parties will not have discussed even the essential terms of the contract (see *Ferguson* v. *John Dawson and Partners Ltd.*, page 298). Nevertheless, once the employment relationship has begun then a contract exists between the parties and it is the courts and tribunals which may be required to put flesh upon the contractual skeleton where the main terms and conditions have remained unwritten or unspoken. In so doing, normal contractual rules of the common law will be applied though with greater flexibility than is usually associated with the interpretation of commercial contracts.

The terms of the contract may be express (*i.e.* formulated by the parties themselves) or implied (*i.e.* incorporated into the contract from an outside source). Increasingly, in fact, the terms of the contract are not settled by the parties themselves but are incorporated from elsewhere. The terms may arise from:

(a) collective agreements;
(b) works rule-books and the custom and practice of the office or factory floor;
(c) statute; and
(d) the common law.

Incorporation of the terms of a collective agreement

A collective agreement is an agreement or arrangement made between a trade union and an employer or employers' association, the subject-matter of which may be wide ranging but could include substantive matters such as the main terms and conditions of employment or procedural matters such as recognition rights. Such collective bargaining between trade union and employer, whether at national, district or plant level, determines in some degree the employment terms of a large part of the working population. However, unless they are in writing and the parties provide to the contrary, such agreements are not themselves legally enforceable (section 18 of the Trade Union and Labour Relations Act 1974) and gain legal effect only by the incorporation of their terms into the *individual* contract of employment. By far the clearest method of incorporation is by *express* reference in the individual contract to the terms of the collective agreement. In *N.C.B.* v. *Galley* the defendant employee's contract expressly provided that his terms and conditions of employment should be subject to the national agreement for the time being in force. The current agreement required pit deputies to work such days or part days as might be required by their employer. By refusing to work a Saturday shift, as required by his employer, the defendant was held to have broken his contract.

A term may also be *impliedly* incorporated from a collective agreement if that is the custom in the trade or industry. However, not every term of a collective agreement may be suited to incorporation (*e.g.* some terms impose obligations on the workforce as a whole and cannot be fulfilled by an individual employee). Moreover, even where a term is suitable for incorporation, further problems may arise where a national agreement is modified at local level since, in the event of conflict between them, the courts have developed no definitive rules to decide which terms should prevail. Nevertheless, this method of incorporation of collectively agreed terms into the individual contract has been boosted since the introduction of a statutory duty upon employers to provide their employees with written particulars of certain terms and conditions of employment (see page 306). By allowing employers to refer to other documents containing those terms and conditions, the legislation has encouraged employers to refer to collective agreements as the source of those particulars.

Works rules and custom and practice

The extent to which works rules and custom and practice become implied terms of the contract will vary greatly from case to case.

Some employers issue to their employees rule-books with instructions on numerous aspects of the workplace such as time-keeping, absenteeism, meal-breaks, discipline and method of work. In most cases the courts (and tribunals) are unlikely to consider such rules as terms of the individual's contract of employment. The employer may therefore be legally free to change them as he thinks fit, although, in practice, such changes will be subject to collective shop-floor acceptance. Moreover, the courts (and tribunals) would undoubtedly be reluctant to enforce rules that are arbitrary or unreasonable.

Equally, it is by no means certain that the customs and practices in a particular industry, trade, district or factory will be viewed by the courts (and tribunals) as constituting legally enforceable terms. In *Sagar* v. *Ridehalgh* a custom that deductions were to be made from the wages of a weaver for bad workmanship was held to be known to all those entering employment in the Lancashire cotton mills and, therefore, was enforceable as a term of the contract of employment. However, not every custom will be so long established, nor every practice so certain or reasonable and every case must be judged on its merits. The fact that employees accept a particular working method may merely be evidence of a willingness to co-operate with management rather than of any contractual obligation to do so.

Statutory employment rights

Increasingly, the terms of the contract of employment are implied from statute. In particular, the Employment Protection (Consolidation) Act 1978 provides rights for most employees, the remedy for infringement of which lies by way of complaint to an industrial tribunal. In some cases these rights exist throughout the period of employment; for example, an employee's entitlement to guaranteed payments when laid off work. In other cases, the right will remain dormant until the termination of employment; for example, the right to receive a redundancy payment. The Employment Protection (Consolidation) Act 1978 is not, of course, the only source of statutory terms implied into the individual contract of employment. As we have seen already legislation on discrimination provides a further example of such statutory protection.

Terms implied by the courts

The common law itself has been a fruitful source of terms to be implied into all contracts of employment. It has long been established that certain terms, giving rise to rights and duties, should be imposed on each and every employer and employee. Further, at a time of increasing statutory intervention, the courts have shown themselves willing to develop new rights and duties based upon the employer-employee relationship. These rights and duties are given greater consideration below.

Written particulars of the terms of employment

The contract of employment is built up in the way that has been outlined. However, given the variety of sources and the informality of many employment situations, employees (and sometimes employers) may not know with certainty the terms of employment. To remedy this situation employers have, since 1963, been obliged to provide their employees with a written statement of the main terms and conditions of employment. This statement must be provided within 13 weeks of the commencement of employment (the obligation is now contained in section 1 of the Employment Protection (Consolidation) Act 1978). The particulars which must be stated (and kept up to date) include details of pay, hours of work, holiday entitlement, sickness or injury provisions, pension schemes, and notice entitlement. The written statement must also provide details of disciplinary rules and disciplinary and grievance procedures. However, an employer may avoid the full rigour of the Act by referring the employee to some document which the employee has a reasonable opportunity of reading in the course of his employment or which is otherwise reasonably accessible. For example, a reference could be made to a collective agreement kept in the personnel manager's office. Even so every employee ought to be given a basic statement specifying his job title, the date of commencement of his employment and whether any earlier period of employment with a previous employer counts as continuous employment (see page 312).

It should be noted that this written statement is not itself the contract of employment nor is it conclusive evidence of the terms of the contract, although, in practice, it may be regarded as such by many employees.

Section B: Common Law Rights and Duties in Employment

As we saw above, the basis of the legal relationship between an employer and his workers is contractual. This contractual relationship gives rise to rights and duties on both sides, not only during the period of employment but also following the termination of the contract. In the case of the self-employed worker these rights and obligations will depend to a large extent upon the express terms of his individual contract. Although even here the scope for negotiation will depend upon the bargaining power of the individual. For the employee the scope for negotiation is even more limited, but the courts have established certain rights and duties which, in the absence of any express agreement to the contrary, will be implied into every contract of employment. Indeed, so well established are these terms that it is likely that the courts would reject any attempt to exclude them as contrary to public policy.

THE DUTIES OF THE EMPLOYER

The duty to pay wages or agreed remuneration

The terms of the contract will determine what remuneration the employee is entitled to. In many cases the rate for the job will be that agreed by collective bargaining between employer and trade union, and will be incorporated, expressly or impliedly, into the individual contract of employment. For his part, the employee promises to be willing and ready for work. Thus, as a general rule, the employer must pay the agreed sum even when no work is available. However, the terms of the contract may provide that the employee can be laid-off or put on short-time when there is no work, and, in this case, there will be no obligation to pay wages. Increasingly, therefore, trade unions are concluding collective agreements guaranteeing the pay of employees where they are laid-off or put on short-time; indeed, there is now limited statutory protection in these circumstances (see page 311). In the absence of a term permitting the employer to suspend the contract without pay, any attempt to do so will, in fact, be a repudiation of the contract amounting to a dismissal. Even where the employer is entitled to take such action, if the period of lay-off or short-term working continues for a long time an employee may be entitled to claim a redundancy payment.

As far as the method of payment of wages is concerned there were a number of statutory controls under the Truck Acts 1831–1940 and the Payment of Wages Act 1960 over the manner of payment and over the power of the employer to make deductions in respect of misconduct or bad workmanship. It was believed that much of this legislation had outlived its original purpose and the Wages Act 1986 has therefore replaced these measures. Under this a deduction from wages must either be authorised by statute (for example, income tax), governed by a contractual term which is in writing, or a term of which the worker has written notice, or it must be accepted by the worker's prior written consent. There is a right of complaint to an industrial tribunal about unauthorised deductions.

There is no longer a statutory right for manual workers to be paid in cash; rather, like non-manual workers, it is the contract of employment which determines whether payment is to be in cash, by cheque or postal order, or direct into a bank account.

Finally, every employee is entitled under the Employment Protection (Consolidation) Act 1978 to receive a written itemised statement of his pay (including any deductions therefrom). Failure on the employer's part to comply may lead to a reference being made to an industrial tribunal.

The duty to provide work

There is generally no duty upon an employer to provide his employees with work, so long as he pays them their contractual remuneration. However, there are exceptions to the general rule. One exception is where the lack of opportunity to work leads to a loss of reputation or publicity. In *Herbert Clayton & Jack Waller Ltd.* v. *Oliver* an actor, who had been given one of the leading parts in a musical comedy, refused a lesser role at the same salary. The court held that the employer had broken the contract in not providing the leading part, since the loss of publicity was just as important to the employee as the payment of salary. Another exception to the general rule is where the employee's remuneration depends on his performing work, as in the case of payment by commission or by piece. Thus in *Devonald* v. *Rosser & Sons* it was held that a workman employed on piece-work, who had received one month's notice of dismissal but no work, should have been provided with work so that he could have earned a reasonable sum.

More recently there have been judicial statements which suggest a general "right to work." This may be no more than a recognition by the courts that as a matter of moral principle a man has the right to have a job to do, but not necessarily the right to work for any particular employer. However, in *Langston* v. *A.U.E.W.* Lord Denning M.R. spoke of the right of a skilled worker to be given work to do in order to enjoy job satisfaction and to maintain his skill and expertise.

The duty to treat the employee with respect

It was observed earlier that the courts have not been reluctant to develop new rights and duties as part of the employment relationship. In some respects these changes have been dictated by the changing social and economic climate. This may be illustrated by reference to the mutual respect with which employer and employee must treat each other. Indeed it is not insignificant that modern statutes (though not all judges) refer to employer and employee rather than master and servant when dealing with the employment relationship. Perhaps the greatest spur for this new attitude came with the statutory protection for dismissed employees (see page 323). Thus, in several unfair dismissal cases tribunals have referred to an employer's duty to act with due regard and respect for employees.

The duty to indemnify

At common law an employee is entitled to be indemnified by his employer for loss or expense incurred in the course of his employment. In most cases such expenses (*e.g.* travelling or lodging expenses) would be provided for expressly or impliedly in the contract of employment. But this would not usually be true of a loss suffered by an employee whilst doing an authorised act for his employer's business, an act that might sometimes be wrongful. In *Re Famatina Development Corporation* a consulting engineer, employed by the company, prepared, at the company's request, a report which led to a libel action being brought against him. He was held to be entitled to an indemnity for the cost of defending the action, since he had been acting in the course of his duties as an employee.

The duty to provide a reference

There is no legal duty on an employer to give a reference to an employee, whatever social pressures might require. Thus, an employer who gives a reference may risk unnecessary liability. If he makes a derogatory statement about an employee he may be sued by the same for defamation and if he gives an unwarrantably good reference to the new employer he may be sued for deceit or negligent misstatement (see page 173). Further, the giving of references may have particular implications for employers in relation to dismissal cases. In *Castledine* v. *Rothwell Engineering Ltd.* the employer had dismissed the employee on the ground of incapability, and yet had given a reference stating he "had carried out his duties satisfactorily, often under difficult conditions." Perhaps one should not be surprised to find that the dismissal was held to be unfair (see page 323).

THE DUTIES OF THE EMPLOYEE

The duty to obey

It is undoubtedly true to say that in the nineteenth century the courts were quite prepared to admit that a single act of disobedience of a lawful order entitled the employer to dismiss. That this is no longer true is indicative of the way that the courts reflect changing social, economic and political attitudes. The duty to obey is now sometimes described as a duty to co-operate. Not every single unco-operative act gives the employer the right to dismiss, unless this lack of co-operation evidences a general attitude on the employee's part. In *Pepper* v. *Webb* a gardener refused an order from his employer in somewhat strong language and was dismissed. His manner and approach to his work over a period of time convinced the court that summary dismissal was justified. In contrast to this in *Wilson* v. *Racher*, a case in which the facts were similar, the court's decision that instant dismissal was unjustified was undoubtedly influenced by the employee's previous satisfactory record and by his employer's own conduct which lacked the necessary mutual respect.

Whatever the legal doubt about a duty to obey lawful orders it is clear that an employee may refuse an unlawful order. In *Morrish* v. *Henlys Ltd.* the employee refused an order from a superior to falsify some records and was dismissed. He was held to be unfairly dismissed, despite his employer's argument that his refusal to accept his superior's orders was unreasonable in view of the fact that "falsification" was common practice. It is less clear, however, whether an employee may refuse an order which is unlawful, in so far as it is not strictly within the terms of his contract, yet reasonable. This issue has arisen particularly in respect of the working of overtime which has not been contractually agreed upon. In some circumstances an employee, who refuses such overtime on the ground that he is not contractually obliged to perform it, may nevertheless find his subsequent dismissal being held to be fair. Such a decision may again turn upon the mutual respect inherent in the employment relationship.

The duty of good faith

Perhaps the most important duty implied into the contract by the courts, so far as the employee is concerned, is the duty of good faith. This duty is not confined to any single aspect but is rather a composite duty embracing a number of different obligations. Included in these obligations are:

(a)   a duty not to receive bribes or make a secret profit;
(b)   a duty to disclose to the employer matters of interest to him;

(c) a duty to respect trade secrets; and
(d) a duty not to disrupt the employer's business.

The duty not to receive bribes or make a secret profit . . . employees who receive bribes or make a secret profit (*i.e.* any financial reward not known to the employer) are in breach of this duty and are liable to account to the employer for the profit, as well as to be dismissed. In *Robb* v. *Green* it was held that it was a breach of this duty for an employee to copy out a list of his employer's customers so that he could trade with them himself.

The duty of disclosure . . . there is an obligation upon an employee to disclose to his employer any information which he acquires that may affect his employer's interests, though not if the disclosure would be detrimental to the employee himself. An employee is in breach of this duty if he attempts to distort information coming to the employer, even if he himself does not benefit (*e.g.* by falsifying the clock-card of a fellow employee).

The duty to respect trade secrets . . . in *Printers and Finishers Ltd.* v. *Holloway* the defendant employee made copies of some secret documents, showed a competitor around his employer's factory where secret processes were being carried out, and obtained for that competitor a secretly designed machine. Injunctions were granted against the employee to prevent him from misusing the copied information and against the competitor from making use of both the information and the machine that he had acquired. If the employee works for a competitor in his spare time this may also be a breach of contract, even if there is no express restriction in the contract.

In *Hivac Ltd.* v. *Park Royal Scientific Instruments Ltd.* the plaintiff's employees worked in their own time for a rival company assembling miniature valves. There was no evidence that the employees had misused any trade secrets, but, in granting an injunction restraining the defendant company from employing the men, the court was clearly swayed by the plaintiff's claim that continued working with the defendant would lead, however innocently, to a transfer of confidential information. The *Hivac* case, however, is not authority for saying that an employee can be prevented from working in his spare time in a different business that does *not* compete with his employer's, so long as such activities do not interfere with his normal work.

The duty of the employee not to disclose information is not confined to his period of employment, but also applies to the ex-employee who has left his former employer's service. How long this duty continues after the end of the contract will be a question of fact in each case.

The duty not to disrupt the employer's business . . . in *Secretary of State for Employment* v. *A.S.L.E.F.* railway employees were "working-to-rule" as part of a pay dispute. In holding such action to be in breach of their contracts, the members of the Court of Appeal spoke of an implied term to serve the employer faithfully and not to carry out lawful orders in such a way as to disrupt the undertaking. The development of this duty is a further example of the willingness of the courts to extend their influence over the contract of employment.

One particular aspect of the duty of good faith relates to the question of inventions and the patents taken out in respect of them. This issue is now regulated by the Patents Act 1977 which replaces the common law rules that largely favoured the employer. Under this Act an invention made by an employee shall belong to his employer if:

(a) it was made in the course of his normal duties or of duties specifically assigned to him, and the circumstances in either case were such that an invention might reasonably be expected to result from his carrying out those duties; or

(b) because of the nature of the employee's duties and the particular responsibilities arising therefrom, he had a special obligation to further the interests of the employer's undertaking.

Any other invention made by an employee shall belong to himself, and no terms in his contract of employment can provide otherwise. Even where the invention belongs to the employer, the employee does not necessarily lose all financial interest in its success. Under the Act he may apply to the Comptroller General of Patents (or the Patents Court) for an award of compensation where the invention is of outstanding benefit to his employer (having regard to the size and nature of the employer's undertaking). Compensation may be awarded in such a case and will be calculated as "a fair share" of the benefit derived by the employer. The criteria to be used in determining what is a fair share include:

(a) the nature of the employee's duties and his remuneration and other benefits;

(b) the effort and skill devoted to the invention by the employee;

(c) the effort and skill devoted by others, and their advice and assistance; and

(d) the employer's contribution (*e.g.* in producing and selling the product).

Where an invention belongs to an employee he may assign his right in the patent or grant a licence under the patent to his employer, in which case he may still apply for compensation where he can show that the benefit he has received from the assignment or licence is inadequate in relation to the benefit derived by his employer, and that it would be just to award compensation in addition to any agreed contractual benefit.

Irrespective of ownership of the invention, an employee cannot apply for compensation if there is in force a relevant collective agreement providing for payment of compensation in respect of inventions of the same description, and the employee is a member of a trade union which is party to that agreement.

Section C: Statutory Employment Rights

In the 1970s the legislature reacting to the changing climate of industrial relations was instrumental in creating rights for employees in general that reflected the existing practices of more progressive and far-sighted employers. It is these rights, statutory implied terms of every contract of employment, which we must now consider. They are to be found principally in the provisions of the Employment Protection (Consolidation) Act 1978, as amended and extended by the Employment Act 1980.

The individual rights

Employees with at least four weeks' service are, in certain circumstances, entitled to guaranteed payments when laid off work or when suspended from work because of particular health hazards. The 1978 Act also provides two rights for employees who become pregnant: a right not to be unfairly dismissed on grounds of pregnancy; and a right to return to work within 29 weeks of confinement. To qualify for the latter a woman must have been continuously employed for at least two years by the eleventh week before the expected week of confinement. She must also have given written notice to her employer of her intention to return to work after confinement. Since 1980 pregnant employees have had an additional right to reasonable paid time off for ante-natal care. The right to maternity pay for women with two years' continuous employment has been combined with a flat rate payment under the Social Security Act 1986 to form a new payment, *statutory maternity pay*.

Time off work is permitted under the Act for reasons other than those related to maternity. An employer must allow an employee who is engaged on public duties (*e.g* as a Justice of the Peace or as a member of a local authority) to take time off to perform those duties. An employee, who is a member of an independent trade union recognised by his employer, is entitled to reasonable time off during working hours to take part in the activities (other than industrial action) of that trade union. Further, if any employee is an official of such a recognised union, he has the right to reasonable time off with pay in order to carry out industrial relations duties and undergo approved training for those duties. (The Advisory, Conciliation and Arbitration Service (A.C.A.S.) has published a *Code of Practice* which sets out good industrial relations practice in this respect.) Further protection from discriminatory action by their employer is given to employees who wish to be members of an independent trade union or to take part in its activities or who do not wish to be members of a trade union. These "employee rights" are not the only statutory terms implied into the contract of employment and the 1978 Act is not the only source; other examples are discussed elsewhere in this book (see pages 300–304 and pages 322–325).

Continuity of employment

In order to qualify for the majority of the rights set out in the 1978 Act, at least, an employee must serve the appropriate period of continuous employment with his employer counted in weeks (see table 2).

It should be noted that the Act lays down specific criteria which must be met before a week of employment will count towards an employee's continuity of employment for these purposes. Broadly, the 1978 Act lays down three different categories of weeks of employment:

    (a)   those weeks which count towards a period of continuous employment;

    (b)   those weeks which do not count, but which do not break continuity;

    (c)   those weeks which break continuity.

Weeks which count . . . include any week during which the employee is employed for 16 hours or more or during which he would, under his contract, normally be employed for 16 hours or more. (Where an employee has been continuously employed for five years or more, the weekly qualifying hours are reduced to eight hours.) A week may also count towards continuity even though the employee is absent from work. Where, for example, an employee is absent on account of a "temporary cessation of work" caused perhaps by a shortage of raw materials or a fire in the factory, the weeks of absence will not only not break continuity but actually count towards it.

Table 2

Employee's right	Minimum period of continuous employment required
Written statement of terms of contract	13 weeks
Itemised pay statement	None
Guarantee payments	4 weeks
Medical suspension payments	4 weeks
Trade union membership and activities	None
Time off work for trade union duties and activities	None
Time off work for public duties	None
Time off work to look for work or arrange retraining	2 years
Time off for ante-natal care	None
Right to return after pregnancy	2 years by the 11th week before confinement
Right to minimum periods of notice	4 weeks
Written statement of reasons for dismissal .	26 weeks
Right not to be unfairly dismissed (general)	2 years
Right not to be dismissed because of trade union membership and activities	None
Right not to be dismissed by reason of pregnancy	2 years
Right to redundancy payment	2 years
Right to payments on insolvency of employer	None
Right to protective award under redundancy consultation provisions	None

Weeks not counting, but not breaking continuity . . . include any week during any part of which the employee took part in a strike or is absent from work because of a lock-out by the employer.

Weeks breaking continuity . . . are those which do not fall into one of the other two categories. For example, where an employee is absent from work in consequence of sickness or injury and his contract of employment does not subsist during that time, not more than 26 weeks of that particular absence may count towards his period of continuity before a break is deemed to occur. Indeed a change of employer will also normally involve a break in continuity, but this is not invariably true. Thus, where two employers are "associated," the change of employer will not break the period of continuity. Similarly, if a trade or business or an undertaking is transferred from one person to another, then this transfer does not necessarily break the continuity of employment of those employed in the business. The cases indicate that a distinction must be drawn between those transfers which involve a sale of the business as a going concern and those which amount only to a sale of some of the assets of the business. It is only in the former situation that continuity is maintained.

Continuity may also be maintained by virtue of the Transfer of Undertakings (Protection of Employment) Regulations 1981 which provide that contracts of employment will be automatically transferred to the new employer where there has been a "relevant transfer," a phrase which seems to equate to that of a "transfer of a business as a going concern."

Section D: Health and Safety at Work

Health and safety at work is in one sense simply a further area where the common law and statute have imposed certain rights and duties upon the parties to the contract. It is an issue which has attracted particular attention in recent years as a result of the enactment of the Health and Safety at Work Act in 1974 and the growing concern about, and increasing awareness of, the long-term consequences to health from prolonged exposure to certain processes or materials. The health and safety of employees and others is, therefore, so crucial that it warrants separate and special treatment.

The duty owed by the employer towards his *independent contractors* is considerably less than that owed to his employees, although this disparity is slowly disappearing, and rightly so. In *McArdle* v. *Andmac Roofing Co.* the plaintiff was employed by one of several sub-contractors who were working on a building site under the direction of a main contractor. The plaintiff was injured because of the negligence of an employee of one of the other sub-contractors. Amongst those held liable were the main contractors, since they had overall responsibility for the site and had taken no steps to ensure the safety of groups of workers working in close proximity, even though these workers were not their own employees.

As far as the safety of the *employee* at work is concerned, protection is provided by the sometimes overlapping but not mutually exclusive rights under:

(a) the common law duty of the employer for his employees' safety;
(b) the framework of protective legislation (*e.g.* the Factories Act 1961); and
(c) the Health and Safety at Work Act 1974.

The employer's common law duty

At common law an employer has a duty to take reasonable care for the safety of his employees. Whilst this duty arises out of the legal relationship between the parties, namely the contract of employment, the action is invariably pursued in the tort of Negligence rather than in contract. The nature and extent of the duty will vary from case to case according to all the circumstances, but some general observations may be made.

The employer's duty is a personal one and delegation of this responsibility to another will not relieve the employer of liability. The duty is a continuing one and standards of safety must be maintained. Further, the duty to safeguard the employee extends not only to activities which the employee is employed to do but also to those which are normal and reasonably incidental to his employment. In *Davison* v. *Handley Page Ltd.*, for example, an employee was injured, as a result of his employer's negligence, whilst on his way to wash his cup after a tea-break. His employer was held to be liable.

The duty is one which the employer fulfils by acting reasonably. In determining what amounts to "reasonable," the courts may have regard to the established practice in a particular trade or industry; or to the state of knowledge about a particular danger (*e.g.* the risk of exposure to a specific chemical process); or to the severity of the possible injury. Moreover, conduct that is reasonable in respect of one employee may not be reasonable in respect of another. Thus, the employer owes a greater duty to the apprentice than to the skilled employee, and to the handicapped employee than to one who has no disability (see *Paris* v. *Stepney Borough Council*, page 177). A further factor that the court may consider when determining whether an employer has acted reasonably is the economic cost of taking safety measures balanced against the risk of injury to employees if those measures are not taken or only taken in part (see *Latimer* v. *A.E.C.*, page 178).

Although the employer owes one duty, the duty to take reasonable care for his employees' safety, this duty can be illustrated by breaking it down into four obligations:

(a) the duty to provide safe and competent fellow employees;
(b) the duty to provide proper and safe plant and machinery;
(c) the duty to provide a safe place of work; and
(d) the duty to provide a safe system of work.

The duty to provide safe and competent fellow employees . . . an employer must exercise reasonable care when selecting and training his workforce. He should ensure that employees are given proper instructions on the work they are employed to do. Further, where an employee is known to carry out practical jokes, his employer may be liable to a fellow-employee who is injured by such behaviour. There may in fact be a positive duty upon an employer to dismiss a known practical joker or an employee who refuses to use safety equipment or to follow safe procedures to the danger not only of himself but others as well. Provided the employer follows fair procedures in these cases, such a dismissal is unlikely to be found to be unfair.

The duty to provide proper and safe plant and machinery . . . means that the tools, machines and equipment to be used by the employee must be reasonably safe and adequate for the purpose for which they are intended. In *Taylor* v. *Rover Company Ltd.* it was held that an employer who knew (either personally or through his representatives) that a piece of equipment was defective, but who failed to withdraw it from use, was liable. Otherwise, at common law, if an employer bought his equipment from a reputable supplier, he was acting reasonably and thus performing his duty. In *Davie* v. *New Merton Board Mills Ltd.* an employee was injured due to a latent defect in a tool which had been purchased from a reputable supplier. His employer, whose system of maintenance and inspection was not at fault, was held to be not liable and the only remedy open to the employee was an action against the manufacturer on the basis of the principle established in *Donoghue* v. *Stevenson* (see page 167). However, this was by no means satisfactory since it would frequently be difficult for an injured employee to prove negligence on the part of a manufacturer. Indeed, the defect might not occur during manufacture but elsewhere in the supply chain. To remedy this the Employer's Liability (Defective Equipment) Act 1969 was passed. This Act provides that where an employee suffers personal injury in the course of employment in consequence of a defect in equipment provided by his employer for the purposes of the employer's business, and the defect is attributable wholly or partly to the fault of a third party, the injury shall be deemed to be attributable also to the negligence of the employer. Thus the harshness of the rule in *Davie's* case is modified to allow the employee to proceed against his employer on the basis of the "deemed" negligence. It is left to the employer to seek a contribution from whomsoever along the supply chain was actually at fault.

The duty to provide a safe place of work . . . is personal to the employer and he cannot escape liability by delegating it even to a skilled and competent contractor. This particular duty is closely related to both the preceding and following duties. It is, for example, often difficult to distinguish between the equipment and plant in a factory and the factory structure itself. Both must, however, be safe.

The duty to provide a "safe system of work" . . . this duty imposes upon the employer an obligation to give thought to: the physical lay-out of work; the sequence in which work is to be done; the giving of warnings and posting of notices; the issue of special instructions; and general working conditions, such as temperature and humidity.

In establishing a system of work an employer should bear in mind that his employees may suffer lapses of concentration or have moments of carelessness and, whilst not every incident may be laid at the employer's door, such frailties should be provided for by the reasonably prudent employer.

In recent years the common law duty of the employer for his employees' safety has shown the growing breadth of the statutory dismissal protection. Thus, an employer who fails to fulfil some aspect of this duty may be faced with a claim for "constructive" unfair dismissal from one or more of those employees. In *British Aircraft Corporation Ltd.* v. *Austin* it was held that an employer had an implied duty to act reasonably in investigating promptly employees' complaints about safety. Failure to do so in the instant case, where the complaint related to non-provision of suitable safety goggles, entitled the employee to resign and claim constructive dismissal (see page 323).

The employer's defences . . . the employer who will attempt to show, when sued by an employee, that he has exercised reasonable care, may also raise defences. These defences, contributory negligence and *volenti non fit injuria*, are discussed in *Unit Two*, page 180.

Employer's insurance against liability . . . since, in practical terms, it would be largely futile for the common law to impose duties upon employers if they could not afford to meet the costs involved in breaking them, it is now established by the Employers' Liability (Compulsory Insurance) Act 1969 that all employers must insure against claims from their employees for personal injury or disease arising out of and in the course of employment.

Protective safety legislation

There are a number of statutes that provide for the protection of specified groups of employees in certain types of employment. The Offices, Shops and Railways Premises Act 1963, the Mines and Quarries Act 1954, and the Factories Act 1961 are but three examples of such protective legislation.

This legislation can be contrasted with the employer's common law duty of care in that the statutory protection deals with issues not touched upon by the common law, such as hours of work and the employment of women and young persons. Moreover, protective legislation is not concerned solely with compensating the injured employee, as the common law is, but also seeks, at least in theory, to enforce prescribed standards upon employers by means of persuasion backed up by criminal sanctions. The common law duty and the statutory duty can also be distinguished on other grounds. The employer's common law duty is one based upon the tort of Negligence (see page 167) and the standard is that of the "reasonable man." The statutory duty, on the other hand, will be based upon a specific provision in a statute that imposes a duty upon a person to take (or not to take) a particular course of action. The standard of care required may be to do all that is "reasonably practicable" to fulfil the duty, or the statute may provide that a person *must* comply with the duty, so that it is no defence for him to say that he did not intend to break the duty, or that he took reasonable care. (This latter situation would be an example of *strict liability*.) An action brought against an employer for breach of an obligation imposed by protective legislation will be one brought for *breach of statutory duty*.

The two duties, common law and statutory, are complementary, the one supporting the other in providing as wide a coverage as possible for the employee's safety. A single incident in a factory that causes injury to an employee may, for example, give rise to civil actions for breach of both common law and statutory duties. An employee would only recover damages once even if he succeeded in both actions. He will, however, proceed against his employer on both grounds to "insure" against his failing to establish either. In *Bux* v. *Slough Metals Ltd.* the plaintiff was hit in the eye by a splash of molten metal whilst working without goggles. These had been provided by his employer but were not worn because they slowed down workers paid by the piece. The employer, who was aware of this problem, was held not to be in breach of his statutory duty which was merely to "*provide* goggles to the prescribed standard." However, the Court of Appeal held that he was in breach of the common law duty of care which required him not only to provide goggles but also to insist on their use and to instruct employees accordingly. The plaintiff, therefore, recovered damages for his injuries, although these were reduced because of his contributory negligence (see page 180).

The Health and Safety at Work Act 1974

The Health and Safety at Work Act 1974 aims at the progressive replacement of most existing legislation on health and safety at work by a system of regulations and approved codes of practice. This framework will seek to secure the health, safety and welfare not only of employees and the self-employed but also of the public generally, particularly in respect of the keeping and using of dangerous substances and of harmful emissions into the atmosphere. The Act imposes general duties on employers as employers; on employers as manufacturers, suppliers and importers of articles and substances for use at work; on the self-employed; and on employees.

An employer must ensure, so far as is reasonably practicable, the health, safety and welfare at work of all his employees; have a written safety policy; and consult with any safety representatives appointed by a recognised trade union under the Safety Representatives and Safety Committee Regulations 1977. He must also establish, if requested to do so by the safety representatives, a safety committee.

The Act imposes upon the employer an obligation to conduct his undertaking so as to ensure, so far as is reasonably practicable, that people *other* than his employees are not exposed to risks to their health and safety. A local authority would, therefore, be under an obligation to protect students in a technical college maintained by the authority, even though the students were not employees of the authority. Similarly an organisation which manufactures chemicals would need to concern itself with the health and safety of the residents of a nearby housing estate. Indeed under the Act regulations may be made requiring an employer to give such persons information on the way in which he conducts his undertaking where their health and safety could be affected.

Enforcement of these duties is generally the responsibility of inspectors appointed by the Health and Safety Executive. Among the powers available to them is the power to issue *improvement notices* or *prohibition notices* by which they may require action to remedy the contravention of any statutory provision or stop any activity which may cause serious personal injury. A person on whom such a notice is served may appeal against the notice, or any of its terms, to an industrial tribunal. Inspectors also have powers to inspect workplaces and to take samples. Employers who fail to perform any of the general duties imposed on them by the Act will also commit a criminal offence, the penalties for which may be a fine and/or imprisonment. Contrary to the usual rule (see page 65) the onus of proving that he took all reasonably practicable steps lies upon the employer. However, the Act does not itself create any new civil liability for personal injury beyond that already existing at common law and for breach of statutory duty. Regulations made under the Act may, however, provide for such liability.

The employee's duty of care

An employee must exercise reasonable care and skill in carrying out his work (a duty arising from an implied term of his contract that he is competent to do the job for which he was engaged). Failure to take such care may be costly for an employee since it has been held that he is under an implied duty to indemnify his employer against the consequences of his negligent acts. In *Lister* v. *Romford Ice and Cold Storage* a lorry driver, whilst carelessly reversing his lorry, injured a fellow employee (his father as it happened). The latter recovered damages from the employer, whose insurance company (suing on behalf of the employer) then successfully sued the son for a breach of his implied contractual duty to take care. In fact, such actions by insurance companies (who normally take over the rights of the employer) have not been common as a result of a "gentlemen's agreement" made after *Lister's* case. In any event, an employee will not generally be bound to indemnify his employer when the negligent act is committed whilst carrying out, on his employer's orders, an activity outside the scope of his employment (since there cannot be a term in his contract that he has any competence in such matters). The common law duty of the employee extends to taking reasonable care of his employer's property when it is entrusted to him.

An employee also has a statutory duty under the Health and Safety at Work Act 1974 to take reasonable care for his own health and safety and that of others who may be affected by his acts or omissions at work. He must also co-operate with his employer so far as is necessary to enable that employer to perform or comply with any duty imposed upon him. Thus, an employee who refuses to wear goggles whilst drilling, or who removes a guard from a machine, may be in breach of his duty and liable to a fine. The Act further provides that employees shall not intentionally or recklessly interfere with or misuse anything provided in the interests of health, safety or welfare.

Breach of the employee's duty of care may involve a further cost to the employee, that of dismissal. In appropriate circumstances after complying with fair procedures an employer may be able to justify as fair the dismissal of an employee who has carried out his work carelessly, or who has acted with disregard for the safety of others or for agreed safety standards.

VICARIOUS LIABILITY

The liability of an employer for the health and safety of others does not stop at his own employees. As we have seen he may also be responsible for the health and safety of the self-employed and the public in general, and if he commits a civil or criminal offence he may be sued by the party affected or prosecuted by the State. In such cases the proceedings will relate to the *primary* liability of the organisation. The employer may, however, find himself a party to proceedings brought not in relation to his own, primary, liability but in relation to the liability of one of his own employees, for whom he is *vicariously* liable. An employer will be vicariously liable for those torts (normally the tort of Negligence, see page 167) of his employees committed in the *course of their employment*. An act is deemed to be in the course of employment if it is either:

(a) a wrongful act authorised by the employer; or

(b) a lawful act authorised by the employer but performed by the employee in a wrongful manner.

(In fact, the first situation is really an example of the *primary* liability of the employer, although it is often treated as a question of *vicarious* liability.)

Various reasons are put forward to justify the application of the vicarious liability doctrine. Suffice it to say that the employer properly bears the loss, since he created the situation in which the employee committed the tort and he is in the better position to pay, having usually insured against such losses. (It ought to be remembered, however, that the cost of such insurance is undoubtedly reflected in the price of the employer's goods or services, and thus at the end of the day it is the customer who pays.) In any event, the employee who commits the wrong is himself liable to any third person who suffers injury or loss as a result. The third party may, then, sue both the employee and the employer (but he cannot recover from both).

Acts in the course of employment

An act will be within the course of employment if it is one which the employee is employed to perform, or one done for the purposes of the employer's business. Even if the employer expressly forbids such an act, he may still be vicariously liable for the employee's activities. In *Limpus* v. *London General Omnibus Co.*, a bus driver employed by the defendants caused an accident, when competing for passengers. He deliberately drove his bus across the path of a bus owned by the plaintiff, despite the fact that he had been expressly forbidden by his employer to compete in this manner. It was held that the driver was employed to convey passengers, which was what he was doing, even though his method of so doing was wrongful. His employer was, therefore, vicariously liable. In *Rose* v. *Plenty*, a boy was injured whilst riding on a milk float driven by a milkman who had asked him to assist on his round. Again, the employers were held to be vicariously liable, despite the strict instructions that had been given to all milkmen not to allow children to travel on floats. In *Beard* v. *London General Omnibus Co.*, on the other hand, the actions of a conductor, who negligently drove a bus whilst at a terminus awaiting the driver, were held to be outside his employment. Driving was not within the class of acts which the conductor was authorised to do.

Even where the employee is performing what appears to be an authorised activity the employer will not be liable for the employee's negligence if the latter has gone off "on a frolic of his own." Thus, the driver who detours from his proper route for some personal objective is not acting within the course of his employment and his employer cannot be burdened with liability for the results of the driver's negligence.

The use of physical force against others, by an employee, does not in itself take an act beyond the scope of employment, but a distinction must be drawn between the action of the over-zealous employee and that of an employee who is seeking personal vengeance. In *Bayley* v. *Manchester, Sheffield and Lincolnshire Railway Co.* the defendants were held liable for the actions of one of their porters who violently pulled a passenger out of a coach when he mistakenly believed the passenger to be on the wrong train. The porter was carrying out his authorised duties, though in a blundering manner. In *Daniels* v. *Whetstone Entertainments Ltd.*, however, the use of force was motivated by personal vengeance. The plaintiff had been evicted from a dance hall by a "bouncer" who had assaulted him in doing so. Once outside the "bouncer" had assaulted the plaintiff again. The employers were liable for the first assault, since the "bouncer" had been acting in the course of his employment, though in an unauthorised manner. The second assault, however, was outside the course of employment since it was motivated by personal vengeance.

For whom is the employer liable . . . an employer is generally liable for the acts of his employees and not for those of any independent contractor who performs services for him. For this reason, and others, the courts have developed tests to distinguish these two categories of worker (see page 296). However, in exceptional circumstances, the employer will also be liable for the tortious acts of his independent contractors. This will be so where, for example, there is a hazardous task to be undertaken, since the employer will, in such a case, be under a non-delegable duty to see that care is taken. Thus, where the employer has engaged a competent contractor to carry out welding operations at his factory and the contractor does so negligently, thereby causing an explosion which damages adjoining property, it will be no defence for the employer to claim that he himself was not negligent and should bear no liability for the fault of the contractor.

Which employer is liable? . . . as we have seen, liability for wrongs committed in the course of employment falls upon both employee and employer, although in practice it is the latter who pays. If, however, an employer lends an employee to another employer, and a tort is committed by that employee whilst working for the temporary employer, which of the employers will be vicariously liable for the act? In *Mersey Docks and Harbour Board* v. *Coggins & Griffith Ltd.*, the harbour board loaned one of its cranes and a driver to a firm of stevedores. The latter had power to instruct the driver where to station his crane, and to decide the order in which cargo should be picked up and removed. But they had no power to direct the manner in which he worked the crane. In negligently working the crane the driver injured a third person. The House of Lords held that the Harbour Board were liable for those injuries, since they had not discharged the burden of showing that the driver was no longer their employee. The issue turned upon the question of who controlled the manner of working of the crane. Control was held not to have passed to the temporary employer since, when lending a valuable piece of machinery such as a crane, the Harbour Board would expect to retain control over the manner of its operation, and hence over its driver. On the other hand, where an unskilled or semi-skilled worker is loaned on his own, it will be easier to show that control and with it, liability, has passed from the general employer to the temporary employer.

Vicarious liability for criminal acts

The employer's vicarious liability is not confined to his employees' tortious acts, but may also encompass his employees' criminal conduct, even though that conduct is aimed entirely for their own benefit. In *Lloyd* v. *Grace, Smith & Co.*, a managing clerk, employed by a firm of solicitors, was allowed by the firm to perform conveyances of land. He fraudulently induced a client to transfer her property to himself, sold the property and absconded with the proceeds. The firm was held liable (even though it stood to gain nothing from that fraud) since the clerk was merely performing the class of duties which he had been given authority to perform. In *Morris* v. *Martin and Sons Ltd.*, the plaintiff took a fur to a furrier for cleaning. The latter handed it to one of its employees, who subsequently stole the fur. The employer was, again, held liable, since its employee had improperly performed his duty which was to look after the fur.

Section E: Termination of the Employment Relationship

Termination by notice

At common law, either party to the contract of employment may terminate the contract by giving due notice. It follows that, unless justified, termination without notice is a breach of the contract. Such action on the part of the employer (*summary dismissal*) may be justified by conduct of the employee which shows that he no longer intends to be bound by the terms of the contract, express or implied. Where an employee has been dismissed without notice (*wrongful dismissal*) he may bring an action for breach of contract and, if successful (*i.e* where the employer cannot show justification), he may be awarded damages.

At common law, in the absence of any express or implied term, an employee is entitled to *reasonable* notice on termination of his employment (unless summary dismissal is justified). His position has, since 1963, been strengthened by statutory provisions laying down minimum periods of notice that an employee must receive. The present Act, the Employment Protection (Consolidation) Act 1978, provides that an employee who has been continuously employed for four weeks or more, but for less than two years, will be entitled to one week's notice. Thereafter an employee will be entitled to one week's notice for every full year of employment up to a maximum of 12 weeks' notice for 12 years' continuous service (see table 3). An employee may be entitled to *longer* notice than the statutory minimum

---

Table 3

STATUTORY PERIODS OF NOTICE

Period of continuous employment	Minimum notice
More than 4 weeks but less than 2 years	1 week
More than 2 years but less than 3 years	2 weeks
More than 3 years but less than 4 years and so on	3 weeks
More than 12 years and over	12 weeks

---

if his contract so provides, but no term of that contract may provide for *shorter* notice. However, at the time of termination an employee may forgo his right to receive notice or may accept payment of wages in lieu of notice. An employee is obliged by the Act to give only one week's notice to an employer, although this period may be extended by a term in his contract.

Unfair dismissal

The common law right of an employer to dismiss an employee by due notice without justifying such dismissal is now severely restricted by the statutory provisions relating to *unfair dismissal* contained in sections 54–80 of the Employment Protection (Consolidation) Act 1978 as amended by the Employment Acts 1980–1982. By these provisions, every employee (with certain exceptions) has the right not to be unfairly dismissed and may enforce this right by way of complaint to an industrial tribunal. The employee's position is further strengthened by his right to a written statement of the reasons for his dismissal. Failure to provide this statement may lead to an award of two weeks' pay being made to him.

The two most basic qualifications for this statutory protection are that an employee must have been continuously employed for the requisite period (presently set at two years for most cases) and he must have been dismissed. An employee will be treated as *dismissed* where:

(a) his contract is terminated by his employer, with or without notice;
(b) a fixed-term contract expires without being renewed; or
(c) the employee justifiably terminates his contract, with or without notice, because of his employer's conduct.

The last category ("constructive dismissal") has given rise to many problems particularly about the kind of conduct on the employer's part which justifies the employee in leaving. In *Western Excavating (ECC) Ltd.* v. *Sharp*, Lord Denning stated that an employee was entitled to treat himself as discharged from the contract where the employer was guilty of conduct which showed that he no longer intended to be bound by one of the essential terms of the contract. Certain actions on the employer's part will clearly entitle an employee to leave (*e.g.* a refusal to pay wages or to demote without justification). However, not every unreasonable act will amount to a breach which goes to the root of the contract. Determination of the terms of the contract of employment may, therefore, assume a vital significance and it is in this context that the willingness of the courts to import terms into the contract becomes important (see *British Aircraft Corporation Ltd.* v. *Austin*, page 316). In particular, in cases of constructive dismissal tribunals have spoken of an employer's obligation to treat his employees with due respect and trust (see page 308). Where an employer's behaviour does not fulfil this requirement, an employee will be entitled to leave, with or without notice, and pursue an unfair dismissal complaint. However, he will lose this right if he delays. Thus, if he continues to work for a short period before leaving, he must make it clear that he is doing so under protest.

An employee will be considered to have been *unfairly* dismissed unless the employer can establish a reason for dismissal, which must be a reason related to any one or more of the following:

(a) the employee's capability or qualifications;
(b) his conduct;
(c) his redundancy;
(d) his continued employment being a breach of any statute; or
(e) some other substantial reason justifying the employee's dismissal.

Decided cases show that these categories are capable of encompassing, prima facie at least, most reasons for which an employee might be dismissed. However, this is only the first step in establishing that a particular dismissal is fair. The tribunal must also determine whether in the circumstances (including the size and administrative resources of the employer's undertaking) the employer acted reasonably or unreasonably in treating the stated reason as a sufficient reason for dismissing the employee. This requirement has proved to be important and, before dismissing an employee, the employer *may* need to take certain further steps (*e.g.* giving a warning to the employee as to future conduct, or allowing him the opportunity of improving his performance, or explaining his behaviour). A *Code of Practice: Disciplinary and Other Procedures in Employment* published by A.C.A.S. gives guidelines concerning the steps employers should take in dismissing their employees.

Dismissal is *automatically* unfair if the reason for it was that the employee had exercised his rights to be a member or to take part in the activities of an independent trade union or had exercised his right not to be a member of any trade union. On the other hand, an employee may lose his right not to be unfairly dismissed where a *union membership agreement* (*i.e.* a closed shop agreement) between trade union and employer is in force and the employee is not a member of that union. However, the employee will not lose the statutory protection where he genuinely objects to membership on grounds of conscience or other deeply held personal conviction, or where the union membership agreement has not been approved by 80 per cent. of those covered by it in a secret ballot.

Redundancy payments

Where the termination of the contract of employment is necessitated by redundancy, an employee is entitled to a redundancy payment. To qualify for such a payment it must be established that:

(a) The employee has been *dismissed* (see above). (He would not, for example, be entitled to a payment if, anticipating redundancy, he gives notice to his employer and finds employment elsewhere.)

(b) The reason for his dismissal was that he was *redundant*.
    (This will be so, if:
    (i)   the business in which he was employed has closed; or
    (ii) the branch of the business in which he was employed has closed; or
    (iii) although the business has not closed, he is now surplus to the requirements of the business.)

(c) He has been *continuously employed* by the organisation that has dismissed him for at least two years since attaining the age of 18.

An employee, who is otherwise entitled to a redundancy payment, will lose that right if he unreasonably refuses an offer of re-employment by his employer, whether on the same terms and conditions as before or on different but suitable terms (in the latter case an employee is allowed a four-week trial period in the new job).

Other rights on redundancy

An employer's duties towards his employees in a redundancy situation are not confined to making a redundancy payment. An employee who believes that he has been *unfairly selected* for redundancy (*e.g.* in breach of an agreed or customary procedure or because of his trade union activities) may bring a complaint of unfair dismissal. Thus, if in a redundancy situation it has been agreed between employer and trade union that the last man to be engaged should be the first to be dismissed (*i.e.* "last in, first out"), then that procedure should be followed. Failure to observe the procedure will give an employee who is dismissed out of turn the right to complain of unfair dismissal. Further, under the Employment Protection Act 1975, an employer must give advance notice of proposed redundancies to the independent trade unions which he recognises and failure to do so may lead to awards being made against him.

Employees with at least two years' service are entitled to reasonable time off with pay, in order to look for new employment or to make arrangements for training, when given notice of dismissal by reason of redundancy. If time off is unreasonably refused, an employee has a right to complain to an industrial tribunal which may award him up to 40 per cent. of his week's pay.

The ex-employee's duties to his employer

The obligations that arise on the termination of the employment relationship are not all one way. As we have seen (see page 309), the employee's implied duty of good faith continues after his employment has ended. Consequently, it would be a breach of the duty of good faith (for which an action for damages or, more likely, an injunction would lie) if an ex-employee was to disclose confidential information about his former employer's business to his new employer. Since it will often be difficult to detect such breaches, employers wishing to protect their interests more usually resort to restraint of trade clauses in their employees' contracts (see page 299).

Section F: Remedies

Where a dispute arises between employer and employee which cannot be resolved by other means (*e.g.* conciliation or arbitration), then any legal action which is subsequently brought will be pursued either through the common law courts or through industrial tribunals.

Common law actions

Actions taken for breach of a common law right or duty owed by or to the parties to the employment relationship will usually be brought in the county courts (subject to their financial jurisdictional limits, see page 34). Such actions could be based directly on the breach of the common law duties owed by the parties to each other. Where the duty alleged to have been broken is the employer's duty to take reasonable care for the safety of his employees, the action will be based on the tort of Negligence and any damages awarded will be calculated according to normal tortious principles (see page 185). More often, however, the employee's claim will be that he has been wrongfully dismissed. If successful damages will be awarded according to normal contractual principles, namely such amount as will place him, financially, in the same position as if the contract had been performed (see page 156). In the case of wrongful dismissal this sum will usually be the wages that the employee should have received during the period of notice, subject to the requirement that the employee must take reasonable steps to *mitigate* his loss by seeking out other suitable employment. This rule was thought not to be inflexible. Thus, in *Cox* v. *Philips Industries Ltd.* the plaintiff's demotion, which was in breach of contract, caused him to become depressed, anxious and ill. Upon his subsequent dismissal he claimed and was awarded damages for the distress caused to him. However, in *Bliss* v. *South Thames Regional Health Authority* the Court of Appeal has overruled that approach and confirmed the general rule that where damages fall to be assessed for breach of contract rather than in tort it is not permissible to award general damages for frustration, mental distress, injured feelings or annoyance occasioned by the breach.

In an action for wrongful dismissal damages are effectively the only remedy, for generally the courts will refuse to specifically enforce the contract of employment by ordering the employer to employ the particular employee. (This may be contrasted with the power to order re-instatement for unfair dismissal, see page 328.) Whilst damages are invariably the remedy in dismissal cases, the courts may grant injunctions on those occasions where damages would be inadequate. Such occasions include breaches of restraint clauses by employees (see page 299) and breaches of the duty to respect the employer's trade secrets (see page 310).

Industrial tribunals

The other common forum for resolution of employment disputes is provided by the system of regionally based industrial tribunals. First established in 1964, the tribunals have since been given by statute extensive jurisdiction over a wide range of employment matters. Appeals from industrial tribunals on points of law go to the Employment Appeal Tribunal. Both the industrial tribunal and the Appeal Tribunal consist of a legally qualified chairman (in the latter case a High Court judge) and two lay members, chosen because of their knowledge and experience of industrial relations.

The complaints brought before the tribunals will usually involve breaches of the various rights presently given to individual employees by statute (*e.g.* rights in relation to pregnancy). Such complaints must generally be brought within three months of the right being infringed. The normal remedy will be one of compensation, calculated according to the principles laid down by statute in relation to that particular right. Thus, where the complaint relates to a failure to allow the employee time off for a permitted purpose (*e.g.* public duties), the Employment Protection (Consolidation) Act 1978 provides that compensation will be "of such amount as the tribunal considers just and equitable in all the circumstances having regard to the employer's default in failing to permit time off to be taken by the employee and to any loss sustained by the employee which is attributable to the matters complained of."

Whilst an award of compensation would be the normal remedy in tribunal proceedings, two other possibilities are worthy of note. The first relates to the employer's duty to provide employees with written particulars of the terms of employment. Where such a written statement has not been provided in whole or in part or a dispute arises as to the contents of a statement, a reference may be made to an industrial tribunal for determination. The tribunal has power to decide what particulars should have been included, or to confirm, amend or substitute those particulars which were included. However, the tribunal cannot seek to interpret those expressed particulars nor, it was once thought, could it rewrite the contract for the parties. But, in *Mears* v. *Safecar Security Ltd.* the Court of Appeal held that a tribunal does have jurisdiction to hear complaints of inaccurate particulars. Moreover, where there is no evidence before a tribunal upon which to base any of the particulars, the tribunal may "invent" a term on the basis of what would be reasonable and sensible, bearing in mind that it will have been the employer at fault. The second possibility involves the consideration of improvement or prohibition notices issued by inspectors under the Health and Safety at Work Act (see page 318). In such cases the tribunal, on an appeal from the person on whom the notice has been served, may either cancel or affirm the notice. In the latter case the notice may be affirmed either in its original form or with such modifications as the tribunal may in the circumstances think fit.

As well as the general observations about the relief available from proceedings before industrial tribunals, the remedies available for breaches of the following rights must be examined in more detail:

(a) discrimination on grounds of sex or race;
(b) unfair dismissal; and
(c) redundancy payments.

Discrimination on grounds of sex or race

All disputes relating to discrimination in the employment field, whether on the grounds of sex or race, may be brought before an industrial tribunal, before which the burden of proof lies, initially at least, upon the complainant. To this end the complainant may seek information not only about his own position or performance but also about other applicants or employees. In *Science Research Council* v. *Nassé* the House of Lords held that where an employer refuses to disclose that information on the ground of confidentiality, the tribunal may order discovery if, after balancing the relevance of the documents against the nature of the confidential information, it is thought that discovery is necessary in order to dispose fairly of the proceedings. The Sex Discrimination Act 1975 and the Race Relations Act 1976 assist the complainant faced with the burden of proving discrimination by providing a "questionnaire procedure" whereby the employer must answer specified questions. Failure to reply, or replies which are evasive or equivocal, may lead to a finding that the employer has unlawfully discriminated against the complainant. The remedies available before the tribunal are a declaration of rights, an award of compensation (including an amount for any injury to feelings), and a recommendation that action be taken within a specified time to remedy the complaint.

The 1975 and 1976 Acts establish two bodies, the Equal Opportunities Commission and the Commission for Racial Equality, to remove discrimination, promote equality of opportunity and review the workings of their respective Acts. These bodies have power to:

(a) issue codes of practice giving practical guidance on equality of opportunity and the elimination of discrimination;
(b) conduct formal investigations; and
(c) issue non-discrimination notices on persons contravening the statutory provisions, which notices require the recipient to act in a lawful way.

Both bodies have in fact issued Codes of Practice whose provisions contain guidance on good employment practices in their respective fields.

Unfair dismissal

On finding that an employee has been unfairly dismissed, an industrial tribunal may order:

(a) that the employee be re-employed; or

(b) that an award of compensation be made.

An order for re-employment is an order that the employee be either *reinstated* in the same job or *re-engaged* in a comparable job with the same employer or an associated employer. The order will also require the employer to give to the employee any arrears of pay. If an order for re-employment is made, but the employer fails to comply with it by refusing to take the employee back, then the employee will be entitled to receive an award of compensation as outlined below. In addition, a further sum may be awarded to him because of the employer's refusal to comply with the re-employment order.

If no order for re-employment is made, the employee will be awarded compensation consisting of a *basic award* and a *compensatory award*. The amount of the basic award, which compensates for the loss of the job itself (and not for consequential financial loss), will be based on age, length of service, and the earnings of the employee. The compensatory award will be based on any loss actually sustained by the employee as a result of the employer's action (*e.g.* loss of earnings during the ensuing period of unemployment).

The amount of compensation awarded to an employee may be reduced because the employee:

(a) failed to mitigate his loss; or

(b) contributed to his dismissal by his conduct.

An employee may mitigate his loss by seeking other suitable employment, although this does not mean that he should necessarily take the first job that comes along. An employee may have contributed to his own dismissal where, for example, he has sworn at a manager and failed to apologise, which action has not been deemed sufficient alone to justify his dismissal.

Redundancy payments

The amount of a redundancy payment is based on:

(a) the number of years of continuous employment served by the employee;

(b) the employee's age during those years; and

(c) the employee's earnings.

When an employee is made redundant, his employer must establish his age and count (backwards) the number of years of continuous employment, to a maximum of 20 years. This period of service must then be divided by reference to the age bands indicated in table 4, which shows that the employee will receive compensation for years served on the basis of his age at that time. His present weekly wage must then be established (there is a maximum allowable—at present it is £155) and the payment must be calculated on the basis indicated in table 4. Thus, a man made redundant at the age of 58, having worked for his employer for ten years at a wage, when dismissed, of £100 per week, will receive £1,500 (10 × 1½ × £100). If that same employee was aged 38 he would receive £1,000 (10 × 1 × £100). The maximum payment possible under the statute is £4,650 (20 × 1½ × £155). In the case of men over 64 (59 for women) there is a deduction of one-twelfth in the total entitlement for every month over that age, so that on dismissal at 65 a man would receive no redundancy payment at all.

Table 4

CALCULATION OF REDUNDANCY PAYMENTS

Relevant age bands	**Pay entitlement for every year in band**
18–21	½ week's pay
22–40	1 week's pay
41–64	1½ week's pay

Part Three

CAPITAL

The visit to the legal office may be prompted, not by a problem in relation to the organisation's workforce (Labour), but by a matter connected with its Capital. Capital is a term that has wide and varied meanings. An organisation must raise *capital finance* as a prerequisite for its expenditure. Having acquired its capital finance the organisation may then spend this on the *capital goods* which will be used in producing the goods or services it wishes to sell or distribute. Capital goods are tangible assets such as factory premises or machinery. An organisation may also acquire intangible assets, an important example of which is *industrial property* (*e.g.* a patent right in an invention).

Thus, the issue that the consumer brings to the legal office may relate to capital in one or other of these meanings and he may be seeking advice or assistance:

(a) in dealing with outside agencies;
(b) in drafting documents;
(c) in response to legal action brought by another person; or
(d) in order to bring a legal action against another person.

Dealing with outside agencies . . . the law consumer who wishes to raise finance for his business may seek advice on the sources and types of finance available to him. It may be necessary to inform him of the legal implications of raising that finance by different means. Moreover, the small businessman in particular may need assistance in preparing his approach to the providers of finance, such as banks and other financial institutions.

Drafting documents . . . one way in which the organisation, large or small, may raise its finance is by means of a charge over its property. This will require the drafting of a mortgage deed creating the charge. The drafting abilities of the legal office may also be called upon where the organisation wishes to assign to another its rights in its industrial property such as a patent. In the same way the sale or purchase of assets in the form of land will require the drafting of a conveyance.

Responding to legal action . . . where the organisation has grown beyond the one-man business there may be occasions when the threat of legal action by a provider of finance, such as a shareholder or debenture holder, induces the visit to the legal office.

Bringing a legal action . . . the commercial or industrial law consumer may consult his lawyers in order to instigate legal proceedings as well as to defend himself against them. Thus, he may wish to protect himself from infringement of *his* rights as a provider of capital to another organisation (*e.g.* where he has not received dividend payments or interest charges

330

which are due), or from infringement of his industrial property rights (*e.g.* where his copyright is being abused).

Section A: Private Sector Capital Finance

SOURCES AND TYPES OF FINANCE

The sources of funds whereby organisations finance their enterprise (whether in establishing the business, in obtaining working capital, or in extending the business by new investment) are varied. The source and availability of funds will be one of the factors that determines the choice of legal status for the organisation, some sources being available only to particular forms of organisation (see page 333). That is not to say that there are no common sources. A sole trader or a partnership may both gain working capital by borrowing from a bank on overdraft or by using trade credit (*i.e.* by obtaining goods or services but deferring payment until a later date), so too may a company. Similarly, a sole trader and a partnership can raise a loan by granting a mortgage over their property, as a company may over its factory. The following discussion will, however, concentrate on the sources of finance available to the company and in particular on two types of finance:

(a) share capital; and
(b) loan capital.

Share capital... is that capital which the company is authorised by its memorandum to issue and to divide into shares of various classes.

Loan capital... is a hybrid collection, including long-term borrowing secured by debenture and short-term borrowing through overdrafts. This will not necessarily be set out in the company's constitution in such detail, although the articles of association may put some limit on the amount of the company's borrowing.

The raising of share and loan capital

One way in which a company may raise either its initial capital, or new capital, is by issuing shares and/or debentures in the company. Such capital may be raised by making an *issue* to the public as a whole or, as has been the common practice of recent years, by a *rights issue*. Under a rights issue, shares (or debentures) in the company are offered first to existing shareholders (or debenture holders) in proportion to their holdings. Only afterwards are they offered to the public as a whole, and then only if not all the shares (or debentures) are taken up by existing shareholders (or debenture holders). Whichever method is adopted the company must comply with the disclosure provisions of the Companies Act, in particular by publishing a *prospectus* (in the case of a quoted public company the issue must also comply with the requirements of the Stock Exchange).

The providers of such finance will usually be either private investors (individuals or other companies) or, increasingly in recent years, the banks and other financial institutions (*e.g.* insurance companies, pension funds or unit trusts).

THE NATURE OF CAPITAL FINANCE

The nature of a share

In *Borland's Trustee* v. *Steel Brothers & Co. Ltd.*, the court defined a share as being:

"The interest of a shareholder in the company, measured by a sum of money, for the purpose of liability in the first place, and of interest in the second, but also consisting of a series of mutual covenants entered into by all the shareholders *inter se* in accordance with [the Companies Act]."

Thus, a share in a company gives its owner rights in the company (*e.g.* the right to receive a dividend) and rights against the company (*e.g.* the right to ensure that the business of the company is conducted according to its constitution). A share also imposes an obligation on its owner, namely the liability to pay for that share.

A *share certificate*, which specifies the shares held by the member and which is prima facie evidence of the member's title to the shares, will be issued to each shareholder. Upon a transfer of shares the company will issue a new share certificate to the new shareholder.

Classes of shares

The share capital of a company may be divided into shares of different classes which are given different rights ("class rights") by the memorandum, articles or terms of issue. Most commonly the share capital will be divided into:

(a) ordinary shares; and

(b) preference shares.

Ordinary shares . . . constitute the class of shares which has the right to all of the company's property, once the special rights of all other classes have been met. For example, once other classes of shares have received their allocation of profits by way of dividends, the remaining distributable profits will belong to the ordinary shareholders. If there is only one class of shares, these will be ordinary shares, although these may be sub-divided into separate classes with differing voting rights. Such voting rights would be class rights, which could only be varied in compliance with the procedures outlined below.

Preference shares . . . the essence of a preference share is that it gives preferential treatment to its holder in some respect. It may give a preferential fixed dividend (*i.e.* the dividend must be paid before other classes of shares receive anything). It may give the preference shareholder the right to have his capital repaid first in the event of the winding up of the company. It may give both rights, and each would be a class right given to holders of that class of share. Preference shares may be *cumulative* or *non-cumulative*. In the case of cumulative preference shares, if the fixed dividend for any year is not paid, then the arrears must be carried into the next year, and any subsequent year, until there are distributable profits. No dividend may be paid to other classes until any such arrears are cleared. If preference shares are non-cumulative, then once a year's dividend is *passed*, it may not be recovered in later years.

Whatever the rights that attach to a particular class of shares, the law seeks to protect the shareholder by providing procedures under which any variation of those rights must be carried out. The variation procedure is often to be found in the memorandum or articles and where this is so any variation of class rights must be enacted according to the prescribed procedure. Even where there is no variation procedure provided by the memorandum or articles, class rights may be altered, but only subject to the strict terms of the Companies Act 1985.

The nature of a debenture

The term "debenture" is, strictly, the name given to particular types of document that evidence the company's debt to the holder. In fact, the term is used generally to refer to any loan which is secured on the company's assets, whether or not any formal document has been issued to the holder. Thus, any financial institution, such as a bank, which lends money to a company, secured on the company's assets, will be regarded as a debenture holder. As well as such separate and individual transactions, the company might decide to raise loan capital by issuing a series of debentures, each conferring the same rights to its holder. Thus a class of debenture holders would be created similar to a class of shareholders. Indeed, where this method is used, the rights of debenture holders will often not differ greatly from those of shareholders.

Whilst a debenture need not necessarily be secured on the company's assets, it usually will be. The two types of security available to the company's creditors are:

(a) the fixed charge; and

(b) the floating charge.

The fixed charge (or fixed debenture)... is a debenture charged over specific identifiable assets, such as the company's land or buildings. In other words, the company may raise a loan by granting a mortgage over its real property. Land is not, however, the only asset which the company has. It might, for example, have a large and valuable stock-in-trade which could be used as security for a loan. Yet a fixed charge on this asset would be impracticable where the stock-in-trade is constantly changing (*i.e.* by raw materials being used to produce finished goods, those goods being sold and new raw materials being bought), since the consent of the mortgagee would have to be obtained everytime any finished good was sold and a new charge made whenever raw materials were bought. This problem is solved as far as the company is concerned by granting a floating charge.

The floating charge (or floating debenture)... is a charge which "floats" over the assets on which it is secured, without restricting the company's power to deal with those assets in the ordinary course of business. Thus, a floating charge over a company's stock-in-trade is particularly appropriate. Floating charges may, however, be granted over any of the company's assets, including its plant and machinery and its land (even if those assets are already subject to a fixed charge). A floating charge will continue to "float" in this way until some event occurs to cause the charge to crystallise (*i.e.* become fixed). A charge might crystallise because the company has defaulted in repayment of the loan or has ceased trading, or because winding-up proceedings have begun. On the occurrence of such an event, if a loan had been secured by a floating charge over, for example, the company's stock-in-trade, the charge would become a fixed charge on whatever goods were in stock at the date of crystallisation. These goods could then be sold and the proceeds used to repay the lender.

For practical reasons, the floating charge is a means of security that is only used by the company and is not used by either the sole trader or the partnership. From the lender's point of view the floating charge is better than no security at all, but in the event of the failure of the company it will rank behind any fixed charge on the same assets when those assets are realised and the proceeds distributed. However, such secured creditors (fixed or floating) will take priority over ordinary unsecured creditors, if their charges have been registered.

Registration of charges . . . any charge upon the company's assets must be registered, within 21 days of its creation, with the Registrar of Companies, otherwise it becomes void against the liquidator or any creditor of the company. Thus, if a bank made a loan to a company secured by a floating charge over all the company's buildings and that charge was not duly registered, then the bank would be unable to claim priority of repayment over unsecured creditors. The duty to register any charge is placed formally upon the company, although, in practice, this task will usually be left to the person in whose favour the charge is created.

[The *"Romalpa* clause" . . . since the decision of the Court of Appeal in *Aluminium Industries B.V.* v. *Romalpa Ltd.*, in 1976, the extent of the protection afforded to a creditor by a floating charge has been the subject of debate. Upon insolvency a floating charge attaches to those assets of the debtor company over which it has been granted and, should a manufacturing company be unable to meet its debts, its stock may form part of those assets. What, however, if it does not own this stock? In the *Romalpa* case, sellers of capital goods to a manufacturing company inserted a term in their contract of sale to the effect that the purchasing company would not become the owner of the goods until it had paid to the sellers all that it owed them; that if the goods (aluminium, in this case) were mixed with other goods in the manufacturing process, the whole of the product manufactured would belong to the sellers of the capital goods; and that if the manufactured product was sold, the proceeds of sale would, likewise, belong to those sellers. In upholding the validity of this clause, the Court of Appeal acknowledged that the sellers of the aluminium had, in the event of the insolvency of their purchasers, a prior claim to the goods, or the proceeds of their sale, to that of secured creditors of the company. If *all* suppliers of capital goods were to use a *Romalpa*-style clause in their contracts of supply, the secured creditors of a company would find, upon insolvency, that there were few goods which could properly be said to form part of the company's assets and in relation to which a floating charge could attach. The *Romalpa* clause gives a supplier, in effect, priority over the goods he is selling to the purchasing company, but, as it is not, in law, a charge over those goods, there is no requirement that his claim over the goods be registered. A creditor could only establish the existence of such priority by examining all of the contracts of purchase entered into by the company to which he lends his money. More recent cases have shown the need for such clauses to be properly drafted if they are to be effective. An improperly drafted clause may be held to create no more than an equitable interest which will be unenforceable for lack of registration.]

THE RIGHTS OF THE PROVIDERS OF CAPITAL FINANCE

In the case of the sole trader, it would be unreal to discuss rights, or duties, since these are no different from those of any individual. In the case of the partnership, the rights of the providers of capital (*i.e.* the partners) will depend upon their partnership agreement and, in the absence of any provision in the agreement, upon the Partnership Act 1890 (see page 264). In the case of the company, the providers of capital are given rights both by the common law and by statute, as well as any contractual entitlement they may have negotiated.

The rights of shareholders

The Companies Act 1985 gives various rights to shareholders including the right to prevent oppression; the right to receive reliable information through the publication of audited accounts; the right to have the interests of directors and large shareholders disclosed; and the right to have the affairs of the company investigated by the Department of Trade and Industry. A shareholder may also have contractual rights based upon the memorandum and articles of association, including the right to attend meetings of the company, the right to vote and the right to receive a dividend. The common law also protects the shareholder. It has imposed certain duties upon the directors of companies (*e.g.* to act in good faith and not to make a secret profit in the conduct of the business). It has prevented majority shareholders from expropriating the property of the company and restricted the alteration of the company's articles in any way that might unfairly deprive the minority of their interest in the company. Further, the common law permits the individual shareholder to bring proceedings to prevent a company acting beyond its stated objects.

[The *public corporation* has no share capital as such, but is funded by government finance (and hopefully by trading profits). Thus the public corporation has no shareholders or board of directors, but it does have a board of management, and it is answerable to the appropriate government department and ultimately to the general public through Parliament.]

The rights of debenture holders

Debenture holders may be given rights under the terms of their loans comparable to those given to shareholders (*e.g.* the right to attend meetings). In addition, both the courts and the legislature have established certain rules for the raising and maintenance of capital that are designed to give some protection to those who give credit to a company on the basis that the company has the share capital which it says it has. Thus, both at common law and by statute, it is provided that shares cannot be issued at a discount but can be treated as paid up only to the extent of cash actually received. In fact, payment in kind rather than in cash is allowed but, in the case of public companies, the 1985 Act provides a compulsory valuation procedure for any such non-cash consideration. Further, once the company's share capital has been raised, the law seeks to ensure that it is maintained. This is a considerable protection, for if the money or assets of the company (which represent the issued capital of the company) could be paid back to shareholders, this would reduce the fund available for payment of the debts of creditors. Thus, a company may not return capital to shareholders except by adhering to the statutory reduction procedure or by winding up, in which case creditors will be protected. Nor may a company normally purchase its own shares nor give any financial assistance towards their purchase, since this too would amount to a reduction in capital. Moreover, dividends can only be paid out of profits, so there is no question of a company returning capital to shareholders in the form of dividend payments.

Section B: Public Sector Capital Finance

Detailed examination of the sources and types of public finance, whether at central government, local authority or nationalised industry level, would be inappropriate in a book of this type. Brief reference to some of the issues arising at local authority level has already been made (see page 293). In the case of nationalised industries finance may be raised on the open market by the issuing of debentures in which case, whilst much will depend upon the terms of issue, the basic principles do not differ from private sector loan capital.

Section C: Capital Goods

One of the meanings given to the term *capital* earlier was that of *capital goods*. Such, in the eyes of an economist, would be those assets which usually last for a long period of time and which are not normally wanted for themselves, but are used in the production of other goods and services (*e.g.* machines and factory buildings). Machines would be accepted as *goods* by lawyers as well as economists, and as such they would be purchased by the organisation entering into a sale of goods contract (see page 362). Factory buildings, on the other hand, would be regarded by lawyers as *land* and as such would be acquired by the organisation as a result of a conveyance of the vendor's freehold estate or by an assignment or grant of a lease (see page 199).

Section D: Industrial Property

There is a further category of capital that an organisation may acquire and which forms an asset of the business. This is a miscellaneous collection of property rights (including patents, copyright, goodwill, trade marks and designs) which is usually referred to as *industrial* or *intellectual property*. Such property may be transferred ("assigned") or mortgaged in the same way as the other property of a business. The whole system of intellectual property rights was the subject of a White Paper in 1986. This proposed the reform of the administration of patents law, the up-dating of copyright law and the introduction of a new property right, the unregistered design right. This last proposal is intended to protect original designs of objects such as car exhausts, designs which the House of Lords held in *British Leyland Motor Corporation Ltd.* v. *Armstrong Patents Co. Ltd.* not to be protected by the Copyright Act 1956.

Patents

A patent gives its proprietor the exclusive right (for a limited period) to use, exercise and sell an invention, and to obtain the profits that accrue from that invention. Under the Patents Act 1977 a patent may be granted for any invention which:

    (a) is new;

    (b) involves an inventive step; and

(c)   is capable of industrial application.

The right to apply for and to obtain a patent will fall upon:

(a)   the person or persons who have invented the subject-matter of the application; or

(b)   anyone who is entitled under any rule of law or valid agreement to the property in the invention.

Where, for example, an invention has been made by an employee during the course of his employment, the invention will be deemed to belong to his employer and he will gain the benefit of a patent, subject to the employee's right to receive compensation (see page 310). Application for a patent is made to the Patents Office, and there the application will be published and duly examined by the Comptroller of Patents. If the invention complies with the requirements of the Act, a patent will be granted and notice to that effect published. The patent will run for a term of 20 years from the time of publication.

A patent may have considerable value for an organisation, which may decide to assign it, mortgage it or grant a licence to others to work the invention. Any such transaction by the proprietor of a patent would be recorded in the Register of Patents, as would the initial granting of the patent.

Copyright

Under the Copyright Act 1956 a copyright may be given in respect of literary, dramatic, musical or artistic works to the author of the work. This will give that person the right:

(a)   to produce multiple copies;

(b)   to prevent unauthorised persons from producing copies; and

(c)   to prevent others from using his work to their advantage.

For example, if a person has written a song he may put that song on record and sell copies of that record. If another person, without authority, attempts to put the song on record, he may be prevented from doing so, as may any person who seeks to take advantage of the song by playing it in public (*e.g.* at a dance). The Copyright (Computer Software) Amendment Act 1985 expressly brought computer programs within the category of literary work under the 1956 Act.

Goodwill

Goodwill is another item of industrial property. It is not easy to define what is meant by "goodwill," but it will include, for example:

(a)   the reputation or connections that a business has built up over its trading life; and

(b)   the personal skill of the owner.

Goodwill is of particular importance to sole traders and partnerships, since it may be the one valuable asset that such forms of organisation possess. Moreover, in the case of a partnership, when a partner leaves the partnership (or retires or dies) he may transfer his share of the goodwill of the business to his partners for a consideration.

Trade marks and designs

Trade marks are used to indicate that goods come from a particular manufacturer or trader (*e.g.* a golliwog on a jar indicates that the jam is made by a particular manufacturer). However, in *Re Coca-Cola Co's*

Applications the House of Lords held that the container or bottle itself, even though it might have a distinctive shape, could not be classed as a trade mark. An organisation may protect its trade mark by:
(a)   an action based on the tort of "passing off";
(b)   registration under the Trade Marks Act 1938.
The benefit of registering trade marks has been extended to organisations providing services.

Designs (*i.e.* features of pattern or ornament applied to an article by industrial process) may be registered under the Registered Designs Act 1949 and this gives protection to the proprietor for a period of five years.

Section E: Remedies

The actions that can be brought and the remedies that may be granted by the courts in respect of the different types of capital are numerous and varied. In this Section, therefore, we will consider the most significant.

PRIVATE SECTOR CAPITAL FINANCE

Shareholders
Where the general meeting has voted to vary the rights attaching to a class of shares section 127 of the Companies Act 1985 provides that the holders of 15 per cent. of the issued shares of the class affected may apply to the court to have the variation cancelled. The court must consider whether the variation would *unfairly prejudice* the shareholders of the class in question and, if it is satisfied that it would, the court must disallow the variation. Otherwise, the variation must be confirmed.

For example, a resolution may be put to vary the preferential dividend to be paid to preference shareholders from ten per cent. to seven per cent. If 80 per cent. of the preference shareholders are also holders of ordinary shares, they are likely to vote in favour of the variation so that more profits will be available for their ordinary dividend. In that case they might not lose anything, but the variation would be unfair to the remaining 20 per cent. of the preference shareholders, whose reduction in preferential dividend would not be balanced by an increase in ordinary dividend. The 20 per cent. would, therefore, have grounds to apply to the court for cancellation of the variation.

Another example of statutory protection for shareholders is to be found in section 459 of the 1985 Act. Under this section any member (or group of members) may petition the court on the ground that the affairs of the company are being or have been conducted in a manner *unfairly prejudicial* to the interests of some part of the members (including himself). Under section 461 the court may make such order as it thinks fit for giving relief in respect of the matters complained of, including an order to:
(a)   regulate the conduct of the company's affairs in the future; or
(b)   provide for the purchase of the shares of any members by others or by the company itself.
The common law has also sought to protect the shareholder by imposing certain duties upon directors. These duties are in fact owed to the company and under the rule in *Foss* v. *Harbottle* it is the company which is the proper person to pursue any action against the director who is in breach of his duties. Where any such action is brought a director may (*inter*

alia) be liable in damages (where, for example, he has not exercised reasonable care in carrying out his duties) or may be liable to account (where, for example, he has made an undisclosed profit from his position as a director). However, such actions may not always be pursued since the day-to-day management of a company (including the bringing and defending of legal actions) lies in the hands of the board of directors. In such cases directors' breaches of duty might have proceeded unchecked had the courts not developed exceptions to the rule in *Foss* v. *Harbottle*. For example, where the directors (or indeed any group of controlling shareholders) attempt to expropriate the company's property, the courts will allow a "wronged" shareholder to bring a *derivative action* by which, whilst nominally suing on behalf of himself and all the members other than the wrongdoers, the plaintiff is really suing on behalf of the company. Should such action be successful, any remedy granted by the court would normally be issued to the company itself and not the individual shareholders.

As well as such civil remedies for breaches of directors' duties, criminal penalties (usually in the form of fines) may be imposed where directors fail to comply with any of the numerous and varied statutory duties imposed upon them.

Debenture holders

The protection afforded to debenture holders and other creditors, secured and unsecured, in the event of the liquidation of a company was outlined earlier. The law also provides protection for such outsiders whilst a company continues to trade. Thus the unsecured creditor may sue for repayment of his principal and any interest if these are overdue. If judgment is given in his favour but not satisfied, then he may levy execution on the debtor's goods. Alternatively, the creditor may petition the court for the compulsory winding up of the company on the ground that the company is unable to pay its debts.

The secured creditor has both of these courses of action available to him in the event of default by the company. In addition, he may exercise any rights conferred by the debenture, for example the right to appoint a receiver. This last step may have advantages over the other, since even the secured creditor may not recover fully in the event of the company's liquidation and it will be in his interests, therefore, to see that the company continues to trade. The function of the receiver will be to gather in the assets subject to the charge, to realise those assets and, as far as possible, to pay off the debenture holders out of the proceeds.

INDUSTRIAL PROPERTY

Patents

To prevent infringement of a patent, the proprietor may bring proceedings from which he may obtain the following remedies:
  (a) an injunction;
  (b) an order for the defendant to deliver up or destroy any infringing article;
  (c) damages;
  (d) an account of any profits made by the defendant;

(e)   a declaration of rights.

Thus, for example, if a person, without the proprietor's consent made and sold a patented product, the proprietor might seek an injunction to prevent future infringements and an account of the profits made so far by the defendant.

Copyright

The owner of a copyright may sue for:

(a)   damages;

(b)   an account of profits;

(c)   injunction.

He may also treat infringing copies as his own and claim delivery up of any others in the defendant's possession. A copyright continues to subsist in a work for 50 years after the year in which the author died.

A recent development in the field of industrial property has been the granting of an *ex parte* injunction (termed an *Anton Piller* order) requiring a defendant, alleged to be in breach of some property right of the plaintiff, to allow entry and inspection of his premises by the plaintiff's solicitor for the purpose of removing material infringing that property right. Such orders have proved to be particularly useful to film and record companies who have suffered "piracy" and "bootlegging" of materials for which they hold the copyright.

Goodwill

When a business is sold, it can be sold along with its goodwill. As part of the sale price, the vendor may receive a sum in consideration of this goodwill and may bind himself not to compete with the new owners. If there is no express agreement not to compete, common law provides that the vendor must not represent to the public that he is continuing the old business, but there is nothing to stop him carrying on a similar business in competition with the new owner. If he does carry on such a business, he may not solicit customers of the old business but may deal with those who come to him voluntarily.

Trade marks and designs

A trader may pursue an action for infringement of his registered trade mark or design and may be granted:

(a)   damages;

(b)   an account of profits;

(c)   an injunction.

He may also bring an action based on the tort of "passing-off," which is considered below (see page 379).

Part Four

COMMERCIAL AND INDUSTRIAL PREMISES

Commercial and industrial premises are purchased in exactly the same way as domestic premises. (See pages 199–205 for a consideration of the way in which land is purchased.) Once purchased it is subject to restrictions on use which are, again, largely the same as those which constrain a private occupier of land. These restrictions are, however, often much more significant to the commercial or industrial occupier for he may wish to undertake processes on the land which are likely to conflict with these restrictions. For this reason the purchaser of commercial or industrial premises is likely to be a regular visitor to the legal office.

Section A: Restrictions on the Use of Land

COMMON LAW AND EQUITABLE RESTRICTIONS

Easements
  The owner of adjoining land may have an *easement* over the land occupied by a commercial or industrial user. If so, such user, like the ordinary private user, may not interfere with the exercise of this right for to do so is actionable as a nuisance.
  Easements are particularly important to a consideration of property for they naturally increase the value of benefited land and diminish the value of land subjected to them. *Halsbury's Laws of England* has described an easement as "a right annexed to land to utilise other land of different ownership in a particular manner (not involving the taking of any part of the natural produce of that land or any part of its soil) or to prevent the owner of the other land from utilising his land in a particular manner." It will be readily appreciated from this description that easements may be either *positive* or *negative* in nature. By way of illustration:
  (a) positively framed easements afford a privilege, such as a right of way, over another's land;
  (b) negatively framed easements, such as a right to light, restrict another in his use of land. Thus a right to light involves a right to prevent another from interfering with the flow of light to windows on the benefited land.
  An easement binds the land over which it is exercised and, thus, may be enforced against successive owners of that land by successive owners of the land benefited by the easement. In *Re Ellenborough Park* the four essential qualities of an easement were identified:
  (a) there must be a dominant and a servient tenement;

341

(b)   an easement must accommodate the dominant tenement;
(c)   the dominant and servient owners must be different persons; and
(d)   the right claimed must be capable of forming the subject-matter of
      a grant.

Each of these characteristics demands explanation.

There must be a dominant and a servient tenement ... an easement cannot
exist *in gross* (*i.e.* independently of the ownership of land) and so if A grants
B a right to walk across A's land, B will not acquire an easement if he owns
no neighbouring land (though B will acquire a *licence* so that his use of A's
land will not constitute trespass). If, however, B owns land which will
benefit from the right of way then an easement will be created. The land
benefited (B's) is called the *dominant tenement*, the land subject to the
easement (A's) is called the *servient tenement*. In *Ackroyd* v. *Smith* a plaintiff's
predecessor in title had granted to an earlier owner of adjoining land a
right to use a road across his land. When this right was subsequently
claimed as an easement it was held to be a mere licence because the right
had been granted to the "owners and occupiers" of the adjoining land and
to "*all persons having occasion to resort thereto.*" This was interpreted as a
right in gross as "no one can have such a way but he who has the land to
which it is appendant."

Where an easement is "appurtenant" to a dominant tenement, it
becomes affixed to that land in just the same way as fixtures become
annexed to it. The result is that the easement passes on subsequent
conveyances or transfers of the land, and may be enjoyed by the occupier
for the time being of the dominant land, even if he is a mere lessee.

An easement must accommodate the dominant tenement ... which means, in
simple language, that the right must confer a benefit upon the dominant
tenement and not merely some purely personal advantage upon the
dominant owner. It is sufficient if the right claimed facilitates or benefits a
trade or business carried on within the dominant tenement so long as the
right makes the dominant tenement a better and more convenient
tenement. Thus a right to use a wall on a servient tenement for advertising
generally and not merely in connection with a business carried on upon the
dominant tenement could not be classed as an easement. But, in *Moody* v.
Steggles, a right to hang a signboard upon an adjoining house was held
claimable as an easement benefiting the public house advertised. There is,
however, no rule that the dominant and servient land must be contiguous,
but the servient land must at least be sufficiently close to the dominant
land for it to confer a practical benefit. It is not sufficient that the claimed
easement increases the market value of the benefited land for, as Lord
Evershed M.R. said in *Re Ellenborough Park*, there must be some "sufficient
nexus between the enjoyment of the right and the use of the dominant
tenement." Thus a grant to a purchaser of free right of entry to a zoo or a
cricket ground cannot, as a matter of law, run with the property as an
easement.

Re Ellenborough Park provides a relatively modern illustration of the
nicety of the judgment that must be made in assessing a claim. Here a
number of owners of residential properties had been given a right of
common enjoyment of a park which was enclosed by their houses. It was
held that the right granted, of "full enjoyment ... of the pleasure
ground," could properly constitute an easement although it was suggested
that mere "recreation and amusement" could not qualify. The court took

the view that use of the park for domestic purposes, such as "taking out small children in perambulators or otherwise," could not be fairly described as mere recreation or amusement and that the facility was clearly of benefit to the dominant properties. It may be assumed that a similar view would be taken of such a facility attached to, say, office accommodation. In contrast, in *Hill* v. *Tupper*, a "sole and exclusive" right to put boats on an adjacent canal was held not capable of existence as an easement. The right, it was considered, did not improve the dominant tenement as land but rather gave a personal advantage to the beneficiary of the right which he wished to exploit as a commercial venture. No doubt a right to cross and re-cross the canal by boat as a means of access would have been treated differently.

The dominant and servient owners must be different . . . an easement is a right *in alieno solo* (in the soil of another) and cannot, therefore, exist over one's own land. However, in order to render the existence of an easement impossible, the same person must not only *own* both tenements but must *occupy* both. For example, if the fee simple of both the dominant and servient tenements is vested in one person, then that unity of ownership will not be fatal to the creation of an easement should the plots be occupied by different lessees. Again, the occupation of both plots by the same tenant will not be fatal to the existence of an easement if the fee simple in each plot is owned by separate individuals, for the easement will merely be suspended during the currency of the lease and will revive on its termination.

The right claimed must be capable of forming the subject-matter of a grant . . . which means that it must be capable of being granted by deed. Such a requirement imposes conditions as to the kinds of right which can constitute easements and also upon the circumstances in which valid easements may be created. These may be considered under three heads.

(a) *There must be a capable grantor and a capable grantee.* Bodies constrained by their constitutions, such as statutory or other corporations, may be incapable of granting easements. Similarly, an alleged dominant owner may be legally incompetent to receive such a grant, as in the case of a fluctuating body of persons such as "the inhabitants for the time being" of a named village. It should be noted, however, that such bodies may claim similar rights through long standing custom.

(b) *The right must be sufficiently definite.* This requirement precludes an easement to a prospect or view, or indeed, to privacy. Similarly, there can be no easement to the uninterrupted access of light or air except through defined apertures in a building, although a greenhouse was in *Allen* v. *Greenwood* treated as "a building with apertures, namely the glass roof and sides." These limitations on the creation of easements may, however, be circumvented by the use of restrictive covenants (considered below) whereby, for example, the owner of neighbouring land may be precluded from building on land so as to obstruct a pleasant prospect.

(c) *The right must be within the general nature of rights recognised as easements.* It is usual to assert that the list of easements is not closed despite the fact that most easements fall within well-known categories, such as rights of way, light or support. Nevertheless, there are limits to the creation of novel easements and it appears unlikely that any new negative easements (*i.e.* beyond rights of light or air) preventing an owner from doing things on his servient land will be allowed. Thus, in *Phipps* v. *Pears* the Court of Appeal disallowed a claim to have the gable end of a property protected from weather by the continued presence of a neighbouring building. Lord Denning indicated that the court should be chary of creating new negative easements for they restrict a servient owner in the enjoyment of his own land and hamper legitimate development (in this case taking the form of demolition). It is not possible to identify with precision the general characteristics of allowable easements but certain observations may usefully be drawn from the case law. The claim to an easement must not amount to a claim to use and enjoyment of the servient land jointly with the servient owner. In *Copeland* v. *Greenhalf* the defendant wheelwright, who had for 50 years used a narrow strip of land belonging to the plaintiff for the purpose of storing vehicles awaiting and undergoing repair, claimed entitlement to an easement. The court rejected the claim as amounting virtually to a right of possession of the servient land. Similarly, in *Grigsby* v. *Melville* a claimed right of storage in a cellar was considered unacceptable where the claim amounted to "an exclusive right of user over the whole of the confined space representing the servient tenement." In contrast, in *Wright* v. *Macadam* the Court of Appeal accepted as an easement a tenant's claim to store coal in a shed provided by her landlord. Moreover, a claim to use of a neighbour's lavatory was accepted in *Miller* v. *Emcer Products Ltd.*, but perhaps the nature of possession was only fleetingly exclusive! Finally, it is unlikely that an easement will be admitted if it involves the servient tenant in the expenditure of money. There is one exception to this principle, the obligation to fence land in order to keep out cattle but even this has been described as a "spurious easement."

An easement can be acquired in the following ways:

(a) by express grant or reservation;

(b) by implied grant or reservation; and

(c) by presumed grant or prescription.

By express grant or reservation . . . to be a legal easement it must be created for an interest equivalent to an estate in fee simple absolute in possession or a term of years absolute and be made by deed. Thus an easement for life can only exist in equity. When a landowner sells part of his land and retains the rest he may *reserve* easements over the part sold and *grant* the purchaser easements over the part retained. The distinction is of significance in the case of ambiguity. In the case of a grant, ambiguity will be resolved in favour of the grantee and against the grantor. But in the case of a reservation any ambiguity is to be resolved in favour of the person who reserved the right albeit that it was doubtless he who created the ambiguity. The reason for this curious rule is that historically reservations were treated as a "regrant" of the easement by the purchaser of the servient tenement. By statute an easement will be created by express grant even though there is no mention of an easement in any deed. Section 62(1) of the Law of Property Act 1925 provides that any conveyance made after 1881 shall, subject to any contrary intention expressed in the conveyance, operate to convey with the land all privileges, easements, rights and advantages appertaining or reputed to appertain to the land or part of it. The effect is that should a landlord grant a tenant a mere licence, as in *Wright* v. *Macadam*, to use a coal shed for domestic purposes then a subsequent conveyance to the tenant will operate to grant him the right as an easement.

By implied grant or reservation . . . because a grantor must not derogate from his grant, the general rule is that a man who sells one plot of land and retains another must *expressly* reserve an easement for the benefit of the land retained, none will be implied. However, the law will imply an *easement of necessity* where the land *retained* is surrounded by the land sold so that there is no means of access to the land. It must be emphasised that implication will only be made so as to accommodate the circumstances existing at the time of the transaction. Thus in *London Corporation* v. *Riggs* the defendant retained a plot used for agriculture which was completely surrounded by land which he had sold to the corporation. It was held that an implied right of way was restricted to agricultural purposes and could not extend to use for the defendant's subsequently conceived plan for tea rooms on the retained land. The law will, however, imply an *intended easement* to give effect to the common intention of the parties; thus upon a sale of a terraced house, the courts will imply an easement of support in favour of an adjoining house which has been retained by the vendor. The law is more willing to imply an easement in favour of the grantee than in favour of the grantor and this may be demonstrated by the complexity of the implied easement in *Wong* v. *Beaumont Property Trust Ltd*. Here a landlord let his basement to a tenant who covenanted that he would carry on business as a restaurateur without creating any nuisance, and that he would control and eliminate all smells and odours in conformity with the health regulations. The tenant then sought to affix a ventilation duct to the outside wall of the landlord's premises. It was held that where a lease is granted which imposes a particular use on the tenant and it is impossible for the tenant to use the premises legally unless an easement is granted, the law will imply such an easement. The rule in *Wheeldon* v. *Burrows* provides a final principle of implication which is said to derive from the doctrine of non-derogation from grant. The rule confers upon the grantee of land the benefit of any user over land retained by the grantor which the grantor had found it convenient to exercise on his own behalf during the time when both the land granted and the land retained were in the common ownership of the grantor. Since the use by the grantor during the period of common ownership may not be recognised as an easement, such incidents of use are known as *quasi-easements*. In order to qualify as easements under this rule the quasi-easements must have been:

(a) continuous and apparent (which means of a constant nature and which are evidenced by some sign on the servient tenement such as a drainpipe from the eaves of a house);

(b) necessary to the reasonable enjoyment of the land (this is probably simply an alternative way of expressing the first requirement); and

(c) at the time of the grant, used by the grantor for the benefit of the part granted.

By presumed grant or prescription . . . long enjoyment of a right might give rise to a grant of an easement. In order to acquire such a right at common law it had to be shown that the right had been exercised *nec vi nec clam nec precario* (without force, without secrecy, without permission) since *time immemorial*, which is fixed at 1189. If it could be shown that the right had been exercised for 20 years there was a presumption that it had existed since 1189, although this presumption could be rebutted by evidence which showed that it had not existed since 1189. The common law also developed an alternative means of prescription by way of the doctrine of *Lost Modern Grant*. Under this doctrine, proof of exercise of a right for 20 years *might* lead the court to conclude that an easement had been granted in modern times but that it had been lost. If so, an easement would be recognised. This mode of prescription suffers from a great deal of uncertainty and, in any event, can only be invoked where common law prescription could not be applied. The Prescription Act 1832 provides a third method by which a prescriptive right may be established. Under this Act a prescriptive right to an easement other than one to light may be established by proof of use as of right for either 20 or 40 years without interruption and immediately preceding some action in which the existence of the easement is raised. (Whilst it may seem odd that the easement may be established by reference to *either* of two periods of time, one of which is longer than the other, the method of computing the two periods is different in that some years of user could count for one period and not for the other.) A claim to an easement of light may be established under the Act by proof of enjoyment of the light for 20 years without interruption and immediately preceding an action which questions the existence of the easement. This claim is easier to establish than those relating to other easements, one reason for this being that there is no need to show that the user was exercised *as of right* (though proof that written consent was provided for the user will defeat the claim).

An easement is extinguished when:
(a) the same person comes to own and possess both the dominant and servient tenements; *or*
(b) there is an express release of the right; *or*
(c) there is an implied release of the right by actions which show that the easement is being abandoned.

Profits à prendre

A profit à prendre is the right to take something from another's land which is part of the soil, part of the produce of the soil or a wild animal existing on it. Examples include the right to take gravel and the right to take fish. The most common profit is the right to pasture cattle on another's land.

Profits and easements are acquired and extinguished in similar ways. But, a profit may exist *in gross*, which means that the owner of the profit need not be the owner of any adjoining or neighbouring land or indeed any land at all. Again, interference with a profit à prendre is actionable as a nuisance.

Licences

Where a person has permission to use another's land in a way which does not constitute a lease, an easement, a profit or any other specific interest, he is said to have a *licence*. The extent to which a user is bound by a licence depends upon the nature of the licence. A licence may be:
(a) *bare* . . . in which case it may be revoked at any time;
(b) *coupled with an interest* . . . as where timber has been sold and the purchaser has to cut it, in which circumstances the licence cannot be revoked whilst the interest subsists;
(c) *for value* . . . as where a person purchases a ticket to a football game and acquires a licence to enter the ground. The licence is not coupled with an interest in the land but is irrevocable during the period that the parties must have intended it to be so (*e.g.* the

duration of the football game) unless the licensee acts in a manner inconsistent with the licence.

The categories of user which are capable of recognition as easements are, as has been seen, fairly limited. However, a licence may be used to permit the conduct of almost any kind of activity on the land of the licensor, for example, the holding of a "hippy festival." There is no requirement to link a licence with any ownership of land and a licence, unlike an easement, generates only contractual rights.

Covenants

In general terms covenants fall within the realm of the law of contract. A covenant is simply a contractual obligation undertaken in a deed. As a result it can be enforced between the original covenantor and the original covenantee. It is usually possible by assignment to transfer the *benefit*, though not the *burden*, to some third party. There is thus "privity of contract" between the original parties (or their personal representatives) and, if the benefit has been assigned, between the assignee and the original covenantor (or his personal representatives). However, land law has special rules which add to the law of contract as regards two classes of covenant: those between landlord and tenant and those between one landowner and another. Tenancies, the reversionary interests of landlords and land itself change hands so it is convenient that the benefits and burdens of covenants should normally change hands at the same time (or should, in legal terminology, run with the land). The extent to which covenants do run with the land is a matter of some complexity. If the covenant is purely personal to the parties then it is only enforceable through privity of contract but if it "touches and concerns" the land, the principles of land law may allow the covenant to become an enduring property interest. The position must be considered in turn, as regards:

(a) covenants between landlord and tenant; and
(b) covenants between landowners.

Covenants between landlord and tenant ... where they have reference to the subject matter of the lease ("touch and concern" the land) are normally either, expressly or impliedly, entered on behalf of the covenantor's successors as well as on his own behalf. When this is allied to basic contractual principles, the liability of the original covenantor (or his personal representatives) continues despite changing landlords or tenants. Thus the original tenant remains liable to the current landlord for breaches by any of his successors and the original landlord remains liable to the current tenant for any breaches by his successors. This follows upon contractual principles but land law adds the dimension of *privity of estate*. Under this doctrine the covenants are enforceable between the person who is *currently the tenant* and the person who is *currently the landlord*. This is likely to be a much more useful notion for as time passes the value of proceeding against the original covenantors may become slight as they die, perhaps become bankrupt, or simply move away. Privity of estate was developed through the common law, rather than in equity, and in consequence both the burden and benefit run with the land. It should be emphasised, however, that covenants which are not reasonably incidental to the relationship of landlord and tenant but which merely confer a personal advantage on a covenantee will not be subject to the principle of privity of estate. For example, covenants to pay rent, to repair a property, not to assign and the landlord's covenant for quiet enjoyment have all been held to touch and concern the land. In contrast, a covenant not to open a public house within half a mile of the demised public house, a covenant to pay the tenant a sum of money unless the lease was renewed and a covenant giving the tenant an option to purchase the reversion have all been held not to touch and concern the land.

Covenants between landowners . . . just as in the case of landlord and tenant covenants, are entered into, expressly or impliedly, on behalf of the covenantor's successors in title as well as on his own behalf. The principle of privity of contract produces a result which is precisely the same as in the situation of landlord and tenant covenants and the *original covenantor* remains liable despite changes in ownership. However, contract law does not make covenants directly enforceable as between the current owners of two pieces of land. The position under land law as between two landowners has been described by the Law Commission as complex and in some respects uncertain. In considering the law it is necessary to differentiate between the *benefit* and *burden* of a covenant and also to consider the position at common *law* and that in *equity*.

Under common law the *burden* of a covenant *does not* run with the land of the covenantor in any circumstances. But the benefit of all covenants entered into for the benefit of land belonging to the covenantee (*i.e.* excluding purely personal covenants) will run with the land enabling successors of the covenantee to enforce positive and negative covenants against the original covenantor. The common law does impose the additional requirement that if covenants were entered before 1926 then the enforcing covenantee must have acquired the same legal estate as the original covenantee. For this technical reason equitable assistance may still be significant (see later under *Tulk* v. *Moxhay*). The failure of the law to allow the burden of covenants to run with the land means that covenants requiring, for example, the erection of boundary walls, the keeping of premises in repair or contributions to the maintenance of roads cannot be enforced against successors of the original covenantor. An inability to ensure compliance with obligations of this nature may cause serious disadvantage in the case of, for example, a covenant by residents on a housing estate to contribute to the maintenance of common facilities. The passage of time will result in the current owners being unable to enforce the obligations against each other.

In equity complex rules have developed allowing the running of covenants but they only apply to *restrictive* covenants and not *positive* covenants. A restrictive covenant has the effect of preventing another from undertaking a certain course of action, for example, such a covenant may restrain another from building or carrying on a particular business on his own land. A positive covenant would require the taking of some action, for example, a covenant to keep a wall in repair. The law looks to the substance and not the form so that a covenant, for example, not to allow a wall to fall into disrepair although negatively expressed will be treated as positive because it requires action.

The equitable development stems from the case of *Tulk* v. *Moxhay* which decided that a covenant to maintain Leicester Square uncovered by any buildings could be enforced by an injunction against a purchaser who bought with notice of the covenant. In its developed form the doctrine of

Tulk v. *Moxhay* now provides that the *burden* of a covenant will run with land provided:

(a) the covenant is restrictive in nature;

(b) the covenant was intended to run with land belonging to the covenantor;

(c) the covenant was entered into for the benefit of land belonging to the covenantee (this seems to be readily established where the restriction adds to the value of the land, as in *Newton Abbott Co-operative Society Ltd.* v. *Williamson and Treadgold Ltd.* where a covenant imposed by the vendor prohibiting dealing in articles of ironmongery in the property sold was clearly of value to a retained ironmonger's shop); and

(d) the person against whom enforcement is sought is not a bona fide purchaser of a legal estate without notice of the covenant (if the burdened land is registered land, the covenant will be void against a purchaser unless *registered* and if the land is unregistered, covenants created after 1925 must also be registered).

Thus, *Tulk* v. *Moxhay* turns a restrictive covenant into an equitable interest in land which those with an interest in the benefited land may enforce by equitable remedies against anyone with an interest in the burdened land.

The doctrine of *Tulk* v. *Moxhay* also, although in a less certain way, extends to the running of the *benefit* of a restrictive covenant. In essence the benefit of a restrictive covenant will run with the benefited land in equity if two requirements are satisfied. The first is that the covenant must touch and concern the land of the covenantee. The second is that at least one of the following is established by the current owner of the benefited land:

(a) that the benefit of the covenant has been "annexed" to the benefited land, which means that it must have been clearly attached or linked to the benefited land;

(b) that the benefit of the covenant has been expressly assigned along with the benefited land;

(c) that the benefit of the covenant has been passed to the current owner under a "building scheme" (a planned development of land under which it is divided into separate plots the purchasers of which have a "community of interest and reciprocity of obligation"—it could, for example, involve restrictions on planting so as to achieve an "open-plan" housing estate).

The major deficiency which can now be seen to exist is that the burden of a positive covenant entered into between nearby landowners does not in any circumstances run with the land of the covenantor. Thus the position as between landowners differs sharply from that existing between a landlord and tenant. In the latter case, of course, the doctrine of privity of estate enables the burden to run automatically with property let.

The discharge of restrictive covenants . . . is provided for under section 84(1) of the Law of Property Act 1925 for it is commonly accepted that it may be undesirable for an inhibition on land use to continue indefinitely. The Act confers a discretionary power on the Lands Tribunal to discharge or modify any restrictive covenant (with or without compensation) on a number of grounds. These include cases where:

(a) by reason of changes in the character of the property concerned or the neighbourhood or otherwise, the restriction is deemed "obsolete";

(b) the continued existence of the restriction would impede some reasonable user of the land for public or private purposes;

(c) the persons entitled to the benefit of the restriction have agreed expressly or by implication to its discharge or modification; and

(d) the proposed discharge or modification will not injure the persons entitled to the benefit of the restriction.

The discretionary power extends to freehold land, and to leasehold land where the lease was made for more than 40 years and at least 25 years have expired.

The law of torts: nuisance

The occupier of land must not commit a *nuisance*. In *Cunard* v. *Antifyre*, a *private nuisance* was defined as "an unreasonable interference for a substantial length of time, by an owner or occupier of property, with the use or enjoyment of neighbouring property." All occupiers of land are likely to annoy their neighbours at some time by the use they make of their land. But not all annoyances will, however, amount to a nuisance. When determining whether a nuisance is committed, the courts will take into account:

(a) the area in which the alleged nuisance takes place;

(b) the frequency of the disturbance;

(c) the motive of the person who is committing the alleged nuisance; and

(d) any undue sensitivity on the part of the complainant.

The area . . . activities which might be regarded as unreasonable in one area may not be so regarded in another. A commercial or industrial organisation located in a rundown inner-city or docks area may, for example, be free to use noisy machinery 24 hours a day, or take (or make) deliveries of consignments carried by heavy lorries late at night or early in the morning. Such activity might, however, be totally unacceptable if undertaken in close proximity to an area previously noted for its peace and tranquillity. In *Sturges* v. *Bridgman* Lord Justice Thesiger asserted that "what would be a nuisance in Belgrave Square would not necessarily be so in Bermondsey" and, in so doing, indicated that the courts are likely to protect the expectations of the inhabitants of a particular area. Those who choose to live close to a vast industrial complex may well expect to experience discomfort as a result of smells or noise. (If they do not they will probably find that they have no redress, for the courts will protect only infringements of reasonable expectations.) If, on the other hand, a person elects to pay a high price for a house on an "exclusive" estate, on the basis that he will, thereby, provide himself and his family with a better life-style, an organisation which carries out its activities in such a way as to frustrate his ambition may find that the expectations of the residents of the estate are advanced by the courts.

In *St. Helen's Smelting Company* v. *Tipping*, the court drew a distinction between nuisances which:

(a) produce "sensible personal discomfort"; and

(b) produce "material injury to the property."

In the case of the former, it was asserted, the area in which the alleged nuisance occurs is relevant; in the case of the latter it is not. The court thus disregarded the nature of the area when the plaintiff complained that fumes from a copper smelting company damaged shrubs and trees on an adjoining estate.

An organisation will not be able to resist the plaintiff's claim by pointing to the fact that it was operating in an area prior to the arrival of the plaintiff. Thus, in *Bliss* v. *Hall*, an organisation which used its premises so as to emit "divers noisome, noxious and offensive vapours, fumes, smells and stenches" was not permitted to defend itself on the basis that it had been carrying out its activities for a period of three years before the plaintiff's arrival in the area. Nor will an organisation be able to defend itself by establishing the value of its activities to others (see *Adams* v. *Ursell, Unit Two, Part Two*, page 184).

The frequency of the disturbance . . . generally an interference with another's use and enjoyment of his land will only constitute a nuisance if it continues for a "substantial length of time." Thus, an isolated interference with the use of neighbouring property will not normally amount to a nuisance. There is, however, no absolute rule that the plaintiff cannot succeed merely because the act which offends him is isolated. A nuisance is committed when an occupier uses his land in an unreasonable way and the frequency of the disturbance to others is, in effect, merely evidence of the reasonableness or otherwise of the use of the land.

The motive of the occupier . . . most people, acting in a spirit of "give and take," are reconciled to the fact that they must ignore occasional interferences with the use and enjoyment of their land and expect that others will, in turn, overlook their transgressions. This approach is recognised by the courts, who are not prepared to accept as a nuisance an activity which is, in effect, a mere irritant. Where, however, there is no spirit of "give and take" and irritating activity is carried out to deliberately annoy a neighbour, the *malice* of the occupier will transform conduct which would not otherwise amount to a nuisance into such (see *Christie* v. *Davey, Unit Two, Part Two*, page 183). Thus, if an organisation deliberately made life unpleasant for its neighbours (hoping, perhaps, to encourage them to sell their land) the bad faith of the organisation would be a factor which the courts would take into consideration.

Undue sensitivity . . . if the complainant irritated is abnormally sensitive, or is particularly vulnerable to loss, he will only be able to establish a nuisance if he can show that the activity in question would amount to a nuisance to another who does not share his sensitivity or vulnerability. Thus, in *Robinson* v. *Kilvert* a manufacturer of paper boxes who, as part of his manufacturing process, heated the cellar of a building, was not liable to the occupier of another floor of the building who discovered that the warm air damaged particularly sensitive brown paper stored in his premises.

Remedies and defences . . . if a commercial or industrial user is found to be committing a nuisance he will be liable in *damages* to the neighbouring occupiers who suffer loss as a result and an *injunction* may be awarded to prevent a continuation of the nuisance. He will, however, have a defence to the action if he can establish:

(a) that the conduct complained of is authorised by statute; or
(b) that the nuisance has been committed for a continuous period of 20 years and that for the whole of that time period the nuisance was known to exist; or

(c)   that the nuisance was due to an unobservable act of nature; or
(d)   that the nuisance resulted from the act of a stranger of which the organisation was unaware; or
(e)   that the complainant consented to the activity.

[See *Unit Two, Part Two*, page 184 for further details.]

Public nuisance . . . a commercial or industrial user must also refrain from committing a *public nuisance*. In *Attorney-General* v. *P.Y.A. Quarries Ltd.* it was said that "any nuisance is 'public' which materially affects the reasonable comfort and convenience of life of a class of Her Majesty's subjects." An activity will, then, only constitute a *public* nuisance if a *class* of persons is affected (*i.e.* such a large group that it would not be reasonable to expect any one person to bring proceedings). Examples of a public nuisance include obstructing the public highway and emitting noxious fumes from a building. A public nuisance is a *crime* and, as such, may result in the imposition of criminal sanctions (*e.g.* a fine). It is only actionable as a civil offence if the plaintiff can establish that he has suffered loss over and above that to which others are subject.

The law of torts: Rylands v. Fletcher

We have seen that some activities may not be carried out on land because they constitute a nuisance. There are other activities which are permitted but which are undertaken at the occupier's risk.

In *Rylands* v. *Fletcher*, an occupier of land engaged the services of an independent contractor to construct a reservoir upon his land. As a result of the negligence of the contractor water from the reservoir flowed into a disused mine-shaft and flooded the plaintiff's coal mine. Even though the occupier had not himself been negligent and was not liable for the actions of the contractor (see page 320) he was found to be liable to the plaintiff. The House of Lords held that a person who brings onto his land something which is not naturally there and which is "likely to do mischief" if it escapes, keeps it at his peril and is "answerable for all the damage which is the natural consequence of its escape."

The decision in this case created a new tort, known as the rule in *Rylands* v. *Fletcher*, which does not depend upon the occupier of land being at fault. If the constituent parts of the rule are satisfied the occupier is liable even though he has not been negligent; such liability is known as *strict liability*.

The constituent parts of the rule are:
(a)   the requirement that the occupier must have brought onto his land something which is not naturally there;
(b)   the requirement that the thing brought onto the land must be "likely to do mischief" if it escapes; and
(c)   the requirement that the thing should escape from the occupier's land onto the land of another.

Non-natural use of land . . . the House of Lords indicated, in *Rylands* v. *Fletcher*, that the rule should only apply where the thing which had been brought onto the land was not naturally there. It is clear that the court intended that an occupier should be liable under the rule where the thing brought onto the land was not of a type which could have been there by act of nature. Water, for example, is naturally found on land, but vast quantities of water stored in a reservoir are not.

The courts constantly modify the common law so as to keep its principles abreast of social and economic development; a very good example of this is the way in which the courts have, over the years, modified the meaning of "non-natural." In *Rickards* v. *Lothian* the court held that it was "an ordinary and reasonable use of such premises" to maintain a water cistern in a block of flats. Obviously such a use is reasonable, but is it natural?—only if "natural use" is equated with "ordinary use" or "that which is to be expected." Such a meaning is quite different to the meaning which originally attached to the phrase. The extent of this change in meaning is emphasised by the view, expressed by the House of Lords in *Read* v. *Lyons*, that the making of munitions is, in war-time, a natural use of land.

There is, today, still a requirement that the occupier must be making a non-natural use of land if he is to be liable in *Rylands* v. *Fletcher*. An organisation will, however, only be making a non-natural use of land if it is making some extraordinary use of land (*i.e.* a use which would not be an "ordinary" use, even in our modern industrialised society). The courts could, by a willingness to accept uses as "natural," virtually eliminate liability under the rule in *Rylands* v. *Fletcher*. No doubt a finding that a use made of land is "natural" or "non-natural" will reflect the court's view as to the desirability of imposing liability in a particular case. A court which wished to impose liability upon an occupier under the rule in *Rylands* v. *Fletcher* would need to find that the use made of the land was "non-natural," whilst a court which did not wish to impose liability could achieve that result merely by finding the use to be a "natural" one.

Things likely to cause damage if they escape . . . there is liability under the rule in *Rylands* v. *Fletcher* only if the thing brought onto the occupier's land is "likely to do mischief if it escapes." Whilst most things which are brought onto land *could* cause damage if they escape onto another's land, it would appear (bearing in mind that liability under this rule is strict) that the courts will only impose liability where the thing brought onto the land was, by its very nature, *likely* to cause damage should it escape.

There must be an escape . . . if there is no escape from the occupier's land there can be no liability under the rule in *Rylands* v. *Fletcher*. In *Read* v. *Lyons* a factory inspector was injured by an explosion at a munitions factory which she was visiting. She was not able to recover damages to compensate her for her injuries, for there had been no escape from the occupier's premises.

Defences to an action in Rylands v. Fletcher . . . although liability under the rule in *Rylands* v. *Fletcher* is strict, it is not absolute. The plaintiff does not need to show that the defendant was at fault, but he will not be able to maintain his action where:

(a) the thing was brought onto the occupier's premises with the plaintiff's consent; or
(b) the escape was due to an *act of God*; or
(c) the escape was due to the *act of a stranger*. Thus, there was, in *Rickards* v. *Lothian*, no liability for an overflow of water which had resulted from the intentional act of some unknown third party.

STATUTORY RESTRICTIONS

In the last 40 years or so a comprehensive framework of statutory provisions has emerged which restricts commercial and industrial users not only in relation to the *manner* in which they carry out their activities, but also as to whether or not they *may* carry out these activities. This framework must be seen as a real restraint upon the activities and policy options of such organisations and, hopefully, as an incentive to carry out their affairs in such a way as to promote a better environment for the society in which they function.

Town and country planning

The Town and Country Planning Act 1947 dramatically affected the right of an organisation (or an individual) to use its land as it pleases. Since that time, indeed, it has been inaccurate to refer to the landowner as having any *right* other than the right to use the land for its present purpose.

The Act currently in force is the Town and Country Planning Act 1971 (as amended). Under this Act, any organisation which wishes to undertake *development* of its land must first obtain *planning permission*. It will, for the purposes of the Act, wish to *develop* its land if it seeks to:

(a) carry out *building operations, engineering operations, mining operations* or other operations upon its land; or

(b) make a *material change in the use of the land* or of any building upon the land; or

(c) *display advertisements* on any external part of a building not normally used for that purpose; or

(d) *deposit refuse or waste materials* on an existing dump so as to extend the area of the dump or increase its height above the level of adjoining land.

In some circumstances even though an activity may prima facie amount to development the General Development Order 1977 as amended provides that it is to be "permitted development" rendering it unnecessary to apply for planning permission. Moreover, under the Use Classes Order 1972 certain *changes of use* are deemed *not* to amount to development. For example, a change of use of a building from a "general industrial building" to use as a "light industrial building," although it is prima facie a material change of use requiring planning permission, is exempted from control by the Order. Appeal against refusal of planning permission lies to the Secretary of State for the Environment who will commonly arrange for determination of the appeal following the holding of a public local inquiry. These inquiries are similar in form to those discussed (at page 210) in relation to compulsory purchase orders but decisions are, today, normally taken by inspectors acting in the name of the Secretary of State.

Although the Town and Country Planning Act is principally concerned with "securing consistency and continuity in the framing and execution of a national policy with respect to the use and development of land," it also deals with further matters of environmental significance lying outside the concept of "development." Thus, it provides for the making of *tree preservation orders* which may secure the preservation of trees, groups of trees or woodlands where this is *in the interests of amenity*. When in force a tree preservation order will prohibit the cutting down, topping or lopping of trees except with the consent of the local planning authority. Similarly *buildings* of special architectural or historic interest may be protected by being formally "listed" whereupon it becomes a criminal offence to "demolish, alter or extend so as to affect the character of a building as a building of special architectural or historic interest."

The restrictive impact of planning on commercial and industrial activity has, in recent times, been viewed with concern by government. In consequence, more relaxed planning regimes have been introduced, for example, in "enterprise zones" and more flexibility is promised.

Statutory nuisances

Some activities have, by statute, been made nuisances. The Public Health Act 1936 (as amended by the Local Government (Miscellaneous Provisions) Act 1982), for example, identifies as a nuisance "any dust or effluvia caused by any trade, business, manufacture or process, being prejudicial to the health of, or a nuisance to the inhabitants of the neighbourhood." If such a nuisance is reported to a local authority by any person who is suffering from it the authority has a statutory duty to eradicate it. The Clean Air Acts 1956–68 provide that the emission of dark smoke from a building is an offence, even though it may not be a nuisance. Where it is a nuisance, it is deemed to be a statutory nuisance for the purposes of the 1936 Act.

Pollution

The Control of Pollution Act 1974 provides that an organisation which deposits poisonous, noxious or polluting waste on land (other than a designated site) so as to create an environmental hazard commits a criminal offence and is also civilly liable for any damage so caused.

Section B: Restrictions Relating to the Safety of the Land

One major restriction on the use which may be made of land results from common law and statutory provisions which impose liability on the occupier or owner of land for injury resulting to others as a result of his land being unsafe. The significance of this potential liability is such that it is appropriate to consider it separately from other restrictions on use.

LIABILITY TO LAWFUL VISITORS

The Occupiers' Liability Act 1957 provides that an occupier of land owes a *common duty of care* to all his lawful visitors.

Duty is imposed upon the occupier

The Act imposes a duty of care upon the occupier, not the owner, of land. In *Wheat* v. *Lacon and Co.*, Lord Denning asserted that a person was an occupier of premises if he "had a sufficient degree of control over premises to put him under a duty of care towards those who came lawfully onto the premises." The test is, then, one of control rather than ownership. He who controls the premises is responsible for the safety of visitors to them. An organisation will, therefore, not be responsible to those who are injured on premises merely because it owns them. Similarly, it will not be immune from liability merely because it does not own the premises it occupies.

Duty is owed to lawful visitors

The duty of care imposed by the 1957 Act extends only to lawful visitors.

It does not extend to trespassers. A person will be within the duty of care, when:

(a) he has been expressly invited onto the premises;
(b) he has implied permission to enter the premises (*e.g.* a postman or refuse collector);
(c) he enters the premises in furtherance of a contract made with the occupier (*e.g.* a driver delivering goods which have been purchased by the organisation);
(d) he enters the premises pursuant to a contract made between the occupier and someone else (*e.g.* where the organisation contracts with a building contractor that sub-contractors may enter its premises).

Whilst a person who is a trespasser will not be within the common duty of care, he may, nevertheless, be within a duty of care arising independently of the 1957 Act (see page 357).

The common duty of care

Section 2(2) of the 1957 Act provides that the common duty of care is, "a duty to take such care as in all the circumstances of the case is reasonable to see that the visitor is reasonably safe in using the premises for the purposes for which he is invited or permitted to be there." The standard of care expected will vary according to the visitor. The occupier of a factory would, for example, be expected to exercise greater care when visited by a party of school-children than when visited by a factory inspector. In any event, the duty imposed is one which requires only that the occupier exercises *reasonable* care. The organisation will not be liable to a visitor who is injured on its premises if it has done all that it reasonably could to prevent such injury. Thus, if the organisation has entrusted repairs to an independent contractor (*e.g.* a joiner or an electrician not employed by the organisation) it will not be liable to a visitor injured as a result of faulty work by the contractor if:

(a) it was reasonable to entrust the work to a contractor;
(b) reasonable steps were taken to ensure that the contractor was competent; and, where appropriate,
(c) reasonable steps were taken to check that the repairs had been properly undertaken.

[The common duty of care extends to damage to property (*e.g.* cars) as well as to personal injuries to visitors.]

Warnings and exclusion of liability

In some situations an organisation may discharge its duty of care simply by warning the visitor of dangers. Thus, if an adult visitor to an office block is informed that the lifts are in a dangerous condition and should not be used, the organisation occupying the block may not be liable to the visitor if he ignores the warning and is injured. The organisation may, in this situation, have done all that is reasonably necessary to protect the visitor. The Act provides, however, that a warning will not prevent an occupier being liable if the warning is not, in all the circumstances, sufficient to enable the visitor to be reasonably safe. Thus a notice attached to the lift door would not protect the occupier if an injured user of the lift was a blind visitor who had not been aware of the warning on the notice. Similarly, notices containing warnings may not be sufficient to ensure the safety of child visitors and may not, therefore, protect the occupier from liability.

Sometimes an occupier may not attempt to *discharge* his duty of care by a warning, he may, instead, attempt to *exclude* his liability by a notice or by a term in a contract with the visitor. Section 2(1) of the 1957 Act provides that a common duty of care is owed to all lawful visitors "except in so far as he [the occupier] is free to and does extend, restrict, modify or exclude his duty to any visitor or visitors by agreement or otherwise." It should be noted that this sub-section does not provide that an occupier will always be free to exclude his liability, it provides only that an exclusion of liability will protect the occupier "in so far as he is free" to rely upon such an exclusion. Sometimes an "exclusion" of liability will be ineffective. Section 2(1) of the Unfair Contract Terms Act 1977 provides that "a person cannot by reference to any contract term or to a notice given to persons generally or to particular persons exclude or restrict his liability for *death or personal injury* resulting from negligence." An occupier is, as a result of this provision, not free to exclude liability for death or personal injury and any such term or notice will not protect him should he be sued by a lawful visitor. (Note, however, that a warning given to a visitor, perhaps by a notice, may *discharge* the occupier's duty—see above—and result in there being *no* negligence. In this case the occupier will not be liable for death or personal injury to the visitor.) The 1977 Act further provides, in section 2(2), that in respect of other loss or damage (*e.g.* damage to a visitor's car) an exclusion of liability will only be valid if it is reasonable to permit such exclusion. An occupier is, therefore, not free to exclude his liability for such loss or damage by an unreasonable exclusion clause and, as a result, will be liable to a visitor despite the attempted exclusion.

Defences available to the occupier

As liability arising from the Occupiers' Liability Act 1957 is, in essence, liability in Negligence, the defences available to the occupier are the same as those available to a defendant in a Negligence action, namely:

(a) contributory negligence; and
(b) *volenti non fit injuria.*

LIABILITY TO TRESPASSERS

The common duty of care imposed by the Occupiers' Liability Act 1957 does not extend to trespassers. After 1957, however, the common law developed so as to impose a more limited duty in relation to trespassers, which duty is now to be found in the Occupiers' Liability Act 1984.

Who is a trespasser?

Anyone who is not a lawful visitor (see page 355) is a trespasser and as such may be removed by use of reasonable force provided he has been asked to leave and has refused to do so. He may be sued if he has damaged the land and an injunction may be awarded to prevent further trespasses. A trespasser was defined, in *Addie & Sons* v. *Dumbreck*, as someone "who goes on the land without invitation of any sort and whose presence is either unknown to the proprietor or, if known, is practically objected to." A visitor may have been invited onto some part of the occupier's land but he will become a trespasser if he enters other parts to which he has not been invited (*e.g.* through a door marked "private" or "staff only"). Similarly, a visitor who has been permitted to enter premises for a specific purpose will become a trespasser if he then begins to act in a manner inconsistent with the occupier's express or implied invitation to enter the land. Thus, the football spectator (a lawful visitor, within the common duty of care) who begins to fight on the terraces becomes, by this act, a trespasser. So does the political agitator who attempts to conduct a demonstration in a shop or restaurant he has entered as a potential customer or patron.

What duty does the occupier owe to trespassers?

Until fairly recent times it was thought that an occupier of land owed only two duties to a trespasser:
  (a)   a duty not to deliberately injure a trespasser (by, for example, the use of spring guns or other traps); and
  (b)   a duty not to act with reckless disregard for the safety of trespassers.
These duties merged into a new duty, recognised in *British Railways Board* v. *Herrington* (1972), a duty *to act with humanity*.

In *Herrington*, the British Railways Board was held to be liable in damages to a child trespasser who had been electrocuted by a live rail. The boy, aged six, had entered the Board's land through a hole in the perimeter fence as, apparently, had other children in the area. Evidence showed that:
  (a)   the fence had been broken, leaving the gap through which the child had entered, for some time;
  (b)   employees of the British Railways Board had, two months before the accident, reported the fact that children were trespassing on the line; and
  (c)   the Board had not acted in response to the report.
When delivering his judgment Lord Reid asserted that an occupier must act in a humane manner in relation to trespassers but that his ability to act humanely will vary according to:
  (a)   his knowledge;
  (b)   his ability; and
  (c)   his resources.
The British Railways Board knew of the danger to child trespassers and, bearing in mind the resources available to the Board, it had not acted as it should have done. As a result it was liable.

Because of the reference to the resources of the occupier the old idea that "a trespasser must take the land as he finds it" gave way to a notion that "he must take the occupier as he finds him." This made organisations with considerable resources particularly vulnerable. Because of the resources at their disposal, that which could reasonably be expected of them might be greater than that which might be expected of other, poorer, occupiers.

The common law duty to act humanely was a less demanding duty than the statutory common duty of care. The common law required that an occupier should not ignore an obvious danger to trespassers, it required little more. Lord Diplock, when delivering his judgment in *Herrington*, distinguished between the duty owed by an occupier of land to a trespasser and the common duty of care owed to a lawful visitor. He emphasised that the duty of humanity, unlike the common duty of care:

(i)   did not arise until the occupier was aware of the presence of the trespasser on his land, or the likelihood of his presence, *and* of the state of affairs which endangered the trespasser. (The occupier was under no duty to inspect his premises to see if they were dangerous to trespassers, he was liable only when he knew of the danger and ignored it.)

(ii) only involved a duty to take reasonable steps to enable the trespasser to avoid the danger.

The framework established by *Herrington* has, in effect, been adopted by statute. The Occupiers' Liability Act 1984, which imposes a duty on occupiers to persons other than their lawful visitors provides, as did *Herrington*, that this duty arises only where:

(a)   the occupier is aware of the danger to trespassers or ought to be aware of the danger;

(b)   the occupier is aware of the presence of the trespasser or is aware that the trespasser may enter his premises;

(c)   it is reasonable, taking into account the type of risk involved, to expect that some protection should be extended to the trespasser.

Where the statutory duty to trespassers exists it involves taking whatever steps are necessary to ensure that the trespasser is not injured by reason of the danger of which the occupier is aware. This duty may involve no more than the giving of warnings.

The duty to trespassers remains a more limited duty than that which extends to lawful visitors. It relates only to *known dangers* and extends only to *known visitors* and to *personal* injury.

LIABILITY FOR NON-REPAIR OF PREMISES

Section 4 of the Defective Premises Act 1972 provides that where premises are let under a tenancy which places upon the landlord an obligation to the tenant for maintenance or repair of the premises (see page 205), the landlord owes a duty of care to anyone who might reasonably be affected by defects in the state of the premises. The duty is expressed to be one which involves taking such care as is reasonable in all the circumstances to see that persons within the duty are reasonably safe from *personal injury* or from *damage to their property* caused by a relevant defect.

A *relevant* defect is a defect in the state of the premises which arises from or continues because of an act or omission of the landlord which constitutes a breach of his obligation to repair. The duty arises only if the landlord knew of the defect or ought reasonably to have known of it.

LIABILITY FOR HEALTH AND SAFETY

The commercial or industrial user as an occupier of land and an employer of labour, owes a duty to his workforce to take care for their safety. This duty is based upon the employer's common law duty of care and upon various statutes, in particular the Health and Safety at Work Act 1974. Under this Act a commercial or industrial user owes duties not only to his employees, but also to others who may be affected by the way he conducts his undertaking. He must ensure, so far as is reasonably practicable, that persons not in his employment are not exposed to risks to their health or safety. (Indeed, he may, in certain circumstances, be under a duty to give such persons information about those aspects of the way in which he conducts his undertaking as might affect their health and safety. This provision would, for example, give those who live next to a chemical factory the right to be informed of hazards emanating from that factory. Moreover, under the 1974 Act an organisation, as the controller of premises, must use the best practicable means for preventing the emission into the atmosphere from those premises of noxious or offensive substances, and for rendering harmless and inoffensive such substances as may be emitted.)

It should be noted that the organisation's liability to its employees (and others) under the Health and Safety at Work Act 1974 is criminal and not civil.

Section C: Business Tenancies

Security of tenure

Part II of the Landlord and Tenant Act 1954 applies to tenancies where the premises are occupied by the tenant for the purposes of any trade, profession, or employment. The commercial or industrial tenant is given security of tenure by section 24 of the Act which provides that the tenancy shall not come to an end unless terminated in accordance with the Act. To terminate under these provisions, the landlord must give notice (of 6–12 months) in the statutory form whereupon the tenant may, if he wishes, serve notice that he does not wish to give up possession of the premises and apply to the court for a new tenancy (section 29). A tenant on a fixed term (which will terminate by expiration of time) may serve on the landlord a statutory request for a new tenancy to begin within 6–12 months. The new lease will be granted by the court unless the landlord can establish one of seven statutory grounds for opposing the application. These grounds are:

(a)   that the tenant has obligations to repair under the current tenancy and has failed to perform them;

(b)   that the tenant has persistently delayed in paying rent;

(c)   that the tenant has committed other substantial breaches of his obligations under the lease;

(d)   that the landlord has offered alternative accommodation for the tenant on reasonable terms;

(e)   that the premises are only a part of larger premises and the landlord, who intends to dispose of the premises as a whole, could obtain a much higher rent for on a letting of the whole premises;

(f)   that the landlord intends to demolish or reconstruct the premises or a substantial part of them and could not reasonably do so without obtaining possession of the holding;

(g)   that the landlord intends to occupy the holding for the purposes of a business to be carried on by him there or at his residence.

The court will either dismiss the tenant's application or make an order for a new tenancy. If a lease is granted it may be for any period up to 14 years (though further renewals are possible) and at a rent which reflects market rent. If a renewal of the tenancy is refused on one of grounds (e) to (g) above, the tenant will receive compensation from the landlord.

The basic principle underlying Part II of the 1954 Act is that a business tenant will be presumed to have a right to continue his business indefinitely on the premises.

Compensation for improvements

The Landlord and Tenant Act 1927 provides that where a business tenant has improved the land he has been occupying in such a way as to increase its letting value he may, in certain circumstances, receive compensation from the landlord for the improvements effected. Compensation will not be awarded unless the tenant had, prior to effecting the improvements, given the landlord notice of his intention to carry out the work. The compensation awarded cannot exceed:

(a) the net increase in value to the land; or

(b) the reasonable cost of effecting the improvements (at the time of the termination of the tenancy) minus any reasonable expense which the landlord must incur in repairing the work effected by the tenant.

Trade fixtures

Normally, upon termination of a lease any items which have become *fixtures* belong to the landlord. (A fixture is an item which has become so affixed to the land that it has, in law, become incorporated into it, for example panelling on an office wall.) A commercial or industrial tenant may, however, remove *trade fixtures* (*i.e.* fixtures which were affixed to the premises for the purposes of the tenant's trade or business). It has, for example, been held that a tenant could, upon termination of a lease of land which he had used as a garage, remove petrol pumps which he had installed.

Part Five

TRADING TRANSACTIONS

Section A: Consumer Protection

As a basic proposition it may be fairly stated that agreements entered into by those in commerce or industry are governed by the same contractual principles as those which govern any other contractual undertaking. For this reason when, in *Unit Two*, consideration was given to the individual in dispute no attempt was made to rigidly separate private and business agreements. However, from the earliest times a distinct body of law developed to govern that most common of all transactions, the contract for the sale of goods, and much of this is specifically referable to trading or business transactions. This area demands special attention as one of the original forms of consumer protection. In addition, however, the rise of consumerism has spawned an almost bewildering series of measures which operate as genuine constraints upon traders who, for example, may otherwise be tempted to use their economic strength to the disadvantage of consumers. These measures have also been selected for consideration in the context of trading transactions for it will frequently be the case that traders will require advice if they are not to transgress through inadvertence.

IMPLIED TERMS

Sale of Goods Act

The 1979 Act indicates a sale of goods contract to be a contract under which the seller transfers ownership in goods to the buyer for a money consideration, called the price. Thus, the buyer's obligation is, basically, to pay for the goods, but the seller's obligations are more extensive. The old common law maxim of *caveat emptor* ("let the buyer beware"), which required buyers to exercise great care and stipulate precisely what they bargained for, has been greatly modified. Today the *implied obligations* of the seller almost warrant the maxim *caveat venditor* ("let the seller beware"). Of course, the buyer must pay a price which reflects the obligations of the seller, When sellers fix prices they take account of the potential liability which each sale represents (in the form of buyers' potential claims) and, although many buyers may be delighted by statutory protection of their bargain, they may not realise the hidden price which they pay in return.

Both express contractual undertakings and implied undertakings may take the form of either *conditions* or *warranties*. Conditions, as previously indicated, are terms going to the very root of the contract, breach of which entitles the innocent party to repudiate the contract and claim damages. In

362

the case of a seller of goods falling into breach of a condition of a contract, the buyer will be entitled to return the goods, demand his money back and claim damages for any loss that he has suffered. Warranties are terms of less significance than conditions, the breach of which merely entitles the innocent party to damages. Thus, in the case of a sale of goods contract in respect of which the seller is in breach of warranty, a buyer will be obliged to keep the goods supplied and recover money compensation.

Although the classification of terms of a contract into conditions and warranties is essentially a question of the intention of the parties to a contract, as regards the important implied undertakings of the seller in a sale of goods contract, the legislature has intervened. The most significant of the statutorily implied undertakings of the seller are all conditions and, as such, give the buyer a right to repudiation and/or damages in the event of breach.

Section 13 of the 1979 Act provides that a seller undertakes, as a condition of his contract, that where he sells goods by description, the goods actually correspond with that description. Thus, should a seller describe goods as a "1984 Ford Escort," then any deviation from this description (as in the case of a car made up of parts of two cars, welded together, one being of an earlier origin) will entitle the buyer to treat the contract as repudiated for breach of condition, without any argument as to whether the seller's undertaking is a condition or a warranty.

Section 14 provides for implied terms as to quality or fitness for the buyer's intended purpose. However, unlike section 13, which applies to all sales, the implied undertakings as to quality and fitness only relate to sales where the seller sells goods in the course of a business. Section 14(2) provides that there is an implied condition that the goods are of *merchantable quality*. The Act provides that goods are of merchantable quality "if they are as fit for the purpose . . . for which goods of that kind are commonly bought as it is reasonable to expect having regard to any description applied to them, the price (if relevant) and all other relevant circumstances." Thus, the standard of merchantable quality varies but, where it is not satisfied, the buyer is entitled to treat the breach of contract as a breach of condition. Moreover, it is no use the seller claiming that the defect in the goods was a manufacturer's error which he, as seller, could not have discovered, for his contractual obligation is strict, it is to supply merchantable goods. Section 14(3) imposes an even greater obligation upon the seller where the buyer explains a particular purpose for which he requires the goods. Here the goods must be "reasonably fit for that purpose, whether or not that is a purpose for which such goods are commonly supplied." Thus, if a buyer explains that he wishes to buy paint to use outdoors, then the seller is under a strict obligation to ensure that the paint he supplies meets this requirement.

Section 15 provides that where goods are sold by reference to a sample, there is an implied condition that the bulk of the goods will correspond with the sample in quality; that the buyer shall be afforded a reasonable opportunity to compare the bulk with the sample; and that the goods will be free from any defect which would render them unmerchantable.

Clearly the right to repudiate and hence reject goods for breach of implied terms classified as conditions is a valuable remedy for a buyer. However, it must be noted that under section 11(4) of the 1979 Act when a buyer has "accepted" goods any breach of condition is thereafter to be treated merely as a breach of warranty and the buyer will have to be content with a claim for damages. What constitutes "acceptance" is a knotty problem but certainly delay in exercising a right of repudiation will bar the right to repudiate.

[The Supply of Goods (Implied Terms) Act 1973 and the Supply of Goods and Services Act 1982 provide for similar terms to those described above to be implied into contracts of hire purchase, and into contracts where goods are supplied other than by way of sale or hire purchase. A contract of hire purchase is simply a contract under which goods are hired to a debtor in return for periodic payments to the creditor. Under the terms of the contract the debtor, provided he makes the payments due under the hire purchase agreement, acquires a right to call upon the creditor to transfer ownership of the goods upon payment of a nominal sum. Contracts covered by the 1982 Act include pure hire or rental agreements and also those where the transfer of ownership in goods is part of a wider service transaction. This latter class would cover, for example, the supply of kitchen units under a contract to supply and install a fitted kitchen.]

Contracts for services

The Supply of Goods and Services Act 1982 implies *terms* into contracts for the supply of services (contracts under which a supplier agrees to carry out a service, excluding a contract of employment) irrespective of whether goods are also supplied under the same contract.

Under section 13, where the supplier acts in the course of a business, there is an implied term that he will carry out the service with "reasonable care and skill." By section 14 there is a term implied in business contracts that, if no time is fixed, then the service will be performed in a reasonable time. Finally, in all contracts for the supply of a service, there is an implied term that where the consideration has not been settled the customer will pay a reasonable charge to the supplier.

The use of the implied *term*, rather than *warranty* or *condition*, in this Act is significant for it leaves flexibility in the hands of the court in the event of dispute (see page 138).

PERFORMANCE OF SALE OF GOODS CONTRACTS

The basic obligation

The basic obligation of a seller is to pass ownership to the buyer for, by definition, a contract for the sale of goods is one under which the seller transfers or agrees to transfer the *property* (the term property is used in the 1979 Act to mean *ownership*) in goods to the buyer in return for the price. Passing of property is a matter of considerable importance for not only does it establish the stage at which the buyer becomes owner of the goods but it will almost certainly, in the absence of contrary agreement, determine which party bears the risk of any loss or deterioration in the goods. The basic obligation of the buyer is to pay for the goods and the Act provides that, unless otherwise agreed, payment and delivery are concurrent conditions. Thus, the seller must pass the property in goods, the buyer must pay for them and the seller must deliver them up to the buyer but only in return for payment of the contract price (other than when credit has been agreed).

Passing of property

The passing of property is an aspect of performance which involves a consideration of a set of rules laid down by the 1979 Act. The time at which property may pass is governed by the *classification of goods*. Goods may be classified as being *specific* goods, *unascertained* goods, or *ascertained* goods. Specific goods are defined by section 61 as "goods identified and agreed on at the time a contract of sale is made." Thus a contract for specific goods may only be performed by delivery of the particular thing agreed (*e.g. the* new Rover 800 on the forecourt and *not* one like it). Unascertained goods are goods which are defined by description only (*e.g. a* new Rover 800) and have yet to become identified as the particular goods which are to become the buyer's under the contract. Ascertained goods are goods which *have become* identified and agreed upon *after* the making of the contract (at the time of the contract they would be unascertained). It should be noted that by definition unascertained goods *can never* become specific goods.

The basic rule is that property passes (and the "agreement to sell" becomes a "sale") when it is intended to pass (s.17) provided that the goods are either specific or ascertained. Section 16 specifically states that no property can pass in unascertained goods unless and until they are ascertained. Section 18 lays down a set of rules for ascertaining the presumed intention of the parties where they have not indicated either expressly or by implication when the property is to pass. Contracting parties ought to be aware of the impact of these rules and if they do not meet their requirements ought to make their wishes plain in agreeing the contract. There are five rules in all but rules 1, 2 and 5 are the most significant.

Rule 1 provides that: "Where there is an *unconditional contract* for the sale of *specific goods*, in a *deliverable state*, the property passes to the buyer when the contract is made, and it is immaterial whether the time of payment or the time of delivery, or both, be postponed."

A contract is *unconditional* when there are no conditions which must be met before the contract comes into effect or which will cause the contract to be terminated subsequent to it coming into existence (*e.g.* an agreement to buy goods in the future at the market price provided it does not rise above a set limit would be a *conditional* contract). Goods are in a *deliverable state* when they are in the state contemplated by the contract as the state in which the buyer would be obliged to take delivery of them. The effect of rule 1 is frequently that the ownership of goods passes to the buyer long before he obtains possession and pays for them.

Rule 2 provides that: "Where there is a contract for the sale of *specific goods* and the seller is bound to do something to the goods, for the purpose of putting them into a deliverable state, the property does not pass until such thing be done, and the buyer has notice thereof." This rule would, for example, postpone the passing of property in a particular piece of antique furniture which the seller has indicated will be polished before it leaves his showroom.

Rule 5 deals with contracts in respect of *unascertained* goods and provides for their being *ascertained* (final identification as being the goods which are to become the subject of the contract). The rule provides that where there is a contract for the sale of unascertained goods and goods of that description and in a deliverable state are *unconditionally appropriated* to the contract either by the seller with the assent of the buyer or by the buyer with the assent of the seller, property passes to the buyer. Unconditional appropriation is a difficult concept in practice for, as Pearson J. said in *Carlos Federspiel and Co.* v. *Twigg (Charles) Ltd.*, "a mere setting apart or selection by the seller of the goods which he expects to use in performance of the contract is not enough. If that is all, he can change his mind and use these goods in performance of some other contract and use some other goods in performance of this contract. To constitute an appropriation of the goods to the contract the parties *must have had or be reasonably supposed to have had an intention to attach the contract irrevocably to those goods* so that those goods and no others are the subject of the sale and become the property of the buyer." In *Twigg's* case it was not sufficient for the seller to have crated up goods of the contract description for he could still have re-allocated the goods in question.

The nature of the performance required under the contract may be fundamentally changed by the operation of section 20 which provides that: "the goods remain at the seller's *risk* until the property therein is transferred to the buyer, but when the property therein is transferred to the buyer the goods are at the buyer's risk whether delivery has been made or not." This provision is again subject to contrary agreement by the parties but its effect may be to require a buyer to pay for goods which have been accidently destroyed or damaged without negligence on the part of the seller. (In effect the seller may require payment for the damaged remains which have never been delivered but which have passed into the ownership of the buyer by operation of the rules discussed above.) The effect on a contract of the perishing of specific goods before the property has passed to the buyer has been discussed in the earlier examination of the doctrine of frustration.

Delivery

Delivery of the goods is, together with the passing of property, an essential element of performance of a contract for the sale of goods. If the seller fails to deliver as required under the contract then he is liable to an action for *damages* or, in appropriate circumstances, an action for *specific performance* (discussed at page 157). Moreover, if a seller merely delays delivery beyond the agreed time this amounts to a breach of contract with serious consequences for the seller, for as McCardie J. asserted in *Hartley* v. *Hymans*, "in ordinary commercial contracts for the sale of goods the rule clearly is that time is prima facie of the essence with respect to delivery." This means that a contractual term relating to delivery will usually be treated as a *condition* (see page 139 for the classification of contractual terms). Again, the delivery made by the seller may be imperfect and section 30 lays down rules to govern this situation. He may, for example, deliver a smaller quantity of goods than that ordered. If so, under the rules, the buyer may reject the whole consignment or accept the smaller quantity and pay a proportionately reduced price. Should the seller deliver more than the quantity required by the contract then the buyer may reject the whole consignment, accept the agreed quantity only or accept the whole and pay a proportionately increased price. If the seller makes a delivery which consists partly of the goods ordered and partly of others (*e.g.* some of the goods fail to correspond with their description as required by s.13), the buyer may reject the whole consignment or accept the goods ordered and reject the others. It is presumed, although the Sale of Goods Act does not deal with the situation, that a buyer may also accept the whole of a consignment of "mixed goods" by treating the delivery of goods not ordered as an offer to sell those goods. The price for the extra goods would, no doubt, be a "reasonable sum."

Payment

Payment for goods is the primary obligation of the buyer and an unpaid seller has a right (a seller's *lien*) to retain possession of the goods until paid. The right of lien subsists: where the goods have been sold without agreement as to credit; where the goods have been sold on credit, but the period of credit has expired; or the buyer has become insolvent (which in this context merely means that the buyer has ceased to pay his debts in the ordinary course of business). In addition, an unpaid seller may stop goods in course of transit and resume possession of them if the buyer has become insolvent. Once the goods have reached the buyer, or his agent, the transit is at an end. These rights against the goods (actions *in rem*) are, of course, in addition to a seller's right to make money claims (actions *in personam*) in respect of a buyer's breach of contract.

EXCLUSION OF LIABILITY

Just as the law has distinguished between sales in the course of a business and other sales as regards the implied terms relating to quality and fitness, so a distinction is drawn between "business" buyers and "consumer" buyers in respect of the freedom which the seller has to contract out of the statutory implied conditions.

Implied terms where goods are supplied

Sections 6 and 7 of the Unfair Contract Terms Act 1977 *negative* any attempt, as against a person "*dealing as consumer*," to exclude or restrict liability in respect of the implied undertakings as to description, quality, fitness and sample contained in sections 13, 14 and 15 of the 1979 Act (and the corresponding provisions of the 1973 and 1982 Acts, see page 364). Thus, exemption clauses relating to these implied terms are totally ineffective against the person who "deals as consumer." As regards anyone dealing *other than* as consumer (*e.g.* the business buyer) the implied terms can only be excluded or restricted by a contractual term which is reasonable. A person "deals as consumer" in relation to another party if:

(a) he does not make the contract in the course of a business; and
(b) the other party (*i.e.* the supplier) does make the contract in the course of a business: and
(c) the goods are of a type "ordinarily supplied for private use or consumption."

This definition of "deals as consumer" applies to the other provisions of the 1977 Act except that qualification (c) is omitted where no goods are involved. Moreover, it is provided that on a sale by auction or competitive tender the buyer is not in any circumstances to be regarded as dealing as consumer.

The requirement of *reasonableness*, to be satisfied in relation to transactions where a party deals "otherwise than as consumer," is to be assessed with regard to the matters specified in Schedule 2 to the 1977 Act.

These "guidelines," which demonstrate the extent to which the doctrine of laissez-faire has been superseded by current legislation, require consideration, for example, of:

(a) the strength of the bargaining positions of the seller and buyer relative to each other, taking into account, among other things, the availability of suitable alternative products and sources of supply;

(b) whether the buyer received an inducement to agree to the term (*e.g.* a reduced price) or in accepting it had an opportunity of entering into a similar contract with other persons, but without having to accept a similar term; and

(c) whether the buyer knew or ought reasonably to have known of the existence and extent of the term.

One may add that this statutory control over exemption clauses will only be relevant where it has first been established that the clause does actually form part of the contract itself (see page 145).

One of the still comparatively few reported cases to apply the reasonableness test, *George Mitchell (Chesterhall) Ltd.* v. *Finney Lock Seeds Ltd.* reveals the balancing of interests undertaken by the courts. Here, cabbage seed was sold for £192 under a contract which limited the seed merchant's liability for the supply of defective seed to either its replacement or a refund of the price. The entire crop of cabbage was a failure and the buyer, a farmer, claimed £61,513 damages. Having found that the exemption clause, which was contained in an invoice, did form part of the contract, because the farmer's regular dealings had made him aware of it, the court considered whether it was a reasonable exemption. In favour of the merchants was noted the low cost of the seed and the high amount of damages. Neither party was insured but it was found that insurance was readily available to the merchants without substantially increasing the price of the seed. Furthermore, the exemption clause had been imposed upon the farmer and not negotiated so that it was not the result of a genuine bargain. It was concluded that the exemption was unreasonable.

This case demonstrates how judicial discretion may be used to allocate risk taking, for no doubt in future such merchants will insure against potential liability, passing on the cost of premiums through farmers and hence to ultimate consumers.

Contractual undertakings generally

The 1977 Act also provides a general means of control over most contractual exemption clauses including those seeking to relieve a supplier of services from the consequences of breach of the implied terms of the 1982 Act or indeed from breach of *express* terms. Section 3 applies where one party *deals as consumer* or on the other party's written *standard terms*. The party in breach cannot by reference to any contract term claim to be entitled:

(a) to render a contractual performance substantially different from that which was reasonably expected of him; or

(b) in respect of the whole or any part of his contractual obligation, to render no performance at all, *except*, in so far as the contract term is reasonable.

In *Woodman* v. *Photo Trade Processing Ltd.*, the court held that a clause was unreasonable which attempted to limit the liability of film processors to the replacement value of a film. No doubt damages would be a small consolation for the loss of the plaintiff's wedding photographs but this and the other reported cases have revealed readiness to disallow exemption clauses. Yet the traffic has not been all one way, for in *Wight* v. *British Railways Board* the Board successfully relied upon a term which restricted its liability for non-delivery "of left luggage" by reference to the weight of the luggage. It was indicated that the Board could not be expected to act as insurer for goods of uncertain value which could readily be valued and insured by the traveller. However, in *Phillips Products Ltd.* v. *Hyland* it was emphasised that the issue of reasonableness must always be resolved in relation to a *particular* contract and that generalised rulings are inappropriate. For example, in *The Zinnia* it was said that a clause was "so convoluted and prolix that one almost needed a law degree to understand it," perhaps such a clause in a contract between those in receipt of legal advice would be unobjectionable.

It should be noted that neither section 3, nor section 2 of the 1977 Act (discussed below) has any application to any contract so far as it relates to the creation or transfer of an interest in land, nor do they extend to contracts of insurance or those concerning intellectual property.

RIGHTS AND LIABILITIES OF THIRD PARTIES

The rights which arise under contracts, whether from express or implied terms, are, of course, of singular importance. However, the rights may in certain circumstances be of little value, for it may be that the party who suffers damage is not a party to the contract (*e.g.* the person who is poisoned by a gift of food which has been sold to a friend). It may happen that the party to suffer damage is the contracting party but his "rights" may be worthless, for the seller may be a "man of straw" who is unable to satisfy a judgment for damages. Fortunately, the consumer need not rely entirely upon his contractual rights. The common law of tort (see page 167) may provide assistance to a consumer who has no contractual link with the supplier and who actually suffers injury to his person or his property. Further, a statute, the Consumer Credit Act 1974, has given consumers in the important area of credit transactions an alternative "target" where their supplier may be of uncertain financial means so making litigation of doubtful value.

Product liability

Where goods of a non-apparent injurious nature have been created and the cause of their injurious nature is the negligence of the manufacturer, a person who is injured by the product may sue the manufacturer for damages in the tort of *Negligence*. The case which established this right is *Donoghue* v. *Stevenson* where the plaintiff and a friend went to a café where the friend bought ginger beer in a dark opaque bottle which concealed the contents. After the plaintiff had consumed some of the ginger beer, the friend poured out the remainder to reveal an apparent corpse of a decomposing snail. The plaintiff claimed to have suffered gastro-enteritis from consumption of the ginger beer and "snail juice." The plaintiff could not, of course, sue the café proprietor in contract, as the contract of sale had been made by the friend. The court held that the manufacturer owed a duty of care to the plaintiff as ultimate consumer of his product. Thus, a manufacturer in such circumstances owes a duty to consumers to exercise reasonable care. Should the manufacturer break that duty of care by negligent conduct, then a consumer suffering injury may sue the manufacturer for damages.

It must be emphasised, however, that whereas a seller owes a strict obligation to a buyer that the goods he supplies will be of merchantable quality, a manufacturer's duty to consumers is an obligation to take *reasonable* care. Moreover, whereas a buyer may claim damages from a seller in respect of the defect in quality in the goods he has purchased (an *economic* loss to the buyer), a consumer must show injury to his person or property (*physical* loss) in an action brought in respect of a manufacturer's negligence if he is to be certain of success. However, the House of Lords has left open the possibility of a consumer succeeding in an action against a manufacturer for pure economic loss. In *Lexmead (Basingstoke) Ltd.* v. *Lewis* their Lordships indicated that where a retailer of a defective towing hitch was liable for contractual damages to a buyer, a claim in tort, based upon the principle of *Donoghue* v. *Stevenson*, for indemnity by the retailer against the negligent manufacturer of the hitch ought not to be dismissed out of hand simply because it arose from pure economic loss. On the facts of *Lexmead* the buyer failed in his action against the retailer and the matter was left unresolved.

In a subsequent case, the House of Lords merely added fuel to the speculation which followed *Lexmead*. In *Junior Books Ltd.* v. *Veitchi Co. Ltd.* a company contracted for the erection of a factory with a contractor but nominated a sub-contractor who was to perform the specific task of installing the floor. The nominated sub-contractor, who had no direct contract with the company, was held liable in the tort of Negligence when the floor proved defective even though safe. The sub-contractor was held liable for the cost of repairing the cracked floor, a pure economic loss to the company.

Their Lordships recognised that this decision, on its facts, extended the duty of care beyond a duty to prevent harm being done by faulty work, to a duty to avoid such faults being present in the work itself. It may seem a short step from the facts of this case to hold a manufacturer liable to an ultimate consumer of his defective (albeit safe) product. However, it would be unwise to draw such a conclusion, for the tenor of the case was to emphasise the close "proximity" and reliance existing between the company and the nominated sub-contractor so as to distinguish it from that of a producer of goods to be offered for sale to the public. One may question whether a consumer relies upon his seller or upon the manufacturer when he purchases brand-name goods, especially following the manufacturer's promotional campaign. Again, if a supplier was to sell goods produced by a manufacturer to a named consumer's specification, could it be that the manufacturer would owe a duty of care to the consumer not to cause economic loss by producing defective goods?

Developments subsequent to the *Junior Books* case have, however, demonstrated an intention to restrict its application to special situations. In *Muirhead* v. *Industrial Tank Specialties Ltd.* a wholesale fish merchant sued a manufacturer of water pumps who had supplied pumps to a contractor who then installed them in the merchant's premises. The pumps were unsuitable for operation in this country and when they failed the merchant lost his stock of live lobsters. The Court of Appeal, after commenting that there were difficulties in extracting the precise *ratio decidendi* from the *Junior Books* case, disallowed the merchant's claim in so far as it was based upon pure economic loss. Their Lordships felt that the only safe principle to be extracted from *Junior Books* was that the nominated sub-contractor was liable because he had assumed a direct responsibility to the building owner.

[The debate about the liability of a manufacturer to the ultimate consumer of his goods may in fact be curtailed by developments not confined to this country. In 1985 the European Communities adopted a Directive upon product liability which member states must assimilate in municipal law within three years. Under the terms of the Directive liability for defective products is no longer to be based upon Negligence but upon proof that the product was defective and that damage ensued. Amongst the defences expected to be available to manufacturers is a "state of the art" claim. This would involve proof that the state of scientific and technical knowledge at the time when the manufacturer put the product into circulation was not such as to enable the existence of the defect to be discovered.]

Exclusion of liability for Negligence

The Unfair Contract Terms Act 1977 provides an important control in the area of both contractual and tortious negligence. Section 2 provides that:

(i) a person cannot by reference to any contract term or to a notice to persons generally or to particular persons exclude or restrict his liability for death or personal injury resulting from negligence; and

(ii) in the case of other loss or damage, a person cannot so exclude or restrict his liability for negligence except in so far as the term or notice is reasonable. Thus the court has—

    (a) power to determine whether an exemption of liability is fair and reasonable in the circumstances which were, or ought reasonably to have been, known to the parties when a relevant contract was made, and

    (b) in relation to tortious liability, power to determine whether it is fair and reasonable to allow reliance upon an exemption of liability.

It ought to be noted that the controls in section 2 over the use of the exemption clauses relate only to *business liability*, that is to say obligations and duties arising from things done or to be done in the course of a business. They would apply, for example, to control attempts to exclude the implied obligation, on the part of a supplier of a service, to use reasonable care and skill but they are not restricted to cases in which a person "deals as consumer."

Consumer credit

The Consumer Credit Act 1974 has recognised that the supplier of goods or services is not necessarily the only person with a moral responsibility to the consumer. A credit card organisation which makes an arrangement with a supplier under which it permits the supplier to display on the door or window of his premises a notice bearing the motif of the organisation, gives that supplier greater standing in the eyes of consumers, who are impressed by the "seal of approval" so provided. If, in such circumstances, the supplier sells unmerchantable goods to the consumer it may seem only reasonable that the creditor should be liable to the consumer in the same way as the supplier. Section 75 of the 1974 Act provides that where the supplier and the creditor have an arrangement under which the creditor will advance credit to the customers of the supplier (subject to their credit-worthiness), the creditor will, in the event of misrepresentation or breach of contract by the supplier, be equally liable to the consumer (see *diagram 7*).

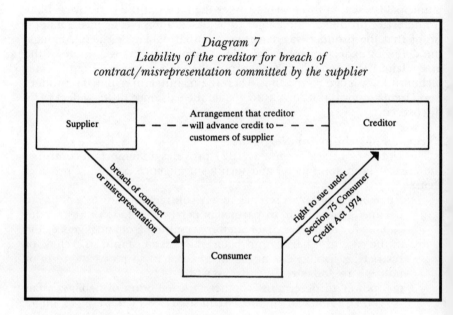

Diagram 7
Liability of the creditor for breach of contract/misrepresentation committed by the supplier

Section 75 only applies, however, where:
(a) the *credit* advanced did not exceed £15,000; and
(b) the *cash* price of the goods was more than £100 but did not exceed £30,000; and
(c) the debtor is an individual (*i.e.* not a corporation); and
(d) the creditor advanced the loan under a business transaction (so a "private" loan between friends would not, for example, render the creditor liable).

As a result of section 75 of the 1974 Act the consumer will, in the event of the supplier proving to be a "man of straw," have a right to proceed against a defendant (the creditor) of substance. The 1974 Act also provides, as did previous legislation, for an extension of the consumer's contractual rights where he enters into a contract of hire-purchase with a finance company or other creditor. Most consumers who enter into hire-purchase agreements for, say, a motor car, do not actually come face to face with the party with whom they will ultimately contract, the finance company. Instead, they negotiate with a dealer who, having persuaded the consumer that he wishes to purchase a particular car, will then sell the car to the finance company. This practice results in a situation in which the party who has a contract with the consumer is not the person who has persuaded the consumer to enter into the contract. What, then, if the statements made by the dealer turn out to have been false? The consumer cannot sue the dealer for breach of contract, for he has no contract with the dealer. Nor can he sue him for misrepresentation, for a misrepresentation is a false statement of fact made by one party to a contract, and the dealer is not a party to the contract. The finance company is a party to the contract with the consumer but it will not be liable under normal contractual principles, for it did not make the statements to the consumer. The common law provided for some redress in this situation in *Andrews* v. *Hopkinson*. In that case the dealer assured the consumer that a vehicle was "a good little bus, I would stake my life on it." The steering mechanism was, in fact, faulty and the consumer was nearly killed in a crash caused by this defect. The court established the right of the consumer to sue the dealer, in such a situation, for breach of a *collateral* contract (see *diagram 8*).

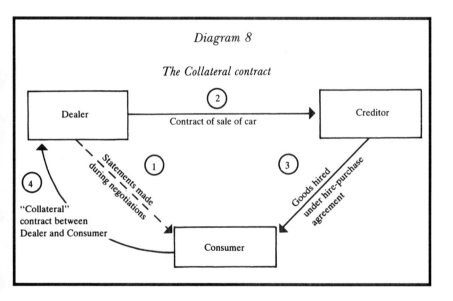

Diagram 8

The Collateral contract

A promise is, of course, only enforceable if supported by consideration and the consideration given by the consumer in this case was his entering into the contract of hire-purchase with the finance company. In effect, the court found that the dealer had made the following, binding, promise: "If you will enter into a contract of hire-purchase with the finance company, I will promise you that the vehicle is 'a good little bus.' " This promise gives rise to a remedy which may be of limited value. The dealer, who is liable in damages, may not be worth suing and the finance company, which may be worth suing, remains immune from liability. However, section 56 of the Consumer Credit Act 1974 provides for an extension of the consumer's rights in the hire-purchase situation. This section provides that statements made by the dealer in pre-contractual negotiations are deemed to have been made by him as agent of the finance company. The consumer may, as a result, proceed against the finance company (with whom he has a contract) as if it had made the false statements to him prior to his having entered into the contract (see *diagram 9*).

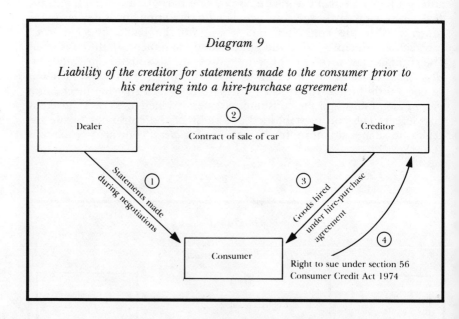

Diagram 9

Liability of the creditor for statements made to the consumer prior to his entering into a hire-purchase agreement

Like section 75, section 56 of the 1974 Act only applies if the consumer is not a company and has borrowed a sum which does not exceed £15,000.

CRIMINAL SANCTIONS

Today, the individual is not protected only by his opportunity for bringing a civil action where he can point to a breach of contract or to breach of any other legal obligation. In certain circumstances the criminal law now provides a framework of protection for the individual which is not necessarily dependent upon a contract having been made and which does not depend for its effectiveness on the individual being willing to invest his time and money in a court action. This is a major concern for the trader for the stigma of conviction is considerable.

Perhaps the best known part of this legislative framework is the Trade Descriptions Act 1968. This Act makes it an offence for any person in the course of trade or business to apply a false trade description to goods, or to supply (or offer to supply) goods to which someone else (*e.g.* the manufacturer) has applied a false trade description. An oral statement may amount to a trade description and a supplier is, for the purposes of this Act, deemed to have offered to supply goods when he exposes them for sale, even though such a display would not amount to a contractual offer. Any supplier who actually sells goods to which he, or someone else, has attached a false trade description may, of course, be liable to the purchaser for breach of section 13 of the Sale of Goods Act 1979. The supplier may, however, be prosecuted under the 1968 Act even where the goods bearing the false trade description have not been sold or where they have been sold but the purchaser is unwilling to sue. Enforcement of the Act is in the hands of Trading Standards Officers employed by local authorities.

There has been a tendency to resort to the sanctions of the criminal law to protect the interests of individuals. The Consumer Credit Act 1974, for example, creates 35 criminal offences which may be committed by those involved in the provision of credit and ancillary services. It is arguable, indeed, that recourse to criminal law is the only effective way of protecting a body of consumers characterised by its ignorance of the rights available through the civil courts. Support for this view may be found in developments in the law relating to the sale of goods. The Sale of Goods Act 1893 which provided implied terms relating, for example, to correspondence with description and merchantable quality, also stipulated that these implied terms could be excluded from contracts of sale by express agreement between the parties. By the middle of the twentieth century the notion that a purchaser could agree to waive his rights under the Act had led to the development of *standard* form contracts. These were couched in terms which were meaningless to the consumer and offered the consumer one alternative; he could "agree" to the terms offered to him or he could "do without" the product. The almost universal use of exemption clauses in contracts for the sale of goods gave rise to excesses such as the "guarantee" under which the unwitting consumer surrendered his rights under the Sale of Goods Act in return for the far more limited rights offered by the supplier. In response to this intolerable situation the Legislature passed the Supply of Goods (Implied Terms) Act 1973. The provisions of this Act (now adopted by the Unfair Contract Terms Act 1977) rendered void any attempt by the supplier to take away the rights afforded to private consumers by the Sale of Goods Act. Suppliers, however, continued to use their now legally ineffective exemption clauses and, unfortunately, consumers, unaware of the protection afforded to them, continued to believe that they had no redress. It was ultimately recognised that if consumers are unaware of their rights they are not likely to be assisted by an extension of those rights. As a result of this realisation it was recognised that an outright prohibition of exemption clauses was the only effective way of dealing with the situation. The Consumer Transactions (Restrictions on Statements) (Amendment) Order 1978 now provides that in a contract of sale (or hire-purchase) it is *illegal* to purport to exclude liability where such an exclusion of liability is ineffective by virtue of the Unfair Contract Terms Act 1977.

It is possible that the consumer will, in the future, be protected more by the imposition of fines upon those who would abuse him than by an extension of his considerable, but largely unused, civil remedies. An increasing use of criminal legislation could, indeed, render a civil action superfluous in certain circumstances. The Powers of Criminal Courts Act 1973 provides that a court may, having convicted the accused of the offence with which he is charged, make an order requiring him to pay compensation to anyone suffering loss as a result of that offence. A supplier who has broken the implied term relating to correspondence with description contained in his contract with the consumer may also have committed a criminal offence under the Trade Descriptions Act 1968. If the consumer can persuade a Trading Standards Officer to initiate a prosecution under the 1968 Act he could, in theory, obtain his compensation by way of an order granted by the criminal court (during proceedings paid for by the state) rather than through an award of damages made by a civil court. Unfortunately, the criminal courts have shown a marked reluctance to encroach upon the jurisdiction of the civil courts in this way. Even amendment of the 1973 Act, by the Criminal Justice Act 1982, enabling compensation orders to be made as the sole or main penalty has failed to make any great change in the numbers of orders made. Nevertheless, it may come to pass that, in the future, attitudes will change and the consumer will receive dual protection from criminal legislation. He may receive the benefit of the deterrent effect of the criminal sanction and, in the event of the deterrent failing to protect him, he may be able to avail himself of a simple, inexpensive method of obtaining his compensation. Certainly Sir Gordon Borrie, Director-General of Fair Trading, has suggested that it may now be time for a "little more boldness."

The criminal sanctions considered thus far have been directed towards protection of consumers' economic interests but it ought not to be forgotten that the criminal law is also used in its traditional role of seeking to deter those who would act so as to cause personal injury. The Consumer Safety Act 1978 enables the making of delegated legislation for the purpose "of securing that goods are safe or that appropriate information is provided . . . in respect of goods." Breach of these safety regulations is a criminal offence and new powers provided by the Consumer Safety (Amendment) Act 1986 allow for confiscation of goods in the absence of an appropriate safety certificate. Similarly, the Public Order Act 1986 provides that it is an offence, *inter alia*, for a person with the intention of causing public alarm or anxiety, or of causing injury to members of the public consuming or using the goods, to contaminate or interfere with goods.

ADMINISTRATIVE SUPERVISION

In addition to the civil remedies available to the individual, and the criminal sanctions which may be applied against the supplier, the consumer's position is now reinforced by the influence and administrative control of the Director-General of Fair Trading.

The Fair Trading Act 1973 requires the Director-General of Fair Trading to keep under review those commercial activities which relate to the supply of goods or services to consumers, so that he may become aware of practices which adversely affect their economic interests. He receives and collates evidence relating to undesirable commercial practices and, if he wishes to suppress such practices, he may act so as to control an individual supplier or suppliers generally. If the Director-General believes that an individual supplier is adopting a practice which is:

(a) detrimental to the interests of consumers; and
(b) unfair to consumers,

he must attempt to obtain from that supplier an *undertaking* that he will refrain from continuing to act in that way. If the Director-General is unable to obtain an undertaking, or if he does obtain one which is subsequently broken, he may bring proceedings before the Restrictive Practices Court. The court will then itself obtain an undertaking or order the supplier to stop acting in a manner inconsistent with an undertaking given to the Director-General of Fair Trading. Any breach of an order made by, or an undertaking given to, the Restrictive Practices Court amounts to a contempt of court and will be punished as such. (Where the supplier is not a company with a paid-up capital of at least £10,000 the Director-General of Fair Trading may bring him before a county court rather than the Restrictive Practices Court.)

It should be noted that the Director-General of Fair Trading may only require a supplier to give an undertaking where the business practice is *unfair*. The Fair Trading Act 1973 provides that a practice will only be unfair if it is, in itself, a breach of civil or criminal law. As such a breach, the practice could, in any event, result in civil proceedings brought by the consumer or in criminal proceedings initiated by a Trading Standards Officer. What, then, is the value of the power of the Director-General of Fair Trading to require and, ultimately, enforce an undertaking? The value of the supervisory function of the Director-General of Fair Trading can only be appreciated when one considers the likelihood of civil or criminal proceedings being initiated. If a door-to-door trader claims that the toothbrushes he is selling are made of nylon, when they are not, he is in breach of section 13 of the Sale of Goods Act 1979 and may be sued by any of the purchasers of his brushes. He also commits an offence under the Trade Descriptions Act 1968 and may be prosecuted. However, because of the fact that each of the items he sells has a low price and because he moves from area to area in plying his trade, there is no real possibility of a civil action being brought against him by a purchaser and there is little prospect of his being pursued by a Trading Standards Officer (who will be employed by a particular local authority). In such cases, the Director-General of Fair Trading is the only person likely to be able to stop this unfair, and illegal, trading practice.

The Director-General of Fair Trading may become aware that an undesirable trading practice is widespread. If so, he may refer the matter to the *Consumer Protection Advisory Committee* and submit proposals for action by the Secretary of State for Trade and Industry. The Consumer Protection Advisory Committee will then report on the practice and, where the Director-General of Fair Trading has submitted proposals for action, indicate whether it approves of the proposals submitted. The Secretary of State may then, by statutory instrument, give legislative effect to the proposals. An example of such an instrument is the Consumer Transactions (Restrictions on Statements) Order 1976, now replaced by the Consumer Transactions (Restrictions on Statements) (Amendment) Order 1978. This Order prohibits notices and advertisements which may mislead consumers as to their rights under the implied terms of the Sale of Goods Act and the Supply of Goods (Implied Terms) Act 1973.

Licensing provides another means of controlling trading malpractice. The Consumer Credit Act 1974 introduced a comprehensive licensing system for those carrying on consumer credit businesses, hire businesses and associated businesses (*e.g.* debt-collecting). The licensing system gives real power to the Director-General of Fair Trading, who administers the system, for he may refuse to grant a licence or withdraw or suspend a licence which has been granted. As it is a criminal offence to carry on without a licence a function for which a licence is required, the withholding of a licence by the Director-General of Fair Trading would,

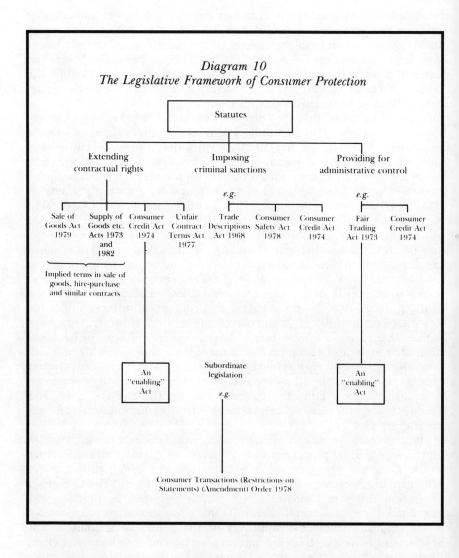

Diagram 10
The Legislative Framework of Consumer Protection

thus, effectively drive the supplier out of the consumer credit, hire or associated business.

Finally, the Director-General has a duty, under section 124 of the Fair Trading Act 1973, to encourage trade associations to prepare and disseminate *Codes of Practice.* Many such codes have been developed under the guidance of the Office of Fair Trading. They cover a wide range of consumer goods and services (*e.g.* footwear, furniture, cars, package holidays and electric appliance servicing). Their purpose is to supplement the law by obtaining the agreement of members of trade associations to raise their standards of trading (*e.g.* the Direct Sales and Services Association Code gives a 14 day cancellation period regardless of whether goods supplied are faulty or not). However, there are obvious weaknesses in voluntary codes since they probably do not apply to those traders most in need of reform. Moreover, expulsion from a trade association following breach of a code will often have little effect, for example, how many would decline to buy from a shoe shop merely because it was unable to display membership of a trade association? Yet codes may on occasions have an impact on the legal rights of consumers for it is possible that in appropriate circumstances their provisions may become incorporated as terms of a consumer's contract either expressly or by implication. The Director-General has said that at present he sees more room for development through the use of codes than through extension of the criminal law.

For an outline of the legislative framework of consumer protection see *diagram 10.*

Section B: Trader Protection

Traders, as well as consumers, may need protection in pursuing their commercial activities and may thus bring their complaints to the legal office. These complaints may relate to faulty goods which they have purchased from another trader or to negligent misstatements of a professional man upon which they have relied. Such complaints by traders would be pursued no differently from those of any other consumer. The trader may also face infringements of his interests which the consumer is unlikely to meet.

Wrongful interference with goods

The protection of a trader's industrial property is achieved largely by legislation which "penalises" infringement of those property rights (*e.g.* Patents Act 1977). Protection of rights to goods is afforded by those torts developed to deal with wrongful interference with goods. Whilst the Torts (Interference with Goods) Act 1977 acknowledges that an actionable interference with goods may arise out of Negligence or any other tort in so far as damage is caused to goods, the two basic torts protecting not only the title to, but also the trader's right to possession of, his goods are trespass to goods and conversion (see page 220).

Passing-off

The exact limits of the tort of passing-off are not clearly discernible, but in the "classic" action one trader passes off his goods or services as those of another trader. In addition the courts have come to recognise that a passing-off action can be maintained by a plaintiff who objects to a trader passing his goods off not as those of the plaintiff but rather as those of a *class* to which those of the plaintiff belong. Thus, in *J. Bollinger* v. *Costa Brava Wine Co. Ltd. (No. 2)* a trader was prevented from identifying his Spanish wines as "champagne" when they were not made by the champenois process from grapes grown in the Champagne district of France. The principle of this case, which protected products which had become identified with a particular geographical area, has been extended to protect goods produced by a particular process. In *Warnink* v. *Townend & Sons* the plaintiffs were one of a group of producers of "advocaat," an egg-based alcoholic drink containing *spirit*. The defendants produced and marketed a drink, described as "Old English Advocaat," which consisted of eggs and imported *wines*; the lower import duty on the latter relative to the duty on spirits allowed the defendants to undercut the plaintiffs' selling price. The House of Lords held that the plaintiffs, as one of a class of producers who benefited from the goodwill which attached to the description of goods as "advocaat," were entitled to protect their property right in the use of that description. Lord Diplock identified five characteristics of the tort of passing-off:

(a) a misrepresentation;

(b) made by a trader in the course of his trade;

(c) to prospective customers of his, or to ultimate consumers of goods or services supplied by him;

(d) which is calculated to injure the business or goodwill of another trader (in the sense that this is a reasonably foreseeable consequence); and

(e) which causes actual damage to that business or will probably do so.

These characteristics embrace not only the "classic" action in passing-off, but also in general the new areas of commercial abuse into which the tort has extended. However, in *Cadbury Schweppes Pty. Ltd.* v. *Pub Squash Co. Pty. Ltd.* a trader failed to sustain a complaint that a rival had deliberately adopted a similar packaging and advertising campaign for its product so as to promote that rival product into the same consumer market as that created by the trader. It is recognised that a successful advertising campaign can so develop an association between a product and a slogan or image that the slogan or image becomes part of the goodwill of the product (*e.g.* the toucan on a bottle of Guinness). But the plaintiff must establish that the slogan or image has become a distinctive part of the intangible property rights in his product. In the present case it was found that the rival's product was sufficiently distinguishable from the plaintiff's and that the public had not been deceived by the deliberate attempt to imitate.

The development of passing-off actions, potentially at least, was given further impetus by the abolition of the Registry of Business Names and the relaxation of controls over company names in 1981. As a result of these moves trading organisations, which believe that their name is being used by others in a way that confuses the public, will be forced to turn to a passing-off action as their means of redress.

Section C: Legislative Control of Competition

It has been, for many years, a basic tenet of government that attempts by commercial organisations to fetter or abolish competitive conditions within their markets should be controlled. A body of law has been developed in relation to trading transactions to safeguard the public interest from the activities of powerful businesses acting either alone or in concert. Traders must be aware of these constraints imposed upon their freedom to transact business.

MONOPOLIES AND MERGERS

The Monopolies and Mergers Commission

The Fair Trading Act 1973 provides for investigation of monopoly situations by the Monopolies and Mergers Commission, upon a reference by the Director-General of Fair Trading or the Secretary of State for Trade and Industry. The members of the Commission are appointed by the

Secretary of State (not less than 10 and not more than 25 regular members) and the principal functions of the Commission are to investigate and report on any question which is referred to it concerning:

(a) the existence, or possible existence of a monopoly situation; or

(b) the transfer of a newspaper or of newspaper assets (where such transfer would result in an undesirable concentration of power in one particular newspaper proprietor); or

(c) the creation, or possible creation, of a merger situation qualifying for investigation.

Monopolies

For the purposes of the Fair Trading Act, a monopoly situation in regard to the supply of either goods or services exists where at least one-quarter of all the goods and services supplied in the United Kingdom are supplied by one person or group, or where, as a result of one or more agreements, the supply of particular goods or services is prevented altogether. A "group" includes two or more persons who, whether voluntarily or not, and whether by agreement or not, so conduct their affairs as in any way to prevent, restrict or distort competition.

Monopoly references to the Commission may be limited to the finding of facts (*e.g.* whether a monopoly situation exists or whether any steps by way of uncompetitive practices or otherwise are being taken for the purpose of maintaining or exploiting a monopoly position) or, more usually, requesting an investigation and report on whether particular activity operates, or may be expected to operate, in a manner contrary to the public interest. The Act directs that references may specify investigation of: prices charged, or proposed to be charged, for goods or services; refusal to supply goods or services; and preferences given to any person (whether by way of discrimination in respect of prices or in respect of priority of supply or otherwise). In determining whether a particular activity operates against the public interest, the Commission is directed to take into account all matters which appear to be relevant and shall, particularly, have regard to the desirability:

(a) of maintaining and promoting effective competition between persons supplying goods and services in the United Kingdom;

(b) of promoting the interests of consumers, purchasers and other users of goods and services in the United Kingdom in respect of the prices charged, the quality and the variety of the goods and services supplied;

(c) of promoting, through competition, the reduction of costs and the development and use of new techniques and new products, and of facilitating the entry of new competitors into existing markets;

(d) of maintaining and promoting the balanced distribution of industry and employment in the United Kingdom;

(e) of maintaining and promoting competitive activity in markets outside the United Kingdom on the part of producers of goods, and of suppliers of goods and services, in the United Kingdom.

The Commission is an advisory body and simply produces a report of its findings and recommendations, following an investigation. The report is submitted to the Secretary of State for Trade and Industry, laid before Parliament and then published. The Secretary of State may make *orders* directed towards remedying situations found to be contrary to the public interest. These powers may even extend to his ordering the transfer of property from one body to another, the adjustment of contracts, or the re-allocation of shares, stocks or securities.

Although orders may direct that certain activities become unlawful, no criminal proceedings may follow contravention of such orders. However, any person may bring civil proceedings in respect of a contravention or apprehended contravention, and the Crown may seek an injunction to prevent contravention.

Finally, a more gentlemanly method of dealing with unsatisfactory competitive conditions is provided by the Act, whereby the Director-General may seek to obtain *voluntary undertakings*, from appropriate parties, as an alternative to the making of formal orders.

Mergers

Power to refer mergers to the Commission is vested in the Secretary of State alone, although a duty to keep conditions under review is placed upon the Director-General. The underlying assumption of the power to control mergers is that such action may prevent an undesirable monopoly situation from arising.

Apart from special provisions relating to newspaper mergers, the preconditions for a merger reference to the Commission are that it must appear to the Secretary of State that:

(a) two or more enterprises (one, at least, being carried on in the United Kingdom) have ceased to be distinct enterprises; and

(b) a monopoly situation is or would be created (see earlier); or

(c) the value of the assets taken over exceeds £30 million (a figure which may be varied by order).

The Commission is required to investigate whether a merger situation, within the Act, exists, and whether it is prejudicial to the public interest. The criteria which the Commission is required to apply are those applicable in the case of a monopoly investigation, and the power of the Secretary of State to make orders is similar to that in the case of monopolies. However, the making of orders is regarded as a measure of final resort and it is more usual for the Director-General to obtain undertakings in the event of an adverse report by the Commission.

Dominant market positions in the European Economic Community

Where inter-State trade within the EEC may be affected by a merger, not only must the Fair Trading Act be considered but also Article 86 of the Treaty of Rome, which prohibits, as incompatible with the Common Market, any abuse by one or more undertakings of a dominant position within the Common Market, or in a substantial part of it (*e.g.* in one member State). Abuse may consist of such matters as directly or indirectly imposing unfair purchase or selling prices, or limiting production or technical development, to the prejudice of consumers.

RESTRICTIVE TRADE PRACTICES

The Restrictive Trade Practices Act 1976 requires all those agreements falling within the Act to be entered upon the register maintained by the Director-General of Fair Trading. It is the function of the Director-General to refer such agreements to the Restrictive Practices Court and the Court is required to declare whether the agreements are void as a result of being contrary to the public interest. (The Court can only act when an agreement has been registered; if, however, an agreement is not registered within the appropriate time, normally three months, the agreement is automatically rendered void.)

The Restrictive Practices Court

The Court is of High Court status, having five judges appointed to it (one of whom is appointed President), together with not more than 10 other members knowledgeable in matters of industry or commerce.

If an agreement is void, then it is unlawful for the parties to adhere to it or to enter a fresh agreement to the same effect. An agreement to which the Act applies is prima facie deemed to be contrary to the public interest and the onus of proving otherwise lies upon the parties to the agreement. The Court has power to make orders restraining the enforcement of agreements rendered void. Unlawful adherence to an agreement is actionable as a breach of statutory duty at the instance of any person suffering loss as a result of its enforcement.

Agreements caught by the Act

The 1976 Act applies to agreements for the provision of goods or services and even to information agreements (under which information as to prices, terms and conditions of supply are exchanged).

Registrable agreements relating to goods ... are those agreements between two or more persons engaged in the production, processing or supply of goods containing restrictions relating to:
 (a) the prices to be charged;
 (b) the terms or conditions as to supply;
 (c) the quantities or descriptions of goods to be produced;
 (d) the processes of manufacture to be applied;
 (e) the persons or classes of person to whom the goods may be supplied or from whom they may be acquired.

Registrable agreements relating to services ... the Secretary of State has power to direct, by statutory instrument, that the Act should apply to designated classes of services. Such an order, the Restrictive Trade Practices (Services) Order 1976, brings all services within the Act unless excepted. In fact there are many important areas excepted from the Act, including the activities of building societies, insurance services and a wide range of professional services the activities of which are governed by associations whose actions in restricting non-qualified practitioners are necessarily restrictive (*e.g.* the services of the legal professions, architects and surveyors).

Proceedings before the Court

In order to maintain an agreement it must be proved that it is not contrary to the public interest. Proving this may only be effected by satisfying the Court that one or more of a number of specified circumstances apply. These specified circumstances are referred to as the *gateways* through which an agreement may pass. Any agreement not passing through one or more gateways will be void. The gateways are:
 (a) that the restrictions are reasonably necessary, having regard to the

character of the goods or services, to protect the public against injury;

(b) that the removal of the restrictions would deny to the public, as purchasers, or consumers, other specified substantial benefits or advantages;

(c) that the restrictions are reasonably necessary to counteract measures taken by a person who is not a party to the agreement;

(d) that the restrictions are reasonably necessary to enable the parties to the agreement to negotiate fair terms of supply from persons who are not parties to the agreement but who control a large part of the trade or business of supplying specified goods or services;

(e) that the removal of the restrictions would be likely to have a serious and persistent adverse effect on the general level of unemployment;

(f) that the removal of the restrictions would be likely to cause a reduction in the volume or earnings of an export business which forms a substantial part of the total export business of the United Kingdom;

(g) that the restrictions are reasonably required for the maintenance of other restrictions not found by the Court to be contrary to the public interest;

(h) that the restrictions do not directly or indirectly restrict or discourage competition to any material degree and are not likely to do so.

Moreover, the Court must also be satisfied that the practices are "not unreasonable having regard to the balance between those circumstances and any detriment to the public likely to result."

RESALE PRICES

The Resale Prices Act 1976 prohibits either collective or individual resale price maintenance. Under its provisions any term of a contract between a supplier and a retailer is void in so far as it seeks to fix a minimum resale price. Moreover, to communicate an indication that a minimum price should be observed is unlawful, that is, it is not a criminal offence, but is an act which may be restrained by injunction or may give rise to a civil action for damages.

Again, as in the case of restrictive trade practices, the Court has a power to exempt particular schemes. Thus, classes of goods may be exempted from the basic prohibition and, if so, resale price maintenance may be enforced against subsequent purchasers of goods who take with notice of the restriction. There are five gateways through which agreements may pass, but, again, there is an additional requirement to be proved: that the detriment resulting from resale price maintenance is, on balance, outweighed by the detriment which would result to the public in the absence of resale price maintenance. The gateways are that in the absence of resale price maintenance:

(a) the quality or variety of the class of goods would be substantially reduced:

(b) the number of retail outlets would be substantially reduced;

(c) the retail price would, ultimately, be higher;

(d) the goods would be sold by retail under such circumstances as would be likely to result in a danger to health as a consequence of misuse by the public;

(e) necessary services currently provided as an after service would cease or be substantially reduced.

A common practice, not outlawed by the 1976 Act, is for suppliers to indicate the "manufacturers' recommended resale price." This practice has, however, been investigated by a number of agencies and now, by order made under the Prices Act 1974, comparisons with manufacturers' recommended retail prices are illegal (constituting criminal offences) for certain products (*e.g.* beds, carpets, domestic electrical appliances and furniture).

ANTI-COMPETITIVE PRACTICES

The legislation governing monopolies, mergers and restrictive trading agreements left untouched (apart from resale price maintenance) individually pursued anti-competitive practices where these were undertaken by persons other than those in a monopolistic position. However, the Competition Act 1980, which defines "anti-competitive practice" by placing emphasis upon its *effect* rather than upon its *form*, lays down a procedure for investigation and control. Section 2 of the Act provides that " . . . a person engages in an anti-competitive practice if, in the course of business, that person pursues a course of conduct which, of itself or when taken together with a course of conduct pursued by persons associated with him has or is intended to have or is likely to have the effect of restricting, distorting or preventing competition in connection with the production, supply or acquisition of goods in the United Kingdom . . . or the supply or securing of services in the United Kingdom . . . ." It is intended that this should encompass such activities as refusals to deal with particular traders (*e.g.* with those involved in discounting), tying to one manufacturer, and full line stock enforcing which requires a trader to take the full range of a manufacturer's products. Section 3 gives power to the Director-General of Fair Trading to make preliminary investigations when it appears to him that an anti-competitive practice is being followed. Upon conclusion of his investigation he must publish a report indicating whether the conduct is found to be anti-competitive. Should this be the case, then he must report whether he believes the matter should be referred, as a *competitive reference*, to the Monopolies and Mergers Commission for fuller investigation to determine whether the activity is contrary to the public interest. The Act provides an alternative to investigation by the Commission, for in appropriate cases the Director-General may accept suitable undertakings for modification or abandonment of a particular practice. Where the Commission does investigate, it may make recommendations as to remedial action should the practice be found to be contrary to the public interest. This remedial action may consist of the giving of undertakings to the Director-General or, indeed, the Secretary of State may make an order prohibiting a practice. Following investigation of T.I. Raleigh's refusal to supply its bicycles to cut-price retailers, the manufacturers were directed to supply "non-branded" bicycles although they were permitted to refuse to supply branded goods.

The Anti-Competitive Practices (Exclusion) Order 1980 provides for specific exemptions from the operation of the legislation and there are

general exclusions. Practices registrable under the Restrictive Trade
Practices Act 1976 are excluded, as are practices carried out by a business
with " . . . an annual turnover less than £5 million and which has less than a
25 per cent. share of a relevant market and which is not a member of a
group with either an annual turnover of £5 million or more or which has a
25 per cent. share of a relevant market."

Enforcement . . . whilst the effect of an order made by the Secretary of
State is to declare further pursuit of an anti-competitive practice unlawful,
the provisions of the Fair Trading Act 1973 apply to enforcement of the
order. Section 93 of that Act provides that no criminal proceedings may be
brought for contravention of the order, but no limitation is placed upon
the right of any person to bring civil proceedings in respect of any
contravention. Moreover, the order may be enforced by the Crown seeking
an injunction to prevent contravention and any person injured by
contravention may seek damages or an injunction.

Statutory corporations . . . in what was a major innovation the 1980 Act, in
section 11, provides that the Secretary of State may refer to the
Commission any question relating to the efficiency and costs of, the service
provided by, or possible abuse of a monopoly situation by any statutory
corporation which supplies goods or services by way of business.

In its report the Commission must give reasons for its conclusions and
may make recommendations to remedy any course of conduct which is
contrary to the public interest. The Secretary of State may make an order
directing persons named to prepare a plan for remedying or preventing
any adverse effects specified in the Commission's report. A major
investigation into the efficiency and costs of the Central Electricity
Generating Board was one of the earliest references made; this of course
involved investigating a body whose only function is to deal with other
nationalised bodies (*i.e.* the Area Electricity Boards) in the supply of
electricity in bulk. Under the Fair Trading Act it is only under very
restricted circumstances that a nationalised industry may be investigated,
but the 1980 Act is designed to ensure competition in both private and
public commercial activities.

INTER-STATE COMPETITION

Finally, where restrictions upon competition affect trade between member
states of the EEC, one must have regard to Article 85 of the Treaty of
Rome. Under its provisions, which are directly applicable in member
States, agreements which have as their object or effect the prevention,
restriction or distortion of competition within the Community are
rendered void. Again, there is provision for reference to a central agency,
the European Commission, which may grant "negative clearance" (or
exemption) to a particular agreement when, on balance, it is not
detrimental to the interests of consumers.

It has been noted earlier, in considering common law controls on
competition through the doctrine of restraint of trade, that "tied public
house" agreements lie outside that doctrine. But E.E.C. law may reach the
parts that the common law does not reach. The European Court of Justice
ruled in *Brasserie de Haecht* v. *Wilken Janssen*, a case coming from a Belgian
court, that exclusive purchasing contracts (solus agreements) *may* infringe
Article 85 if they affect trade between member states. In 1983 the

European Commission issued a Regulation which is directly effective in all member states concerning both "beer supply agreements" and "service-station agreements." It applies to agreements made after 1983 so that earlier agreements which satisfy the common law on restraint of trade will gradually fall into line with the European perspective on competition. The basic position is that the two types of agreement will be exempt from Article 85 unless: (a) in the case of beer, the tie is for more than 10 years but if it applies to beer and other drinks the maximum period is five years (although if the supplier is the landlord of the seller, the tie may be of indefinite duration); (b) in the case of motor fuels (other goods are not provided for) the tie is for more than 10 years (again the landlord proviso applies).

It will now be appreciated that today preservation of the public interest in the context of restrictive business practices is almost entirely a matter of legislative rather than common law development.

INDEX